The Art and Science of Counseling and Psychotherapy

MICHAEL S. NYSTUL
New Mexico State University

Merrill,
an imprint of Prentice Hall
Upper Saddle River, New Jersey   Columbus, Ohio

Library of Congress Cataloging-in-Publication Data

Nystul, Michael S.
     The art and science of counseling and psychotherapy / Michael S.
  Nystul.
        p.   cm.
     Includes bibliographical references
     ISBN 0-675-21212-X
     1. Counseling.   2. Psychotherapy.   I. Title
  BF637.C6N97   1993
     158' .3—dc20

92-8509
CIP

Cover art: Linda Childers
Editor: Linda A. Sullivan
Production Editor: Christine M. Harrington
Art Coordinator: Lorraine Woost
Artist: Jane Lopez
Photo Editor: Anne Vega
Cover Designer: Russ Maselli
Production Buyer: Pamela D. Bennett
Electronic Text Management: Ben Ko, Marilyn Wilson Phelps

This book was set in Garamond by Macmillan Publishing Company and was printed and
bound by R. R. Donnelley & Sons Company. The cover was printed by Phoenix Color.

Photo credits: The Bettman Archive, pp. 120, 128, 137; Center for Studies of the Person,
Carl Rogers Memorial Library, p. 150; Stanford University, p. 185; Institute for Rational Emotive
Therapy, p. 188; University of Pennsylvania, p. 192; all other photos supplied by Michael S.
Nystul.

Printed in the United States of America
10 9 8 7 6 5 4 3

ISBN: 0-675-21212-X

Prentice-Hall International (UK) Limited, *London*
Prentice-Hall of Australia Pty. Limited, *Sydney*
Prentice-Hall of Canada, Inc., *Toronto*
Prentice-Hall Hispanoamericana, S. A., *Mexico*
Prentice-Hall of India Private Limited, *New Delhi*
Prentice-Hall of Japan, Inc., *Tokyo*
Simon & Schuster Asia Pte. Ltd., *Singapore*
Editora Prentice-Hall do Brasil, Ltda., *Rio de Janeiro*

This book is dedicated to my mother and father.

They helped me believe in myself and gave me the capacity to give of myself to others.

Preface

A career in counseling can be exciting and rewarding, and there are many reasons for becoming a counselor. You might think that helping a client work through a crisis or develop a more effective and meaningful lifestyle would be personally gratifying. Perhaps you find people interesting, or you are curious about how the mind functions or even fascinated by abnormal conditions such as schizophrenia. You might view the challenge of working in a relatively new profession as appealing. Counseling offers numerous opportunities for its practitioners to make a significant contribution to the profession. You can develop new approaches to counseling or become involved in professional issues such as licensure. There are many ways to involve yourself in the counseling profession, and this book may help you identify some facet of counseling you would like to explore.

This book provides a survey of the counseling professions, with an objective overview of major topics. I have also added personal thoughts and feelings in the form of "Personal Notes," which are based on more than 20 years of clinical experience. These notes are boxed off for the reader, so they can be appreciated as supplementary to the text. I hope these Personal Notes will bring to life some of the basic counseling principles as well as provide practical guidelines relating to the counseling process.

In this text, I use the term *counselor* to refer to members of all the disciplines represented by the helping profession: psychologists, psychiatrists, counselors, and social workers, psychiatric nurses, and others.

The text has been divided into four parts. Part One is an overview of counseling and the counseling process. Chapters 1 and 2 discuss various models for understanding counseling, including counseling as an art and a science, describe the stages in the counseling process and common problems that beginning counselors face. Chapters 3 and 4 provide information on two phases of the counseling process that reflect the science of counseling model—assessment and diagnosis and research and evaluation.

Part Two provides information that counselors can use to formulate a personal approach to counseling. Chapter 5 presents guidelines for developing a personal approach that is responsive to a multicultural society. Chapters 6, 7, and 8 provide information on the major counseling theories.

Part Three focuses on counseling specialties. Information is provided on marriage and family counseling (Chapter 9), child counseling (Chapter 10), group counseling (Chapter 11), and career counseling (Chapter 12).

Part Four addresses professional settings and issues. It begins by providing an overview of two common settings where counselors work—schools (Chapter 13) and mental health settings (Chapter 14). The last chapter of the book provides information on professional issues such as becoming licensed, and ethical and legal principles (Chapter 15).

ACKNOWLEDGMENTS

I want to extend my deepest thanks and appreciation to several people. I extend a very special thanks to Dr. Gerald Becker of Oregon State University, who has been my mentor since I began studying counseling. Over the years he has also become a very dear friend. His encouragement and suggestions regarding this manuscript were invaluable. I also express appreciation to the reviewers: Harold Leon Gillis, Jr., Georgia College; Larry Golden, University of Texas; Janet Heddesheimer, George Washington University; Daniel Kennedy, Florida International University; Courtland Lee, University of Virginia; J. Jeffries McWhirter, Arizona State University; Jeffrey Messing, West Virginia University; Eugene R. Moan, Northern Arizona University; Thomas Russo, University of Wisconsin; Gerald Spadafore, Idaho State University; Holly A. Stadler, University of Missouri, Kansas City; Aaron B. Stills, Howard University, and William Welch, Memphis State University, all of whom provided constructive feedback on the manuscript. They made numerous suggestions that were very helpful in the development of this text. I would like to extend a special acknowledgment to Aaron B. Stills of Howard University. His suggestions and encouragement played a major role in the evolution of this text. In addition, experts in the field provided excellent suggestions regarding individual chapters. These individuals included: Duane Bown (Chapter 12); Charles Gelso (Chapter 2, Chapter 4); Charles Huber (Chapter 9, Chapter 15); Elaine LeVine (Chapter 10); Robert Myrick (Chapter 13); and Paul Pedersen (Chapter 5). I am also indebted to the staff of Merrill/Macmillan Publishing Company, in particular to Linda Sullivan, Kevin Davis, David Faherty, Christine Harrington, and Anne Vega, whose suggestions were invaluable. I would also like to thank my typists, Yvonne Perez and Laura Nystul. I truly appreciate their patience, dedication, and willingness to work under the pressure of deadlines. Most of all, I would like to thank my wife Laura for her love and encouragement.

Brief Contents

PART 1

PART 2

PART 3

PART 4

Contents

CHAPTER EIGHT
Cognitive-Behavioral Theories

PART 3

Counseling Specialties   209

CHAPTER ELEVEN
Group Counseling   261

CHAPTER TWELVE
Career Counseling   277

An Overview of Counseling and the Counseling Process

Part One of this text provides an overview of counseling and the counseling process. Chapter 1 presents several models that can be used to conceptualize counseling. These models include the art and science of counseling and psychotherapy, formal versus informal helping, counseling from a historical perspective, and future trends in counseling. Chapter 2 provides an overview of the stages of counseling as well as special skills that can be used in counseling. Chapters 3 and 4 provide a more detailed description of two of the stages of the counseling process: assessment and diagnosis (Chapter 3) and counseling research (Chapter 4). These two chapters provide important information on the science of counseling in terms of how objective information can be obtained from assessment and diagnosis and research strategies.

CHAPTER ONE

An Overview of Counseling

CHAPTER OVERVIEW

This chapter provides several models that can be used to conceptualize counseling. Highlights of the chapter include

- The art and science of counseling and psychotherapy
- Counseling versus psychotherapy
- Formal versus informal helping
- Personal qualities of effective helpers
- The helping profession
- Counseling from a historical perspective
- Future trends in counseling

WHAT IS COUNSELING?

No simple answer addresses the question, "What is counseling?" Counseling can more appropriately be understood as a dynamic process associated with an emerging profession. It involves a professionally trained counselor assisting a client with particular concerns. In this process, the counselor can use a variety of counseling strategies such as individual, group, or family counseling to assist the client. These strategies can generate a variety of outcomes. Some of these are facilitating behavior change, enhancing coping skills, promoting decision making, and improving relationships.

This chapter will provide several conceptual models through which the different facets of counseling can be understood. It will begin by describing counseling as an art and a science. The chapter will then differentiate counseling from psychotherapy and formal from informal helping; describe the personal qualities of effective helpers; identify members of the helping profession; and provide information on past and future trends in counseling.

The Art and Science of Counseling and Psychotherapy

One way to conceptualize counseling is as an art and a science. The art of counseling relates to the subjective dimension of counseling, and the science of counseling relates to the objective dimension. The focus of counseling can shift back and forth between these two dimensions as one proceeds through the counseling process. For

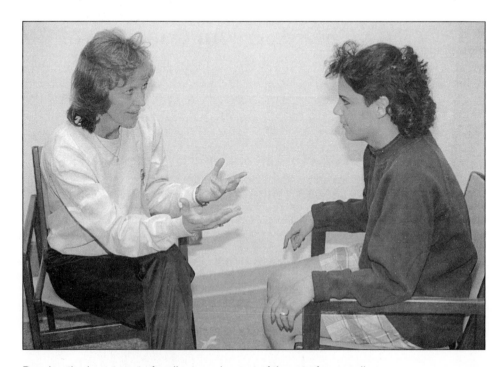

Drawing the beauty out of a client can be part of the art of counseling.

example, during the initial sessions, the counselor may function more like an artist, using listening skills to understand the client. Later, the focus might shift to the science dimension as the counselor uses psychological tests to obtain an objective understanding of the client. Together, the art and science can create a balanced approach to counseling. A more detailed description of each of these two dimensions to counseling follows.

The Art of Counseling.   I believe to a large degree counseling is an art. To call counseling an art suggests it is a *flexible, creative process* whereby the counselor adjusts the approach to the unique and emerging needs of the client. The following Personal Note provides an illustration of how a counselor can be flexible and creative in working with a client.

a personal note

As a psychologist working for the Public Health Service on a Navajo Indian Reservation, I was asked to work with an autistic child as part of my consultation with the public schools. School personnel had placed the young girl in a classroom for the mentally retarded, not knowing she was autistic. The child was referred to me for counseling and self-concept development. When she came into my office, I had some puppets ready to use with her that were part of a self-concept program called Developing an Understanding of Self and Others (DUSO) (Dinkmeyer & Dinkmeyer, 1982). I soon realized that she seemed oblivious to me and the puppets. My counseling plans appeared to be useless.

I wanted to make contact with the child and find a way to reach into her world and develop a special relationship with her. I decided to let her be the guide, and I would follow. She walked over and threw the puppets into a neat pile. If she missed the pile, she threw it until it landed right on top of the others. She was very good at throwing puppets into a pile, and she seemed to enjoy doing it. I had identified one of her assets—something she felt good about, something she felt secure with. It was an extension of her world, her way of doing things. It made sense to her.

I wanted to become part of her world, to reach into it. I walked over and put my arms around her pile of puppets, becoming a puppet-basketball net. She continued to throw her puppets on the pile and through my net. For the next 20 minutes, the child threw the puppets into a pile. When she ran out of puppets, she would gather them up and start over, throwing them into a new pile. I would move the "net" as necessary. During this time, she never made eye contact with me or said a word. I became discouraged and walked back to my seat. As I did, I noticed that her eyes followed my movement. At that instant, I knew I had made contact. I had found a way into her world.

Over the next year, she let me further into her world. For the most part, she was the guide and I the follower—a guest in her home. As the relationship grew stronger, she became willing to explore my world. Through our relationship, I helped her reach out into the world of others. For example, I helped her with language development and encouraged her to move away from her ritualistic behavioral patterns. (A more detailed description of this case can be found by referring to Nystul, 1986.)

Another aspect of the art of counseling is the concept of giving of oneself in counseling. This concept is derived from humanistic psychology and emphasizes the importance of counselors being authentic and human in the counseling approach.

Counselors can give of themselves on many levels. They can give concern and support as they empathize with their client. A more intense form of giving is an existential encounter, which involves the process of self-transcendence. In this experience, the counselor moves beyond the self and feels at one with the client (Nystul, 1987). The experience can help a client overcome feelings of aloneness and alienation.

Giving of oneself in counseling may be especially appropriate in situations that involve working with neglected and abused children. These children may be wards of a court, without parents or "significant others." They may feel unloved and lost, lacking a reason to live. In these cases, the counselor may attempt to communicate compassion, kindness, tenderness, and perhaps even love. The following Personal Note illustrates the concept of giving of oneself in counseling.

a personal note

A 5-year-old child was abandoned by her parents and placed in a residential facility for neglected and abused children. On one occasion, the caretakers of the institution became concerned when the child stayed up all night crying and vomiting. They brought her to a hospital the next morning. A pediatrician found nothing physically wrong with the child and referred her to me for mental health services.

After introducing myself to the child, I asked her how she was feeling. She sat down, put her face between her legs, and began to cry. It was the most deep-sorrowful sobbing I had ever heard. I leaned forward and gently touched her head, trying to comfort her. I could feel her pain. She looked up at me and appeared frightened and alone. I reached over and held her hand and told her I wanted to help her feel better. My heart reached out to her. I looked at her and said I thought she was a beautiful person, and I wanted to work with her every day. She nodded in agreement. I worked with her in play therapy for several weeks. During that time, her depression gradually lifted.

Counselors must use safeguards when expressing intense feelings to a client. They must clearly establish their role as a counselor and not a parent. They must avoid becoming overly involved to the point where they lose professional objectivity. Counselors must also be aware that excessive concern or worry about a child could lead to burnout. Giving of oneself in counseling is a very delicate process. It can be enriching and rewarding for the counselor and the child, but it can also be exhausting. Communicating intense emotion may not be practical for some counselors. For others, it is an art that must be developed over time.

The Science of Counseling.   The science of counseling provides a balance to the art of counseling by creating an objective dimension to the counseling process. Claiborn (1987) noted that science provides an important aspect to the identity of counselors in that it can differentiate professional counselors from nonprofessional helpers. He suggested that counselors should strive to be counselors-as-scientists (i.e., someone who functions as a counselor and thinks as a scientist). Thinking as a scientist requires the counselor to have the skills to formulate objective observations and inferences, test hypotheses, and build theories (Claiborn, 1987).

Claiborn (1987) also suggested that the scientist-practitioner model, set forth by Pepinsky and Pepinsky (1954), could provide useful guidelines for contemporary counselors. Pepinsky and Pepinsky's model conceptualized science and practice as integrated, mutually dependent, and overlapping activities. The interrelationship between theory, research, and practice provides an illustration of the complementary nature of science and practice. For example, practice can test a counseling theory that can, in turn, be evaluated by research.

The science of counseling also proposes that counselors develop skills that can promote professional objectivity in the counseling process. These include the observation, inference, hypothesis-testing, and theory-building skills that Claiborn (1987) suggested are necessary for counselors to think as scientists. Other strategies include the use of psychological tests; a systematic approach to diagnosis; and research methods to establish counseling accountability and efficacy. We should not view these as separate entities of counseling. Instead, counselors should integrate these skills and strategies into their overall role and function.

Counseling and Psychotherapy

The counseling literature has not made a clear distinction between counseling and psychotherapy (Patterson, 1980), perhaps because the two processes are more similar than different. We can probably best understand their relationship within a continuum, with counseling at one end and psychotherapy at the other. A counselor may actually do both counseling and psychotherapy in one session. The two processes can therefore blend.

We can identify some subtle differences between these two processes. The main difference is that counseling addresses the conscious mental state, whereas psychotherapy also ventures into the client's unconscious processes. An example of relating to unconscious processes is providing insight to a client. Several other differences exists between counseling and psychotherapy in terms of clients, goals, treatment, and setting. These differences are shown in Table 1.1.

As depicted in Table 1.1, counseling is used with clients whose problems do not stem from a serious mental disorder such as a major depression. Instead, it is more appropriate for clients who have "problems of living," for example, parent-child conflicts or marital difficulties. Goals of counseling tend to focus on resolving immediate concerns such as helping clients work through a relationship difficulty or make a career decision.

Treatment programs in counseling vary according to the client's concern. For example, counseling might involve a parent education program to help parents learn how to establish a positive relationship with their child. Other counseling strategies might help a client work through marital difficulties. Counseling approaches are usually short-term, involving one session each week for 3 to 12 weeks. Counseling services may take place in a variety of settings such as schools, churches, and mental health clinics.

Table 1.1
Comparison of Counseling and Psychotherapy

	Counseling	Psychotherapy
Clients	Clients tend to have "problems of living" such as relationship difficulties, or need assistance with specific problems such as career choice.	Client's problems are more complex and may involve using formal diagnostic procedures to determine if there is a mental disorder.
Goals	The focus is more on the short-term goals (resolution of immediate concerns).	The focus is on short- and long-term goals. Long-term goals can involve processes such as helping the client overcome a particular mental disorder.
Treatment Approaches	The treatment program can include preventative approaches and various counseling strategies to assist with the client's concerns.	Psychotherapeutic approaches are complex. They utilize strategies that relate to conscious and unconscious processes.
Setting	Counseling services can be provided in a variety of settings such as schools, churches, and mental health clinics.	Psychotherapy is typically offered in settings such as private practice, mental health centers and hospitals.

Psychotherapy is a process that can be used to assist a client who is experiencing more complex problems such as a mental disorder. Psychotherapy can involve both short- and long-term goals. The focus of short-term goals may be similar to problems addressed in counseling, for example, dealing with marital problems. Long-term goals relate to more deep-seated or involved problems such as depression or schizophrenia.

Psychotherapy is complex, and relates to both conscious and unconscious processes. Hypnosis, projective tests, and dream analysis are all examples of techniques that relate to unconscious processes. Psychotherapy requires expertise in several areas such as personality theory and abnormal psychology. Psychotherapeutic approaches are usually long-term, occurring once each week for 3 to 6 months, and sometimes even longer. Typical settings for psychotherapy are private practice, mental health centers, and hospitals.

Differentiating Formal from Informal Helping

One way to answer the question, "What is counseling?" is to differentiate counseling from the informal helping that can take place between friends. Some individuals who have had no formal training in counseling can provide valuable assistance. These informal helpers usually have some of the personal qualities associated with effective counselors such as being caring, nonjudgmental, and utilizing listening skills. Professional counselors may differ from informal helpers in a number of ways.

First, counselors can maintain a degree of objectivity because they are not directly involved in the client's life. Though there are exceptions, informal helpers usually have a personal relationship with the individual, so the assistance they provide is likely to reflect a personal bias. A related fact is that counselors usually don't have a preconceived idea of how a client should behave. Having no previous experience with the counselor, the client is free to try new modes of behaving and relating. This often does not occur with informal helpers, who may expect the person they are trying to help to act in a certain way. The person being helped might easily fall into the habits established in the relationship. This can create a restrictive environment.

Second, counselors are guided by a code of ethics, which is designed to protect the rights of clients (see American Counseling Association [ACA] code of ethics in Appendix F and American Psychological Association [APA] code of ethics in Appendix G). For example, the information that a client presents to a counselor must be held in confidence, except in extreme circumstances such as when the client plans to do serious harm to self or others. Knowing this, a client might feel more free to share thoughts and feelings with a professional counselor than an informal helper.

Third, formal counseling can be an intense and emotionally exhausting experience. After establishing a rapport, the counselor may find it necessary to confront the client with painful issues. Informal helpers may avoid confrontation to avoid jeopardizing the friendship. They often play a more supportive and reassuring role, at times even attempting to rescue the person they are helping. In doing so, the helper, despite good intentions, does not communicate the all-important belief that the client is a capable person. The helper may also rob the individual of an opportunity to get in touch with feelings.

A final difference lies in the repertoire of counseling strategies and techniques available to professional counselors and their ability to systematically utilize these strategies and techniques to promote client growth. For example, a client may have a phobia such as a fear of heights. The counselor may use a behavioral technique called systematic desensitization, which helps the client replace an anxiety response to heights with a relaxation response. Some clients may not be able to stand up for their rights or state their opinions and could therefore benefit from assertive training. Other clients may have marriage or family problems, and the professional counselor may utilize the various schools of marriage and family therapy. Lacking formal counselor training, informal helpers are unfamiliar with and thereby unable to utilize these strategies. Instead, they typically rely on advice giving as their main method of helping.

Personal Qualities of Effective Helpers

The following *Helping Formula* developed by Brammer (1988) provides another conceptual model for answering the question, "What is counseling?"

$$\underset{\text{of the Helper}}{\text{Personality}} + \underset{\text{Skills}}{\text{Helping}} = \underset{\text{Conditions}}{\text{Growth-Facilitating}} \rightarrow \underset{\text{Outcomes}}{\text{Specific}}$$

This formula suggests that taking the personality of the helper and adding some helping skills like counseling techniques can generate growth-facilitating conditions.

A feeling of mutual trust, respect, and freedom between the counselor and client characterize these growth-facilitating conditions (Brammer, 1988). When such conditions exist, desirable outcomes tend to emerge from the counseling process.

The Helping Formula emphasizes the importance of the personality of the helper (Brammer, 1988). Combs et al. (1969) suggested that the central technique of counseling is to use the "self as an instrument" of change. In other words, counselors use their personality to create a presence that conveys encouragement for, belief in, and support of the client. Rogers (1981) also commented on the importance of the counselor's personal qualities. He noted that the client's perception of the counselor's attitude was more important than the counselor's theories and methods. Rogers' point underscores the fact that clients are interested in and influenced by the personal style of the counselor.

A number of attempts have been made to identify the personal characteristics that promote positive outcomes in counseling. The Association for Counselor Education and Supervision (1964) suggested that counselors should have six qualities: belief in each individual, commitment to individual human values, open-mindedness, professional commitment, understanding of self, and alertness to the world. Combs et al. (1969) found that effective counselors perceived other people as dependable, friendly, worthy, and capable of solving their own problems. The authors also stated that effective counselors were more likely to identify with people, rather than things, and were more self-revealing than self-concealing. Allan (1967) emphasized the importance of the counselor's emotional stability as a prerequisite to effective counseling. It would not be realistic to imply that an effective counselor must be a certain type of person. At the same time, the literature does suggest certain basic qualities tend to be important to the counseling process. I have incorporated these basic qualities into what I believe are the 12 personal characteristics of an effective counselor.

1. *Encouraging.* Being encouraging may be the most important quality of an effective counselor. Encouragement helps clients learn to believe in their potential for growth and development. A number of Adlerian counselors have written about the power of encouragement (e.g., Dinkmeyer & Losoney, 1980).

2. *Artistic.* As mentioned, I believe that effective counselors tend to be sensitive and responsive to their clients. Being artistic implies being creative and flexible and adjusting counseling techniques to the unique needs of the client. Just as true artists give something of themselves to each thing they create, counselors must give of themselves to the counseling process. Effective counselors cannot insist on maintaining an emotional distance from the client if such a distance inhibits client growth. If necessary, counselors must allow themselves to experience the client's world directly and be personally affected by the counseling process, as they bring their humanness and vulnerability to the moment. Counselors who allow themselves to be human may also promote authenticity and genuineness in the counseling process.

3. *Emotionally Stable.* An emotionally unbalanced counselor will probably do more harm than good for the client. Unfortunately, some counselors enter the counseling profession in an attempt to work through serious mental

problems. These counselors may attempt to meet their own needs at the expense of their clients. Langs (1985) went as far as to suggest that a substantial number of clients spend much of their energy adjusting to the mood swings of their counselor. In some instances, clients might even believe they have to provide temporary counseling for the counselor (Langs, 1985). Role reversals of this type are obviously not in the best interest of the client. An inconsistent counselor will not only waste valuable time but create confusion and insecurity within the client.

4. *Empathic and Caring.* Effective counselors care about people and have the desire to help those in need. They are sensitive to the emotional states of others and can communicate an understanding of their struggles with life. Clients experience a sense of support and kindness from these counselors. This can help the client have the courage to face life realistically and explore new directions and possibilities.

5. *Self-Aware.* Being self-aware enables counselors to become aware of their limitations. Self-awareness can also help counselors monitor their needs, so they can gratify those needs in a manner that doesn't interfere with the counseling process. Self-awareness requires an ongoing effort by the counselor. The various ways counselors can promote their self-awareness include using meditation techniques and taking time for personal reflection.

6. *Self-disclosure.* Effective counselors are constructively open with their thoughts and feelings. When counselors model openness, they encourage their clients to be open. The resulting candidness can be critical to the counseling process.

7. *Courageous.* While it is important for clients to perceive their counselors as competent, counselors are not perfect, and they should not be viewed as perfect. Instead, they should try to model the courage to be imperfect (Dreikurs & Soltz, 1964). Counselors with the courage to communicate their weaknesses as well as their strengths are disclosing an authentic picture of themselves. They are also presenting a realistic view of the human condition and can help clients avoid self-defeating perfectionist tendencies. Another facet of the courage to be imperfect is the willingness of counselors to seek out counseling services for themselves if the need arises. Counselors should not feel they are too good for counseling, or they might develop a condescending attitude about counseling that could result in looking down at their clients. Obtaining counseling can also help counselors understand what it feels like to be in the role of client, contributing to a better understanding of the counseling process.

8. *Positive Self-Image.* A positive self-image can help counselors cope with their personal and professional life and maintain the emotional stability that is central to their job. Also, counselors who don't feel positive about themselves may look for the negative in their clients. Even worse, such counselors might attempt to degrade the client to enhance their own self-image.

9. *Patient.* Being patient can be valuable in the counseling process. Helping someone change is a complex process and requires significant effort. Clients

Table 1.2
Types of Professional Helpers

Type of Helper	Licensure and Degree Requirements	Skills and Responsibilities	Work Setting
Mental health counselor	Master's degree in counseling or related field.	Use of counseling and psychotherapeutic strategies.	Community mental health centers.
Private practitioners in counseling or marriage, child, and family counseling	Usually a master's degree in counseling; marriage, child, or family counseling; or related field. An increasing number of states require licensure of counseling.	Personal, marriage, child, or family counseling.	Private practice.
Psychiatric social worker	Usually a master's degree in social work. Many states require licensure.	Counseling and psychotherapy usually from a family perspective; knowledge about psychiatric service, and ability to assist with social services (food, shelter, child abuse and neglect, foster and nursing care).	Most work in hospitals, and social service agencies. Some have their own private practice.
Pastoral counselor	Master's degree in counseling or related field. Few states require certification or licensure.	Counseling and psychotherapy from a religious perspective. Some focus their practice on issues pertaining to marriage and the family (e.g., marital enrichment).	Churches or agencies with church affiliation.
Clinical and counseling psychologist	Psy.D., Ph.D., or Ed.D (Doctor of Psychology, Philosophy, or Education). All states require licensure or certification.	Counseling and psychotherapy, psychological testing, and mental health specialist.	University counseling centers, community mental health centers, hospitals, and private practice.

Psychiatrist	M.D. (Medical Degree) and 3–4 years specialized training in psychiatry in a full residency program. All states require licensure.	Treatment of serious mental disorders usually involving the use of medications, some counseling and psychotherapy, and consultation. Supervision of other mental health workers is usually involved.	Hospitals, community mental health centers, and private practice.
Psychiatric nurse	R.N. (Registered Nurse) degree. All states require licensure.	Assist in the psychiatric treatment of mental disorders by monitoring medication and providing counseling and psychotherapy.	Hospitals, community mental health centers.
School counselor	Many states require a master's degree in counseling. All states require certification in school counseling.	Personal and career counseling and consultation with school staff and parents.	Elementary, middle, and senior high schools.
School psychologist	Many states require master's degree in school psychology or related field. All states require certification as a school psychologist.	Psychological testing, counseling, consulting.	Elementary, middle, and high schools.

may make some progress and then regress to old habits. Counselors must be patient with the goal of achieving overall positive therapeutic movement.

10. *Nonjudgmental.* Counselors must be careful not to impose their values or beliefs on the client, even though they might wish to expose clients to new ideas at times. Being nonjudgmental communicates a respect for clients and allows them to actualize their unique potential.

11. *Self-Realization.* Bob Dylan (1971) captured the spirit of this personal characteristic when he said, "Those that aren't busy being born are busy dying." Effective counselors are busy being born. They reach out in new directions and explore new horizons. As they do, they realize that growth requires commitment, risk, and suffering. They discover they have to stretch to grow. Counselors can welcome life experiences and learn from them. They develop a broad outlook on life that can help their clients put their problems in perspective. Being alive also means counselors have an enthusiasm for life. This enthusiasm can create energy and optimism that can energize and create hope for a client.

12. *Tolerance for Ambiguity.* This can be an important characteristic of effective counselors. Ambiguity is often associated with the art of counseling. For example, the counselor never knows for sure what is the best technique for a client or exactly what was accomplished during a session. While the science of counseling can contribute to the objective understanding of the counseling process, counselors must be able to tolerate some ambiguity.

The Helping Profession

Counseling can also be understood within the context of the helping profession. The term *helping profession* encompasses several professional disciplines, including psychology, counseling, and psychiatry. Each discipline can be distinguished by its unique training programs and resulting specialties. Many individuals from these various groups provide similar services, such as counseling and psychotherapy.

Members of the helping profession often work together on multidisciplinary teams. For example, school counselors and school psychologists join forces to provide counseling services in school settings. Psychiatrists, psychiatric nurses, psychiatric social workers, psychologists, and mental health counselors blend their specialized skills to provide a comprehensive treatment plan in mental health settings. An overview of the degree requirements, specialized skills, and work settings for the members of the helping profession is provided in Table 1.2.

COUNSELING: PAST, PRESENT, AND FUTURE

The counseling profession has been characterized by a dynamic evolution. This section will describe some of these key events as well as attempt to predict some of the future trends in counseling.

Counseling from a Historical Perspective

A number of prominent individuals have made unique and lasting contributions to the counseling profession. The pioneering work of Freud, Adler, and Jung can be credited with establishing the foundation for modern clinical practice. These three men were colleagues in Vienna in the early 1900s, and each went on to develop a unique school of counseling and psychotherapy.

Freud developed psychoanalysis, which emphasized the role of sexuality in personality development. Adler developed his own school of psychology that he called individual psychology, which emphasized the importance of social interest in mental health. Jung is credited with originating the school of psychology called analytic psychology. Jung's work was influenced by various disciplines, including theology, philosophy, and anthropology. His theory is probably best known for its recognition of a collective unconscious, which suggested that all people share some common memories.

Numerous other schools of counseling have emerged since the pioneering work of Freud, Adler, and Jung. Perhaps more than any other theorist, Rogers has influenced the development of contemporary counseling approaches. His person-centered approach was a testament to the belief in the dignity and worth of the individual (Rogers, 1981). Rogers' approach has held wide appeal among individuals in the helping professions. He was particularly influential in the development of the third force, or humanistic school of counseling and psychotherapy.

A recent trend in counseling theory has related to the popularity of cognitive-behavioral approaches (e.g., Beck, 1976). These approaches emphasize the role of cognition and behavior in creating and maintaining emotional distress. Techniques that focus on modifying cognitions and behaviors have been developed to treat a wide range of mental disorders such as depression and anxiety.

Many other individuals have played significant roles in the evolution of the counseling profession. Table 1.3 identifies these individuals and their unique contributions to counseling as well as important events affecting the profession.

Key Historic Events.   Several historic events have played important roles in the evolution of counseling. Among these are the vocational guidance movement, the standardized testing movement, the mental health movement, and key legislative acts.

The vocational guidance movement had its inception in the efforts of Frank Parson, a Boston educator who started the Vocational Bureau in 1908. Parson contended that an individual who took the time to choose a vocation, as opposed to a job, would be more likely to experience success and work satisfaction (Brown & Brooks, 1990). Career counseling, which focuses on helping clients explore their unique potential in relation to the world of work, evolved from the vocational movement.

The standardized testing movement can be traced to Sir Frances Golton, an English biologist, and his study of heredity. Golton developed simple tests to differentiate characteristics of genetically related and unrelated people (Anastasi, 1988).

Table 1.3 (pp. 16 – 18)
Individuals and Events Central to the Evolution of Counseling

Individual	Contribution
Hippocrates (400 B.C.)	Classified types of mental illnesses and personality disorders
Socrates (400 B.C.)	Encouraged self-awareness as the purest form of knowledge
Plato (350 B.C.)	Postulated human behavior in terms of internal states
Aristotle (350 B.C.)	Designed first rational psychology to manage emotions
St. Augustine (400 A.D.)	Prescribed introspection to master emotions
Leonardo da Vinci (1500)	Combined science with art to recreate human reality
Shakespeare (1600)	Created a literature of psychologically complex characters
Philippe Pinel (1800)	Described various forms of neurosis and psychosis
Anton Mesmer (1800)	Used hypnotic suggestion to cure psychological symptoms
Fyodor Dostoyevsky (1850)	Wrote novels with complex character studies of anxiety and dread
Charles Darwin (1850)	Set forth an evolutionary theory of individual differences
Jean Charcot (1850)	Scientifically studied hypnosis to give it respectability
Soren Kierkegaard (1850)	Developed an existential concept of giving meaning to being
G. Stanley Hall (1880)	Began first child guidance clinic
James Cattell (1890)	Coined the term *mental tests;* in 1903 became known for research on mental tests and individual differences
Jesse Davis (1890)	Became the first school counselor
Emil Kraepelin (1900)	Systematized the classification of mental disorders
William James (1900)	Postulated comprehensive theory of emotions
Ivan Pavlov (1900)	Described behavioral theory of conditioned reflexes
Sigmund Freud (1900)	Developed the first systematic form of therapeutic counseling
Alfred Binet (1908)	Developed first intelligence test
Clifford Beers (1905)	Published *A Mind That Found Itself;* became acknowledged leader of mental hygiene movement
Eugen Bleuler (1908)	Proposed the name *schizophrenia* and related the prognosis to the extent of the symptoms
Frank Parsons (1908)	Established field of vocational guidance
Carl Jung (1920)	Developed the school of Analytic Psychology, which included the concept of the collective unconscious

Individual	Contribution
Alfred Adler (1920)	Developed a school of psychology that emphasized the importance of social interest
J. L. Moreno (1920)	Proposed an approach to therapy that he called *psychodrama*
John Watson (1920)	Proposed a behavioristic theory to predict and control behavior
Hermann Rorschach (1921)	Published *Psychodiagnostics,* initiating usage of ink blots to assess mental disorders
Robert Hoppock (1930)	Studied levels of job satisfaction
Gordon Allport (1937)	Introduced a personality theory that positioned personality traits as the basic components
B. F. Skinner (1940)	Formulated theory of operant conditioning
E. G. Williamson (1940)	Published standard text on school counseling
Stark R. Hathaway & J. C. McKinley (1942)	Published the Minnesota Multiphasic Personality Inventory
Clark Hall (1943)	Introduced the Theory of Learning
Gregory Batson (1945)	Emphasized family influence on psychological disturbances
Kurt Lewin (1945)	Used training group format for personal development
Wolfgang Kohler (1947)	Founded the Gestalt psychology movement along with Kurt Kollka and Max Werhheimer
Rollo May (1948)	Expanded work on existential therapy
David Wechsler (1949)	Developed the Wechsler Intelligence tests
Erick Erikson (1950)	Proposed theory of personality development
Jean Piaget (1950)	Proposed theory of cognitive development
Victor Frankl (1950)	Introduced system of existential therapy
Milton Erickson (1950)	Focused on linguistic aspects of therapeutic encounter
Carl Rogers (1950)	Proposed theory of client-centered counseling
Donald Super (1950)	Proposed career development theory
Abraham Maslow (1955)	Studied self-actualized individuals
Arnold Lazarus (1958)	First used terms "behavior therapy" and "behavior therapist"
Passage of National Defense and Education Act (NDEA) (1958)	Provided financial assistance for training counselors
J.P. Guilford (1959)	Proposed a three-dimensional "structure of intellect"

Table 1.3 *continued*

Individual	Contribution
Joseph Wolpe (1960)	Devised systematic theory of behavior therapy
Jay Haley (1960)	Started family counseling movement
Eric Berne (1960)	Introduced Transactional Analysis
Albert Ellis (1960)	Introduced Rational-Emotive Therapy
Albert Bandura (1960)	Emphasized the importance of social modeling in learning
Rudolf Dreikurs (1964)	Related Alfred Adler's theory to parent education and child counseling
Fritz Perls (1965)	Popularized Gestalt therapy
George Gazda (1965)	Described methods of group counseling
Robert Carkhuff (1965)	Identified specific skills of helping
John Krumboltz (1965)	Published theory of behavioral counseling
William Glasser (1965)	Founded Reality Therapy
American Psychological Association (1966)	Published *Standards for Educational and Psychological Tests and Manuals*
Donald Blocher (1966)	Presented a model for developmental counseling
Allen Ivey (1971)	Introduced microcounseling as a method of learning counseling skills
Aaron Beck (1976)	Developed a cognitive model for treating depression
Hilde Bruche (1979)	Published work on eating disorders
Derald Sue (1981)	Published work in cross cultural counseling
Counselor Certification (1982)	American Association for Counseling and Development (APGA) establishes the National Board for Certified Counselors to certify counselors
APGA name change to AACD (1983)	APGA changed name to American Association for Counseling and Development (AACD)
AACD ethical standards (1988)	AACD revised its ethical standards
Licensure-Certification for counselors (1992)	Thirty-five states instituted licensure or certification laws in professional counseling
AACD name change to ACA (1992)	AACD changed name to American Counseling Association (ACA)

Note. From *Introduction to Therapeutic Counseling* (pp. 15–16) by J. A. Kottler and R. W. Brown, 1985, Monterey, CA: Brooks/Cole. Copyright 1985 by Brooks/Cole. Reprinted by permission.

Many others have made significant contributions to the testing movement. Cattel set forth the concept of mental testing in 1890 (Anastasi), and Binet developed the first intelligence scale in 1905.

World Wars I and II played important roles in the testing movement. The army's need to classify new recruits for training programs resulted in the development of mass intelligence and ability testing. Examples are the Army Alpha and Army Beta tests during the First World War and the Army General Classification Test in the Second World War. After World War II, the use of tests proliferated throughout American society. Testing soon became an integral part of the public school system. Tests were also used in a variety of other settings, including mental health services and employment agencies. The testing movement slowed to some extent during the 1960s, when it became apparent that many standardized tests reflected a cultural bias (Minton & Schneider, 1981). Since that time, there appears to be an increased sensitivity to multicultural issues pertaining to the use of tests.

The mental health movement resulted from the contributions of several forces. In 1908, Clifford Beers wrote *A Mind that Found Itself*, describing the horrors of his 3 years as a patient in a mental hospital. Beers' efforts resulted in an increase in public awareness of the issues relating to mental disorders. Beers later formed the Society for Mental Hygiene, which promoted comprehensive treatment programs for the mentally ill (Baruth & Robinson, 1987).

Another major factor in the mental health movement was the development of medications in 1952 that could treat serious disorders such as schizophrenia (Rosenhan & Seligman, 1989). Today, it is uncommon for psychiatric patients to remain in a hospital for more than 1 or 2 months. Although these medications do not cure mental disorders, they often can control symptoms to the degree that a person can function in society.

Unfortunately, it has been difficult to develop effective follow-up programs for psychiatric patients after their discharge from a hospital. The result has been an alarming number of mentally disturbed people wandering the streets as homeless "street people." Several studies have estimated that 25–50 percent of homeless people are mentally ill (Frazier, 1985; Ball & Harassy, 1984). Many mental health professionals are attempting to develop more effective follow-up and outreach services for the chronically mentally ill.

Key legislative acts have also contributed to the evolution of the counseling profession, in particular, the National Defense Education Act (NDEA) of 1958. This act was designed to improve the teaching of science in public schools, motivated by a popular belief that the United States was lagging behind Russia's achievements in science. This belief developed after Americans learned of the Soviet Union's success in launching the first space satellite, Sputnik. The NDEA had a major impact on the counseling profession by providing funds to train school counselors, resulting in a marked increase in the number of counselors employed in U.S. schools.

Future Trends

In this section, we go beyond describing what counseling is and attempt to predict some trends as we enter the 1990s and beyond. Although it is difficult to speculate what the future will entail, several researchers have identified possible trends in research, ethics, multicultural counseling, mental health services, and mental disorders.

Research.   Gelso and Fassinger (1990) provided a comprehensive review of the counseling research conducted during the 1980s. They noted that the decade was characterized by increased interest in alternative research methodologies, which incorporate more field-based and fewer laboratory-based designs. These authors suggested that the interest in alternative research designs will continue into the 1990s along with "a trend toward the use of more refined methodological strategies and, in particular, advanced statistical procedures" (p. 374).

Ethics.   Goodyear and Sinnett (1984) identified emerging ethical issues that need to be addressed. Some of these issues are appropriate use of the media to promote

An infant's genetic makeup may be useful in the identification and treatment of mental disorders.

private practice, the use of sexual surrogates in sex therapy, and the role of the counselor in cases involving the question of euthanasia with terminally ill patients.

Multicultural Counseling.   Heath, Neimeyer, and Pedersen (1988) surveyed 53 experts to obtain their predictions regarding future trends in multicultural counseling. Results of the survey suggested the experts were optimistic there would be an increase in the quality of training in multicultural counseling characterized by greater use of skill development and role-playing techniques. The experts also predicted that future trends in multicultural research would focus on gaining a better understanding of the ethnic groups that are increasing most rapidly in proportion of the population, especially Hispanic and Asian Americans. In addition, the experts surveyed expect positive changes in terms of professional networking and recognition of multicultural issues.

Mental Health Services.   Watkins (1988) contended that there will be a increase in Health Maintenance Organizations (HMOs) and Independent Providers Associations (IPAs). He believed the trend will create opportunities for members of the helping professions to provide services to these organizations. According to Watkins, counselors who focus on short-term treatment, accountability, and symptom relief will be especially valuable to these organizations.

Marx, Shaughnessy, and Riley (1990) provided projections regarding mental health trends in the 1990s. They contended that one of the major challenges will relate to monetary resources. These authors suggested that the federal government would reduce its support for mental health programs, requiring state and local communities to make up the differences.

West, Hosie, and Mackey (1988) commented on future needs relating to the training of counselors who plan to work in mental health services. They suggested that counselors would be better prepared if graduate programs required additional courses in psychopathology, assessment and diagnosis, and psychotropic medications.

Mental Disorders.   Yager (1989) and Pincus et al. (1989) made projections about the impact of advances in science on the diagnosis and treatment of mental disorders. A summary of their predictions follows.

- Genetics will play an increasingly important role in the diagnosis and treatment of mental disorders. For example, scientists could use genetic engineering to alter the gene structure to prevent or treat mental disorders, and clinicians will be able to identify children who are at risk to develop mental disorders.

- Neurobiologists will gain a more complete understanding of the role of neurotransmitters, or agents that facilitate communication between neurons, in the development and treatment of mental disorders.

- Psychopharmacology researchers will develop more effective medications with fewer unwanted side effects to treat mental disorders. Scientists will also develop new medications that will successfully treat mental disorders previously unresponsive to medication. Examples are substance abuse disorders including alcoholism, personality disorders, and sexual disorders.

- Sociobiologists will identify factors that trigger the onset of mental disorders.
- Advances in computer technology and software development will enable clinicians to make better use of computers in the diagnosis and treatment of mental disorders.

CHAPTER SUMMARY

This chapter provided our overview of counseling. It began by addressing the question, "What is counseling?" Counseling was described as a complex process that does not afford a simple definition. The chapter did provide several models that can be used to conceptualize counseling. Counseling was described as both an art and science emphasizing the importance of the subjective and the objective dimensions. Counseling was then differentiated from psychotherapy in terms of clients, goals, treatment, and settings. Counseling was also presented as part of the helping profession which included psychiatrists, psychologists, mental health counselors, and school counselors.

The chapter concluded by conceptualizing counseling from historical and futuristic perspectives. A description of some of the key individuals and historic events in the evolution of counseling was provided. Several studies were also used to predict future trends in the counseling profession.

REFERENCES

Allan, T. (1967). Effectiveness of counselor trainees as a function of psychological openness. *Journal of Counseling Psychology, 14,* 35–40.

Anastasi, A. (1988). *Psychological testing* (6th ed.). New York: Macmillan.

Ball, F. L. J., & Harassy, B. E. (1984). A survey of the problems and needs of homeless consumers of acute psychiatric services. *Hospital and Community Psychiatry, 35,* 917–921.

Baruth, L. G., & Robinson, E. H. (1987). *An introduction to the counseling profession*. Englewood Cliffs, NJ: Prentice-Hall.

Beck, A. T. (1976). *Depression: Clinical, experimental and theoretical aspects*. New York: Harper & Row.

Beers, C. (1908). *A mind that found itself*. New York: Longman Green.

Brammer, L. M. (1988). *The helping relationship: Process and skills* (4th ed.). Englewood Cliffs, NJ: Prentice-Hall.

Brown, D., & Brooks, L. (1990). Introduction to career development: Origins, evolution and current approaches. In D. Brown and L. Brooks (Eds.), *Career Choice and Development* (2nd ed.). San Francisco: Jossey-Ball.

Claiborn, C. D. (1987). Science and practice: Reconsidering the Pepinskys. *Journal of Counseling and Development, 65*(6), 286–288.

Combs, A., Soper, D., Gooding, C., Benton, J., Dickman, J., & Usher, R. (1969). *Florida studies in the helping professions*. Gainesville: University of Florida Press.

Dinkmeyer, D. C., & Dinkmeyer, D. C., Jr. (1982). *Developing an understanding of self and others* (DUSO). Circle Pines, MN: American Guidance Service.

Dinkmeyer, D. C., & Losoney, L. E. (1980). *The encouragement book: Becoming a positive person*. Englewood Cliffs, NJ: Prentice-Hall.

Dreikurs, R., & Soltz, V. (1964). *Children the challenge*. New York: Hawthorn Books.

Dylan, B. (1971). *It's alright ma* [Song]. Los Angeles, CA: Columbia Records.

Frazier, S. H. (1985). Responding to the needs of the homeless mentally ill public. *Health Reports, 100,* 462–469.

Gelso, C. J., & Fassinger, R. E. (1990). Counseling psychology: Theory and research on intervention. *American Review of Psychology, 41*, 355–386.

Goodyear, R. K., & Sinnett, E. R. (1984). Current and emerging ethical issues for counseling psychology. *The Counseling Psychologist, 12*, 87–98.

Heath, A. E., Neimeyer, G. J., & Pedersen, P. B. (1988). The future of cross-cultural counseling. *Journal of Counseling and Development, 67*, 27–30.

Kottler, J. A., & Brown, R. W. (1985). *Introduction to therapeutic counseling*. Monterey, CA: Brooks/Cole.

Langs, R. (1985). *Madness and cure*. New York: Newconcept Press.

Marx, D. J., Shaughnessy, M. F., & Riley, J. R. (1990). Mental health issues in the 1990s. *National Social Science Journal, 1*, 112–122.

Minton, H. L., & Schneider, F. W. (1981). *Differential Psychology*. Monterey, CA: Brooks/Cole.

Nystul, M. S. (1986). Reaching in—reaching out: Counseling an autistic child. *American Mental Health Counselors Association Journal, 8*, 18–26.

Nystul, M. S. (1987). Creative arts therapy and the existential encounter. *The Creative Child and Adult Quarterly, 12*(3), 243–249.

Patterson, C. H. (1980). *Theories of counseling and psychotherapy* (3rd ed.). New York: Harper & Row.

Pepinsky, H. B., & Pepinsky, P. N. (1954). *Counseling: Theory and practice*. New York: Ronald Press.

Pincus, H. A., Goodwin, F. K., Barchas, J. D., Cohen, D. J., Judd, L. L., Meltzer, H. Y., & Vaillant, G. E. (1989). The future of the science of psychiatry. In J. A. Talbott (Ed.), *Future directions for psychiatry*. Washington, DC: American Psychiatric Press.

Rogers, C. (1981). *A way of being*. Boston: Houghton Mifflin.

Rosenhan, D. L., & Seligman, M. E. P. (1989). *Abnormal Psychology* (2nd ed.). New York, NY: W. W. Norton.

Watkins, C. E. (1988). Contemporary issues in counseling psychology: A selected review. *Professional Psychology: Research and Practice, 19*, 441–448.

West, J. D., Hosie, T. W., & Mackey, J. A. (1988). The counselor's role in mental health: An evaluation. *Counselor Education and Supervision, 27*, 233–289.

Yager, J. (1989). A futuristic view of psychiatry. In J. Yager (Ed.), *The future of psychiatry as a medical specialty*. Washington, DC: American Psychiatric Press.

CHAPTER TWO

The Counseling Process

CHAPTER OVERVIEW

This chapter provides an overview of the counseling process as well as a description of some of the common problems that beginning counselors experience. It will explore what can occur in a counseling session as well as some of the special skills utilized in counseling.

Highlights of the chapter include

- A description of the six stages of the counseling process
- Common problems for beginning counselors such as having unrealistic expectations, getting lost in the counseling process, rescuing clients, and using inappropriate phrases

THE SIX STAGES OF THE COUNSELING PROCESS

Most counseling sessions last approximately 50 minutes (Linder, 1954). A counseling session is therefore sometimes referred to as the 50-minute hour. What actually takes place in a session depends on the client's needs and the counselor's personal approach to counseling. Although there is some variation during a session, there is a basic structure that most counseling approaches have in common. This structure was described by Cormier and Hackney (1987) as a five-stage process: relationship building, assessment, goal setting, interventions, and termination and follow-up. These stages have been expanded in the following six-stage model of the counseling process.

Stage one: Relationship building

Stage two: Assessment and diagnosis

Stage three: Formulation of counseling goals

Stage four: Intervention and problem solving

Stage five: Termination and follow-up

Stage six: Research and evaluation

Counseling can be conceptualized as a series of stages or steps that lead one through the counseling process

A typical counseling session can involve all six stages except termination. The focus of counseling may shift as the counseling process progresses over time. For example, during the first few sessions with a client, a counselor may place the primary emphasis on building a positive counseling relationship, assessment and diagnosis, and formulating counseling goals. During the later phase of the counseling process, the counselor may shift the emphasis to intervention and problem solving, termination and follow-up, and research and evaluation. A more complete description of these six stages follows.

Stage One: Relationship Building

The counseling relationship is the heart of the counseling process. It supplies the vitality and the support necessary for counseling to work. It is the critical factor associated with successful outcomes in counseling (Kokotovic & Tracey, 1990). Gelso and Carter (1985) commented on the importance of the counseling relationship when they said, ". . . theoreticians and practitioners probably all currently agree that the counselor-client relationship is important to the outcome of most or all therapeutic efforts" (p. 185).

Although there appears to be a general consensus that the counseling relationship is important, it is less clear how important it is and in what way (Gelso & Carter, 1985). Research efforts that have attempted to address these issues can be grouped into two general categories, counselor-offered conditions and counselor- and client-offered conditions.

Counselor-Offered Conditions.   Counselor-offered conditions relate to how the counselor influences the counseling process. The majority of the literature on the counseling relationship has focused on counselor-offered conditions relating to core conditions for effective counseling and the Social Influence Model. An overview of the issues associated with these two important topics follows.

Core Conditions.   Rogers (1957) identified what he believed were core conditions for successful counseling: empathic understanding, unconditional positive regard, and congruence. Rogers (1957) suggested that these core conditions were necessary and sufficient for constructive personality change to occur. No other conditions were necessary. Later, Carkhuff (1969, 1971) expanded the core conditions to include respect, immediacy, confrontation, concreteness, and self-disclosure. Carkhuff (1969, 1971) also pioneered the development of listening skills that could be used to promote these core conditions. See Appendix A for information on listening skills. An overview of the eight conditions is provided in Table 2.1. This table is followed by a description of each of these core conditions.

Empathy.   Egan described empathic understanding as a process that "involves both listening and understanding *and* communicating understanding to the client." (1990, p. 123). Empathy is considered the most important core condition in terms of promoting positive outcomes (Orlando & Howard, 1986). Gelso and Fretz (in press) observed that virtually all major schools of counseling note the importance of empathy in the counseling process. Empathic understanding can be understood as a multistage process (Barrett-Lennard, 1981; Gladstein, 1983) consisting of different types

Table 2.1
Core Conditions

Core Conditions	Description	Purpose
Empathy	Communicating a sense of caring and understanding	To establish rapport; gain an understanding of the client; and encourage self-exploration in the client
Unconditional positive regard	Communicating to clients that they have value and worth as individuals	To promote acceptance of the client as a person of worth as distinct from accepting the client's behavior
Congruence	Behaving in a manner consistent with how one thinks and feels	To be genuine (not phony) in interactions with the client
Respect	Focusing on the positive attributes of the client	To focus on the client's strengths (not weaknesses)
Immediacy	Communicating in the here-and-now about what is occurring in the counseling session	To promote direct mutual communication between the counselor and client
Confrontation	Pointing out discrepancies in what the client is saying and doing (between statements and nonverbal behavior); and how the client is viewed by the counselor and client	To help clients clearly and accurately understand themselves and the world around them
Concreteness	Helping clients discuss themselves in specific terms	To help clients focus on pertinent issues
Self-disclosure	Making the self known to others	To promote increasing counseling relevant communication from the client; enhancing the client's evaluation of the counselor; and increasing the client's willingness to seek counseling

of empathy. Gladstein (1983) identified the following stages of empathy: the counselor has an emotional reaction to the client's situation; the counselor attempts to understand the client's situation from the client's perspective; the counselor communicates empathy to the client; and the client feels a sense of caring and understanding from the counselor. Several kinds of empathy have also been identified, for example, primary and advanced empathy (Egan, 1990). Egan described primary empathy as a process that involves the counselor attending, listening, and communicating accurate perceptions of the client's messages. Advanced empathy involves the characteristics associated with primary empathy as well as utilizing the skills of self-disclosure, directives, or interpretations.

Unconditional Positive Regard.   Unconditional positive regard involves the counselor communicating to clients that they are of value and worth as individuals. This concept has been referred to by several other names, including nonpossessive warmth, acceptance, prizing, respect, and regard. There has been some controversy regarding the core condition of unconditional positive regard. Gelso and Fretz (in press) contend that this concept is neither desirable nor obtainable. Martin (1989) counters the critics by suggesting that the concept has been misunderstood. According to Martin, unconditional positive regard does not imply that the counselor reacts permissively, accepting all the client's behavior. Instead, it means that the counselor's unconditional positive regard involves acceptance of the client while setting limits on certain behaviors (see Rogers, Gendlin, Kiesler, & Truax, 1967 for additional information on unconditional positive regard).

Congruence.   Congruence involves counselors behaving in a manner consistent with how they think and feel. This condition has also been referred to as genuineness. An example of not functioning congruently is a counselor who says, "I'm glad to see you," when a client arrives for an appointment, even through the counselor does not like the client.

Respect.   Respect is similar to unconditional positive regard in that it focuses on the positive attributes of the client. Counselors can communicate respect by making positive statements about the client and openly and honestly acknowledging, appreciating, and tolerating individual differences (Okun, 1987).

Immediacy.   Carkhuff (1969, 1971) developed the concept of immediacy, which is similar to Ivey's (1971) notion of direct, mutual communication. Immediacy involves communication between the counselor and client that focuses on the here-and-now. It allows the counselor to directly address issues of importance to the counseling relationship. Immediacy can involve counselors describing how they feel in relation to the client in the moment. For example, if a client does not appear interested in counseling, the counselor might say, "I'm getting concerned that you are not finding our sessions meaningful. How are you feeling about what is going on in counseling now?"

Confrontation.   The core condition of confrontation involves the counselor pointing out discrepancies in what a client is saying. There can be discrepancies between what the client is saying and doing (Gazda, Asbury, Blazer, Childress, & Walters, 1979); between statements and nonverbal behavior (Ivey, 1988); and between how clients see themselves versus how the counselor sees them (Egan, 1990).

Confrontation is a difficult and risky counseling technique that is used most effectively by high-functioning counselors (Berenson & Mitchell, 1968). Confrontation can have a negative effect on the counseling process, for example, when a client misreads the confrontation and feels attacked or rejected by the counselor (Egan, 1990).

Concreteness.   Concreteness refers to the counselor helping clients discuss their concerns in specific terms. Clients can feel overwhelmed with their problems and have difficulty putting things into perspective. When this occurs, concreteness can help the counselor create a focus for the client in the counseling process.

Self-Disclosure.   Jourard (1958) developed the concept of self-disclosure, which involves making the self known to another. Danish, D'Augelli, and Brock (1976) differentiated two types of self-disclosure statements: self-disclosing and self-involving. In self-disclosing statements, counselors disclose factual information about themselves. In self-involving statements, counselors describe what they are experiencing in relation to the client in the counseling process.

The research literature has provided some support for the efficacy of self-involving as compared to self-disclosing statements. Self-involving statements tended to promote increased counseling-relevant communication from clients (McCarthy, 1979, 1982); clients having a more positive evaluation of the counselor (McCarthy, 1982; Reynolds & Fischer, 1983); and an increased willingness of clients to seek counseling from the counselor (Weiner, 1978).

Research on Core Conditions.   As mentioned, Rogers (1957) contended that the core conditions are all that is necessary or sufficient for constructive personality change. Many researchers have conducted studies to evaluate this premise. The early research of Truax and Carkhuff (1967) and Truax and Mitchell (1971) provided support for Rogers' theory. During the 1970s, researchers began to report negative results with criticism of earlier studies for methodological flaws or failure to test the efficacy of core conditions in non-Rogerian approaches (Garfield & Bergin, 1971; Mintz, Luborsky, & Auerbach, 1971; Sloane, Staples, Cristol, Yorkston, & Whipple, 1975).

More recent research has provided moderate support for Rogers' theory, especially when the establishment of core conditions is based on the perceptions of the client versus outside judges (Gurman, 1977; Orlando & Howard, 1986; Beutler, Cargo, & Arizmendi, 1986). After reviewing the vast amount of literature on this topic, several scholars have concluded that the core conditions are neither necessary nor sufficient but do facilitate the promotion of positive counseling outcomes (Gelso & Carter, 1985; Gelso & Fretz, in press).

Social Influence Model.   Strong's (1968) Social Influence Model is another theory that emphasizes the importance of counselor-offered conditions in the counseling process. Strong's model has two stages, representing an integration of social psychology into counseling theory. During the first stage, the counselor attempts to be perceived by the client as expert, attractive, and trustworthy. When this occurs, the counselor establishes a power base. In the second stage of Strong's model, the counselor uses the power base to exert positive influence on the client within the counseling process. Extensive research efforts have been conducted to test both stages of Strong's model (see Corrigan, Dell, Lewis, & Schmidt, 1980; Heppner & Dixon, 1981; Heppner & Claiborn, 1989 for literature reviews). For example, Heppner and Claiborn provided an overview of studies that have evaluated each stage of Strong's model.

Studies evaluating the first stage of Strong's model attempted to identify what factors promote the client's perception of the counselor as expert, attractive, and trustworthy. Counselors tended to be perceived as *expert* when they had objective evidence of training and utilized prestigious cues (Angle & Goodyear, 1984; Littrell, Caffrey, & Hopper, 1987); used frequent, consistent, and responsive nonverbal behavior such as touch, smiling, and body leans (Roll, Crowley, & Rappl, 1985; Strohmer & Biggs, 1983; Tyson & Wall, 1983); and used narrative analogies and empathic responses (Suit & Paradise, 1985). Counselors were perceived as *attractive* when they had objective evidence of training (Angle & Goodyear; Paradise, Conway, & Zweig, 1986); had status (McCarthy, 1982); and were self-disclosing (Andersen & Andersen, 1985; Curran & Loganbell, 1985). Counselors appeared more *trustworthy* when they used credible introductions and reputational cues (Bernstein & Figioli, 1983; Littrell, Caffrey, & Hopper, 1987); responsive nonverbal behavior (Hackman & Claiborn, 1982); and verbal and nonverbal cues associated with confidentiality (La Fromboise & Dixon, 1981; Merluzzi & Brischetto, 1983).

As noted, the second stage of Strong's model suggests that once counselors establish a power base by appearing expert, attractive, and trustworthy, they can exert a positive influence on the client. The majority of the studies reviewed by Heppner and Claiborn (1989) provided support for the second stage of Strong's model. For example, expertness, attractiveness, and trustworthiness are related to client satisfaction (Heppner & Heesacker, 1983; McNeill, May, & Lee, 1987); changes in the client's self-concept (Dorn & Day, 1985); favorable counseling outcomes (La Crosse, 1980); and less premature terminators (McNeill, May, & Lee, 1987).

Counselor- and Client-Offered Conditions.   The working alliance is another concept that can be used to describe the counseling relationship. It goes beyond focusing on counselor-offered conditions and includes counselor- and client-offered conditions. Several models of the working alliance have emerged from the literature (Greenson, 1967; Bordin, 1979; and Gelso & Carter, 1985). Bordin's model has received considerable attention (Kokotovic & Tracey, 1990). Bordin (1979) suggested that the working alliance was composed of three parts: agreement between the counselor and client in terms of the goals of counseling; agreement between the counselor and client in terms of the tasks of counseling; and the emotional bond between the counselor and client. Gelso and Fretz (in press) expanded on Bordin's model by noting that the strength of the working alliance depends on the degree of agreement relating to goals and tasks of counseling and the level of emotional attachment between the counselor and client.

Several studies have investigated counselor and client characteristics associated with the working alliance and the relationship between the working alliance and counseling outcomes. Gelso and Fretz (in press) noted that counselor characteristics included concern, compassion, and willingness to persist as well as promoting the core conditions described earlier. Client characteristics included having a past history of positive interpersonal relationships (Moras & Strupp, 1982); being able to formulate positive attachment and trust with others and willing to assume responsibility in the counseling process (Gelso & Carter, 1985); and not being prone to hostile or negative behavior (Marziali, Marmar, & Krupnick, 1981; Strupp, 1980). Outcome research has provided evidence that a positive working alliance is associated with counseling efficacy (Horvath & Greenberg, 1986; Hartley & Strupp, 1983).

Stage Two: Assessment and Diagnosis

Assessment and diagnosis contribute to several important aspects of the counseling process. They can help a counselor develop an in-depth understanding of a client and identify mental disorders that require attention. This understanding can facilitate goal setting and also suggest types of intervention strategies.

Assessment procedures can be divided into two categories: standardized and non-standardized measures (Kottler & Brown, 1985). Standardized measures include psychological tests that have a standardized norm group. Nonstandardized measures do not have a standardized norm group and include strategies such as the clinical interview and assessment of life history.

Diagnosis is a medical term that means ". . . identification of the disease-causing pathogens responsible for a physical illness" (Nathan & Harris, 1980, p. 110). Rosenhan and Seligman (1989) identified four reasons for making a diagnosis: facilitating communication shorthand, indicating possible treatment strategies, communicating etiology, and aiding in scientific investigation. Additional information regarding assessment and diagnosis can be found in Chapter 3.

Stage Three: Formulation of Counseling Goals

Cormier and Hackney (1987) described three functions that goals serve in the counseling process: motivational, educational, and evaluative.

First, goals can have a motivational function, especially when clients are involved in establishing the counseling goals. Clients appear to work harder on goals they helped create (Cormier & Hackney, 1987). They may also be more motivated when they have specific, concrete goals to work toward. Concrete goals can help clients focus their energy on specific issues. It is also important for counselors to encourage clients to make a verbal commitment to work on a specific counseling goal. Clients tend to be more motivated to work when they have made a commitment to do so (Strong & Claiborn, 1982).

The second function of a counseling goal is educational. From this perspective, clients can learn new skills and behaviors that they can use to enhance their functioning. For example, a counseling goal might be to become more assertive. During assertiveness training clients can learn skills to enhance their functioning in interpersonal situations.

The third function of a counseling goal is evaluative. Clear goals allow the counselor and client an opportunity to evaluate progress. Goals can also be useful in implementing research strategies, and they provide a means for counselor accountability.

We can also conceptualize counseling goals as either process or outcome goals (Cormier & Hackney, 1987). *Process goals* establish the conditions necessary to make the counseling process work. These goals relate to the issues of formulating a positive relationship by promoting the core conditions, as described earlier in this chapter. Process goals are primarily the counselor's responsibility. *Outcome goals* specify what the client hopes to accomplish in counseling. The counselor and client should agree on these goals and modify them as necessary. George and Cristiani

(1990) identified five types of outcome goals: facilitating behavior change, enhancing coping skills, promoting decision-making, improving relationships, and facilitating the client's potential. The following overview expands on these five outcome goals.

1. *Facilitating behavior change.* Some form of behavior change is usually necessary for clients to resolve their concerns. The amount of change necessary varies from client to client. For example, one client might need counseling to learn how to deal effectively with a child, while another might require psychotherapy to change an unhealthy, stressful lifestyle.

2. *Enhancing coping skills.* Erikson (1968) identified several developmental tasks and associated coping mechanisms unique to the various stages of development. Blocher (1974) later created a developmental counseling approach that identified coping skills necessary to proceed through the life span. For example, intimacy and commitment are developmental tasks of young adulthood. Coping behaviors necessary to meet these developmental tasks include appropriate sexual behavior, risk-taking behavior, and value-consistent behavior such as giving and helping. In more general terms, many clients may require help coping with life. They may have problems dealing with stress, anxiety, or a dysfunctional lifestyle. In these situations, clients may benefit from a stress management program that includes relaxation, meditation, and exercise.

3. *Promoting decision-making.* Some clients have difficulty making decisions. They may feel that no matter what they decide, it will be wrong. They may even think they are "going crazy." Difficulty making decisions is often a normal reaction to a stressful life situation, for example, a recent divorce. In these situations, the counselor may want to reassure clients that they are not going crazy. Helping clients feel normal can encourage them and alleviate unnecessary worry. For clients who need help developing decision-making skills, the counselor may wish to take a more active role. It may be appropriate to involve family members if the client is suffering from a serious mental disorder such as an organic brain syndrome.

4. *Improving relationships.* Adler (1964) once suggested that the barometer of mental health is social interest. He believed that a person who did not have a close relationship with anyone was at risk for mental problems. Glasser (1965) supported this notion when he noted that all people needed one or more reciprocal relationships in which they feel loved and understood and experience a sense of caring. Counselors can use a variety of counseling strategies to help clients improve their interpersonal relations. These strategies include social-skill training programs (Argyle, 1981); group counseling that focuses on interpersonal relations (Rogers, 1970); couple therapy (Sager, 1976); and marital therapy (Humphrey, 1983).

5. *Facilitating the client's potential.* Goals in this category are more abstract and relate to the concepts of self-realization and self-actualization. Self-realization implies helping clients become all they can be as they maximize their creative potential. There can be roadblocks to self-realization that require the

counselor's attention. For example, clients might become discouraged and want to quit at the first sign of failure. In these instances, the counselor can help clients gain a more realistic understanding of what is required to be successful. Maslow (1968) developed the concept of self-actualization, which related to the need to fulfill one's potential. He believed that as people's basic needs were met, they would move toward self-actualization. Rogers (1980) incorporated the concept of self-actualization into his person-centered counseling approach. He believed that if the counselor established certain conditions, such as communicating nonpossessive warmth, unconditional positive regard, and empathy, then the client could move toward self-actualization and become a healthy, integrated person.

Stage Four: Intervention and Problem Solving

Once the counselor and client have formulated a counseling goal, they can determine what intervention strategy to implement. They may choose from a variety of interventions, including individual, group, couples, and family counseling. It may be best to begin with individual counseling for clients with problems of an intrapersonal nature. As clients become more secure, they may be able to benefit from the open dialogue that often characterizes group counseling. Couples or family counseling may be more appropriate for clients with difficulties of an interpersonal nature, as in a marital or parent-child conflict.

Involving clients in the process of selecting intervention strategies has some advantages. For example, Devine and Fernald (1973) noted that this approach can help counselors avoid using strategies that a client has already tried without apparent success. Instead, the counselor and client together can select a strategy that seems realistic in terms of its strengths and weaknesses.

Cormier and Cormier (1991) provided the following guidelines that encourage client involvement in selecting the appropriate intervention strategy. The counselor should provide an overview of the different treatment approaches available; describe the role of the counselor and client for each procedure; identify possible risks and benefits that may result; and estimate the time and cost of each procedure. In addition, it is important for the counselor to be sensitive to client characteristics such as values and beliefs when selecting an intervention strategy (Cormier & Hackney, 1987). This sensitivity should extend to multicultural issues. Counselors should also be aware of a client's personal strengths and weaknesses in selecting a counseling approach. For example, counselors should determine whether a client has the necessary self-control or ego strength to utilize a counseling strategy (Cormier & Hackney, 1987).

Problem-Solving Strategies.   One way to conceptualize intervention is within the framework of problem solving. Dixon and Glover (1984) suggested that all counseling or psychotherapy is a problem-solving process, whether it involves individual, group, marriage, or family counseling. They noted that since the counseling process is focused on helping a client resolve problems, counselors should develop a systematic approach to problem solving. Dixon and Glover also believed that counselors should attempt to teach clients how to use problem-solving skills in their daily lives.

This approach would enable clients to learn skills that could contribute to their personal autonomy.

Several problem-solving approaches can be used in the counseling process (e.g., D'Zurilla & Goldfried, 1971; Heppner & Krauskopf, 1987; Kanfer & Busemeyer, 1982; Urban & Ford, 1971). For example, Kanfer and Busemeyer identified a six-stage model for problem solving: problem detection, problem definition, identification of alternative solutions, decision-making, execution, and verification. This model is a behaviorally oriented approach that involves describing a particular problem in behavioral terms; identifying possible solutions associated with the problem; deciding on a course of action relative to the various alternative solutions; implementing the decision; and verifying if the outcome is consistent with the expected outcome.

I have developed a six-step problem-solving approach that can be used to incorporate techniques from the various schools of counseling. Counselors should adjust this approach to the unique and emerging needs of the client. It is also important to note that it may take more than one session to utilize the six steps.

1. The counselor assists the client in selecting a goal to work on in counseling. More than one goal can be worked on at the same time if necessary.

2. The counselor and client identify what problems they must overcome to achieve the counseling goal. They also identify the client's assets that can be used to overcome these problems.

3. The counselor attempts to increase the client's motivation for change by helping the client understand the "cost" of not changing. For example, they might discuss what life will be like if the counseling goal is not achieved, or they might determine the benefits of changing. The counselor obtains a commitment from the client to make the necessary changes.

4. The counselor assists the client in selecting a particular problem from Step 2 to work on.

5. The counselor and client utilize the counseling techniques necessary to assist with the problem.

6. The counselor gives the client a homework assignment to practice away from the counseling session what was learned in Step 5. The counselor can begin the next session with a follow-up on how the client did with the assignment.

The following example illustrates how these six steps might be used in counseling.

1. The counselor and client identify two counseling goals: improve interpersonal skills and explore career options. They decide to work first on interpersonal skills.

2. The counselor and client identify the following problems associated with poor interpersonal skills: lack of assertion, poor listening skills, low self-image, and impatience. They also identify the client's assets: hard-working, dependable, and interested in personal growth.

3. The counselor attempts to increase the client's motivation for changing by identifying the cost of not changing. For example, the client will continue to have interpersonal difficulties and will feel lonely and lack meaning in life.

The counselor also identifies as a benefit of changing the development of skills that will promote a meaningful relationship. The counselor then obtains a commitment from the client to make the necessary changes.

4. The counselor assists the client in identifying a particular problem to work on from Step 2: develop more effective listening skills.

5. The counselor uses a particular counseling strategy for the problem selected in Step 4: the counselor teaches the client how to use basic listening skills.

6. The client is given a homework assignment to practice listening skills outside of counseling. At the beginning of the next session, the counselor and client review how the homework assignment went and then do additional work developing listening skills as required.

Stage Five: Termination and Follow-Up

Perhaps the ultimate goal in counseling is for counselors to become obsolete or unnecessary to their clients. This result can occur when clients have worked through their concerns and are able to proceed forward in their lives without the counselor's assistance. At this point, counseling can be terminated. It is usually best for the counselor and client to agree on a termination date, reducing the chance of premature termination or feelings of ambivalence.

It is also advantageous to plan for termination several weeks in advance to provide the client an opportunity to prepare psychologically. The final session can be used to review what has occurred over the counseling process; what the client has learned; and how the client will use that information in the future. The counselor should also arrange for appropriate follow-up with the client. An appointment for a formal follow-up counseling session can be made 2 to 4 weeks after the final session. This can allow the counselor and client adequate time to evaluate how things are going without counseling. Clients should be reassured that they will be able to obtain additional counseling services if the need arises. They should also be informed as to how they can request these services in the future.

Stage Six: Research and Evaluation

Research and evaluation can occur at any time during the counseling process or after termination. Some behavioral approaches utilize single-case or small-group research designs that require counselors to evaluate counseling whenever they implement an intervention strategy. These research procedures involve face-to-face interaction between the counselor and client. Other research procedures that may or may not involve direct interaction between counselor and client are empirical research involving hypothesis testing and alternative methodology such as the discovery approach. These procedures may be used before or after a client has terminated (see Chapter 4 for a description of research methods).

Research and evaluation are an integral part of the counseling process. They contribute to the science dimension of counseling by promoting an objective understanding of what is occurring in counseling. Counselors can also use research and evaluation to communicate accountability.

COMMON PROBLEMS FOR BEGINNING COUNSELORS

It has been my observation that beginning counselors tend to experience similar problems in counseling. These problems can manifest themselves as roadblocks to the counseling process. In this section, I present a discussion of 15 typical road-blocks that can impede counseling effectiveness with suggestions for overcoming each problem.

Focusing on the First Issue in a Session

Some beginning counselors tend to focus on the first problem the client presents in a session, even though a client may not want to work or be capable of working on this problem. The counselor may then spend the rest of the session trying to help the client resolve this particular problem. Counselors can overcome this roadblock by first obtaining an overview of the client's concerns and then selecting a counseling goal with the client.

Overlooking Physical or Medical Issues

Beginning counselors may assume that when a client seeks their services for counseling, counseling is all the client needs (Nystul, 1981). For example, a client may seek counseling to obtain stress management to help alleviate migraine headaches. In this instance, it would be important for the counselor to ensure the client has had a recent physical examination. This will enable the counselor to rule out possible organic causes of the headache such as a brain tumor. A substance abuse problem may be another medical issue that counselors may overlook. A counselor may assume that clients do not have substance abuse problems if they do not raise the issue. Counselors can avoid this problem by obtaining a history of alcohol and drug use when they gather other important background information.

Wanting to Rescue Clients from their Unhappiness

Some beginning counselors have a naive notion that counseling is a process that makes clients feel happier. It is true that a major goal of counseling could be self-realization and inner peace. The road to that goal, however, will undoubtedly have ups and downs, and emotional highs and lows.

Counseling is a process that requires the client to take risks and have the courage to face difficult issues. For example, a client may need to become aware of personal inadequacies or self-defeating patterns of behavior. This can make a client feel uncomfortable or sad and may even result in the client crying. Counselors may falsely conclude that since their client cried, they must have done something wrong. When this occurs, the counselor should consider that helping a client get in touch with inner feelings is an important part of the counseling process.

There are several ways that a counselor may rescue a client. Three common examples follow.

- *Reassuring clients.* When clients feel bad about their situation, the counselor may be tempted to say, "Don't worry, things will get better." It is important, however, for the counselor and client to have a realistic view of the counseling process. If the client does not make necessary changes, things probably will not get better. In fact, the client's situation may worsen.

- *Offering instant advice.* When clients are uncomfortable with their situation, the counselor may attempt to rescue the client by offering advice. In counseling, giving advice is usually unproductive, can foster dependency, and can be a superficial solution to a complex problem.
- *Rescuing clients from intense emotions.* Some beginning counselors tend not to allow clients to experience any intense emotions. When clients express intense emotions such as anger or grief, the counselor may want to calm them or get them to think about something else. This type of rescuing prevents clients from getting in touch with and working through their feelings.

Having Perfectionist Tendencies

Some beginning counselors may have perfectionist tendencies. They may fear making mistakes or looking bad. These tendencies may cause several problems, including counselors being reluctant to explore a new idea or technique because they fear not learning or using it correctly; avoiding supervision because they believe seeking assistance might reflect their inadequacy; and being hesitant to refer a client because they think a referral might imply they could not handle the situation.

The following Personal Note provides some of my suggestions for helping beginning counselors overcome perfectionist tendencies.

a personal note

I have found several ways to help counselors overcome perfectionist tendencies. First, counselors should avoid absolutistic, or right-versus-wrong, views of the counseling process. Once counselors realize there is not a right or wrong way of doing counseling, then they can stop worrying about making mistakes. The model of counseling as an art maintains a realistic, pragmatic view of counseling. This model suggests that when the client seems to be making progress, the counselor and client should continue using that counseling approach. When the client does not appear to be making gains in counseling, the counselor and client should make the necessary adjustments to the counseling process.

I identified the "monkey on the back" phenomenon as another way to help student counselors overcome perfectionist tendencies. The "monkey on the back" symbolizes why it is not productive to try to look perfect while learning new counseling skills. I begin by explaining to students that a counselor training program is in some ways like having a "monkey" put on their back. The "monkey"—instructions from the professor—may tell students to do some things differently from what they would ordinarily do. For example, the instructions might be to use open rather than closed questions during active listening.

When the "monkey" suggests that students stop to consider different ways of responding, they may feel the "monkey" is interfering with their spontaneity. If they focus on their professor perceiving them as spontaneous, they may avoid trying new behaviors. Unfortunately, these students will also not learn much from their counseling program.

I tell students that the feeling of the "monkey" interfering with their spontaneity is a good sign. It indicates that they are trying some new skills and are in the process of becoming a more effective counselor. In time, the new skills will become integrated into their natural way of working with clients and their spontaneity will be restored.

Having Unrealistic Expectations

Some beginning counselors have unrealistic expectations for their clients. They may therefore become frustrated when their client does not make steady progress. When a client has a setback and regresses to old negative patterns of behavior, counselors may feel they have failed the client. In time, the counselor may project these negative feelings onto the client (Nystul, 1979). The art of counseling model suggests that counselors develop a balanced set of expectations blending optimism with realism. These expectations involve believing that clients can improve and realizing that change can take time.

Getting Carried Away with the Latest Technique

Some beginning counselors tend to get carried away after learning a new technique, wanting to use this technique with all clients (Nystul, 1981). For example, after attending an extensive training program in hypnosis, a counselor may believe that every client could benefit from hypnosis. This enthusiasm may continue for a period of time until the counselor gets excited about another new technique.

It is important for counselors to get excited and be enthusiastic about their education. At the same time, they must learn to channel these energies into a positive direction, rather than imposing their current interest on the client.

Getting Lost in the Counseling Process

Clients often feel overwhelmed with issues when they begin counseling. Each time they come to a counseling session, they may talk about many different concerns. They may describe these concerns in a very interesting manner, and the concerns may begin to seem like an ongoing soap opera from television.

As counselors hear these "stories," they may find themselves taking a passive role in counseling. I call this the *popcorn syndrome* (Nystul, 1981). It is as if counselors are eating popcorn at the movies, listening to their client's latest struggle with life. Counselors who find themselves in the popcorn syndrome usually enjoy the counseling sessions, but they often have the feeling they are not accomplishing much. When this occurs, counselors can feel lost in the ongoing storytelling. To overcome this problem, the counselor can create a focus in the counseling process by exploring with the client what has happened in counseling—where they have been, what they are currently working on, and where they seem to be headed. Together they can make the necessary adjustments for future sessions. If the popcorn syndrome is occurring, the counselor may also want to create more of a shared responsibility in the counseling process and work toward clearer counseling goals.

Using Inappropriate Phrases

Although I contend there are no right or wrong ways to approach counseling, I believe that certain phrases are usually inappropriate and unproductive in counseling. Three examples follow.

- *"Why" questions.* "Why" questions usually provoke a defensive response, causing people to believe they need to justify their behavior. Instead of asking, "Why did you and Tim break up?" the counselor might ask, "Could you tell me what happened regarding your break-up with Tim?"

- *I know how you feel.* Counselors may use this phrase to show that they have been through a similar situation and can therefore understand the client. Actually, no two people have exactly the same reaction to a situation. For example, take the varied reactions to a house burning down. One person might feel relief at the prospect of insurance money, while another might be heartbroken because of losing priceless family mementos. A client may have negative reactions to a counselor saying, "I know how you feel." The client may think, "No, she does not. She is not me. Who does she think she is?" Another client might react by thinking, "If this counselor knows how I feel, why bother exploring my feelings with him?"

- *Let me tell you what I would do.* This phrase can lead to instant advice. As mentioned earlier, advice giving usually does not promote positive outcomes in counseling.

Having an Excessive Desire to Help

Many students are drawn to counseling because they truly want to help others. Wanting to help can be beneficial to the counseling process because it communicates enthusiasm, desire, and caring. Some counselors can be excessive in their need to help, however, to the point of being overly invested in the counseling process. A useful indicator that counselors may have gone too far in wanting to help is when they feel they are working harder than the client. Students should also explore their motives for wanting to become counselors. A positive motive would be to enjoy helping a client overcome self-defeating forces to move toward self-realization. A negative motive would be an excessive desire to feel needed by someone. This desire could foster unnecessary dependency in the counseling relationship. Another negative motive would be a need to feel power or control over others. This need could lead to a counselor intimidating clients, undermining their self-esteem, and fostering dependency. When counselors discover they have inappropriate motives for providing counseling services, they should refer the client and seek out counseling for themselves.

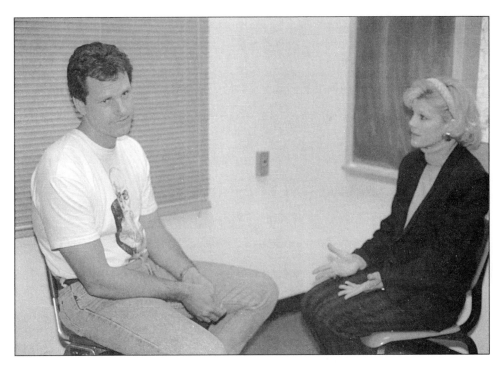

It's not a good sign when the counselor is working harder than the client.

Having an Excessive Need to be Liked

Most people, including counselors, enjoy being liked. At times, however, the counselor may need to do things that could make the client angry or unhappy, such as during a confrontation. It is therefore not necessary for the client always to like the counselor. Instead, it is essential to establish mutual respect to maintain a rapport throughout the counseling process.

Getting Too Emotionally Involved

Some beginning counselors tend to get too emotionally involved with the counseling process. There can be many reasons for developing this tendency. One is what I call the *stray cat syndrome*, which involves counselors wanting to take responsibility for the client's welfare. These counselors may have tendencies to want to go out of their way to help all living creatures—including stray cats—that appear to need assistance. As a result, whenever they see a client suffering, they may want to find a way to take away the pain and fix things, leading to the rescuing process described earlier.

Counselors can become so emotionally invested in their clients that they can lose professional objectivity. They can also become emotionally exhausted and burned out. The art of counseling model suggests that for counseling to be effective, the counselor must be affected. At the same time, counselors should not assume ownership of the client's problems. They should instead help clients become capable of resolving their own problems.

Taking Things Too Personally

Beginning counselors may take things too personally when a client expresses intense emotions. For example, a client may react as if the counselor were another person with whom the client has had a close relationship, for example, a father or mother figure. During this process of transference, the client may become angry with the counselor. It would be inappropriate for the counselor to take this personally and retaliate against the client. Instead, the counselor should view the transference as an important part of therapy. For example, Freudian psychoanalysis contends that transference is therapeutic in that it allows the client to work through unresolved emotional trauma (Freud, 1969).

Having Difficulty Differentiating between Normal and Abnormal

Beginning counselors often have a difficult time deciding whether clients suffer from some form of psychopathology. For example, a counselor may wonder if a client is acutely suicidal and needs hospitalization or mildly suicidal and only requires monitoring. Another dilemma may be differentiating a clinical depression, such as a major depression, from a normal depressive reaction to a life event relating to the death of a loved one.

The reason some beginning counselors have trouble differentiating between normal and abnormal may be their lack of exposure to psychopathology. Student counselors may overcome this obstacle by taking advantage of internships and other clinical placements during their educational placement to obtain experience working with clients who suffer from mental disorders.

Being Uncertain about Self-Disclosure

Another problem that beginning counselors commonly experience is determining how much they should self-disclose. Although there are no hard-and-fast rules on this issue, the following suggestions may be useful.

- Answer questions about yourself that you feel comfortable with—just answer the questions without elaborating. Feel free to offer information about your professional qualifications. Be willing to share immediate reactions to what is taking place in the session.
- Don't tell your life story to your clients—they are there to tell you their story, not listen to yours. Don't say, "This is how I handled it." It could lead to ineffective advice giving.

Being Uncertain about Confidentiality

Many beginning counselors are unclear about the limits of confidentiality. One of the most common sources of confusion relates to the question, "With whom can I discuss a client, and what information can I disclose?" The following are my suggestions regarding this issue. A counselor may discuss a case with a supervisor or when required by law, such as reporting child abuse or neglect. It is also permissible to break confidentiality when clients pose a serious threat in terms of harming themselves or others. It is not appropriate to discuss a case with a secretary, friends, or family members even if you change the name of the client.

CHAPTER SUMMARY

In this chapter, I have provided an overview of the counseling process. I described counseling as a six-stage approach, which involves relationship building, assessment and diagnosis, goal setting, intervention and problem solving, termination and follow-up, and research and evaluation. The art of counseling model suggests the counselor utilize a flexible, creative approach to proceed through these stages. It is also important for counselors to adjust their approach to the unique and changing needs of the client.

In the final analysis, counseling is a process that varies in length and content according to the concerns of the client. In this process, the client may appear to make some progress and then regress to self-defeating habits. When things appear to be going wrong, the counselor, like a navigator on a ship, can adjust course. Counseling may be considered successful when the overall direction of therapy is positive.

In this chapter, I also described 15 problems that beginning counselors experience and provided guidelines for dealing with each. The problems are focusing only on the first issue in a session, overlooking medical issues, wanting to rescue clients, having perfectionist tendencies or unrealistic expectations, getting carried away with the latest technique learned, getting lost in the counseling process, using inappropriate phrases, having an excessive desire to help or to be liked, getting too emotionally involved or taking things too personally, and being uncertain about psychopathology issues, self-disclosure, or confidentiality.

REFERENCES

Adler, A. (1964). *Social interest: A challenge to mankind.* New York: Capricorn Books. (Original work published 1929)

Andersen, B., & Andersen, W. (1985). Client perceptions of counselors using positive and negative self-involving statements. *Journal of Counseling Psychology, 32,* 462–465.

Angle, S. S., & Goodyear, R. K. (1984). Perception of counselors' qualities: Impact of subjects' self-concepts, counselor gender, and counselor introductions. *Journal of Counseling Psychology, 31,* 576–579.

Argyle, M. (1981). The contribution of social interaction research to social skills training. In J. D. Wine & M. D. Syme (Eds.), *Social Competence.* New York: Guilford.

Barrett-Lennard, G. T. (1981). The empathy cycle: Refinement of a nuclear concept. *Journal of Counseling Psychology, 28,* 91–100.

Berenson, B., & Mitchell, K. (1968). Therapeutic conditions for therapist-initiated confrontation. *Journal of Clinical Psychology, 24,* 363–364.

Bernstein, B. L., & Figioli, S. W. (1983). Gender and credibility introduction effects on perceived counselor characteristics. *Journal of Counseling Psychology, 30*, 506–513.

Beutler, L. E., Cargo, M., & Arizmendi, T. G. (1986). Therapist variables in psychotherapy process and outcome. In S. L. Garfield & A. E. Bergin (Eds.), *Handbook of psychotherapy and behavior change*. New York: John Wiley & Sons.

Blocher, D. H. (1974). *Developmental counseling* (2nd ed.). New York: Ronald Press.

Bordin, E. S. (1979). The generalizability of the psychoanalytic concept of the working alliance. *Psychotherapy: Theory, Research and Practice, 16*, 252–260.

Carkhuff, R. R. (1969). *Helping and human relations* (Vols. 1–2). New York: Holt, Rinehart, & Winston.

Carkhuff, R. R. (1971). *The development of human resources*. New York: Holt, Rinehart, & Winston.

Cormier, W. H., & Cormier, L. S. (1991). *Interviewing strategies for helpers* (3rd ed.). Monterey, CA: Brooks/Cole.

Cormier, L. S., & Hackney, H. (1987). *The professional counselor: A process guide to helping*. Englewood Cliffs, NJ: Prentice-Hall.

Corrigan, J. D., Dell, D. M., Lewis, K. N., & Schmidt, L. D. (1980). Counseling as a social influence process: A review [monograph]. *Journal of Counseling Psychology, 27*, 395–441.

Curran, J., & Loganbell, C. R. (1985). Factors affecting the attractiveness of a group leader. *Journal of College Student Personnel, 24*, 250–255.

Danish, S. J., D'Augelli, A. R., & Brock, G. W. (1976). An evaluation of helping skill training: Effects on helpers' verbal responses. *Journal of Counseling Psychology, 23*, 259–266.

Devine, D. A., & Fernald, P. S. (1973). Outcome effects of receiving a preferred, randomly assigned, or non-referred therapy. *Journal of Consulting and Clinical Psychology, 41*, 104–107.

Dixon, D. N., & Glover, J. A. (1984). *Counseling: A problem solving approach*. New York: John Wiley & Sons.

Dorn, F. J., & Day, B. J. (1985). Assessing change in self-concept: A social psychological approach. *American Mental Health Counselors Association Journal, 7*, 180–186.

D'Zurilla, T. J., & Goldfried, M. R. (1971). Problem-solving and behavior modification. *Journal of Abnormal Psychology, 78*, 107–126.

Egan, G. (1990). *The skilled helper: A model for systematic helping and interpersonal relating* (4th ed.). Monterey, CA: Brooks/Cole.

Erikson, E. H. (1968). *Identity, youth, and crises*. New York: W. W. Norton.

Freud, S. (1969). *A general introduction to psychoanalysis*. New York: Simon & Schuster.

Garfield, S. L., & Bergin, A. E. (1971). Therapeutic conditions and outcome. *Journal of Abnormal Psychology, 77*, 108–114.

Gazda, G. M., Asbury, F., Blazer, F., Childress, W., and Walters, R. (1979). *Human relations development: A manual for educators*. Boston: Allyn & Bacon.

Gelso, C. J., & Carter, J. A. (1985). The relationship in counseling and psychotherapy: Components, consequences, and theoretical antecedents. *The Counseling Psychologist, 13*, 155–243.

Gelso, C. J., & Fretz, B. R. (in press). *Counseling psychology*. Orlando, Florida: Holt, Rinehart, & Winston.

George, R. L., & Cristiani, T. S. (1990). *Counseling: Theory and practice* (3rd ed.). Englewood Cliffs, NJ: Prentice-Hall.

Gladstein, G. (1983). Understanding empathy: Integrating counseling, developmental and social psychology perspectives. *Journal of Counseling Psychology, 30*, 467–482.

Glasser, W. (1965). *Reality therapy*. New York: Harper & Row.

Greenson, R. R. (1967). *Technique and practice of psychoanalysis*. New York: International University Press.

Gurman, A. S. (1977). The patient's perception of the therapeutic relationship: In A. Gurman & A. Razin (Eds.), *Effective psychotherapy: A handbook of research* (pp. 503–543). New York: Pergamon.

Hackman, H. W., & Claiborn, C. D. (1982). An attributional approach to counselor attractiveness. *Journal of Counseling Psychology, 29*, 224–231.

Hartley, D. E., & Strupp, H. H. (1983). The therapeutic alliance: Its relationship to outcomes in brief psychotherapy. In J. Masling (Ed.), *Empirical studies in analytical theories* (Vol. 1, pp. 1–37). Hillsdale, NJ: Earlbaum.

Heppner, P. P., & Claiborn, C. D. (1989). Social influence research in counseling: A review and critique [monograph]. *Journal of Counseling Psychology, 36*, 365–387.

Heppner, P. P., & Dixon, D. N. (1981). A review of the interpersonal influence process in counseling. *Personnel and Guidance Journal, 59*, 542–550.

Heppner, P. P., & Heesacker, M. (1983). Perceived counselor characteristics, client expectations, and client satisfaction with counseling. *Journal of Counseling Psychology, 30*, 31–39.

Heppner, P. P., & Krauskopf, C. J. (1987). An information-processing approach to personal problem solving. *The Counseling Psychologist, 15*, 371–447.

Horvath, A. O., & Greenberg, L. (1986). The development of the Working Alliance Inventory. In L. Greenberg & W. Pinsoff (Eds.), *The psychotherapeutic process: A resource handbook* (pp. 529–556). New York: Guilford.

Humphrey, F. G. (1983). *Marital therapy*. Englewood Cliffs, NJ: Prentice-Hall.

Ivey, A. (1971). *Microcounseling: Innovations in interviewing training*. Springfield, IL: Charles C. Thomas.

Ivey, A. E. (1988). *Intentional interviewing and counseling: Facilitating client development* (2nd ed.). Pacific Grove, CA: Brooks/Cole.

Jourard, S. M. (1958). *Personal adjustment: An approach through the study of healthy personality*. New York: Macmillan.

Kanfer, F. H., & Busemeyer, J. R. (1982). The use of problem solving and decision making in behavior therapy. *Clinical Psychology Review, 2*, 239–266.

Kokotovic, A. M., & Tracey, T. J. (1990). Working alliance in the early phase of counseling. *Journal of Counseling Psychology, 37*, 16–21.

Kottler, J. A., & Brown, R. W. (1985). *Introduction to therapeutic counseling*. Monterey, CA: Brooks/Cole.

La Crosse, M. B. (1980). Perceived counselor social influence and counseling outcomes: Validity of the Counselor Rating Form. *Journal of Counseling Psychology, 27*, 320–327.

La Fromboise, T. D., & Dixon, D. N. (1981). American Indian perceptions of trustworthiness in a counseling interview. *Journal of Counseling Psychology, 28*, 135–139.

Linder, R. (1954). *The fifty-minute hour*. New York: Bantam Books.

Littrell, J. M., Caffrey, P., & Hopper, G. C. (1987). Counselor's reputation: An important precounseling variable for adolescents. *Journal of Counseling Psychology, 34*, 228–231.

Martin, D. G. (1989). *Counseling and therapy skills*. Prospect Heights, IL: Therapy Press.

Marziali, E., Marmar, C., & Krupnick, J. (1981). Therapeutic alliance scale: Development and relationship to therapeutic outcome. *American Journal of Psychiatry, 138*, 361–364.

Maslow, A. H. (1968). *Toward the psychology of being* (2nd ed.). New York: Van Nostrand Reinhold.

McCarthy, P. R. (1982). Differential effects of counselor self-disclosure versus self-involving counselor statements across counselor-client gender pairings. *Journal of Counseling Psychology, 26*, 538–541.

McCarthy, P. R. (1979). Differential effects of self-referent responses and counselor status. *Journal of Counseling Psychology, 29*, 125–131.

McNeill, B. W., May, R. J., & Lee, V. E. (1987). Perceptions of counselor source characteristics and successful terminators. *Journal of Counseling Psychology, 34*, 86–89.

Merluzzi, T. V., & Brischetto, C. S. (1983). Breach of confidentiality and perceived trustworthiness of counselors. *Journal of Counseling Psychology, 30*, 245–251.

Mintz, J., Luborsky, L., & Auerbach, A. (1971). Dimensions of psychotherapy: A factor-analytic study of ratings of psychotherapy sessions. *Journal of Consulting and Clinical Psychology, 36*, 106–120.

Moras, K., & Strupp, H. H. (1982). Pretherapy interpersonal relations, patient's alliance, and outcomes in brief therapy. *Archives of General Psychiatry, 39*, 405–409.

Nathan, P. E., & Harris, S. L. (1980). *Psychopathology and society*. New York: McGraw-Hill.

Nystul, M. S. (1981). Avoiding roadblocks in counseling. *The Individual Psychologist, 18*, 21–28.

Nystul, M. S. (1979). Three levels of a counseling relationship. *The School Counselor, 26*, 144–148.

Okun, B. F. (1987). *Effective helping interviewing and counseling techniques* (3rd ed.). Monterey, CA: Brooks/Cole.

Orlando, D. E., & Howard, K. I. (1986). Process and outcome in psychotherapy. In S. L. Garfield & A. E. Bergin (Eds.), *Handbook of psychotherapy and behavior change*. New York: John Wiley & Sons.

Paradise, L. V., Conway, B. S., & Zweig, J. (1986). Effects of expert and referent influence, physical attractiveness, and gender on perceptions of counselor attributes. *Journal of Counseling Psychology, 33*, 16–22.

Reynolds, C. L., & Fischer, C. H. (1983). Personal versus professional evaluations of self-disclosing and self-involving counselors. *Journal of Counseling Psychology, 30*, 451–454.

Rogers, C. R. (1957). The necessary and sufficient conditions of therapeutic personality change. *Journal of Counseling Psychology, 21*, 95–103.

Rogers, C. R. (1970). *On encounter groups*. New York: Harper & Row.

Rogers, C. R. (1980). *A way of being*. Boston: Houghton Mifflin.

Rogers, C. R., Gendlin, E. T., Kiesler, D. J., & Truax, C. B. (1967). *The therapeutic relationship and its impact: A study of psychotherapy with schizophrenics*. Madison: University of Wisconsin Press.

Roll, S. A., Crowley, M. A., & Rappl, L. E. (1985). Client perceptions of counselor's nonverbal behavior: A reevaluation. *Counselor Education and Supervision, 24*, 234–243.

Rosenhan, D. L., & Seligman, M. E. P. (1989). *Abnormal Psychology*. New York, W. W. Norton.

Sager, C. (1976). *Marriage contracts and couple therapy*. New York: Brunner/Mazel.

Sloane, B., Staples, F., Cristol, A., Yorkston, N., & Whipple, K. (1975). *Psychotherapy versus behavior therapy*. Cambridge, MA: Harvard University Press.

Strohmer, D. C., & Biggs, D. A. (1983). Effects of counselor disability status on disabled subjects' perceptions of counselor attractiveness and expertness. *Journal of Counseling Psychology, 30*, 202–208.

Strong, S. R. (1968). Counseling: An interpersonal influence process. *Journal of Counseling Psychology, 15*, 215–224.

Strong, S. R., & Claiborn, C. D. (1982). *Change through interaction*. New York: John Wiley & Sons.

Strupp, H. H. (1980). Success and failures in time-limited psychotherapy. A systematic comparison of two cases: Comparison 2. *Archives of General Psychiatry, 376*, 708–716.

Suit, J. L., & Paradise, L. V. (1985). Effects of metaphors and cognitive complexity on perceived counselor characteristics. *Journal of Counseling Psychology, 32*, 23–28.

Truax, C. B., & Carkhuff, R. R. (1967). *Toward effective counseling and psychotherapy*. Chicago: Aldine.

Truax, C. B., & Mitchell, K. M. (1971). Research on certain therapist interpersonal skills in relation to process and outcome. In A. E. Bergin & S. L. Garfield (Eds.), *Handbook of psychotherapy and behavior change*. New York: John Wiley.

Tyson, J. A., & Wall, S. M. (1983). Effect of inconsistency between counselor verbal and nonverbal behavior on perceptions of counselor attributes. *Journal of Counseling Psychology, 30*, 433–437.

Urban, H. B., & Ford, D. H. (1971). Some historical and conceptual perspectives on psychotherapy and behavior change. In A. E. Bergin & S. L. Garfield (Eds.), *Handbook of psychotherapy and behavior change: An empirical analysis*. New York: Wiley.

Weiner, M. F. (1978). *Therapist disclosure: The use of self in psychotherapy*. Boston: Butterworths.

CHAPTER THREE

Assessment and Diagnosis

CHAPTER OVERVIEW

This chapter will provide an overview of assessment and diagnosis. Highlights of the chapter include

- Evaluation of tests
- Administration and interpretation of tests
- Test bias
- Types of tests
- Historical perspective of diagnosis
- Uses of diagnosis
- The DSM-III-R
- The clinical interview

Assessment and diagnosis are important aspects of the counseling process for most schools of counseling. Exceptions to this include person-centered counseling (Rogers, 1981) and reality therapy (Glasser, 1965). Person-centered counseling avoids assessment and diagnosis because of the focus on the counselor rather than the client. As Glasser contends, reality therapy avoids diagnosis because it results in inaccurate or harmful labels. Aside from these exceptions, the vast majority of counselors do engage in assessment and diagnosis, largely because of the numerous functions these tools can fulfill in the counseling process. For example, Hansen, Stevic, and Warner (1982) identified the following four functions of assessment. Assessment procedures can be used for

- *Prediction*, by predicting a client's success in a course of study or career
- *Diagnosis*, by contributing information that can assist in making a diagnosis
- *Monitoring*, by determining the level of progress a client is making
- *Evaluation*, by providing a means for evaluating the effectiveness of the counseling process

Assessment and diagnosis serve interrelated functions. This chapter will provide an overview of some of the key issues associated with these two important aspects of the counseling process.

ASSESSMENT

Sundberg (1977) noted that *assessment* first appeared as a psychological term in *Assessment of Men* (Office of Strategic Services, 1948). The term was used to describe the process of selecting men to serve on special missions in World War II. Since that time, its meaning has broadened to include a wide range of techniques and processes. These include standardized psychological tests, interviewing and observation strategies, socio-cultural assessment, behavioral assessment, and environmental assessment. This section will provide a description of these assessment procedures as well as information on evaluating tests and administration and interpretation of test results.

Evaluation of Tests

Anastasi (1988) described several sources of information on tests, which provide a valuable means of evaluating tests. These are summarized as follows.

- *Mental Measurement Yearbook*, edited by Burros, provides information on most tests as well as a critique of each test.
- *Test Collection Bibliographies*, produced by the Educational Testing Service, provides information on tests pertaining to a particular content such as physical disabilities.
- *Test and Microfiche*, distributed by Test Collection, Educational Testing Service, provides important information about tests such as reliability and validity.

- *The APA's Standards for Educational and Psychological Testing* provides guidelines for proper test use and interpretation of test results.

Three concepts are especially important in evaluating tests: validity, reliability, and norms. An overview of these concepts follows.

Validity.   Validity is the degree to which a test measures what it is intended to measure (Anastasi, 1988). According to Anastasi (1988), validity is the most important characteristic of a test and provides a check on how well the test fulfills its intended function. For example, the Graduate Record Examination could be used to help select students for Ph.D. programs in counseling psychology. The test would have a high validity if these students were successful in their graduate programs.

The three major types of validity are content, construct, and criterion-related. Anastasi (1988) provided a description of these types of validity.

1. *Content validity* involves the examination of a test's content to determine whether it covers a representative sample of the behavior to be measured. Content validity is often used in achievement tests to determine if the test content is representative of the information that an individual was exposed to (e.g., biology concepts in a biology course).

2. *Construct validity* refers to the degree to which a test measures a theoretical construct or trait such as neuroticism or anxiety.

3. *Criterion-related validity* provides an indication of how well a test predicts an individual's performance on a particular criterion. For example, a mechanical aptitude test might be used to predict how well a person will perform as a machinist. There are two types of criterion-related validity. *Concurrent validity* is determined when the criterion is available at the time of testing. *Predictive validity* can be assessed when the criterion is available only after the testing has occurred.

Reliability.   Reliability is another important factor that should be considered in test evaluation. It ". . . refers to the consistency of scores obtained by the same person when reexamined with the same test on different occasions, or with different sets of equivalent items, or under variable examining conditions" (Anastasi, 1988, p. 109). Reliability can be determined by the following three methods.

1. *Test-retest reliability* involves administering the same test again to an individual.

2. *Alternate-forms reliability* refers to administering equivalent forms to the individual on separate occasions.

3. *Split-half reliability* involves dividing a test into two equivalent halves and administering each half to the individual. It provides a measure of the test's internal consistency.

Norms.   Sundberg (1977) noted that to understand an individual's score, it is necessary to have information on scores made by other people (i.e., the norm group). In evaluating the norms used in a test, it is important to determine if the norm group is representative of the population for whom the test was designed (Sundberg). For example, a test with norms derived from an upper-class white group may be inappropriate to use with a minority client.

Administration and Interpretation of Tests

Only qualified individuals should administer and interpret tests. Many tests such as the Wechsler Intelligence Test require specialized training in test administration and interpretation. In addition, the counselor should carefully review the test manual to determine procedures to use in test interpretation. For example, it is important to determine the strengths and limitations of the test and if the norm group is representative of the individual being tested.

Miller (1982) provided the following guidelines for interpreting test results to clients.

- The counselor should explore how the client felt about taking the test.
- The counselor should review the purpose of taking the test and provide information necessary for test interpretation (e.g., norms and percentiles).
- The counselor and client should examine the test results and discuss what the results mean to the client.
- The counselor should help the client integrate the test scores into other aspects of the client's self-knowledge.
- The counselor should encourage the client to develop a plan to utilize the test results.

More recently, Goodyear (1990) suggested that counselors should introduce test materials and interpretations in response to specific concerns raised by the client throughout the counseling process, rather than at one particular point in counseling. Goodyear contends that a client will achieve better assimilation of information from an approach to interpretation that occurs at various phases of the counseling process.

Several research studies provide useful information regarding interpretation. Jones and Gelso (1988) found that clients perceived tentative interpretations as more helpful than absolute interpretations. Clients were also more willing to see counselors who used tentative interpretations. Goodyear (1990) cited a study by Taylor and Brown (1988) that found mentally healthy individuals were more likely to harbor unrealistic positive self-perceptions. Based on these findings, Goodyear warned that clients may be prone to distort test interpretations in an unrealistically positive manner. Other studies have shown that clients prefer individual test interpretations over group interpretations in terms of clarity (Miller & Cochran, 1979); favorability (Oliver, 1977); and helpfulness (Wilkerson, 1967).

Computer-based test interpretation (CBTI) is an increasingly popular resource for testing and assessment (Sampson, 1990). A variety of computer software programs have been designed to assist counselors in interpreting the most commonly used tests, such as the Minnesota Multiphasic Personality Inventory (MMPI-II) and the Wechsler Intelligence scales. CBTI systems are not intended to replace the counselor's role in the assessment process. Instead, counselors should view CBTI as a source for an objective second opinion to aid in assessment, diagnosis, and treatment planning (Sampson).

Test Bias

Watkins and Campbell (1990) noted increasing concern in the literature regarding the fairness of tests and assessment methods for clients of culturally diverse backgrounds. Evidence of cultural bias has been found in numerous assessment procedures such as projective techniques, intelligence tests, and self-report measures (Jewell, 1989). Reynolds (1982) identified the following factors that are often associated with test bias.

- *Inappropriate content.* Test content is biased toward values and experiences of white, middle-class individuals.
- *Inappropriate standardization samples.* Most norm groups, which tend to be underrepresented by ethnic minorities, are not realistic reference groups for minorities.
- *Examiner and language bias.* Psychologists tend to be white and speak only standard English. As test examiners, they can therefore intimidate ethnic minorities and create communication barriers, which can account for lower performance on tests.
- *Inequitable social consequences.* Ethnic minorities receive unfair labels from tests (e.g., low intelligence), which can relegate them to dead-end educational tracks.
- *Measurement of different constructs.* Tests measure significantly different attributes when used with ethnic minorities, for example, the degree of their adherence to the value system of the dominant culture.
- *Differential predictive validity.* While tests can accurately predict outcomes such as academic attainment for whites, they are much less effective in terms of predicting outcomes for ethnic minorities.

In response to the potential problems in multicultural assessment, Anastasi (1985) suggested that "all testing should be considered within a framework of cultural diversity" (p. 29). Culture-fair tests have been developed in an attempt to overcome the problems associated with test bias. Penrose and Raven (1936) developed one of the first culture-fair intelligence tests called the Raven Matrices Test. This test has three versions, allowing for the evaluation of mentally retarded individuals up to normal adults. Each version consists of a nonverbal test in which the examinee must choose which matrix completes a particular pattern. Cattell (1949) developed another culture-fair intelligence test called the Cattell Culture-Fair Intelligence Test. The test is primarily nonpictorial and nonverbal and can be used with individuals from age 4 through adult.

A more current approach to culture-fair testing is the System of Multicultural Pluralistic Assessment (SOMPA) developed by Mercer (1977). This system can be used with children from 5 to 11 years of age. The SOMPA approach has several unique qualities. First, the child is administered several tests including the Wechsler

Intelligence Test for Children-Revised (WISC-R). Second, an interview is conducted with the child's primary caregiver to obtain information on how the child functions in various activities and settings (McMillan, 1984). The WISC-R score is then "corrected" after consideration of other test scores and the interview. Mercer contends that the "uncorrected" test scores can be useful in making educational and instructional decisions, but the "corrected" score more accurately reflects the child's intellectual aptitude (McMillan, 1984).

Types of Tests

Assessment procedures can be divided into two major categories: standardized and nonstandardized measures (Kottler & Brown, 1985). *Standardized measures* are tests that have a standardized norm group. This category includes a wide variety of psychological tests such as intelligence tests, personality tests, interest tests, aptitude tests, achievement tests, and neuropsychological tests. Nonstandardized measures do not have a standardized norm group and include procedures such as observations, behavioral assessment, and environmental assessment.

Each form has advantages and disadvantages. Standardized assessment procedures provide the counselor with objective information regarding the client. In addition, these tests contain information on validity and reliability, which can be used to evaluate the results. The disadvantages include tendencies toward having cultural bias, promoting harmful labels, and producing scores that may be oversimplified or misleading.

Table 3.1
Comparison of Standardized and Nonstandardized Measures

Type of Test	Advantages	Disadvantages
Standardized	1. Provides objective information regarding the client	1. Is prone to cultural bias
	2. Provides specific information about a client relative to a norm group	2. Often results in "labels"
	3. Contains information on validity and reliability that can be used to evaluate the test	3. Leads to oversimplified and misleading test results (e.g., IQ scores)
Nonstandardized	1. Provides a flexible, individualized approach that yields information unique to the individual client	1. Lacks information on validity and reliability
	2. Fosters an active role for the client in the assessment process	2. Lacks objectivity and ability to generalize to a reference group
	3. Can be easily modified to accommodate individual differences	3. Lack specific scores and reference groups, which may make assessment results appear confusing to clients

Testing can provide counselors with objective information regarding the client's psychological functioning.

Nonstandardized assessment procedures also have inherent strengths and weaknesses. One strength of these measures is providing a flexible and individualized approach, which yields information unique to the individual. They can also be easily modified to accommodate individual differences, thereby minimizing cultural bias. Weaknesses include a lack of information on reliability and validity to evaluate the assessment procedures and a lack of objectivity in terms of test results. The advantages and disadvantages of standardized and nonstandardized assessment procedures are summarized in Table 3.1.

Standardized Measures.   Standardized measures include a wide range of psychological tests. Anastasi (1988) defined a psychological test as "an objective and standardized measure of a sample behavior" (p. 23). "Standardization implies uniformity of procedure in administering and scoring a test" (Anastasi, 1988, p. 25). Psychological tests can be administered to an individual or a group to assess a wide range of traits and attributes such as intelligence, achievement, aptitude, interest, personality, and neuropsychological impairment. Some commonly used tests in these domains are intelligence tests, achievement tests, aptitude tests, interest inventories, personality inventories, projective techniques, and neuropsychological tests. Intelligence tests provide information regarding the client's intellectual functioning. The most common individually administered intelligence tests are the Stanford Binet and three Wechsler scales: The Wechsler Pre-School and Primary Scale of Intelligence-Revised (WPPSI-R), The Wechsler Intelligence Scale for Children-Revised (WISC-R), and The Wechsler Adult Intelligence Scale-Revised (WAIS-R). Two of the more commonly used group-administered intelligence tests are the Otis-Lennon Mental Ability Test and the California Tests of Mental Maturity. Nonverbal intelligence tests are also available, such as the Raven Progressive Matrixes and the Test of Nonverbal Intelligence (TONI). These are especially useful in multicultural testing to overcome language barriers. They can also be used if the counselor has limited time available and only needs to have a rough estimate of the client's intellectual level (Anastasi, 1988).

Achievement tests are used primarily in school settings. They provide information on what a person has learned. Three of the more popular achievement tests are the Iowa Test of Basic Skills, the Wide Range Achievement Test, and Woodcock Johnson Psycho-Educational Battery (Anastasi, 1988).

Aptitude tests focus on the client's potential in an attempt to predict success. As mentioned, the Graduate Record Examination is an example of an aptitude test, and it is designed to predict if a person will be able to successfully complete graduate study. Another example is the Differential Aptitude Test, which counselors use frequently in educational and vocational counseling of students in Grades 8 through 12 (Anastasi, 1988).

Interest inventories help the counselor determine where the client's interests lie. This information can be especially useful to career counselors. Three of the most commonly used interest inventories are the Kuder Preference Record, The Career Assessment Inventory, and the Strong Campbell Inventory.

Personality inventories provide information about personality dynamics and can also be part of the diagnostic process to determine if there is a mental disorder. The two types of personality tests are objective and subjective. Objective tests require more rigid responses, such as true-false or multiple-choice responses. The most widely used objective personality test is the Minnesota Multiphasic Personality Inventory (MMPI-II). It is especially useful in identifying tendencies toward certain mental disorders, for example, depression or schizophrenia. Two popular objective personality tests that provide an overview of the personality are the California Psychological Inventory (CPI) and the 16 Personality Factors Questionnaire (16 PF).

Projective techniques are subjective tests that allow clients to project their thoughts and feelings into a variety of ambiguous stimuli, such as the ink blots of the Rorschach Test or pictures in the Thematic Apperception Test. Projective tests are sometimes more appropriate in multicultural settings since they minimize the use of words, thereby decreasing tendencies toward cultural bias. Two examples are the Draw-a-Person and House-Tree-Person Tests.

Neuropsychological tests ". . . are used to evaluate the neurologically impaired patients' cognitive, behavioral, and psychological strengths and weaknesses and to determine their relationship to cerebral functioning" (Newmark, 1985, p. 383). Several popular neuropsychological tests and test batteries are in use. One example is the Bender-Gestalt Test, which involves having the client copy nine separate designs. This test can be scored by subjective intuitive means or by utilizing an objective scoring procedure (Anastasi, 1988). Another neuropsychological test that clinicians use is the Benton Visual Retention Test, which requires the client to reproduce 10 different geometric figures. Although these two tests can provide an indication of brain damage, they should not be used as a sole means of making a diagnosis. Bigler and Ehrfurth (1981) even suggested that the Bender should be banned as a single neuropsychological technique.

Several neuropsychological test batteries have been developed in an attempt to create a more comprehensive approach to assessment and diagnosis. The two most popular test batteries are the Halstead-Reitan Neuropsychological Test Battery and the Luria Nebraska Neuropsychological Battery. The Halstead-Reitan Neuropsychological Test can be used with individuals ages 15 and older. It is technically comprised of 10 tests, 2 of which are considered allied procedures (Newmark, 1985). The main battery is comprised of the Category Test, Speech-Sounds Perception, Seashore Rhythm, Tactual Performance Test (TPT), Finger Oscillation, Trail Making A and B, Aphasia Screening, and Sensory Perceptual Examination. The allied procedures are the WAIS-R and the MMPI-II. Compared with the Halstead-Reitan, the Luria Nebraska Battery requires less time to administer (2 1/2 hours versus 6 or more hours), is more highly standardized, and provides a fuller coverage of neurological deficits (Anastasi, 1988).

Nonstandardized Measures.   Goldman (1990) referred to nonstandardized measures as qualitative assessment, noting that for the most part these forms of assessment do not yield quantitative raw scores as are found in standardized measures. Goldman suggested that qualitative assessment has a number of advantages over standardized approaches. Some advantages of qualitative assessment procedures are as follows.

- They foster an "active role for the client in the process of collecting and teasing meaning out of data, rather than the role of a passive responder who is being measured, predicted, placed, or diagnosed" (Goldman, 1990, p. 205).

- They emphasize "the *holistic study* of the individual rather than the isolation and precise measurement of narrowly defined discrete elements of ability, interest, or personality" (Goldman, 1990, p. 205).

- They encourage clients to learn about themselves within a developmental framework.

- They are especially effective in group work whereby clients can learn about individual differences as well as gain an understanding about themselves in relation to others in the group.

- They reduce the distinction between assessment and counseling by stimulating rather than hampering counseling methods, as can be the case with standardized assessment.

- They can be easily modified to accommodate individual differences such as cultural diversity and gender since they do not attempt precise measurements from normative samples.

A variety of nonstandardized measures can be used in the counseling process. These include observation skills, behavioral assessment, and environmental assessment. A description of each of these procedures follows.

Observation Skills.   The power of observation can be a very revealing aspect of clinical assessment. Freud attested to the power of observation when he said, "He that has eyes to see and ears to hear may convince himself that no mortal can keep a secret. If his lips are silent, he chatters with his fingertips; betrayal oozes out of him at every pore" (Freud, 1953, p. 77–78). As Freud noted, the skilled clinician can learn much from observing what occurs during the counseling session.

Baruth and Huber (1985) expanded on Ivey's (1983) work by identifying different aspects of nonverbal behavior that can be observed by counselors. These aspects have been summarized as follows.

- *Eye contact.* Pupils tend to dilate when clients are discussing an interesting topic and contract when they are bored or uncomfortable. In addition, clients tend to look away when discussing something that is depressing or disturbing.
- *Body language.* Much can be learned from a client's body language. For example, crossing the arms can suggest reluctance or resistance; leaning forward can imply interest; and leaning away can imply fear or boredom.
- *Autonomic physiological behavior.* Autonomic responses are very expressive and provide uncensored information about the client. For example, rapid breathing can suggest anxiety or nervousness, and blushing can indicate embarrassment.
- *Vocal qualities.* A client's voice quality can provide important information to the counselor. Changes in rate, volume, or pitch can communicate different messages. For example, hesitations and breaks can suggest confusion or stress.
- *Facial expressions.* Grimaces, frowns, smiles, and raised eyebrows all communicate something important about the client's emotional state.

Counselors can also learn from observing clients in their natural habitat. Goldman (1990) referred to this process as *shadowing*, which he defined as "following someone through a day or part of a day to observe how the person acts and reacts in various places and in various interactions" (p. 210). Shadowing can provide information on how the client functions in a "real-life" situation. Numerous possibilities exist for making observations in the field. Some examples include observing a student in a classroom, on a school bus, or on a playground to assess the child's interpersonal skills; observing a mother or father with a newborn to determine the degree of bonding; conducting a marriage or family session in a client's home to observe the family in their natural habitat; and observing a manager role-play administrative functions in an organizational setting.

Sundberg (1977) identified systematic methods for observing and recording behavior in organizational settings. These methods include the situational test, in-basket test, and critical incidence technique.

The situational test involves a contrived situation in which the subject is given a task to accomplish, for example, as a perspective policeman attempting to find a person

Observing prosocial behavior
can be part of the assessment
process.

who has mysteriously vanished. Specific measures of observation are identified to facilitate accurate recording of information.

The in-basket test is a method used to select and train managers and executives (Vernon & Parry, 1949; Lopez, 1966; Bray, Campbell, & Grant, 1974). This test entails observing an individual role-play various administrative tasks. Systematic procedures are then identified for observing and recording behavior.

The critical incidence technique involves an observer recording instances of behavior that indicate good or poor performance. From this information, procedures are identified to chart performance or plan training.

Behavioral Assessment.   Behavioral assessment, which evolved from behavioral psychology, involves the systematic measurement of behaviors broadly defined to include attitudes, feelings, and cognitions (Sundberg, 1977). In behavioral assessment, counselors may use a wide variety of procedures, including direct observation in the natural environment, problem checklists, self-reports, and record-keeping (Sundberg, 1977; Anastasi, 1988).

Behavioral assessment can be tied directly into treatment by using single-subject designs, such as A-B and A-B-A designs. The *A* phase involves obtaining a baseline of a problem behavior before treatment. The *B* phase assesses behavior after treatment. The behaviors recorded during the *A* and *B* phases are usually graphed to provide a measure of behavior change before and after treatment. Additional information on single-subject designs such as A-B and A-B-A can be found in Chapter 4.

Environmental Assessment.   Walsh (1990) observed that any assessment is incomplete without some assessment of the environment. Walsh suggested that counselors include an environmental assessment to determine how clients perceive their environment and how these perceptions influence their behavior. Environmental assessment can be particularly important when determining the etiology, or cause, of psychopathology. A counselor who does not consider environmental factors may attribute a mental disorder to intrapsychic forces, that is, forces within the person, instead of considering environmental factors such as living in poverty.

As counseling becomes increasingly multicultural, it is particularly important to include an assessment of socio-cultural factors when conducting an environmental assessment. Social forces that may warrant attention include how clients feel about where they live and whom they live with and their attitudes toward their job, family, and friends. Topper (1985) identified cultural factors that counselors should address during the assessment process. He noted that it is particularly important to evaluate the client's level of acculturation to determine if traditional Western counseling approaches would be appropriate. In addition, he suggested it would be advantageous to determine how the client's condition would be viewed by members of the client's culture and then evaluate the client in terms of patterns of psychological development that are normative to that culture.

DIAGNOSIS

This section will present an overview of diagnosis. It will include a historical perspective of diagnosis, uses of diagnosis, and a description of the Diagnostic Statistical Manual of Mental Disorders, Third Edition Revised (DSM-III-R) (American Psychiatric Association, 1987).

Historical Perspective

Nathan and Harris (1980) provided information that showed the process of diagnosis has been traced to the preclassical period in Greece. The Greeks were able to identify the behavioral consequences associated with the aging process and the mental health consequences of alcoholism. Somewhat later during classical times, the Greeks went on to identify and describe psychological disorders that are still recognized today, for example, mania, melancholia, and paranoia.

It was not until much later that a formal classification of psychological disorders was developed. Rosenhan and Seligman (1989) identified several key individuals who contributed to this process. Philippe Pinel (1745–1856), the psychiatric reformer, divided psychological disorders into melancholia, mania (with and without delirium), dementia, and idiotism. In 1896, Emil Kraepelin (1855–1926) developed the first comprehensive system of classifying psychological disorders. He based this system of diagnosis on a medical model. In this regard, Kraepelin believed all medical disorders had a physical origin and diagnosis required a careful assessment of symptoms. Rosenhan and Seligman identified several other individuals, such as Eugene Blueler and Adolf Meyer, who proposed their own systems of diagnosis.

Although there were merits in the various diagnostic systems, the need for one coherent system of diagnosis became apparent. This led to the development of the Diagnostic Statistical Manual of Mental Disorders (DSM) in 1952. The DSM has undergone several revisions since that time, including the DSM-III-R (3rd Edition Revised), the most recent revision in 1987.

Uses of Diagnosis.   Diagnosis is an important aspect of the counseling process. Rosenhan and Seligman (1989) described four reasons for making a diagnosis.

1. *It provides communication shorthand among clinicians.* Diagnosis enables the clinician to incorporate the various symptoms of a client into a single diagnosis that other clinicians can easily understand.

2. *It suggests treatment possibilities.* Diagnosis can help clinicians narrow down the treatment possibilities. For example, a paranoid schizophrenic will usually not respond well to verbal therapies.

3. *It can communicate information about etiology.* Mental disorders are associated with different types of etiology. For example, one of the major causative factors associated with schizophrenia is an excess of the neurotransmitter dopamine in the brain.

4. *It aids scientific investigation.* Diagnosis helps group symptoms together so they can be systematically studied to determine etiology and treatment strategies.

Woody, Hansen, and Rossberg (1989) noted that some counselors shy away from diagnosis because they believe it is a judgmental process that labels clients. These authors counter that diagnosis is more than a process of labeling. It also provides an analysis of the client's functioning to determine the most appropriate treatment.

The DSM-III-R

The DSM-III-R is a classification system of all recognized mental disorders. It is a multiaxial evaluation system, which provides information on five separate axes. An overview of these axes follows.

Axes I and II.   These two axes comprise the entire system of mental disorders. All recognized mental disorders will be on either Axis I or Axis II. The DSM-III-R provides "decision trees," which describe the symptoms associated with various mental disorders. Clinicians can use decision trees to rule out certain disorders when conducting a differential diagnosis to determine if a patient has a particular mental disorder.

Axis I is used for all mental disorders except for personality disorders and developmental disorders, which are placed on *Axis II*. Axis I can also be used to record counseling problems that are not mental disorders but require professional attention

Clinicians often refer to the DSM to formulate a diagnosis.

or treatment. These are called *V-codes* and include many so-called "problems of living," such as marital difficulty or parent-child problems. It is also important to note that multiple diagnoses can be recorded on both Axis I and II. For example, a 54-year-old male with a history of alcohol abuse is currently experiencing a major depression. In addition, the patient has an antisocial personality disorder. These disorders will be recorded on each axis as follows.

Axis I	296.22	Major depression, single episode, moderate
	305.00	Alcohol abuse
Axis II	301.70	Antisocial personality disorder

Clinicians record the presence or absence of a diagnosis on Axis I and Axis II, as illustrated in the following examples.

A 12-year-old client who is mentally retarded

Axis I	V71.09	No diagnosis or condition on Axis I
Axis II	317	Mild mental retardation

A client who does not have a mental disorder but is receiving help for a marital problem

| Axis I | V61.10 | Marital problem |
| Axis II | V71.09 | No diagnosis or condition on Axis II |

Another factor for clinicians to consider when making an Axis I or Axis II diagnosis is to determine the principal diagnosis or condition. The principal diagnosis is the condition that was primarily responsible for the evaluation and will be the main focus of attention. When making two or more diagnoses on the same axis, the clinician should list the primary diagnosis first on that axis. When making diagnoses on both axes, the clinician should indicate which is the primary diagnosis, as illustrated in the following example.

| Axis I | 309.24 | Adjustment disorder |
| Axis II | 301.20 | Schizoid personality disorder (principal diagnosis) |

The DSM-III-R also provides a mechanism for the clinician to indicate the degree of diagnostic certainty. There may be inadequate information to make a diagnosis on either Axis I or Axis II. When this occurs, the clinician can use the notation, "799.90 Diagnosis or condition deferred," on the appropriate axis, as illustrated in the following example.

| Axis I | 799.90 | Diagnosis or condition deferred |
| Axis II | 799.90 | Diagnosis or condition deferred |

The clinician can also make a provisional diagnosis on either axis. This enables the clinician to formulate a tentative diagnosis, which requires additional assessment before a final diagnosis can be made. The following example shows how the clinician indicates a provisional diagnosis.

| Axis I | 296.22 | Major depression, single episode, moderate (provisional) |

Axis III.   Axis III allows the clinician to indicate if there is a current physical disorder or condition that may be relevant to the particular case. For example, a person may be suffering from syphilis, which could be responsible for producing hallucinations. If this were the case, the clinician would record a diagnosis of untreated syphilis on Axis III.

Axis IV.   Axis IV provides information relating to pertinent psychosocial stressors. These are stressors a client has experienced during the preceding year that have contributed to the development of some new mental disorder; recurrence of some prior mental disorder; or exacerbation of a currently existing mental disorder (American Psychiatric Association, 1987).

The DSM-III-R provides examples of the types of psychosocial stressors that clinicians should consider. These include parenting problems, interpersonal difficulties, and financial problems. In addition, the DSM-III-R requires clinicians to rate the severity of psychosocial stressors for each client, using the Psychosocial Stressors Scale. The ratings on this scale range from "none" to "catastrophic."

Axis V.   Axis V allows the clinician to indicate a client's current level of functioning and the highest level of functioning during the past year. The DSM-III-R provides the Global Assessment of Functioning Scale (GAF) for clinicians to assign numerical ratings to both current and past levels of functioning. The scale ranges from 1 for "severe impairment of functioning" to 90 for "no impairment of functioning."

A Case Study.   Spitzer, Gibbon, Skodol, Williams, and First (1989) provided an excellent learning tool for counselors to gain expertise in using the DSM. For numerous case studies involving children, adolescents, and adults, the authors followed a format of describing each case study, giving a DSM-III-R diagnosis, and explaining the rationale for the diagnosis. The following excerpt from *The DSM-III-R Casebook* (Spetzer, et al., 1989, pp. 285–287) provides an example of how to apply the DSM diagnostic process to a case (reprinted by permission).

"Sniper"

Leah, age 7, was referred by her teacher for evaluation because of her tearfulness, irritability, and difficulty concentrating in class. Three months earlier Leah had been among the children pinned down by sniper fire on her school playground. Over a period of 15 minutes, the sniper killed one child and injured several others. After the gunfire ceased, no one moved until the police stormed the sniper's apartment and found that he had killed himself. Leah did not personally know the child who was killed, or the sniper.

According to her teacher, before the shooting, Leah was shy but vivacious, well-behaved, and a good student. Within a few days after the incident, there was a noticeable change in her behavior. She withdrew from her friends. She began to bicker with other children when they spoke to her. She seemed uninterested in her schoolwork and had to be prodded to persist in required tasks. The teacher noticed that Leah jumped whenever there was static noise in the public address system and when the class shouted answers to flashcards.

Leah's parents were relieved when the school made the referral, because they were uncertain about how to help her. Leah was uncharacteristically quiet when her parents asked her about the sniping incident. At home she had become moody, irritable, argumentative, fearful, and clinging. She was apprehensive about new situations and fearful of being alone and insisted that someone accompany her to the bathroom. Leah regularly asked to sleep with her parents. She slept restlessly and occasionally cried out in her sleep. She appeared always to be tired, complained of minor physical problems, and seemed more susceptible to minor infections. Her parents were especially worried after Leah nearly walked in front of a moving car without being aware of it. Although she seemed less interested in any of her usual games, her parents noticed that she kept engaging her siblings in nurse games, in which she was often bandaged.

When asked about the incident in the interview, Leah said that she had tried desperately to hide behind a trash can when she heard the repeated gunfire. She had been terrified of being killed, and was "shaking all over," her heart pounding and her head hurting. She vividly told of watching an older child fall to the ground, bleeding and motionless. She ran to safety when there was a pause in the shooting. Leah described a recurring image of the injured girl lying bleeding on the ground. She said that thoughts of the incident sometimes disrupted her attention, though she would try to think about something else. Lately, she could not always remember what was being said in class. She no longer played in the area where the shooting had occurred during recess or after school. She avoided crossing over the playground on her way home from school each day and avoided the sniper's house and street. She was particularly afraid at school on Fridays, the day the shooting had occurred. Although her mother and father had comforted her, she did not know who to tell what it was she was feeling.

Leah continued to be afraid that someone would shoot at her again. She had nightmares about the shooting and dreams in which she or a family member was being shot at or pursued. She ran away from any "popping noises" at home or in the neighborhood. Although she said that she had less desire to play, when asked about new games, she reported frequently playing a game in which a nurse helped an injured person. She began to watch television news about violence, and recounted news stories that demonstrated that the world was full of danger.

Discussion of "Sniper"

Leah's experience was clearly outside the range of usual human experience. Within a few days of the trauma, she began to exhibit the characteristic symptoms of a severe Post-Traumatic Stress Disorder.

Although adults sometimes have "flashback" experiences in which they actually experience the situation as if it were currently happening, children rarely reexperience trauma in this way. As is typical for her age, Leah reexperienced the trauma in the form of recurrent, intrusive images and recollections of the event and recurrent, distressing dreams about it. She also incorporated themes from the event into repetitive themes in play.

Leah attempted to avoid thoughts and feelings associated with the trauma and places that reminded her of the event. This formerly vivacious little girl exhibited numbing of general responsiveness. She became apathetic and uninterested in her schoolwork and detached from her former friends. She displayed persistent symptoms of increased arousal, including exaggerated startle reaction (to loud noises), irritability, difficulty concentrating, and sleep disturbance.

In making a multiaxial assessment, we rate the severity of the stress of witnessing a murder and being in danger of being killed as Extreme. Because of the impairment in her social relationships and schoolwork, we assign a current GAF of 45.

DSM-III-R Diagnosis

Axis I 309.89	Post-traumatic stress disorder
Axis II V71.90	No diagnosis or condition on Axis II
Axis III	None
Axis IV	Psychosocial stressors: Witnessing a killing and in danger of being killed
	Severity: 5—extreme (acute event)
Axis V	Current GAF: 45
	Highest GAF past year: 85

The Clinical Interview

The clinical interview provides a structure for assimilating information pertaining to assessment and diagnosis. May (1990) noted that the clinical interview is one of the most widely used assessment procedures. It serves a variety of purposes such as providing information on the client's presenting problem and concerns; enabling the counselor to gain necessary historical information, including organic factors that could contribute to the client's condition; and aiding in the process of making a differential diagnosis to determine if a client suffers from a particular mental disorder.

The clinical interview normally takes place early in the counseling process, usually during the first or second session. It allows the counselor to gain important background information and determine if the client suffers from a mental disorder or is in a state of crisis that requires immediate attention. The clinical interview can be structured according to the counselor's theoretical orientation and the client's unique issues and concerns.

I have developed a four-stage model for the clinical interview: using listening skills, taking the client's history, conducting a mental status exam, and using standardized and nonstandardized measures. These four stages serve overlapping functions and should not be perceived as discrete entities. For example, a counselor may gain useful information about the client's history and mental status while using listening skills. An overview of these four stages follows.

Stage One: Using Listening Skills.   Counselors can begin the clinical interview by using listening skills to obtain a phenomenological understanding of the client (see Appendix A for a description of listening skills). Counselors can also use listening skills to determine if the client was self-referred; what prompted the appointment; and a description of the presenting problem and underlying concerns.

Stage Two: Taking the Client's History.   The counselor may take an in-depth history after clients have had a chance to discuss their situation with the counselor. The history can be divided into two parts. The first part involves the client providing background information regarding work, family, social relationships, health, and other areas of interest such as important turning points in the client's life. Counselors may develop or use forms to solicit information on these topics as an efficient method of gathering this part of the history. The second part of the history involves exploring the client's symptoms and concerns, such as difficulty sleeping, loss of appetite, or marital problems, in terms of onset, duration, and severity. This information can help the counselor gain a better overall understanding of the client's condition. It can also be particularly useful in diagnosis, since major systems of diagnosis such as the DSM-III-R require this information to make a differential diagnosis.

It is particularly important when conducting a history to explore possible organic factors that could contribute to mental disorders. These factors include the use of alcohol or drugs, prescription medications, and existing or past medical conditions. For example, excessive use of alcohol can create hallucinations, resulting in a mental disorder called alcohol hallucinosis. Many prescription drugs have been known to contribute to the symptoms associated with mental disorders (Othmer & Othmer, 1989). Examples of these drugs and their associated disorders are: estrogen can cause anxiety and depression; diuretics can produce irritability, restlessness, insomnia, and delirium; and insulin can induce psychosis and confusion. Medical conditions may also be accompanied by symptoms of psychological distress. For example, gout or brain tumors can produce depression; head injury can cause anxiety; and multiple sclerosis can foster anxiety, depression, and episodic psychiatric symptoms. Othmer and Othmer (1989) provide a more complete list of prescription drugs and medical conditions and their associated psychiatric symptoms.

Stage Three: Conducting a Mental Status Exam.   Counselors can conduct a mental status exam to help make a differential diagnosis. For a client who claims to hear voices, a counselor may consider schizophrenia as a possible diagnosis. The counselor could then use the mental status exam to explore whether the client has other symptoms associated with schizophrenia, such as delusions, flat or inappropriate affect, and evidence of a thought disorder.

Nathan and Harris (1980) noted six components of behavior that counselors should assess when conducting a mental status exam. These components are summarized as follows.

1. *The client's general appearance and manner.* The counselor assesses what kind of overall impression the client makes during the interview and if that impression corresponds to the client's position in life. In addition, the counselor observes if the client's nonverbal behavior is congruent with verbal behavior.

2. *The client's speech characteristics.* The counselor assesses the content of the client's speech to determine if there is evidence of abnormality, such as flight of ideas (jumping from one topic to another), which is a characteristic of schizophrenia.

3. *The client's level and quality of mood.* The counselor assesses the client's mood to determine if it is appropriate (e.g., sad when things have gone wrong) or inappropriate (e.g., laughing when discussing a death in the family). Inappropriate mood or "flat affect" (expressionless) can be signs of psychosis. Profound sadness could indicate depression.

4. *The client's content of thought.* The counselor may want to assess if there is a thought disorder, especially if psychosis is suspected. For example, paranoid thoughts or loose association (rambling, disjointed thoughts) can be associated with schizophrenia. The preoccupation with fearsome thoughts beyond a client's control could indicate an obsessive compulsive disorder.

5. *The client's memory, learning, attention, concentration, and general information.* The counselor can assess how well the client is able to take in, process, and utilize data from the environment. Impairment of these functions could indicate a brain disorder such as intoxication or acute brain trauma. Clients with these disorders also tend to be disoriented in terms of not knowing where they are, why they are there, or what time it is. Chronic brain disorders such as alcoholism or senility are characterized by memory impairment, especially short-term memory. For example, the client may not recall what occurred in the previous hour or even the past few minutes.

6. *The client's insight and judgment.* The counselor can attempt to determine if the client is capable of utilizing insight and sound judgment. For example, a client with a serious mental disorder who denies having any problems and refuses any treatment may be considered incapable of utilizing sound judgment or insight. Alcoholics typically lack insight or ability to use sound judgment in this regard.

Stage Four: Using Standardized and Nonstandardized Measures.   Counselors can use standardized and nonstandardized measures to refine diagnostic considerations and plan treatment. For example, a client's MMPI-II profile might include elevated scales on 2 (depression) and 9 (mania), which could contribute to a diagnosis of manic-depression. In terms of nonstandardized measures, environmental assessment might show that the client feels depressed about living on the East coast, hates working in a retail job, and wants to go back to school. Information from the environmental assessment can be useful in terms of understanding the etiology or cause of the mental disorder as well as in planning treatment. In this example, the client could consider moving and going to school.

CHAPTER SUMMARY

Assessment and diagnosis are important parts of the counseling process. They provide critical background information that is necessary before the counselor and client can establish counseling goals. Assessment and diagnosis also contribute to the science dimension of counseling by providing objective information regarding the counseling process.

This chapter provided a description of standardized and nonstandardized assessment procedures. Standardized assessment procedures include psychological tests that have a standardized norm group, such as the MMPI-II. Nonstandardized tests do not have standardized norm groups, are more subjective in nature, and include a variety of procedures such as observation and environmental assessment. Standardized and nonstandardized assessment procedures have their inherent strengths and weaknesses. For example, the major strength of nonstandardized measures lies in the ease of adjusting these procedures to the unique characteristics of the individual, thereby avoiding tendencies to induce test bias.

The chapter also covered issues relating to diagnosis, including a historical perspective, the uses of diagnosis, the DSM-III-R, and the clinical interview. Particular attention was directed at the DSM-III-R and how it can be used to formulate a multi-axial diagnosis. The clinical interview was also described as a valuable tool for counselors to use in assessment and diagnosis. Counselors can use the interview to establish positive relationships and provide a structure for assessment and diagnosis. The clinical interview can also help the counselor avoid overlooking important issues such as a medical condition, past history of alcohol or drug abuse, and symptoms associated with a mental disorder.

REFERENCES

American Psychiatric Association. (1987). *Diagnostic and statistical manual of mental disorders* (3rd ed.). Washington, DC: American Psychiatric Association.

Anastasi, A. (1985). Mental measurement: Some emerging trends. In J. V. Mitchell, Jr. (Ed.), *The ninth mental measurement yearbook* (pp. xxiii—xxix). Lincoln, NE: University of Nebraska Press.

Anastasi, A. (1988). *Psychological testing* (6th ed.). New York: Macmillan.

Baruth, L. G., & Huber, C. H. (1985). *Counseling and psychotherapy: Theoretical analyses and skill application*. Columbus, OH: Merrill/Macmillan.

Bigler, E. D., & Ehrfurth, J. W. (1981). The continued inappropriate singular use of the Bender Visual Motor Gestalt Test. *Professional Psychology, 12*, 562–569.

Bray, D. W., Campbell, R. J., & Grant, D. L. (1974). *Formative years in business: A long-term AT&T study of managerial lives*. New York, NY: John Wiley & Sons.

Cattell, R. B. (1949). *Culture-fair intelligence tests*. Champaign, IL: Institute for Personality and Ability Testing.

Freud, S. (1953). Fragment of an analysis of a case of hysteria. In J. Strachey (Ed.), *The standard edition of the complete psychological works of Sigmund Freud* (Vol. 7, pp. 3–122). London: Hogarth.

Glasser, W. (1965). *Reality Therapy*. New York: Harper & Row.

Goldman, L. (1990). Qualitative assessment. *The Counseling Psychologist, 18*, 205–213.

Goodyear, R. K. (1990). Research on the effects of test interpretation: A review. *The Counseling Psychologist, 18*, 240–257.

Hansen, J. C., Stevic, R. R., & Warner, R. W., Jr. (1982). *Counseling theory and process* (2nd ed.). Boston: Allyn & Bacon.

Ivey, A. E. (1983). *Intentional interviewing and counseling*. Monterey, CA: Brooks/Cole.

Jewell, D. A. (1989). Cultural and ethnic issues. In S. Wetzler and M. M. Katz (Eds.), *Contemporary approaches to psychological assessment* (pp. 299–309). New York: Brunner/Mazel.

Jones, A. S., & Gelso, C. J. (1988). Differential effects of style of interpretation: Another look. *Journal of Counseling Psychology, 35*, 363–369.

Kottler, J. A., & Brown, R. W. (1985). *Introduction to therapeutic counseling*. Monterey, CA: Brooks/Cole.

Lopez, F. M., Jr. (1966). *Evaluating executive decision making*. New York: American Management Association.

May, T. M. (1990). An evolving relationship. *The Counseling Psychologist, 18*, 266–270.

McMillan, J. H. (1984). Culture-fair tests. In R. Corsini (Ed.), *Encyclopedia of Psychology* (pp. 335–336). New York: John Wiley & Sons.

Mercer, J. R. (1977). *SOMPA: System of Multicultural Pluralistic Assessment*. New York: Psychological Corp.

Miller, G. M. (1982). Deriving meaning from standardized tests: Interpreting test results to clients. *Measurement and Evaluation in Guidance, 15*, 87–94.

Miller, M. J., & Cochran, J. R. (1979). Evaluating the use of technology in reporting SCII results to students. *Measurement and Evaluation in Guidance, 12*, 166–173.

Nathan, P. E., & Harris, S. L. (1980). *Psychopathology and society* (2nd ed.). New York: McGraw-Hill.

Newmark, C. S. (1985). *Major psychological assessment instruments*. Boston: Allyn & Bacon.

Office of Strategic Services. (1948). *Assessment of men*. New York: Holt, Rinehart, & Winston.

Oliver, L. W. (1977). Evaluating career counseling outcome for three modes of test interpretation. *Measurement and Evaluation in Guidance, 10*, 153–161.

Othmer, E., & Othmer, S. C. (1989). *The clinical interview: Using DSM-III-R*. Washington, DC: American Psychiatric Press.

Penrose, L. S., & Raven, J. C. (1936). A new series of perceptual tasks: Preliminary communication. *British Journal of Medical Psychology, 16*, 97–104.

Reynolds, C. R. (1982). The problem of bias in psychological assessment. In C. R. Reynolds and T. B. Gutkin, *The Handbook of School Psychology*. New York: John Wiley & Sons.

Rogers, C. (1981). *A way of being*. Boston: Houghton Mifflin.

Rosenhan, D. L., & Seligman, M. E. P. (1989). *Abnormal Psychology* (2nd ed.). New York: W. W. Norton.

Sampson, J. P. (1990). Computer-assisted testing and the goals of counseling psychology. *The Counseling Psychologist, 18*, 227–239.

Spitzer, R. L., Gibbon, M., Skodol, A. E., Williams, J. B., & First, M. B. (1989). *The DSM-III-R Casebook*. Washington, DC: American Psychiatric Press.

Sundberg, N. D. (1977). *Assessment of persons*. Englewood Cliffs, NJ: Prentice-Hall.

Taylor, S. E., & Brown, J. D. (1988). Illusion and well-being: A social psychological perspective on mental health. *Psychological Bulletin, 103*, 193–210.

Topper, M. D. (1985). Navajo "alcoholism": Drinking, alcohol abuse, and treatment in a changing cultural environment. In L. A. Bennett & G. M. Ames, (Eds.), *The American experience with alcohol: Contrasting cultural perspectives*. New York: Plenum Press.

Vernon, P. E., & Parry, J. B. (1949). *Personnel selection in the British forces*. London: University of London Press.

Walsh, W. B. (1990). Putting assessment in context. *The Counseling Psychologist, 18*, 262–265.

Watkins, C. E., & Campbell, V. L. (1990). Testing and assessment in counseling psychology. *The Counseling Psychologist, 18*, 189–197.

Wilkerson, C. D. (1967). The effects of four methods of test score presentation to eighth-grade students. *Dissertation Abstracts International*, 1318A (order number 67–12661).

Woody, R. H., Hansen, J. C., & Rossberg, R. H. (1989). *Counseling psychology: Strategies and services*. Pacific Grove, CA: Brooks/Cole.

CHAPTER FOUR

Counseling Research and Evaluation

CHAPTER OVERVIEW

This chapter provides an overview of the issues relating to counseling research and evaluation. In addition to discussing traditional research methodologies, particular attention will be focused on field-based methodologies such as alternative and single-subject research designs. These newer methodologies are attracting considerable attention in the literature as being particularly relevant to the practitioner. Highlights of the chapter include

- The purpose of research and evaluation relative to theory and practice, counselor accountability, and the body of knowledge in the counseling field
- Overview of the types of research such as alternative research methodologies and single-subject designs

The section on single-subject design was written by Dr. Steven Stile.

THE PURPOSE OF RESEARCH AND EVALUATION

Counseling research serves many functions in the counseling process. This section will review several of these uses such as evaluating the efficacy of a counseling approach through the interaction of theory, practice, and research; providing a means for communicating counselor accountability; and contributing to the body of knowledge in the counseling field.

Research, Theory, and Practice

The art and science of the counseling model is similar to the scientist-practitioner model. Barlow, Hayes, and Nelson (1984) described the scientist-practitioner as a counselor who uses the methods of scientific inquiry to shape and guide clinical practice. The scientist-practitioner emphasizes the interrelationship between theory, practice, and research as illustrated in Figure 4.1 below.

Figure 4.1 shows theory at the apex of the triangle, thus placing it in the upper-most position. The interrelationship between theory, practice, and research can be illustrated in the following example. The counseling theory of behavior therapy develops techniques such as assertion training. A counselor may then use this technique in clinical practice and later implement research strategies to evaluate its effectiveness. The results of this research can provide useful information to refine the theoretical origins of assertion training.

Research and Counselor Accountability

Research and evaluation can also be used to communicate counselor accountability. One way to conceptualize how this occurs is through the interaction of research, evaluation, and accountability, as shown in Figure 4.2.

This model suggests that counselors can use research strategies to evaluate their individual clinical skills or an entire counseling program. The information obtained from the evaluation process can then provide professional accountability. Once accountability has been established, however, the process is not complete. The counselor should then set up an ongoing accountability program. This may require additional research strategies to evaluate the various facets of one's professional activities. Gibson (1977) provided the following guidelines for conducting evaluation research.

Figure 4.1
The Relationship Between
Theory, Practice, and Research

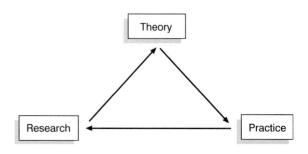

Figure 4.2
The Relationship Between
Research, Evaluation, and
Accountability

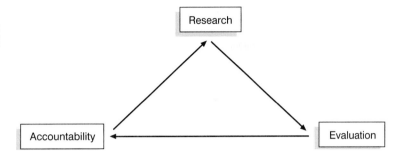

- *Effective evaluation begins with a recognition of program goals.* The first step is to determine what the program is trying to accomplish and which goals need to be evaluated. These goals must be stated in clear, measurable terms.
- *Effective evaluation uses valid measuring criteria.* Once goals have been identified, criteria for measuring these goals must be established. For example, a goal in a mental health center might be to have all counselors initiate a follow-up contact with each client within 1 to 2 months after termination of counseling services. The measuring criterion might be the percentage of clients whose follow-up activities were initiated.
- *Effective program evaluation depends on accurate application of the measuring criteria.* Appropriate research strategies should be used to collect and analyze the data.
- *Program evaluation should obtain input from all people involved in the program.* Opportunities for input from all levels of the organization should be provided. In a mental health center, for example, the evaluation might include information from administrators, clerical staff, counselors, and clients.
- *The evaluation should include feedback and follow-through.* Once the evaluation is complete, the results may be communicated to the staff in a clear and concise fashion. Recommendations should be included to facilitate future program planning and development.
- *Evaluation should be a planned and continuous process.* A program should have an ongoing evaluation process. This enables the staff to monitor strengths and weaknesses. Accountability does not imply that a program has only strengths. Rather, it implies also becoming aware of weaknesses and attempting to rectify them.

The Contribution of Research to the Counseling Field

Another purpose of conducting research is to contribute to the body of knowledge in the counseling field so that theories can be tested and practices refined. Gelso and Fassinger (1990) reviewed the counseling research conducted during the 1980s. These authors noted the following important trends.

- Research on Strong's (1968) Social Influence Model tapered off as interest began to shift to client factors and counselor-client factors important to the counseling process
- Research activity increased on behavioral, cognitive, and cognitive-behavioral interventions
- The number of studies relating to core conditions (e.g., empathy, respect) declined significantly
- Extensive research was conducted on vocational theory
- Research on clinical judgment represented an integration of diverse literature and offered much promise for future research activity
- A substantial increase in research on gender and racial/ethnic minority issues occurred during the review period

Additional research will need to be conducted on these topics as well as others if counseling is to continue to evolve in a meaningful fashion. Counselors can play a vital role in contributing to their profession by engaging in an ongoing research program. The following guidelines can be used to formulate a research program.

1. Do research on topics that interest you, rather than selecting a topic to impress someone else.
2. Develop some tenacity when doing research. Once you believe in a project, stick with it and follow it through. There will always be someone to tell you what you can't do. Your job is to tell yourself what you can and will do.
3. Make a detailed outline before starting to write the research report. This will help you organize your ideas and make your paper easier to read and understand.
4. Don't get discouraged with the publishing process. Once you submit a paper to a journal, it may be accepted; accepted provisionally; rejected with suggestions for resubmission; or rejected. Don't give up if you are requested to revise and resubmit your paper. Only 4% of the articles submitted to American Counseling Association journals are accepted without necessary revisions (Seligman, 1986).
5. Finally, never assume your idea is so simple that someone must have published it already. There is a good chance that your idea has not been published, and your contribution might be valuable to the counseling profession.

In the following Personal Note, I share some of my personal rewards and struggles with the publishing process.

a personal note

I've had my share of ups and downs in conducting research. Some highs include having my first paper accepted for publication and feeling excited about contributing to an area of investigation. I was particularly pleased that this was a theoretical paper about a new dimension to social interest. I remember thinking, "Wow, now I'm part of the evolution of Adlerian theory development." I've also had my share of lows in conducting research. The letters of rejection and critical reviews of articles are still painful to receive today.

To survive the research and publication process, I have had to develop a lot of tolerance, patience, perseverance, and self-discipline. But it's been worth it. I've been able to gain a better understanding of a wide range of topics from stuttering to why children soil their pants. Research has also helped me continually develop my personal approach to counseling, as I carefully examine what occurred in a case study. In addition, research has been a helpful tool to communicate accountability. For example, I am currently using a single-subject design, a topic discussed later in this chapter, to assess what is occurring with a program I'm using to treat encopresis (soiling the pants).

OVERVIEW OF THE TYPES OF RESEARCH

Research can be classified in several ways. One classification system differentiates basic research from applied research. *Basic research* is usually conducted under controlled conditions in a laboratory setting, often in a university. Basic research usually involves university students acting as subjects. Although basic research studies tend to use rigorous research designs, it may be risky to generalize the results of this type of research to the "real world." *Applied research* typically tests theories in a field setting. Applied research is therefore reflective of people in their natural habitat. Unfortunately, field studies are not always easy to control and may provide misleading results. Regardless of these limitations, applied research may provide a more realistic alternative for clinicians.

Types of Research Methodologies

Research can also be classified in terms of design. Some of the more common types of research designs are as follows.

Survey Studies.   This research design uses interviews and questionnaires to determine attitudes, preferences, and behaviors of a specific group of people (La Fleur, 1983). For example, an investigator might survey a representative sample of professional counselors to determine what counseling approaches are used most often.

Correlational Studies.   These studies are used to determine if two factors are related. A counselor may wish to determine if there is a relationship between gender and age of clients. A review of the counselor's clients over a 2-year period may show that clients over 40 years of age tended to be female and those under 15 tended to be male.

Experimental Methods.   This methodology attempts to determine if a cause-and-effect relationship exists. An experimental design usually involves evaluating a particular treatment effect under controlled conditions. For example, an investigator may wish to evaluate the effects of a parent education program on parent attitudes and

Counseling research can involve statistical analysis of data.

parent-child behavioral interactions. Traditional experimental designs involve randomly assigning a group of subjects to a treatment group (subjects receiving parent education) and a control group (subjects who do not receive parent education). The two groups can then be compared before and after the program on attitudes, behaviors, or other measures. Statistical analysis is used to evaluate the degree of change in the particular measures to determine the effects of the parent education program.

Longitudinal Studies.   These studies are designed to evaluate a particular group of subjects over an extended period of time. For example, a counselor may wish to analyze how well a group of immigrants adjust to American society. Using this research design, the counselor might periodically check on variables such as the percent who graduate from high school and college or tendencies toward physical or mental health problems.

Large-Scale Reviews.   This methodology involves reviewing many published research studies, and it has usually been conducted in an attempt to assess the efficacy of counseling. Some of the early work of this type did much to challenge the efficacy of counseling. This was especially true for Eysenck (1952, 1965), who claimed that counseling was not effective and that people tended to get better regardless of whether they received counseling. Levitt (1957) also challenged the efficacy of counseling in a large-scale review of studies that evaluated the effectiveness of child counseling and concluded that Eysenck's findings were essentially correct.

Several recent large-scale reviews of outcome research provided support for the effectiveness of counseling (Andrews & Harvey, 1981; Miller & Berman, 1983; Smith & Glass, 1977; Smith, Glass, & Miller, 1980). These large-scale reviews employed a sophisticated form of statistical analysis called meta-analysis in an attempt to reduce some of the methodological problems that can result from grouping together numerous studies for analysis. Smith and Glass conducted the first large-scale review that demonstrated strong empirical support for the effectiveness of counseling. Their investigation of 400 studies showed that treated individuals were better off than 75% of those who did not receive counseling. Smith, Glass, and Miller reviewed 475 studies and found that treated individuals were better off than 80% of those who did not receive counseling. Lambert, Shapiro, and Bergin (1986) provided a comprehensive overview of the literature relating to counseling effectiveness.

Qualitative Methods (Alternative Methods).   This design attempts to understand people and events in their natural setting. It has therefore been referred to as a naturalistic approach. Qualitative methods typically employ nonstandardized measures such as interviews and observations as a means of collecting data. Qualitative methods are oriented to the discovery of insights rather than confirmation of hypotheses. More recently qualitative methods have been called *alternative methods* because they provide an alternative to more traditional experimental designs. A more in-depth description of alternative methods will be provided later in this chapter.

Case Studies and Single-Subject Designs.   This method involves an intensive study of one individual or a single group of individuals. According to Borg and Gall (1989), "Most case studies are based on the premise that a case can be located that is typical of many other cases" (p. 402). Freud was one of the first clinicians to use case studies to illustrate a particular therapeutic technique. A case study usually involves a detailed description of the client: information about the counseling strategy used; and an evaluation of the counseling outcomes.

Case studies can be expanded to incorporate some of the principles of experimental design. These designs are sometimes referred to as *single-subject designs* (Goldman, 1978), which are presented later in this chapter. They can increase the counselor's ability to evaluate counseling outcomes objectively. Goldman (1978) suggested that case studies and single-subject research conducted in the field can be very useful for counselors.

Shortcomings of Traditional Counseling Research

Although the scientist-practitioner model appears to be a goal in the counseling profession, it is not yet a reality. Unfortunately, as Rogers noted, few counselors do any research and few researchers do little if any counseling (Heppner, Rogers, & Lee, 1984). Brown (1989) also commented on the apparent split between counselors and researchers, observing that they do not appear to be working together. The author said that counselors pay little attention to research findings, and researchers publish studies that are of little relevance to counselors (Brown).

Sprinthall (1975) and Goldman (1976; 1977) cited several problems with counseling research, which may in part account for the split between researchers and practitioners. These observations include claims that counseling research

- Has done little to influence how counseling is conceptualized or practiced
- Relies too much on laboratory experiments and not enough on applied research in the field
- Uses research methodology that was designed for the physical and biological sciences and is therefore inappropriate for analyzing intangible qualities such as attitudes and feelings
- Does not investigate topics that are relevant or interesting to practitioners
- Has focused too much on the average person and not enough on individuals

Considering these shortcomings, it is not surprising that practitioners find research to have little relevance to their practice (Minor, 1981; Howard, 1985). In addition, practitioners often avoid doing research and rarely read counseling journals (Goldman, 1976). There is even a tendency for counseling students at the graduate level to resent having to take research courses (Winfrey, 1984).

Many changes appear necessary in counseling research. Goldman (1978) suggested that practitioners need to be equipped with less formal, more practical tools for conducting research. Two strategies that are attracting considerable interest in the counseling literature are (a) alternative research strategies and (b) case studies that employ single-subject and small-group designs.

Alternative Research Methodologies

As mentioned, alternative research strategies, also referred to as qualitative methods, have evolved in response to disillusionment with traditional basic research methodologies that typically utilize experimental designs, for example, subjects and control groups. In addition, advocates of alternative research methodologies suggest that basic research designs are unnecessarily restrictive and yield results that have little relevance to practitioners (Mahrer, 1988).

Hoshmand (1989) provided an extensive overview of alternative methodologies in a 1989 special issue on alternative research in *The Counseling Psychologist*. She presented information relating to the purpose of alternative methods; the roles of the researcher and subjects; the process of inquiry; the types of inquiry; and data analysis. This information has been summarized as follows.

- *Purpose.* Alternative research designs are characterized by the purpose of developing an understanding of the essence of human experience. They emphasize description and discovery as opposed to theory testing. In this regard, Goldman (1989) pointed out that researchers using alternative methods are more concerned with what topics they want to learn about and explore than with what instruments to use or how to obtain subjects.
- *Role of the researcher and subjects.* The researcher takes a more active role in the research process than simply observing and recording data. This role may involve engaging in dialogue and interacting with the subject as a means of exploring and discovering significant events that the client has experienced. Subjects also take a more active role, becoming co-investigators in a collaborative and reciprocal relationship with the researcher. From this perspective,

research activity is not controlled by the researcher. In addition, subjects are consulted as to what they consider meaningful and relevant research questions and if the interpretations and conclusions are valid for the subject.

- *The process of inquiry*. Inquiry is characterized as an emergent, ongoing process that includes responsiveness to feedback from the subject. The course of inquiry is therefore determined by collaboration between the researcher and subject.

- *Data gathering*. Data gathering procedures vary according to the methodology employed. Typical methods include observation in the client's natural setting for extended periods of time; in-depth interviews from a phenomenological perspective; and oral histories such as recording myths and legends.

- *Data analysis*. The methods of data analysis can be described as interpretive with the goal of recognizing meaningful patterns.

Types of Alternative Research Methodologies.   This section will present three types of alternative methodologies: naturalistic-ethnographic, discovery-oriented, and representative-case methods.

Hoshmand (1989) described *naturalistic-ethnographic* methodologies as involving the observation of subjects in their natural context to obtain an understanding of the factors that influence human behavior. This approach requires prolonged contact and immersion in a particular setting to enable the researcher to obtain an understanding of the members in that setting. Data gathering may incorporate activities such as observation, interviews, oral histories, reviews of existing research documents and literature, and the use of critical incidence. Kidder, Judd, and Smith (1986) and Lincoln and Guba (1985) provide detailed descriptions of these procedures. The selection of a particular data-gathering procedure involves a consideration of how to relate effectively to the population under study. For example, one investigation used "rap" groups in a data-gathering method with mentally retarded adults (Hoshmand, 1985). Data analysis entails constant recording, categorizing, sorting, and re-sorting in an attempt to create emergent core categories of meaning. Field notes are transcribed verbatim and analyzed during repeated readings of the data to identify key phrases and concepts. Independent judges identify categories of meaning and sort them into themes to check for reliability. The researcher then collaborates with the participants for their opinion on the data that were generated.

McKenzie (1986) provided an example of a naturalistic-ethnographic study, which investigated the attitudes of West Indian-American youths toward counseling. In the first phase of the study, a counselor spent 6 months immersing himself in the schools, homes, peer groups, and other activities of students under study. The researcher spent an average of 40 hours with each student. During the second phase, the researcher conducted in-depth interviews with the students and counseling staff, exploring issues such as development and attitudes toward counseling and toward seeking help. The data were then analyzed to identify meaningful patterns. Results of the study showed that West Indian-Americans had strong taboos against seeking counseling; their cultural background affected their career choices; and biculturalism induced conflict within their families.

Research can involve in-depth analysis of a case to discover important aspects of what may be occurring in counseling.

Mahrer (1988) developed another type of alternative methodology, which he called *discovery-oriented psychotherapy research*. The purpose of the discovery-oriented approach is to take an in-depth look at psychotherapy and attempt to discover important aspects of what is occurring in counseling, for example, what prompted a personality change in a client. Mahrer described the following method for using the discovery-oriented approach.

1. Select the target of investigation. Start off by identifying some aspect of counseling of interest, no matter how large or insignificant it may seem. Avoid getting sidetracked by technical jargon such as transference or locus of control.

2. Obtain instances of the target being investigated. Obtain as many instances as possible of the target under investigation. For example, a researcher may be interested in exploring what can be discovered about early childhood memories. The researcher can attempt to obtain examples of these memories in a variety of ways, such as video recordings of sessions and narratives provided by clients.

3. Obtain an instrument to take a closer look. Once incidences of target behavior are obtained, the researcher can develop an instrument to take a closer look at the target being investigated (e.g., early memories). A category system can be used for this purpose. This can begin with a search of the literature. Next, a group of judges can review the sample incidences of the target under

investigation (e.g., videotapes) and continuously review this material until meaningful themes or categories of data emerge. The themes and categories obtained can provide the researcher with an instrument to systematically evaluate the target of investigation (e.g., early memories).

4. Gather data. This step involves obtaining the necessary data for the study and applying the instrument to the data. This may involve analyzing the original data obtained during Step 2 or obtaining new examples of the target of investigation (e.g., additional early memories).

5. Make discovery-oriented sense of the data. This step involves interpreting the data to determine what can be learned from the study. This process requires the characteristics associated with the art of counseling. The investigator must be sensitive to the discoverable by being open to what appears new, unexpected, challenging, or disconcerting in the data.

Gordon and Shontz (1990) developed a case-study type of alternative methodology called *representative-case research*. This method can be used to gain an in-depth understanding of people with various problems, such as children who are terminally ill, school dropouts, and single parents. Gordon and Shontz described representative-case research as a process that involves carefully examining "chosen persons one at a time, in depth, to learn how each experiences and manages an event, situation, or set of circumstances or conditions that is important in human life" (p. 62).

Representative-case research is considered an alternative methodology because it requires the active involvement of the client, who is considered to be an expert on the problem under study and a co-investigator. It is a process that attempts to discover what a client has learned about a particular experience or set of circumstances. The assistance of supervisors or advisors can also promote objectivity and monitor different aspects of the research process. These individuals can help with various activities such as data analysis and interpretation. They can also assist with the relationship between the counselor and client—the investigator and co-investigator.

Evaluation of Alternative Methodologies

Alternative methods appear to offer much promise for practitioners as a viable research method, but they also seem to pose some potential problems. One way to assess this new form of research is to relate it to nonstandardized measures, as described in Chapter 3. The same strengths and weaknesses apply to both, since alternative research methods typically utilize nonstandardized measures, such as observation and environmental assessment.

In terms of weaknesses, both nonstandardized assessment and alternative research methods lack objectivity and ability to generalize to a reference group; can create confusing results; and often lack acceptable levels of validity and reliability. The advantages common to both nonstandardized measures and alternative research methods are that they provide a flexible, individualized approach, which generates information unique to the individual; can be easily modified to accommodate individual differences; and foster an active role between the counselor (researcher) and the client (subject).

These advantages make alternative research methods particularly attractive to multicultural counseling research (Helms, 1989). Another advantage of alternative methods is that they require some of the same skills associated with effective counseling, as Goldman (1989) wrote.

> . . . these new methods are not for the faint of heart. They demand imagination, courage to face the unknown, flexibility, some creativeness, and a good deal of personal skill in observation, interviewing, and self-examination—some of the same skills, in fact, required for effective counseling, but now systematically directed toward the education of principles and generalizations, rather than effective change in individuals (pp. 83–84).

Alternative research methodologies can be viewed as an emerging form of counseling research. These methods should be viewed as alternatives, not as replacements for other forms of research. Additional research and development is necessary to refine these methodologies. In particular, investigators need guidelines for data gathering and analysis. At present, these procedures appear vague, lacking in structure, and confusing. In addition, clinicians may get the impression that these alternative research methods must involve a lengthy investigative process that includes living in the particular setting under study. These impressions could discourage active clinicians from considering this form of research. Hopefully, the problems associated with alternative methodologies can be overcome since many benefits may evolve from this intriguing new approach.

Single-Subject Designs

Single-subject designs constitute another emerging form of research that offers much promise to the practitioner. Single-subject designs may be used to investigate the effectiveness of counseling with one client or a small group of clients. These designs may be classified into three distinct families or groups: ABA or "withdrawal" designs, multiple baseline designs, and comparative intervention designs (Tawney & Gast, 1984). Stile (1987) described eight major steps involved in applying single-subject design strategies to counseling research or evaluation, as shown in Table 4.1. These steps are the same regardless of the design used.

ABA Designs.   This family of designs gets its name from the simplest design, which allows withdrawal of a treatment in order to measure its effects at introduction and after removal (Barlow & Hershen, 1984).

The five most common ABA designs are the A, the B, the A-B, the A-B-A, and the A-B-A-B. The first three designs have been termed *pre-experimental* (the A and B designs) and *quasi-experimental* (the A-B design) in relation to their abilities to establish cause-and-effect relationships. The A-B-A and A-B-A-B designs are classified as *experimental* designs, since they can be used to establish cause and effect with single subjects or small groups.

The A Design.   This design has also been referred to as the *case study method*. According to Borg and Gall (1989), "the case study . . . involves an investigator who makes a detailed examination of a single subject or group or phenomenon" (p. 402). Although case studies have long been considered unscientific because of a lack of control and subjectivity, Borg and Gall have recently noted an increased acceptance of

Table 4.1
Steps in Applying Single-Subject Strategies

Step	Procedure
1. Identification	Identify which skills or behaviors will be targeted for change (e.g., "irresponsibility").
2. Definition	Define the targeted skill or behavior in such a way that it can be observed and measured (e.g., "staying out late" provides a more adequate unit of measurement than "irresponsibility").
3. Selection of dependent variable or measure	Select the characteristic of the behavior to be measured and the counseling objective. For example, the *number* of occurrences of staying out late can be measured in relation to a particular treatment. Zero occurrences may be established as the outcome.
4. Identification of independent variable or treatment	Identify the treatment (e.g., counseling technique) to be applied to the dependent variable. For example, logical consequences may be applied to occurrences of staying out late.
5. Completion of planning	Complete all related planning. Decisions made at this step should include who will record the occurrence of the behavior (e.g., staying out late) and how the occurrence of the behavior will be recorded (e.g., tally marks on a simple recording instrument).
6. Training	Train (if appropriate) all other participants to consistently carry out data collection/treatment procedures. For example, all observers should practice collecting data until they reach close agreement on recording of the dependent variable.
7. Intervention and data collection	Intervene by withholding, applying, or withdrawing the treatment while continuously collecting data on the dependent variable (e.g., number of occurrences).
8. Graphing	Graph the results of the treatment by plotting data points on graph paper and connecting the points to represent trends.

qualitative methods such as "ethnography and participant observation." The A design can be thought of as an extended period during which data are collected on the dependent variable—the behavior you hope to change—but treatment is withheld.

The B Design.   The B design is closely related to the A design. In this design, no baseline observations are made, but dependent variables are monitored throughout the course of a treatment. As Barlow and Hersen (1984) described it, the B design is "a very modest improvement over the uncontrolled case study method" (p. 141).

The A-B Design.   The A-B design corrects for some of the weaknesses of the A and B designs. The inquirer begins by selecting a subject or subjects, pinpointing a problem, selecting a dependent variable, and choosing a treatment. Next, the dependent variable is measured during a minimum of three baseline (A) observations. In the second and final phase of this design, the investigator applies the treatment (B) and measures its effect on the dependent variable. In this design the baseline can be thought of as a control since it predicts future behavior without intervention. The major objection to this design is the possibility that some other variable may be operating simultaneously with the treatment to bring about change in skills or behavior.

The A-B-A Design.   The A-B-A design addresses objections to the A-B design by employing a second baseline (A2) as a control. If withdrawal of treatment results in trends in A2 that approximate A1, arguments for a cause-and-effect relationship between the independent and dependent variables gain considerable support.

The A-B-A-B Design.   The A-B-A-B design addresses the major shortcoming of the A-B-A design because it ends in a second treatment condition, or B2. Tawney and Gast (1984) have observed that the A-B-A design is rarely the original design of choice anymore. In fact, it is used only when attrition prevents the final phase of the A-B-A-B design. Since no limitation exists regarding the length of B2, a successful treatment may be left in place for a lengthy period to help ensure maintenance of change. The major shortcoming of the A-B-A design is that it often ends on a "negative note" (Borg and Gall, 1989), since a presumably effective treatment is withdrawn.

The following case illustrates the steps in the application of a member of the ABA family of single-subject designs (the A-B) to evaluate the efficiency of a counseling program. The steps refer to those listed in Table 4.1. The A-B design was chosen because it is easy to apply. Beginning counselors may wish to use this design in a pilot study of a new counseling technique.

The Case of Ann.   Ann was a 17-year-old girl enrolled in a large urban high school. The target behavior identified (Step 1 in Table 4.1) in this case was "school phobia." The school principal defined Ann's behavior (Step 2) as often refusing to go to school or failing to remain there once she arrived. Ann was referred to the school counselor for assistance with this problem. Before seeing Ann, the school counselor examined her attendance records. These records showed that she had attended school for the entire day only 40%, 60%, and 20% during the first, second, and third weeks of school, respectively. At this point, the counselor identified percent of attendance as the dependent variable and established the therapeutic objective (Step 3) that Ann would attend school 95% of the time every week unless she had a legitimate excuse such as a family emergency. Next, the counselor identified a treatment package consisting of individual and group counseling sessions as the independent variable and completed all prior planning (Steps 4 and 5). Since training (Step 6) was not necessary in this case, the next step was to begin the intervention and data collection (Step 7).

A behaviorally oriented approach was used in individual sessions. In these sessions, Ann was helped to understand how school had become threatening to her and how certain physical symptoms including nausea, diarrhea, and dizziness were related to her anxiety. After four sessions, Ann was able to enter the counselor's office and attend one class independently. She was then invited to attend weekly group sessions with the school's five other school-phobic students to discuss feelings toward school and related issues.

Over a 4-month period, the counselor observed that Ann developed a caring attitude toward other group members. She met with them before school, and they often walked home together. Beginning with the first group session, Ann was asked to monitor her own school attendance. By the beginning of Christmas vacation (Week 15), she reported to the group that her attendance (i.e., the dependent variable) had increased to 100%. Periodic checks at monthly intervals revealed that her attendance remained at this level. The graph developed by Ann and her counselor (Step 8) is shown as Figure 4.3.

Multiple-Baseline Designs.   A variation of the A-B design is the multiple-baseline design. Frequently, withdrawal designs such as A-B-A or A-B-A-B are inappropriate for a given behavior. For example, a counselor might be viewed as unethical for beginning a second baseline phase when it appears that treatment (e.g., self-monitoring) is associated with a significant reduction of aggressive behavior in the client. In such cases, multiple-baseline designs should be considered.

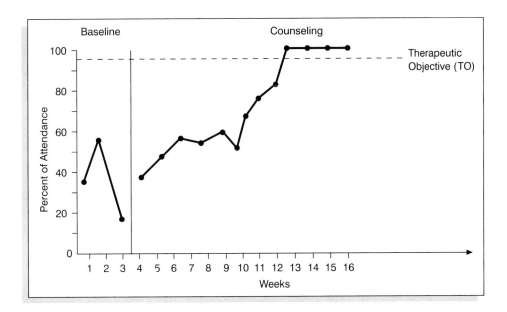

Figure 4.3
A-B Design for the Case of Ann

The three major multiple-baseline designs are multiple baseline across behaviors, multiple baseline across settings, and multiple baseline across subjects. All three may be thought of as extensions of the A-B design illustrated by the Case of Ann.

Multiple Baseline Across Behaviors.   This design is intended for use with single subjects or groups. When used with groups, data are summed or averaged, and the group is treated as a single organism (Barlow & Hersen, 1984). When using the across-behaviors design, the inquirer is cautioned to select behaviors that are independent of one another. Borg and Gall (1989) explained as follows.

> Independence is demonstrated by a change in the target behavior to which the treatment is being applied while other target behaviors (or controls) maintain a stable baseline rate. If other behaviors change reliably from baseline, the multiple-baseline design is invalid (p. 585).

Multiple Baseline Across Settings.   The across-settings design is also intended for use with single groups or subjects. In this design, the effect of a treatment on a dependent variable is studied in independent temporal and/or physical settings.

Multiple Baseline Across Subjects.   The across-subjects design is used for inquiry with matched groups. For example, Peck, Apolloni, Cooke, and Raver (1978) used this methodology to examine imitation of free-play behavior in a group of three preschool students with mental disabilities.

The following case illustrates the steps in implementing the design of multiple baseline across behaviors in a counseling situation. As shown in Figure 4.4, this design requires that the counselor apply a treatment (B) to a *succession* of behaviors that are being baselined (A). The steps refer to those shown in Table 4.1.

The Case of Drew.   Drew was an 18-year-old college freshman living at home with his mother and father. The target behavior identified (Step 1) by counselor and parents was "irresponsibility." Irresponsible behavior was defined as (a) staying out too late on school nights, (b) not parking the car in the garage, and (c) not putting his father's tools away after use (Step 2). After closely observing these behaviors for 5 days, Drew's father established the number of occurrences of irresponsible behavior as the dependent variable and set zero occurrences of the behavior as the therapeutic objective (Step 3). After a lengthy discussion, the counselor and family decided that logical consequences (Dreikurs & Soltz, 1964) would be the treatment approach used in response to Drew's irresponsible behaviors (Step 4). Logical consequences involve experiencing the consequences of one's behavior, as in losing the use of a car if one gets a citation for driving while intoxicated. Planning was completed (Step 5) when it was decided that Drew would experience a logical consequence immediately upon occurrence of an irresponsible behavior. In addition, application of the logical consequences would be applied sequentially as follows: (a) first only with staying out late; (b) second, it would be applied to inappropriate car parking; and (c) finally it would be applied to all three behaviors (staying out late, parking the car, and not putting away the tools). Drew's father and mother were then trained by the counselor to tally occurrences of the three behaviors on a simple record-keeping instrument (Step 6).

The treatment began (Step 7) with Drew being told that he would lose the privilege of going out on school nights (Sunday through Thursday) if he came home after 11:00 p.m. After 5 more days, the logical consequence treatment was also applied to his parking the car. That is, if he did not park the car in the garage, he would be unable to use it. Finally, after an additional 5 days (Day 16), the logical consequence strategy was applied to putting his father's tools away. If Drew failed to put his father's tools away after using them, he would be unable to borrow them. Thus beginning on day 16, the treatment was applied to all three behaviors with Drew's mother and father continuing observations and data collection. His father charted Drew's progress on a graph (Step 8), as shown in Figure 4.4. The use of logical consequences appears to have resulted in the elimination of each of the problem behaviors targeted for change. In addition, the zero rate of occurrence was maintained until the treatment and monitoring were withdrawn after 40 days.

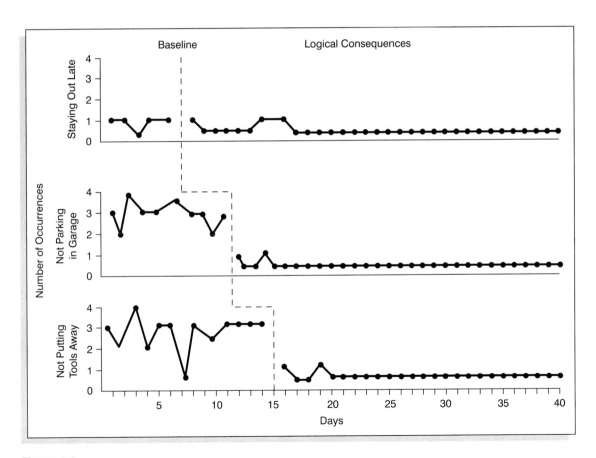

Figure 4.4
Multiple Baseline Across Behavior Design for the Case of Drew

Evaluation of Single-Subject Designs

Single-case designs offer much value to the active clinician. They provide an objective means to evaluate what is occurring in the counseling process with one client at a time. A counselor can use this information to adjust the treatment program throughout the counseling process. It also can provide a useful tool to keep the client informed as to what is occurring in counseling. These designs have been used primarily in conjunction with behavioral approaches. Additional research and development is necessary to expand their use to accommodate other schools of counseling.

CHAPTER SUMMARY

Research and evaluation are an ongoing facet of the counseling process. Research strategies serve several functions, such as offering a means to evaluate the efficacy of a counseling approach; communicate accountability: and contribute to the body of knowledge relating to the counseling profession. Research and evaluation can also be conceptualized as contributing to the science of counseling model by providing objective information regarding the counseling process. The practice of research and evaluation is both an art and science with approaches such as alternative methodologies and single-subject designs encouraging clinicians to develop flexible, creative strategies of evaluation.

REFERENCES

Andrews, G., & Harvey, R. (1981). Does psychotherapy benefit neurotic patients? A re-analysis of the Smith, Glass, and Miller data. *Archives of General Psychiatry*, 38, 1203–1508.

Barlow, D. H., Hayes, S. C., & Nelson, R. O. (1984). *The scientist practitioner*. New York, NY: Pergamon.

Barlow, D. H., & Hersen, M. (1984). *Single-case experimental designs: Strategies for studying behavior change*. New York: Pergamon Press.

Borg, W. B., & Gall, M. D. (1989). *Educational research: An introduction* (5th ed.). New York: Logman.

Brown, M. T. (1989). Healing the split: Mental health counseling research and practice. *Journal of Mental Health Counseling, 11*, 116–121.

Dreikurs, R., & Soltz, V. (1964). *Children: The challenge*. New York: Hawthorn.

Eysenck, H. J. (1965). The effects of psychotherapy. *Journal of Consulting Psychology, 16*, 319–324.

Gelso, C. I., & Fassinger, R. E. (1990). Counseling psychology: Theory and research on intervention. *American Review of Psychology, 41*, 354–386.

Gibson, R. L. (1977). Counseling and annual guidance committee report. Unpublished manuscript, North Central Association of Colleges and Schools.

Goldman, L. (1976). A revolution in counseling research. *Journal of Counseling Psychology, 23*, 543–552.

Goldman, L. (1977). Toward more meaningful research. *Personnel and Guidance Journal, 55*, 363–368.

Goldman, L. (1978). *Research methods for counselors: Practical approaches in field settings*. New York: John Wiley & Sons.

Goldman, L. (1989). Moving counseling research into the 21st century. *The Counseling Psychologist, 17*, 81–85.

Gordon, J., & Shontz, F. (1990). Representative case research: A way of knowing. *Journal of Counseling and Development, 69,* 62–66.

Helms, J. E. (1989). At long last: Paradigms for cultural psychology research. *The Counseling Psychologist, 17,* 98–100.

Heppner, P. P., Rogers, M. E., & Lee, L. A. (1984). Carl Rogers: Reflections on his life. *Journal of Counseling and Development, 64,* 14–20.

Hoshmand, L. L. S. (1989). Alternate research paradigms: A review and teaching proposal. *The Counseling Psychologist, 17,* 3–80.

Hoshmand, L. T. (1985). Phenomenological-based groups for developmentally disabled adults. *Journal of Counseling and Development, 64*(2), 147–148.

Howard, G. S. (1985). Can research in the human sciences become more relevant to practice? *Journal of Counseling and Development, 63,* 539–544.

Kidder, L. H., Judd, C. M., & Smith, E. R. (1986). *Research methods in social relations.* New York: Holt, Rinehart, & Winston.

Lambert, M. J., Shapiro, D. A., & Bergin, A. E. (1986). The effectiveness of psychotherapy. In S. L. Garfield & A. E. Bergin (Eds.), *Handbook of psychotherapy and behavior change* (3rd. ed.). New York: John Wiley & Sons.

La Fleur, K. N. (1983). Research and evaluation. In J. A. Brown & R. A. Pate, *Being a counselor.* Monterey, CA: Brooks/Cole.

Levitt, E. E. (1957). The results of psychotherapy with children: An evaluation. *Journal of Consulting Psychology, 21.* 189–196.

Lincoln, Y. S., & Guba, E. G. (1985). *Naturalistic inquiry.* Beverly Hills, CA: Sage.

Mahrer, A. R. (1988). Discovery-oriented psychotherapy research: Rationale, aims, and methods. *American Psychologist, 43,* 694–702.

McKenzie, V. M. (1986). Ethnographic findings on West Indian-American clients. *Journal of Counseling and Development, 65.* 40–44.

Miller, R. C., & Berman, J. S. (1983). The efficacy of cognitive behavior therapies: A quantitative review of the research evidence. *Psychological Bulletin,* 94, 39–53.

Minor, B. J. (1981). Bridging the gap between research and practice. *Personnel and Guidance Journal, 59.* 485–486.

Peck, C. A., Apolloni, T., Cooke, T. P., & Raver, S. A. (1978). Teaching retarded preschoolers to imitate the free-play behavior of non-retarded classmates: Trained and generalized effects. *Journal of Special Education,* 12, 195–207.

Seligman, L. (1986). The manuscript evaluation process used by AACD journals. *Journal of Counseling and Development,* 65(4), 189–192.

Smith, M. L., & Glass, G. J. (1977). Meta-analysis of psychotherapy outcome studies. *American Psychologist, 32,* 752–760.

Smith, M. L., Glass, G. V., & Miller, T. I. (1980). *The benefits of psychotherapy.* Baltimore: Johns Hopkins University Press.

Sprinthall, N. A. (1975). Fantasy and reality in research: How much to move beyond the unproductive paradox. *Counselor Education and Supervision, 14,* 310–332.

Stile, S. W., (1987). Alternating treatment designs (ATD) for inquiry in early childhood education programs. *Journal of the Division for Early Childhood, 11,* 233–237.

Strong, S. R. (1968). Counseling: An interpersonal influence process. *Journal of Counseling Psychology, 15,* 215–224.

Tawney, J. W., & Gast, D. L. (1984). *Single-subject research in special education.* Columbus, OH: Merrill/Macmillan.

Winfrey, J. K. (1984, Oct.). Research as an area of renewal for counselor educators and supervisors. *Measurement and Evaluation in Counseling and Development,* 139–141.

2

Developing a Personal Approach to Counseling

The process of formulating a personal approach to counseling is both an art and science. It is an art in that the counselor must adjust the approach to accommodate the ever-changing forces that occur in the counseling process. It is a science in that research methodologies can be used to determine what works and what aspects of theory need to be modified. Part 2 provides guidelines for developing a personal approach to counseling as well as a description of the major theories of counseling. In addition, Chapter 5 emphasizes the importance of incorporating a multicultural perspective when formulating a personal approach to counseling.

CHAPTER FIVE

Developing a Personal Approach to Counseling with a Multicultural Perspective

CHAPTER OVERVIEW

This chapter provides guidelines for formulating a personal approach to counseling and addresses issues relating to multicultural counseling. Highlights of the chapter include

- Developing a personal approach to counseling
- An eight-stage model for developing a personal approach
- Multicultural counseling
- Potential problems in multicultural counseling
- Suggestions for incorporating a multicultural perspective

DEVELOPING A PERSONAL APPROACH TO COUNSELING

All counselors have a personal approach to counseling. Some put a considerable amount of time and effort into the process, while others simply "do counseling." Using a personal approach that results from careful planning enhances the complex process of counseling. Developing a personal approach is both an art and a science. The art of counseling model suggests that the counselor develop an approach responsive to clients in a multicultural society. The science of counseling model recognizes that a well-developed personal approach provides the structure necessary to obtain an objective understanding of the counseling process.

Over the years, there has been a proliferation of counseling approaches. Lynn and Garske (1985) observed more than 130 different approaches, many of which they said were far from the mainstream and of questionable value. The authors believed there appeared to be a shift in emphasis from more to fewer theories, creating an optimal climate for integrating theories. Patterson (1989) supported this view by noting that the 1980s were characterized by a movement toward eclecticism and integration. Baruth and Huber (1985) described the merits of an integrative approach. They believed that counselors who align themselves with one theoretical orientation have limitations because no single approach can apply to all situations.

Baruth and Huber (1985) said an effective approach must be more than randomly borrowing ideas from here and there. They recommended that counselors develop an integrative counseling approach that is grounded primarily in one theoretical school of counseling. Counselors then systematically apply techniques from other theories and integrate them into a pragmatic therapeutic position. In this regard, Baruth and Huber (1985) suggested a two-stage approach to developing a personal approach to counseling. Stage One involves surveying the major schools of counseling and then selecting the one most compatible with the counselor's personal theory of counseling. The counselor can then undertake an in-depth study of the selected school of counseling. Stage Two involves systematically integrating techniques from other theories into the school of thought selected in Stage One.

AN EIGHT-STAGE MODEL FOR DEVELOPING A PERSONAL APPROACH

The following eight-stage model is an extension of the Baruth-Huber model. It can be used to develop a personal approach to counseling. The eight stages of this model are self-assessment; survey of supportive disciplines; overview of major counseling theories; intensive study of one counseling theory; sensitivity to individual differences; integration of techniques from counseling theories; implementation; and research and evaluation.

Stage One: Self-Assessment

Self-assessment helps counselors understand their values, beliefs, strengths, and weaknesses. With self-awareness, counselors can avoid overreacting in counseling and use their strengths to maximize their effectiveness. Vontress (1988) noted that self-knowledge may be the best predictor of effective living because it provides a clear direction in life and is necessary to make meaningful decisions. Counselors can undertake a self-assessment in numerous ways. Perhaps the most comprehensive approach is to obtain formal counseling. Through the use of tests and other counseling strategies, counselors can gain information about their self-concept, personality, interests, values, aptitude, and other important aspects of the self. Many training programs, for example, in psychiatry require students to undertake analysis by a psychotherapist for 1 year or longer. The underlying belief in this requirement is that the experience can help provide students with personal insights necessary to become effective helpers.

Stage Two: Survey of Supportive Disciplines

A variety of disciplines can contribute to the development of a personal approach to counseling. but psychology and medicine are perhaps the most relevant. Other disciplines that may be useful are philosophy, theology, anthropology, sociology, and literature. A brief description of each of these disciplines follows.

Psychology.   Psychology is vital as a discipline for counselors to draw from since it encompasses the major schools of counseling and psychotherapy, which are the topics of Chapters 6, 7, and 8. Psychology also has a number of specialties that can contribute to a counselor's personal theory. The following summarizes the relevant aspects of some of these specialties.

- *Clinical and counseling psychology* investigates how psychological tests and other helping skills can be used in the counseling process.
- *Developmental psychology* helps counselors gain an understanding of how human growth and development take place over the life span. The counseling profession emphasizes the importance of utilizing a developmental perspective. This perspective enables counselors to adapt their approaches to the unique needs of clients progressing through the life span.
- *Experimental psychology* provides an important link to the science of counseling model by identifying research strategies to evaluate counseling approaches and processes.
- *Abnormal psychology* provides an overview of mental disorders and helps counselors learn how to use that information in the process of assessment and diagnosis.
- *Multicultural psychology* explores how psychology varies across cultures. This knowledge can be particularly important in developing a counseling perspective.
- *School psychology* focuses on the use of psychological tests in the school setting to assess personality, intelligence, aptitude, and achievement.
- *Physiological psychology* explores the physiological foundations of psychology. It can contribute a frame of reference for understanding physiological factors associated with behavior, cognition, and emotions.
- *Social psychology* explores psychology from a social perspective. It provides much promise to counseling research in terms of identifying paradigms relating to the social forces that influence the counseling process.

Medicine.   Medicine is another important discipline for counselors to study to develop some theoretical grounding. The mind and body are not separate entities but are an interrelated whole. To understand one, it is essential to have some knowledge of the other. The following Personal Note illustrates how some physical illnesses can cause psychiatric symptoms such as hallucinations.

a personal note

A doctor suspected that a female patient was schizophrenic, since she was having auditory hallucinations (hearing voices), and referred the woman to me. My psychological evaluation of the patient did not suggest that she was suffering from schizophrenia. In reviewing her hospital chart, however, I noticed that she had been diagnosed as having syphilis more than 10 years earlier and that there was no record of her successfully completing treatment for the condition. I knew that syphilis can cause hallucinations, so I referred the patient back to the physician to begin medical treatment for syphilis. I also arranged for the patient to see a consulting psychiatrist, who gave her medication for the auditory hallucinations.

Psychiatry is a medical specialty that has direct relevance to counseling. The three "classic" theorists who will be discussed in Chapter 6 were all psychiatrists. Psychiatry is the study of human behavior from a medical perspective. Psychiatrists have a special interest in how pathology, or abnormality, in the brain and nervous system can cause mental disorders, such as schizophrenia and major depression. They also have special training in the use of medications to treat these mental disorders. A basic background in psychiatry can help counselors differentiate a medical problem from a psychological problem so the client can receive the appropriate treatment. It can also assist counselors in understanding physiological factors associated with mental disorders.

Philosophy.   Philosophy can provide a valuable foundation for counselors in developing a personal approach. It can help them broaden and enrich how they see life and clarify beliefs, attitudes, and values. The following issues may be useful to explore in undertaking a study of philosophy.

1. Do people have free will?

2. What is the purpose of anxiety in life? Is it something to be avoided at all cost?

3. In order to experience love and joy, must one also be able to bear pain and sorrow?

4. Are people inherently good or bad, or is their nature primarily determined by environmental forces?

The study of philosophy can help counselors explore these and other relevant issues. It can also help counselors become aware of personal biases to avoid imposing them on clients.

Existentialism is a major school of philosophy that may be particularly interesting to counselors. Existentialism contends that people are self-determined and have free will, which they can use to make choices in life. Shakespeare summed up the spirit of existentialism when he wrote, "To be or not to be—that is the question."

The writings of several noted philosophers can be used to develop a philosophical perspective. A list of recommended reading is provided at the end of this chapter. One example is Gibran's (1965) popular book *The Prophet*, which expresses philosophical views that are easy to understand. It covers a wide variety of topics from children to love. The following is an excerpt from the section on children.

On Children

And a woman who held a babe against her bosom said, Speak to us of Children. And he said: Your children are not your children. They are the sons and daughters of life's longing for itself. They come through you but not from you. You may give them your love but not your thoughts, for they have their own thoughts. You may house their bodies but not their souls, for their souls dwell in the house of tomorrow, which you cannot visit, not even in your dreams. You may strive to be like them, but seek not to make them like you. For life goes not backward nor tarries with yesterday. You are the bows from which your children as living arrows are sent forth. The archer sees the mark upon the path of the infinite, and he bends you with his might that his arrows may go swift and far. Let your bending in the archer's hand be for gladness; for even as he loves the arrow that flies, so he loves also the bow that is stable. (pp. 17–18)

Theology.   Theology is the study of religion, and various schools of theology incorporate theories of philosophy. Theological concepts have not played a significant role in counseling. Most counselors view the client's religion as a personal, private matter that is not necessary or appropriate to explore with a client. An exception to this view is pastoral counseling, in which counselors practice from a particular religious perspective. In those situations, the client often seeks counseling from a religious orientation. Many churches employ counselors for this purpose. Worthington (1989) identified five reasons why counselors should make more of an effort to include religious considerations in formulating a counseling approach.

1. A high percentage of people in the United States are religious.
2. People often turn to religion during an emotional crisis.
3. Clients (especially religious clients) are reluctant to mention religious issues during secular therapy.
4. Counselors do not tend to be as religiously oriented as their clients.
5. Since many counselors are not as religiously oriented as their clients, they tend to be less informed about religion and are therefore less helpful to these clients.

Theological issues can play an important role in formulating a personal approach to counseling.

Worthington (1989) provided guidelines for incorporating religious issues into the counseling process. In these guidelines, he provided information on religious faith across the life span in terms of implications for counseling and research.

Anthropology.   Cultural anthropology is the study of cultures. Mental health cultural anthropology is a specialty that investigates mental health issues unique to a particular culture. For example, Topper (1985) explored Navajo alcoholism in terms of drinking, alcohol abuse, and treatment in a changing cultural environment. The mental health cultural anthropology perspective can be particularly useful in addressing cross-cultural issues in counseling.

Sociology.   Sociology is the study of social group behavior. A basic premise is that behavior is primarily determined by a person's social interaction. For example, during the socialization process, a person is encouraged to conform to the norms and laws of society. Many different groups and institutions can exert a significant influence on personality development. Some of these are family, friends, church, the work place, and school. A counselor may be interested in how these forces affect the client.

Literature.   The roads of literature and psychology have often crossed, creating new perspectives for understanding the psychology of people and exploring the counseling process. Adler emphasized the importance of literature in the development of individual psychology, as illustrated in the following excerpt.

> Some day soon it will be realized that the artist is the leader of mankind on the path to the absolute truth. Among poetic works of art which have led me to the insights of Individual Psychology, the following stand out as pinnacles: fairy tales, the Bible, Shakespeare, and Goethe. (Ansbacher & Ansbacher, 1956, p. 291)

Numerous possibilities exist for exploring the implications for counseling to be found in literature. For example, I related Adlerian psychotherapy and the life-style analysis to the investigative strategies employed by Sherlock Holmes (Nystul, 1978). Kopp (1971) provided another example of understanding literature from a counseling perspective in his analysis of *The Wizard of Oz*. He noted that Dorothy was similar to a client in search of herself, and the Wizard could be perceived as her counselor. As Dorothy journeyed through the Land of Oz, she encountered the Scarecrow, the Tin Woodsman, and the Cowardly Lion, who became her support system.

Kopp (1971) identified several insights into life that Dorothy and her friends may have realized, as the following excerpt shows.

> Acquiring wisdom involves risking being wrong or foolish; being loving and tender requires a willingness to bear unhappiness; courage is the confidence to face danger, though afraid; gaining freedom and power requires only a willingness to recognize their existence and to face their consequences. We can find ourselves only when we are willing to risk losing ourselves to another, to the moment, to a quest, and love is the bridge. (p. 98)

Bibliotherapy provides another example of how the roads of literature and counseling cross (see Chapter 7). Bibliotherapy involves having clients read books or other literary works to promote different outcomes associated with counseling, for example, anxiety reduction or stress management. Gelso and Fassinger (1990) suggested that counselors should consider client characteristics to determine the appropriateness of self-help literature.

Stage Three: Overview of Major Counseling Theories

It is necessary to study the major schools of counseling to obtain an overview of the various counseling theories (see Chapters 6, 7, and 8). This understanding alerts counselors to the various theoretical perspectives that are available to use with different clients. One central or core theory can then be selected as the foundation of an integrative approach.

Stage Four: Intensive Study of One Counseling Theory

A solid foundation in theory is necessary for developing a personal approach. The importance of a theoretical foundation is evident in all disciplines. For example, music students usually benefit from studying music theory and learn to read music before creating their own musical composition. The same is true in counseling. After students have established an in-depth theoretical foundation, they are ready to develop their own personal style and approach.

Stage 4 suggests that counselors undertake an in-depth study of the particular school they have selected. The core theory should include a comprehensive theory of personality to provide an understanding of the dynamics of behavior. The theory should be a well-thought-out approach to counseling that includes an understanding of the counseling process. The core theory can provide internal consistency in terms of how counselors understand and work with a client. Counselors who do not have a well-thought-out core theory are prone to superficial and fragmented personality assessment. They are likely to have a technique-oriented approach to counseling, thinking, for example, "With this client, I'll use this theory's suggested technique." It is important for counselors to read books and articles written by the founder of the school they have selected. Reading about an approach in a textbook will not provide an in-depth understanding. Training in an institute associated with the theory, such as the Gestalt Institute in Arizona, can also help counselors develop expertise in a particular school of counseling. It may be useful to join a professional organization associated with the chosen theory. An example is the North American Society of Individual Psychology for counselors interested in Adlerian psychology.

Stage Five: Sensitivity to Individual Differences

Counselors should not force a client to fit into their personal approach. I referred to this as "forcing square pegs into round holes" (Nystul, 1981). On the contrary, a counselor's approach should be adjusted to the unique and emerging needs of the client. In this regard, the counselor should be sensitive to the individual differences of clients. It is particularly important to address multicultural issues to make the counseling process relevant to the needs of the client. The next section of this chapter describes multicultural issues that can be used to formulate one's personal approach to counseling.

It is also important to assess the client's personal characteristics to help determine what type of counseling approaches may be appropriate. One way of doing this is by trying to identify how the client tends to engage in problem solving in terms of "spaces of perception." This theory suggests there are three spaces of perception: near-, mid-, and far-spaced (Nystul, 1981). *Near-spaced* clients tend to want a lot of detail in problem solving. For example, they want to know exactly what and how they are supposed to do something. These clients may be better able to utilize behavioral approaches that incorporate the monitoring of behavior with graphs and other objective procedures.

At the other extreme are *far-spaced* clients. These are people who hate to be pinned down with a lot of details. They do not want to be locked into a preconceived method of problem solving. An existential or humanistically oriented approach may be more in keeping with their mode of problem solving.

Mid-spaced clients are characterized by having difficulty making decisions. They tend to want others to make decisions and resolve problems for them. Reality therapy or Gestalt therapy may help these clients become aware of choices and accept responsibility for their behavior.

Stage Six: Integration of Techniques from Counseling Theories

To develop an integrative counseling approach, counselors may draw from different counseling theories to add to their repertoire of counseling techniques. In reviewing the various schools of counseling, students may find that these theories have more in common than they have differences. Subtle differences do exist, however, enabling counselors to adjust their approach to the particular problems that present themselves in the counseling session.

Stage Seven: Implementation

As counselors make the transition from theory to practice, they will begin to implement their approach. The application of one's approach is an art. It is a creative process that varies according to the particular clinical situation.

Stage Eight: Research and Evaluation

Research and evaluation enable counselors to determine the efficacy of their approach; use the literature to refine their approach; and contribute to the literature on a topic of interest. Chapter 4 provides information pertaining to this important topic.

MULTICULTURAL COUNSELING

In the preceding discussion, I suggested that a personal approach to counseling should incorporate a multicultural perspective sensitive to the individual differences that reflect contemporary society. In this regard, Pedersen (1991) contends that multicultural counseling has become a fourth force, which follows psychodynamic, behavioral, and humanistic counseling. It is relevant to all aspects of counseling as a generic rather than exotic perspective (Pedersen, 1991).

I will now provide an overview of some of the major issues in multicultural counseling. In this section, I will describe key terms and concepts. In the next two sections, I will identify potential problems associated with multicultural counseling and provide guidelines for developing a multicultural perspective.

Terms and Concepts

Many terms relating to multicultural counseling can be difficult to differentiate and can therefore obscure its meaning. The following explanations help clarify some common terms and concepts.

- *Culture* is an ambiguous concept that defies definition. In a broad sense, it can be thought of as "things a stranger needs to know to behave appropriately in a particular setting" (Pedersen, 1988, p. viii).
- *Race* "refers to a pseudobiological system of classifying persons by a shared genetic history or physical characteristics such as skin color (Pedersen, 1988, p. viii).
- *Minority* "generally refers to a group receiving differential and unequal treatment because of collective discrimination" (Pedersen, 1988, p. viii).
- *Ethnicity* "includes a shared socio-cultural heritage that includes similarities of religion, history, and common ancestry" (Pedersen, 1988, p. viii).
- *Cross-cultural counseling* is "any counseling relationship in which two or more of the participants differ with respect to cultural background, values, and life style" (Sue et al., 1982, p. 47).
- *Multicultural counseling* has a broader definition of culture than implied in cross-cultural counseling. Pedersen (1988) defined multicultural counseling as

"a situation in which two or more persons with different ways of perceiving their social environment are brought together in a helping relationship" (p. viii). Pedersen (1991) prefers the broader definition of culture associated with multicultural counseling, because it ". . . helps counselors become more aware of the complexity in cultural identity patterns, which may or may not include the obvious indicators of ethnicity and nationality" (p. 11).

POTENTIAL PROBLEMS IN MULTICULTURAL COUNSELING

Many studies have identified potential problems in multicultural counseling. This research addresses a wide range of topics, including counseling as a white middle-class activity; social class; gender; the intrapsychic perspective; stereotyping; communication problems; faulty assumptions; test bias; and the efficacy of multicultural counseling.

Counseling as a White Middle-Class Activity

A major criticism of contemporary counseling is that its theories and techniques have been developed primarily by people from a white, middle-class culture. As a result, contemporary counseling is not directly applicable to ethnic minorities because its theories and techniques do not address their specific issues and concerns (Wilson & Stith, 1991). In addition, Ponterotto and Casas (1991) noted that traditionally trained counselors are encapsulated in a culturally biased framework and consequently tend to engage in culturally conflicting and oppressive counseling approaches. It is therefore not surprising that counseling services are not utilized as much by minorities as by whites (Sue & Sue, 1990). In addition, the rate of dropping out of counseling after attending one session is 50% for ethnic minorities versus 30% for whites (Sue & Sue, 1990).

Social Class

Social-class differences may be more profound than cultural differences (Baruth & Manning, 1991). For example, whites in the lower socioeconomic class may have more in common with Hispanics in the same class than with whites in the middle or upper class.

Diagnostic and treatment bias is one problem that has been associated with social class. In one of the earliest studies on this subject, Lee (1968) found that clients from the lower socioeconomic class received a diagnosis of mental illness at a higher rate than clients from the upper socioeconomic class. Some evidence also suggests that counselors become more involved with clients from the upper class than with clients from the lower class (Garfield, Weiss, & Pollack, 1973). Considering these findings, it is not surprising that clients with a lower socioeconomic status tend to drop out of counseling after one or two sessions (Berrigan & Garfield, 1981; Weighill, Hodge, & Peck, 1983). With these concerns in mind, Atkinson, Morten, and Sue (1989) noted that social class is an important variable to consider when formulating a treatment approach.

Gender

Gender factors associated with the counseling process pertain to potential advantages and disadvantages of same- versus opposite-sex pairings between the counselor and client. The central issue has been a possible tendency for male counselors to dominate and control women clients and direct them into stereotypical career choices (Cayleff, 1986; Jones, Krupnick, & Kerig, 1987). Although the research on this topic has been inconclusive, there is some evidence that women clients prefer women counselors. For example, Jones, Krupnick, and Kerig (1987) found that women counselors elicited less negative affect and fewer interpersonal difficulties in women clients than men counselors did.

The Intrapsychic Perspective

An *intrapsychic* counseling approach, which conceptualizes the client's problems from within the individual, may not be appropriate for minority clients (Sue, 1988). The intrapsychic model does not take into account oppressive forces such as racism, sexism, and discrimination, which can explain or contribute to the client's problems (Banks, 1972; Sue & Sue, 1990; Williams & Kirkland, 1971).

Several studies have shown that the effects of racism, oppression, and discrimination can have an adverse effect on the counseling process. Boyd-Franklin (1989) found that African-Americans have reacted to racism, discrimination, and oppression by not trusting people who are different in terms of values, color, or life style. Poston, Craine, and Atkinson (1991) noted a direct relationship between African-American clients' mistrust of white counselors and their perceived credibility of white counselors.

Stereotyping

Stereotyping can be defined as "rigid preconceptions we hold about *all* people who are members of a particular group, whether it be defined along racial, religious, sexual, or other lines" (Sue & Sue, 1990, pp. 47–48). Examples of stereotyping are: Native Americans live on reservations and get drunk; African-Americans are musical; and Asians are good with numbers. Stereotyping has negative effects on the counseling process (Sue, 1988). Some potential problems are that stereotyping causes counselors to apply a perceived characteristic of a group to all members of that group without regard for individual differences; fail to take logic or experience into consideration; and distort all new information to fit preconceived ideas (Sue & Sue, 1990).

Communication Problems

Pedersen (1988) noted that much of the criticism directed at multicultural counseling relates to communication problems that interfere with the counseling process. Language differences can result in a variety of problems in counseling (Sue, 1988). For example, Vontress (1973) found that counselors who experience language difficulties with a client have trouble establishing a positive counseling relationship with the client. Sue and Sue (1977) also warned that counselors who use only standard

English with a bilingual client may make an inaccurate assessment of the client's strengths and weaknesses.

The style of nonverbal communication may also vary across cultures, creating communication problems. For example, African-Americans tend to utilize more direct eye contact when speaking than whites and as a result have been labeled as more angry (Sue & Sue, 1990). Native Americans tend to avoid direct eye contact when listening, causing them to be incorrectly perceived as inattentive (Sue & Sue, 1990). Herring (1990) noted the particular importance of counselors being able to assess nonverbal communication accurately, because this type of communication is more ambiguous and culturally bound than verbal communication.

Westwood and Ishiyama (1990) provided the following guidelines regarding the communication process in multicultural counseling.

1. Counselors should check with the client on the accuracy of their interpretation of nonverbal communication.

2. Counselors can promote catharsis by encouraging clients to use their own language to express a particular feeling when another language cannot accurately describe it.

3. Counselors should try to learn culturally meaningful expressions of the client to accurately describe the client's inner process.

4. Counselors should use alternate modes of communicating such as art, music, and photography.

Faulty Assumptions

Pedersen (1987) identified 10 faulty assumptions that can impede progress in counseling. Later in this chapter, these assumptions are used to evaluate the appropriateness of counseling theory in multicultural counseling. These 10 faulty assumptions are summarized as follows.

Misconceptions of Normal Behavior.   A tendency exists for people to assume that the definition of *normal* is universal across social, cultural, economic, and political backgrounds. Pedersen (1987) suggested that "what is considered normal will vary according to the situation, the cultural background of a person or persons being judged, and the time during which a behavior is being displayed or observed" (p. 17). Counselors can make an error of diagnosis if they fail to consider how the definition of normalcy can vary.

Emphasis on Individualism.   Counselors with a traditional Western approach tend to emphasize the importance of the welfare of the individual. Self-awareness, self-fulfillment, and self-discovery are often used as indices of success in counseling. In addition, the task of the counselor is often perceived as ". . . changing the individual in a positive direction even at the expense of the group in which that individual is a member" (Pedersen, 1987, p. 18).

This emphasis on the interests of the individual over the group may not be consistent with the value system of some cultures. In the Chinese culture, it would be inappropriate to put the welfare of an individual before the welfare of that individual's family (Pedersen, 1987). Counselors should therefore take cultural issues into consideration before promoting the virtues of individualism in counseling.

Fragmentation by Academic Disciplines.   Some tendency exists for counselors to isolate themselves from related disciplines such as sociology, anthropology, theology, and medicine. This can result in a narrow view of people and an inability to understand individual differences. Cultural anthropology can be a particularly useful area for a counselor to study in terms of addressing multicultural issues.

Use of Abstract or Out-Of-Context Concepts.   Many counseling principles contain abstract concepts, which can be easily misunderstood across cultures. In addition, the meaning of a concept will vary from one context or situation to another. It is therefore important to determine what a concept means as it relates to a particular client.

Overemphasis on Independence.   A common goal in counseling is to help the client become autonomous and independent. Pedersen (1987) warned that some cultures, such as the Japanese, believe that dependency is not only healthy but necessary. Some examples of relationships in which the Japanese culture views dependency as appropriate are those between employer and employees, mother and son, and teacher and student. Counselors should therefore be sensitive to cultural issues in determining if a client's dependency is excessive.

Neglect of Client's Support System.   A client who enters counseling may want the counseling relationship to become a substitute for existing support systems. To ensure that this does not occur, counselors should include the client's support system in treatment planning. This can be especially important for a minority client who may already feel a high degree of isolation because of cultural differences.

Dependence on Linear Thinking.   Traditional Western counseling approaches tend to be characterized by linear thinking whereby each cause has an effect and each effect has a particular cause. Some cultures are not tied to the linear model of analysis. The concept of Yin and Yang from Eastern culture does not differentiate between cause and effect but sees them as interrelated. In counseling, it is therefore important to attempt to communicate in a manner that is consistent with the client's way of viewing the world.

Focus on Changing the Individual, Not the System.   "In many minority groups counseling has a bad reputation for taking the side of the status quo in forcing individuals to adjust or adapt to the institutions of society" (Pedersen, 1987, p. 22). To overcome this obstacle, counselors should broaden their intervention strategies to include a community psychology perspective. This can include trying to change the system if it appears the system is having a detrimental effect on the client. If a client's depression appears to be related to high unemployment in the community, the counselor may become active in efforts to create employment opportunities.

Neglect of History.   Counselors may focus only on the most recent precipitating events that lead up to a crisis or mental disorder and fail to consider the client's problems from a historical perspective. For some minority clients, a historical perspective may be more appropriate because it can help the counselor understand socio-cultural forces that have contributed to shaping a client's approach to problem solving and outlook on life. Many African-Americans, for instance, have experienced years of poverty, oppression, prejudice, racism, and exploitation. This can cause some to develop limited horizons and affect the way they view themselves and others, for example, with a sense of despair, helplessness toward self, or hostility or suspicion toward others.

Dangers of Cultural Encapsulation.   *Cultural encapsulation* is a process whereby counselors cannot see beyond their belief system and fail to address cultural issues with the client. Multicultural counselors must move beyond "parochial concerns and perspectives" and develop a comprehensive perspective that integrates contrasting assumptions from other cultures (Pedersen, 1987, p. 23).

Test Bias

Lonner (1985) provided a comprehensive overview of testing and assessment in multicultural counseling. The author identified a variety of potential problems in multicultural testing that could contribute to test bias. These include difficulties in reactions to test-taking situations and problems that relate to validity, reliability, and norms.

Regarding test-taking situations, Lonner (1985) noted there could be cultural differences in terms of use of time, language difficulties, and the manner of response to test questions. As an example of the effect of culture on an individual's manner of response, it may be culturally appropriate for some to agree with nearly every statement out of politeness. For others, it may be appropriate to give only socially desirable answers. Some individuals may view tests as unimportant and respond carelessly (Lonner, 1985).

Validity, reliability, and norms are critical in determining the use and effectiveness of tests, as discussed in Chapter 3. Validity may be the most important factor in evaluating a test. Construct validity is one type of validity that may vary across cultures (Lonner, 1985). Construct validity is the extent to which a test measures a theoretical construct or trait such as intelligence and verbal fluency (Anastasi, 1988). The meaning and importance of these constructs may vary from one culture to another. Tests that utilize the same constructs across cultures may therefore have invalid construct validities.

Socio-cultural factors may influence a test's reliability. Different opportunities in learning may vary across cultures, affecting a test's reliability. One culture may require formal education, for instance, and another may not (Lonner, 1985). It is therefore best to develop separate indices of reliability for each culture (Lonner, 1985).

Another potential problem in using psychological tests multiculturally relates to norms. Most standardized tests utilize a white, middle-class norm group in determining standards or points of comparison. These standards often vary considerably across cultures. The norms are therefore only relevant for the particular reference group or culture in which they were developed. If the test is to be used multiculturally, new norms should be established based on the population (Lonner, 1985).

It is also important to ensure that the test results are used in an appropriate fashion. Cronbach (1984) warned that the central issue in the test-bias controversy relates to decision making and how the inappropriate use of a test can create an unfair advantage for one culture over another. For example, using a culturally biased test in job selection could create an unfair advantage for some prospective employees. Culture-fair tests have been developed in an attempt to overcome some of the problems associated with test bias. Several of these tests were described in Chapter 3.

The Efficacy of Multicultural Counseling

After reviewing the potential problems in multicultural counseling, one may wonder if any counselor could overcome these barriers. Research in this area has focused on investigating if white counselors are effective in treating ethnic minorities. Sue (1988) provided a review of the literature on this topic, noting a divergence of opinions: white counselors are effective in treating minorities (Sattler, 1977); white counselors are frequently ineffective (Griffith & Jones, 1978); and it does not seem to matter if the counselor and client are of different ethnic backgrounds (Atkinson, 1985). A review of these studies suggests a tendency for minority clients to prefer counselors with a similar ethnic background. At the same time, a competent white counselor who is sensitive to multicultural factors can provide effective counseling services. In addition, multicultural counseling can be enriching for the counselor and the client by creating a "cultural exchange" (Draguns, 1976).

The following Personal Note illustrates how a counselor can turn potential problems in multicultural counseling into an advantage.

a personal note

I was surprised to discover that some of the problems I envisioned in multicultural counseling turned out to be benefits. When I was a psychologist at a public health hospital on the Navajo Indian reservation, I was especially concerned about language barriers. I was told that I would need an interpreter since some Navajos could not speak English. This proved to be true in individual counseling with clients who did not speak English. In family therapy, however, I often found that some family members could not speak English but others were bilingual. In these situations, I would have the bilingual family members act as interpreters, so an "outside" interpreter was not necessary.

Several positive outcomes resulted from having clients act as interpreters. First, they seemed to listen very carefully since they did not know when I would ask them to interpret. These clients seemed to take their responsibility as interpreter very seriously. Perhaps it allowed them to show respect for what other family members said. Second, clients were taking an active role in the counseling process, since interpreting is basically paraphrasing.

I believe that many of the potential problems in multicultural counseling can be overcome if the counselor develops a positive attitude and is sensitive in adjusting the approach to the unique needs of the client.

Gaining knowledge about a culture can be important to multicultural counseling.

SUGGESTIONS FOR INCORPORATING A MULTICULTURAL PERSPECTIVE

This section will identify suggestions for counselors to incorporate a multicultural perspective into their personal approach to counseling. It presents information on beliefs, knowledge, and skills necessary for multicultural counseling; describes the concept of *world view* as a construct that can be used to individualize multicultural counseling; provides an overview of identity development; presents methods for determining the appropriateness of traditional counseling theory; and provides general guidelines for implementing a multicultural approach.

Beliefs, Knowledge, and Skills

The Division of Counseling Psychology of the American Psychological Association established a task force that identified beliefs and attitudes, knowledge, and skills of the culturally skilled counselor (Sue et al., 1982). The following overview provides a summary of the task force's findings.

Beliefs and Attitudes.   To be effective in a multicultural setting, counselors should be aware of how their beliefs and attitudes may impact the counseling process. Sue (1981) noted that counselors who are not aware of their beliefs and attitudes may unknowingly impose their values and standards on others and engage in cultural oppression. It is therefore important to develop appropriate attitudes and beliefs. Sue et al. (1982) suggested that culturally skilled counselors

- Are aware of and sensitive to their cultural heritage and have learned to value and respect differences

- Are aware of their own values and biases and how those attitudes may affect minority clients
- Are comfortable with differences that exist between themselves and their client in terms of race and beliefs
- Are sensitive to circumstances such as personal biases, stages of ethnic identity, and socio-political influences that may dictate a referral of a minority client to a counselor of the client's culture (Sue et al., 1982)

Knowledge.   An effective multicultural approach to counseling requires some knowledge about the client's culture. In addition, Sue et al. (1982) noted that culturally skilled counselors

- Have a good understanding of the socio-political system's operation in the United States with respect to its treatment of minorities
- Possess specific knowledge and information about a particular group they are working with
- Have clear, explicit knowledge and understanding of the generic characteristics of counseling and therapy
- Are aware of institutional barriers that prevent minorities from using mental health services

Skills.   Some counseling strategies, such as being a good listener, are usually effective regardless of the culture. At the same time, as Sue (1981) warned, different cultural groups usually have different counseling goals and therefore require different counseling strategies to be effective. In addition, Sue et al. (1982) suggested that culturally skilled counselors

- Are able to generate a wide variety of verbal and nonverbal responses
- Are able to send and receive both verbal and nonverbal messages accurately
- Are able to exercise institutional intervention skills on behalf of their clients when appropriate (Sue et al., 1982)

World View

Although it is important to have a knowledge of the client's culture, it is also essential to be able to understand the client as a unique individual. World view, a concept with increasing recognition in the multicultural literature, is a construct that can be used to individualize the counseling process (Ibrahim, 1991; Sue, 1978, 1981).

World view, which extends beyond culture or ethnic group, can be defined as assumptions and perceptions regarding the world (Sire, 1976; Sue, 1978). World view is directly related to thoughts, feelings, and perceptions of social relations and the world (Ibrahim, 1991). It also has a direct effect on ability to solve problems, make decisions, and resolve conflicts (Ibrahim, in press). Knowledge of a client's world view can promote a better understanding of the client and can lead to more sensitive and effective counseling strategies (Ibrahim, 1991).

Ibrahim (1991) suggested that a client's world view should be determined during the initial client assessment. One effective tool for determining a client's world view is The Scale to Assess World Views (SAWV) (Ibrahim & Kahn, 1984, 1987). The SAWV assesses information regarding the client's view of human nature, social relations, relations with nature, time orientation, and activity orientation. The SAWV can help the counselor explore the client's values, beliefs, and assumptions; gain an understanding of the client's concerns; and differentiate between the client's world view and cultural views (Ibrahim, 1991).

Identity Development

Identity development is "a process of integrating and expanding one's sense of self" (Myers et al., 1991, p. 54). Establishing a positive self-identity can be difficult to attain (Myers et al., 1991). Helping clients clarify or enhance their self-identity can be a central task in counseling.

Identity development models have emerged as a means of understanding the process of identity formation and determining where clients are functioning in that process. Several models have emerged to describe the stages of identity development for racial-ethnic groups, for example, African-Americans (Parham, 1989); Latinos (Keefe & Padilla, 1987); Asian Americans (Sue, 1981); and whites (Helms, 1990).

Myers et al. (1991) noted that the racial-ethnic identity development models have several inherent limitations. For example, they do not take into account multiple oppressive factors such as socio-economic status and minority status (e.g., lower-class Mexican Americans) or multiracial backgrounds (e.g., Amerasians). In an attempt to overcome some of these limitations, these authors developed the Optimal Theory Applied to Identity Development model (OTAID) . The OTAID model does allow for consideration of multiple oppressive factors that can influence identity development. In addition, it is based on a world view, rather than being restricted to racial-ethnic considerations.

Myers et al. (1991) described the OTAID model as a six-phase process. An overview of these phases follows.

- *Phase 0: Absence of Conscious Awareness*. In this phase, individuals lack a sense of the self as a separate individual. Individuals do not develop self-awareness until 1 or 2 years of age (Dworetzky, 1990).

- *Phase 1: Individuation*. During this phase, individuals adhere to a personal identity that was generated by early familial and societal experiences. They utilize an egocentric view of themselves, which does not take into account the negative views of others.

- *Phase 2: Dissonance*. In Phase 2, individuals begin to consider the opinions of others regarding who they are, even if these opinions are negative. Their perceptions of negative views from others create dissonance, and they begin to wonder who they really are.

- *Phase 3: Immersion*. Individuals who feel devalued by others may immerse themselves in the customs and way of life of the devalued group and react angrily toward the dominant group. For example, a 20-year-old Asian-American woman who had identified with anglo customs now rejects those customs and immerses herself in Asian customs if she hear whites talking about her in derogatory ways (e.g., "silly chink").

- *Phase 4: Internalization.* During this phase, individuals incorporate a number of salient aspects of the self in formulating their personal identity. This broadened self-image enables them to be more tolerant and accepting of the criticisms of others.

- *Phase 5: Integration.* As individuals gain deeper self-understanding, they begin to change their assumptions regarding the world. Their world view is broad and accepting of individual differences. At this point, they choose friends on the basis of shared values and interest instead of ethnic-racial criteria.

- *Phase 6: Transformation.* In the transformation phase, the self is redefined according to a world view that appreciates the interrelatedness of all aspects of life. This emerging personal identity incorporates a spiritual awareness regarding the order of life and the universe and fosters a sense of wholeness or completeness in the individual.

Methods to Evaluate Counseling Theories

To formulate a personal approach to counseling, it is necessary to determine the appropriateness of traditional counseling theory in multicultural counseling. Several methods can be used to assist with this process.

One model suggests that it is important for counselors to identify a client's level of acculturation to the majority society. This method contends that the more acculturated a client is, the more appropriate it is to use traditional approaches (Topper, 1985). Counselors can estimate a client's level of acculturation by examining how much the client has assimilated into the mainstream society. Lee (1991) noted the factors that influence acculturation include educational level, socio-economic status, length of time lived in the United States, and extent of exposure to racism.

Usher (1989) presented another method to evaluate the appropriateness of a theory. She suggested that the 10 faulty assumptions identified by Pedersen (1987) can be used to determine if a traditional counseling theory can be used in multicultural counseling. A counseling theory that appears to foster one or more of these faulty assumptions could either be modified or avoided in a multicultural context. Usher (1989) illustrated this method by using the 10 faulty assumptions to evaluate Rogers' (1951) person-centered therapy. Her analysis showed Rogers' theory to have some strengths and weaknesses in terms of its use in multicultural counseling.

Usher (1989) identified two facets of Rogers' theory that appeared to promote multicultural counseling. First, since clients define the goals and determine the evaluation process, there is less chance of their being judged in terms of the dominant culture's view of normality. Second, Rogers' approach contains elements of circularity, allowing clients to express themselves within a framework that is nondirective and nonjudgmental.

Usher (1989) also identified some potential problems with person-centered counseling in multicultural settings. One problem related to Rogers' emphasis on individualism and independence from others. He did not recognize the view of healthy dependencies that some cultures hold for authorities and family members. A second problem could arise from Rogers' belief that the locus of control and responsibility resides within the client. This position does not take into account environmental factors such as poverty which could contribute to the client's growth process. Another potential problem related to Rogers' emphasis on the here-and-now. Such a frame of reference may not be adequate to understand problems such as oppression that may impact on culturally different clients.

A third method that can be used to evaluate the efficacy of counseling theory in multicultural counseling involves the concepts of *etic* and *emic*, terms linked to linguistics. Etic relates to phonetics, which is something common to all languages. Emic relates to phonemics, which is something unique to that particular language.

These terms have been related to multicultural counseling (Lee, 1984). Etic is associated with concepts in counseling theory that are universal to all cultures. An example of an etic concept is the contention in Rational Emotive Therapy (RET) that irrational beliefs contribute to negative emotional consequences (Ellis, 1983). Emic is associated with concepts that emphasize individuality. An example of an emic concept is neurolinguistic programming, since it is an approach that varies with each individual (Bandler & Grinder, 1975).

There may be some advantages in using emic concepts versus etic concepts in multicultural counseling. Emic concepts encourage the counselor to treat each client as an individual, thereby avoiding tendencies to engage in prejudice or stereotyping. Etic concepts, on the other hand, must be truly universal to be applied to different cultures without bias. Problems can surface with etic concepts when the theory assumes the concept is universal when in fact it is not. This could occur in RET, since it suggests that irrational thinking will generate emotional difficulties regardless of the culture (Bandler & Grinder, 1975). RET does not appear to take into consideration the possibility that the definition of irrational ideas may vary from one culture to another. The efficacy of RET would therefore be significantly reduced in situations where a counselor was imposing inappropriate standards regarding what is rational, irrational, and self-defeating.

Guidelines for Multicultural Counseling

This section provides 10 guidelines for incorporating multicultural counseling strategies into a personal approach to counseling.

Establish Mutual Respect.   Mutual respect forms the foundation for all relationships (Dinkmeyer & McKay, 1989). This may be especially important in multicultural counseling when a counselor from the majority culture counsels a minority client. In these situations, clients may feel they are being looked down upon and consequently resist participating in counseling.

Counselors can create opportunities to communicate respect to the client by honoring the client's unique way of perceiving and interacting with the world. Counselors can also communicate an acceptance of their client whenever possible. For example, some clients may become embarrassed because they have difficulty speaking English.

When this occurs, a counselor can tell these clients that it is impressive that they are becoming bilingual when most people can speak only one language.

As clients experience acceptance and respect, they may become more relaxed with and accepting of their counselor. The resulting mutual respect can contribute to a relationship of equality in the counseling process.

Don't Impose Your Belief System.   When working in multicultural counseling, it is important for the counselor to be nonjudgmental. Each culture has its own norms and value system. This may influence how clients see important issues pertaining to counseling such as their understanding of mental health. For example, the Navajos do not differentiate between physical and mental health (Harrar, 1984). They see mental problems resulting when a person is "out of harmony" with the traditional Navajo culture (Harrar, 1984).

Treat Clients as Unique Individuals First and as People from a Particular Culture Second.   It is important to consider that all people are unique, even in terms of what it means to be part of a particular culture. Focusing on the unique characteristics of a particular client will help counselors overcome stereotyping and other self-defeating processes.

Determine if Traditional Counseling Approaches Would be Appropriate for a Particular Client.   The counselor can use the three methods described in this chapter to determine the appropriateness of traditional counseling theory in multicultural settings.

Provide Accessible, Dependable Services.   It is important for counseling services to be adequately staffed so clients will know someone will be there if they come for help. This is especially important in rural areas, where a client may have traveled a long distance to come for counseling services. On the Navajo reservation, it was not uncommon that clients may have journeyed 100 miles and may have had to get a ride from a friend or hitchhike. It would not be very welcoming for these clients to be told that they would have to come back the next day or wait a long time to receive help. It is essential for the counseling center to develop a reputation for being reliable and responsive, or clients will stop coming.

Some clients may feel that their problems are not "big enough" to warrant counseling services. These are often the clients who need help the most. They need to be reassured that the counseling service is there for them to use and that they are not "in the way," as they might feel, but are welcome.

Use a Flexible Approach.   Counselors should adjust their approach to the client's unique needs in all cases, but flexibility is especially important in multicultural counseling. In many minority cultures, such as Mexican Americans, African-Americans, and Native Americans, a high percentage of people are struggling against the elements of poverty. These individuals may therefore need assistance with basic needs such as food, shelter, and safety. When this occurs, counselors should adjust their approach to meet these needs, becoming more action-oriented and focused in the present (Sue, 1981). Counselors may even function to some degree as advocates for the client's basic rights. This may involve helping clients obtain benefits from social services or other agencies.

Be Perceived as a Doer, Not Just a Talker.   Counselors should show they are capable of accomplishing something concrete with the client as early as possible in the counseling relationship. A counselor who is perceived as a doer and not just a talker will be valued and sought after by clients, especially those struggling to fulfill basic needs.

Conduct an Environmental Assessment.   It is important to avoid an overemphasis on intrapsychic forces in assessment and diagnosis. An environmental assessment will enable the counselor to explore socio-cultural factors that could also be contributing to the client's problems. This will not only contribute to more accurate assessment and diagnosis but also help the counselor and client identify realistic treatment goals.

Allow Yourself to be Enriched by The Client's Culture.   Multicultural counseling can be rewarding and exciting. It can involve living and working in a different culture or simply providing a multicultural counseling service. Regardless of the degree of a counselor's multicultural experience, many opportunities exist for cultural enrichment. A counselor may soon discover some of the special facets of a culture such as types of food, styles of dress, differences in family life, and approaches to physical and mental health.

Each culture also has its special customs, beliefs, heritages, and creative arts. It may be helpful to study a culture to appreciate its special beauty. This can involve reading, going to art exhibits and other cultural events, and, of course, learning from clients.

You Don't Have to be a Minority to Counsel a Minority.   There can be potential problems in multicultural counseling such as language barriers, stereotyping, and a lack of awareness of the value systems of a cultural group. At the same time, counselors can overcome these problems by being sensitive to the unique needs of the client and attempting to gain the beliefs, knowledge, and skills necessary to counsel in multicultural settings.

CHAPTER SUMMARY

Developing a well-thought-out personal approach to counseling creates the necessary structure to work within the counseling process. Guidelines for formulating a personal approach responsive to a multicultural society were provided in an eight-stage model, including the merits of using an integrative approach. This model suggested that counselors who utilize a central or core theory will have a solid foundation to approach the counseling process. This foundation will provide internal consistency for the counselor's approach.

The chapter also identified some of the potential problems associated with multicultural counseling such as a tendency for diagnostic and treatment bias. It was suggested that these problems could be overcome when the counselor treats the client as a person first and a member of a particular culture second; sensitively relates to the special needs and circumstances of the client; and gains the necessary beliefs, knowledge, and skills associated with the populations the counselor intends to serve.

SUGGESTED READINGS RELATING TO PHILOSOPHY

Binswanger, L. (1963). *Being-in-the-world. Selected papers of Ludwig Binswanger* (J. Needleman, Trans.). New York: Basic Books.

Bugental, J. F. T. (1965). *The search for authenticity*. New York: Holt, Rinehart, & Winston.

Gibran, K. (1965). *The prophet*. New York: Alfred A. Knopf.

Kierkegaard, S. (1944). *The concept of dread* (W. Lowrie, Trans.). Princeton, NJ: Princeton University Press.

Sartre, J. P. (1956). *Being and nothingness* (H. Barnes, Trans.). New York: Philosophical Library.

REFERENCES

Anastasi, A. (1988). *Psychological testing* (6th ed.). New York: Macmillan.

Ansbacher, H. L., & Ansbacher, R. R. (Eds.). (1956). *The individual psychology of Alfred Adler*. New York: Basic Books.

Atkinson, D. R. (1985). A meta-review of research on cross-cultural counseling and psychotherapy. *Journal of Multicultural Counseling and Development, 1*, 138–153.

Atkinson, D. R., Morten, G., & Sue, D. W. (1989). *Counseling American minorities: A cross-cultural perspective* (3rd ed.). Dubuque, IA: William C. Brown.

Bandler, R., & Grinder, J. (1975). *The structure of magic* (Vol. 1). Palo Alto, CA: Science and Behavior Books.

Banks, W. (1972). The black client and the helping professionals. In R. I. Jones (Ed.), *Black psychology*. New York: Harper & Row.

Baruth, L. G., & Huber, C. H. (1985). *Counseling and psychotherapy: Theoretical analyses and skills applications*. Columbus, OH: Merrill/Macmillan.

Baruth, L. G., & Manning, M. L. (1991). *Multicultural counseling and psychotherapy: A lifespan perspective*. New York: Macmillan.

Berrigan, L. P., & Garfield, S. L. (1981). Relationships of missed psychotherapy appointments to premature termination and social class. *The British Journal of Clinical Psychology, 20*, 239–242.

Boyd-Franklin, N. (1989). *Black families in therapy: A multisystems approach*. New York: Guilford Press.

Cayleff, S. E. (1986). Ethical issues in counseling gender, race, and culturally distinct groups. *Journal of Counseling and Development, 64*, 345–347.

Cronbach, L. J. (1984). *Essentials of psychological testing*. New York: Harper & Row.

Dinkmeyer, D., & McKay, G. (1989). *Systematic training for effective parenting (parent's handbook)* (3rd ed.). Circle Pines, MN: American Guidance Service.

Draguns, J. G. (1976). Counseling across cultures: Common themes and distinct approaches. In P. B. Pedersen, W. J. Lonner, & J. G. Draguns (Eds.), *Counseling across cultures*. Honolulu: University of Hawaii Press.

Dworetzky, J. P. (1990). *Introduction to child development* (4th ed.). New York: West.

Ellis, A. (1983). *Rational-emotive and cognitive behavior therapy*. New York: Springer.

Garfield, J. C., Weiss, S. I., & Pollack, E. A. (1973). Effects of the child's social class on school counselors' decision-making. *Journal of Counseling Psychology, 20*, 166–168.

Gelso, C. J., & Fassinger, R. E. (1990). Counseling psychology: Theory and research on intervention. *Annual Review of Psychology, 41*, 387–416.

Gibran, K. (1965). *The Prophet*. New York: Alfred A. Knopf.

Griffith, M. S., & Jones, E. E. (1978). Race psychotherapy: Changing perspectives. In J. H. Masserman (Ed.), *Current psychiatric therapies* (Vol. 18, pp. 225–235). New York: Grune & Stratton.

Harrar. L. (Producer). (1984). *Make my people live: The crises in Indian health* [Television broadcast]. Boston, MA: Public Broadcasting System, NOVA.

Helms, J. E. (Ed.). (1990). *Black and white racial identity theory, research, and practice*. Westport, CT: Greenwood Press.

Herring, R. D. (1990). Nonverbal communication: A necessary component of cross-cultural counseling. *Journal of Multicultural Counseling and Development, 18*(4), 172–179.

Ibrahim, F. A., & Kahn, H. (1984). *Scale to assess world views*. Unpublished manuscript, University of Connecticut, Storrs, CT.

Ibrahim, F. A., & Kahn, H. (1987). Assessment of world views. *Psychological Reports, 60*, 163–176.

Ibrahim, F. A. (1991). Contribution of cultural worldview to generic counseling and development. *Journal of Counseling and Development, 70*(1), 13–19.

Ibrahim, F. A. (in press). Multicultural counseling: An existential world view perspective. In A. B. Stills (Ed.), *Theories of multicultural counseling*.

Jones, E. E., Krupnick, J. L., & Kerig, P. K. (1987). Some gender effects in a brief psychotherapy. *Psychotherapy, 24*, 337–352.

Keefe, S. F., & Padilla, A. M. (1987). *Chicano ethnicity*. Albuquerque: University of New Mexico Press.

Kopp, S. B. (1971). *Guru: Metaphors from a psychotherapist*. Palo Alto, CA: Science and Behavior Books.

Lee, C. C. (1991). Cultural dynamics: Their importance in multicultural counseling. In C. C. Lee & B. L. R. Richardson (Eds.), *Multicultural issues in counseling: New approaches to diversity*. Alexandria, VA: American Association for Counseling and Development.

Lee, D. (1984). Counseling and culture: Some issues. *Personnel and Guidance Journal, 62*, 592–597.

Lee, S. D. (1968). *Social class bias in the diagnosis of mental illness*. Doctoral dissertation, University of Oklahoma. Ann Arbor, MI: (University Microfilms No. 68–6959).

Lonner, W. J. (1985). Issues in testing and assessment in cross-cultural counseling. *The Counseling Psychologist, 13*(4), 599–614.

Lynn, S. J., & Garske, J. P. (1985). *Contemporary psychotherapies: Models and methods*. Columbus, OH: Merrill/Macmillan.

Myers, L. J., Speight, S. L., Highlen, P. S., Cox, C. I., Reynolds, A. L., Adams, E. M., & Hanley, C. P. (1991). Identity development and worldview: Toward an optimal conceptualization. *Journal of Counseling and Development, 70*(1), 54–63.

Nystul, M. S. (1978). Adler as a Sherlockian. *The Individual Psychologist, 15*(1), 41–45.

Nystul, M. S. (1981). Avoiding roadblocks in counseling. *The Individual Psychologist, 18*, 21–28.

Parham, T. A. (1989). Cycles of psychological nigrescence. *The Counseling Psychologist 17*, 187–226.

Patterson, C. H. (1989). Eclecticism in psychotherapy: Is integration possible? *Psychotherapy, 26*(2), 157–161.

Pedersen, P. B. (1987). Ten frequent assumptions of cultural bias in counseling. *Journal of Multicultural Counseling and Development, 15*(1), 16–24.

Pedersen, P. (1988). *A handbook for developing multicultural awareness*. Alexandria, VA: American Association for Counseling and Development.

Pedersen, P. B. (1991). Multiculturalism as a generic approach to counseling. *Journal of Counseling and Development, 70*(1), 6–12.

Ponterotto, J. G., & Casas, J. M. (1991). *Handbook of racial/ethnic minority counseling research*. Springfield, IL: Charles C. Thomas.

Poston, W. S. C., Craine, M., & Atkinson, D. R. (1991). Counselor dissimilarity, confrontation, client cultural mistrust, and willingness to self-disclose, *Journal of Multicultural Counseling and Development, 19*(2), 65–74.

Rogers, C. (1951). *Client-centered therapy*. Boston: Houghton Mifflin.

Sattler, J. M. (1977). The effects of therapist-client racial similarity. In A. S. Gurman & A. M. Razin (Eds.), *Effective psychotherapy: A handbook of research* (pp. 252–290). Elmsford, NY: Pergamon.

Shakespeare, W. (1938). *The works of William Shakespeare: Gathered into one volume*. New York: Oxford University Press.

Sire, J. W. (1976). *The universe next door*. Downers, IL: Intervarsity.

Sue, D. W. (1978). World views and counseling. *The Personnel and Guidance Journal, 56*, 458–462.

Sue, D. W. (1981). *Counseling the culturally different: Theory and practice*. New York: John Wiley & Sons.

Sue, D. W., Bermier, T. E., Durran, A., Feinberg, L., Pedersen, P., Smith, E. T., & Vasquez-Nuttall, E. (1982). Position paper: Cross-cultural counseling competencies. *The Counseling Psychologist, 10*(2), 45–52.

Sue, D. W., & Sue, D. (1977). Barriers to effective cross-cultural counseling. *Journal of Counseling Psychology, 24*, 420–429.

Sue, D. W., & Sue, D. (1990). *Counseling the culturally different* (2nd. ed.). New York: John Wiley & Sons.

Sue, S. (1988). Psychotherapeutic services for ethnic minorities. *American Psychologist, 43*(4), 301–308.

Topper, M. D. (1985). Navajo "alcoholism": Drinking, alcohol abuse, and treatment in a changing cultural environment. In L. A. Bennett & G. M. Ames (Eds.), *The American experience with alcohol: Contrasting cultural perspectives*. New York: Plenum Press.

Usher, C. H. (1989). Recognizing cultural bias in counseling theory and practice: The case of Rogers. *Journal of Multicultural Counseling and Development, 17*, 62–71.

Vontress, C. E. (1973). Counseling the racial and ethnic minorities. *Focus on Guidance, 5*(6), 1–10.

Vontress, C. E. (1988). An existential approach to cross-cultural counseling. *Journal of Multicultural Counseling and Development, 16*, 73–83.

Weighill, V. E., Hodge, J., & Peck, D. F. (1983). Keeping appointments with clinical psychologists. *British Journal of Clinical Psychology, 22*, 143–144.

Westwood, M. J., & Ishiyama, F. I. (1990). The communication process as a critical intervention for client change in cross-cultural counseling. *Journal of Multicultural Counseling and Development, 18*(4), 163–171.

Williams, R. L., & Kirkland, J. (1971). The white counselor and the black client. *The Counseling Psychologist, 2*, 114–117.

CHAPTER SIX

The Classic Theories of Freud, Adler, and Jung

CHAPTER OVERVIEW

This chapter provides a description of the three classic theories of Freud, Adler, and Jung. Highlights of the chapter include information regarding these three theorists in terms of

- Background information
- View of human nature
- Key concepts
- The counseling process
- Techniques
- Contemporary issues
- Summary and evaluation

AN OVERVIEW OF FREUD, ADLER, AND JUNG

The classic psychological theories of Sigmund Freud, Alfred Adler, and Carl Jung laid the foundation for modern clinical practice. Their influence transcended psychology, making a significant impact on the arts, education, child-rearing practices, and numerous other aspects of daily living.

Freud's masterpiece *The Interpretation of Dreams*, which was published in 1900, caught the interest of Adler and Jung. Adler and Jung became colleagues of Freud and went on to become central figures in the psychoanalytic organization. They eventually broke ranks with Freud when they believed he overemphasized the role of sexuality in personality development. Adler and Jung proceeded to develop their own personal theories. The three distinct schools of psychology that evolved have a number of commonalities. Each emphasized the importance of early life experiences on personality development and also viewed insight as an important prerequisite to change.

The Freudian, Adlerian, and Jungian schools of psychology can be considered the "classic schools," because each developed its own comprehensive theory of personality and approach to psychotherapy. They can be used as the central or core theory from which to develop an integrative counseling approach. Table 6.1 presents an overview of these three theories. In the remainder of this chapter, I will describe the theories in terms of background information, view of human nature, key concept, the counseling process, techniques, contemporary issues, and summary and evaluation. A more in-depth understanding of these schools of counseling can be gained from the references found in the reading list at the end of this chapter.

FREUD'S PSYCHOANALYTIC THEORY

Background Information

Patterson (1986) described some of the significant events of Freud's life. These observations have been incorporated into the following overview.

Sigmund Freud (1856–1939) was born in Freiberg, Moravia, a town in what is now Czechoslovakia. He was the oldest of eight children and moved with his family to Vienna when he was 4.

Freud obtained a medical degree in 1881 from the University of Vienna. After graduation, he went to Paris to study with Charcot, who was known for his work with hypnosis in the treatment of hysteria. Freud then returned to Vienna and married Martha Bernays. They had six children; the youngest was Anna, who later became a distinguished child analyst.

In 1882, Freud began a private practice in medicine, initially specializing in nervous diseases. He later broadened his practice into what is known today as psychiatry. At this point in his career, Freud became interested in the "talking cure," which was being developed by the prominent Viennese physician, Joseph Breuer. Breuer believed that a client could be helped by simply talking about his problem. This concept contributed to Freud's free association technique and is an important part of the evolution of the counseling profession.

The most creative period in Freud's life was also a period during which he experienced serious emotional problems. He was tormented by psychosomatic disorders

Table 6.1
Freud, Adler, and Jung

Theory	Key Concepts	The Counseling Process	Techniques
Freud's Psychoanalytic Theory	Endopsychic conflicts resulting from the id, ego, and superego; defense mechanisms; the conscious–unconscious continuum; and the effects of traumatic experiences in childhood on personality development.	Has the major aim of resolving intrapsychic conflicts to restructure the personality as necessary.	Dream analysis and free association can be used to explore unconscious processes; confronting, clarification, and interpretation provide necessary insight.
Adler's Individual Psychology	The creative self; behavior as goal directed and purposeful; social interest; and striving for significance as a motivational force; and the family constellation.	Is educationally oriented; provides information; guides and attempts to encourage discouraged clients	The life-style analysis as an assessment technique; motivation modification to modify underlying motivational forces; and techniques to reorient clients from basic mistakes
Jung's Analytic Psychology	The collective unconscious; archetypes; and personality types.	Explores unconscious processes to help the self emerge so clients can be free to move toward self-realization.	Analysis of the interrelationship of several dreams for their symbolic content and cues to the various systems of the personality

Sigmund Freud

and phobias such as an exaggerated fear of dying. At one point, he was even afraid to cross the street. During this time Freud engaged in extensive self-analysis by studying his dreams. The insights Freud gained from his self-analysis became very influential in the development of his own theories such as the Oedipus complex. He remembered that as a child he felt hostility toward his father, whom he perceived as an overbearing authority figure. On the other hand, Freud had sexual feelings for his mother, whom he remembered to be loving, attractive, and protective.

Freud's rise to prominence required perseverance and an ability to withstand severe criticism. As Freud developed his revolutionary theory, he was initially met with scorn and ridicule from all corners of the academic and scientific community. Alone, he forged on, typically working for 18 hours a day. Finally, with his publication of *The Interpretation of Dreams* in 1900, he became "respectable" again. Shortly thereafter, Freud was welcomed back to the intellectual community and regarded with great esteem.

In his later years, Freud's struggles turned to his personal health. His fondness for cigars apparently contributed to the development of jaw cancer. During the last 20 years of his life, he was in almost constant pain and underwent 33 operations. Somehow, he still managed to maintain an active professional life. Hall and Lindzey (1978) noted that Freud was a prolific writer, with his collective works filling 24 volumes. His work also stands out from a literary point of view. Freud's eloquent writing style did much to popularize his ideas.

View of Human Nature

Freud had a deterministic view of human nature. He was convinced that behavior was determined by unconscious biological urges of sex and aggression and psychosexual experiences during the first 6 years of life.

Key Concepts

Freud's theory of personality is characterized by several key concepts (Strachey, 1953–1974). Some of these are the structure of the personality, endopsychic conflicts, defense mechanisms, the conscious-unconscious continuum, and psychosexual stages of development. These concepts, as described by Freud (Strachey, 1953–1974) are incorporated into the following overview.

The Structure of the Personality.   In Freud's view, the personality is made up of three autonomous yet interdependent systems: the id, ego, and superego.

The *id* is the original system of the personality from which the ego and superego emerge (Hall & Lindzey, 1978). It is the reservoir of psychic energy, supplying energy to the other two systems. The id can be considered the "hedonistic branch" of the personality (Hall, 1954). It is driven by the pleasure principle, which attempts to reduce tension by gratification of sexual and aggressive impulses.

The *superego* is the other extreme of the personality. It can be considered the "judicial branch" and is concerned with moralistic issues determining what is right or wrong (Hall, 1954). It represents the values and ideals of society as handed down from parent to child. The superego has three purposes: to inhibit the impulses from the id; to alter the ego's orientation from realistic to moralistic; and to encourage the personality to strive for perfection.

The *ego* can be considered the "executive branch" of the personality (Hall, 1954). It is ruled by the reality principle, which attempts to exert a realistic, reality-based influence over the id and superego.

Endopsychic Conflicts.   An *endopsychic* conflict is a conflict within (from *endo*) the psyche. Endopsychic conflicts result from the interaction of the three parts of the personality: the id, ego, and superego. According to Freud, there is only so much "psychic energy" for the three parts of the personality to function. All three systems are therefore in constant competition for this energy to take control and dominate the personality. As the three parts of the personality compete for psychic energy, they create conflicts within the psyche called endopsychic conflicts. These conflicts create anxiety, which the organism can attempt to alleviate by creating defense mechanisms. Examples of endopsychic conflicts are

- *Id versus ego:* (Id:) "I want to rape or murder." (Ego:) "If you do, you will go to jail."

- *Id versus superego and ego:* (Id:) "I want to rape or murder." (Superego:) "You shouldn't because it is wrong" and (Ego:) "You will go to jail."

- *Ego versus superego:* (Ego:) "I would like to go to bed with my lover." (Superego:) "Don't do it, because it is a sin to have sex unless you are married."

denial

included in these choices

Defense Mechanisms.   Freud's concept of defense mechanisms was one of his most important theoretical achievements. Defense mechanisms develop unconsciously when the ego feels threatened by an endopsychic conflict. When this occurs, defense mechanisms can be utilized to deny, falsify, or distort reality so the ego can cope. Some of the more common defense mechanisms are projection, reaction formation, fixation, regression, and repression.

Projection is an attempt to attribute to another person one's own thoughts or feelings. For example, instead of saying you hate someone, you say, "That person hates me." In this example, projection occurs because the ego is threatened by aggressive id impulses. Projection can therefore be seen as an attempt to "externalize the danger."

Reaction formation is a way of coping by creating an extreme emotional response that is the opposite of how one actually feels. This results in a "falsification of reality." For example, a man may hate his wife and want a divorce. At the same time, he may have intense feelings of guilt, since he believes divorce is morally wrong. If the man tells others how wonderful his wife is and how much he loves her, a reaction formation may be operating.

Fixation can occur if the demands of life become too threatening. In an attempt to avoid new responsibilities, a person can avoid growing up and fixate, or stand still, in terms of development. When this occurs during adolescence, the individual's personality would remain like an adolescent for the remainder of life.

Regression is an attempt to cope by moving back to a point in one's development that was less threatening. For example, a person who has a major business failure may feel life is falling apart. In an attempt to cope, the person may try to escape these feelings of failure by moving back to a point in time that was not so threatening. When this occurs, the person may assume the role of a child to avoid adult responsibilities.

Repression is an attempt to cope by creating an avoidance response. In repression, the stressful situation is pushed from the conscious to the unconscious dimension of the mind.

The Conscious-Unconscious Continuum.   Freud was one of the first to explore the unconscious dimension of the human psyche. He believed it held the key to understanding behavior and problems within the personality. It is therefore not surprising that the majority of the techniques associated with psychoanalysis are used to explore unconscious processes (e.g., free association and dream analysis).

Freud conceptualized conscious and unconscious processes in terms of a continuum. The analogy of the iceberg can be used to understand this continuum, as illustrated in Figure 6.1.

As shown in Figure 6.1, most of the psyche involves unconscious processes. The *conscious* dimension contains material that the person is aware of and can readily retrieve. The *preconscious* relates to material that the person is almost consciously aware of but that is just out of mental awareness (e.g., almost being able to remember a person's name). The *unconscious proper* includes all memory traces that the person is not consciously aware of (e.g., a repressed traumatic experience such as childhood incest).

Figure 6.1
Iceberg Analogy

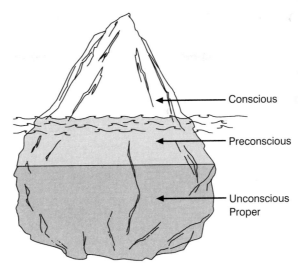

- Conscious
- Preconscious
- Unconscious Proper

Psychosexual States of Development.   Freud contended that personality development was determined to a large degree by early life experiences. His theory suggests that problems in the personality could result if the child had a traumatic experience or the child's basic needs were not met. When this occurs, the person could attempt to achieve indirect gratification by displacement or sublimation to restore equilibrium to the organism. Displacement is indirect gratification, such as a baby sucking a thumb when not allowed to eat. Sublimation is also indirect gratification, but it results in some form of social recognition. An example of sublimation is a sexually frustrated person creating a beautiful, sensuous painting.

Freud was one of the first theorists to identify stages of development that a person progresses through. He called them psychosexual stages, emphasizing the role of sexuality in the developmental process. Freud divided these stages into three periods: the pregenital period, which lasts until age 6; the latency period, which spans from age 6 to adolescence; and the genital period, which continues for the rest of a person's life.

A brief overview of these stages will now be provided as well as an explanation of how problems can occur at each stage. The pregenital period is composed of the oral, anal, and phallic stages and latency period. Freud believed that the *oral stage* occurs during the first 18 months of life. It was called the oral stage because the child appears preoccupied with oral functions (e.g., sucking mother's breast and exploring objects by putting them into the mouth). Problems that occur during the oral stage (such as extreme frustration of oral gratification) could result in the individual developing an oral personality as an adult. Adult nail-biting could be an example of displacement of latent oral needs. Becoming a teacher or orator could result from sublimation of oral needs.

The *anal stage* occurs from 18 months to 3 years of age. This stage emphasizes the impact of toilet training on personality development. Problems that can occur during the anal stage may result in a anal-explosive or anal-retentive personality. The anal-explosive personality is an aggressive type of person. This style of personality could result when a child went to the toilet all the time as a means of keeping a parent's attention. The anal-explosive personality could develop skills in football or boxing as a form of sublimation. An anal-retentive personality could occur if a parent used severe punishment when the child had an "accident." Out of fear, the child could develop a pattern of not going to the toilet. An example of sublimation for the anal-retentive personality could be a person who is good at saving money.

The *phallic stage* occurs between the ages of 3 and 6. According to Freud, it is a time when male children become sexually interested in their mothers (the Oedipus complex), and female children become attracted to their fathers (the Electra complex). The boy eventually resolves his Oedipus complex out of fear of castration from his father. Problems could occur if a father had jealous tendencies and threatened to hurt his son if the boy did not stop "pestering mother." This threat could intensify the boy's fear of castration. According to Freud, this fear could then inhibit any future thoughts of the opposite sex, promoting homosexual tendencies.

Unlike the male child, the female does not have a dramatic means of resolving her Electra complex, such as fear of castration. Instead, she may resolve her sexual feelings by reacting to the realistic barriers that are established to prohibit incestuous relationships. A problem could result during this stage if a child felt emotionally rejected by her father, possibly causing her to avoid relationships with males in the future. On the other hand, if an incestuous relationship were allowed to occur, the child could experience even more profound difficulties in her personality such as low self-image and perhaps promiscuity.

The *latency period*, which occurs between the ages of 6 and 12, is a period of relative calm. The child has emerged from the turbulence of the pregenital period with the basic structure of the personality largely formed. During this period, the child develops new interests to replace infantile sexual impulses. Socialization takes place as the child moves from a narcissistic preoccupation to a more altruistic orientation. Problems could occur during this period if the parents did not encourage the child's interest in establishing positive social relationships. As a result, the child might not be able to develop the social skills necessary for successful interpersonal relationships.

The *genital period* begins at puberty and continues for the rest of life. The focus of this period is an opposite-sex relationship leading to the experience of intimacy. Problems during this period could occur for an individual who was discouraged from socializing or began sexual relationships before being emotionally ready to handle them.

The Counseling Process

Freud's approach to counseling and psychotherapy is called psychoanalysis, emphasizing the analysis of the mind. It is a time-consuming approach that can typically involve four 1-hour sessions each week over a period of several years (Arlow, 1989).

The major aim of psychoanalysis is to restructure the personality by resolution of intrapsychic conflicts. The actual process of traditional psychoanalysis involves the patient lying on a couch and engaging in free association, saying whatever comes to mind. In this process, the analyst is seated out of the patient's view behind the couch and listens and reacts in a noncritical manner. Arlow (1989) described four phases of psychoanalysis: the opening phase, the development of transference, working through, and the resolution of transference.

The Opening Phase.   The analyst obtains important history from the patient. Gradually, over a period of 3 to 6 months, the analyst obtains a broad understanding of the patient's unconscious conflicts.

The Development of Transference.   During this phase, the patient begins to experience a transference relationship with the analyst. This involves projecting thoughts and feelings onto the analyst that are associated with significant others such as a father or mother.

Analysis of the transference is a cornerstone of the psychoanalytic process. It provides the patient with insight into how past relationships and experiences are creating problems in present relationships. Analysis of transference also helps the patient learn how to use insight to have appropriate, mature decisions regarding current relationships.

Countertransference may also occur in therapy and results when analysts unconsciously begin to see qualities in the client that remind them of someone from their past. Countertransference can interfere with the analyst's objectivity and destroy the therapeutic process. When this occurs, the analyst may need psychoanalysis to work through these tendencies.

Working Through.   This phase is essentially a continuation of the previous phase. It involves additional analysis of transference aimed at generating more profound insights and consolidating what can be learned from them.

Resolution of Transference.   During the final phase of therapy, the analyst and patient work toward termination. This can involve working through resistance from the patient regarding termination or preparing the patient to function independently once termination is complete.

Techniques

Freud developed many techniques that could be used in psychoanalysis (Strachey, 1953–1974). Their primary purpose is to make the unconscious conscious. Some of the more commonly used techniques are as follows.

- *Free association* is the primary technique used in psychoanalysis. As discussed earlier, it is used throughout the counseling process. Free association encourages the patient to discuss whatever comes to mind, thereby overcoming the patient's tendencies to suppress or censor information.

- *Dream analysis* is a technique Freud developed as a means to explore unconscious processes. He suggested that elements of dreams contained symbolic meaning, such as a screwdriver being a phallic symbol, representing a penis.

- *Confrontation and clarification* are feedback procedures to help the patient become aware of what is occurring and in need of further analysis (Prochaska, 1984).

- *Interpretation* involves providing insight to the patient regarding inner conflicts reflected in resistance, transference, and other processes.

Contemporary Issues

Contemporary Freudian psychology reflects several changes and modifications from Freud's original theory. These changes evolved primarily in response to what was considered to be his overemphasis on the role of sexuality in personality development and the excessive time required to complete psychoanalysis. Two emerging trends characterize these new dimensions to Freud's approach: the ego-analytic position and brief psychodynamic psychotherapy.

Ego-Analytic Theory.   The ego-analytic position incorporates theories associated with ego-psychology and object-relations theory. Ego psychology is associated with the work of Erikson (1950) and Rapaport (1958) and represents a shift in focus from the id to the ego as the primary driving force of personality (Prochaska, 1984). In this new role, the ego is viewed as capable of functioning independently from the id in its attempt to adapt to reality and master the environment (Prochaska, 1984).

Object-relations theory, as proposed by Kernberg (1976) and Kohut (1971), emphasizes the self and objects (i.e., people) as the primary organizing force in personality functioning (Prochaska, 1984). Object relations are intrapsychic structures based on the mental representations of the self and others (Prochaska, 1984).

Baker (1985) identified the following six characteristics of the ego-analytic position.

1. Noninstinctual factors are emphasized

2. The ego is conceptualized as a separate autonomous structure that operates independently of the id

3. The function of the ego has been expanded to include the role of adaptation to the environment by developing coping and mastery skills

4. Psychosocial and interpersonal variables are emphasized over biological-instinctual variables

5. Developmental stages that occur after puberty are considered as important as those occurring before puberty

6. Psychopathology occurs as a result of not meeting the needs associated with developmental tasks and other forces that could cause defects in the personality structure of the individual

Brief Psychodynamic Psychotherapy.   Brief psychodynamic psychotherapy evolved as an alternative to classic psychoanalysis. Among the brief psychodynamic approaches are Malan's (1976, 1980) focal therapy; Mann's (1973, 1981) time-limited psychotherapy; Sifneos's (1979, 1984) short-term dynamic psychotherapy; and Davanloo's (1978, 1984) short-term dynamic psychotherapy. Garske and Molteni (1985) noted that all brief psychodynamic approaches shared several characteristics.

The approaches are all based on psychoanalytic theory, suggest similar efficacy, and modify psychoanalytic procedures for use in a briefer format.

The aim of brief psychodynamic psychotherapy is to go beyond symptom relief and bring out necessary changes in the client's personality (Garske & Molteni, 1985). The number of sessions required in brief psychodynamic psychotherapy tends to be limited to 12 sessions and depends on the nature of the client's problem and the type of therapy utilized (Garske & Molteni, 1985). Mann's (1973) time-limited model has a duration of between 1 and 12 sessions. Davanloo's (1978, 1984) short-term dynamic approach varies the number of recommended sessions from 2–5 sessions, 6–15 sessions, 16–25 sessions, and 26–40 sessions depending on the nature of the client's problem.

Garske and Molteni (1985) identified the following six factors that are seen to promote change in brief psychodynamic psychotherapy.

1. A contract is established with the client, which includes a description of the client's problems in psychoanalytic terms.

2. A statement of goals and objectives is established, along with a time limit on the number of sessions.

3. The therapist takes an active, probing approach, clarifying and confronting the client's resistance.

4. The therapist interprets the links between the client's current problems, relationship with the therapists and significant others, and past conflicts.

5. The time-limited aspect of therapy arouses issues relating to separation and individualization within the client.

6. The termination phase of therapy is characterized by working through problems associated with separation and individualization.

Research efforts have attempted to determine what factors contribute to efficacy of brief psychodynamic psychotherapy. Nergaard and Silberschatz (1989) found that high measures of shame and guilt (especially guilt), as measured by the Therapy Shame and Guilt Scale, correlated with positive therapy outcomes. Mills, Bauer, and Miars (1989) noted that transference reactions should be addressed quickly and energetically by the therapist to maximize their impact.

Goldfried, Greenberg, and Mormar (1990) reviewed the literature on brief psychodynamic psychotherapy. They noted the approach has been effective for treating stress and bereavement disorders (Mormar & Horowitz, 1988); late-life depression (Thompson, Gallagher, & Breckenridge, 1987); and adjustment, affective, and personality disorders (Marziali, 1984). In addition, Barth et al. (1988) evaluated 34 short-term dynamic psychotherapy cases. They found significant gains in symptom relief, adaptive functioning, and personality change at termination and over a 2-year follow-up period.

Summary and Evaluation

Sigmund Freud's place in history is secure. He is widely regarded as one of the most prominent intellectual figures of all time. His contributions to psychology and other fields are phenomenal. His most remarkable achievements include the concept of defense mechanisms as a means for coping with anxiety; the mapping of the conscious-unconscious continuum; and his methods for exploring unconscious processes in psychoanalysis. Weaknesses of Freud's theory are what has been considered his overemphasis of the role of sexuality in personality development and the excessive length of time required to achieve the aims of psychoanalysis. New advances in Freudian theory as reflected in the ego-analytic position and in brief psychodynamic psychotherapy are attempts to overcome these problems.

ADLER'S INDIVIDUAL PSYCHOLOGY

Background Information

Alfred Adler (1870–1937) received a medical degree from the University of Vienna in 1895. In 1902, he began what was to develop into a rather stormy relationship with Sigmund Freud. Adler quickly took an active role in Freud's psychoanalytic society and was elected as its president in 1910. He and Freud co-founded and became co-editors of the *Journal of Psychoanalysis*. Shortly thereafter, Adler broke ranks with Freud over several important theoretical issues. These differences culminated in Freud asking Adler to resign from his positions as president of the society and co-

Alfred Adler

editor of the journal. At this point, Adler disassociated himself from the Freudian circle and founded his own school, which he called individual psychology.

After serving as a medical officer during World War I, Adler returned to practice medicine in Vienna. In 1922, he turned his attention to the problems of children and established a child guidance clinic in the Vienna public schools (Dinkmeyer & Dinkmeyer, 1985). Eventually, more than 50 similar guidance clinics were opened before political turmoil restricted the growth of Adlerian psychology in Europe (Dinkmeyer & Dinkmeyer, 1985). By 1935, political unrest forced Adler to flee Europe, and he settled in the United States. Adler died 2 years later while on a lecture tour in Aberdeen, Scotland.

Adler maintained a busy schedule throughout his career. He was particularly known for his extensive lecture tours, during which he would often work with a client in front of an audience. This was revolutionary at the time, because therapy was not practiced with such openness (Dinkmeyer & Dinkmeyer, 1985). Today, Adlerians continue the tradition of demonstrating counseling strategies in front of live audiences.

Adler was a prolific writer, publishing more than 100 books and articles during his lifetime. *The Practice and Theory of Individual Psychology* (Adler, 1969) is an excellent introduction to Adlerian psychology.

View of Human Nature

Adler held an optimistic view of people. He believed people were basically positive with the capability of self-determination. This view of human nature stimulated the development of the humanistic movement in psychology, which focuses on the dignity and worth of the individual. Adler also emphasized that behavior is holistic, or interrelated; teleological, in that it has a purpose and is directed toward a goal; and phenomenological, because it can best be understood from the client's frame of reference.

Key Concepts

Adler (1969) and Ansbacher and Ansbacher (1956, 1964) described a number of key concepts that make up the structure of Adler's theory of personality. The following 10 principles are central to this theory.

The Creative Self.   This concept was Adler's "crowning achievement as a personality theorist" (Hall & Lindzey, 1978, p. 165). It lies at the heart of Adlerian theory of personality. The creative self is the center or nucleus from which all life movement generates (Ansbacher & Ansbacher, 1956). Freud called this center the ego. For Adler, the creative self emphasized that each person has the potential to creatively interact with the world. Adler expressed the potential for self-determined behavior when he said:

> . . . the important thing is not what one is born with, but what use one makes of that equipment . . . To understand this we find it is necessary to assume the existence of still another force, the creative power of the individual. (Ansbacher & Ansbacher, 1964, pp. 86–87)

The Concept of Teleological Movement.   Adler saw all behavior in terms of movement; nothing was static. This movement is teleological in nature since it has a purpose and is directed toward a goal. According to Adler, a person can move on the useful or useless side of life. Movement on the useful side is characterized by cooperative efforts, whereas movement on the useless side is narcissistic in nature (Ansbacher & Ansbacher, 1956).

Adler also believed that life movement was from a sensed minus to a sensed plus. According to their private logic, individuals would behave in a manner that appears to improve their position (Ansbacher & Ansbacher, 1956). This concept can be useful to understand the motivation behind misbehavior. For example, a child may move toward a goal of power to gain recognition. In this instance, the private logic may be, "I can be somebody if I fight with others."

Behavior Can be Understood From an Interpersonal Perspective.   Adler emphasized that behavior can best be understood from an interpersonal perspective (Ansbacher & Ansbacher, 1956). This spirit was captured by the poet John Donne (1952) when he said, "No man is an island" (p. 441). Adler believed that people do not behave in isolation from others but in relation to others. This reasoning can be used to identify goals of misbehavior. For example, parents can develop a tentative hypothesis by asking themselves how they feel when their child misbehaves. Feeling annoyed could indicate their child has a goal of attention; feeling angry or threatened could suggest a goal of power; feeling hurt could indicate a goal of revenge; and feeling desperate or hopeless could suggest a goal of a display of inadequacy (Dinkmeyer & McKay, 1989; Dreikurs & Soltz, 1964).

The Psychology of Use.   Adler stressed that all behavior has a use or payoff that is usually unconscious in nature (Ansbacher & Ansbacher, 1956). Emotions serve a use in helping propel a person toward a goal. This concept can also be used to understand the symptoms associated with psychopathology, as the following Personal Note illustrates.

a personal note

Don was a 22-year-old assistant accountant. One day while he was working, his hand became numb and he was unable to move it. Don was taken to a hospital where I was the staff psychologist. The patient received a complete medical evaluation, including numerous neurological tests. After the doctors decided there was nothing physically wrong with the patient's hand, they referred him to me. When I asked Don how he liked his work, he said he hated it, largely because he wanted to go to medical school. After some additional assessment, I decided to hypnotize him. I told him he was a doctor and asked him to take my blood pressure. At this point, he was able to move his hand.

The psychology of use was quite apparent in this case, since the patient's inability to move his hand could help him avoid a job he hated. It is important to point out that Don wasn't consciously aware of trying to avoid his job. He was actually relieved to discover there was nothing physically wrong with his hand.

Together, we decided that Don would try to go back to college, so he could be doing something he wanted to do. With this in mind, I spent the next few sessions helping him apply for admission into college. It is interesting to note that Don could not voluntarily move his hand until he received a letter of acceptance from the college.

Don's disorder is known in the literature as a *conversion disorder*. It involves losing a bodily function such as the use of a hand or sight due to psychological, not physical, reasons. As illustrated in this case, the disorder can also be understood in terms of the psychology of use.

A Phenomenological Psychology.   The phenomenological perspective provides an understanding of clients from their internal frame of reference. Adler suggested that what individuals perceive is biased according to past experiences (Ansbacher & Ansbacher, 1964). He referred to this phenomenon as an apperception. A phenomenological perspective is therefore necessary to understand clients' interpretations of their experiences.

Emphasis on Social Interest.   Adler's term *Gemeinschaftsgefühl* has been translated into English as social interest (Ansbacher & Ansbacher, 1964). It refers to an inborn tendency to cooperate and work with others for the common good (Ansbacher & Ansbacher, 1964). Adler related this concept to mental health when he observed that social interest is the barometer of mental health (Ansbacher & Ansbacher, 1964). Glasser (1965) supported this position when he suggested that all people need love and affection to be fulfilled.

The Life Style.   Hall and Lindzey (1978) suggested that life style became the recurrent theme in Adler's later writings and the most distinctive feature of his psychology. "The term *life style* refers to the person's basic orientation to life—the set of patterns of recurrent themes that run through his or her existence" (Dinkmeyer & Dinkmeyer, 1985, p. 123). According to Adler, the life style is relatively fixed by age 4 or 5. Once established, the individual's life style guides the assimilation and utilization of future experiences (Hall and Lindzey, 1978).

A Holistic Psychology.   Adler's individual psychology means the individual is indivisible and undivided. It is therefore a holistic psychology, which attempts to understand the overall life style as a unified whole. Adlerians are interested in assessing how the person organizes the self as a whole person with interrelated and coherent beliefs, perceptions, and goals (Dinkmeyer & Dinkmeyer, 1985). This position is similar to the holistic health concept, which views the mind and body as an interacting system, not as separate entities.

Striving for Significance.   Adler believed that people have a basic tendency to avoid feelings of inferiority by striving for superiority (Ansbacher & Ansbacher, 1956). A person could therefore compensate for feelings of inadequacy in one area by excelling in another aspect of life. In this example, striving for superiority should not be viewed as an attempt to feel superior over others. Instead, it amounts to a striving for significance and worth as an individual and is a major motivational force (Dinkmeyer & Dinkmeyer, 1985).

The Family Constellation.   The family constellation encompasses many factors associated with a person's family of origin, such as birth order, family size, and the relationship between family members. Adler believed that each person's family constellation was unique and could therefore make a significant impact on the development of the life style. Adler was particularly interested in birth order and how it would affect a person's development (Ansbacher & Ansbacher, 1956). For example, first-born children tend to be bossy and talkative, since they are used to telling their brothers and sisters what to do. They also tend to be conservative, since they are born into a world of adults and therefore tend to affiliate with adults and adult values.

With the arrival of a second child, first-born children can feel temporarily dethroned, since they have to share their parent's attention. This can cause them to be suspicious and have tendencies to protect themselves from sudden reversals of fortune. Middle-born children tend to be very ambitious as they attempt to compete with the oldest. This can result in the "racecourse syndrome," which can foster an achievement orientation in middle-born children. It can also promote sibling rivalry or competition between siblings, which is another Adlerian principle. In addition, middle-born children can grow up having difficulty feeling a sense of belonging, since they don't have the special place of being the oldest or youngest. They also tend to be observers and mediators interested in what is going on between the siblings and willing to mediate when a conflict occurs.

The youngest child of the family is the "baby." Parents tend to be more lenient and give special favors to the baby. Youngest children usually appreciate these special considerations and learn early in life that other people will take care of them and protect them from life's difficulties.

Dinkmeyer and Dinkmeyer (1985) noted that birth-order characteristics are only tendencies, which may or may not occur. Whether they manifest themselves depends on how parents relate to a child and how children interpret their ordinal position. When a person does not have the typical characteristics of a particular birth order, it can be interesting to determine what familial factors could account for the differences. For example, a middle-born female with three brothers and no sisters will usually not lack a sense of belonging, because she feels special as the only girl. A middle-born male may act like a first-born child as a result of the first-born being disowned from the family because of doing something extreme, such as committing murder.

The Counseling Process

Adlerians attempt to go beyond overt behavior and understand the motivation behind the behavior (Nystul, 1985). This approach is therefore more concerned with modifying motivation than with modifying behavior. Sonstegard, Hagerman, and Bitter (1975) elaborated on this position when they said:

> The Adlerian counselor is not preoccupied with changing behavior, rather he is concerned with understanding the individual's subjective frame of reference and the

identification of the individual's mistaken notion or goal within that framework. Indeed, the behavior of an individual is only understood when the goals are identified . . . (p. 17)

Mosak (1989) summarized the major goals of Adlerian psychotherapy as

- Increasing clients' social interest
- Helping clients overcome feelings of discouragement and reducing inferiority feelings
- Modifying clients' views and goals and changing their life scripts
- Changing faulty motivation
- Helping clients feel a sense of equality with others
- Assisting clients to become contributing members of society

The counseling process is educationally oriented, providing information, guiding, and attempting to encourage discouraged clients. The approach attempts to reeducate clients, so they can live in society as equals, both giving and receiving from others (Mosak, 1989).

The counseling relationship is based on equality. Adlerians avoid placing the client in a subservient position as in a doctor-patient relationship. They consider a sense of mutual respect to be vital to all relationships, including the counseling relationship.

Dinkmeyer and Dinkmeyer (1985) identified four phases of Adlerian psychotherapy: establishing the relationship; performing analysis and assessment; promoting insight; and reorientation. The authors observed that these phases are not intended to be separate or distinct processes but instead tend to overlap and blend in clinical practice. This can be especially true in the process of establishing a positive relationship. Adlerians believe it is important to maintain a positive relationship throughout the counseling process.

Techniques

Adlerian techniques can be described in terms of the four phases of Adlerian psychotherapy.

Phase One: Establishing the Relationship.   Adlerians utilize many techniques to establish a positive relationship. Three of these techniques are

1. *Use of listening skills.* Dinkmeyer, Dinkmeyer, and Sperry (1987) noted that effective listening skills were necessary to promote mutual trust and mutual respect—two essential elements of the Adlerian counseling relationship.

2. *Winning respect and offering hope.* Nystul (1985) suggested that a counselor could increase the client's motivation for becoming involved in counseling by winning the client's respect and offering hope.

3. *Encouragement.* Encouragement communicates a sense of support and can also help clients learn to believe in themselves. Dinkmeyer and Losoncy (1980) identified important skills that are involved in the encouragement pro-

cess. Some of these skills are focusing on the client's assets; communicating respect and confidence; being enthusiastic; helping the client become aware of choices; combating self-defeating, discouraging processes; and promoting self-encouragement.

Phase Two: Analysis and Assessment.   Adlerians typically do an in-depth analysis and assessment as early as the first session. This usually involves conducting a life-style analysis to explore how early life experiences can contribute to the adult personality.

Dream analysis can be a part of the life-style analysis (Mosak, 1989). Adlerians do not attempt to analyze dreams in terms of their symbolic content, as do Freudians. Instead, they see dreams as an attempt to deal with the difficulties and challenges of life. In this sense, dreams become a problem-solving activity, allowing the person a chance to rehearse for some future action (Mosak, 1989).

The life-style analysis can also be used to identify faulty or irrational views that may interfere with the client's growth. These are referred to as *basic mistakes*, and the following descriptions of these statements by Mosak (1989) are listed with examples.

- *Overgeneralizations*: "People can't be trusted."
- *False or impossible goals of security*: "I must please everybody."
- *Misrepresentations of life and life's demands*: "I never get any breaks."
- *Minimization or denial of one's worth*: "I'm dumb."
- *Faulty values*: "It doesn't matter how you play the game as long as you win."

Phase Three: Promoting Insight.   Adlerians believe that insight is an important prerequisite to long-term change. Insight allows clients to understand the dynamics of self-defeating patterns so they can be corrected during the reorientation process. The main tool for providing insight is interpretation, which focuses on creating awareness of basic mistakes that are impeding the client's growth.

Counselors can use confrontation techniques during the insight process if they encounter resistance from clients. Shulman (1973) noted that confrontation can challenge a client to make an immediate response or change or examine some issue. It can also foster immediacy in the relationship by enabling a client to know how the therapist is experiencing the client in the moment (Dinkmeyer & Dinkmeyer, 1985).

Phase Four: Reorientation.   The final phase of Adlerian psychotherapy involves putting insight into action. Clients are encouraged to make the necessary changes in their life as they develop more functional beliefs and behaviors. Counselors can use the following techniques during the reorientation phase.

1. *Spitting in the client's soup.* This technique can be used when clients engage in manipulative games, such as acting like a martyr. Spitting in their soup involves determining the payoff of the game and interpreting it to the client. For instance, a client may say, "My husband is such a drunk, I don't know why I put up with him." The counselor could respond by saying, "You must get a lot of sympathy from others, because you have to put up with so much." As

this client realizes that someone is aware of the payoffs she is receiving from her martyr syndrome, the game may seem less enjoyable.

2. *The push-button technique*. This technique is based on Ellis' (1962) Rational Emotive Therapy. It involves having clients concentrate on pleasant and unpleasant experiences and the feelings they generate (Dinkmeyer & Dinkmeyer, 1985). When clients discover that their thoughts influence their emotions, they recognize that they can take control of their emotional responses. The push-button concept symbolizes the amount of control clients can exert when they "push the button" and put a stop to self-defeating processes. They can then create a constructive way of reacting to their situation, producing a more positive emotional response.

3. *Catching oneself*. Clients can use this technique to avoid old self-defeating patterns. Initially, clients may catch themselves in the process of self-defeating behavior, such as playing a manipulative game. Eventually, they can catch themselves just before they start playing the game. Clients can be encouraged to use humor when they catch themselves, learning to laugh at how ridiculous their self-defeating tendencies are.

4. *Acting as-if*. This technique involves clients acting as if they could do whatever they would like to do, such as being more confident or being a better listener. The technique promotes a positive "can-do" spirit and a self-fulfilling prophecy, which can help clients experience success.

5. *Task setting and commitment*. Adlerians do not believe that change occurs by osmosis. They believe instead that it takes work and effort to change. Task setting and commitment are therefore essential aspects of Adlerian psychotherapy. Homework assignments can be useful in this regard by providing a structure through which clients can try out new modes of behaving.

Contemporary Issues

Many contemporary Adlerian concepts derive from the work of Rudolph Dreikurs (1897–1972). Dreikurs was a student of Adler's. In 1939, just 2 years after Adler's death, Dreikurs moved to Chicago and established the Alfred Adler Institute of Chicago (Dinkmeyer & Dinkmeyer, 1985). In many ways, he picked up where Adler left off (Dinkmeyer & Dinkmeyer, 1985). He continued the development of Adlerian theory, especially in terms of parent education and child guidance. Dreikurs had a gift for taking Adler's writings and reworking them into concepts that are easy to understand and apply. In addition, he developed his own concepts based on Adlerian principles, such as the four goals of misbehavior (Dreikurs, 1949; Dreikurs & Soltz, 1964); encouragement (Dinkmeyer & Dreikurs 1963); logical and natural consequences (Dreikurs & Soltz, 1964) and social equality (Dreikurs, 1971). Dreikurs maintained an active lecture tour during which he would demonstrate his approach. He is credited with having much to do with the popularization and acceptance of Adlerian psychology as a major school of counseling and psychotherapy (Dinkmeyer & Dinkmeyer, 1985).

Don Dinkmeyer is another key individual in the evolution of Adlerian psychology. Dinkmeyer and his associates have incorporated a number of Adlerian and Dreikurserian concepts into programs relating to children, adolescents, parents, and teachers. These programs have gained popularity and wide usage among counselors and other members of the helping professions. Some of these programs are: Systematic Training for Effective Parenting (STEP) (Dinkmeyer & McKay, 1989); Systematic Training for Effective Teaching (Dinkmeyer, McKay, & Dinkmeyer, 1980); Training in Marital Enrichment (TIME) (Dinkmeyer & Carlson, 1984); and Developing Understanding of Self and Others (DUSO-R) (Dinkmeyer & Dinkmeyer, 1982).

Several other individuals have made significant contributions to contemporary Adlerian psychology. Ray Corsini (1977, 1979) developed an educational system based on Adlerian principles, which he called individual education. Dreikurs, Corsini, Lowe, and Sonstegard (1959), Sherman and Dinkmeyer (1987), and Oscar Christenson have done much to promote the popularity of Adlerian family counseling.

A recent trend is a movement toward integrating Adlerian psychology with other schools of thought. In this regard, Shulman suggested that Adlerian psychology needs to develop further to incorporate new advances in the field of child development, neurochemical processes in the brain, and cognitive psychology (Nystul, 1988).

The movement toward integration appears to be gaining momentum among the Adlerian ranks. A special issue of *Individual Psychology: The Journal of Adlerian Theory, Research, and Practice* focused on exploring the issues relating to "beyond Adler." In this special issue, Carlson (Nystul, 1991) suggested that the Adlerian movement has become isolated, focusing too much on well-developed concepts such as the four goals of misbehavior and logical consequences. Carlson contended that broader, more permeable boundaries are needed for Adlerian psychology to become part of the mainstream of contemporary psychology (Nystul, 1991). Carlson also suggested that Adlerian approaches could be developed to reach nontraditional, non-YAVIS (young, attractive, verbal, intelligent, and sensitive) clients; clients who are victims of family violence; clients infected with the AIDS virus; and clients who require sex therapy. Mosak (1991) echoed the call for change by noting that Adlerian theory focuses too much on the psychology of abnormalcy and not enough on the psychology of normalcy.

Summary and Evaluation

Adler was a man ahead of his time. His psychological insights stressed the importance of phenomenology, holism, and social interest. These concepts are incorporated into most contemporary counseling theories. Adlerian psychology is perhaps best known for concepts that can be used to understand individual differences such as lifestyle, family dynamics, birth order, and sibling rivalry. Another strength of Adlerian psychology is its influence on programs such as STEP, TIME, and other guidance programs.

A criticism is that Adlerian counselors may be trying too hard to adhere to Adler's original concepts in terms of theory, research, and practice. As Shulman recommended, Adlerian psychology must be responsive to ongoing advances in counseling and psychology if it is to remain a viable theory for contemporary practitioners (Nystul, 1988).

Carl Jung

JUNG'S ANALYTIC PSYCHOLOGY

Background Information

Carl Gustav Jung (1875–1961) was born in Kesswil, Switzerland. His father was a pastor, which may have contributed to his fondness for religion. Jung's intellectual interests were by far the most varied of the three classic theorists. As a young man, he became intrigued by mythology, philosophy, religion, history, literature, and archeology. While Jung was struggling to decide what to study at the university, he had an unusual dream that somehow compelled him to pursue medicine (Hall & Lindzey, 1978). Jung went on to obtain a medical degree from the University of Basel in 1900, the same year Freud published *The Interpretation of Dreams*. Freud's work may have influenced his decision to specialize in psychiatry. Shortly thereafter, Jung obtained a position at the University of Zurich and worked under Eugene Bleuler, who was well known for his theories on schizophrenia. During this time, Jung was also fortunate to study with Pierre Janet, who was conducting research on hysteria and multiple personality disorders.

By 1907, Jung had his first meeting with Freud. They found many areas of common interest as they talked continuously for 13 hours. Freud believed that Jung was his crown prince and successor (Hall & Lindzey, 1978). It was therefore not surprising that in 1910 Jung became the first president of the International Psychoanalytic Association. Their initial compatibility was short-lived, as Jung began to differ with Freud on important theoretical issues. Like Adler, Jung became particularly disenchanted with Freud's emphasis on the role of sexuality in personality development. By 1914, Jung felt he could no longer participate in the Freudian movement and resigned from the presidency of the Psychoanalytic Association.

At this point, Jung decided to develop his own school of psychology, which he called analytic psychology. It is interesting to note that some of Jung's most creative years occurred during a time of personal distress between 1913 and 1916, as with Freud. Jung was able to make the most of difficult times. During this period, Jung did extensive self-analysis through the interpretation of his dreams. He obtained a number of insights that had a profound effect on the development of his theory. An example is the importance of gaining an understanding of unconscious processes during psychotherapy.

Jung's analytic theory was unique in its varied theoretical foundation. Jung was able to integrate his early interests in religion, mythology, archeology, literature, history, and philosophy into the study of psychology. This work resulted in what may be the most comprehensive understanding of the human condition (Hall & Lindzey, 1978). His collective works are extensive, filling 20 volumes (Read, Fordham, & Adler, 1953–1978). Jung's work holds particular interest for those who wish to integrate mystical ideas from the Far East with analytical concepts from the Western European and American traditions.

View of Human Nature

Jung (1928) had a positive view of the human condition, believing that people had inherent tendencies toward individualization—becoming unique individuals capable of wholeness and self-realization. This process of individualization is characterized by a union or integration of conscious and unconscious processes (Jung, 1928).

Key Concepts

Jung identified the following concepts, which were associated with his theory of personality (Read, Fordham, & Adler, 1953–1978).

The Ego, the Personal Unconscious, and the Collective Unconscious.   According to Kaufmann (1989), Jung believed that the psyche is made up of autonomous yet interdependent subsystems of the ego, the personal unconscious, and the collective unconscious. The ego represents the conscious mind and the personal unconscious and collective unconscious make up the unconscious domain of the psyche. An overview of these three subsystems of the psyche will now be provided.

The *ego* is the center of consciousness and is made up of conscious perceptions, memories, thoughts, and feelings (Kaufmann, 1989). It provides consistency and direction in people's lives (Fadiman & Frager, 1976).

The *personal unconscious* is similar to Freud's preconscious, containing thoughts based on personal experience just beyond the reach of conscious recall (Feist, 1985). It contains forgotten or repressed material that had once been conscious and could become conscious in the future (Hall & Lindzey, 1978). The information in the personal unconscious clusters around several complexes (Kaufmann, 1989). Complexes revolve around themes such as prestige or control, which can interfere with effective living (Corey, 1982). For example, a client could have a "mother complex," whereby he behaves as if he were under his mother's domination or control.

The *collective unconscious* is sometimes referred to as the transpersonal or nonpersonal unconscious, since it is not associated with personal experiences. It is considered the most provocative yet controversial aspect of Jung's theory (Hall & Lindzey, 1978). The collective unconscious is made up of memory traces inherited from one's ancestral past. Jung called it *collective* because he believed that all people shared common images and thoughts regarding such things as mother, earth, birth, and death.

Jung referred to these universal thoughts as archetypes. He believed that the collective unconscious creates the foundation for the personality. Starting from birth, the collective unconscious guides an individual's life experiences, thereby influencing perceptions, emotions, and behavior. It is therefore the most powerful and influential aspect of the personality (Hall & Lindzey, 1978).

Jung suggested that the collective unconscious was not directly amenable to the conscious but could be observed indirectly through its manifestations in eternal themes in mythology, folklore, and art (Kaufmann, 1989). Jung visited numerous "primitive" cultures to test his theory in Africa and the American southwest. He found that even though these cultures evolved independently, they shared intricate memories that could have been transmitted only by a collective unconscious.

Archetypes.   Jung discovered that several archetypes evolved so completely that they could be considered separate systems within the personality (Hall & Lindzey, 1978). These are the persona, the anima and animus, the shadow, and the self. An overview of these archetypes follows.

The *persona* is the public self one projects as opposed to the private, personal view of oneself. The persona is reflected in various roles such as work, marriage and family, and social situations. According to Jung, awareness of the persona has an inverse relation to awareness of one's personal self or individuality. For example, the more aware one is of the persona, the less aware that person will be of individuality and the private, personal self.

The *anima* and *animus* refer to the suggestion that people have both masculine and feminine dimensions to their personality. The *anima* is the feminine archetype in men, and the *animus* is the masculine archetype in women. Jung believed these archetypes resulted from years of men and women living together (Hall & Lindzey, 1978). Fadiman and Frager (1976) noted that this archetype appears in dreams and fantasies as figures of the opposite sex and functions as the primary mediator between unconscious and conscious processes.

The *shadow* represents the negative or evil side of the personality that people do not want to recognize. The shadow is associated with thoughts that originate from animal instincts inherited through the evolutionary process.

The *self* is the center of the personality including the conscious and unconscious parts of the mind (Feist, 1985). The self provides the personality a sense of unity, equilibrium, and stability (Hall & Lindzey, 1978). The self cannot emerge until the other systems of the personality have fully developed, which is usually not until middle age (Corey, 1982). The emergence of the self occurs when the center of the individual shifts from the conscious ego to the midpoint between conscious and unconscious (Hall & Lindzey, 1978). This midpoint region becomes the domain of the self. It is not surprising that Jung discovered the existence of the self when he was studying Eastern meditation practices, which emphasize the interaction between conscious and unconscious processes.

Personality Types.   Jung noted that personality types could be differentiated in terms of attitudes and functions. He identified two types of attitudes: extroverted, or outgoing; and introverted, or introspective. According to Jung, people have both attitudes in their personality makeup. The dominant attitude is represented in the conscious mind and the subordinate attitude exists in the unconscious psyche (Hall & Lindzey, 1978).

Jung also describes four functions that provide additional means to differentiate personality types. These functions include thinking, feeling, sensation, and intuition. Jung contended that although people rely on all these functions to react to events, the function that is the best developed will be relied on most and becomes the superior function.

The Counseling Process

The overall aim of analytic psychotherapy is to help the self emerge so the client can be free to move toward self-realization. For this to occur, the analyst must help the client develop the other major systems of the personality. Much of psychotherapy therefore involves exploring unconscious processes in order for clients to gain insight into the structure of their personality (Kaufmann, 1989). In time, clients can learn how to make the various systems develop to their fullest and function in a complementary fashion. For example, a client who describes himself as a real "macho-type" person seeks help for marital problems. The analytic psychotherapist may encourage the client to recognize the feminine (anima) dimension to his personality. According to analytic theory, this will help the client become a more fully functioning person and develop a better understanding of life.

Jung had a unique conception of psychopathology. He did not view it as a disease or abnormal state (Kaufmann, 1989). Instead, he believed the symptoms associated with psychopathology could be instructive for both the client and analyst (Kaufmann, 1989). They could serve as warning signals that something was wrong and could also provide clues into the functioning of the personality (Kaufmann, 1989). Jung was therefore reluctant to use medication to treat mental disorders, because he was afraid it might mask important messages that symptoms could communicate.

The nature of the therapeutic relationship is also unique in analytic psychotherapy. Analysts are required to undertake their own analysis, which helps them gain a respect for what is involved in being a client. They do not see the counseling relationship as a healthy therapist treating a sick patient. Instead, Jungian analysts view therapy as one person who has journeyed into the unconscious helping another person develop a meaningful dialogue with unconscious processes (Kaufmann, 1989). The Jungian analyst also believes it is critical for the client to feel a sense of acceptance during therapy (Kaufmann, 1989).

Fadiman and Frager (1976) described two major stages utilized in Jungian psychotherapy. In the *analytic stage*, clients attempt to identify unconscious material. This is followed by the *synthetic stage*, which initially involves helping clients use insight to formulate new experiences. The final phase of the synthetic stage is called transformation, in which clients engage in self-education and thus become more autonomous and responsible for their own development.

Techniques

Jung advocated a flexible approach to psychotherapy, believing that the method of treatment should be determined by the unique features of each client (Maduro & Wheelwright, 1977). His approach shares the characteristics associated with the art of counseling model, as described in Chapter 1, in that he recommended the analyst be creative and flexible in working with the client.

Jungian psychotherapy is a practical approach based on the guiding principle that anything goes, as long as it seems to work (Kaufmann, 1989). When one patient complained of difficulty falling asleep, for example, Jung simply sang the client a lullaby (Kaufmann, 1989).

Jung was skeptical of using techniques in therapy, because he thought they could be unnecessarily restrictive. At the same time, he believed dream analysis could be a useful vehicle for helping clients explore unconscious processes. Unlike Freud, Jung found little value in analyzing a single dream. He believed it was essential to investigate the interrelationship of several dreams recorded over a period of time. In this process, Jung would help the client understand the symbolic meaning of dreams, and how they provide clues to the various systems of the personality.

Contemporary Issues

Current trends in Jungian psychology are directed at diversification and integration. Samuels (1985) noted that there are three schools of Jungian psychology: classical, developmental, and archetypal. The classical school emphasizes the role of the self as the major personality construct; the developmental school focuses on the use of transference and interpretation to work through problems associated with childhood experiences; and the archetypal school relates primarily to issues pertaining to archetypes (Spiegelman, 1989). Samuels (1989) suggested that the emerging schools of Jungian psychology need not be viewed as a form of conflict. He believed differences should be encouraged to foster creative developments in Jungian psychology. Jungian psychology is also expanding its horizons in an attempt to incorporate other theories and approaches. Saayman, Faber, and Saayman (1988) provide an example of this by exploring how family systems theory could be integrated into Jungian marital therapy.

Jungian concepts have also been incorporated into other psychological theories and systems. Myers and McCaulley (1985) incorporated Jung's concept of attitudes and functions (e.g., introvert, extrovert, thinking, feeling) into the development of the Myers-Briggs Type Indicator (MBTI). The MBTI has become a popular personality instrument for individuals who want to gain self-understanding and for use in organizational and industrial psychology (McCrae & Costa, 1989). Unfortunately, research evidence has emerged suggesting that Jung's theory was inaccurately incorporated into the MBTI and therefore should not be used to interpret test results (McCrae & Costa, 1989).

Summary and Evaluation

The fundamental strength of Jung's approach lies in his comprehensive view of the human condition. In this regard, Hall and Lindzey (1978) observed:

The originality and audacity of Jung's thinking have few parallels in recent scientific history, and no other person aside from Freud has opened more conceptual windows into what Jung would choose to call the "soul of man." (p. 149)

The impact of Jung's work transcends psychology. Progoff (1953) noted that Jung has had a major impact on modern religious thought. Jung also did much to help build a meaningful bridge between Eastern and Western concepts, bringing new meaning to such concepts as self-transcendence, altered states of consciousness, meditation, and mysticism.

Several criticisms have been directed at Jungian psychology. The existence of a collective unconscious has been challenged more than any other. Glover (1950) insisted that the concept is metaphysical and incapable of proof. Glover (1950) further suggested that Jung's theory lacks developmental concepts necessary to explain the growth of the mind. Hall and Lindzey (1978) observed that many psychologists have found Jung's writing to be ". . . baffling, obscure, confusing, and disorganized. . . " (p. 148).

CHAPTER SUMMARY

This chapter provided an overview of the theories of Freud, Adler, and Jung. These are considered classic theories because of their historical significance and comprehensiveness. These theories shared some elements. Freud and Adler both noted the importance of early life experiences on adult personality formation. Freud and Jung both emphasized the role of unconscious forces in personality functioning.

Each theory also has its unique psychological constructs and orientation. Freud stressed the role of sexuality and developed a psychosexual model for personality development. Adler favored the importance of social interest as a major motivating force for understanding the dynamics of personality. Jung was known for his formulation of the collective unconscious, proposing that all people inherited a common set of memories from birth that were passed on from generation to generation.

The three classic schools of psychology continue to evolve in terms of theory, research, and practice. In addition, each has had a major impact on the evolution of current psychotherapies. Most contemporary counseling theories have incorporated psychological constructs from Freud, Adler, and Jung. Most noticeable is the wide recognition of the importance of early life experiences and the existence of unconscious processes. Some of the principles of Adlerian psychology have been particularly influential in the evolution of modern clinical practice (Corey, 1991). Adlerian concepts of holism and phenomenology are reflected in experiential theories. Adler's emphasis on cognition (e.g., basic mistakes) has also contributed to the current cognitive behavioral approaches.

The strength of the classic schools is their foundation in personality theory. They tend to be more limited in terms of their approaches to counseling and psychotherapy. In this regard, the classic schools of psychotherapy need further development and integration with modern counseling practice to enable practitioners to develop comprehensive treatment programs.

SUGGESTED READING

Freud

Freud, S. (1953). The interpretation of dreams. In J. Strachey (Ed.), *The standard edition of the complete psychological works of Sigmund Freud* (Vols. 4 and 5). London: Hogarth Press.

Freud, S. (1953). Three essays on sexuality. In J. Strachey (Ed.), *The standard edition of the complete psychological works of Sigmund Freud* (Vol. 7). London: Hogarth Press.

Freud, S. (1960). The psychopathology of everyday life. In J. Strachey (Ed.), *The standard edition of the complete psychological works of Sigmund Freud* (Vol. 6). London: Hogarth Press.

Freud, S. (1963). Introductory lectures on psycho-analysis. In J. Strachey (Ed.), *The standard edition of the complete psychological works of Sigmund Freud* (Vols. 15 and 16). London: Hogarth Press.

Hall, C. (1954). *A primer of Freudian psychology*. Cleveland, OH: World.

Hall, C., & Lindzey, G. (1978). *Theories of personality* (3rd ed.). New York: John Wiley & Sons.

Strachey, J. (Ed.). (1953–1974). *The standard edition of the complete psychological works of Sigmund Freud*. London: Hogarth Press.

Adler

Adler, A. (1931). *What life should mean to you*. Boston: Little, Brown.

Adler, A. (1969). *The practice and theory of individual psychology*. Patterson, NJ: Littlefield, Adams.

Ansbacher, H. L., & Ansbacher, R. R. (Ed.). (1956). *The individual psychology of Alfred Adler*. New York: Basic Books.

Ansbacher, H. L., & Ansbacher, R. R. (Ed.). (1964). *Superiority and social interest*. Evanston, IL: Northwestern University Press.

Jung

Hall, C. S., & Norby, J. J. (1973). *A primer of Jungian psychology*. New York: New American Library.

Jung, C. G. (1964). *Man and his symbols*. London: Aldus Books Ltd.

Read, H., Fordham, M., & Adler, G. (Eds.). (1953–1978). *Jung's collected works*. Princeton: Princeton University Press.

REFERENCES

Adler, A. (1969). *The practice and theory of individual psychology*. Patterson, NJ: Littlefield, Adams.

Ansbacher, H. L., & Ansbacher, R. R. (Ed.). (1956). *The individual psychology of Alfred Adler*. New York: Basic Books.

Ansbacher, H. L., & Ansbacher, R. R. (Ed.). (1964). *Superiority and social interest*. Evanston, IL: Northwestern University Press.

Arlow, J. A. (1989). Psychoanalysis. In R. J. Corsini (Ed.), *Current psychoanalysis*. Itasca, IL: F. E. Peacock.

Baker, E. L. (1985). *Psychoanalysis and psychoanalytic psychotherapy*. In S. J. Lynn & J. P. Garske (Eds.), *Contemporary psychotherapies: Models and methods*. Columbus, OH: Merrill/Macmillan.

Barth, K., Nielson, G., Haver, B., Havik, O. E., Molstad, E., Rogge, H., & Statun, M. (1988). Comprehensive assessment of change in patients treated with short-term dynamic psychotherapy: An overview. *Psychotherapy Psychosomatic, 50*, 141–150.

Corey, G. (1982). *Theory and practice of counseling and psychotherapy* (2nd ed.). Pacific Grove, CA: Brooks/Cole.

Corey, G. (1991). *Theory and practice of counseling and psychotherapy* (4th ed.). Pacific Grove, CA: Brooks/Cole.

Corsini, R. J. (1977). Individual education. *Journal of Individual Psychology, 33*, 295–349.

Corsini, R. J. (1979). Individual education. In E. Ignas & R. J. Corsini (Eds.), *Alternate educational systems* (pp. 200–256). Itasca, IL: F. E. Peacock.

Davanloo, H. (1978). *Basic principles and techniques in short-term dynamic psychotherapy.* New York: SP Medical and Scientific Books.

Davanloo, H. (1984). Intensive short-term dynamic psychotherapy. In H. Kaplan and B. Sadock (Eds.), *Comprehensive textbooks of psychiatry.* Baltimore, MD: Williams & Wilkins.

Dinkmeyer, D., & Carlson, J. (1984). *Training in marriage enrichment.* Circle Pines, MN: American Guidance Service.

Dinkmeyer, D. C., & Dinkmeyer, D., Jr. (1982). *Developing understanding of self and others.* DUSO-1 Revised, DUSO-2 Revised. Circle Pines, MN: American Guidance Service.

Dinkmeyer, D., & Dinkmeyer, D. C., Jr. (1985). Adlerian psychotherapy and counseling. In S. Lynn & J. P.Garske (Eds.), *Contemporary psychotherapies: Models and methods.* Columbus, OH: Merrill/Macmillan.

Dinkmeyer, D., Dinkmeyer, D., Jr., & Sperry, L. (1987). *Adlerian counseling and psychotherapy.* Columbus, OH: Merrill/Macmillan.

Dinkmeyer, D., & Dreikurs, R. (1963). *Encouraging children to learn: The encouragement process.* Englewood Cliffs, NJ: Prentice-Hall.

Dinkmeyer, D., & Losoncy, L. (1980). *The encouragement book: Becoming a positive person.* Englewood Cliffs, NJ: Prentice-Hall.

Dinkmeyer, D., & McKay, G. (1989). *Systematic training for effective parenting (STEP)* (3rd ed.). Circle Pines, MN: American Guidance Service.

Dinkmeyer, D., McKay, G. D., & Dinkmeyer, D., Jr. (1980). *Systematic training for effective teaching.* Circle Pines, MN: American Guidance Service.

Donne, J. (1952). *The complete poetry and selected prose of John Donne.* New York: Random House.

Dreikurs, R. (1949). The four goals of children's misbehavior. *Nervous Child, 6*, 3–11.

Dreikurs, R. (1971). *Social equality: The challenge of today.* Chicago: Henry Regnery.

Dreikurs, R., Corsini, R. J., Lowe, R., & Sonstegard, M. (1959). *Adlerian family counseling.* Eugene, OR: University of Oregon Press.

Dreikurs, R., & Soltz, N. (1964). *Children: The challenge.* New York: Hawthorn.

Ellis, A. (1962). *Reason and emotion in psychotherapy.* New York: Lyle Stuart.

Erikson, E. H. (1950). *Childhood and society.* New York: W. W. Norton.

Fadiman, J., & Frager, R. (1976). *Personality and personal growth.* New York: Harper & Row.

Feist, J. (1985). *Theories of personality.* New York: Holt, Rinehart, & Winston.

Freud, S. (1972). *The interpretation of dreams.* New York: Avon Books.

Garske, J. P., & Molteni, A. L. (1985). Brief psychodynamic psychotherapy: An integrative approach. In S. J. Lynn & J. P. Garske (Eds.), *Contemporary psychotherapies.* Columbus, OH: Merrill/Macmillan.

Glasser, W. (1965). *Reality therapy: A new approach to psychiatry.* New York: Harper & Row.

Glover, E. (1950). *Freud or Jung.* New York: W. W. Norton.

Goldfried, M. R., Greenberg, L. S., & Mormar, C. (1990). Individual psychotherapy: Process and outcome. *Annual Review of Psychology, 41*, 659–688.

Hall, C. S. (1954). *A primer of Freudian psychology.* New York: World Publishing.

Hall, C. S., & Lindzey, G. (1978). *Theories of personality* (3rd ed.). New York: John Wiley & Sons.

Jung, C. (1928). *Contributions to analytic psychology.* New York: Harcourt.

Kaufmann, Y. (1989). Analytical psychotherapy. In R. J. Corsini (Ed.), *Current psychotherapies* (4th ed.). Itasca, IL: Peacock.

Kernberg, O. F. (1976). *Object-relations theory and clinical psychoanalysis.* New York: Jason Aronson.

Kohut, H. (1971). *The analysis of the self.* New York: International University Press.

Maduro, R. J., & Wheelwright, J. B. (1977). *Analytical psychology.* In R. J. Corsini (Ed.), *Current personality theories.* Itasca, IL: Peacock.

Malan, D. (1976). *The frontier of brief psychotherapy.* New York: Basic Books.

Malan, D. H. (1980). The most important development since the discovery of the unconscious. In H. Davanloo (Ed.), *Short-term dynamic psychotherapy*. New York: Aronson.

Mann, J. (1973). *Time-limited psychotherapy*. Cambridge, MA: Harvard University Press.

Mann, J. (1981). The core of time-limited psychotherapy: Time and central issue. In S. H. Budman (Ed.), *Forms of brief therapy*. New York: Guilford Press.

Marziali, E. (1984). Predictions of outcomes of brief psychotherapy from therapist interpretive interventions. *Archives of General Psychiatry, 41,* 301–304.

McCrae, R. R., & Costa, P. T., Jr. (1989). Reinterpreting the Myers-Briggs Type Indicator from the perspective of the five-factor model of personality. *Journal of Personality, 57,* 1, 17–40.

Mills, J. A., Bauer, G. P., & Miars, R. D. (1989). Use of transference in short-term dynamic psychotherapy. *Psychotherapy, 26*(3), 112–119.

Mormar, C. R., & Horowitz, M. J. (1988). Diagnosis and phase-oriented treatment of post-traumatic stress disorder. In J. F. Wilson, Z. Harel, & B. Kahana (Eds.), *Human adaption to extreme stress: From Holocaust to Viet Nam*. New York: Plenum.

Mosak, H. (1989). Adlerian psychotherapy. In R. J. Corsini (Ed.), *Current psychotherapies* (4th ed., pp. 65–118).

Mosak, H. (1991). Where have all the normal people gone? *Individual Psychology: The Journal of Adlerian Theory, Research, and Practice, 47*(4), 437–446.

Myers, I. B., & McCaulley, M. H. (1985). *Manual: A guide to the development and use of the Myers-Briggs Type Indicator*. Palo Alto: Consulting Psychologist Press.

Nergaard, M. O., & Silberschatz, G. (1989). *The effects of shame, guilt, and the negative reaction in brief dynamic psychotherapy*.

Nystul, M. S. (1985). The use of motivation of modification techniques in Adlerian psychotherapy. *Individual Psychology: The Journal of Adlerian Theory, Research, and Practice, 44,* 2, 199–209.

Nystul, M. S. (1991). An interview with Jon Carlson. *Individual Psychology: The Journal of Adlerian Theory, Research, and Practice, 47*(4), 498–503.

Patterson, C. H. (1986). *Theories of counseling and psychology*. New York: Harper & Row.

Prochaska, J. O. (1984). *Systems of psychotherapy: A transtheoretical analysis*. Chicago, IL: The Dorsey Press.

Progoff, I. (1953). *Jung's psychology and its social meaning*. New York: Julian.

Rapaport, D. (1958). The theory of ego autonomy: A generalization. *Bulletin of Menninger Clinic, 22,* 13–35.

Read, H., Fordham, M., & Adler, G. (Eds.). (1953–1978). *Jung's collected works*. Princeton: Princeton University Press.

Saayman, G. S., Faber, P. A., & Saayman, R. V. (1988). Archetypal factors revealed in the study of marital breakdown: A Jungian perspective. *Journal of Analytical Psychology, 33,* 253–276.

Samuels, A. (1985). *Jung and the post-Jungians*. London: Routledge & Kegan Paul.

Samuels, A. (1989). Analysis and pluralism: The politics of psyche. *Journal of Analytical Psychology, 34,* 33–51.

Sherman, R., & Dinkmeyer, D. (1987). *Systems of family therapy: An Adlerian integration*. New York: Brunner/Mazel.

Shulman, B. H. (1973). *Contributions to individual psychology*. Chicago: Alfred Adler Institute.

Sifneos, P. E. (1979). *Short-term dynamic psychotherapy*. New York: Plenum.

Sifneos, P. (1984). The current status of individual short-term dynamic psychotherapy and its future. *American Journal of Psychotherapy, 38,* 4, 472–483.

Sonstegard, M. A., Hagerman, H., & Bitter, J. (1975). Motivation modification: An Adlerian approach. *The Individual Psychologist, 12,* 17–22.

Spiegelman, J. M. (1989). The one and the many: Jung and the post-Jungians. *Journal of Analytical Psychology, 34,* 53–71.

Strachey, J. (Ed.). (1953–1974). *The standard edition of the complete psychological works of Sigmund Freud*. London: Hogarth Press.

Thompson, L. W., Gallagher, D., & Breckenridge, J. S. (1987). Comparative effectiveness of psychotherapies for depressed elders. *Journal of Consulting and Clinical Psychology, 55,* 385–390.

CHAPTER SEVEN

Experiential Theories and Approaches

CHAPTER OVERVIEW

This chapter provides an overview of three major experiential counseling theories: person-centered, Gestalt, and existential. The information on these three theories is presented in terms of

- Background information
- View of human nature
- Key concepts
- The counseling process
- Techniques
- Summary and evaluation

The chapter also provides an overview of creative arts therapy (CAT) and the various modalities associated with it: music, art, drama, and dance therapy, bibliotherapy, and multimodality CAT. The material on these theories is organized in terms of

- Key concepts
- Procedures and outcomes
- Special populations

At the end of the discussion of the various modalities of CAT, I present a summary and evaluation of creative arts therapy as a whole.

This chapter presents theories and approaches to counseling that emphasize experiential processes. It begins by providing an overview of three major schools of counseling: person-centered, Gestalt, and existential. The last part of the chapter describes the major creative arts therapy (CAT) modalities of music, art, drama, and dance therapy, bibliotherapy, and multimodality CAT. The common thread among these theories is their emphasis on the importance of the *experiential* aspect of counseling, or what is experienced in the counseling session.

EXPERIENTIAL THEORIES

The experiential theories focus on what the client is experiencing in the counseling process. In person-centered counseling, the client is encouraged to experience the self in an open and flexible manner (Raskin & Rogers, 1989). The focus of Gestalt counseling is to help clients become aware of what they are thinking and feeling in the here-and-now. Existential therapy suggests that a client can obtain personal meaning by experiencing both the joys and sorrows of life. From an existential point of view, even anxiety can be instructive.

The experiential theories maintain a humanistic orientation regarding the nature of people. These theories tend to view people as inherently positive with self-actualizing tendencies. The experiential theories can therefore be particularly attractive to counselors who share this optimistic point of view. An overview of these three theories is provided in Table 7.1.

PERSON-CENTERED THERAPY

Background Information

Carl Rogers (1902–1987) was the fourth of six children. He was raised in a closely knit family with strict religious standards (Rogers, 1961). In 1931 Rogers obtained a Ph.D. Degree in clinical psychology from the Teachers College of Columbia University.

Rogers then embarked on his professional career, taking a position as a psychologist with the Child Guidance Clinic of Rochester, New York. Shortly thereafter, in 1939, he wrote his first book, *The Clinical Treatment of the Problem Child,* which was based on his experience at the guidance center. This led to his appointment as a full professor in psychology at The Ohio State University. It was there during the

Table 7.1
Overview of Experiential Approaches

Theory	Founder(s)	Key Concepts	The Counseling Process	Techniques
Person-Centered	Carl Rogers	Trust in the inherent self-actualizing tendencies of people; the role of the self and the client's internal frame of reference in personality dynamics.	Involves an if-then process: if certain conditions are established (such as communicating empathic understanding), then the client will move toward self-actualization.	Although no techniques are identified, the approach requires the use of listening skills to communicate empathic understanding and establish other core conditions.
Gestalt	Fritz Perls	An existential–phenomenological perspective; moving from dependence to independence; and being integrated and centered in the present.	Involves a dialogue between the therapist and client whereby the client becomes aware of what is occurring in the here-and-now.	The therapist models authenticity and uses techniques to help the client become aware and centered in the present. Some of the techniques include the empty-chair technique and the use of personal pronouns.
Existential Therapy	Victor Frankl, Rollo May, and James Bugental	Uniqueness of the individual, search for meaning, role of anxiety; freedom of responsibility; and being and nonbeing.	Emphasizes the role of the counseling relationship over techniques. Counseling goals can include searching for personal meaning and becoming aware of choices.	Paradoxical reflection, dereflection, and existential encounter.

Carl Rogers

1940s that Rogers began to formulate his own approach to counseling and psychotherapy, culminating in the publication of *Counseling and Psychotherapy* in 1942.

From 1945 to 1964 Rogers held academic positions at the University of Chicago and the University of Wisconsin. During this time, he was able to continue developing his personal approach and explore its implementation in education, group process, and counseling and psychotherapy. Rogers noted that he had a somewhat negative experience with his academic peers at the Ohio State University and the University of Wisconsin (Heppner, Rogers, & Lee, 1984). He felt he was not liked by his colleagues, although he did not have a particularly high regard for them either. Not surprisingly, he preferred graduate students or people outside the department as friends (Heppner, Rogers, & Lee, 1984). In 1964 Rogers left academia permanently. During the last years of his career, he worked at the Institute for the Study of the Person in La Jolla, California. Today, the institute continues to provide training opportunities in person-centered counseling.

View of Human Nature

Rogers (1951) held a positive view of human nature, noting the inherent self-actualizing tendencies of people. He believed that if the right conditions existed, people would naturally proceed toward self-actualization. In addition, Rogers' theory emphasized the phenomenological perspective by suggesting that an individual's internal frame of reference was the best vantage point to understand the person.

Key Concepts

Raskin and Rogers (1989) noted that trust is the most fundamental concept in person-centered therapy. This theory contends that clients can be trusted to establish their own goals and monitor their progress toward these goals. In addition, counselors trust that all individuals have inherent self-actualizing tendencies.

Many other key concepts can be derived from Rogers' (1951) theory of personality, which is described in 19 propositions. The key concepts emphasize the role of a person's internal frame of reference and the self in understanding the dynamics of behavior. Four propositions that characterize Rogers' personality theory are

1. *People react to the phenomenal field as they experience and perceive it.* A person's phenomenal field is the internal frame of reference for perceiving the world. This proposition suggests that what a person perceives will be influenced according to past experiences.

2. *The best point to understanding behavior is the internal frame of reference of the person.* This proposition is logically related to the first proposition. Since each person's perception is unique, it can only be understood from the person's internal frame of reference. Rogers therefore advocated developing a phenomenological perspective when working with clients, which involves understanding things from the client's perspective.

3. *People tend to behave in a manner consistent with their concept of self.* The self is the center of the organism and consists of how a person sees the self in relation to others. The self attempts to foster consistency within the organism by promoting behavior that is compatible to one's view of the self.

4. *The more people perceive and accept experiences, the more they will tend to be accepting and understanding of others.* Self-acceptance and understanding are viewed as contributing factors in understanding and accepting others as unique individuals.

The Counseling Process

The counseling process can be described as an "if-then" approach. If certain conditions exist in the counseling relationship, then the client will move toward self-actualization (Rogers, 1961). Rogers (1957) identified the following three core conditions as necessary and sufficient for personal growth to occur:

1. *Counselor congruence.* Counselor congruence means counselors are congruent in terms of what they are experiencing and what they communicate. For example, when counselors feel threatened by a client, it would be inappropriate for them to say they enjoy being with the client. This would communicate a confusing double message and the counselor would not be genuine or authentic.

2. *Empathic understanding*. The counselor attempts to understand the client from the client's internal frame of reference. This phenomenological perspective involves understanding what the client is thinking, feeling, and experiencing and communicating this understanding to the client.

3. *Unconditional positive regard*. Rogers believed it is essential for the counselor to communicate a sense of acceptance and respect to the client. There has been some misunderstanding of what Rogers meant by unconditional positive regard. He did not mean the counselor should tolerate and accept anything the client did (Martin, 1989). He instead believed the counselor should try to "separate the deed from the doer" (Martin, 1989). The counselor should accept the client as a person worthy of respect even though the client's behavior may be inappropriate (Rogers, Gendlin, Kiesler, & Truax, 1967).

In addition to these therapist-offered core conditions, Rogers (1957) identified three other conditions that must occur for successful counseling to occur. The first two are considered preconditions for therapy: the therapist and client are in psychological contact, or aware of each other's presence, and the client is experiencing some discomfort in life to be motivated for therapy. The third condition is that the client must be able to accurately perceive and experience the core conditions set forth by the therapist.

A number of goals and therapeutic outcomes emerge from the person-centered therapy. This style of counseling is unique in that it does not attempt to resolve the client's presenting problem (Rogers, 1977). It instead assists the client in the growth process to become a fully functioning individual. Rogers (1961) identified the following changes that tend to occur as the client moves toward self-actualization.

- *Open to experience*. Clients are capable of seeing reality without distorting it to fit a preconceived self-structure. Instead of operating from a rigid belief system, clients are interested in exploring new horizons.
- *Self-trust*. Initially clients tend to have self-doubts. Clients may believe that no matter what they decide, it will be wrong. As therapy progresses, clients can learn to trust their own judgment and become more self-confident.
- *Internal source of evaluation*. Person-centered therapy fosters the development of an internal locus of control. This occurs as clients are encouraged to explore their inner choices and discouraged from looking to others for a sense of direction or locus of evaluation.
- *Willingness to continue growing*. As a result of person-centered therapy, clients will realize that self-actualization is a process and not an end goal. In this sense, no one ever becomes self-actualized. Instead, a fully functioning person is always in the state of becoming.

Techniques

Rogers (1951, 1961) minimizes the importance or use of techniques. Instead of relying on techniques, he emphasized the importance of the counseling relationship. He believed that the counseling relationship can create the necessary and sufficient conditions for the client's self-actualization. In addition, the person-centered therapist uses listening skills to communicate empathic understanding and help the client explore inner choices.

Summary and Evaluation

Carl Rogers has made a phenomenal contribution to counseling. He was the major figure behind the humanistic movement in counseling. In addition, many principles of his person-centered therapy have been incorporated into other current psychotherapies. For example, listening skills are frequently used to help establish a positive relationship, obtain a phenomenological understanding of the client, and promote the core conditions identified by Rogers.

One limitation associated with the person-centered approach is that counseling goals are unclear, creating ambiguity in the counseling process. Usher (1989) also noted the person-centered approach could be prone to cross-cultural bias in terms of its emphasis on independence and individualism. In addition, research suggests that Rogers' core conditions are not necessary and sufficient but can more accurately be viewed as facilitative for personality change (Gelso & Carter, 1985; Gelso & Fritz, in press).

GESTALT THERAPY

Background Information

Frederick "Fritz" S. Perls (1883–1970) was the founder of Gestalt therapy. Born in Berlin, Perls was initially a student of psychoanalytic theory. In 1946, he moved to the United States and began to develop Gestalt therapy. Perls went on to help establish a Gestalt Institute in New York in 1952 and another one in Cleveland in 1954.

Perls is best known for the work he did at the Esalen Institute of Big Sur, California. He was a resident associate psychiatrist at Esalen from 1964 to 1969. This was Perls' most productive and creative period. In 1969, he published two of his most popular books, *Gestalt Therapy Verbatim* and *In and Out of the Garbage Pail*. Perls died a year later, after leaving the Esalen Institute to establish a Gestalt community on Vancouver Island in British Columbia.

View of Human Nature

The Gestalt view of human nature is similar to the person-centered position. According to Perls, people are self-determined, striving for self-actualization, and best understood from a phenomenological perspective. The term Gestalt also relates to a particular view of human nature. It draws from the principles of Gestalt psychology, which suggests that people are a whole compiled of interrelated parts of body, emotions, thoughts, sensations, and perceptions. Each of these aspects of a person can be understood only within the context of the whole person.

Key Concepts

Perls (1969a, 1969b) described the following three key concepts associated with Gestalt therapy

1. *An existential-phenomenological perspective*. The Gestalt therapist functions from an existential-phenomenological perspective. From this perspective, the therapist attempts to understand clients from the clients' perspective and help clients gain personal meaning to their existence.

2. *Helping a client move from dependence to independence*. Perls (1969a) referred to this concept when he said Gestalt therapy helps clients make the transcendence from environmental support to self-support. When clients seek counseling, they tend to expect environmental support such as reassurance from the counselor. The Gestalt therapist avoids reinforcing clients' dependency needs and helps the client become an independent person. Clients will often resist moving toward self-support because change is threatening. When this occurs, the Gestalt therapist will usually frustrate and confront clients to help them work through the impasse.

3. *Being integrated and centered in the now*. Perls (1969a) believed that nothing exists except the now, since the past is gone and the future is yet to come. From this perspective, self-actualization is centered in the present rather than oriented to the future. It requires that clients become centered in the now and aware of what they are experiencing. Anxiety can result when clients are not centered in the now but are preoccupied with the future (Perls, 1969a). When this occurs, clients may develop excessive worry about what might happen and lose touch with what is happening. Unresolved difficulties from the past can also cause problems resulting in emotional reactions such as anger, guilt, or resentment. Being unaware of this "unfinished business" can interfere with one's functioning in the now. Resentment is seen as the most frequent and worst kind of unfinished business. Perls (1969a) believed that unexpressed resentment often converts to guilt. For example, a man finds out his wife has had an affair and becomes angry and resentful. Unfortunately, he doesn't express his resentment. Instead, he wonders what he could have done to prevent the affair, resulting in feelings of guilt.

The Counseling Process

The counseling process in Gestalt therapy is experiential. It focuses on what is occurring in the here-and-now of the moment (Yontey & Simkin, 1989). "Explanations and interpretations are considered less reliable than what is directly perceived and felt" (Yontey & Simkin, 1989, p. 323). Gestalt therapy involves a dialogue between the therapist and client whereby the client experiences from the inside what the therapist observes from the outside (Yontey & Simkin, 1989).

The goals that emerge from Gestalt therapy are not specific to a client's concerns. The only goal is awareness, which includes knowledge of the environment, taking responsibility for choices, self-knowledge, and self-acceptance (Yontey & Simkin, 1989).

Passons (1975) identified common problems that can impede a client's progress in Gestalt therapy. Problems can occur with clients who are overly dependent on others and lack self-responsibility; become out of touch with the world around them; allow unresolved experiences from the past to interfere with being aware of what is occurring in the now; disown their own needs; or define themselves in absolutistic, *either-or* terms.

Techniques

Levitsky and Simkin (1972) noted that authenticity symbolized the Gestalt approach. These authors suggest that it is essential for therapists to be authentic since they cannot teach what they do not know. Gestalt institutes focus their training efforts on trainees playing the role of client. Aside from being authentic, the Gestalt therapist also utilizes several techniques: assuming responsibility, using personal pronouns, and using the *now I'm aware* and empty-chair techniques.

Assuming responsibility is a technique that requires the client to rephrase a statement to assume responsibility. For example, a client can be asked to end all statements with: ". . . and I take responsibility for it." The client may also be requested to change "can't" to "won't" or "but" to "and." For example, instead of saying, "I want to get in shape *but* I don't exercise", the client says, "I want to get in shape *and* I don't exercise."

Using personal pronouns encourages clients to take responsibility by saying *I* or *me* instead of making generalizations using *we* or *us*, or *people*, for example. Clients will tend to feel they own their thoughts and feelings more by saying, "It scares *me* to think of going to college" than by saying, "It scares *people* to go to college."

Now I'm aware is a technique that can help clients get in touch with the self. One way to use this technique is to have clients close their eyes to encourage them to get in touch with their inner world and say, "Now I'm aware" before each statement. For example, "Now I'm aware of my breathing"; "Now I'm aware of some tension in my stomach"; "Now I'm aware of feeling embarrassed and self-conscious of having my eyes closed"; "Now I'm aware of feeling afraid of something, but I don't know what." The exercise can continue after clients open their eyes to help them become aware of themselves in relation to their environment.

The *empty-chair* technique can be used to help clients work through conflicting parts of the personality, such as in an approach avoidance conflict. For example, a client wants to ask a girl out but is afraid of rejection. The empty-chair technique involves placing an empty chair in front of the client. The client is then told that sitting in the empty chair is the part of his personality that does not want to ask the girl out. The client is then encouraged to start a conversation with the empty chair by stating the reasons why he wants to ask the girl out. After the client expresses the positive side of the argument, he is asked to sit in the empty chair and respond with the reasons why he does not want to ask her out. The client continues to move back and forth until he has resolved the issue. The empty-chair technique can be useful in helping clients work through unfinished business so they can be centered in the now.

Summary and Evaluation

Gestalt therapy can be particularly appropriate for clients who lack self-awareness and feel "out of touch" with themselves. Several research studies provide some support for the efficacy of Gestalt therapy. Guinan and Foulds (1970) found clients to have increased self-actualization and self-concepts after Gestalt therapy. Clarke and Breeberg (1986) found the empty-chair technique to be more effective than problem-solving techniques in resolving decisional conflict.

The main weakness of the Gestalt approach is that it lacks a strong theoretical base. It appears to emphasize techniques of therapy, rather than providing an in-depth theoretical foundation for understanding human behavior or providing a comprehensive approach to psychotherapy. Additional research on Gestalt techniques and principles appears warranted.

EXISTENTIAL THERAPY

Background Information

No single individual is responsible for the development of existential therapy. The theoretical origins of existential therapy can be traced to existentially oriented philosophy. In this regard, Nietzsche, Heidegger, Sartre, and Buber have played influential roles. For example, Buber (1970) proposed an interesting view of existence. He contended that people do not exist as isolated individuals but instead function in a state of existence that is between the I or oneself and others. In addition, several individuals have written books on existential therapy: Victor Frankl (1963, 1967, 1971, & 1978); Rollo May (1953, 1961, & 1977); and James Bugental (1976). To a large degree, the basic concepts and other tenets of existential therapy identified in this section represent an integration of these major existential theorists.

View of Human Nature

Existential therapy focuses on attempting to understand the human condition. It rejects a fixed view of human nature but instead contends that each person must ultimately define his or her own personal existence.

Key Concepts

The following five key concepts form the basis for existential therapy.

1. *Uniqueness of the individual.* The existential position suggests that no two people are alike—each one is unique. To become aware of one's uniqueness, it is necessary to encounter oneself as a separate and distinct individual. An important part of this process is to have the experience of existential aloneness. This can be a painful experience as a person attempts to encounter the meaning of one's existence. It can also help a person discover the capability of becoming autonomous.

2. *The search for meaning*. Victor Frankl's (1963, 1967, 1971, 1978) logothera-peutic approach evolved out of his experience as a prisoner of war in a Jewish concentration camp during World War II. He described these experiences as well as the basic principles of logotherapy in his book *Man's Search for Meaning* (Frankl, 1963). Logotherapy suggests that the most prominent psychological problem facing people is a lack of meaning in life, which he called the *existential vacuum*. Frankl (1978) believed that a person can experience meaning by feeling valued or needed, which in turn can create a purposeful existence. In this regard, Frankl (1963) cited the words of Nietzsche, who said, "He who has a *why* to live can bear almost any *how*" (p. 121).

3. *The role of anxiety*. Existential therapy differentiates between two types of anxiety. One is normal or healthy anxiety called *existential anxiety*, and the other is unhealthy anxiety referred to as *neurotic anxiety*. Neurotic anxiety is not healthy because it is an anxiety reaction that is not in proportion to the situation and can overwhelm the person. Existential anxiety suggests that some degree of anxiety can be positive, since it can motivate a person to make the necessary changes in life. Another positive aspect of anxiety is that it often occurs when a person faces a difficult situation. A person that flees from this anxiety will not be able to learn from the challenges of life. From this perspective, existentialists believe one can draw meaning from pain and suffering. Nietzsche also related to this point when he said, "That which does not kill me, makes me stronger" (Hollingdale, 1978, p. 23).

4. *Freedom and responsibility*. Existential therapy contends that freedom and responsibility are interrelated. Although people are free to choose their own destiny, they must take responsibility for their actions. Existentialists help clients become aware of their choices and the control they can exert over their own destiny.

5. *Being and nonbeing*. Being and nonbeing are also interrelated. The reality of death brings meaning to life. Being and nonbeing are also related to freedom and responsibility. People are free to be or not to be. If individuals choose to be, they must assume responsibility for their existence.

The Counseling Process

The goals of existential therapy relate directly to the key concepts. They can be directed at helping clients (a) discover their own uniqueness; (b) find personal meaning in life; (c) use anxiety in a positive sense; (d) become aware of their choices and the need to take responsibility for choices; and (e) not see death as a nemesis but as an eventual reality that gives meaning and significance to life.

The actual process of existential therapy emphasizes the role of the counseling relationship over the use of specific techniques. This approach is similar to the person-centered position in that both attempt to obtain a phenomenological understanding of the client and encourage the client to become aware of inner choices. The two approaches differ on the nature of the counseling relationship. Whereas Rogers focused on the client, the existentialists focused on the therapist and the client. Counseling from an existential point of view is therefore a shared responsibility. Buber's (1970) *I-thou* concept epitomizes this position. It emphasizes the importance of the therapist sharing the self as an authentic human being with the client.

Techniques

Some existential theories such as Frankl's (1963, 1967, 1971, 1978) logotherapy utilize specific techniques. Frankl (1963, 1978) described two techniques that are central to his approach. The first is *paradoxical intention*, which involves asking clients to do what they fear doing, such as asking them to stutter if they fear stuttering. It is not entirely clear what makes this technique existential. Paradoxical intention is simply a technique that helps a client overcome anticipatory anxiety by redefining success and failure. Several research studies provide support for the efficacy of paradoxical intention. It appears to be particularly effective for cases that did not respond to behavior therapy (Ascher, 1979; Ascher & Efran, 1978). One particularly well-controlled study by Turner and Ascher (1979) also showed paradoxical intention to effectively treat insomnia. The second technique Frankl described is *dereflection*, which is a procedure that involves helping clients focus on strengths rather than weaknesses. This technique seems more closely aligned to the cognitive school of counseling than to existential theory.

Frankl (1963) also refers to the process of self-transcendence, which means moving beyond the self. This is a uniquely existential concept, which can allow the therapist to transcend the limit of the self and directly experience the client's inner world of pain or joy. When this occurs, it can be referred to as an existential encounter. Unfortunately, Frankl (1963) did not describe a technique that can facilitate the existential encounter.

Summary and Evaluation

Existential therapy focuses on how clients feel about their existence. Since many clients who seek counseling feel a lack of meaning or direction in their lives, it can be a popular and productive approach.

The major weakness of this approach lies in its lack of a well-formulated theoretical foundation. Another weakness is that there are few, if any, unique existential techniques that can be utilized in the counseling process. In addition, Goldfried, Greenberg, and Mormar (1990) noted a significant decline in research on experiential therapies and thus a danger of their becoming extinct or being integrated into other schools of counseling.

CREATIVE ARTS THERAPY

Creative arts therapy (CAT) can be defined as promoting psychological and physiological well-being through the use of creative modalities, for example, art, music, dance, or drama. Two groups of individuals use CAT: members of the helping professions who use CAT as an adjunct to counseling and psychotherapy, such as counselors and psychologists; and CAT professionals who are certified or registered in a particular CAT modality, such as music or art therapists.

According to Fleshman and Fryrear (1981), CAT has been referred to by many names over the years. These include expressive therapy, expression therapy, and creative therapy. CAT has been shown to (a) facilitate communication of cognitively impaired and nonverbal patients with their therapists, (b) enable therapists to readily explore patients' affect, and (c) foster therapeutic bonding (Johnson, 1984a; Robbins, 1985).

CAT is not a recognized school of counseling because it lacks a clear theoretical foundation. It does share some commonalities with existential theory in terms of the concepts of self-transcendence and the existential encounter. In this regard, CAT can foster self-transcendence, enabling the counselor to feel at one with the client (Nystul, 1987). When this occurs, the counselor directly experiences the client's inner emotional state, resulting in an existential encounter. The case of Ron, described in a Personal Note later in this chapter, provides an illustration of the use of CAT and the existential encounter.

Professional Issues

The profession of CAT is made up of individuals who have undertaken formal study in the therapeutic use of a particular creative arts modality such as music or drama. Professional recognition is achieved by obtaining certification or registration in a particular CAT modality. Requirements for registration or certification vary according to the CAT specialty from a bachelor's to a master's degree and from 6 months to 2 years of supervised clinical training. Current requirements for certification or registration can be obtained by writing to the CAT professional organizations listed in Table 7.2.

Certified and registered CAT professionals work in a variety of settings that include hospitals, nursing homes, and private practice. Their role in mental health services has been primarily as "an adjunctive, secondary form of psychotherapeutic treatment" (Johnson, 1984a, p. 212). Johnson (1984a) identified several changes that need to be made for CAT to emerge as an independent profession. These include (a) using CAT to advance the knowledge of psychology, (b) identifying the unique contribution CAT can make in the helping process, (c) overcoming CAT's dependency on other disciplines such as psychology and psychiatry by broadening the role and function of professional creative art therapists, and (d) taking a more assertive position with other professional groups and legislative agencies.

In the remaining sections of this chapter, I will present an overview of the prominent modalities associated with CAT. Information will be provided in terms of key concepts, procedures and outcomes, and special populations. These are summarized in Table 7.3.

Table 7.2

Addresses for CAT Professional
Organizations

Music

    Music Educators National Conference
    1902 Association Drive
    Reston, VA 22091

    National Association for Music Therapy and Company
    P.O. Box 610
    Florence, KS 66044

Art Therapy

    American Art Therapy Association and Company
    428 East Preston Street
    Baltimore, MD 21202

    National Art Education Association
    1916 Association Drive
    Reston, VA 22091

Dance

    American Dance Therapy Association
    2000 Century Place
    Columbia, MD 21044

Drama

    National Association for Drama Therapy
    c/o Barbara Sandberg, Recording Secretary
    Theatre Department
    William Paterson College
    Wayne, NJ 07470

    American Theatre Association
    1000 Vermont Avenue NW
    Washington, DC 20005

Bibliotherapy

    Association of Hospital and Institution Libraries
    Committee on Bibliotherapy

    American Library Association
    50 East Huron Street
    Chicago, IL 60611
    (Division of Health and Rehabilitative Library Services)

Miscellaneous CAT Addresses

    American Association for Psychotherapy and the Arts
    175 Fifth Avenue
    New York, NY 10010

    Institute for Psychotherapy and the Arts
    175 Fifth Avenue
    New York, NY 10010

MUSIC THERAPY

Music is the oldest form of art associated with curing the ill according to Fleshman and Fryrear (1981), who cited instances of primitive tribes and other people using songs and chants to obtain divine assistance.

Key Concepts

Fleshman and Fryrear (1981) identified the following three key concepts associated with music therapy.

1. Music is intrinsically part of a culture.
2. Music can help clients get in touch with thoughts and feelings and communicating emotions that cannot be described by words.
3. Music has a basic structure characterized by rhythm, melody, pitch, and tempo that can be used to promote structure in clients whose thoughts are disorganized and chaotic (e.g., schizophrenics).

Procedures and Outcomes

Bruscia (1987) noted that music therapy involves using musical experiences and the therapeutic relationship to enhance the client's state of well-being. According to Bruscia (1987), musical experiences can include a wide range of activities that include improvising, performing, composing, and listening to music. Bruscia (1987) contended that improvising is the fundamental approach to music therapy and involves creating and playing simultaneously.

Fleshman and Fryrear (1981) suggested that music therapy involves four basic activities: (a) recreational and entertainment-oriented experiences to foster socialization; (b) therapeutic listening groups to promote group cohesion; (c) an adjunct activity to psychotherapy to stimulate emotions, encourage discussions, promote self-understanding, and facilitate socialization; and (d) individual and group music therapy to address a client's particular problem, for example, asking clients to play a duet to foster cooperation.

Several studies have been conducted on music therapy and its implication for the counseling process. Some of this research shows music therapy facilitates the counseling process in terms of assessment and diagnosis (Isenberg-Grzeda, 1988; Wells & Stevens, 1984). Others studies have found music therapy exerts positive influence on perceived locus of control (James, 1988) and as a stimulus to promote group cohesion (Wells & Stevens, 1984). Moreno (1988) suggested that all procedures used in music therapy should reflect a multicultural sensitivity since musical traditions vary from culture to culture.

Special Populations

Music therapy can be used with people of all ages. Gibbons (1988) suggested that music therapy can be particularly effective when working with the elderly. Gibbons (1984) noted that elderly people prefer active involvement in music and can learn

Table 7.3
CAT Modalities

CAT Modality	Key Concepts	Procedures and Outcomes	Special Populations
Music Therapy	1. Music is intrinsically part of a culture. 2. Music can help clients get in touch with their thoughts and feelings. 3. Music has a basic structure in terms of rhythm, melody, et al., which helps clients overcome problems with thought disorders.	Use of a musical experience to enhance and facilitate counseling goals.	Can be used with all types of clients of all ages but can be particularly effective with young children and the elderly.
Art Therapy	1. Art offers a form of sublimation whereby clients can achieve indirect gratification of unconscious needs. 2. Visual symbols in art can be useful diagnostic tools. 3. Art allows for the expression of unconscious thoughts and feelings. 4. Art promotes a sense of internal equilibrium.	The process of art therapy varies according to theoretical orientation but typically includes color analysis and spontaneous drawings.	Can be used with clients of all ages but can be particularly useful with children and adolescents.

	Description	Procedures	Clients
Drama Therapy	1. Offers an opportunity to externalize and learn from experiences. 2. Allows for the expression of strong feelings. 3. Deals directly and openly with functions of the personality. 4. Emotional conflicts can be better understood by expressing them in action through drama.	Spontaneous role-play is the heart of drama therapy. A variety of procedures are used in drama therapy such as movement, mime, and puppet plays.	Drama therapy can be used with clients of all ages. Its main use is with children who are physically, emotionally, or mentally handicapped.
Dance Therapy	1. Dance therapy involves the integration of mind and body. 2. Can reflect a client's mood and indicate flexibility or rigidity. 3. Clients can channel self-expression into dance.	Dance procedures vary according to the outcomes desired. It can involve spontaneous or structured dance experiences. It can be used to improve motor skills and interpersonal relationships; facilitate expression of moods, attitudes, and ideas; and stimulate, energize, and relax the body.	Dance therapy can be used with clients of all ages.
Bibliotherapy	Bibliotherapy can be used to foster universalizing, identification, catharsis, and insight.	Books or some form of literature are read to promote particular counseling outcomes.	Any client who can read can benefit from bibliotherapy.
Multimodality CAT	Multimodality CAT involves using the full range of CAT modalities. It can broaden the client's ability to respond to creativity.	Procedures vary according to the theoretical orientation and can include: counselors setting the stage for creativity, setting an example, setting themselves at ease, and developing insights from creativity after a client has finished a creative expression.	All clients can benefit from multimodality CAT.

new musical skills such as the guitar or piano at a level comparable to much younger people.

Music therapy has also been used successfully with children and adolescents. Eidson (1989) utilized a behaviorally oriented music therapy program to help emotionally disturbed middle school students improve their classroom behavior. Cripe (1986) provided guidelines for how to use music therapy with children with attention deficit disorder. Wells and Stevens (1984) found music stimulates creative fantasy in young adolescents during group psychotherapy.

Fleshman and Fryrear (1981) identified other special populations, such as the mentally retarded and physically disabled, who could be served by music therapy. According to Fleshman and Fryrear (1981), music therapy can be useful with mentally retarded individuals to provide stimulation and teach social skills. In addition, regimental music, such as a march, can be used to help mentally retarded individuals obtain control over their impulses. Physically disabled clients can also benefit from music therapy. Fleshman and Fryrear (1981) cited examples such as using wind instruments to help clients with lung disorders and using certain instruments that require finger dexterity to help clients overcome motor control dysfunctions.

ART THERAPY

Art therapy is one of the oldest and most established forms of CAT. Some of the earliest examples of art therapy can be traced to the prehistoric era when people painted pictures on the walls of their caves to express their relationship with the world (Wadeson, 1980). Art therapy encompasses many of the visual art forms including painting, sculpture, crafts, and photography (Kenny, 1987).

Key Concepts

The key concepts associated with art therapy are that art

1. Offers a form of sublimation whereby clients can achieve indirect gratification of unconscious needs (Kramer, 1987)
2. Has visual symbols that can be useful diagnostic tools (Wilson, 1987)
3. Allows for the expression of unconscious thoughts and feelings (Rubin, 1987)
4. Promotes a sense of internal equilibrium (Fleshman & Fryrear, 1981)

Procedures and Outcomes

The origins of art therapy can be traced to psychoanalytic theory (Rubin, 1987). More recently, however, it has been applied to most other major schools of psychology and counseling. Some examples are Gestalt (Rhyne, 1987); behavioral (Roth, 1987); and cognitive (Silver, 1987). A brief review of these applications follows.

Psychoanalytic.   Art can be analyzed for its symbolic content (Fleshman & Fryrear, 1981; Rubin, 1987).

Gestalt.   Art allows the client "to experience and express immediate perceptions and awareness" (Rhyne, 1987, p. 173).

Behavioral.   The behavioral approach to art therapy involves applying the principles of behavior modification to traditional art therapy techniques (Roth, 1987). In this process, principles of reinforcement are used to involve the client in art therapy and other desirable behaviors (Roth, 1987).

Cognitive.   Cognitive art therapy involves both the assessment and development of cognitive processes (Silver, 1987). Based primarily on Piaget and other cognitive psychologists, Silver (1987) identified different ways art can be used to foster cognitive and creative skills. For example, Silver (1987) described how the concept of sequential order can be developed through painting. Several other individuals have described procedures that are common to all approaches to art therapy. For example, color analysis can be traced to the work of Jung (1959) who noted that the use of color was related to perceptions and judgment. According to Jung (1959), yellow was associated with intuition, red was related to feeling; green suggested sensation; and blue represented thinking. In addition, Kenny (1987) suggested that color selection is also associated with emotional states, with blacks and grays indicating depression and white suggesting emotional rigidity.

Stabler (1984) provided additional guidelines for analyzing art. He noted that proportion, form, detail, movement, and theme could be used to obtain an estimate of a client's psychosocial and cognitive development and level of maturity (see Chapter 10).

Stabler (1984) also identified three types of drawings that could be useful in art therapy: self-portraits, free drawings, and family drawings. Bertoia and Allan (1988) emphasized the role that *spontaneous drawings*, which are essentially free drawings, can play in art therapy by providing a direct link to unconscious processes.

Special Populations

Art therapy can be used with clients of all ages. Fleshman and Fryrear (1981) noted it can be particularly useful with disadvantaged ghetto youth, children with sexual identity problems, mentally retarded children, schizophrenics, and suicidal patients. For example, the "suicide slash", which is a slip of the pen or an inappropriate line in a picture, and powerful repetitious images can indicate suicide ideations (Fleshman & Fryrear, 1981).

The following Personal Note provides an example of how I used art therapy as an adjunct to my counseling approach.

a personal note

"Sam" was a 21-year-old self-referred client I saw at a university counseling center in Australia. He had a severe stuttering problem and also complained of loneliness and boredom. During our second session, I asked Sam to draw whatever came to his mind. Sam drew the picture shown in Figure 7.1.

After Sam finished drawing, I asked him to describe himself in terms of his picture. Soon we began to acquire information regarding Sam's motivation for therapy, possible

Figure 7.1
Sam's Picture

counseling goals, and barriers to the goals. The picture seemed to provide an overview of what Sam wanted from counseling. He mentioned that he had never had a girlfriend and hadn't even kissed a girl. The catapult suggested he was very motivated to have a girl-friend. Unfortunately, he didn't believe this was possible since there were several barriers standing in his way, as illustrated by the sharks swimming between him and the girl.

We went on to identify what these barriers were in terms of *basic mistakes*, as dis-cussed in Chapter 6. For example, he thought he could not get a girlfriend if he was a stutterer. I then helped Sam overcome the basic mistakes as well as other self-defeating processes during the reorientation phase of counseling. (See Nystul and Musynska, 1976, for a more detailed description of this case.)

DRAMA THERAPY

Moreno (1946) was the founder of psychodrama, which was one of the first system-atic uses of drama as a form of therapy. Later, drama therapy emerged as a more flex-ible alternative to psychodrama. Irwin (1987, p. 277) noted that drama therapy was less verbal, less structured, and less oriented toward the theater than psychodrama. Johnson (1984b, p. 105) defined drama therapy "as the intentional use of creative drama toward the psychotherapeutic goals of symptom relief, emotional and physi-cal integration, and personal growth." Drama therapy includes any use of role-play-ing, but it is especially associated with the use of creative theater as a medium for self-expression (Johnson, 1984b).

Key Concepts

Although drama therapy is in its formative stage of development, the following four key concepts characterize its current status.

Various moods can be expressed in drama therapy.

1. Drama offers an opportunity to externalize and learn from experiences, both real and imagined (Irwin, 1987).

2. Drama allows for the expression of strong feelings, thinking, impulses, and action (Irwin, 1987).

3. Drama deals directly and openly with different functions of the personality (Fleshman & Fryrear, 1981).

4. Emotional conflicts can be better understood by expressing them in action through drama (Irwin, 1987).

Procedures and Outcomes

As in all CAT Modalities, the procedures of drama therapy will vary according to the theoretical orientation of the practitioner. Irwin (1987) noted that drama therapists draw from a variety of theoretical orientations such as psychoanalytic, behavioral, Gestalt, Jungian, and Rogerian.

Several authors have identified what can be considered common procedures associated with drama therapy. First, spontaneous role-playing is the heart of drama therapy and can be found in all its forms (Fleshman & Fryrear, 1981). Second, the therapist uses a variety of procedures such as movement, mime, and puppet plays to involve the client in action so inner conflicts can be expressed and better understood (Irwin, 1987). Third, drama therapy contributes to assessment and diagnosis by analyzing roles that were enacted or rejected; themes and conflicts that emerged in fantasies and stories; and the process of the session in terms of emotional release (Irwin, 1987).

Special Populations

Drama therapy can be used with people of all ages. Its main use appears to be with children, and numerous programs have been developed for children who are physically, emotionally, or mentally disabled (Fleshman & Fryrear, 1981). Drama therapy can be particularly useful in school settings to teach students how to deal with pressures relating to dating or drug and alcohol use.

DANCE THERAPY

The origins of dance therapy can be traced to modern dance, which began early in the 20th century (Fleshman & Fryrear, 1981).

Key Concepts

Fleshman and Fryrear (1981) identified these three key concepts associated with dance therapy.

1. The fundamental concept in dance therapy is the integration, or more specifically the reintegration, of mind and body.
2. Movement can reflect a client's mood and indicate either flexibility or rigidity.
3. Dance therapy provides an opportunity for clients to express themselves in movement, channeling self-expression into dance form.

Procedures and Outcomes

Dance therapy may involve clients dancing by themselves or with other clients. The dance method can be spontaneous or more structured in nature. Particular attention is paid to what the client communicates or discovers from the dance. Other factors worth noting are how the client interacts with others, the client's awareness of space, and how the dance may relate to a particular problem that the client is experiencing.

Fleshman and Fryrear (1981) and Lasseter, Privette, Brown, and Duer (1989) identified goals associated with dance therapy, which include

- Improving motor skills
- Enhancing the relationship between the client and therapist
- Increasing the client's movement repertoire to facilitate expression of moods, attitudes, and ideas
- Allowing for the sublimation of erotic and aggressive impulses
- Encouraging interpersonal relationships
- Stimulating, energizing, and relaxing the client's body

Special Populations

Dance therapy can be used with people of all ages. Lasseter, Privette, Brown, and Duer (1989) noted that dance therapy has been a primary treatment strategy for children with mental, physical, and emotional problems. In this regard, dance therapy has been used successfully with autistic children (Cole, 1982); psychotic children (Gunning & Holmes, 1973); children with cerebral palsy (Clark & Evans, 1973); mentally retarded children (Boswell, 1983); and emotionally disturbed and learning-disabled children (Polk, 1977; Wislocki, 1981).

BIBLIOTHERAPY

The earliest uses of bibliotherapy can be traced to the Grecian times where a sign was hung over the entrance of a library proclaiming "the healing place of the soul" (Zaccaria & Moses, 1968). Riordan and Wilson (1989, p. 506) defined bibliotherapy as "the guided reading of written materials in gaining understanding or resolving problems relevant to a person's therapeutic needs." There appears to be an increase in use of bibliotherapy as an adjunct to counseling (Riordan & Wilson, 1989), with 60% of psychologists prescribing self-help books occasionally; 24% often, and 12% regularly (Starker, 1988).

Key Concepts

According to Fleshman and Fryrear (1981), the key concepts of bibliotherapy are derived from psychoanalytic theory and include

1. *Universalizing*. Clients minimize feelings of guilt, shame, and isolation when they discover others share similar problems in life.
2. *Identification*. Clients can identify with characters in books, which provide a positive role model regarding attitudes and values.
3. *Catharsis*. Bibliotherapy group discussions provide clients opportunities for self-disclosure and catharsis.
4. *Insight*. Clients can obtain insight by having an external frame of reference for comparison.

Procedures and Outcomes

Bibliotherapy involves asking clients to read a book or some form of literature to promote certain outcomes associated with the counseling process (e.g., career awareness and exploration). The nature of the reading assignment will depend on the desired outcomes. For example, *What Color Is Your Parachute?* could be used to assist a client with career choice. Four of the most commonly prescribed books by psychologists are *What Color Is Your Parachute? The Relaxation Response, Your Perfect Right*, and *Feeling Good* (Starker, 1988). Once clients have read a book or other literature, they can discuss what they learned with the counselor.

Special Populations

Bibliotherapy can be used with any client who knows how to read. Research on the efficacy of bibliotherapy has provided mixed results. The most recent studies showed support for bibliotherapy in effecting behavioral change (Riordan & Wilson, 1989).

Counselors can share their creative outlets in multimodality creative arts therapy (CAT).

MULTIMODALITY CAT

A relatively recent addition to the CAT approaches involves the use of multiple CAT modalities instead of relying on a single modality such as dance or music. This broad-based approach to CAT has been called various names, including creative-expressive arts, mixed-media arts, and multimedia approach to the expressive arts (Fleshman & Fryrear, 1981; Talerico, 1986). In this chapter, I will use the term *multimodality CAT* because it involves using whatever CAT modality the therapist and client want to use.

Key Concepts

The major premise behind multimodality CAT is that it creates limitless possibilities for creative expression, whereas using one modality can be unnecessarily restrictive, discouraging creative responses from the client (Talerico, 1986).

Procedures and Outcomes

I proposed a four-phase model of CAT that can be used with all types of creative media, for example, art, music, or dance, with clients of all ages (Nystul, 1980, 1985, 1987). The four phases of this model are

1. *Set the stage*. The counselor sets the stage for creative process by either hav-ing creative arts material available to use or encouraging the client to bring a creative outlet (e.g., guitar) to the next counseling session.

2. *Set an example.* The counselor may wish to share a creative outlet with the client to set an example of risk taking and self-disclosure.

3. *Set yourself at ease.* The counselor should initially avoid analyzing a client's creative expression for psychological insights before the client is finished. This can cause a client to become self-conscious and interfere with the counselor directly experiencing the client's creative expression.

4. *Obtain a phenomenological understanding of the client.* Once the client has completed the creative expression, for example, a song or drawing, the counselor can attempt to gain a phenomenological understanding of the client. This can be accomplished by asking clients to describe what the creative expression said about them or describe themselves in terms of the creative expression.

I noted that the use of multiple CAT modalities in counseling and psychotherapy could promote the following outcomes (Nystul, 1980, 1985, 1987). The use of multimodality CAT can provide assessment and diagnostic information by having clients project their thoughts and feelings into a creative expression; promote self-disclosure in counselors and clients as they share their creative outlets; increase clients' social interest as they discover the support that can result from sharing a creative expression; develop a phenomenological understanding of clients as they describe themselves in terms of their creative expression; and promote an existential encounter as counselors directly experience their clients' emotions through the release of their creative expressions.

Special Populations

Multimodality CAT can be used with clients of all ages. Some examples are autistic children (Nystul, 1985); emotionally disturbed children (Nystul, 1978, 1980); a young adult stutterer who felt socially isolated (Nystul & Musynska, 1976); and a student in a university counseling center who had a sexual identity problem (Nystul, 1979). In addition, the counselor is not restricted to one modality such as art therapy, so clients have more opportunities to explore and discover creative outlets.

The following Personal Note provides an example of how I used multimodality CAT.

a personal note

One case that was very special to me involved a first-grader named Ron. I was an elementary school counselor and Ron was referred to me for counseling services. The reason for the referral was that he spent most of his time daydreaming in class and appeared to have no friends at school.

Ron was unresponsive to my questions during our first counseling session, so I decided to see him in a play therapy setting. As described later in Chapter 10, my approach to play therapy involves two parts: a self-concept program and the four-stage model associated with multimodality CAT (Nystul, 1980).

After we finished our self-concept program, Ron was humming a song. I asked him to make up a song about how he was feeling. I attempted in accompany him on the guitar, and he responded by singing a deep, sorrowful song. These were the words to Ron's song

My mom comes home and daddy stays home
Momma goes home, daddy stays
Momma stays in the city when she wants to
Momma stays in the city when she wants to

Momma daddy, Momma daddy
I just can't seem to go.

Daddy keep care of the baby
Daddy keep care of the baby
Daddy keep care of the baby

Please help me
I want no!
I need help!

I can't seem to stop
Daddy keep care of the baby
Good-bye, good-bye.

As Ron sang, I did not try to identify any psychological insights from the words of the song. Instead, I went with the music and allowed myself to get caught up with his creative energy. When Ron finished singing, I felt I had gone beyond attempting to understand or empathize with Ron's pain or sorrow. Instead, I had to some degree experienced these feelings as he sang.

As a result of our existential encounter, Ron and I had established a special counseling relationship. He therefore felt free to discuss his thoughts and feelings with me. Later that day, we listened to his song again, which I had tape-recorded. This time, I was interested in exploring the song for possible psychological significance. I asked Ron what the song might say about him. He responded by telling me different facets of his past.

As I listened, I began to identify basic mistakes, which were described in Chapter 6— faulty views that may interfere with what a person wants out of life. For example, he said his father was black, and his mother said black men are all no good. This was a basic mistake, since his view of being black would have a detrimental effect on feeling good about himself and others (something he wanted out of life).

To help reorient Ron from this basic mistake, I enlisted the help of Bill, a black counselor from another school, who agreed to co-lead some of my play therapy groups. The students loved Bill. Soon Ron began to believe that being even part black could be beautiful. (See Nystul, 1980, for a more complete description of this case.)

SUMMARY AND EVALUATION OF CAT

Creative arts therapy is a dynamic and powerful tool. CAT can be viewed as an emerging profession or adjunctive strategy associated with counseling and psychotherapy. It can have many uses such as promoting socialization; communicating thoughts and emotions; enhancing the counseling relationship; and as a projective device in assessment and diagnosis. A weakness is the lack of empirical research to determine its precise effect on psychological functioning and the counseling process.

CHAPTER SUMMARY

In this chapter, I provided an overview of theories and approaches that are called *experiential* because of their common view that therapeutic gains result from what the client experiences during the counseling session. The chapter began by providing an overview of three major experiential theories: person-centered, Gestalt, and existential. These schools of counseling reflect the spirit of humanistic psychology in conceptualizing human nature as inherently positive, self-determined, and having self-actualizing tendencies.

The strength of experiential therapies lies in their ability to help clients become aware of their thoughts and feelings, discover their inner choices, and promote personal responsibility. The weakness of experiential therapies could be their overemphasis on feelings and underemphasis on cognition and behavior. Experiential therapies may therefore lack some of the counseling strategies necessary to promote a comprehensive treatment program.

Later in the chapter, I provided an overview of counseling approaches that utilize the creative arts. CAT was described as an emerging profession with opportunities for professional certification and registration in various CAT modalities such as music, art, and drama. CAT was also conceptualized as an adjunctive counseling strategy, which can be used to facilitate the counseling process.

An overview of prominent CAT modalities—music therapy, art therapy, drama therapy, dance therapy, and bibliotherapy—was provided in terms of key concepts, procedures and outcomes, and special populations. Multimodality CAT was described as a relatively new addition to the CAT field. It has the advantage of utilizing whatever CAT modality the counselor or client preferred to use. Specific guidelines for its use were also provided.

SUGGESTED READING

Person-Centered Counseling
American Psychological Association. (1975). Carl Rogers on empathy (Entire Issue). *The Counseling Psychologist, 5*(2).
Rogers, C. (1951). *Client-centered therapy*. Boston: Houghton Mifflin.
Rogers, C. (1961). *On becoming a person*. Boston: Houghton Mifflin.

Gestalt Therapy
Passons, W. R. (1975). *Gestalt approaches in counseling*. New York: Holt, Rinehart, & Winston.
Perls, F. (1969). *Gestalt therapy verbatim*. Moab, UT: Real People Press.
Perls, F. (1969). *In and out of the garbage pail*. Moab, UT: Real People Press.

Polster, E., & Polseer, M. (1973). *Gestalt therapy integrated: Contours of theory and practice*. New York: Brunnel/Mazel.

Existential Therapies

Buber, M. (1970). *I and thou* (W. Kaufmann, Trans.). New York: Scribner's.

Frankl, V. (1963). *Man's search for meaning*. New York: Simon and Schuster (Touchstone).

Frankl, V. (1971). *The doctor and the soul*. New York: Bantam.

Laing, R. D. (1965). *The divided self*. Baltimore: Pelican.

May, R. (Ed.). (1961). *Existential psychology*. New York: Random House.

Van Kaam, A. (1967). Counseling and psychotherapy from the viewpoint of existential psychology. In D. Arbuck (Ed.), *Counseling and psychotherapy: An overview*. New York: McGraw-Hill.

Yalom, I. D. (1980). *Existential psychotherapy*. New York: Basic Books.

REFERENCES

Ascher, L. M. (1979). Paradoxical intention in the treatment of urinary retention. *Behavior Research and Therapy, 17*, 267–270.

Ascher, L. M., & Efran, J. S. (1978). The use of paradoxical intention in a behavioral program for sleep onset insomnia. *Journal of Consulting and Clinical Psychology, 46*, 547–550.

Bertoia, J., & Allan, J. (1988). Counseling seriously ill children: Use of spontaneous drawings. *Elementary School Guidance and Counseling*, 206–221.

Boswell, B. (1983). Adapted dance for mentally retarded children: An experimental study (Doctoral dissertation, Texas Women's University, 1983). *Dissertation Abstracts International, 43*(9–A), 2925.

Bruscia, K. E. (1987). *Improvisational models of music therapy*. Springfield, IL: Charles C. Thomas.

Buber, M. (1970). *I and thou* (W. Kaufmann, Trans.). New York: Scribner's.

Bugental, J. (1976). *The search for existential identity*. San Francisco: CA: Jossey-Bass.

Clarke, K., & Breeberg, L. (1986). Differential effects of the Gestalt two chair intervention and problem solving in resolving decisional conflict. *Journal of Counseling Psychology, 33*, 48–53.

Clarke, J., & Evans, E. (1973). Rhythmical intention as a method of treatment for cerebral-palsied patients. *Australia Journal of Physiotherapy*, 19–20, 57–64.

Cole, I. (1982). Movement negotiations with an autistic child. *Arts in Psychotherapy, 9*, 49–53.

Cripe, F. F. (1986). Rock music as therapy for children with attention deficit disorder: An exploratory study. *Journal of Music Therapy, 23*, 30–37.

Eidson, C. E., Jr. (1989). The effects of behavioral music therapy on the generalization of interpersonal skills from sessions to the classroom by emotionally handicapped middle school students. *Journal of Music Therapy, 26*, 4, 206–221.

Fleshman, B., & Fryrear, J. L. (1981). *The arts in therapy*. Chicago, IL: Nelson-Hall.

Frankl, V. (1963). *Man's search for meaning*. New York: Washington Square Press.

Frankl, V. E. (1967). *Psychotherapy and existentialism: Selected papers on logotherapy*. New York: Simon and Schuster (Touchstone).

Frankl, V. E. (1971). *The doctor and the soul*. New York: Bantam.

Frankl, V. (1978). *The unheard cry for meaning*. New York: Simon & Schuster (Touchstone).

Gelso, C. J., & Carter, J. A. (1985). The relationship in counseling and psychotherapy: Components, consequences, and theoretical antecedents. *The Counseling Psychologist, 13*, 155–243.

Gelso, C. J., & Fritz, B. R. (in press). *Counseling Psychology*, Orlando, FL: Holt, Rinehart, & Winston.

Gibbons, A. C. (1984). A program for noninstitutionalized, mature adults: A description. *Activities, Adaptation, and Aging, 6*, 71–80.

Gibbons, A. C. (1988). A review of literature for music development/education and music therapy with the elderly. *Music Therapy Perspectives, 5*, 33–40.

Goldfried, M. R. Greenberg, L. S., & Mormar, C. (1990). Individual psychotherapy: Process and outcome. In M. R. Rosenzweig & L. W. Porter (Eds.), *Annual review of psychology*, Palo Alto, CA: Annual Reviews.

Guinan, J., & Foulds, M. (1970). Marathon groups: Facilitator of personal growth? *Journal of Consulting Psychology, 17*, 145–149.

Gunning, S., & Holmes, T. (1973). Dance therapy with psychotic children. *Archives of General Psychiatry, 28*, 707–713.

Heppner, P. P., Rogers, M. E., & Lee, L. A. (1984). Carl Rogers: Reflections on his life. *Journal of Counseling and Development, 63*, 14–20.

Hollingdale, R. J. (1978). *Twilight of the idols and the anti-christ*. New York: Penguin Books.

Irwin, E. C. (1987). Drama: The play's the thing. *Elementary School Guidance and Counseling*, 276–283.

Isenberg-Grzeda, C. (1988). Music therapy assessment: A reflection of professional identity. *Journal of Music Therapy, 25*(3), 156–169.

James, M. R. (1988). Music therapy values clarification: A positive influence on perceived locus of control. *Journal of Music Therapy, 25*(4), 206–215.

Johnson, D. R. (1984a). Establishing the creative arts therapies as an independent profession. *The Arts in Psychotherapy, 11*, 209–212.

Johnson, D. R. (1984b). Perspectives, projects, and training facilities. *Journal of Mental Imagery, 7*(1), 105–109.

Jung, C. G. (1959). *The archetypes and the collective unconscious*. Princeton, NJ: Princeton University Press.

Kenny, A. (1987). An arts activity approach: Counseling the gifted, creative, and talented. *The Gifted Child Today, 10*(3), 22–37.

Kramer, E. (1987). Sublimation and art therapy. In J. A. Rubin (Ed.), *Approaches to art therapy: Theory and technique*. New York: Brunner/Mazel.

Lasseter, J., Privette, G., Brown, C. G., & Duer, J. (1989). Dance as treatment approach with a multidisabled child: Implications for school counseling. *The School Counselor, 36*, 310–315.

Levitsky, A., & Simkin, J. S. (1972). Gestalt therapy. In L. N. Solomon & B. Berzon (Eds.), *New perspectives on encounter groups* (pp. 245–253). San Francisco, Jossey-Bass.

Martin, D. G. (1989). *Counseling and therapy skills* (2nd ed.). Prospect Heights, IL: Therapy Press.

May, R. (1953). *Man's search for himself*. New York: Norton.

May, R. (1961). *Existential psychology*. New York: Random House.

May, R. (1977). *The meaning of anxiety* (rev. ed.). New York: Norton.

Moreno, J. L. (1946). *Psychodrama* (Vol. 1). Beacon, NY: Beacon House.

Moreno, J. (1988). Multicultural music therapy: The world music connection. *Journal of Music Therapy, 25*(1), 17–27.

Nystul, M. S. (1977). The use of music in counseling and psychotherapy. *The Individual Psychologist, 14*, 45–50.

Nystul, M. S. (1978). The use of creative arts therapy within Adlerian psychotherapy. *The Individual Psychologist, 15*, 11–18.

Nystul, M. S. (1979). Integrating current psychotherapies into Adlerian psychotherapy. *The Individual Psychologist, 16*, 23–29.

Nystul, M. S. (1980). Nystulian play therapy: Applications of Adlerian psychology. *Elementary School Guidance and Counseling, 15*, 22–30.

Nystul, M. S. (1985). Reaching in—reaching out: Treatment of an autistic child. *Mental Health Counselor's Association Journal, 8*, 18–26.

Nystul, M. S. (1987). Creative arts therapy and the existential encounter. *The Creative Child and Adult Quarterly, 12*(3), 243–249.

Nystul, M. S., & Musynska, E. (1976). Adlerian treatment of a classical case of stuttering. *Journal of Individual Psychology, 32*, 194–202.

Passons, W. R. (1975). *Gestalt approaches in counseling.* New York: Holt, Rinehart, & Winston.

Perls, F. (1969a). *Gestalt therapy verbatim.* Moab, UT: Real People Press.

Perls, F. (1969b). *In and out of the garbage pail.* Moab, UT: Real People Press.

Polk, E. (1977). Dance therapy with special children. In K. Mason (Ed.), *Dance therapy: Focus on dance VII* (pp. 56–58). Washington, DC: American Alliance for Health, Physical Education, and Recreation.

Raskin, N. J., & Rogers, L. R. (1989). Person-centered therapy. In R. J. Corsini (Ed.), *Current psychotherapies* (pp. 154–194). Itasca, IL: F. E. Peacock.

Rhyne, J. (1987). Gestalt art therapy. In J. A. Rubin (Ed.), *Approaches to art therapy: Theory and technique.* New York: Brunner/Mazel.

Riordan, R. J., & Wilson, L. S. (1989). Bibliotherapy: Does it work? *Journal of Counseling and Development, 67*, 506–508.

Robbins, A. (1985). Working towards the establishment of creative arts therapies as an independent profession. *The Arts in Psychotherapy, 12*, 67–70.

Rogers, C. (1939). *The clinical treatment of the problem child.* Boston: Houghton Mifflin.

Rogers, C. (1942). *Counseling and psychotherapy.* Boston: Houghton Mifflin.

Rogers, C. (1951). *Client-centered therapy.* Boston: Houghton Mifflin.

Rogers, C. (1957). The necessary and sufficient condition of therapeutic personality change. *Journal of Consulting Psychology, 21*, 95–103.

Rogers, C. (1961). *On becoming a person.* Boston: Houghton Mifflin.

Rogers, C. R., Gendlin, E. T., Kiesler, D. J., & Truax, C. B. (1967). *The therapeutic relationship and its impact: A study of psychotherapy with schizophrenics.* Madison: University of Wisconsin Press.

Roth, E. A. (1987). A behavioral approach to art therapy. In J. A. Rubin (Ed.), *Approaches to art therapy: Theory and technique.* New York: Brunner/Mazel.

Rubin, J. A. (1987). Freudian psychoanalytic theory: Emphasis on uncovering and insight. In J. A. Rubin (Ed.), *Approaches to art therapy: Theory and technique.* New York: Brunner/Mazel.

Rubin, J. A. (1988). Art counseling an alternative. *Elementary School Guidance and Counseling*, 180–185.

Silver, R. A. (1987). A cognitive approach to art therapy. In J. A. Rubin (Ed.), *Approaches to art therapy: Theory and technique.* New York: Brunner/Mazel.

Stabler, B. (1984). *Children's drawings.* Chapel Hill, NC: Health Science Consortium.

Starker, S. (1988). Psychologists and self-help books: Attitudes and prescriptive practices of clinicians. *American Journal of Psychotherapy, 42*, 448–455.

Talerico, C. J. (1986). The expressive arts and creativity as a form of therapeutic experience in the field of mental health. *The Journal of Creative Behavior, 20*(4), 229–247.

Turner, R. M., & Ascher, L. M. (1979). Controlled comparison of progressive relaxation, stimulus control, and paradoxical intention therapies for insomnia. *Journal of Consulting and Clinical Psychology, 47*, 500–508.

Usher, C. H. (1989). Recognizing cultural bias in counseling theory and practice: The case of Regus. *Journal of Multicultural Counseling and Development, 17*, 62–71.

Wadeson, H. (1980). *Art psychotherapy.* New York: John Wiley & Sons.

Wells, N. F., & Stevens, T. (1984). Music as a stimulus for creative fantasy in group psychotherapy with young adolescents. *The Arts in Psychotherapy, 11*, 71–76.

Wilson, L. (1987). Symbolism and art therapy: Theory and clinical practice. In J. A. Rubin (Ed.), *Approaches to art therapy: Theory and technique.* New York: Brunner/Mazel.

Wislocki, A. (1981). Movement is their medium: Dance movement methods in special education. *Milieu Therapy, 1*, 49–54.

Yontey, G. M., & Simkin, J. S. (1989). Gestalt therapy. In R. J. Corsini (Ed.), *Current psychotherapies* (pp. 323–361). Itasca, IL: F. E. Peacock.

Zaccaria, J. S., & Moses, J. A. (1968). *Facilitating human development through reading: The use of bibliotherapy through teaching and counseling.* Champaign, IL: Stipes.

CHAPTER EIGHT

Cognitive-Behavioral Theories

CHAPTER OVERVIEW

This chapter provides a description of prominent cognitive-behavioral theories. The theories covered in this chapter are behavior therapy, rational-emotive therapy, cognitive therapy, transactional analysis, and reality therapy. Highlights include information about each theory in terms of

- Background information
- View of human nature
- Key concepts
- The counseling process
- Techniques
- Summary and evaluation

Cognitive-behavior theories emphasize the role of cognition and/or behavior in psychological functioning and well-being. The recent trend toward diversifying and integrating counseling theories has altered the focus of some cognitive-behavior theories. Theories that originally had a cognitive focus have incorporated behavioral techniques (e.g., cognitive therapy and rational-emotive therapy) and behaviorally oriented theories have incorporated cognitive techniques and concepts (e.g., behavior therapy and reality therapy).

The integration of theories represents an attempt to develop a more comprehensive approach as opposed to highlighting what is unique about a particular school of counseling. It is hoped that this trend will continue, replacing unnecessary barriers between theories with compatible concepts and procedures.

This chapter will provide a description of the following theories: behavior therapy, rational-emotive therapy, cognitive therapy, transactional analysis, and reality therapy. Table 8.1 provides an overview of these theories in terms of key concepts, the counseling process, and techniques.

BEHAVIOR THERAPY

Background Information

The historical roots of behavior therapy can be traced to three learning theories: classical conditioning, operant conditioning, and social learning theory. Classical conditioning evolved from Ivan Pavlov's experiments with dogs. In these experiments, Pavlov (1906) demonstrated that he could condition a dog to salivate to the sound of a bell. This was the first demonstration of what Pavlov called *classical conditioning*, the principle of conditioning people to respond to a stimulus. Pavlov's principles of classical conditioning were later applied to counseling. Joseph Wolpe (1958, 1973) played a key role in this process, integrating the principles of classical conditioning into a systematic desensitization process to treat phobias. This technique continues to be one of the most popular approaches for the treatment of phobias.

B. F. Skinner developed the second major field of learning theory, operant conditioning. Skinner (1938, 1953, 1961) proposed that learning cannot occur without some form of reinforcement. He contended that behaviors that are reinforced will tend to be repeated, and those that are not tend to be extinguished. Compared to classical conditioning, operant conditioning is a more active process of learning in that the person must do something to be reinforced.

Skinner developed the principles of operant conditioning in his now-famous Skinner Box experiments, which involved training a rat to press a bar for food. More recently, the principles of operant conditioning have been utilized in programmed learning, self-control, behaviorally oriented discipline procedures, and management of clients in institutions by use of token economies.

The third major learning theory that helped formulate behavior therapy is social learning theory. Along with the various cognitive theories, social learning theory represents a more recent dimension to the behavioral school. Among the individuals associated with these new trends are Beck (1976); Meichenbaum (1977); Mahoney

Table 8.1
The Cognitive-Behavioral Theories

Theory	Founder(s)	Key Concepts	The Counseling Process	Techniques
Behavior Therapy	Palov, Skinner, Bandura, Wolpe, and Meichenbaum	Incorporation of principles from learning theories; grounding in the scientific method; focus on overt, observable behavior; view of psychopathology primarily in behavioral terms.	Attempts to establish clear and precise counseling goals such as modifying maladaptive behavior, strengthening desired behavior, and helping clients learn effective decision making.	Assertive training, systematic desensitization, token economy, cognitive behavior modification, and self-control.
Rational-Emotive Therapy	Ellis	Basic premise that emotional disturbance results from illogical or irrational thought processes.	Helps the client learn how to dispute irrational or illogical thoughts.	Cognitive restructuring emotive techniques, shame attacking exercises, bibliotherapy, and behavioral techniques.
Cognitive Therapy	Beck	The role of cognition in mental health, cognitive vulnerability, cognitive distortions, systematic bias in information processing, cognitive triad of depression, and the cognitive model of anxiety.	Offers a short-term treatment program for depression, anxiety, and other mental disorders. Its ultimate goal is elimination of systematic bias in thinking.	Cognitive techniques such as decatastrophizing, reattribution, redefining, decentering; and behavioral techniques such as skill training, progressive relaxation, behavioral rehearsal, and exposure therapy.
Transactional Analysis (TA)	Berne	The three ego states (parent, adult, child), transactional analysis, games people play, life scripts, the four life positions, and strokes.	Educative method to teach the client how to use TA concepts to make positive decisions regarding their lives.	Structural analysis, transactional analysis, script analysis, and analysis of games.
Reality Therapy	Glasser	Success and failure identity, emphasis on responsibility, avoidance of labels associated with mental disorders, positive addiction, and control theory.	Has primary aim to help client develop a success identity through responsible action; teaches clients how to use control theory to fulfill basic needs and not interfere with the rights of others.	Incorporates an 8-step approach that includes: create a relationship, focus on current behavior, have client evaluate behavior, make an action plan, obtain a commitment, don't accept excuses, don't use punishment, and refuse to give up.

(1974); and Bandura (1974, 1977a, 1989). In particular, Bandura was instrumental in the integration of cognition into behavior therapy.

Bandura's (1977a) early work on social learning theory focused on how learning occurs from observation, modeling, and imitation. The idea that learning could occur entirely as a function of cognitive control was a direct challenge to the traditional behavioral stimulus-response model (Mahoney & Lyddon, 1988). In addition, Bandura's (1974) "endorsement of an interactional reciprocity between person and environment marked a pivotal shift from exclusive environmental determinism" (Mahoney & Lyddon, 1988, p. 196).

More recently Bandura (1977b, 1982, 1986, 1989) developed a theory of self-efficacy, which related to a person's belief in the ability to successfully accomplish a particular task. Perceived self-efficacy plays a central role in mediating constructive behavior change (Bandura, 1986). Bandura's theory contends that self-efficacy can directly influence what activities people will choose to engage in; how much effort they will exert; and how long they will continue when faced with adversity (Johnson, Baker, Kapola, Kiselica, & Thompson, 1989).

View of Human Nature

Historically, behaviorists viewed human nature as neutral. A person was not inherently good or bad but would become what the environment dictated. This position was in direct contrast to the humanistic stance, which suggested people were capable of self-determination. The more recent behavioral point of view recognizes the possibility of self-determined behavior (Bandura, 1974, 1977b; Meichenbaum, 1977). In this regard, individuals can take an active role in their destiny.

Key Concepts

Behavior therapy is currently in a state of rapid change and evolution (Wilson, 1989). Rimm and Cunningham (1985) identified common elements that characterize behavior therapy. I have incorporated five of their observations into the following overview.

1. *Behavior therapy concentrates on overt, observable behavioral processes and cognitions*. The early behaviorist focused on overt behavior. More recently, the cognitive realm is also viewed as an important mediating factor in relation to behavior.

2. *Behavior therapy focuses on the here-and-now*. Information about past experience is considered important only as it relates to current treatment issues. The focus is on understanding and treating current problems relating to behavior and cognitions.

3. *Maladaptive behaviors are primarily the result of learning*. Models of learning (operant, classical, and social learning theories) can be used to understand the etiology of maladaptive behavior. Learning principles can therefore be used to change maladaptive behavior.

4. *Well-defined, concrete goals are used*. Goals are stated in observable, measurable terms whenever possible.

5. *Behavior therapy is committed to the scientific method*. Behavior therapy utilizes the principles of scientific method to evaluate techniques and procedures. Assessment and treatment are viewed as part of the same process, creating a built-in mechanism for research and accountability.

The Counseling Process

The counselor utilizes an active and directive approach, which often incorporates problem-solving strategies (Wilson, 1989). The client is also expected to take an active role in the counseling process in terms of assessment by engaging in processes such as self-monitoring and treatment by acquiring new skills and behaviors through work and practice.

A misconception regarding behavior therapists is that they view a positive counseling relationship as unimportant to the counseling process (Wilson, 1989). Brady (1980) noted, however, that the nature of the counseling relationship can have a direct bearing on the outcome of behavior therapy. In addition, Swan and MacDonald (1978) found that behavior therapists reported that relationship-building procedures were among the most frequently used.

Behavior therapy has concrete, specific goals that include acquiring necessary behaviors and coping skills and overcoming self-defeating cognitive processes. When possible, clients assume primary responsibility for determining treatment goals. The therapist's role and function are therefore directed at how to accomplish goals in therapy, rather than focusing on which goals to work on (Wilson, 1989).

Techniques

Most behavior therapy procedures are short-term in duration, although some may extend as long as 25 to 50 sessions (Wilson, 1989). Behavior therapists use a wide variety of techniques and procedures: cognitive behavior modification, self-management and self-control, self-efficacy, participant modeling, assertiveness training, systematic desensitization, and token economy.

Cognitive Behavior Modification.   Meichenbaum's (1977) cognitive behavior modification is a form of self-control therapy whereby clients learn to use tools to take control of their lives. Behavior change occurs "through a sequence of mediating processes involving the interaction of inner speech, cognitive structures, and behaviors, and their resultant outcomes" (Meichenbaum, 1977, p. 218).

This theory suggests that people have a set of beliefs or cognitive structures that influence how they react to events in terms of an inner speech or self-talk. To a large degree, cognitive structures and inner speech determine how people behave. The focus of therapy is on restructuring faulty cognitive structures, altering inner speech so that it triggers coping behaviors, and if necessary using behavior therapy to teach coping responses.

Self-Management and Self-Control.   Three individuals associated with self-management and self-control are Kaufer (1975, 1977), Bandura (1977b), and Meichenbaum (1977). Self-management and self-control procedures are directed at helping clients become their own agents for behavior change (Gintner & Poret,

1987). In this process, the therapist provides support and expertise in terms of behavioral management. The client assumes responsibility for implementing and carrying out the program (Kaufer, 1975).

A wide range of skills can be used to promote self-management and self-control. For example, Kaufer (1975) identified skills in (a) self-monitoring, (b) establishing rules of conduct by contracting, (c) obtaining environmental support, (d) self-evaluating, and (e) generating reinforcing consequences for behaviors that promote the goals of self-control. Wilson (1989) described other self-control skills such as progressive relaxation to reduce stress; biofeedback to treat psychophysiological disorders; and self-instructional training for control of anger, impulsivity, and other coping problems.

Self-Efficacy.   As noted earlier, self-efficacy is a theory developed primarily by Bandura (1977b, 1982, 1986, 1989). which relates to a person's belief in the ability to accomplish a particular task. Self-efficacy is not a behavioral technique. It can be better viewed as a concept that should be considered when implementing a technique. Rimm and Cunningham (1985) noted that treatments that foster the greatest change in self-efficacy should be the most effective. They suggested that treatment efficacy could be increased by promoting methods that foster efficacy information to clients. In this regard, Bandura, Reese, and Adams (1982) noted that efficacy information can be transferred to clients by (a) actual performance, which is the most powerful information source; (b) vicarious learning or modeling; (c) verbal persuasion; and (d) psychological arousal.

Self-efficacy theory has stimulated a proliferation of research activity. It has been shown to predict many behaviors such as depression (Davis-Berman, 1988); cessation after treatment (Gooding & Glasgow, 1985; Nicki, Remington, & MacDonald, 1984); recovery from heart attacks (Bandura, 1982); sports performance (Lee, 1982; McAuley, 1985); and success in weight reduction programs (Weinberg, Hughes, Critelli, England, & Jackson, 1984). Based on a review of the literature on self-efficacy, Johnson et al. (1989) concluded that "across varied behavioral domains, self-efficacy has predicted differences in the degree to which people choose, present, and succeed in performing targeted behaviors" (p. 206).

Participant Modeling.   Participant modeling is based on Bandura's (1974, 1977a) social learning theory, which emphasizes the role of observation and imitation in learning. It is used primarily to treat phobias and fears (Rimm & Cunningham, 1985). Participant modeling involves two stages, observation and participation. During the observation stage, the client observes a model engaged in the feared behavior, for example, petting a dog. Research suggests that efficacy increases when the model is similar to the client in terms of age and gender (Raskin & Israel, 1981) and the manner in which the model approaches the feared task (Meichenbaum, 1972). The second stage involves the client participating or engaging in the feared behavior. During this process, the counselor guides the client through a series of exercises relating to the feared task (Rimm & Cunningham, 1985).

Assertiveness Training.   Assertiveness training can be used for clients who find it difficult to stand up for their rights or who are unable to express their feelings in a

Albert Bandura

constructive manner (Wilson, 1989). Rimm and Cunningham (1985) described the following steps involved in assertiveness training. First, the therapist and client determine if there is a need for assertiveness training. Second, the therapist describes how increased assertiveness can be beneficial. The third step is the most important and involves a process of behavioral rehearsal. During behavioral rehearsal, the therapist models an assertive behavior, then asks the client to "rehearse" the assertive behavior, and finally provides feedback and appropriate reinforcement.

Systematic Desensitization.   Systematic desensitization is a technique developed by Wolpe (1958, 1973) to treat problems resulting from classical conditioning such as phobias. It has also been used to treat a variety of other maladaptive behaviors including excessive fears about issues such as death, injury, and sex (Kazdin, 1978).

The following steps can be used to implement this technique.

1. *Teach deep relaxation*. Systematic desensitization utilizes the principle of counterconditioning by introducing a relaxation response to replace the previously conditioned adversive response. It is based on the assumption that a person cannot be anxious and relaxed at the same time. The client is therefore taught to experience a state of deep relaxation when the therapist describes a relaxing scene.

2. *Develop a hierarchy*. The therapist and client develop a hierarchy of situations that elicit a fear response. The situation that elicits the lowest level of anxiety is the first item in the hierarchy, and the one that elicits the highest level of anxiety is last. It is important that the statements are specific enough that the client will be able to visualize the situation. An example is, "I walked up a flight of stairs to the fourth floor and looked out the window."

3. *Proceed through the hierarchy*. The therapist helps the client enter into a state of deep relaxation. The therapist then asks the client to imagine the first item in the hierarchy. By introducing a relaxation response to a situation that previously elicited a fear response, the therapist helps the client become desensitized by the counterconditioning process.

4. *Address the fear in vivo*. This step involves desensitizing the client to *in-vivo* or real-life situations associated with the fears. For example, if the client has a snake phobia, an item on the hierarchy may be to imagine looking at a snake. During the *in-vivo* experience, the client will be asked to look at a real snake.

5. *Follow up and evaluate*. The final step is to evaluate the client's success in dealing with the fear response in a variety of situations over an extended period of time.

Token Economy.   Ayllon and Azrin (1968) developed the technique of *token economy* to teach psychiatric patients to become more responsible. It has been used primarily in hospitals, residential settings, and schools. The technique is based on the principles of operant conditioning and involves giving tokens to reinforce a desired behavior such as cleaning one's room. After collecting enough tokens, clients can exchange them for goods or privileges such as being able to watch TV. To increase intrinsic motivation, the tokens must be gradually eliminated and replaced by social reinforcers such as encouragement. This will enable clients to maintain newly acquired behaviors after they leave the treatment setting.

Summary and Evaluation

Behavior therapy is an approach to counseling that focuses on overt behavior. The counseling process emphasizes the importance of establishing clear goals stated in behavioral terms. Progress in therapy is indicated when there is a change or modification in behavior. Treatment and assessment are seen as part of the same process, creating a built-in mechanism for research and accountability.

Some weaknesses are associated with the behavioral approach. Behavior therapy tends to disregard the importance of feelings and emotions in the counseling process; ignore historical factors that can contribute to a client's problem; and minimize the use of insight in the counseling process.

RATIONAL-EMOTIVE THERAPY (RET)

Albert Ellis (b. 1913) received M.A. and Ph.D. degrees in clinical psychology from Columbia University and went on to practice in the areas of marriage, family, and sex therapy. In 1962, Ellis published *Reason and Emotion in Psychotherapy*, which laid the foundation for rational-emotive therapy (RET). Ellis founded the Institute for Rational-Emotive Therapy in 1959 and has been its executive director since 1960. The following Personal Note provides additional information about his interests and professional activities.

a personal note

I had the privilege of interviewing Albert Ellis when he was 71 years old, and I found him to be very energetic (Nystul, 1985). He noted that his typical daily schedule involves providing individual and group counseling and psychotherapy from 9:30 a.m. until 11:30 p.m. Ellis' other activities include directing his institute, supervising numerous therapists, making many presentations, conducting workshops, and writing approximately 20 articles and 1 or 2 books each year.

Although Ellis had already written more than 45 books and 500 articles, he had no intention of retiring. At the end of our interview, he said:

> All this activity is infinitely more enjoyable to me than would be lying on a beach, sightseeing, or reading romantic novels. I hope that my good health continues, in spite of the diabetes that I have had for the last 30 years, and that I shall die in the saddle a few decades from now.
>
> Many years ago, I reluctantly came to the conclusion that when I die I shall still have at least 100 books unwritten and that is a frustration I had better realistically accept. I would prefer to live forever and to keep exploring the realm of human disturbance and potential realms to happiness and self-fulfillment for eons to come, but no such luck! One of these days in the not-too-distant future, I shall run down. Too damned bad! But hardly awful and terrible. (Nystul, 1985, p. 254)

View of Human Nature

Ellis (1989) believes that humans have a potential to be rational or irrational—to be self-preserving or self-destructive. He contends that people perceive, think, emote, and behave simultaneously. Thus, to understand self-defeating conduct, it is necessary to "understand how people perceive, think, emote, and act" (Ellis, 1989, p. 198).

Key Concepts

The major concepts in RET (Ellis, 1962, 1989) relate to the role of cognition and how irrational thoughts can create self-defeating, emotionally disturbing outcomes.

Albert Ellis

The Role of Cognition.   The basic premise of RET is that emotional disturbance results primarily from cognitive processes that are fundamentally irrational or illogical in nature (Ellis, 1989). Ellis and Harper (1975) defined *rational* as anything that promotes happiness and survival for the individual and *irrational* as anything that inhibits personal happiness and survival.

One way to identify illogical or irrational thought processes is to look for statements that contain the unconditional *should* or the absolutistic *must* or *ought* (Ellis, 1989; Ellis & Harper, 1975). Examples of these self-defeating statements are

- "I should get all A's, and if I don't, I'm stupid."
- "I ought to know better when it comes to choosing a boyfriend. The ones I pick are all duds."
- "I must do well at my job, and if I don't, I'm no good."

Ellis (1977, 1989) noted that not all statements of irrational beliefs contain shoulds, oughts, and musts. For example, some focus on what is awful, as illustrated in the statement, "Life is awful; I don't get any breaks."

The A-B-C-D-E Acronym.   In part, RET's popularity is due to its simplicity. The basic procedures associated with RET can be taught to the client by using the A-B-C-D-E acronym. The letter "A" in the acronym stands for the activating event. This can be whatever the client may be reacting to, such as a recent phone conversation or a report that was received by a supervisor. "B" represents the client's belief system or cognitive reaction to the activating event. "C" is the emotional consequence that the client is experiencing such as feeling anxious or depressed. "D" suggests that the client learn to dispute self-defeating thought processes, and "E" is the effect of the disputing process.

Ellis (1962, 1989) contends that it is not "A" that causes a serious emotional reaction ("C"). For "C" to occur, a self-defeating thought process must occur at "B." The client is therefore taught how to dispute self-defeating processes ("D") to generate a positive effect ("E").

Ellis (1962, 1989) also suggested that self-defeating cognitive reactions follow a predictable pattern. People usually start with a sane or rational reaction to the activating event. Next, they tend to engage in self-talk that is illogical or irrational. Finally, they grossly overreact to the situation, making it seem like a catastrophe.

The following Personal Note provides an illustration of RET.

a personal note

Tim was a 30-year-old, self-referred male who came to a mental health clinic complaining of anxiety and depression and threatening suicide. Tim told me he had recently started a new job as an accountant for a firm. Two days earlier, his boss had returned a report he had written with several suggestions and one or two indications of possible errors in his statistics. His boss had asked him to look over the suggestions and revise the report accordingly. Tim told me all he could think about since then was the report and how his boss "*must* be out to get me."

I decided to use RET, so I provided Tim with an overview of the A-B-C-D-E acronym. Together, we decided that the activating event "A" was the boss returning the report; "B" was his cognitive reaction to "A" (i.e., My boss must be out to get me); and "C" represented his feelings of being anxious, depressed, and suicidal. Since RET focuses on cognition, we then explored his cognitive reactions to "A." Tim's thought process followed the predictable pattern described earlier. He started with a sane reaction, "It looks like there are some mistakes here." He then began to think irrationally and said things like, "He *must* be out to get me. I know he has decided he made a mistake in hiring me and is looking for a way to let me go." Finally, his thoughts became catastrophic as he concluded, "It's just a matter of time until he fires me, and I'll never get another job. I guess there is just no hope for me."

When I asked Tim how he felt when he said these things to himself, he replied, "Terrible." He began to realize that his thoughts could cause an intense emotional reaction at "C." Tim and I then attempted to restructure his cognitive reactions. We disrupted "D" his irrational reactions with rational reactions. For example, he changed "My boss *must* be out to get me" to "My boss seems to have some concerns about my report."

By the end of our first counseling session, Tim no longer had intense feelings of being anxious, depressed, or suicidal. He said he had no idea how much power thoughts could have on emotions, and he was glad he had a tool he could use to help control his emotional reactions. Tim also commented that he still felt somewhat uncomfortable about his relationship with his boss. He wanted to know how his boss thought he was doing in his job. Tim agreed to ask his boss this question as a homework assignment. At the start of our next session, Tim smiled and said, "I guess I caused myself a lot of needless worry. My boss said he thought I was doing just fine, and he really appreciated me revising my report." Counseling was terminated shortly thereafter.

The Counseling Process

The primary goal of RET is "minimizing the client's central self-defeating cognitions" and helping the client acquire "a more realistic, tolerant philosophy of life" (Ellis, 1989, p. 214). The actual process of therapy is educational and confrontational in nature. The therapist teaches the client how to dispute irrational thoughts and also confronts and even attacks, if necessary, the client's self-defeating belief system. Once clients become aware of negative self-talk, they can create a cognitive reaction that generates a more positive emotional consequence.

In terms of the counseling relationship, Ellis (1989) does not believe that a warm relationship is a necessary or sufficient condition for personality change. He believes the therapist must fully accept clients but must also point out discrepancies in their behavior when necessary (Ellis, 1989).

Techniques

The techniques that Ellis (1962, 1989) identified for therapists to utilize in RET include the following cognitive, emotive, and behavioral techniques.

Cognitive Restructuring.   The main technique of RET is to teach the client how to restructure irrational or illogical cognitions by utilizing the A-B-C-D-E acronym.

Shame-Attacking Exercises.   These exercises help clients realize the ridiculous nature of adhering to some of their self-limiting tendencies. For instance, a client may be afraid to play racquetball because of what other people think. As a homework assignment, the client might be asked to play racquetball and observe other people's reactions. As a result, the client may realize that other people are not even paying attention, that they have better things to do than stand around and watch one person play racquetball.

Bibliotherapy.   RET often requests the client to read books and listen to tapes to learn about the basic principles of RET.

Behavioral Techniques.   RET utilizes the full range of behavioral techniques such as desensitization, assertiveness training, and operant conditioning to supplement the basic RET approach. Contemporary RET contends that a change in behavior may facilitate cognitive restructuring. For example, a therapist might use assertiveness training to help clients stand up for their rights. The training will not only help clients become more assertive but will also reduce their tendency to engage in irrational thinking evidenced by a statement like, "If I talk, nobody will listen to me anyway."

Summary and Evaluation

RET is an educationally oriented approach that attempts to teach a client how to overcome self-defeating cognitive reactions. One of the strengths of RET is its simplicity. It can be taught to the client in terms as simple as the A-B-C-D-E acronym. In time, clients can learn to use the tools necessary to become their own self-therapists and gain control over their mental health.

The major weakness of RET may be to overemphasize the role of cognition in the etiology of mental disorders and emotional disturbances. In addition, it may be an oversimplified approach in terms of what is required to effectively restructure cognition. For many clients, much more may be required than simply changing irrational statements to rational statements. RET also avoids exploring other factors such as traumatic early-life experiences, which could represent important treatment considerations. Ellis (1989) identified limitations of RET in that it is not appropriate for clients who are not capable of engaging in a cognitively oriented process, for example, people who have mental retardation, brain injuries, psychosis, or mania.

COGNITIVE THERAPY

Background Information

During the mid-1950s Aaron Beck developed a cognitive-oriented approach to treat mental disorders, rejecting his early training in psychoanalysis. Beck is best known for his work on depression (Beck, 1963, 1964, 1967) and, more recently, anxiety (Beck & Emery, 1985). Beck's early work on depression resulted in the development of the Beck Depression Inventory, which is widely used as a clinical and research instrument.

View of Human Nature

Beck contends that people are a product of the interaction of innate, biological, developmental, and environmental factors (Beck & Weishaar, 1989). He also suggests that people have the capacity for self-determination by emphasizing the role of cognition in mental health (Beck, 1976).

Key Concepts

Beck (1976) and Beck and Weishaar (1989) described the following key concepts associated with cognitive therapy.

The Role of Cognition in Mental Health.   Emotions and behaviors are determined primarily by how a person perceives, interprets, and assigns meanings to events.

Cognitive Vulnerability.   Personality structures have vulnerabilities that predispose them to psychological distress. These vulnerabilities are characterized by

Aaron Beck

schemata, which are fundamental beliefs and assumptions that develop early in life and are reinforced by learning situations throughout life. They create beliefs, values, and attitudes about oneself, others, and the world. A schema can be functional or dysfunctional. Examples of statements indicating dysfunctional schemes of a border-line personality are: "There is something fundamentally wrong with me" or "People should support me and should not criticize, abandon, disagree with, or misunderstand me and my feelings" (Beck & Weishaar, 1989, p. 294). A dysfunctional schema can contribute to cognitive distortions, systematic bias in information processing, and other problems associated with emotional distress.

Cognitive Distortions.   A cognitive distortion is a systematic distortion in reasoning that results in psychological distress. Cognitive distortions identified by Beck and Weishaar (1989) include

- *Arbitrary inference*, which involves making a conclusion that has no supportive evidence or contradicts existing evidence.
- *Selective abstraction*, which occurs when taking information out of context or ignoring other information.
- *Overgeneralization*, which results when making a general rule on the basis of one or more isolated incidents and then applying it to unrelated situations.

- *Magnification and minimization*, which involves viewing something out of proportion as either less or more significant than it actually is.
- *Personalization*, which occurs when attributing external events to oneself without evidence of a causal connection.
- *Dichotomous thinking*, which involves conceptualizing an experience in either-or terms, such as seeing it as good or bad.

Systematic Bias in Information Processing. Mental disorders are characterized by a bias in information processing. Typically, the bias begins when a person "misreads" external events, thereby creating dysfunctional responses. For instance, someone who suffers from claustrophobia may "misread" taking an elevator as a very dangerous situation. The systematic bias then tends to shift to internal messages such as physiological responses. In this example, the person may "misread" feelings of tension and apprehension as an impending anxiety attack.

Cognitive Triad of Depression. The cognitive triad is characterized by a negative view of the self, the world, and the future. Psychological and physical symptoms of depression can evolve from the cognitive triad. Beck and Weishaar (1989) cited several examples of this phenomenon. A feeling of being unable to cope or control events can lead to a paralysis of will. Negative expectations about life can contribute to physical symptoms of depression such as low energy, fatigue, and inertia.

Cognitive Model of Anxiety. Anxiety results when a person's information processing is faulty, resulting in perceptions of danger when no danger exists. People with this anxiety have difficulty correcting their misconception by recognizing safety cues or other evidence. The cognition of anxious individuals is characterized by themes of danger and the likelihood of harm.

The Counseling Process

Beck summed up the major thrust of cognitive therapy in an interview by Weinrach (1988, p. 160).

> Cognitive therapy is a short-term treatment that was developed primarily for the treatment of depression and anxiety. It is now being used for personality disorders, eating disorders, and some of the other types of problems that have been more refractory to psychotherapy in the past. It is based on a view of psychopathology that stipulates that people's excessive affect and dysfunctional behavior is due to excessive or inappropriate ways of interpreting their experiences. It is also based on the notion that people who are depressed or anxious have in some way a distorted image of themselves and their external situation. (p. 160)

Beck (1976) and Beck and Weishaar (1989) provided information relevant to the counseling process, which I have incorporated into the following overview. The counselor initially attempts to promote a positive relationship by establishing the core conditions identified by Rogers: warmth, accurate empathy, and genuineness. The client is then encouraged to take an active role in the counseling process in setting goals, recounting cognitive and behavioral reactions to problem situations, and doing homework assignments.

The counselor functions as a guide in the counseling process by helping the client understand the role of cognition in emotions and behaviors. The counselor also acts as a catalyst by promoting corrective experiences that result in necessary cognitive restructuring and skill acquisition. In this process, counselors avoid the role of passive expert. They instead engage in a process of collaboration with the client with the ultimate goal of eliminating systematic biases in thinking. In addition, counselors do not tell the client that a particular belief is irrational or wrong. Instead, they explore with the client the meaning, function, usefulness, and consequences associated with the belief. The client then decides whether to retain, modify, or reject a belief.

Techniques

Beck (1976) and Beck and Weishaar (1989) described the following techniques associated with cognitive therapy.

Decatastrophizing.   This process is also known as the *what-if* technique and involves preparing clients for feared consequences by identifying problem-solving strategies.

Reattribution Technique.   This technique encourages challenging thoughts and assumptions by exploring other possible causes of events.

Redefining.   Redefining helps mobilize clients who feel they have no control over a problem by rephrasing the problem in a manner that promotes action. For instance, a student could change "I'm not a good student" to "I'm going to study more."

Decentering.   This technique involves having the client make observations to obtain a more realistic understanding of other people's reactions. It can alleviate anxiety by helping clients realize that they are not the center of attention.

Behavioral Techniques.   Cognitive therapy utilizes a wide range of behavioral techniques to help clients acquire necessary skills (e.g., skill training); relax (e.g., progressive relaxation); prepare for difficult situations (e.g., behavioral rehearsal); and expose themselves to feared situations (e.g., exposure therapy).

Summary and Evaluation

Cognitive therapy has become an increasingly popular form of counseling. This is especially true for the treatment of depression and anxiety. Its popularity is due in part to the massive research efforts that have evaluated the efficacy of cognitive therapy in the treatment of depression.

Beck and Weishaar (1989) conducted a literature review, which showed that cognitive therapy is superior to drug therapy (Blackburn, Bishop, Glen, Whalley, & Christie, 1981; Dunn, 1979; Maldonado, 1982; Rush, Beck, Kovacs, & Hollon, 1977) or equal to drug therapy (Blackburn, Eunson, & Bishop, 1986; Hollon, Evans, & DeRubeis, 1983; Murphy, Simons, Wetzel, & Lustman, 1983; Simons, Murphy, Levine,

& Wetzel, 1986). Studies indicate that a combination of cognitive therapy and antide-pressant medication is the most effective treatment for depression (Blackburn et al., 1981; Blackburn et al., 1986; Maldonado, 1982; Teasdale, Fennell, Hibbert, & Amies, 1984). Cognitive therapy also appears to have stronger long-term effects than drug therapy (Blackburn et al., 1986; Hollon et al., 1983; Kovacs, Rush, Beck, & Hollon, 1981; Maldonado, 1982).

Dobson (1989) conducted a meta-analysis of the efficacy of cognitive therapy for the treatment of depression. He analyzed 28 studies that used the Beck's Depression Inventory as the outcome measure. Results of Dobson's (1989) study indicate that cognitive therapy clients do better than 98% of the control subjects; 70% of the drug-therapy clients; and 70% of the other psychotherapy clients. These results were con-sistent with the results of an earlier meta-analysis study by Nietzel, Russell, Hemmings, and Gretter (1987).

Aside from the research support, cognitive therapy has other advantages. First, the approach is short-term, usually 12 to 16 weeks for depression and anxiety. Second, cognitive therapy has specific treatment programs for common mental dis-turbances such as anxiety and depression. These attributes promote cost-effective treatment planning.

All approaches have inherent strengths and weaknesses, and cognitive therapy is no exception. In fact, Beck and Weishaar (1989) pointed out that cognitive therapy is not recommended as the exclusive treatment of people with bipolar affective disor-ders, psychotic depression, and psychosis (including schizophrenia). These clients would tend not to benefit from cognitive therapy because it requires that clients have good concentration and memory (Beck & Weishaar, 1989).

TRANSACTIONAL ANALYSIS (TA)

Background Information

Eric Berne (1910–1970) is the originator of transactional analysis (TA). He received an M.D. degree from McGill University in Montreal in 1935 and then completed psy-chiatry training at Yale University.

TA is unique in its effort to avoid psychological jargon. Instead, the language of TA is easy to understand, using terms such as parent, adult, child, strokes, games, rack-ets, decisions, and redecisions. Its use of clear, simple language helped TA become attractive not only as a form of therapy but also as a self-help approach. As evidence of its popularity, two major books on the topic were international best sellers at vari-ous times: *Games People Play* (Berne, 1964) and *I'm OK, You're OK* (Harris, 1967).

View of Human Nature

Berne (1961, 1964) believed that people have the capacity to determine their own destiny. He contended that few people acquire the necessary self-awareness to become autonomous. Berne (1961) also stressed the importance of early-life experi-ences in contributing to personality development. His theory suggests that people develop scripts that are played throughout life. These scripts are derived from parental messages and other sources such as fairy tales and literature.

Key Concepts

Berne (1961, 1964) and Dusay and Dusay (1989) described the following concepts that are unique to the TA approach.

Ego States.   Berne identified the three ego states of the parent, adult, and child. The *parent ego state* represents the person's morals and values and can be either critical or nurturing. The critical parent attempts to find fault, whereas the nurturing parent is supportive and promotes growth. The *adult ego state* is the rational-thinking dimension. It is devoid of feelings and acts as a mediator between the child and parent ego states. The *child ego state* is the uninhibited side of the personality, characterized by a variety of emotions such as fear, happiness, and excitement. The child ego state has two dimensions, the free child and the adapted child. The *free child* is uninhibited and playful whereas the *adapted child* is rebellious and conforming.

An egogram can be used to assess the relative strengths and weaknesses of the various ego states. The egogram "reflects the type of person one is, one's probable types of problems, and the strengths and weaknesses of the personality" (Dusay & Dusay, 1989, p. 420). Interpreting an egogram is a complex process that requires specialized training. Clinicians are especially interested in ego states that are particularly high or low relative to the client's other ego states. For example, low critical parent (CP) suggests problems with exploitation; low nurturing parent (NP) implies loneliness; low adult (A) indicates difficulty concentrating; low free child (FC) suggests a lack of zest for life; and low adapted child (AC) indicates a person who is rigid and difficult to get along with (Dusay & Dusay, 1989). A healthy egogram is indicated when there is relative balance between the strength of the ego states as illustrated in Figure 8.1.

Transactional Analysis.   The concept of transactional analysis involves analyzing the transactions between people. It entails assessing the three ego states of parent, adult, and child of each person to determine whether the transactions between the people are complementary, crossed, or ulterior.

Complementary transactions occur when each person receives a message from the other person's ego state that seems appropriate and expected. Figure 8.2 provides three examples of complementary transactions. In each example, both people are sending and receiving messages as expected.

Figure 8.1
An Egogram with Relative
Balance

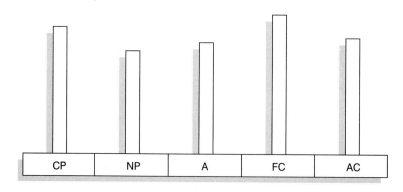

| CP | NP | A | FC | AC |

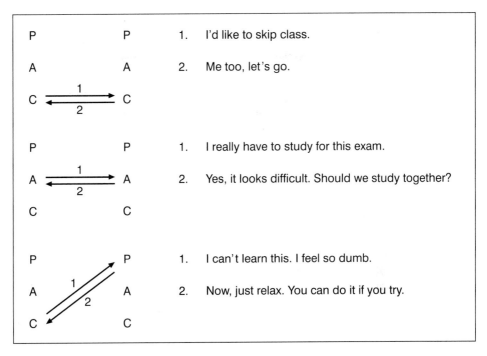

Figure 8.2
Complementary Transactions

Crossed transactions occur when one or more of the individuals receives a message from the other person's ego state that does not seem appropriate or expected. Figure 8.3 illustrates two examples of crossed transactions.

Ulterior transactions occur when a person's communication is complex and confusing. In these transactions, a person sends an overt message from one ego state and a covert ulterior message from another ego state. The ulterior message can be communicated verbally, nonverbally via body language, or by tone of voice. Figure 8.4 gives examples of each possibility.

Games People Play.   Berne (1964) defined *games* as "an ongoing series of complementary ulterior transactions progressing to a well-defined, predictable outcome" (p. 48). These games are usually played at an unconscious level, with the people not aware they are playing a particular game. Some of the different games people can play are "Now I've got you, you SOB" and "Kick me."

Although game playing results in bad feelings for both players, it also offers payoffs for the participants (Dusay & Dusay, 1989). The following example illustrates what might occur during the game of "Kick me."

Mary fears dating because she believes things will never work out. She reluctantly accepts a date with John, whom she finds attractive. Within the first 10 minutes of the date, she criticizes John's hair style and then complains about the movie they are going to see. After the movie, John gets tired of Mary's insults and takes her home.

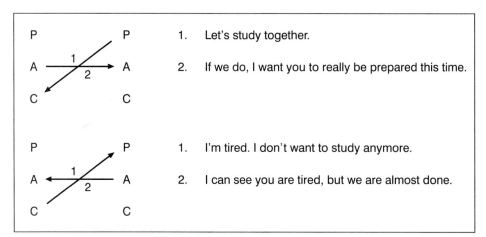

Figure 8.3
Crossed Transactions

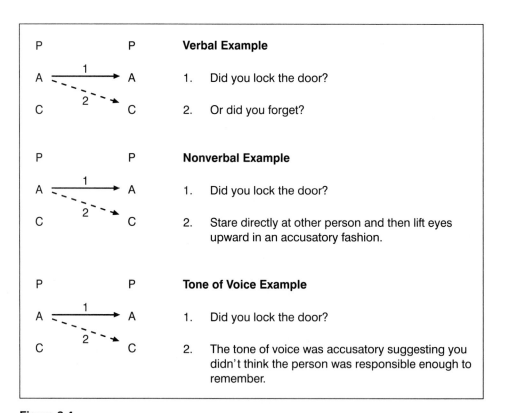

Figure 8.4
Ulterior Transactions
Note: Solid lines indicate overt messages; dotted lines indicate covert messages.

As he pulls up to her house, he proceeds to tell her off ("kicks her"), saying what an ungrateful person she is.

Although Mary initially feels hurt by John's comments, she will receive a payoff from her game. As she goes into the house, she can ask herself, "Why do I always get rejected? Things never work out. I guess dating isn't for me." The game therefore provides Mary with the payoff of having an excuse to avoid dating in the future. John also receives a payoff in that her rudeness made him feel free to "kick her."

Life Scripts.   A major part of personality structure relates to the life scripts that are created beginning in childhood. A life script is composed of parental messages, for example, a parent saying, "You're my darling angel", and complementary messages from other sources that may include fairy tales, movies, and literature. These messages create a role that a person identifies with and acts out throughout life. For instance, a person could identify with the Superman character and play the role of the "good person who comes to the rescue" in interpersonal relations. Another possible life script is identifying with the Cinderella character, which might lead to feelings of self-pity, being taken advantage of, and never having a chance to get out and have fun.

The Four Life Positions.   Berne (1961) said that in developing life scripts, people put themselves in the role of being "OK" or "not OK." They also tend to see others as basically friendly (OK) or hostile (not OK). The following four possible life positions represent combinations of how people define themselves and others.

1. "I'm OK, you're OK" represents people who are happy with themselves and others.

2. "I'm OK, you're not OK" suggests people who are suspicious of others; could have a false sense of superiority; or may be suffering from a mental disorder such as paranoia.

3. "I'm not OK, you're OK" indicates people who have a low self-concept and feel inadequate in relation to others.

4. "I'm not OK, you're not OK" implies people who have given up on themselves and life and may even be suicidal.

Strokes.   TA suggests that the basic motivation for social interaction is related to the need for human recognition or *strokes* (Dusay & Dusay, 1989). Strokes can be physical, verbal, or psychological and can be positive, negative, conditional, or unconditional. Positive strokes tend to communicate affection and appreciation and are essential to psychological development.

TA attempts to identify what types of strokes are important to clients and encourages them to take an active role in getting these strokes. For instance, after having a rough day, people could tell their partner that they need some extra strokes that evening.

The Counseling Process

Berne (1961) noted that the ultimate goals of TA are to help clients become autonomous, self-aware, and spontaneous, and have the capacity for intimacy. To promote these ultimate goals, some of the short-term goals of TA are that it helps clients

- Make new decisions, called *redecisions*, regarding their behavior and approach to life
- Rewrite their life script so they feel OK about themselves and can relate effectively with others
- Stop playing games that confuse communication and interfere with authentic interpersonal functioning
- Understand their three ego states of parent, adult, and child and how they can function in an effective and complementary fashion
- Avoid communicating in a manner that promotes crossed or ulterior transactions
- Learn how to obtain and give positive strokes

The counseling process in TA is educative in nature. The therapist takes on the role of teacher, providing clients information on how to use the TA concepts. TA emphasizes cognition in its approach by showing clients how they can use their intellect in applying TA principles to overcome mental disorders.

TA utilizes an active counseling process that emphasizes the importance of clients doing something outside of counseling via homework assignments. TA also relies on the use of a counseling contract, which the therapist and the client develop together. The contract is very specific in identifying the counseling goals, treatment plan, and roles and responsibilities for achieving these goals.

Techniques

The following techniques of TA relate to the key concepts described earlier.

- *Structural analysis* is a technique that helps clients become aware of their three ego states and learn to use them effectively.
- *Transactional analysis* helps clients learn to communicate with complementary transactions (e.g., adult to adult).
- *Script analysis* is a process that explores the type of life script the client has developed and how it can be rewritten in a more effective manner.
- *Analysis of games* involves clients identifying what games they play and how the games interfere with interpersonal functioning.

Summary and Evaluation

The fundamental goal of TA is to help the client develop as an autonomous individual. TA attempts to help clients achieve this goal by utilizing TA principles and concepts to restructure the functioning of the personality. It is an educative, cognitively oriented process whereby clients learn to apply TA principles so they can become self-therapists and lead autonomous, fully functioning lives. The strength of TA is that the concepts are written in easily understandable words, such as parent, adult, child, strokes, and games, instead of psychological jargon.

One weakness of TA is the possibility of focusing too much attention on self-analysis and intellectualization. When this occurs, clients may become self-absorbed and calculating in their relationships with others.

REALITY THERAPY

Background Information

William Glasser (b. 1925) is the founder of reality therapy. Glasser was a consulting psychiatrist for the Ventura School for Girls in California when he attempted his first large-scale implementation of reality therapy. His program was well-received, prompting an interest in the merits of reality therapy. It appeared to be a realistic approach, especially for clients who had a pattern of being irresponsible, for example, delinquent children and substance abusers.

In 1961 Glasser published his first book, *Mental Health or Mental Illness?* He took an antipsychiatry position, exploring how labels such as *mental disorder* or *schizophrenia* could be harmful to a client. Glasser has since persisted with this position by not recognizing the various mental disorders described in the DSM-III-R.

Glasser wrote several other books that contributed to the evolution of reality therapy. In 1965, he published *Reality Therapy*, which established his approach as a major force in counseling and psychotherapy. *In Schools Without Failure*, Glasser (1969) attempted to apply the principles of reality therapy to education. His more recent publications have attempted to broaden the theoretical base of his approach. In *Positive Addiction*, he described how positive addictions can be substituted for negative addictions (Glasser, 1976). In *Stations of the Mind*, he described the neurological and psychological basis of reality therapy (Glasser, 1981). In the mid-1980s, Glasser's interests began to focus on the role of control in mental health. Reality therapy has therefore been expanded to include control theory (Glasser, 1984, 1985). More recently, Glasser has applied the concepts of control theory to education (1986, 1990).

View of Human Nature

Glasser believes that the primary motivational force of people is directed at fulfilling basic physiological and psychological needs (Glasser, 1986). He emphasized the control that people have over fulfilling their needs and creating their own destiny.

Key Concepts

Glasser (1961, 1965, 1976, 1984) identified several key concepts that characterize reality therapy.

Success and Failure Identity.   A *success identity* results when a person is able to fulfill the psychological needs of loving and of feeling worthwhile to the self and others in a manner that does not interfere with the rights of others. When a person is unable to meet these basic psychological needs, a *failure identity* results. Failure identities are associated with problematic approaches to life such as delinquency and mental disorders.

Emphasis on Responsibility.   Reality therapy encourages clients to evaluate their behavior in terms of whether it is helping or hurting themselves and others. When people make an honest evaluation of their behavior, they can assume responsibility for it. Glasser believes that responsibility is critical to mental health and therefore a primary goal of reality therapy.

View of Psychopathology.   As mentioned earlier, Glasser (1961) set the stage for his antipsychiatry stance regarding mental disorders with the publication of his first book, *Mental Health or Mental Illness?* Since that publication, he has consistently maintained that there are no mental disorders and that the labeling process can do more harm than good.

In addition, Glasser (1984) believes that people are in control of their mental health. According to this theory, a person must behave in a manner associated with depression in order to be depressed. In addition, when clients say they are depressed, Glasser would suggest that they say instead, "I'm depressing." As a result, clients will realize the control they have over their mental health.

Positive Addiction.   Glasser's (1976) *Positive Addiction* was an innovative attempt to redefine the concept of addiction. Up to that time, the tendency was to understand addiction as something negative and to be avoided. Glasser observed that there were some positive behaviors, for example, jogging and meditation, that appeared addictive, since the person would become uncomfortable if these behaviors were not allowed to occur. Glasser (1976) suggested that people with a negative addiction such as alcoholism could try to discover a positive addiction that could become a substitute for it.

Control Theory.   Glasser (1984, 1985) noted that control theory is the central concept in reality therapy. This theory suggests that each person has a control system that serves to exert control over the environment. It represents a direct challenge to the traditional stimulus—response notion, which suggests that people's responses are conditioned by the environment. Glasser (1986) insisted that "what goes on in the outside would never 'stimulate' us to do anything. All of our behavior, simple to complex, is our best attempt to control ourselves to satisfy our needs. . . " (p. 17). Simply stated, people feel good when they believe they have control of their lives and feel bad when they feel their lives are out of control.

Glasser (1984, 1986) noted that the basic tenet of control theory is that all behavior results from people attempting to satisfy basic needs. These include the psychological needs that relate to survival and reproduction as well as the needs of belonging, love, power, freedom, and fun.

The Counseling Process

The primary goal of reality therapy is to help clients take effective control of their lives in a manner that is responsible and does not interfere with the rights of others.

The counseling process is educational in nature whereby clients learn how to apply control theory to effective living. Reality therapy contends that a positive counseling relationship will promote efficacy in the counseling process. In addition, reality therapy focuses on present behavior and makes no attempt to explore past events such as childhood trauma. It also does not recognize mental disorders, because they represent harmful labels.

Techniques

The main technique in contemporary reality therapy is teaching clients how to use control theory to meet their basic needs in a responsible manner (Glasser, 1984). Glasser (1980, 1984) set forth an eight-step approach for implementing reality therapy: create a relationship; focus on current behavior; invite clients to evaluate their behavior; make a plan of action; get a commitment; refuse to accept excuses; refuse to use punishment; and refuse to give up. Glasser (1984) suggested using a flexible approach when applying these steps and noted that the steps are interrelated and overlapping processes, rather than discrete steps.

Summary and Evaluation

Reality therapy is a popular short-term form of intervention that focuses on behavior that is occurring in the present. It is a particularly attractive type of treatment with people who have a pattern of acting irresponsibly, such as delinquent children, students with school-related behavioral problems, and people with substance abuse problems.

Although there is much merit to the role of control in human functioning, additional research and development on Glasser's control theory seems warranted. In its present form, it is difficult to understand exactly what it entails, how it functions, and more importantly how it can be applied in the counseling process.

CHAPTER SUMMARY

This chapter provided an overview of theories that emphasize the role of cognition and/or behavior in the counseling process. Cognitive-behavior approaches utilize an integration of concepts and counseling strategies. This is especially true for behavior therapy, rational-emotive therapy (RET), and cognitive therapy. These three theories have a common focus on the integral role that cognition plays in the development of mental disorders. They also incorporate behavioral techniques to teach the skills and behaviors necessary for a comprehensive treatment program. Subtle differences also exist among these three theories. Ellis' RET focuses on confronting and disputing the client's irrational and illogical thoughts. Beck's cognitive therapy is concerned with whether a client is making a functional or dysfunctional interpretation of an event. For Meichenbaum, the central issue in behavior therapy is the nature of the client's inner speech or self-talk. He contends that a client must learn self-talk that triggers effective coping mechanisms.

All the cognitive-behavior approaches discussed in this chapter, with the possible exception of transactional analysis, have strengths that should extend their appeal into the 1990s and beyond. First, they employ short-term approaches that can be used to treat specific mental disorders. These attributes will become increasingly attractive as health organizations and third-party insurers continue to press for cost-effective treatment programs. A second advantage is their strong foundation in research. In this regard, Mahoney and Lyddon (1988) noted that during the past decade, cognitive theories have dominated psychological research.

A potential disadvantage of most of these approaches is that they do not allow for exploring and working through early-life experiences that could be contributing to a client's emotional problem. The exception is transactional analysis, which identifies life scripts that develop during the formative years and influence personality formation.

SUGGESTED READING

Behavior Therapy

Bandura, A. (1977). Self-efficacy: Toward a unifying theory of behavioral change. *Psychological Review, 84*, 191–215.

Bandura, A. (1986). *Social foundations of thought and action: A social cognitive theory.* Englewood Cliffs: NJ: Prentice-Hall.

Franks, C. M., Wilson, G. T., Kendall, P., & Brownell, K. D. (1982). *Annual review of behavior therapy: Theory and practice* (Vol. 8). New York: Guilford Press.

Goldfried, M. R., & Davison, G. C. (1976). *Clinical behavior therapy.* New York: Holt, Rinehart, & Winston.

Meichenbaum, D. (1977). *Cognitive behavior modification.* Cambridge, MA: Ballinger.

Thorenson, C. E. (Ed.). (1980). *The behavior therapist.* Monterey, CA: Brooks/Cole.

Rational-Emotive Therapy

Beck, A. T. (1976). *Cognitive therapy and emotional disorders.* New York: International Universities Press.

Ellis, A. (1962). *Reason and emotion in psychotherapy.* New York: Lyle Stuart.

Ellis, A. (1973). *Humanistic psychotherapy: The rational-emotive approach.* New York: Julian Press.

Ellis, A., & Harper, R. (1975). *A new guide to rational living* (rev. ed.). Hollywood: Wilshire Books.

Cognitive Therapy

Beck, A. T. (1976). *Cognitive therapy and emotional disorders.* New York: International Universities Press.

Beck, A. T., & Emery, G. (1985). *Anxiety disorders and phobias: A cognitive perspective.* New York: Basic Books.

Beck, A. T., Rush, A. J., Shaw, B. F., & Emery, G. (1979). *Cognitive therapy of depression.* New York: Guilford Press.

Transactional Analysis

Berne, E. (1961). *Transactional analysis in psychotherapy.* New York: Grove Press.

Berne, E. (1964). *Games people play.* New York: Grove Press.

Goulding, R., & Goulding, M. (1978). *The power is the patient: A TA/Gestalt approach to psychotherapy*. San Francisco: TA Press.

Goulding, R., & Goulding, M. (1979). *Changing lives through redecision therapy*. New York: Brunner/Mazel.

Harris, T. (1967). *I'm OK, you're OK*. New York: Avon.

Reality Therapy

Glasser, W. (1965). *Reality therapy: A new approach to psychiatry*. New York: Harper & Row.

Glasser, W. (1976). *Positive addictions*. New York: Harper & Row.

Glasser, W. (1981). *Stations of the mind*. New York: Harper & Row.

Glasser, W. (1984). *Take effective control of your life*. New York: Harper & Row.

REFERENCES

Ayllon, T., & Azrin, N. (1968). *The token economy: A motivation system for therapy and rehabilitation*. New York: Appleton-Century-Crofts.

Bandura, A. (1974). Behavior theory and the models of man. *American Psychologist, 29*, 859–869.

Bandura, A. (1977a). *Social learning theory*. Englewood Cliffs, NJ: Prentice-Hall.

Bandura, A. (1977b). Self-efficacy: Toward a unifying theory of behavioral change. *Psychological Review, 84*, 191–215.

Bandura, A. (1982). Self-efficacy mechanism in human agency. *American Psychologist, 37*(2), 122–167.

Bandura, A. (1986). *Social foundations of thought and actions: A social cognitive theory*. Englewood Cliffs, NJ: Prentice-Hall.

Bandura, A. (1989). Human agency in social cognitive theory. *American Psychologist, 44*(9), 1175–1184.

Bandura, A., Reese, L., & Adams, N. E. (1982). Microanalysis of actions and fear arousal as a function of differential levels of perceived self-efficacy. *Journal of Personality and Social Psychology, 43*(1), 5–21.

Beck, A. T. (1963). Thinking and depression. 1. Idiosyncratic content and cognitive distortions. *Archives of General Psychiatry, 9*, 324–333.

Beck, A. T. (1964). Thinking and depression. 2. Theory and therapy. *Archives of General Psychiatry, 10*, 561–571.

Beck, A. T. (1967). *Depression: Clinical, experimental, and theoretical aspects*. New York: Hoeber.

Beck, A. T. (1976). *Cognitive therapy and emotional disorders*. New York: International Universities Press.

Beck, A. T., & Emery, G. (1985). *Anxiety disorders and phobias: A cognitive perspective*. New York: Basic Books.

Beck, A. T., & Weishaar, M. E. (1989). Cognitive therapy. In R. J. Corsini (Ed.), *Current psychotherapies* (4th ed., pp. 285–320). Itasca, IL: F. E. Peacock.

Berne, E. (1961). *Transactional analysis in psychotherapy*. New York: Grove Press.

Berne, E. (1964). *Games people play*. New York: Grove Press.

Blackburn, I. M., Bishop, S., Glen, A. I. M., Whalley, L. J., & Christie, J. E. (1981). The efficacy of cognitive therapy in depression: A treatment trial using cognitive therapy and pharmacotherapy, each alone and in combination. *British Journal of Psychiatry, 139*, 181–189.

Blackburn, I. M., Eunson, K. M., & Bishop, S. (1986). A two-year naturalistic follow-up of depressed patients treated with cognitive therapy, pharmacotherapy, and a combination of both. *Unpublished manuscript*. Royal Edinburgh Hospital, Scotland.

Brady, J. P. (1980). Some views on effective principles of psychotherapy. In M. Goldfried (Ed.)., *Cognitive Therapy and Research, 4*, 271–306.

David-Berman, J. (1988). Self-efficacy and depressive symptomatology in older adults: An exploratory study. *International Journal of Aging and Human Development, 27*(1), 35–43.

Dobson, K. S. (1989). A meta-analysis of the efficacy of cognitive therapy for depression. *Journal of Consulting and Clinical Psychology, 57*(3), 414–419.

Dunn, R. J. (1979). Cognitive modification with depression-prone psychiatric patients. *Cognitive Therapy and Research, 3*, 307–317.

Dusay, J., & Dusay, K. M. (1989). Transactional analysis. In R. Corsini (Ed.), *Current psychotherapies* (4th ed.). Itasca, IL: Peacock.

Ellis, A. (1962). *Reason and emotion in psychotherapy*. New York: Lyle Stuart.

Ellis, A. (1977). The basic clinical theory of rational-emotive therapy. In A. Ellis & R. Grieger (Eds.), *RET handbook of rational-emotive therapy* (pp. 3–34). New York: Springer.

Ellis, A. (1989). Rational-emotive therapy. In R. Corsini (Ed.)., *Current psychotherapies* (4th ed.). Itasca, IL: Peacock.

Ellis, A., & Harper, R. (1975). *A new guide to rational living* (rev. ed.). Hollywood: Wilshire Books.

Gintner, G. G., & Poret, M. K. (1987). Factors associated with maintenance and relapse following self-management training. *The Journal of Psychology, 122*(1), 79–87.

Glasser, W. (1961). *Mental health or mental illness?* New York: Harper & Row.

Glasser, W. (1965). *Reality therapy: A new approach to psychiatry*. New York: Harper & Row.

Glasser, W. (1969). *Schools without failure*. New York: Harper & Row.

Glasser, W. (1976). *Positive addiction*. New York: Harper & Row.

Glasser, W. (1980). Reality therapy. An explanation of the steps of reality therapy. In N. Glasser (Ed.), *What are you doing? How people are helped through reality therapy*. New York: Harper & Row.

Glasser, W. (1981). *Stations of the mind*. New York: Harper & Row.

Glasser, W. (1984). *Take effective control of your life*. New York: Harper & Row.

Glasser, W. (1985). *Control theory: A new explanation of how we control our lives*. New York: Harper & Row (Perennial Paperback).

Glasser, W. (1986). *Control theory in the classroom*. New York: Harper & Row.

Glasser, W. (1990). *The quality school*. New York: Harper & Row.

Gooding, P. R., & Glasgow, R. E. (1985). Self-efficacy and outcome expectations as predictors of controlling smoking status. *Cognitive Therapy and Research, 9*, 583–590.

Hollon, S. D., Evans, M. D., & DeRubeis, R. (1983). The cognitive-pharmacotherapy project: Study design, outcome, and clinical follow-up. Paper presented at the World Congress of Behavior Therapy. Washington, DC.

Johnson, E., Baker, S. B., Kapola, M., Kiselica, M. S., & Thompson, E. C. III. (1989). Counseling self-efficacy and counseling competency in preparaticum training. *Counselor Education and Supervision, 28*, 205–218.

Kaufer, F.H. (1975). Self-management methods. In F. H. Kaufer & A. P. Goldstein (Eds.), *Helping people change*. New York: Pergamon Press.

Kaufer, F.H. (1977). The many faces of self-control, or behavior modification changes its faces. In R. B. Stuart (Ed.), *Behavioral self-management*. New York: Brunner/Mazel.

Kazdin, A. E. (1978). *History of behavior modification: Experimental foundations of contemporary research*. Baltimore: University Park Press.

Kovacs, M., Rush, A. J., Beck, A. T., & Hollon, S. D. (1981). Depressed outpatients treated with cognitive therapy or pharmacotherapy. *Archives of General Psychiatry, 38*, 33–39.

Lee, C. (1982). Self-efficacy as a predictor of performance in competitive gymnastics. *Journal of Sports Psychology, 4*, 405–409.

Mahoney, M. J. (1974). *Cognitive and behavior modification*. Cambridge, MA: Ballinger.

Mahoney, M. J., & Lyddon, W. J. (1988). Recent developments in cognitive approaches to counseling and psychotherapy. *The Counseling Psychologist, 16*(2), 190–234.

Maldonado, A. (1982). Terapia de conducta y depresion: Un analisis experimental de los modelos conductal y cognitivo (Cognitive and behavioral therapy for depression. Its efficacy and interaction with pharmacological treatment). *Revista de psicologia general y aplicada, 37*(1), 31–56.

McAuley, E. (1985). Modeling and self-efficacy: A test of Bandura's model. *Journal of Sports Psychology, 7*, 283–295.

Meichenbaum, D. H. (1972). Cognitive modifications of test-anxious college students. *Journal of Consulting and Clinical Psychology, 39*, 370–390.

Meichenbaum, D. (1977). *Cognitive-behavior modification: An integrative approach*. New York: Plenum.

Murphy, G. E., Simons, A. D., Wetzel, R. D., & Lustman, P. J. (1983). Cognitive therapy and pharmacotherapy: Singly and together in the treatment of depression. *Archives of General Psychiatry, 41*, 33–41.

Nicki, R. M., Remington, R. M., & MacDonald, G. A. (1984). Self-efficacy, nicotine fading/self-monitoring and cigarette-smoking behavior. *Behavior Research and Therapy, 22*, 477–485.

Nietzel, M. T., Russell, R. L., Hemmings, K. A., & Gretter, M. L. (1987). The clinical significance of psychotherapy for unipolar depression: A meta-analytic approach to social comparison. *Journal of Consulting and Clinical Psychology, 55*, 156–161.

Nystul, M. S. (1985). An interview with Dr. Albert Ellis. *Individual Psychology: The Journal of Adlerian Theory, Research and Practice, 41*(2), 243–254.

Pavlov, I. P. (1906). The scientific investigation of the psychical faculties of processes in the higher animals. *Science, 24*, 613–619.

Raskin, P. A., & Israel, A. C. (1981). Sex role imitation in children: Effects of sex of child, sex of model, and sex role appropriateness of modeled behavior. *Sex Roles, 7*(11), 1067–1077.

Rimm, D. C., & Cunningham, H. M. (1985). Behavior therapies. In S. J. Lynn & J. P. Garske (Eds.), *Contemporary psychotherapies*. Columbus, OH: Merrill/Macmillan.

Rush, A. J., Beck, A. T., Kovacs, M., & Hollon, S. (1977). Comparative efficacy of cognitive therapy and imipramine in the treatment of depressed outpatients. *Cognitive Therapy and Research, 1*, 17–37.

Simons, A. D., Murphy, G. E., Levine, J. L., & Wetzel, R. D. (1986). Cognitive therapy and pharmacotherapy: Sustained improvement over one year. *Archives of General Psychiatry, 43*, 43–48.

Skinner, B. F. (1938). *The behavior of organisms*. New York: Appleton-Century-Crofts.

Skinner, B. F. (1953). *Science and human behavior*. New York: Macmillan.

Skinner, B. F. (1961). *Cumulative record*. New York: Appleton-Century-Crofts.

Swan, G. E., & MacDonald, M. D. (1978). Behavior therapy in practice: A national survey of behavior therapists. *Behavior Therapy, 9*, 799–807.

Teasdale, J. D., Fennell, M. J. V., Hibbert, G. A., & Amies, P. L. (1984). Cognitive therapy for major depressive disorder in primary care. *British Journal of Psychiatry, 144*, 400–406.

Weinberg, R. S., Hughes, H. H., Critelli, J. W., England, R., & Jackson, A. (1984). Effects of pre-existing and manipulated self-efficacy on weight loss in a self-control program. *Journal of Research in Personality, 18*, 352–358.

Weinrach, S. G. (1988). Cognitive therapist: A dialogue with Aaron Beck. *Journal of Counseling and Development, 67*(3), 159–164.

Wilson, G. T. (1989). Behavior therapy. In R. J. Corsini (Ed.), *Current psychotherapies* (4th ed.). Itasca, IL: Peacock.

Wolpe, J. (1958). *Psychotherapy by reciprocal inhibition*. Stanford, CA: Stanford University Press.

Wolpe, J. (1973). *The practice of behavior therapy* (2nd ed.). New York: Pergamon Press.

PART

3

Counseling Specialties

In Part One and Part Two, I provided a conceptual overview of counseling and its theoretical foundations. In Part Three, I describe four counseling specialties: marriage and family counseling, child counseling, group counseling, and career counseling. Each of these specialties reflects the art and science of counseling. For example, child counselors practice the art of counseling when they are able to adjust their approach to a child. Counselors in each specialty implement the science of counseling by using the research and theoretical information available on a wide range of topics such as cognitive, physical, and emotional development of children. Chapters 9 through 12 provide an overview of the major issues associated with marriage and family counseling, child counseling, group counseling, and career counseling as well as a description of their unique treatment approaches.

CHAPTER NINE

Marriage and Family Counseling

CHAPTER OVERVIEW

This chapter provides an overview of the field of marriage and family counseling. Highlights of the chapter include

- The evolution of marriage and family counseling
- Theoretical foundations including systems theory and the family life cycles
- Marriage counseling
- Family counseling
- Evaluation of marriage and family counseling

EVOLUTION OF MARRIAGE AND FAMILY COUNSELING

The field of marriage and family counseling has evolved over the last 60 years (Everett, 1990). Goldenberg and Goldenberg (1991) identified key events associated with this evolution, and I have incorporated their observations into the following overview.

Psychoanalysis.   Nathan Ackerman's (1937) work on the family as an important psychosocial unit set the stage for the adaptation of Freudian concepts to family counseling. Prior to Ackerman's work, psychoanalysis was strictly a process of individual psychotherapy.

General Systems Theory.   Ludwig Von Bertalanffy developed general systems theory in the 1940s. This theory contended that seemingly unrelated phenomena represent interrelated facets of a larger system (Von Bertalanffy, 1968). General systems theory was later applied to marriage and family counseling, providing an important theoretical foundation.

Research on Schizophrenia.   Since the late 1940s numerous studies have been conducted to investigate the relationship between family dynamics and schizophrenia. Although this massive research effort has determined nothing conclusive as yet, it has drawn much interest to family therapy as a potentially useful treatment modality.

Marriage Counseling and Child Guidance.   Marriage counseling and child guidance represent the first counseling approaches recognizing that problems relate to both intrapersonal (within the person) and interpersonal (between people) forces. The inclusion of the interpersonal perspective prompted the necessity for counselors to work with the parent and child or husband and wife together in a counseling session.

Group Therapy.   Around 1910, Morino developed what can be considered the earliest uses of group processes in counseling. Since then, many other forms of group counseling have evolved. The evolution of group counseling influenced marriage and family counseling in terms of how marriage and family counselors could use effective group-leadership skills; how the knowledge of group process could contribute to the understanding of interactions between family members; and how the concept of "the group" as a change agent could be applied to "the family" as a change agent.

Changing Family Structure.   The traditional intact family characterized by a wage-earning father, a homemaker mother, and biological children is now in the minority. Current family structures in the United States represent a wide range of alternative family systems that include single parents rearing children; blended families, where the husband and wife live with children from a previous marriage; cohabiting couples, or unmarried individuals living together for an extended period of time; and gay couples living together rearing children.

Numerous problems emerge as family members attempt to adjust to changing family structures. For example, a family often experiences financial problems following a divorce (especially women with children). Marriage and family counseling has to some degree evolved as a means of assisting with these common problems of modern family life.

The field of marriage and family counseling is both a professional discipline and a specialized counseling strategy practiced by various members of the helping profession. The two main professional organizations for marriage and family counselors are the American Association for Marriage and Family Therapy (AAMFT) and the American Counseling Association (ACA)—formerly known as the American Association for Counseling and Development (AACD). The AAMFT has a much longer history; it was originally called the American Association of Marriage Counselors in 1942. As of 1990, there were approximately 15,000 members (Everett, 1990). In 1989, the ACA established division status to the International Association of Marriage and Family Counselors. As of 1991, there were approximately 4,000 members.

The AAMFT and ACA have done much to promote the professionalism of marriage and family counseling. Some of these activities have been to establish ethical codes (see Chapter 13 and Appendix B) and promote state licensure in marriage and family counseling. By 1990, 18 states had licensure laws regarding marriage and family counseling (Cummings, 1990).

THEORETICAL FOUNDATIONS

Several important theoretical foundations have contributed to marriage and family counseling. Theories described in this section include systems theory and the family life cycle.

Systems Theory

Systems theory is the foundation and integrating force in marriage and family counseling (Brown-Standridge, 1986; Everett, 1990). The systems perspective is based on the principle of circular causality (Everett, 1990). According to this principle, actions caused by one family member influence the actions of all other family members, affecting the functioning of the family system, including the person who was responsible for the initial action (Goldenberg & Goldenberg, 1991). In addition, systems theory focuses on the function of the system versus the individual. From this perspective, problematic individuals are understood in terms of family interaction patterns and are therefore conceptualized within the social context in which their problems occurred (Hazelrigg, Cooper, & Borduin, 1987).

Key Concepts

Goldenberg and Goldenberg (1991) and Sperry and Carlson (1991) identified key concepts associated with systems theory. The following overview of these concepts incorporates their descriptions.

Organization.   The organizational structure of the family system can be understood in terms of wholeness, hierarchies, and boundaries (Gurman & Kniskern, 1981). *Wholeness* relates to the recurrent patterns reflected in the family system as opposed to individual elements of the family (Sperry & Carlson, 1991). Wholeness suggests that the family is more than the sum of its parts, with the family system having a life of its own (Everett, 1990). *Hierarchies* involve the different levels of subsystems that make up the family system, for example, parents, siblings, and relatives. *Boundaries* are "the invisible lines of demarcation that separate a system, subsystem, or individual from outside surrounding" (Goldenberg & Goldenberg, 1991, p. 45). Extreme separateness between family members can occur when boundaries are rigid, and extreme togetherness is associated with diffuse boundaries (Sperry & Carlson, 1991).

Communication.   All behaviors, verbal and nonverbal, are considered important aspects of communication. Systems theory also attempts to identify and assess familial communication patterns.

Family Rules.   Families are governed by rules that influence how family members interact and how well the family functions. For example, an alcoholic family might have an unwritten rule that no one may talk about a family member's drinking problem.

Family Homeostasis.   Family homeostasis is the tendency of family systems to maintain equilibrium or restore balance if the system becomes disrupted. Family systems can resist change in an attempt to maintain homeostasis.

Information Processing.   Information processing involves the exchange of information between the family and the outside world. It provides essential feedback for families to make necessary alterations in functioning. A family system is considered open if there is sufficient opportunity for information processing and closed if there is insufficient opportunity. Healthy family systems are neither too open nor too closed (Sperry and Carlson, 1991).

Change.   Watzlawick, Weakland, and Fisch (1974) noted that there can be first-order or second-order change. First-order changes are alterations that leave the organizational structure unchanged, whereas second-order changes result in fundamental change to the system's organization (Sperry & Carlson, 1991).

The Functional Family System.   It would be presumptuous to set forth a definitive description of what constitutes a functional family, since any definition would vary from culture to culture and family to family. Therefore, I present findings from the following studies on this topic with that caution.

Fisher and Sprinkle (1978) surveyed 310 members of AAMFT in terms of what they believed constituted a healthy family. The results of the survey suggested that the fully functioning family is one in which the family members feel valued, supported, and safe. In addition the researchers noted that "They can express themselves without fear of judgment, knowing that opinions will be attended to carefully and emphatically. Family members are also able to negotiate when necessary" (Fisher & Sprinkle, 1978, p. 9).

Ebert (1978) and Stinnet and DeFrain (1985) identified many additional characteristics of healthy family functioning. These characteristics are summarized as follows.

- *Sharing of feelings.* Family members feel free to openly share positive and negative feelings with each other.

- *Understanding of feelings*. All members of the family sense that they are being understood by the other family members.
- *Acceptance of individual differences*. Individual differences among family members are permitted and even encouraged so all family members can develop their unique potential.
- *Highly developed sense of caring*. Family members communicate a sense of love and caring to each other. This contributes to family members feeling valued and having a sense of belonging within the family.
- *Cooperation*. Each family member is willing to work in a cooperative manner to help the family function effectively.
- *Sense of humor*. Family members are capable of laughing at themselves and joking about family events.
- *Provision for survival and safety needs*. The basic needs of food, shelter, and clothing are provided.
- *Nonadversary problem solving*. Problems are usually solved in a democratic fashion.
- *Overall philosophy*. The family has a set of values that provides a structure for family living.
- *Commitment*. Family members are committed to each other's well-being.
- *Expression of appreciation*. Family members regularly express appreciation to each other.
- *Communication*. Good communication patterns are established between family members.
- *Time spent together*. Family members spend time together to foster positive relationships and a sense of family unity.
- *Spirituality*. Family members can draw strength from their spirituality.
- *Coping skills*. The family has the coping skills necessary to meet the challenges of family life.

These characteristics collectively suggest that a functional family system creates a positive environment for individuals to grow and develop. It is characterized by love, caring, and mutual respect. Family members can effectively communicate with each other and be responsive to forces outside the family. The family has the necessary coping mechanisms to be successful in meeting the developmental tasks of family life.

Evaluation of Systems Theory

Systems theory has added an important dimension to the counseling literature. It has contributed to the understanding of how systems function and their influence on psychological functioning.

Enns (1988) and Epstein and Loos (1989) also identified five weaknesses of systems theory. First, systems theory has been accused of overlooking the importance of intrapsychic issues; ignoring clients' emotions and affect; and failing to address issues of responsibility (Golann, 1987; Nichols, 1987a, 1987b). Second, feminists contend that systems theory does not take into account important familial issues such as power, equality, and sex roles function (Enns, 1988; Goldner, 1985). Third, the systems perspective does not adequately consider factors that occur outside the family system, such as at a job or in school (Elkaim, 1982). Fourth, the systems approach is not realistic in that it attempts to "heal the cracked bones of a whole number of people rather than stop the hand of those delivering the blows" (Elkaim, 1982, p. 345). Fifth, systems concepts and practices are in need of empirical validation (Liddle, 1982; Shields, 1986).

The Family Life Cycle

Duvall (1957) proposed an eight-stage model for understanding family life, which provides another important theoretical foundation for marriage and family counselors. The eight stages begin with marriage and end with the death of both spouses. The model identifies developmental tasks associated with each stage as well as the approximate number of years that each stage will last. Table 9.1 provides an overview of Duvall's family life cycle model.

More recently Duvall's family life cycle model has been integrated into theories of marriage and family counseling (Carter & McGoldrick, 1988; Haley, 1971, 1973; Kovacs, 1988; Solomon, 1973). Carter and McGoldrick (1988) noted that Duvall's model could be useful for practitioners to identify past, present, and future developmental tasks associated with family life. Solomon (1973) suggested that failure to master the developmental tasks associated with a particular stage could have adverse effects on family's functioning. Wilcoxon (1985) also noted that marriage and family counselors could play an important role in assisting families to develop the necessary coping skills associated with particular developmental tasks.

Haley (1973) provided additional information on the therapeutic implications of the family life cycle. He noted that the transition points between stages were the most stressful times for the family and that familial problems typically occurred during these periods. In addition, Haley (1973) contended that a central therapeutic task is to help families resolve developmental issues so they can move forward in the family life cycle.

Evaluation of the Family Life Cycle

The family life cycle is a valuable model for understanding how family life proceeds through time. It has also been used extensively in family research, including how it can be integrated with systems concepts (Kovacs, 1988). In addition, the family life cycle provides a focus for counseling by identifying developmental tasks that require assistance from the counselor.

Goldenberg and Goldenberg (1991) also identified weaknesses of the family life cycle model. They pointed out that it did not take into account the wide array of contemporary family structures that result from divorce and remarriage. In addition, Goldenberg and Goldenberg (1991) noted that Duvall's model does not provide

Table 9.1
Duvall's Model of the Family Life Cycle

Stage of the Family Life Cycle	Positions in the Family	Stage-Critical Family Developmental Tasks	Approximate Number of Years in Stage
1. Married Couples (without children)	Wife Husband	Establishing a mutually satisfying marriage. Adjusting to pregnancy and the promise of parenthood.	2 years
2. Childbearing families (oldest child birth–30 months)	Wife-mother Husband-father Infant daughter or son or both	Giving birth to, adjusting to, and encouraging the development of infants.	2–5 years
3. Families with preschool children (oldest child 30 mos–6 years)	Wife-mother Husband-father Daughter-sister Son-brother	Adapting to the critical needs and interests of preschool children. Coping with energy depletion and lack of privacy as parents.	3–5 years
4. Families with school children (oldest child 6–13 years)	Wife-mother Husband-father Daughter-sister Son-brother	Fitting into the community of school-age families. Encouraging children's educational achievements.	7 years
5. Families with teen-agers (oldest child 13–20 years)	Wife-mother Husband-father Daughter-sister Son-brother	Balancing freedom with responsibility as teen-agers mature. Establishing postparental interests and careers as parents of growing children.	7 years
6. Families as launching centers (first child gone to last child leaving home)	Wife-mother-grandmother Husband-father-grandfather Daughter-sister-aunt Son-brother-uncle	Releasing young adults into work, military service, college, marriage, with appropriate rituals and assistance. Maintaining a supportive home base.	8 years
7. Middle-aged parents (empty nest to retirement)	Wife-mother-grandmother Husband-father-grandfather	Rebuilding the marriage relationship. Maintaining kin ties with older and younger generations.	15± years
8. Aging family members (retirement to death of both spouses)	Widow/widower Wife-mother-grandmother Husband-father-grandfather	Coping with bereavement and living alone. Closing the family home or adapting it to aging needs. Adjusting to retirement.	10–15± years

Note. From *Marriage and Family Development* (5th ed.), by E. Duvall, 1977, Philadelphia, PA: Lippincott. Copyright 1977 by Lippincott. Reprinted by permission.

enough information on the transition points between stages, which can be especially problematic for families.

MARRIAGE COUNSELING

Marital problems rank highest as the reason for referral to mental health services (Sperry & Carson, 1991). Sholevar (1985) estimated that 75% of all clients entering counseling are seeking assistance with marital difficulties, as well as help with other problems. Goldenberg and Goldenberg (1991) noted that people tend to seek marriage counseling when a family system is experiencing a state of disequilibrium due to problems such as infidelity, sexual incompatibility, disagreements over child-rearing practices, concerns of divorce, ineffective communication, and issues relating to power and control.

The Counseling Process

Marriage counseling tends to be brief, problem-centered, and pragmatic (Goldenberg & Goldenberg, 1991). The most popular form of marriage counseling currently is *conjoint marriage counseling* (Nichols & Everett, 1986), which involves the counselor working with the couple together. Humphrey (1983) described a slight modification of the conjoint session, suggesting that the counselor see each individual separately before the conjoint session. He contends that when the individuals are seen separately, they will more openly discuss sensitive issues such as an extramarital affair. When this approach is used, the counselor must establish a clear policy regarding confidentiality. The counselor must clarify with the client what information from individual sessions can be introduced during conjoint sessions, and how it will be conveyed.

The actual process of marriage counseling will vary according to the theoretical orientation of the counselor. Marriage counselors utilize a wide variety of counseling theories, such as psychoanalytic, cognitive-behavioral, strategic, and structural (Sperry & Carlson, 1991). To a large degree these theories can be considered adaptations of those utilized in individual counseling, as discussed in Chapters 6, 7, and 8, and those associated with family counseling, as presented later in this chapter.

There also appear to be some commonalities in marriage counseling. Sperry and Carlson (1991) noted that all approaches utilize a systems perspective. Goldenberg and Goldenberg (1991) suggested that marriage counselors "address the affective, cognitive, and behavioral aspects of the husband-wife relationship within the context of marital and family systems" (p. 68).

In addition, several integrative models of marriage counseling have been developed that provide a broad, flexible approach. For example, Glick, Clarkin, and Kessler (1987) and Nichols (1988) contended that marriage counseling has three stages: early, middle, and termination. Nichols' (1988) model has three tasks associated with the early stage: establishing a positive relationship, assessment and goal setting, and providing immediate assistance to the couple. The middle stage is primarily concerned with using intervention strategies to resolve counseling goals. The termination stage allows for the transition toward termination once the counseling goals have been achieved.

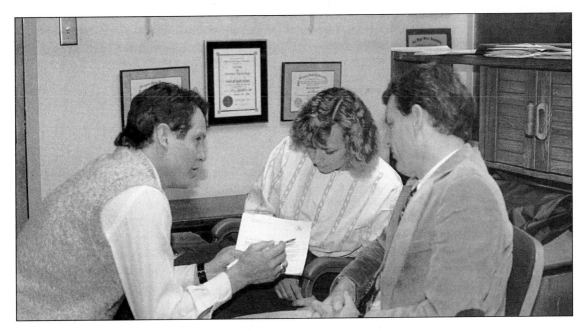

Marriage counseling can involve reviewing marital assessment inventories.

Marital Assessment

Marital assessment is one aspect of the counseling process that deserves special attention. Comprehensive assessment is essential in marriage and family counseling (Sperry & Carlson, 1991), since 83% of treatment failures are associated with inadequate assessment (Coleman, 1985). Sperry (1989) suggested that comprehensive assessment in marriage counseling involves assessing the situation, the system, each spouse, and the suitability of the couple for marriage counseling. A description of these four factors follows.

1. *The situation.* Assessing the situation involves identifying stressors, precipitating factors to marital discord, and other factors that affect the situation.

2. *The system.* Systems theory can be used to assess the marital system to gain an understanding of its functional and dysfunctional characteristics.

3. *Each spouse.* Each spouse is evaluated to determine the level of physical and psychological health and the personality style.

4. *Suitability for treatment.* It is also important to determine if marriage counseling is appropriate for a couple. Beutler (1983) suggested that clients need to be motivated to change and have reasonable expectations regarding outcomes to be suitable for marriage counseling.

Commonly used assessment procedures include the clinical interview in marriage counseling (Framo, 1981); the use of enactment, which involves getting clients to act out conflicts or problems during a counseling session (Nichols, 1988); and the use of standardized tests designed for marriage counseling (Boen, 1988).

Marital assessment instruments have become popular in marriage counseling. These instruments are especially useful during the initial counseling sessions, but they can also be used throughout the counseling process as the need arises (Boen, 1988). Boen (1988) provided an overview of the most widely used marital assessment instruments.

Stuart's Couples Precounseling Inventory (SCPI).   The SCPI was developed by Stuart (1983). It identifies 15 areas where the couple is satisfied or dissatisfied, for example, child-rearing practices or sexual practices. The SCPI also identifies the amount of commitment each member has to the relationship, and which individual has more to gain or lose by maintaining the relationship.

Russell and Madsen's Marriage Counseling Report (MCR).   The MCR was developed by Russell and Madsen (1985). It is based on the 16 Personality Factors Questionnaire, which was developed by Raymond Cattell, as discussed in Chapter 3. The MCR provides information on the personalities of each spouse; how these personalities may be contributing to marital difficulties; and how the marriage may be exacerbating psychological problems of the spouses.

Taylor-Johnson Temperament Analysis (TJTA).   The TJTA (Taylor & Morrison, 1984) represents a revision of the Johnson Temperament Analysis developed by R. H. Johnson in 1941. It "can be used to show where a couple are similar or different to the normal population as well as where they are similar or different to each other and the degree of understanding they have for each other's personality characteristics" (Boen, 1988, p. 485).

Snyder's Marital Satisfaction Inventory (MSI).   The MSI was developed by Snyder (1981). It identifies basic areas where the couple is satisfied or dissatisfied, for example, communication or problem solving. The MSI is particularly useful for couples who do not know where to begin in terms of dealing with their concerns.

Skills-Based Marriage Counseling

Sperry and Carlson (1991) described a skill-based approach to marriage counseling adapted from Dinkmeyer and Carlson's (1984) earlier work on marital enrichment. It is a practical approach that could be utilized by practitioners of different theoretical orientations. The skill-based approach to marriage counseling evolved from the following principles: (a) Healthy productive marriages require time and commitment; (b) The skills necessary for a satisfying marriage can be learned; (c) Change requires each partner to assume responsibility: (d) Positive feelings such as love and caring can return with behavior change; and (e) Small changes can help bring about big changes.

According to Sperry and Carlson (1991, p. 45), the 10 skills that are believed to contribute to effective marriages are that both partners

1. Individually accept responsibility for their behavior and self-esteem

2. Identify and align their personal and marital goals

3. Choose to encourage each other

4. Communicate their feelings with honesty and openness

5. Listen emphatically when feelings are expressed

6. Seek to understand the factors that influence their relationship

7. Demonstrate that they accept and value each other

8. Choose thoughts, words, and actions that support the positive goals of their marriage

9. Solve marital conflicts together

10. Commit themselves to the ongoing process of maintaining an equal marriage

The skill-based approach to marriage counseling is educative in that it provides the couple opportunities to learn how to use the 10 skills associated with effective marriages. For example, the couple can learn how to use some of these skills, for example, in a four-step approach to conflict resolution. The four steps are: show mutual respect; pinpoint the real issue; seek areas of agreement; and mutually participate in decisions. Additional guidelines for conflict resolution include: be specific and oriented in the present and future; use good communication skills such as "I" messages and active listening; avoid using absolutes; and avoid attempting to determine who was right or wrong (Sperry & Carlson, 1991).

FAMILY COUNSELING

No clear definition of family counseling has emerged. Its hallmark, however, is that the process involves problems experienced by an individual that seem to indicate more fundamental problems within the family system (Horne & Ohlsen, 1982). The systems perspective continues to characterize family counseling in that family counselors treat problems within a relationship context rather than working separately with individuals (Goldenberg & Goldenberg, 1991).

This section first provides an overview of five prominent theories used by family counselors, as summarized in Table 9.2. Following this overview, I present a discussion of the counseling process in family counseling.

Psychodynamic Family Counseling

Ackerman (1937, 1956, 1966, 1970) is credited with integrating Freud's psychoanalytic theory into family counseling. His model emphasized the importance of both intrapersonal and interpersonal forces. Ackerman (1970) viewed the family as a system of interacting personalities, with each family member representing a subsystem. The primary aim of Ackerman's approach is to promote change and growth by altering patterns of communication, resolving pathological inner conflicts, and helping family members define their roles in a complementary manner (Goldenberg & Goldenberg, 1991).

More recently Framo (1981, 1982) integrated object relations theory (see Chapter 6) into psychodynamic family counseling. The basic premise of object relations theory is that the fundamental motivation in life is the drive to satisfy object relations, for example, satisfying relationships (Goldenberg & Goldenberg, 1991). In addition,

Table 9.2
Theories of Family Counseling

Theory	Founder(s)	Key Concepts	Process	Goals
Psychodynamic Family Counseling	Ackerman, Framo	Intrapsychic forces are believed to play a key role in family dysfunction; object relations such as meaningful relationships are primary motivational force in life.	Focuses on intrapersonal and interpersonal forces (e.g., strengthening the ego, clarifying roles, helping clients obtain more satisfying relationships).	Promote change and growth by altering patterns of communication; resolving pathological inner conflicts; and defining roles of family members in complementary fashion.
Experiential Family Counseling	Satir Whitaker, Bumberry	Self-actualization, awareness, choice, and responsibility.	Free family members to move toward self-actualization; experiential focus; relates to here-and-now rather than past issues.	Promote clear communication; help family members become authentic–autonomous individuals; promote a positive family climate.
Structural Family Counseling	Minuchin	Systemic concepts such as boundaries and reframing.	Counselor joins the family to alter structure of the interaction between family members.	Clarify boundaries; increase flexibility of family interactions; modify dysfunctional family structure.
Strategic Family Counseling	Haley, Madanes	Communication patterns and power struggles determine the nature of the relationships between family members.	Attempts to directly resolve presenting problems with little attempt to provide insight from past events.	Resolve symptomology of family members by redefining relationship between family members.
Adlerian/Dreikursian Family Counseling	Adler, Dreikurs	Family constellation, mutual respect, goals of misbehavior, use of consequences, encouragement, communication.	Educational focus to help parents learn skills to foster positive parent–child relationships.	Understand the dynamics of problems occurring within the family and promote positive parent–child relationships.

object relations theory contends that intrapsychic conflicts that evolved from the family of origin play a key role in relationship difficulties. As part of the overall treatment program, psychodynamic family counselors may conduct individual counseling, couples counseling, and family counseling that includes members of the client's family of origin (Goldenberg & Goldenberg, 1991).

Experiential Family Counseling

The theoretical origins of experiential family counseling can be traced to the humanistic-existential schools of counseling, as discussed in Chapter 7. Satir (1967, 1972, 1982), Whitaker (1976, 1977), and Bumberry (Whitaker & Bumberry, 1988) are credited with incorporating the major concepts of the humanistic-existential schools into family counseling. The basic premise of this approach is that if the individual family member can be freed to move toward self-actualization, then the family will function effectively. The goals of experiential family counseling include promoting clear communication among family members; helping family members become authentic, autonomous individuals; assisting the family in developing a positive family climate characterized by encouragement, caring, and intimacy; and promoting awareness of choice and responsibility in family members.

The counseling process in experiential family counseling focuses on the here-and-now instead of dealing with problems from the past. The emphasis within counseling is on experiencing rather than intellectualizing. In this regard, the counselor uti-

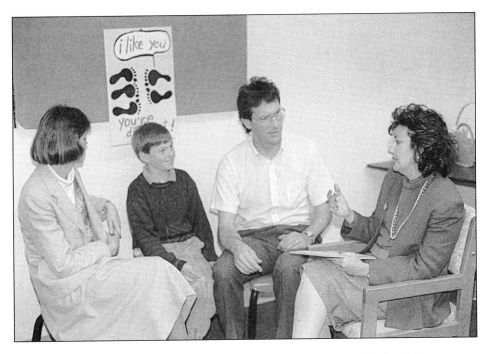

Family counseling can help family members enhance their communication skills.

lizes a variety of techniques such as sculpting, confrontation, communication skill training, and Gestalt exercises to help family members become aware of their feelings. For example, the technique of *sculpting* involves having one person physically arrange the other family members to create a "sculpture." The person creates the sculpture by using space and form to represent perceptions of family relationships, for instance, placing a child between the mother and father to symbolize interference between the marital dyad. All family members are then invited to discuss the creation. Typical themes that result from such discussions are closeness, isolation, alignment, intimacy, and power.

Structural Family Counseling

Salvador Minuchin (1974, 1984) is credited with developing structural family counseling. The role of the counselor in this approach is to join the family in a position of leadership. The goals are to clarify boundaries between family members; increase flexibility of family interactions; and modify dysfunctional family structure (Goldenberg & Goldenberg, 1991).

Minuchin (1974, 1984) developed several innovative concepts that have played a key role in the evolution of systems theory (Goldenberg & Goldenberg, 1991). One example is the concept of *boundaries*, which are the unwritten rules that help define roles and functions of family members. Boundaries determine what will be allowed to occur between family members, and they can insure privacy or allow for intimacy. Family dysfunctioning can result when boundaries become rigid, confused, or conflicting.

Another concept that Minuchin (1974, 1984) developed is *reframing*, a family counseling technique to help the family see things from a more positive perspective. For example, an adolescent might complain that his mother spends too much time working. Using the technique of reframing, the counselor might help the adolescent focus on the fact that his mother enjoys her job and that it makes her a pleasant person to be with.

Strategic Family Counseling

Jay Haley (1963, 1971, 1973, 1976, 1980) and more recently individuals such as Madanes (1981, 1984) played key roles in the development of strategic family counseling. This approach focuses on communication patterns between family members and views intrapsychic forces as unimportant. Haley (1976, 1980) contended that the relationship between family members can be determined by the manner in which they communicate and how they position themselves in terms of power issues.

This approach is considered strategic because it focuses on resolving the presenting problem directly, with little attempt to provide insight from past events. To resolve the presenting problem, counselors use procedures oriented to concrete actions including homework assignments, teaching new skills, and advice giving. They also use paradoxical techniques, which involve prescribing the symptom. For example, if a husband and wife have a habit of yelling at each other, the counselor might ask them to spend 10 minutes yelling at one another every day.

Strategic family counseling can be a powerful and effective form of counseling. Strategies such as advice giving and paradoxical techniques must be used carefully, however, or they may do more harm than good to the family (Nichols, 1984).

Adlerian Family Counseling

Alfred Adler's school of psychology and the later writings of Rudolph Dreikurs (see Chapter 6) have been applied to a variety of helping processes including family counseling and parent education. Adlerian family counseling focuses on individual family members as well as the overall functioning of the family. The main goal of this approach is to improve parent-child relationships (Lowe, 1982).

The role and function of the counselor are to help parents learn principles and understand the dynamics of problems occurring within the family (Lowe, 1982). The approach is therefore educative in nature. In this process, the counselor identifies basic mistakes; teaches the parents concepts that will help them understand misbehavior; helps parents deal effectively with discipline problems; and assists in establishing positive parent-child relations.

The key concepts of this approach are family constellation, goals of misbehavior, use of natural and logical consequences, encouragement, and communication. Although I discussed these Adlerian concepts in Chapter 6, I present them here in light of the family counseling approach.

Family Constellation.   The family constellation relates to the overall structure of the family. Particular attention is paid to how birth-order characteristics can be used to understand the personality of the children (e.g., first-born children tend to be bossy).

Goals of Misbehavior.   Children's misbehavior is seen as movement toward one of four goals of misbehavior: attention, power, revenge, and display of inadequacy. Additional goals of misbehavior for teen-agers include excitement, peer acceptance, and superiority (Dinkmeyer & McKay, 1990).

Use of Natural and Logical Consequences.   Parents are taught to use natural and logical consequences as opposed to punishment to discipline children. Among the advantages of this approach over punishment are that consequences are more logically tied to misbehavior; promote responsibility in the child; and minimize animosity between the parent and child.

Encouragement.   Parents are taught to use encouragement with their child. Offering encouragement focuses on effort and helps build self-esteem and confidence.

Communication Skills.   Parents learn how to use effective communication skills with their child. A philosophy of mutual respect is essential for effective communication. When parents respect the child, they will tend to communicate empathic understanding of the child's point of view. Parents may also be taught listening skills and problem-solving skills, which can be used to help their child deal with personal problems.

Parent education can be beneficial to all parents.

The concepts utilized in Adlerian family counseling have also been incorporated into parent education programs such as Dinkmeyer and McKay's (1989, 1990) Systematic Training for Effective Parenting (STEP) programs. Parent education programs typically involve small groups of individuals meeting to discuss parenting concepts and concerns, usually for approximately 1 1/2 hours each week over a 10-week period. Research efforts show that the effectiveness of parent educators is not related to whether the educators have been parents themselves (Schultz, Nystul, & Law, 1980). Research also suggests that it is important to include role-play activities to allow for the internalization and transfer from attitudes to behaviors (Schultz & Nystul, 1980).

I developed an approach to family counseling called *marathon family counseling* while working on the Navajo Indian reservation. The approach evolved out of my work with Katherine Hillis, a Navajo mental health counselor. Marathon family counseling shares the following characteristics with Mara Selvini-Palazzoli's (1980) approach. Both utilize extended family sessions lasting up to 8 hours approximately once a month, and both serve clients who live in rural areas and have had to travel hundreds of miles for the session.

Marathon family counseling is based on the principles of Adlerian family counseling, including the use of encouragement, establishing mutual respect, identifying basic mistakes, and reorientation from basic mistakes. The following Personal Note illustrates this approach.

A 74-year-old grandmother arrived at the mental health center at the Navajo Indian reservation where I was working. Accompanied by a daughter, the woman appeared depressed and tearful during the initial interview. She lived with her husband 100 miles from the center and had three daughters, two sons, and twelve grandchildren.

The grandmother complained that two of her grandchildren had wrecked four of her automobiles over the years. She thought that the situation was hopeless and it would probably happen again because "kids will be kids. . . " While she talked, my Navajo mental health aide and I identified some basic mistakes. As discussed in Chapter 6, the Adlerian concept of a basic mistake is a self-defeating idea, such as an overgeneralization, false goals of security, misconception of life's demands, or minimization of one's worth.

The client's basic mistakes were as follows

1. Others can't survive without me.
2. The children of my family aren't responsible, so I'll have to take care of everything.
3. I'm not important. Other people are more important than me.

At this point, my aide and I decided that the client could benefit from marathon family counseling because of the great distance she and her daughter had traveled and the depth of her distress. We then discovered that the grandchild who had most recently wrecked her car was in jail for a D.W.I. citation. Since we wanted to include that family member in the session, we decided that we would have the family counseling session at the local jail. We phoned several other family members, and they agreed to meet us there.

We began the session by asking the grandmother to share how she was feeling. She started to cry and said she was so sad. She didn't feel her grandchildren cared about her but just wanted to use her and her cars. She said she felt they had no respect for her or her feelings. I asked how the family members felt about what grandmother was saying. The two grandchildren that had wrecked her cars seemed uneasy and defensive. After these feelings were explored, they were able to make some statements that seemed to express genuine concern.

I mentioned that all people make mistakes and have room for improvement. The family members agreed. My aide and I then explored ways each family member had contributed to the current problem and what they could do to help. With much encouragement, each person was able to make a specific plan for improvement.

At the end of the session, I asked the family members to express how the session affected them and what they wanted to do differently to help their family. I arranged to see them all in 2 weeks at the grandmother's house. We finished the session by thanking the family members and shaking their hands. Several family members also shook hands with one another and gave each other warm embraces.

We then talked with the grandmother privately and explored how she was feeling. She said she was relieved but still felt somehow responsible for her family's behavior. At this point, we discussed the basic mistakes we had identified earlier. We then used a variety of procedures to reorientate the grandmother from her basic mistakes. For example, we read the section on children from *The Prophet* (Gibran, 1965). This helped her realize that she was not responsible for her grandchildren. Her job was to provide guidance and love and let them—like arrows—fly freely into the challenges of life. She began to realize that if she didn't let go, they wouldn't have the opportunity to become responsible people. She had a very positive response to the reading from *The Prophet* and wanted a copy of the book. I let her borrow mine until she could get a copy. She then left for home with her daughter.

After the initial marathon counseling session, my mental health aide and I provided counseling services for the family over an 18-month period. The grandmother was eventually able to let go of her tendency to feel responsible for her grandchildren's behavior. Her signs of depression were gone after one month. The two grandchildren who had wrecked her cars both had minor problems with the law (e.g., public intoxication) during the counseling period. On the positive side, however, they didn't wreck any more cars during that time.

Note. From "Marathon Family Counseling" by M. Nystul, 1988, *Individual Psychology: The Journal of Adlerian Theory, Research, & Practice, 44*(2), pp. 210–216. Copyright 1988 by the University of Texas Press. Excerpts reprinted by permission.

The Counseling Process

The counseling process in family counseling will vary according to the theoretical orientation of the practitioner. Many aspects, however, are common to family counseling approaches regardless of the theoretical perspective. Friedlander and Highlen (1984) and Friedlander, Highlen, and Lassiter (1985) identified some commonalitites associated with family counseling. Some of these are that family counselors

- View the marital subsystem as the most stressed
- Align themselves with the family's established hierarchy, interacting more with parents than children
- Focus on the nuclear family, especially the parental subsystem
- Avoid direct confrontation with family members, preferring to direct messages to other family members (such as asking the wife why she thinks her husband is afraid of her)
- Actively engage in interpretation and educational processes
- Avoid the use of silence, restatements, empathic comments, or self-revealing comments

In addition, the authors found that family counselors make few references to the future; parents emphasize current issues; and children tend to relate to here-and-now issues regarding sibling relationships.

Goldenberg and Goldenberg (1991) noted that the challenge for the 1990s is to develop integrative models for family counseling that can be responsive to different populations. L'Abate (1986) set forth the following four-stage integrative model for family counseling.

Stage One: Stress Reduction.   The tasks associated with this stage are establishing a positive relationship, reducing stress and conflict, resolving an existing crisis if necessary, and reducing symptomatic behavior to a tolerable level.

Stage Two: Training and Education.   This stage involves helping the family learn the skills necessary to function effectively. Counselors frequently use homework assignments during this stage for family members to practice the skills they are learning.

Stage Three: Issue of Termination.   During this stage, the family is given an opportunity to deal with issues that have not been resolved, such as dealing effectively with intimacy. When all issues have been resolved, the counselor helps the family move toward termination of the counseling process.

Stage Four: Follow-Up.   Follow-up involves determining the efficacy of counseling and allowing for additional counseling as needed.

EVALUATION OF MARRIAGE AND FAMILY COUNSELING

At least 20 literature reviews of marriage and family counseling have been conducted since 1970, involving the analysis of approximately 300 studies (Raffa, Sypek, & Vogel, 1990). Early investigations appeared promising, as summarized by Bednar, Burlingame, and Masters (1988). Their summary showed that family counseling was at least as effective as other therapeutic techniques such as individual counseling (Gurman, Kniskern, & Pinsof, 1986; Gurman & Kniskern, 1978, 1981); deterioration in marriage counseling occurs at the same rate as it does in other types of counseling (Gurman et al., 1986; Jacobson & Bussod, 1983); and family counseling has become an acceptable form of treatment for mental health problems (Gurman et al., 1986; Jacobson & Bussod, 1983; Russel, Olson, Sprenkle, & Atilano, 1983).

Unfortunately, more recent studies have challenged these findings primarily due to weaknesses in methodology and the lack of a clear description of intervention strategies used in marriage and family counseling studies (Bednar et al., 1988; Raffa et al., 1990). Problems cited by Raffa et al. (1990) include a lack of controlled studies; failure to adequately describe the treatment approaches employed; inadequate research design; an absence of descriptive statistics in reporting and analyzing results; the use of assessment instruments with questionable reliability and validity; and a complete absence of any replication studies.

These concerns indicate that additional research on the efficacy of marriage and family counseling is warranted. Particular emphasis should be given to clearly defining and differentiating systemic approaches from traditional counseling approaches and addressing methodological weaknesses (Bednar et al., 1988).

CHAPTER SUMMARY

The field of marriage and family counseling is both an emerging profession and a counseling specialty practiced by various members of the helping profession. In this chapter, I began by describing systems theory and the family life cycle model as important theoretical foundations for marriage and family counseling.

Following these topics, I provided an overview of marriage counseling and family counseling in terms of theory, research, and practice. I presented different theories outlining the key concepts, goals, and counseling process of each. Although the theories differ, commonalities in the field were also identified. In this regard, marriage and family counseling focus on the relationship between family members and the overall family system rather than individual family members. There also appears to be a trend toward integration of theories in an attempt to meet the needs of different populations.

I concluded the chapter by summarizing major reviews of the research that has been conducted on marriage and family counseling. Recent reviews have raised concerns that suggest additional research is warranted to gain a clearer understanding of the efficacy of marriage and family counseling.

REFERENCES

Ackerman, N. W. (1937). The family as a social and emotional unit. *Bulletin of the Kansas Mental Hygiene Society, 12*(2).

Ackerman, N. W. (1956). Interlocking pathology in family relationships. In S. Rado & G. Daniels (Eds.), *Changing conceptions of psychoanalytical medicine.* New York: Grune & Stratton.

Ackerman, N. W. (1966). *Treating the troubled family.* New York: Basic Books.

Ackerman, N. W. (1970). *Family therapy in transition.* Boston: Little, Brown.

Bednar, R. L., Burlingame, G. M., & Masters, K. S. (1988). Systems of family treatment: Substance or semantics? *Annual Review of Psychology, 39,* 401–434.

Beutler, L. (1983). *Eclectic psychotherapy: A systematic approach.* New York: Pergamon Press.

Boen, D. L. (1988). A practitioner looks at assessment in marital counseling. *Journal of Counseling and Development, 66*(10), 484–486.

Brown-Standridge, M. D. (1986). Family therapy: New profession or professional specialty? *Family Therapy, 13*(2), 133–142.

Carter, B., & McGoldrick, M. (1988). Overview: The changing family life cycle—A framework for family therapy. In B. Carter & M. McGoldrick (Eds.), *The changing family life cycle: A framework for family therapy* (2nd ed.). New York: Allyn & Bacon.

Coleman, S. (1985). *Failures in family therapy.* New York: Guilford Press.

Cummings, N. A. (1990). The credentialing of professional psychologists and its implication for the other mental health disciplines. *Journals of Counseling and Development, 68,* 485–490.

Dinkmeyer, D., & Carlson, J. (1984). *Time for a better marriage.* Circle Pines, MN: American Guidance Service.

Dinkmeyer, D., & McKay, G. (1989). *Systematic training for effective parenting (STEP): The parent's handbook* (3rd ed.). Circle Pines, MN: American Guidance Service.

Dinkmeyer, D., & McKay, G. (1990). *Systematic training for effective parenting of teens* (2nd ed.). Circle Pines, MN: American Guidance Service.

Duvall, E. M. (1957). *Family development.* Philadelphia: Lippincott.

Duvall, E. M. (1977). *Marriage and family development* (5th ed.). Philadelphia: Lippincott.

Ebert, B. (1978). The healthy family. *Family Therapy*, 5(3), 227–232.

Elkaim, M. (1982). From the family approach to the socio-political approach. In F. Kaslow (Ed.), *The international book of family therapy* (pp. 337–357). New York: Brunner/Mazel.

Enns, C. Z. (1988). Dilemmas of power and equality in marital and family counseling: Proposals for a feminist perspective. *Journal of Counseling and Development*, 67(4), 242–248.

Epstein, E. S., & Loos, V. E. (1989). Some irreverent thoughts on the limits of family therapy: Towards a language-based explanation of human systems. *Journal of Family Psychology*, 2(4), 405–421.

Everett, C. A. (1990). The field of marital and family therapy. *Journal of Counseling and Development*, 68, 498–502.

Fisher, B. L., & Sprinkle, D. H. (1978). Therapists' perceptions of healthy family functioning. *International Journal of Family Counseling*, 19(4), 9–18.

Framo, J. L. (1981). The integration of marital therapy with family of origin sessions. In A. Gurman & D. Kniskern (Eds.), *Handbook of family therapy*. New York: Brunner/Mazel.

Friedlander, M. L., & Highlen, P. S. (1984). A spatial view of the interpersonal structure of family interviews: Similarities and differences across counselors. *Journal of Counseling Psychology*, 31, 477–487.

Friedlander, M. L., Highlen, P. S., & Lassiter, W. L. (1985). Content analytic comparison of four expert counselors' approach to family treatment: Ackerman, Bowen, Jackson, and Whitaker. *Journal of Counseling Psychology*, 32(2), 171–180.

Gibran, K. (1965). *The Prophet*. New York: Harper & Row.

Glick, I., Clarkin, J., & Kessler, D. (1987). *Marital and family therapy* (3rd ed.). Orlando, FL: Grune & Stratton.

Golann, S. (1987). On description of family therapy. *Family Process*, 26, 331–340.

Goldenberg, I., & Goldenberg, H. (1991). *Family therapy: An overview* (3rd ed.). Monterey, CA: Brooks/Cole.

Goldner, V. (1985). Feminism and family therapy. *Family Process*, 24, 31–47.

Gurman, A. S., & Kniskern, D. P. (1978). Research on marital and family therapy: Progress, perspective, and prospect. In S. L. Garfield & A. E. Bergin (Eds.), *Handbook of psychotherapy and behavior change: An empirical analysis* (2nd ed.). New York: John Wiley & Sons.

Gurman, A. S., & Kniskern, D. P. (1981). Family therapy outcome research: Knowns and unknowns. In A. S. Gurman & D. P. Kniskern (Eds.), *Handbook of family therapy*. New York: Brunner/Mazel.

Gurman, A. S., Kniskern, D. P., & Pinsof, W. M. (1986). Research on marital and family therapies. In S. L. Garfield & A. E. Bergin (Eds.), *Handbook of psychotherapy and behavior change* (3rd ed., pp. 565–624). New York: Wiley.

Haley, J. (1963). *Strategies of psychotherapy*. New York: Grune & Stratton.

Haley, J. (1971). Approaches to family therapy. In J. Haley (Ed.), *Changing families: A family therapy reader*. New York: Grune & Stratton.

Haley, J. (1973). *Uncommon psychiatric techniques of Milton H. Erickson*. New York: W. W. Norton.

Haley, J. (1976). *Problem-solving therapy*. San Francisco: Jossey-Bass.

Haley, J. (1980). *Leaving home*. New York: McGraw-Hill.

Hazelrigg, M. D., Cooper, H. M., & Borduin, C. M. (1987). Evaluating the effectiveness of family therapies: An integrative review and analysis. *Psychological Bulletin*, 101(3), 428–442.

Horne, A. M., & Ohlsen, M. M. (1982). Introduction: The family and family counseling. In M. Horne & M. M. Ohlsen (Eds.), *Family counseling and therapy*. Itasca, IL: Peacock.

Humphrey, F. G. (1983). *Marital therapy*. Englewood Cliffs, NJ: Prentice-Hall.

Jacobson, N. S., & Bussod, N. (1983). Marital and family therapy. In M. Hersen, A. E. Kazdin, & A. S. Bellack (Eds.), *The clinical psychology handbook* (pp. 611–630). New York: Pergamon.

Kovacs, L. (1988). Couple therapy: An integrated developmental and family system model. *Family Therapy*, 15(2), 133–155.

L'Abate, L. (1986). *Systematic family therapy*. New York: Brunner/Mazel.

Liddle, H. (1982). On the problems of eclecticism: A call for epistemological clarification and human-scale theories. *Family Process*, 21, 243–250.

Lowe, R. N. (1982). Adlerian/Dreikursian family counseling. In A. M. Horne & M. M. Ohlsen (Eds.),

Family counseling and therapy. Itasca, IL: Peacock.

Madanes, C. (1981). *Strategic family therapy*. San Francisco: Jossey-Bass.

Madanes, C. (1984). *Behind the one-way mirror: Advances in the practice of strategic therapy*. San Francisco: Jossey-Bass.

Minuchin, S. (1974). *Families and family therapy*. Cambridge, MA: Harvard University Press.

Minuchin, S. (1984). *Family kaleidoscope*. Cambridge, MA: Harvard University Press.

Nichols, M. (1984). *Family therapy: Concepts and methods*. New York: Gardner Press.

Nichols, M. (1987a). The individual in the system. *Family Therapy Networker, 11*(2), 33–38, 85.

Nichols, M. (1987b). *The self in the system: Expanding the limits of family therapy*. New York: Brunner/Mazel.

Nichols, W. (1988). *Marital therapy: An integrative approach*. New York: Brunner/Mazel.

Nichols, W. C., & Everett, C. A. (1986). *Systematic family therapy: An integrative approach*. New York: Guilford Press.

Nystul, M. S. (1988). Marathon family counseling. *Individual Psychology: The Journal of Adlerian Theory, Research, & Practice, 44*(2), 210–216.

Raffa, H., Sypek, J., & Vogel, W. (1990). Commentary on reviews of "outcome" studies of family and marital psychotherapy. *Contemporary Family Therapy, 12*(1), 65–73.

Russel, C. S., Olson, D. H., Sprenkle, D. H., & Atilano, R. B. (1983). From family symptom to family system: Review of family therapy research. *American Journal of Family Therapy, 11*, 3–14.

Russell, T., & Madsen, D. H. (1985). *Marriage counseling report user's guide*. Champaign, IL: Institute for Personality and Ability Testing.

Satir, V. M. (1967). *Conjoint family therapy*. Palo Alto, CA: Science and Behavior Books.

Satir, V. M. (1972). *Peoplemaking*. Palo Alto, CA: Science and Behavior Books.

Satir, V. M. (1982). The therapist and family therapy: Process model. In A. M. Horne & M. M. Ohlsen (Eds.), *Family counseling and therapy*. Itasca, IL: Peacock.

Schultz, C., & Nystul, M. S. (1980). Mother-child interaction behavior as an outcome of theoretical models of parent group education. *Journal of Individual Psychology, 36*, 16–29.

Schultz, C., Nystul, M. S., & Law, H. (1980). Attitudinal outcomes of theoretical models of parent group education. *Journal of Individual Psychology, 37*, 107–112.

Selvini-Palazzoli, M. (1980). Why a long interval between sessions? The therapeutic control of the family-therapist suprasystem. In M. Andolfi & I. Zwerling (Eds.), *Dimensions of family therapy*. New York: Guilford Press.

Shields, C. G. (1986). Critiquing the new epistemologies: Towards minimum requirements for scientific theory of family therapy. *Journal of Marital and Family Therapy, 12*, 359–372.

Sholevar, G. (1985). Marital therapy. In H. Kaplan & B. Sadock (Eds.), *Comprehensive textbook of psychiatry IV* (Vol. 2). Baltimore: Williams & Wilkins.

Snyder, D. K. (1981). *Marital Satisfaction Inventory (MSI)*. Los Angeles: Western Psychological Services.

Solomon, M. A. (1973). A developmental, conceptual premise for family therapy. *Family Process, 12*, 179–188.

Sperry, L. (1989). Assessment in marital therapy: A couples-centered biopsychosocial approach. *Individual Psychology: The Journal of Adlerian Theory, Research, and Practice, 45*, 446–451.

Sperry, L., & Carlson, J. (1991). *Marital therapy: Integrating theory and technique*. Denver, CO: Love.

Stinnet, N., & DeFrain, J. (1985). *Secrets of strong families*. Boston: Little, Brown.

Stuart, R. B. (1983). *Couples' pre-counseling inventory, counselor's guide*. Champaign, IL: Research Press.

Taylor, R. M., & Morrison, L. P. (1984). *Taylor-Johnson temperament analysis manual*. Los Angeles: Psychological Publications.

Von Bertalanffy, L. V. (1968). *General systems theory: Foundations, development, application*. New York: Braziller.

Watzlawick, P., Weakland, J. H., & Fisch, R. (1974). *Change: Principles of problem formation and problem resolution*. New York: Norton.

Whitaker, C. A. (1976). The hindrance of theory in clinical work. In P. J. Guerin (Ed.), *Family therapy: Theory and practice*. New York: Gardner Press.

Whitaker, C. A. (1977). Process techniques of family therapy. *Interaction, 1*, 4–19.

Whitaker, C. A., & Bumberry, W. M. (1988). *Dancing with the family: A symbolic-experiential approach*. New York: Brunner/Mazel.

Wilcoxon, S. A. (1985). Healthy family functioning: The other side of family pathology. *Journal of Counseling and Development, 63,* 495–499.

CHAPTER TEN

Child Counseling

CHAPTER OVERVIEW

This chapter provides an overview of child counseling. Highlights of this chapter include

- Children from a historical perspective
- Developmental theories
- Treatment issues, including assessment procedures, research on child counseling, and play therapy
- Special problems of children, including child abuse and neglect, depression, and antisocial behavior

Child counseling is an emerging specialty within the counseling profession. Some of the most promising advances in counseling and psychology are occurring in this field. These are reflected in our understanding and treatment of common problems that children experience, including child abuse and neglect, childhood depression, and antisocial behavior. In this chapter, I present information on these types of problems as well as other conceptual and treatment issues.

CHILDREN FROM A HISTORICAL PERSPECTIVE

The concept of childhood as a distinct developmental stage is relatively new (LeVine & Sallee, 1986). Children had been viewed as miniature adults and forced to work alongside adults in the fields and in factories and to fight in wars. Children had no special privileges, lacking the protection of child labor laws or the advantage of formal education. They were to be "seen and not heard" and used in whatever way the parents dictated (LeVine & Sallee, 1986).

Children were often lucky to survive long enough to become adults. Until the 19th century, parents had the right to kill a newborn child who was deformed, sickly, retarded, or even the "wrong" sex (Radbill, 1980). If children survived that possibility, there was still a very good chance they would die of illness or accident. In the 1600s, 59% of the children in London died before they were 5 years old, and 64% died before they turned 10 (LeVine & Sallee, 1986).

Kanner (1962) presented the following story of Emerentia to illustrate how a 7-year-old girl was viewed and treated in 1713.

> This 7-year-old girl, the offspring of an aristocratic family, whose father remarried after an unhappy first matrimony, offended her "noble and god-fearing" stepmother by her peculiar behavior. Worst of all, she would not join in the prayers and was panic-stricken when taken to the black-robed preacher in the dark and gloomy chapel. She avoided contact with people by hiding in closets or running away from home. The local physician had nothing to offer beyond declaring that she might be insane. She was placed in the custody of a minister known for his rigid orthodoxy. The minister, who saw in her ways the machinations of a "baneful and infernal" power, used a number of would-be therapeutic devices. He laid her on a bench and beat her with cat-o'-nine-tails. He locked her in a dark pantry. He subjected her to a period of starvation. He clothed her with a frock of burlap. Under these circumstances, the child did not last long. She died after a few months, and everybody felt relieved. The minister was amply rewarded for his efforts by Emerentia's parents (p. 97).

LeVine and Sallee (1986) cited the following events as forces that contributed to the recognition of children as a distinct stage of development. In 1744, Pestalozzi published the first scientific record of the development of a young child. In the late 19th century, two books served as models for observational and experimental approaches to analyze child development: Charles Darwin's *Biographical Sketch of an Infant* in 1877 and Wilhelm Preyer's *The Mind of a Child* in late 1892. Also during the latter part of the 19th century, G. Stanley Hall studied the physical and mental capabilities of children at Clark University. In the early 1900s, child guidance clinics emerged to provide counseling and guidance services to children. In 1910, the Stanford-Binet IQ tests were published. In 1917, John B. Watson conducted his now-famous "Little Albert" experiments, which demonstrated that a child could be conditioned to cry at the sight of a furry object.

Although children have come a long way from the "dark ages" of yesteryear, there are still signs that being a child is not easy. Current estimates suggest that from 15% to 19% of the children in the United States suffer from emotional problems that warrant mental health services (Tuma, 1989). Studies also estimate that 3% to 18% of these children are considered seriously emotionally disturbed and require intensive care (Knitzer, 1982; Tuma, 1989). Unfortunately, only 20% to 30% of the children who have emotional problems receive mental health services (Tuma, 1989). Children are therefore considered one of the most neglected groups in terms of receiving mental health services (Tuma, 1989).

DEVELOPMENTAL THEORIES

Providing counseling services to children differs dramatically from working with adults. Unlike adults, children are undergoing constant change in their physical, cognitive, and psychosocial abilities. A child may therefore express certain symptoms at one stage of development and entirely different symptoms at another stage (LeVine & Sallee, 1986). For example, a child at age 3 may resort to temper tantrums when under stress. The same child at age 13 may turn to drugs as a means of dealing with stress (LeVine & Sallee, 1986).

It is therefore important to utilize a developmental perspective when working with children. This section will provide an overview of developmental theories relating to cognitive, moral, and psychosocial development as well as issues that relate to psychopathology, as summarized in Table 10.1.

Cognitive Theories

Many theories have attempted to explain how cognitive development occurs throughout the life span (Piaget, 1952; Bruner, 1973). Among these, Piaget's theory has received significant attention in literature. Piaget (1952) divided cognitive development into four distinct stages: sensorimotor (birth to 2 years of age); preoperational (2 to 6 years of age); concrete operational (ages 7 to 11); and formal operational (age 12 through adulthood).

According to Piaget, children's cognitive development becomes more sophisticated as they progress from one stage to the next. For example, children are usually unable to understand cause and effect during the preoperational stage. Concepts such as divorce or death may therefore be difficult for children to understand during this stage, from 2 to 6 years old. When faced with divorce or death during this stage, they may become confused and even blame themselves. It is important for counselors to be aware of a child's level of cognitive development during the counseling process.

Theories of Moral Development

Counselors are faced with an increasing number of children who are "out of control" and engaging in various acts of misbehavior (McMahon & Forehand, 1988). Theories of moral development can be used to gain a better understanding of children who misbehave in terms of their moral reasoning.

Piaget (1965) and more recently Kohlberg (1963, 1973, 1981) presented theories of moral development. Kohlberg's theory is based on Piaget's work and is widely accepted in the literature. Kohlberg suggested that moral development could be conceptualized in terms of three levels, with each level containing two stages. These levels and stages are hierarchical, requiring a person to move through them one at a time without skipping any of them.

Table 10.1
Developmental Theories

Developmental Theories	Founder	Key Concepts	Implications for Counseling
Cognitive Theory	Piaget	Divided cognitive development into four distinct stages: sensorimotor (birth to 2), preoperational (2 to 7), concrete operations (7 to 11), and concrete operations (begins after 11).	Counselors should adjust the counseling approach to the child's level of cognitive functioning.
Theory of Moral Development	Kohlberg, Gilligan	Identified three levels of moral development beginning with an egocentric view regarding morality (i.e., a child controls behavior out of a fear of punishment).	An understanding of moral reasoning can be useful to promote self-control.
Psychosocial Development Theory	Erikson	Identified seven psychosocial stages and their associated developmental tasks (e.g., from birth to 1 year of age the central task is trust).	Counselors can help clients obtain the coping skills necessary to master the developmental tasks so they can move forward in their development.
Developmental Psycho-pathology	Kazden, Kovacs, and others	Study of childhood psychopathology in the context of maturational and developmental processes.	Provides a framework for understanding childhood psychopathology as unique from adult psychopathology and to aid in accurate assessment, diagnosis, and treatment.

According to Kohlberg, children functioning at Level 1 have an egocentric point of view regarding morality. They control their behavior out of fear of punishment. Children who have reached Level 2 of moral development control their behavior and abide by laws out of a concern about how others will view them as a person, and also how they will view themselves. At Level 3, children control their behavior and abide by laws out of a rational decision to contribute to the good of society. Children who have reached the age of 11 or 12 are often capable of functioning at Level 3.

Carol Gilligan (1982, 1987) contends that Kohlberg's theory does not take into account gender issues associated with moral development. According to Gilligan (1982, 1987), Kohlberg's theory is based primarily on the way males perceive morality, as a set of values and moral principles that can be applied to all situations regardless of the social context and that are concerned with what is fair and equitable. Female moral reasoning is more concerned with caring for the needs of others than with equity. It is also directly related to the social context in that an individual's moral reasoning is influenced by how one will be viewed by significant others.

Psychosocial Theories

Children's psychosocial development is another important issue in counseling. Erikson (1963, 1968) identified seven psychosocial stages from birth to death. In his theory, each stage involves a particular task that must be accomplished before the individual can proceed effectively to the next developmental task. From birth to age 1, for example, the central task is to experience a sense of trust from the environment. Without that experience, an infant will develop a mistrustful attitude toward the environment. To accomplish each task, the individual must master various coping skills associated with that task. Counselors can help a child develop these coping skills to promote positive psychosocial development (Blocher, 1987). Chapter 13 provides a more detailed description of the role of developmental tasks in the counseling process.

Developmental Psychopathology

A recent trend in counseling is an attempt to view psychopathology from a developmental perspective (Kazdin, 1989; Kovacs, 1989). Kazdin (1989) defined developmental psychopathology as "the study of clinical dysfunction in the context of maturational and developmental processes" (p. 180). Kovacs (1989) noted that developmental psychopathology attempts to address three issues: (a) how the developing organism mediates the development of mental disorders; (b) the impact of mental disorders on age-appropriate abilities; and (c) whether mental disorders develop continually or in stages.

According to Kazdin (1989), the greatest advance in developmental psychopathology occurred with the publication of the DSM-III and later DSM-III-R (American Psychiatric Association, 1980, 1987). "It represented a quantum leap in the attention accorded disorders of infancy, childhood, and adolescence" (Kazdin, 1989, p. 183). Advances in the DSM include recognizing the variations from childhood to adulthood in the nature and course of psychopathology. For example, the DSM-III-R notes that it is common for a depressed child also to experience problems that are usually not found with adult depression. Some of these are somatic, or bodily, complaints; psychomotor agitation; and mood-congruent hallucinations.

Developmental psychopathology holds much promise in terms of refining the process of assessment and diagnosis in child counseling. Additional research is required to determine how different developmental levels may influence symptom expression and treatment (Kazdin, 1989).

TREATMENT ISSUES

This section will address treatment issues in child counseling. It will begin by describing some of the commonly used assessment procedures. The chapter will then provide information on treatment in terms of research findings and a description of play therapy.

Assessment Procedures

Child counseling encompasses the full range of standardized and nonstandardized assessment procedures described in Chapter 3. In addition, two child assessment procedures warrant additional attention. The first involves the use of children's drawings as an assessment tool, a procedure clinicians have used for some time. The second is the use of clinical interviews with children and parents. Although clinical interviews have been used with adults for many years, their use with children has begun more recently (Edelbrock & Costello, 1988), representing a major advance in the assessment of childhood disorders (Kazdin, 1989).

Children's Drawings.   Children's drawings can be used both in standardized and nonstandardized assessment procedures. One standardized procedure is the Goodenough-Harris Drawing Test (Harris, 1963). This test requires children to make a picture of a man or woman depending on the sex of the child and a picture of themselves. Another commonly used standardized test is the House-Tree-Person Test (Buck, 1949), in which children first draw a house, then a tree, and last a person. More recently, Knoff and Prout (1985) developed The Kinetic Drawing System for Family and School. Children draw one picture of their family and another that relates to school. This test assesses important relationships at home and school.

Stabler (1984) provided information on the nonstandardized use of children's drawings. He noted that children's drawings could be used to obtain an estimate of a child's cognitive and psychosocial development and level of maturity. Stabler (1984) identified the following five factors that are important in assessing children's drawings.

1. *Proportion or form*. Do figures in the drawings have appropriate proportion or form?
2. *Detail*. What is the degree of detail in the drawing (e.g., Are there ears, eyes, mouth, and a nose on the face?)
3. *Movement or action*. Is there movement or action depicted in the drawing, such as having the appearance of a three-dimensional person?
4. *Theme*. Is there a theme or story conveyed in the picture, such as two people in love or Superman stopping a villain?

Children's drawings can provide valuable assessment information.

   5. *Gender identity.* Is there evidence that the child has a clear concept of gender identity?

Stabler (1984) also provided guidelines for assessing children's drawings in terms of cognitive functioning and overall maturity for children in three age groups: 5 to 7, 8 to 9, and 10 to 12. For example, children from age 5 to 7 tend to be able to draw pictures that are more or less proportional; have limited detail; some evidence of gender identity emerging; rather poor movement or action; and typically little or no form. Figure 10.1 provides an illustration of a typical drawing by a 6-year-old.

   Stabler (1984) also noted three types of drawings that are particularly useful in the assessment process. These are free drawings, where children are encouraged to draw whatever they like; self-portraits; and family drawings, in which children draw themselves with their family. These drawings enable the counselor to make hypotheses about what to explore with a child. Some possibilities follow. A free drawing may have themes that represent children's concerns. For example, a child who repeatedly draws a house with a child by a mother and father in the home could suggest the child is concerned with issues relating to home and family life. A self-portrait with no arms or legs could indicate a sense of lack of control over the environment. Children who draw a self-portrait without a mouth may think that others do not value their views. A family drawing that has a significant distance between the child and other family members could suggest a feeling of isolation or alienation.

Figure 10.1
Typical Drawing by a 6-Year-Old
Child

Note. From *Children's Drawings* (p.
5) by B. Stabler, 1984, Chapel Hill,
NC: Health Sciences Consortium.
Copyright 1984 by Health Sciences
Consortium. Reprinted by permis-
sion.

Clinical Interviews.   The clinical interview has become an increasingly popular
tool to assist with assessment and diagnosis (see Chapter 3 for a description of the
clinical interview). The clinical interview is not designed to replace other forms of
assessment but can be best viewed as an adjunct to the process of assessment and
diagnosis. In this regard, the clinical interview has been shown to increase diagnostic
reliability (Robins, Helzer, Croughan, & Ratcliff, 1981).

Although clinical interviews have been used with adults for some time, their
development and use with children have occurred primarily during the last 10 to 15
years. Interest in the utilization of clinical interviews for children corresponds to the
increased differentiation of mental disorders for children during the past decade.

Edelbrock and Costello (1988) identified several advantages and disadvantages of
clinical interviews as compared to other childhood assessment procedures, such as
observation and psychological tests. Advantages of clinical interviews include establishing rapport, clarifying misunderstandings, and obtaining self-report data from
parents and children. The primary disadvantages relate to questionable levels of
validity and reliability due to the newness of these instruments and the consequent
lack of time to empirically evaluate them.

Many clinical interviews for children are currently available. Edelbrock and
Costello (1988) described commonly used clinical interviews for children. They vary
in terms of structure, and the more structured interviews require less training to
administer (Edelbrock & Costello, 1988). Three examples are

1. *The Diagnostic Interview for Children and Adolescents* (Herjanic & Reich,
1982). This is a highly structured diagnostic interview that can be used with
children 6 years of age or older. It covers a broad range of childhood symptoms in terms of frequency and duration. There is also a version for parents,
which solicits pertinent developmental and family history.

2. *The Interview Schedule for Children* (Kovacs, 1982). This is a semistructured interview for children ages 8 to 17. It is a symptom-oriented interview that focuses primarily on depression, although it also assesses other diagnostic criteria. A separate interview can be conducted with parents and children.

3. *The Diagnostic Interview Schedule for Children* (Costello, Edelbrock, Kalas, Kessler, & Klaric, 1982). This is a highly structured interview for children ages 6 to 18. It provides information on a wide range of symptoms and behaviors in terms of onset, duration, and severity. A parallel version can be used with parents and children.

Research on Child Counseling

Many research studies have identified current trends in child counseling treatment approaches. This section will provide a review of some of this literature.

Casey and Berman (1985) conducted a meta-analysis of 75 studies published between 1952 and 1983 that evaluated the efficacy of child counseling strategies. Results of their study showed that treated children were better off than two thirds of untreated children regardless of the type of treatment. Weisz, Weiss, Alicke, and Klotz (1987) conducted another meta-analysis study of 108 studies involving youths 4 to 18 years of age. Their results provided additional support for the efficacy of child counseling. They found that treated children were better off than nontreated children; behavioral approaches were superior to nonbehavioral techniques; younger children, ages 4 to 12, improved more than adolescents; and there were no differences in outcomes for boys versus girls.

Tuma (1989) identified childhood problems and disorders that responded best to cognitive-behavioral approaches (see Chapter 8 for a description of cognitive-behavioral theories). Behavior therapy was shown to be effective with phobias and enuresis; cognitive methods were shown to be successful with fears, hyperactivity, disruptive behavior, and self-control; group therapy was effective with delinquent adolescents; and behaviorally orientated family therapy promoted positive outcomes with conduct-disordered and delinquent children in terms of reducing aggression and antisocial behavior.

Tuma (1989) also surveyed the literature on the efficacy of drug treatment for mental disorders of children. Stimulants were shown to be useful in treating attention-deficit hyperactivity disorder (ADHD). The drug decreased attention deficits but did not improve academic achievement. Antipsychotic drugs were effective in treating psychotic children; reducing hyperactivity in children with ADHD, although less effectively than stimulants; and treating tic disorders. Antidepressant drugs were effective in treating depressed children, ADHD, enuresis, separation anxiety, and school phobia.

Play Therapy

Most counseling approaches currently used in child counseling, such as behavioral and cognitive approaches, are adaptations of strategies used with adults (Tuma,

Puppets can help children express themselves in play therapy.

1989). Play therapy represents one of the few approaches developed specifically for child counseling. Hellendorn (1988) provided an overview of the uses of play therapy. He concluded that it can be used to treat a wide range of childhood problems but appears to work best with neurotic children. In another study, Reams and Friedrich (1983) conducted a meta-analysis of 15 research reports on play therapy. Results of their investigation showed that play therapy was superior to nontreatment and promoted general adaptation and intellectual skills.

Two major schools of play therapy are currently in use. The first is the psychoanalytic school developed by Anna Freud (1928) and further refined by Melanie Klein (1960). These clinicians incorporated the major principles of psychoanalysis in their approach, for example, strengthening the ego to minimize endopsychic conflicts and utilizing the transference relationship to help children overcome traumatic experiences.

The psychoanalytic counselor conceptualizes play in a manner similar to free association. From this perspective, play allows children to express themselves freely and spontaneously. The counselor's role in this process is passive and interpretive. For example, if a child painted a picture with dark objects, the counselor might ask, "Are you feeling sad or gloomy today?"

The second major school of play therapy was developed by Virginia Axline (1974). Its theoretical foundation can be traced to Carl Rogers' person-centered school of counseling, and it is therefore a humanistic-phenomenological approach. Axline's (1964, 1974) approach suggested that the counselor conveys a warm and accepting attitude toward the child and encourages the child to freely explore the different play materials. The role of the counselor is similar to that in person-centered counseling. As the child plays, counselors attempt to convey empathic understanding by reflecting what they sense the child is experiencing. A more detailed description of Axline's approach can be found in *Dibs: In Search of Self* (Axline, 1964).

The following Personal Note provides a description of an approach to play therapy that I developed.

a personal note

I developed an approach to play therapy called Nystulian play therapy (Nystul, 1980). It incorporates Adlerian psychology and utilizes the four phases of multimodality creative arts therapy described in Chapter 7: set the stage, set an example, set yourself at ease, and obtain a phenomenological understanding of the child.

My approach to play therapy (Nystul, 1980) is based on the following seven assumptions

1. The counselor attempts to establish a feeling of mutual respect with the child.
2. The counselor uses encouragement whenever possible.
3. The counselor attempts to understand the child by exploring the child's private logic.
4. The counselor tries to redirect the child's teleological movement to increase the child's motivation for change.
5. The session starts with 15 to 30 minutes of self-concept development and ends with 15 to 30 minutes of multimodality creative arts therapy.
6. The counselor uses logical and natural consequences to establish realistic limits.
7. The counselor recognizes the importance of parent and teacher involvement as an adjunct to play therapy.

Guidelines for Play Therapy.   The following guidelines may be useful when implementing a play therapy program.

Play therapy can be conducted individually or in small groups of two or three children. The play therapy room should be approximately 15 by 15 feet. It should be big enough for two adults and four children, but small enough to promote a sense of closeness between the counselor and the child. If the room is too large, for example, the child may wander off. The counselor should ensure privacy. No one should be permitted to come into the play therapy room while a session is in progress. Interruptions can be a major distraction from the counseling process.

The counselor should obtain different play materials, for example, play houses, puppets, babies, and an inflatable "bozo clown" to punch. It is also useful to have art supplies such as molding clay and watercolors and musical instruments such as bongo drums and a tambourine.

The counselor should establish limits with the child during the first session regarding time and behavior. In terms of time, the session length can vary according to the time available but should not exceed 1 hour. The length of time should be determined before the first session and adhered to as much as possible. Regarding behavior, the counselor should restrain a child who acts in an aggressive, hostile manner. It may even be necessary to discontinue the play therapy session if the child persists in being hostile. When a child abuses a toy, the counselor can use a logical consequence. For example, a counselor might say, "It looks like you're not ready to use the drum today. I'll put it up for now. Some other time, you can try to use it the way it is supposed to be used."

In communicating, counselors should use a friendly, kind voice, especially if they sense a child feels insecure; not talk down to a child in terms of tone of voice; and use an appropriate vocabulary level so that the child will understand the words. While it may be necessary to be firm with a child, it is probably counterproductive to be stern. Counselors should let themselves laugh and have fun with the child, and they should talk from a positive perspective, using encouragement whenever possible.

SPECIAL PROBLEMS OF CHILDREN

This section provides an overview of some of the special problems experienced by children: child abuse and neglect, depression, and antisocial behavior. For each type of problem, I present information on incidence, assessment, causes, effects, and treatment.

Child Abuse and Neglect

Children have been abused and neglected throughout history, but it was not until the early 1960s that child abuse and neglect became recognized as social problems that require comprehensive treatment (Wolfe, 1988). This section will review some of the issues associated with child abuse and neglect.

Incidence.   The incidence of child abuse and neglect continues to increase at an alarming rate in the United States (Talbutt, 1986). Breezer (1985) estimated that between 1 and 2 million children in the U.S. are abused each year. Brockman (1987) noted that reports of physical abuse have increased 158% since 1976, with 1,726,649 cases reported in 1984. Approximately 1,000 children die as a result of physical abuse each year (Burgdoy, 1981). The incidence of sexual abuse in the United States is also staggering. Current estimates suggest that 1 in every 4 girls and 1 in every 7 to 10 boys will have a sexual experience with an adult before reaching 18 years of age (England & Thompson, 1988). In addition, psychological abuse may be the most prevalent and destructive form of child abuse (Dworetzky, 1990).

Assessment.   Early identification and treatment of child abuse and neglect is critical to minimize negative effects on the child. Salkind (1990) identified the following warning signs of the various forms of child abuse and neglect

- *Physical abuse*. Signs of bruises, burns, and broken bones
- *Child neglect*. Poor health and hygiene and excessive school absenteeism
- *Sexual abuse*. Use of sexually explicit terminology, nightmares, genital injury, and sexually transmitted disease
- *Psychological (emotional) abuse*. Depression, self-deprecation, somatic (bodily) complaints such as headaches or stomachaches, and fear of adults

The assessment of child abuse and neglect is a multistage process (Wolfe, 1988). The process usually begins with impressionistic data from the reporting and referral source. That stage is followed by a refinement of information during interviews with parents and the child (Wolfe, 1988). Much of the initial information regarding the functioning of the parent and child can be obtained in a semistructured interview with the parent (Wolfe, 1988). The Parent Interview and Assessment Guide can be used to structure the interview and provide information on family background, marital relationship, areas of stress and support, and symptomatology (Wolfe, 1988). Several instruments have been developed that can be used to survey the attitudes of parents on topics relating to marriage and the family. The Child Abuse Potential Inventory (Milner, 1986) identifies familial patterns associated with child abuse. The Childhood Level of Living Scale (Polansky, Chalmers, Buttenwieser, & Williams, 1981) measures the degree of positive and negative influences in the home and is particularly useful for assessing neglect (Wolfe, 1988).

Causes.   Current research shows that child abuse results from a complex interaction of events. Wolfe (1988) summarized the research by noting that child abuse is a special type of aggression resulting from proximal and distal events.

Proximal events are those that precipitate abuse. A proximal event can involve a child's behavior or an adult conflict that triggers the abuse. Common child behaviors that can trigger child abuse are aggression, unspecified misbehavior, lying, and stealing (Kadushin & Martin, 1981). Straus, Gelles, and Steinmetz (1980) suggested that marital problems and violence are also associated with child abuse.

Distal events are those that are indirectly associated with child abuse. Indirect factors that have been shown to contribute to child abuse include low socio-economic status and poverty; restricted educational and occupational opportunities; unstable family environment; excessive heat; overcrowding; ambient noise level; and unemployment (Wolfe, 1988).

Other research efforts have attempted to identify characteristics of abusive parents as a means of understanding the causes of child abuse. Talbutt (1986) summarized this research by noting that abusive parents tend to be abused as children; have difficulty coping with stress; suffer from substance abuse problems; be immature and hold unrealistic expectations of children; and have children with special needs that require extra time and energy.

Sroufe and Cooper (1988) described a typical profile of parents at high risk for child abuse. They tend to be young, poorly educated, single, living in poverty, and socially isolated, and feel little support from a significant other. The authors also noted that abusive mothers tend to have a negative attitude toward their pregnancy.

Compared to nonabusive parents, they had less understanding of what was involved in caring for an infant; were less prone to plan for pregnancy; did not attend child-birth classes; did not have special living quarters for the baby to sleep; and had unrealistic expectations about raising an infant.

Effects.   Sroufe and Cooper (1988) described the effects of child abuse and neglect on the child. Physical neglect that results from not meeting the child's basic needs, such as food and shelter, tends to produce a lack of competency in dealing with the tasks of daily living, such as personal hygiene. Physical abuse and emotional unavailability often result in behavioral and emotional problems, for example, avoidance of intimacy in relationships, aggressiveness with peers, and blunted emotions. Psychologically abused children can develop neurotic traits, conduct disorders, negative self-image, and distorted relations with others (Craig, 1989; Hart & Brassard, 1987).

Sexual abuse can have traumatic and enduring effects. Feinauer (1990) noted that children who have been sexually abused can develop symptoms associated with posttraumatic stress disorder, for instance, flashbacks of the trauma and nightmares. These symptoms also tend to persist into adulthood (Feinauer, 1990). In addition, sexually abused individuals have a high risk of developing psychiatric problems as adults (Herman, 1986).

O'Brien (1983) identified several ways that sexual abuse can damage a child.

- *Psychological effects.* Sexual experiences can be confusing for children because they are unable to understand the strong emotional feelings associated with sex.

- *Low self-esteem.* Children may blame themselves for permitting the sexual contact or may feel dirty or ashamed as a result of the experience.

- *Exploitation.* Sexually abused children may feel used and develop a hostile, suspicious attitude toward others.

- *Vulnerability.* Because children are dependent on adults, they are vulnerable to and trusting of adults. When that trust is broken, children may develop a negative attitude toward vulnerability, making it difficult to develop trust and intimacy in relationships.

- *Distorted view of sexuality.* It is common for sexually abused children to develop a very negative or perverted attitude toward sex. As they grow up, they may avoid sex or become sexually promiscuous.

- *Violation of the child's privacy.* After an incestuous relationship is discovered, the abused child must cooperate with the authorities. This violation of the child's privacy can be very traumatic and anxiety-provoking.

- *Distorted moral development.* Sexual abuse often occurs between the ages of 9 and 11 when a child's moral development is also being formulated. Children can become quite confused about what is right and wrong when an adult is allowed to violate them sexually.

The following Personal Note illustrates how difficult it can be for a child to deal consciously with the trauma of sexual abuse.

When I was a psychologist at a hospital, I worked with several girls who had babies as a result of incestuous relationships with their fathers. These girls tended to use denial as a means of coping with what had happened.

For example, I met a 14-year-old girl the day before she had her baby. She insisted that she was not even pregnant. After she had the baby, she said that the baby was not hers. This patient required extensive counseling and psychotherapy to develop a realistic approach to her situation.

Treatment.   Brockman (1987) noted that the most hopeful treatment for abusive parents involves "resocialization" tasks, which help parents overcome isolation and foster interpersonal relations and support. These efforts can include encouraging parents to join Parents Anonymous or other self-help groups. Brockman (1987) also identified several preventive programs that could be promoted in schools. These programs include adult education, interpersonal training for students, courses on sexuality and parenting in high school, and guest speakers for students from organizations such as Parents Anonymous.

Treatment efforts can also be directed at the abused child. Group counseling can be especially effective in working with abused and neglected children (Damon & Waterman, 1986) and adolescents (Hazzard, King, & Webb, 1986). Kitchur and Bell (1989) noted that group counseling can be useful with this population to foster self-esteem, overcome problems with trust, correct distorted cognitions, and enhance self-control skills.

Orenchuk-Tomiuk, Matthey, and Christensen (1990) identified special treatment considerations relating to sexual abuse. The authors proposed a three-stage model for treating sexual abuse called The Resolution Model. The three stages are (a) the noncommittal or oppositional stage, (b) the middle stage, and (c) the resolution stage. The model differentiates treatment issues for the child, the nonoffending parent, and the offending parent at each stage, as follows.

The child feels responsible for the abuse during the noncommittal or oppositional stage; feels angry and experiences symptoms associated with posttraumatic stress disorder during the middle stage; and no longer feels responsible for the sexual abuse or experiences problematic symptoms during the resolution stage.

The nonoffending parent denies occurrence of sexual abuse, blames the child for disclosure, and defends the offender during the noncommittal or oppositional stage; believes the abuse has taken place and begins to become an ally for the child during the middle stage; and becomes a positive ally for the child and works through guilt associated with not protecting the child during the resolution stage.

The offender refuses to accept responsibility for abuse and/or denies its occurrence during the noncommittal or oppositional stage; is able to admit to the abuse but may blame the child during the middle stage; and assumes responsibility for the abuse and establishes a more positive parental role during the resolution stage.

The Resolution Model recommends that individual and group counseling can be useful during the noncommittal or oppositional stage. Couples and family counseling should not be used until the middle or resolution stages and should involve the child only if the child is ready.

England and Thompson (1988) provided additional guidelines that counselors can use with children who have been sexually abused. Counselors should take on the role of advocate for sexually abused children; help them overcome feelings of guilt and shame, emphasizing that the abuse was not their fault and that it will stop; use open-ended questions when assessing for sexual abuse and thus avoid leading questions; and take their accusations seriously, since children tend not to lie about sexual abuse, and psychological harm can occur if they are not taken seriously.

Depression

The recognition of childhood depression is a relatively recent occurrence (Sakolske & Janzen, 1987). This section will review some of the major issues associated with depression in children.

Incidence.   Research investigations suggest that children are as capable of experiencing clinical depression as adults (Alper, 1986; Kovacs, 1989). Serious depression has been found in infants (Field et al., 1988; Spitz, 1946) and preschool and school-age children (Digdon & Gotlib, 1985; Kazdin, 1988; Kovacs, 1989). The average duration of a major depression in children is 7 to 9 months, and a dysthymic depression lasts an average of 3 or more years (Kovacs, 1989). Manic disorders for children are rare and hard to diagnose accurately (Strober, Hanna, & McCracken, in press).

Assessment.   Sakolske and Janzen (1987) identified some major symptoms associated with childhood depression. Changes in mood and affect are the most obvious indications. Examples are children who were relatively happy and had positive self-images suddenly saying they are sad, miserable, and no good. Another indication is that depressed children tend to lack interest in activities that were previously enjoyable, such as hobbies and sports. They may also lose interest in friends and family members. Other symptoms include physical complaints such as headaches and abdominal discomfort; sleep disturbances including nightmares; changes in appetite; impaired cognitive processes such as difficulty concentrating; and problems in school, work, and interpersonal relationships.

Multiple diagnosis is common with depressed children, complicating the diagnostic process. The two mental disorders that occur most frequently with childhood depression are conduct and anxiety disorders (Kovacs, 1989). Multiple diagnosis can create a *masked depression*, which occurs when the symptoms of depression are obscured by an additional diagnosis (Kovacs, 1989).

Several instruments have been designed specifically to assess childhood depression. The most widely used instrument is the Children's Depression Inventory (Kovacs, 1981), which was developed from the Beck Depression Inventory. It assesses the cognitive, affective, and behavioral signs of depression. Other instruments include the Short Children's Depression Inventory (Carlson & Cantwell, 1979); the

Children's Depression Scale (Lang & Tisher, 1978); and the Schedule for Affective Disorders and Schizophrenia for School-Age Children (Chambers, Puig-Antich, & Tabrizi, 1978). Kazdin (1988) provides a description of each of these instruments.

Causes.   Several factors have been associated with childhood depression. These include parents who have high standards and do not express positive affect to the child (Cole & Rehm, 1986); children who have negative cognitive schemata characterized by self-depreciation, hopelessness, and despair (Hammer & Zupan, 1984); and social-skill and problem-solving deficits (Altmann & Gotlib, 1988).

Effects.   Depression in children can have serious consequences. Some problems associated with childhood depression are suicidal tendencies (Pfeffer, 1981); impaired cognitive development (Kovacs, Gatsonis, Marsh, & Richards, 1988); and problems with social and educational progress (Kovacs, Gatsonis, Marsh, & Richards, 1988). Even if a person does not become depressed as a child, childhood experiences can make the individual prone to depression as an adult. Brown and Harris (1978) found that children who experienced the death of their mother before they were 11 years of age were more prone than other children to develop depression as adults.

Treatment.   Several counseling approaches are available to treat childhood depression. Cognitive approaches have been shown to be particularly effective (Reynolds & Coats, 1986). Another approach is parent education, which can be used to help parents learn skills to promote a positive environment for the family. Play therapy is another option, which enables children to work through traumatic experiences and enhance their social skills and self-image. Antidepressant medication can also be considered in the treatment of depression, although there are mixed reports regarding its efficacy for children (Puig-Antich et al., 1987).

Antisocial Behavior

The majority of studies in the child counseling literature relate to children whose behavior can be described as "out of control" (McMahon & Forehand, 1988). These children are prone to engage in antisocial behavior and acts of delinquency. This section provides an overview of the issues associated with antisocial behavior.

Incidence.   Antisocial behavior can include acts that violate major social rules, including aggression, lying, stealing, and truancy (Kazdin, Bass, Siegel, & Thomas, 1989). The incidence of children engaging in antisocial behavior is high and involves one third to one half of all mental health clinical referrals (Kazdin, Bass, Siegel, & Thomas, 1989).

The incidence of antisocial behavior and delinquency in the United States is staggering. Of all serious crimes such as murder, rape, and robbery, 47% involve people under 21 years of age (U.S. Department of Justice, 1984). In addition, the likelihood of being arrested is greater at age 16 than at any other age (Berger, 1988).

Assessment.   Children who engage in a well-established pattern of antisocial behavior, for at least 6 months, tend to receive a DSM-III-R diagnosis of either conduct disorder or oppositional defiant disorder. Conduct disorder is the more serious mental disorder and requires that the individual has violated the rights of others and age-appropriate norms or rules of society. McMahon and Forehand (1988, p. 107) noted that most behaviors associated with conduct disorder involve "direct confrontation or disruption of the environment" and "are basically the same type of behavior that Patterson (1982) and Loeber and Schmaling (1985) have labeled 'overt antisocial behavior'." The major feature of oppositional defiant disorder is a "pattern of negativistic, hostile, and defiant behavior without the more serious violations of the basic rights of others" (American Psychiatric Association, 1987, p. 56).

McMahon and Forehand (1988) identified instruments that can be used to assess antisocial behavior. Several structured interviews have been developed for children. For example, the Diagnostic Interview Schedule for Children is a highly structured interview that can be used with children ages 6 to 18 and their parents (Costello, Edelbrock, Dulcan, & Kalas, 1984). It provides scores that correspond to DSM-III-R diagnosis of conduct disorder and oppositional defiant disorder.

Several behavioral rating scales are also available for assessing antisocial behavior in children. The Child Behavior Checklist (Achenback & Edelbrock, 1983) is one of the most popular rating scales in use. It can be used with children ages 2 to 16 and provides a comprehensive assessment of behaviorally disordered children (McMahon & Forehand, 1988). An advantage of this scale is that it has parallel forms for the child, parent, teacher, and observer. The Revised Behavior Problem Checklist (Quay & Petersen, 1983) is a rating scale that can be used to detect tendencies toward conduct problems, personality problems, inadequacy and immaturity, and socialized delinquency. This scale is completed by parents or teachers.

Causes.   Patterson, DeBaryshe, and Ramsey (1989) suggested that antisocial behavior is a developmental trait that begins in childhood and often continues into adolescence and adulthood. These authors utilize a social-interactional perspective, which suggests that family members train children to engage in antisocial behaviors (Patterson, 1982; Snyder, 1977; Wahler & Dumas, 1984). According to this theory, parents do not adequately reinforce prosocial behavior or effectively punish deviant behavior. On the contrary, these children learn to use antisocial behaviors to stop aversive intrusions from other family members. From this perspective, antisocial behavior can be viewed as the manifestation of survival skills necessary to cope with a dysfunctional family.

McMahon and Forehand (1988) provided an overview of studies that identified factors associated with conduct disorders and antisocial behaviors. These studies suggested that children with conduct disorders also tend to exhibit impaired peer relationships (Achenback & Edelbrock, 1983); misattribute hostile intentions to others (Milich & Dodge, 1984); have deficits in social problem-solving skills (Asarnow & Calan, 1985); lack empathy (Ellis, 1982); are prone to hyperactivity (Loeber & Schmaling, 1985) and depression (Chiles, Miller, & Cox, 1980); have low levels of academic achievement; and have a genetic predisposition to develop antisocial tendencies (Kazdin, 1985). Kazdin, Bass, Siegel, and Thomas (1989) also noted that antisocial children had deficits in interpersonal cognitive problem-solving skills (such as formulating solutions to problems); impaired cognitive development (such as moral reasoning); and maladaptive cognitive strategies (such as impulsiveness). Another series of studies found a link between the influence of the peer group and acts of delinquency and substance abuse (Elliott, Huizinga, & Ageton, 1985; Huba & Bentler, 1983; Kandel, 1973).

Effects.   Kazdin, Bass, Siegel, and Thomas (1989) suggested that the effects of anti-social behavior tend to prevail from childhood to adulthood. In addition, individuals diagnosed with antisocial behavior disorders tend to experience disproportional problems as adults, including criminal behavior, alcoholism, and antisocial personality disorders.

Patterson, DeBaryshe, and Ramsey (1989) noted that children who engage in antisocial behavior are also prone to become delinquents. Approximately one half of antisocial children become delinquent adolescents, and one half to three fourths of delinquent adolescents become adult offenders. The cost of delinquency transcends the offender, with $500 million spent annually on school vandalism alone (Feldman, Caplinger, & Wodarski, 1981).

Patterson, DeBaryshe, and Ramsey (1989) also suggested that many factors that are typically seen as causes of antisocial behavior, for example, academic failure and peer rejection, can more accurately be understood as effects. For example, research has shown that childhood aggression leads to rejection by the peer group, not the reverse (Cole & Kupersmidt, 1983; Dodge, 1983).

Treatment.   Many treatment approaches have been used with antisocial children, including individual and group counseling, family therapy, residential treatment, and use of psychotropic medication. Unfortunately, these interventions tend to lead to negative outcomes or at best improvement for 1 to 2 years before returning to pre-treatment levels (Kazdin, 1985, 1987; Wilson & Herrnstein, 1985).

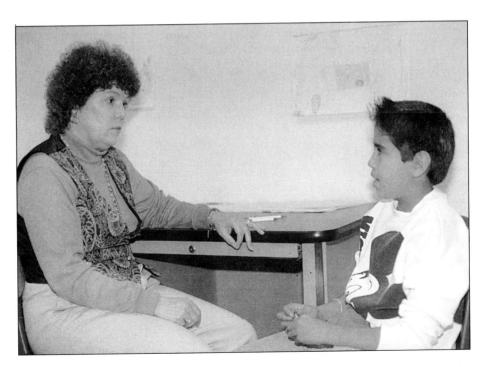

Child counseling can focus on helping children take responsibility for their behavior.

More recently Kazdin, Bass, Siegel, and Thomas (1989) reported the effectiveness of cognitive-behavioral problem-solving skill training. They found it was effective in reducing antisocial behavior and increasing prosocial behavior at home and school upon completion of treatment and at a 1-year follow-up assessment. Patterson, DeBaryshe, and Ramsey (1989) noted that the literature shows support for utilizing parent-training interventions to treat preadolescents (Kazdin, 1987). Patterson, DeBaryshe, and Ramsey (1989) also suggested that successful preventive approaches are possible. They recommended that interventions should attempt to identify children in elementary school who are antisocial and unskilled and provide them with social-skill training and academic remediation. In addition, they suggested that parent education could be used with these students' parents.

CHAPTER SUMMARY

This chapter provided an overview of the major issues associated with child counseling. It was described as an emerging counseling specialty with many new trends and innovations in the assessment and treatment of childhood disorders. The chapter began by describing child counseling from a developmental perspective. It was noted that the concept of children as a distinct developmental stage is relatively new and that previously the special needs of children were generally ignored. More recently, theories of child development have been formulated, providing information on the cognitive, moral, psychosocial, and mental health development of children. These theories provide an important conceptual framework for understanding and treating children.

This chapter also described some of the special treatment issues in child counseling. Particular attention was directed at assessment procedures unique to child counseling, such as the use of children's drawings and clinical interviews. Other treatment issues were addressed including play therapy, cognitive-behavioral therapy, and the use of psychotropic medications.

The last section of the chapter provided information on three special problems of children: child abuse and neglect, childhood depression, and antisocial behavior. Information was provided in terms of incidence, assessment, causes, effects, and treatment to illustrate some of the current trends in child counseling.

REFERENCES

Achenback, T. M., & Edelbrock, C. S. (1983). *Manual for the child behavior checklist and revised child behavior profile*. Burlington, VT: University of Vermont, Department of Psychiatry.

Alper, J. (1986, May). Depression at an early age. *Science, 86*, 44–50.

Altmann, E. O., & Gotlib, I. H. (1988). The social behavior of depressed children: An observational study. *Journal of Abnormal Child Psychology, 16*, 29–44.

American Psychiatric Association. (1980). *Diagnostic and statistical manual of mental disorders* (3rd ed.). Washington, DC: Author.

American Psychiatric Association. (1987). *Diagnostic and statistical manual of mental disorders* (3rd ed. revised). Washington, DC: Author.

Asarnow, J. R., & Calan, J. W. (1985). Boys with peer adjustment problems: Social cognitive processes. *Journal of Counseling and Clinical Psychology, 53*, 80–87.

Axline, V. M. (1964). *Dibs: In search of self*. Boston: Houghton Mifflin.

Axline, V. M. (1974). *Play therapy*. New York: Houghton Mifflin.

Berger, K. S. (1988). *The developing person through childhood and adolescence* (3rd ed.). New York: Worth.

Blocher, D. H. (1987). *The professional counselor*. New York: Macmillan.

Breezer, B. (1985). Reporting child abuse and neglect: Your responsibility and your protection. *Phi Delta Kappa, 66*, 434–436.

Brockman, M. P. (1987). Children and physical abuse. In A. Thomas & J. Grimes (Eds.), *Children's needs: Psychological perspectives* (pp. 418–427). Washington, DC: The National Association of School Psychologists.

Brown, G. W., & Harris, T. (1978). *Social origins of depression*. London: Tavistock.

Bruner, J. S. (1973). *Beyond the information given: Studies in the psychology of knowing*. New York: Norton.

Buck, J. N. (1949). The H-T-P technique: A qualitative and scoring manual, Part 2. *Journal of Clinical Psychology, 5*, 37–76.

Burgdoy, K. (1981). Recognition and reporting child maltreatment: Study findings. *National study of the incidence and severity of child abuse and neglect*. (DHHS Publication No. 80–30325). Washington, DC: National Center on Child Abuse and Neglect.

Carlson, G. A., & Cantwell, D. P. (1979). A survey of depressive symptoms in a child and adolescent psychiatric population. *Journal of the American Academy of Child Psychiatry, 18*, 587–599.

Casey, R. J., & Berman, J. S. (1985). The outcome of psychotherapy with children. *Psychological Bulletin, 98*, 388–400.

Chambers, W. J., Puig-Antich, J., & Tabrizi, M. A. (1978, Oct.). *The ongoing development of the Kiddie-SADS (schedule for affective disorders and schizophrenia for school-age children)*. Paper presented at the meeting of the American Academy of Child Psychiatry, San Diego, CA.

Chiles, A., Miller, M. L., & Cox, G. B. (1980). Depression in an adolescent delinquent population. *Archives of General Psychiatry, 37*, 1179–1184.

Cole, J. D., & Kupersmidt, J. B. (1983). A behavioral analysis of emerging social status in boys' groups. *Child Development, 54*, 1400–1416.

Cole, O. A., & Rehm, L. P. (1986). Family interaction patterns and childhood depression. *Journal of Abnormal Child Psychology, 14*, 297–314.

Costello, A. J., Edelbrock, C. S., Dulcan, M. K., & Kalas, R. (1984). *Testing of the NIMH Diagnostic Interview Schedule for Children (DISC) in a Clinical Population* (Contract No. DB–81–0027, final report to the Center for Epidemiological Studies, National Institute for Mental Health). Pittsburgh: University of Pittsburgh.

Costello, A. J., Edelbrock, C., Kalas, R., Kessler, M. D., & Klaric, S. H. (1982). *The NIMH Diagnostic Interview Schedule for Children (DISC)*. Unpublished interview schedule, Department of Psychiatry, University of Pittsburgh.

Craig, C. J. (1989). *Human development* (5th ed.). Englewood Cliffs, NJ: Prentice-Hall.

Damon, L., & Waterman, J. (1986). Parallel group treatment of children and their mothers. In K. MacFarlane & J. Waterman (Eds.), *Sexual abuse of young children*. New York: Guilford Press.

Digdon, N., & Gotlib, I. H. (1985). Developmental considerations in the study of childhood depression. *Developmental Review, 5,* 162–199.

Dodge, K. A. (1983). Behavioral antecedents of peer social station. *Child Development, 54,* 1386–1399.

Dworetzky, J. P. (1990). *Introduction to child development* (4th ed.). St. Paul, MN: West.

Edelbrock, C., & Costello, A. J. (1988). Structured psychiatric interviews for children. In M. Rutter, A. H. Tuma, & I. S. Lann (Eds.), *Assessment and diagnosis in child psychopathology* (pp. 82–112). New York: Guilford Press.

Elliott, D. S., Huizinga, D., & Ageton, S. S. (1985). *Explaining delinquency and drug use*. Beverly Hills, CA: Sage.

Ellis, P. L. (1982). Empathy: A factor in antisocial behavior. *Journal of Abnormal Child Psychology, 10,* 123–133.

England, L. W., & Thompson, C. L. (1988). Counseling child sexual abuse victims: Myths and realities. *Journal of Counseling and Development, 66,* 370–373.

Erikson, E. H. (1963). *Childhood and society* (2nd ed.). New York: Norton.

Erikson, E. H. (1968). *Identity, youth, and crisis*. New York: Norton.

Feinauer, L. L. (1990). Relationship of treatment to adjustment in women sexually abused as children. *The American Journal of Family Therapy, 17*(4), 326–334.

Feldman, R. A., Caplinger, T. E., & Wodarski, S. S. (1981). The St. Louis conundrum: Prosocial and antisocial boys together. Unpublished manuscript.

Field, T., Healy, B., Goldstein, S., Perry, S., Bendell, D., Schanberg, S., Zimmerman, E. A., & Kuhn, C. (1988). Infants of depressed mothers show "depressed" behavior even with nondepressed adults. *Child Development, 59,* 1569–1579.

Freud, A. (1928). Introduction to the technique of child analysis. *Nervous and Mental Disease Monograph No. 48*. New York.

Gilligan, C. (1982). *In a different voice: Psychological theory and women's development*. Cambridge, MA: Harvard University Press.

Gilligan, C. (1987). Adolescent development reconsidered. In C. Irwin (Ed.), *Adolescent social behavior and health*. San Francisco: Jossey-Bass.

Hammer, C., & Zupan, B. A. (1984). Self-schemas, depression, and the processing of personal information in children. *Journal of Experimental Child Psychology, 37,* 598–608.

Harris, D. E. (1963). *Children's drawings as measures of intellectual maturity*. A revision and extension of Goodenough Draw-A-Man Test. San Diego, CA: Harcourt Brace Jovanovich.

Hart, S. N., & Brassard, M. R. (1987). A major threat to children's mental health: Psychological maltreatment. *American Psychologist, 42,* 160–165.

Hazzard, A., King, H. E., & Webb, C. (1986). Group therapy with sexually abused adolescent girls. *American Journal of Psychotherapy, 40*(2), 213–223.

Hellendorn, J. (1988). Imaginative play technique in psychotherapy with children. In C. E. Schaefer (Ed.), *Innovative interventions in child and adolescent therapy*. New York: John Wiley & Sons.

Herjanic, B., & Reich, W. (1982). Development of a structured psychiatric interview for children: Agreement between child and parent of individual symptoms. *Journal of Abnormal Child Psychology, 10,* 307–324.

Herman, J. L. (1986). *Father-daughter incest*. Cambridge, MA: Harvard University Press.

Huba, G. J., & Bentler, P. M. (1983). Causal models of the development of law abidance and its relationship to psychosocial factors and drug use. In W. S. Lauger & J. M. Day (Eds.), *Personality theory, moral development, and criminal behavior* (pp. 164–215). Lexington, MA: Lexington Books.

Kadushin, A., & Martin, J. A. (1981). *Child abuse: An interactional event*. New York: Columbia University Press.

Kandel, D. B. (1973). Adolescent marijuana use: Role of parents and peers. *Science, 181,* 1067–1081.

Kanner, L. (1962). *Child psychiatry* (3rd ed.). Springfield, IL: Charles C. Thomas.

Kazdin, A. E. (1985). *Treatment of antisocial behavior in children and adolescents*. Homewood, IL: Dorsey Press.

Kazdin, A. E. (1987). Treatment of antisocial behavior in children: Current status and future directions. *Psychological Bulletin, 102,* 187–203.

Kazdin, A. E. (1988). Childhood depression. In E. J. Mash & L. Terdal (Eds.), *Behavioral assessment of childhood disorders* (2nd ed., pp. 157–196). New York: Guilford Press.

Kazdin, A. E. (1989). Developmental psychopathology: Current research, issues, and directions. *American Psychologist, 44*(2), 180–187.

Kazdin, A. E., Bass, D., Siegel, T. & Thomas, C. (1989). Cognitive-behavioral therapy and relationship therapy in the treatment of children referred for antisocial behavior. *Journal of Consulting and Clinical Psychology, 57*(4), 522–535.

Kitchur, M., & Bell, R. (1989). Group psychotherapy with preadolescent sexual abuse victims: A literature review and description of an inner-city group. *International Journal of Group Psychotherapy, 39*(3), 285–310.

Klein, M. (1960). *The psychoanalysis of children*. New York: Grove Press.

Knitzer, J. (1982). *Unclaimed children*. Washington, DC: Children's Defense Fund.

Knoff, H. M., & Prout, H. T. (1985). *The kinetic drawing system for family and school*. Los Angeles, CA: Western Psychological Services.

Kohlberg, L. (1963). Development of children's orientation towards a moral order. 1. Sequence in the development of moral thought. *Vita Human, 6,* 11–36.

Kohlberg, L. (1973). Continuities in childhood and adult moral development revisited. In P. B. Baltes & K. W. Schair (Eds.), *Life-span developmental psychology: Personality and socialization*. New York: Academic Press.

Kohlberg, L. (1981). *The philosophy of moral development*. New York: Harper & Row.

Kovacs, M. (1981). Rating scales to assess depression in school-aged children. *Acta Parlopsychiatrica, 46,* 305–315.

Kovacs, M. (1982). *The Interview Schedule for Children (ISC)*: Unpublished interview schedule, Department of Psychiatry, University of Pittsburgh.

Kovacs, M. (1989). Affective disorders in children and adolescents. *American Psychologist, 44,* 209–215.

Kovacs, M., Gatsonis, C., Marsh, J., & Richards, C. (1988). Intellectual and cognitive development in childhood-onset depressive disorders: A longitudinal study. Manuscripts submitted for publication.

Lang, M., & Tisher, M. (1978). *Children's depression scale*. Victoria, Australia: Australian Council for Educational Research.

Loeber, R., & Schmaling, K. B. (1985). Empirical evidence for overt and covert patterns of antisocial conduct problems: A meta-analysis. *Journal of Abnormal Child Psychology, 13,* 337–352.

McMahon, R. J., & Forehand, R. (1988). Conduct disorders. In E. J. Mash & L. G. Terdal (Eds.), *Behavioral assessment of childhood disorders* (2nd ed., pp. 105–156). New York: Guilford Press.

Milich, R., & Dodge, K. A. (1984). Social information processing in child psychiatric population. *Journal of Abnormal Child Psychology, 12,* 471–490.

Milner, J. S. (1986). *The child abuse potential inventory: Manual* (rev. ed.). Webster, NC: Psytec Corporation.

Nystul, M. S. (1980). Nystulian play therapy: Applications of Adlerian psychology. *Elementary School Guidance & Counseling, 15*(22), 30.

O'Brien, S. (1983). *Child pornography*. Dubuque, IA: Kendall/Hunt.

Orenchuk-Tomiuk, N., Matthey, G., & Christensen, C. P. (1990). The resolution model: A comprehensive treatment framework in sexual abuse, *Child Welfare, 69*(5), 417–431.

Patterson, G. R. (1982). *Coercive family process*. Eugene, OR: Castalia.

Patterson, G. R., DeBaryshe, R. D., & Ramsey, E. (1989). A developmental perspective on antisocial behavior. *American Psychologist, 44*(2), 329–335.

Pfeffer, C. R. (1981). Suicidal behavior of children: A review with implications for research and practice. *American Journal of Psychiatry, 138*, 154–159.

Piaget, J. (1952). *The origins of intelligence in children* (M. Cook, Trans.). New York: Norton.

Piaget, J. (1965). *The moral judgment of the child* (M. Gabain, Trans.). New York: Free Press. (Original work published 1936)

Polansky, N., Chalmers, M., Buttenwieser, E., & Williams, D. (1981). *Damaged parents: An anatomy of child neglect*. Chicago: University of Chicago Press.

Puig-Antich, J., Perel, J. M., Lupatkins, W., Chambers, W. J., Tabrizi, M. A., King, J., Goetz, R., Davies, M., & Stiller, R. L. (1987). Imipramine in prepubertal major depressive disorders. *Archives of General Psychiatry, 44*, 81–89.

Quay, H. C., & Petersen, D. R. (1983). *Interim manual for the revised behavior problem checklist*. Unpublished manuscript, University of Miami.

Radbill, S. X. (1980). Children in a world of violence: A history of child abuse. In C. H. Kempe & R. E. Helfer (Eds.), *The battered child*. Chicago: University of Chicago.

Reams, R., & Friedrich, W. N. (1983). *Play therapy: A review of outcome research*. Seattle: University of Washington, Department of Psychology.

Reynolds, W. M., & Coats, K. I. (1986). A comparison of cognitive-behavioral therapy and relocation training for the treatment of depression in adolescents. *Journal of Counseling and Clinical Psychology, 54*, 653–660.

Robins, L., Helzer, J. E., Croughan, J., & Ratcliff, K. S. (1981). National Institute of Mental Health diagnostic interview schedule: Its history, characteristics, and validity. *Archives of General Psychiatry, 38*, 381–389.

Sakolske, D. H., & Janzen, H. L. (1987). Dependency. In A. Thomas & J. Grimes, (Eds.), *Children's needs: Psychological perspectives* (pp. 157–166). Washington, DC: The National Association of School Psychologists.

Salkind, N. (1990). *Child development* (6th ed.). Orlando, FL: Holt, Rinehart, & Winston.

Snyder, J. J. (1977). Reinforcement analysis of interaction in problem and nonproblem families. *Journal of Abnormal Psychology, 86*, 528–535.

Spitz, R. (1946). Anaditic depression. *Psychoanalytic Study of the Child, 2*, 113–117.

Sroufe, L. A., & Cooper, R. G. (1988). *Child development: Its nature and course*. New York: Alfred A. Knopf.

Stabler, B. (1984). *Children's drawings*. Chapel Hill, NC: Health Sciences Consortium.

Straus, M. A., Gelles, R. J., & Steinmetz, S. (1980). *Behind closed doors: Violence in the American family*. Garden City, NY: Doubleday/Anchor.

Strober, M., Hanna, G., & McCracken, J. (in press). Bipolar illness. In C. Last & M. Hersens (Eds.), *Handbook of child psychiatric diagnosis*. New York: Wiley.

Talbutt, L. C. (1986). The abused child. In L. B. Golden & D. Capuzzi (Eds.), *Helping families help children*. Springfield, IL: Charles C. Thomas.

Tuma, J. M. (1989). Mental health services in children: The state of the art. *American Psychologist, 44*(2), 188–199.

U.S. Department of Justice. (1984). *Crime in the United States*. Washington, DC: Federal Bureau of Investigation.

Wahler, R. G., & Dumas, J. E. (1984). Family factors in childhood psychopathology: Toward a coercion neglect model. In T. Jacob (Ed.), *Family interaction and psychopathology*. New York: Plenum Press.

Weisz, J. R., Weiss, B., Alicke, M. D., & Klotz, M. L. (1987). Effectiveness of psychotherapy with children and adolescents: Meta-analytic findings for clinicians. *Journal of Consulting and Clinical Psychology, 55,* 542–549.

Wilson, J. Q., & Herrnstein, R. J. (1985). *Crime and human nature.* New York: Simon & Schuster.

Wolfe, D. A. (1988). Child abuse and neglect. In E. J. Mash & L. G. Terdal (Eds.), *Behavioral assessment of childhood disorders* (2nd ed., pp. 627–679). New York: Guilford Press.

CHAPTER ELEVEN

Group Counseling

CHAPTER OVERVIEW

This chapter provides an overview of group counseling. Highlights of the chapter include

- Group counseling from a historical perspective
- Comparison to individual and family counseling
- Goals and types of groups
- Problem solving and group process
- Group size, composition, and duration
- Use of co-leaders
- Pregroup screening and orientation
- Stages in group counseling
- Dealing with disruptive group members
- Common mistakes of group leaders
- Qualities of effective group leaders

Group counseling is an important specialty within the counseling profession. The practice of group counseling is found in most counseling programs and is therefore an integral part of the counselor's identity (Fuhriman & Burlingame, 1990). Several organizations have done much to advance the professionalization of group counseling. The American Counseling Association (ACA) charted a special division for group counseling in 1973 called the Association for Specialists in Group Work (ASGW). Ethical guidelines were established in 1980 and revised in 1989 (see Appendix C). Several other professional organizations have furthered the cause of group counseling, including the American Group Psychotherapy Association, the International Group Psychotherapy Association, and the American Association of Group Psychotherapy, Psychodrama, and Sociometry.

This chapter provides an overview of group counseling. It begins by describing group counseling from a historical perspective. Group counseling is then differentiated from individual and family counseling. Information on the practice of group counseling and a description of the stages of group counseling are also provided.

GROUP COUNSELING FROM A HISTORICAL PERSPECTIVE

Group counseling has a rich and fascinating history. The group movement can be traced to the pioneering work of J. L. Morreno and Kurt Lewin in the 1920s and 1930s (Bonner, 1959). Lewin's field theory provided an important theoretical foundation for group work, and Morreno developed a unique approach to group counseling called psychodrama.

Initially, group counseling was met with skepticism in the professional community. Some perceived this new technique as a radical, unorthodox procedure that would undermine confidentiality. In addition, it conflicted with the basic definition of counseling, that of counselors working with individual clients. Gradually, however, group counseling gained respectability. In 1946, the National Training Laboratory (NTL) was founded in Bethel, Maine (Baruth & Robinson, 1987) and soon became a major training institute for group work. The institute focused on how to use group dynamics to promote personal growth and interpersonal functioning.

During the 1960s encounter and sensitivity groups became popular in general, and the "in" thing on many college campuses. The spirit of the group movement seemed to blend with the cultural revolution also taking place in the 1960s. Both encouraged self-exploration, mind expansion, spontaneity, openness, honesty, and confrontation when necessary.

Perhaps in part due to its association with the "hippies" of the 1960s, the group movement came under criticism. Because of a few unusual encounter groups that were conducted in Northern California with nude participants, implications were made that all group counseling evolved into sex orgies. In addition, charges were made that the group movement was a contributing factor to social unrest among youth. As a result, an anti-group movement began in California in the late 1960s.

Some of its leaders even suggested that group counseling was part of a communist conspiracy to undermine the minds of youth. Patterson contended that there were legitimate criticisms of many of the groups run in the 1960s (Vacc, 1989). He believed that problems resulted from inadequate training of group leaders; too much emphasis on uncovering people's problems and doing whatever "feels right" without concern for one's effect on other group members; and the use of gimmicky, manipulative techniques and games.

During the 1970s and 1980s, several factors contributed to group counseling's return to respectability. The major factor was a shift away from the lack of structure associated with sensitivity and encounter groups, which was seen as a contributing factor not only to negative perceptions about the specialty but also to "casualties" in counseling. Professionals believed that groups based on clear goals and objectives could generate more productive outcomes.

Commenting on the future of group counseling as we enter the 1990s, Gazda (Elliot, 1989) said there will be a continuing emphasis on family group work, social-skills training, and life-skills training groups. In addition, he believes that the popularity of self-help groups will grow faster than that of any other type.

COMPARISON TO INDIVIDUAL AND FAMILY COUNSELING

Group counseling is a specialty that has unique features in terms of theory and practice. At the same time, it has common elements with other forms of counseling such as individual and family counseling. This section will describe the similarities and differences between group counseling and individual or family counseling. It will also identify advantages and disadvantages of group counseling.

Group Versus Individual Counseling

Fuhriman and Burlingame (1990) suggested there are few differences between group and individual counseling. This is not surprising, since theories and techniques tend to be transferred from individual to group counseling (Fuhriman & Burlingame, 1990).

Although the techniques used in group and individual counseling are similar, the counseling process varies in group counseling to accommodate the increased complexities that result from multiple clients. Drawing primarily from Yalom's (1985) 11 therapeutic factors for group work, Fuhriman and Burlingame (1990) identified the following six factors that differentiate group counseling from individual counseling.

1. *Vicarious learning.* Group counseling offers opportunities for members to learn from observing other group members as they explore their concerns.

2. *Role flexibility.* Clients in group counseling can function both as helpers and helpees. Clients in individual counseling can only maintain the role of helpee.

3. *Universality.* Group counseling creates opportunities for clients to discover that other group members have similar concerns, fears, and problems. This experience of universality can help clients put their problems in perspective and not overreact to them.

4. *Altruism.* During group counseling, members are encouraged to offer help to other group members. Clients who engage in altruistic behavior can provide support for other group members and enhance their self-image.

5. *Interpersonal learning.* Interaction between group members creates opportunities to enhance interpersonal skills.

6. *Family reenactment.* The therapeutic climate created in a group can be similar to what was experienced in a client's family of origin. Group counseling can therefore be particularly useful in working through early familial conflicts.

The following Personal Note is an illustration of how I helped a client work through an early familial conflict in group counseling.

a personal note

I was a counseling psychologist at a university counseling center, and a client in the group was a young man in his early 20s. "Tom" was having problems, feeling a lack of confidence and courage.

During one session, Tom told the group about an experience he had as a teen-ager. He said his father was an alcoholic, who verbally and physically abused Tom's mother. Tom described one instance that he often thought about. He and his mother were sitting in the living room when his father started yelling terrible things at his mother, then went over and slapped her on the face. Tom just sat and watched. He felt angry at his father, but also at himself because he couldn't help his mother. As he reflected on the incident, he said he just wished he would have had the courage to "stand up like a man" and come to the aid of his mother.

I suggested that we reenact the situation. I arranged to have a group member play the role of mother; Tom would be himself; I would play the role of father; and the rest of the group members would be the audience and provide feedback.

When we started the scene, Tom initially had a difficult time taking his role seriously. He started to laugh and said, "You don't look like my father." I intensified my yelling and abusive language toward his "mother." I then went over and started to shake her. The next thing I realized was that Tom was standing in front of me. He grabbed my shoulders and told me to leave his mother alone. His face was bright red with anger. He was breathing hard and then started to cry.

At this point, I stopped the reenactment and held the client for a few moments and encouraged him to cry and get his feelings out. We then discussed the experience with the group members. Tom said something seemed to snap in him when I began to yell at his "mother." He really felt he was there with his mother and father. Tom said it made him feel better to be able to tell his father how he felt and stand up for his mother. He went on to say that his tears were tears of relief, that he was finally able to let go of his feelings of helplessness and shame.

This case provides an illustration of the intense emotions that can result from group counseling procedures. The procedures should therefore be used carefully. It is especially important not to push clients to the point where they are forced to deal with emotions that they are not ready to handle.

Group Versus Family Counseling

Group and family counseling also have similarities and differences. In terms of similarities, both "bring people together to resolve problems by emphasizing interpersonal relationships" (Hines, 1988, p. 174). The processes of group and family counseling are also similar. The focus of the initial sessions in both is for the counselor to define the presenting problem from an interpersonal perspective (Hines, 1988; Whitaker & Keith, 1981; Yalom, 1985). In addition, the working stage in both is an interactive process whereby the client and counselor are actively engaged (Hines, 1988; Whitaker & Keith, 1981; Yalom, 1985).

Hines (1988) identified differences between group and family counseling in terms of inclusion, structure, and interrelatedness. According to Hines (1988), inclusion must be gained by participation in a group, whereas it is a biological given in a family. Structurally, group members have equal power, while family members have hierarchical power (Couch & Childers, 1989; Hines, 1988). Group members have a lesser degree of interrelatedness than family members, who have spent years living together (Hines, 1988). As a result, family members have well-established interpersonal processes, whereas group members are strangers to one another when they form the group (Couch & Childers, 1989).

Another difference between group and family counseling is the role of the counselor. During the initial stage of group counseling, the leader attempts to assist group members with the process of inclusion (Hines, 1988; Schultz, 1977). The reverse is true in family counseling, since the counselor initially feels like an outsider and attempts to be included in the family (Hines, 1988). The counselor's role also varies between group and family counseling in terms of establishing norms (Couch & Childers, 1989; Hines, 1988). During the initial phase of group counseling, the leader plays an active role establishing group norms (Couch & Childers, 1989; Hines, 1988). This is not the case in family counseling because the family already has a well-established norm system (Couch & Childers, 1989; Hines, 1988).

Perhaps the biggest difference between group and family counseling lies in the goals of each process. Couch and Childers (1989) noted that group counseling has goals for the group, such as creating a climate of trust and acceptance, as well as specific goals for each individual member. In contrast, the goal of family counseling is to improve the overall functioning of the family unit.

Advantages and Disadvantages of Group Counseling

As with any counseling strategy, group counseling has potential advantages and disadvantages. The main advantage of group counseling is that it provides a safe environment for clients to try out and experience new behaviors with other group members. Other advantages are that

- Clients can learn from other group members as they explore their personal concerns
- The process is more economical in terms of time, since several clients can be seen during a session

- Clients can have an opportunity to help others during the session, thereby minimizing tendencies to be overly concerned with their own problems
- Problem solving for a client can be enhanced by the ideas generated by other group members
- The group can foster energy and enthusiasm, which can help motivate a client to pursue personal goals

The main disadvantage of group counseling is that it may be inappropriate for some clients. This is especially true for clients with a serious mental disorder or a low self-concept. It may even be dangerous for these clients to participate in a group because they may feel threatened or personally attacked by the feedback they receive from other group members. In these cases, the client may first need to participate in individual counseling to be able to utilize group counseling successfully. Corey and Corey (1987) also identified risks associated with group counseling, including problems with confidentiality that can arise in groups; inappropriate self-disclosing due to group pressure; feeling attacked as a result of confrontation; and negative emotional consequences that can occur from scapegoating.

GOALS AND TYPES OF GROUPS

Couch and Childers (1989) noted there are group goals as well as individual goals. Group goals include fostering trust and acceptance and promoting self-disclosure,

Group counseling involves fostering trust and acceptance between group members.

feedback, and risk taking (Corey & Corey, 1987). Most approaches to group counseling also encourage group members to formulate individualized goals (Couch & Childers, 1989). Members are then assisted in learning problem-solving strategies they can utilize outside the group setting (Couch & Childers, 1989).

Goals will also vary according to the type of group. Nelson-Jones (1992) and Jacobs, Harvill, and Masson (1988) identified common types of groups and their goals. These include life-skills training, mutual-sharing, growth, counseling and psychotherapy, family, discussion, and task groups.

Life-skills training groups, also called education groups, are defined as "time-limited, structured groups in which one or more leaders use a repertoire of didactic and facilitative skills to help participants develop and maintain one or more specific life skills." (Nelson-Jones, 1992, p. 6). These groups are characterized by an emphasis on wellness versus sickness; systematic instruction; an experiential focus; and participant involvement. Life-skills training groups promote skills relating to all aspects of life, for example, parenting, intellectual development, self-management, and physical development.

Mutual-sharing groups, also called support or self-help groups, are composed of people with similar concerns providing support for one another. The fundamental goal of mutual-sharing groups is to provide support to members. Examples of these groups are children of divorced parents, adult children of alcoholics, and adults who are prone to engage in child abuse.

Growth groups are designed to help group members increase self-awareness. Their goal is to assist members in improving their lives by clarifying their values, personal concerns, and interpersonal relationships.

Counseling and psychotherapy groups can be used to promote personal growth through members sharing their own concerns and listening to the concerns of others. The primary goal is to provide a therapeutic climate that enables group members to share personal concerns and work toward resolving them.

Family groups involve inviting different families to a group setting to discuss issues of concern. The primary goal is to enhance the functioning of the family system. Multiple-family group work can be used when a counselor wants to work with several families at a time. Family network groups can be established with the goal of providing information and support to families.

Discussion groups provide an opportunity to discuss a topic of interest rather than the personal concerns of group members. Examples of discussion group topics are the pros and cons of having children; the effects of drug abuse; and attitudes toward marriage. The goal of discussion groups is to have members share ideas and knowledge regarding a particular topic.

Task groups can be appropriate when individuals have a specific task to accomplish, for example, students wanting to change a policy at their school. The goal of these groups is to accomplish the task.

PROBLEM SOLVING AND GROUP PROCESS

Group counseling is characterized by two dimensions that are critical to the success of the group: problem solving and group process. These dimensions are interrelated, and success in one dimension fosters success in the other.

The problem-solving strategies of individual counseling, as discussed in Chapter 2, can also be used in group counseling. These strategies typically involve the group leader and members first listening to a particular concern of a group member and then helping that member resolve the concern. The member taking action and assuming responsibility is an important part of the problem-solving process (Burlingame & Fuhriman, 1990).

Burlingame and Fuhriman (1990) identified the following four factors associated with group process.

1. *Engagement.* Engagement entails members sharing their feelings with one another. This practice is believed to foster cohesion (Aiello, 1979) and universality (Brabender, 1985).

2. *Group versus individual focus.* Opinions vary as to whether the process in group counseling should focus on the group, the individual, or alternately on the group and the individual (Burlingame & Fuhriman, 1990). A more equitable position might be to focus simultaneously on the individual and the group. Having co-leaders is a useful format, with one leader focusing on the concerns of an individual client and the other on issues that relate to the group process.

3. *Here-and-now focus.* Most approaches to group counseling emphasize the importance of maintaining a focus on the here-and-now in terms of group process (Burlingame & Fuhriman, 1990). Yalom (1985) suggested that a primary task of the group leader is to encourage group members to relate in the here-and-now, and then to have the group reflect on the here-and-now behavior that has just transpired. The here-and-now focus is believed to help group members learn about themselves through self-disclosure and feedback as they interact with each other (Sklare, Keener, & Mas, 1990).

4. *Goals of the group.* To some degree, a group's goals will determine the nature of the group. For example, a group designed to discuss parenting may have a didactic emphasis, where groups designed to improve interpersonal relationships will tend to be experiential in nature.

GROUP SIZE, COMPOSITION, AND DURATION

The appropriate group size varies according to the type of group and the ages of its members. For example, a play therapy group should not exceed four children for the counselor to be effective. In contrast, an education group may have an entire classroom full of people and the counselor can still work effectively with the group. For group counseling and psychotherapy, the average group size ranges from 4 to 10 members (Burlingame & Fuhriman, 1990). This range is large enough to create a diversity of ideas, yet small enough to provide an opportunity for each member to participate.

Group composition is another important issue to consider in formulating a group. Groups can be either heterogeneous or homogeneous. Heterogeneous groups are composed of a diversity of individuals of different ages, gender, cultures, socio-economic status, and so forth. These groups can help promote a diversity of ideas for group members to consider. Heterogeneous groups are also believed to foster greater individualization due to the wide range of issues they can address (Unger, 1989). Heterogeneous groups are commonly used in schools, where a counselor might conduct a session on alcohol and drug use with an entire classroom, or in community mental health centers, where a counselor might have several clients participate in group counseling to resolve personal problems. Homogeneous groups are composed of individuals who have something in common, for example, parents who want to learn about parenting or clients who suffer from eating disorders. An advantage of homogeneous groups is that they enhance universality by bringing together individuals with similar problems or concerns. Homogeneous groups are also believed to promote more cohesion and identification than heterogeneous groups (Unger, 1989).

Duration relates to three issues: whether the group is open or closed, the length of each session, and the number of sessions. *Open groups* are ongoing with no termination date, and they allow new members to join at any time. Alcoholics Anonymous uses an open-group format, encouraging new members to start attending sessions whenever they can. *Closed groups* have a specific starting date, and they do not allow new members to join after the first session. Closed groups are often utilized when the members want to learn certain principles and do not want to have to keep reviewing what was covered in an earlier session. A parent education group designed to help members learn about parenting might be an example of a closed group. Burlingame and Fuhriman (1990) found that hospital outpatient groups tend to be about half open and half closed, whereas inpatient groups tend to be open to accommodate new patients as they are admitted to the hospital.

For most groups, each session lasts approximately 90 minutes (Burlingame & Fuhriman, 1990). The group leader and members should determine the length of the session in advance and adhere to it as much as possible so group members can plan accordingly.

The number of sessions associated with group work varies according to the type of group, the needs of the group members, and the theoretical orientation of the group leader. Education groups might require from 6 to 10 sessions or extend over an entire school year. For counseling and psychotherapy groups, the number of sessions varies according to the setting. Groups for inpatient psychiatric patients usually meet at least once each day while the patients are in the hospital. Counseling and psychotherapy groups that are conducted in schools, private practice, and counseling centers typically meet once a week over a period of several months, with an average of 13 sessions (Burlingame & Fuhriman, 1990).

USE OF CO-LEADERS

Several advantages are associated with having a leader and co-leader in group counseling. First, group members can benefit from the expertise of two counselors. Second, there may be an advantage in having male and female counselors to create a more balanced perspective. Third, at the end of a session, the leader and co-leader can spend time debriefing, or sharing ideas about the session. As a result, they can gain a more comprehensive understanding of what occurred. A fourth advantage is that the leader can focus on helping a client work through a personal problem while the co-leader focuses on the group process. Facilitating the group process can involve creating a positive, trusting climate; keeping the group on task; helping each member feel valued; assisting reluctant clients in becoming involved in the group; and dealing with difficult members who may want to monopolize or sabotage the group.

PREGROUP SCREENING AND ORIENTATION

There appears to be a positive correlation between the amount of time spent in preparation for a group and positive outcomes occurring from the group (Lynn & Frauman, 1985). A pregroup interview is typically utilized to help screen and orientate prospective group members. The screening process typically excludes individuals who suffer from severe psychopathology such as psychoses, extreme paranoia, or sociopathy (Burlingame & Fuhriman, 1990). The same qualities that are considered desirable for inclusion in individual counseling apply to groups. These include high motivation, adequate ego strength, a satisfactory past relationship with other individuals, the presence of an acute problem, and realistic expectations (Burlingame & Fuhriman, 1990).

Pregroup orientation is designed to help members prepare for entry into the group. Corey and Corey (1987) provided a list of the following issues that should be discussed with prospective group members before they join the group.

- Describe the purpose of the group
- Provide information on the group format, procedures and ground rules
- Determine if the group is appropriate for the client
- Explore client concerns
- Provide information regarding the leader's education, training, and qualifications
- Discuss possible psychological risks that could result from the group
- Provide information on fees and expenses
- Discuss limits of confidentiality
- Clarify what services can be provided by the group

STAGES IN GROUP COUNSELING

Several authors have attempted to delineate stages in group counseling (Budman & Gurman, 1988; Corey, 1990; Brabender, 1985; Gazda, 1984; Poey, 1985). These authors contend that a model of the stages in group counseling provides a structure to the process that helps us better understand it.

Corey (1990) developed the following model, which consists of four stages: the initial, transition, working, and final stages.

Stage 1: The Initial Stage.   The initial stage of group counseling involves screening, orientation, and determining the structure of the group. The major functions of the group leader during this stage are establishing ground rules and norms for the group; helping members express their fears and expectations; being open and psychologically present; assisting group members in identifying concrete personal goals; and sharing expectations and hopes for the group. During the initial stage, members attempt to create trust; learn to express their feelings and thoughts, including fears or reservations about the group; become involved in establishing group norms; establish personal goals; and learn about the dynamics of the group process.

Stage 2: The Transition Stage.   The transition stage is characterized as a time when group members experience anxiety and defensiveness as they begin to question the value of the group. The major functions of the leader during this phase are encouraging members to express their anxiety, dealing openly with conflicts that occur in the group, and helping group members become autonomous and independent. During this stage, it is common for group members to become concerned about being accepted by the group. A central task for members is to recognize and express feelings of resistance toward the group process.

Stage 3: The Working Stage.   The working stage occurs when group members feel free to explore their thoughts and feelings and work on their concerns. The major functions of the group leader are encouraging members to translate insight into action and helping them make the necessary changes to achieve their goals. The working stage is characterized by group members introducing personal issues that they are willing to work on; providing and receiving feedback; applying what they learn in the group to their daily lives; and offering support and encouragement to other group members.

Stage 4: The Final Stage.   The final stage is a time that should offer members a smooth transition toward termination of the group. The major functions of the leader during the final stage are to assist clients in working toward termination; provide opportunities for them to receive additional counseling if necessary; and help them gain a useful understanding of what they have learned. This stage is often characterized by sadness and anxiety regarding the termination of the group. Members may begin to decrease their intensity of participation to prepare for termination, and they may also evaluate how they experienced the group.

Some authors have questioned whether group counseling actually has stages. Yalom (Forester-Miller, 1989) claimed that stages are merely a way of imposing a type of structure that does not exist in groups. Patterson (Vacc, 1989) also expressed a negative view of the stage model of group counseling. He contended that group counseling is a continuous process that does not have discrete stages (Vacc, 1989). In addition, Patterson believed that the stage model creates expectations for group members that can interfere with the normal development process of the group (Vacc, 1989). Burlingame and Fuhriman (1990) also noted that the various stage models of group counseling have not been supported by research. Additional research on this topic appears warranted.

DEALING WITH DISRUPTIVE GROUP MEMBERS

Occasionally, a group member can become disruptive to the group process. The following discussion presents typical behaviors that may surface and the steps coun-

Group members can obstruct group progress by acting as if they are not interested.

selors can take to avert disruption of the group process. The behaviors are those observed in people acting as aggressors, obstructors, story tellers, and attention-seekers.

Aggressors may be overt or covert in their aggressive behavior toward other group members or the leader. When this occurs, the leader should try not to become angry or threatened. The aggressor is often trying to create a conflict, so an angry reaction may only reinforce that behavior. An approach that may be more productive is to inform the aggressor firmly but kindly that group process is based on a philosophy of encouragement and support. It may also be productive to explore and work through the aggressor's feelings.

Obstructors tend to be negative and obstruct the group process. They often find ways to sidetrack the issues being discussed and prevent the group from staying on task. This may involve a variety of disruptive behaviors, for example, constantly trying to change the topic or complaining that nothing seems to be happening in the group. Obstructors often engage in their disruptive behavior as a means of gaining power and control. It is therefore important for the counselor avoid reacting with anger, since that reaction may only create a power struggle. When the obstructor tries to change the topic, the leader might say, "No, let's not change the focus of our work. We need to spend more time with this so we can reach a meaningful conclusion."

Story tellers often like to monopolize the group by telling drawn-out stories about things that have happened months ago. What they say usually holds little interest for the group, because they typically have already resolved the issue or have no desire to do anything about it. When this occurs, the leader can ask what the story teller is thinking and feeling at the moment. The leader can emphasize that it is important to try to stay in the here-and-now so the group can have something concrete to work on.

Attention-seekers find different ways to draw attention to themselves. Since their goal is typically gaining attention, the counselor must be careful not to reinforce the behavior. Two strategies can be used in working with attention-seekers. The leader should first attempt to channel the attention-seeker's need for attention in a positive direction by asking for assistance when possible. When that fails, the leader should ask the attention-seeker to refrain from the behaviors that are creating a problem. For example, if the behavior is making frequent, inappropriate jokes, the leader might say, "Turning a serious issue into a joke does not allow the group to work on issues realistically."

COMMON MISTAKES OF GROUP LEADERS

Jacobs, Harvill, and Masson (1988) identified the following common mistakes group leaders make in therapy groups.

- *Attempting to conduct therapy without a contract.* It is important to ensure that a member wants help with a particular problem by directly inquiring if the client would like assistance. Assuming a client wants help may waste valuable time with a member who is not ready to make a commitment to work on his problem.

- *Spending too much time on one person.* Group time can be dominated by difficult group members or members who are interesting and attractive and are eager for assistance during *each* session. Group leaders have an ethical responsibility to ensure that all members have an opportunity to participate.

- *Spending too little time with one person.* Group leaders can spend too little time with a member during the problem-solving process in an attempt to give everyone a chance to talk. While it's important to ensure that all members be encouraged to participate, this does not mean they all need to talk. Problem solving requires that one member be the focus of attention for a sufficient period of time.

- *Letting members rescue each other.* There can be a tendency for group members to rescue other members when they sense pain or sorrow. Emotional rescuing is not productive in any form of counseling, because it communicates sympathy. Group counselors should instead encourage members to convey support, concern, and empathy.

- *Letting the session turn into advice-giving.* Premature advice-giving can be particularly prevalent when group members attempt to offer help to other members during problem solving. Premature advice-giving is not productive in any counseling including group counseling. When this occurs, the leader could suggest that members take more time using listening skills to gain a better understanding of the problem before attempting to solve it.

QUALITIES OF EFFECTIVE GROUP LEADERS

Perhaps the most important factor in effective group counseling is the personal qualities of the group leader. The art of counseling model emphasizes the role of the self as an instrument of change. Several authors have identified leadership qualities that promote positive outcomes in group counseling. Ohlsen (1970) noted that effective group counselors are in tune with the group process. They can then make the necessary changes to ensure positive therapeutic movement. Corey (1990) identified personal qualities associated with effective group leadership, which include presence, personal power, courage, willingness to confront oneself, self-awareness, sincerity, authenticity, a sense of identity, belief in the group process, enthusiasm, inventiveness, and creativity. Yalom and Lieberman (1971) suggested that the group leader sets the emotional climate for the group. When the leader acts in an autocratic, confrontational, or emotionally distant fashion, the group experience may actually do more harm than good to members. These authors recommended that a leader with moderate amounts of executive function and emotional stimulation and high amounts of caring and meaning attribution contributes to improvements in group members. Taken collectively, the literature suggests that the qualities of effective group leaders are having a positive presence, which can instill trust and enthusiasm; being sensitive to the group process and capable of making adjustments as necessary; and setting a positive and encouraging therapeutic climate.

CHAPTER SUMMARY

Group counseling is becoming an increasingly popular counseling specialty. This chapter addressed some of the major issues associated with group counseling. It began by describing group counseling from a historical perspective. Group counseling was then differentiated from individual and family counseling. A description of the process of group counseling was also provided including information on goals and types of groups; problem solving and group process; group size, composition, and duration; use of co-leaders; pregroup screening and orientation; stages in group counseling; dealing with disruptive group members; common mistakes of leaders; and qualities of effective group leaders.

REFERENCES

Aiello, T. J. (1979). Short-term group therapy of the hospitalized psychotic. In P. Olsen & H. Grayson (Eds.), *Short-term approaches to psychotherapy*. New York: Human Sciences Press.

Baruth, L. G., & Robinson, E. H. III. (1987). *An introduction to the counseling profession*. Englewood Cliffs, NJ: Prentice-Hall.

Bonner, H. (1959). *Group dynamics*. New York: Ronald Press.

Brabender, V. (1985). Time-limited impatient group therapy: A developmental model. *International Journal of Group Psychotherapy, 35,* 373–390.

Budman, S. H., & Gurman, A. S. (1988). *Theory and practice of brief therapy*. New York: Guilford Press.

Burlingame, G. M., & Fuhriman, A. (1990). Time-limited group therapy. *The Counseling Psychologist, 18*(1), 93–118.

Corey, G. (1990). *Theory and practice of group counseling* (3rd ed.). Monterey, CA: Brooks/Cole.

Corey, M. S., & Corey, G. (1987). *Groups: Process and practice* (3rd ed.). Monterey, CA: Brooks/Cole.

Couch, R. D., & Childers, J. H., Jr. (1989). A discussion of differences between group therapy and family therapy: Implications for counselor training and practice. *The Journal for Specialists in Group Work, 14*(4), 226–231.

Elliot, G. (1989). An interview with George M. Gazda. *The Journal for Specialists in Group Work, 14*(3), 131–140.

Forester-Miller, H. (1989). Dr. Irvin Yalom discusses group psychotherapy. *The Journal for Specialists in Group Work, 14*(4), 196–201.

Fuhriman, A. & Burlingame, G. M. (1990). Consistency of matter: A comparative analysis of individual and group process variables. *The Counseling Psychologist, 18*(1), 6–63.

Gazda, G. M. (1984). *Group counseling: A developmental approach* (3rd ed.). Boston: Allyn Bacon.

Hines, M. (1988). Similarities and differences in group and family therapy. *The Journal for Specialists in Group Work, 13*(4), 173–179.

Jacobs, E. E., Harvill, R. L., & Masson, R. L. (1988). *Group counseling: Strategies and skills*. Pacific Grove, CA: Brooks/Cole.

Lynn, S. J., & Frauman, D. (1985). Group psychotherapy. In S. J. Lynn & F. P. Garske (Eds.), *Contemporary psychotherapies: Model and methods* (pp. 419–458). Columbus, OH: Merrill.

Nelson-Jones, R. (1992). *Group leadership: A training approach*. Pacific Grove, CA: Brooks/Cole.

Ohlsen, M. M. (1970). *Group counseling*. New York: Holt, Rinehart, & Winston.

Poey, K. (1985). Guidelines for the practice of brief, dynamic group therapy. *International Journal of Group Psychotherapy, 35*, 331–354.

Schultz, W. C. (1977). *FIRO-B* (2nd ed.). Palo Alto, CA: Consulting Psychologists Press.

Sklare, G., Keener, R., & Mas, C. (1990). Preparing members for "here and now" group counseling. *The Journal for Specialists in Group Work, 15*(3), 141–148.

Unger, R. (1989). Selection and composition criteria in group psychotherapy. *The Journal for Specialists in Group Work, 14*(3), 151–157.

Vacc, N. A. (1989). Group counseling: C. H. Patterson—A personalized view. *The Journal for Specialists in Group Work, 14*(1), 4–15.

Whitaker, C. A., & Keith, D. V. (1981). Symbolic-experiential family therapy. In A. S. Gurman & D. P. Kniskern (Eds.), *Handbook of family therapy* (pp. 187–225). New York: Brunner/Mazel.

Yalom, I. D. (1985). *The theory and practice of group psychotherapy* (3rd ed.). New York: Basic Books.

Yalom, I. D., & Lieberman, M. (1971). A study of encounter group casualties. *Archives of General Psychiatry, 25*, 16–30.

CHAPTER TWELVE

Career Counseling

CHAPTER OVERVIEW

This chapter provides an overview of career counseling, a challenging and evolving specialty that helps individuals with career planning and decision making throughout the life span. This chapter provides information on the following topics

- Evolution of career counseling
- Theoretical foundations in terms of career development and decision-making
- Treatment issues, including personal versus career counseling, assessment instruments, intervention strategies, and the process of career counseling
- Special issues including career counseling for women and computer-assisted career counseling

EVOLUTION OF CAREER COUNSELING

The world of work has changed dramatically over the centuries along with the evolution of the human species. Our early ancestors had limited opportunities and choices regarding work (Axelson, 1985). What people did was primarily restricted to preserving the survival of the species. Today, people work for many reasons that go beyond obtaining money for food and shelter. Some work to enhance their self-esteem; others have a goal of independence; some want to help people; while others work to experience power and control. As people's needs change over the life span, so too does the type of work they find rewarding. This in turn can account for the career changes that can take place throughout one's life.

Career counseling has evolved as a means of assisting individuals in developing career planning and decision-making skills to facilitate career choice. It has been referred to by several different names over the years, including occupational counseling, vocational guidance, and vocational counseling. These names tended to have a narrower focus than career counseling, since they emphasized the importance of obtaining occupational information in selecting a particular career. Career counseling is a more comprehensive concept incorporating the various career development theories to formulate a strong theoretical foundation. Super (1951) defined career counseling as

> . . . helping a person to develop and accept an integrated and adequate picture of himself and his role in the world of work, to test this concept against reality, and to convert it into a reality, with satisfaction to himself and benefit to society (Super, 1951, p. 92).

Career counseling is practiced by professional counselors in schools and agencies. Some counselors incorporate career counseling into their repertoire of helping skills to assist clients in exploring career issues and personal problems. Counselors can also specialize in this field and identify themselves as career counselors or career development professionals. In 1952, the American Counseling Association (ACA) recognized the special skills and professional interests associated with career counseling by creating a special division for career counselors called the National Career Development Association (NCDA).

The NCDA took an active role in establishing credentials for career counseling. These efforts resulted in career counseling becoming the first specialty designation offered by the National Board of Certified Counselors. Requirements for certification include

- Becoming certified by the National Board of Certified Counselors (see requirements in Chapter 15)
- Earning a graduate degree in counseling or a related profession
- Working at least part-time in career counseling for 3 years following graduate study
- Passing the National Career Counselor Examination

THEORETICAL FOUNDATIONS

Several individuals have provided theories of career development and career decision making. These theories provide a description of how career development occurs over the life span and what is entailed in the process of career choice and decision making.

Career Development Theories

Career development theories relate to how career issues develop over the life span. This section will provide an overview of three prominent career development theories, those of Super, Holland, and Roe.

Super's Theory.   Super (1990, p. 199) described his theory as "a loosely unified set of theories dealing with specific aspects of career development, taken from developmental, differential, social, personality, and phenomenological psychology." Super's (1957, 1980, 1990) theory emphasized the role of self-concept in career development. He contended that how individuals define themselves will have a major effect on their career choices. For example, a person with a self-image of a strong, hard worker but not particularly intellectual may be attracted to a "physical job" such as an auto mechanic.

Super's (1957) theory can be considered developmental because he suggested there are five stages of career development, each with corresponding developmental tasks: growth, exploration, establishment, maintenance, and decline. An overview of these stages follows.

The *growth stage* spans from birth to 14 years of age. The self-concept develops as the individual identifies with significant others. Developmental tasks during the growth stage include gaining self-understanding and obtaining an overall understanding of the world of work.

The growth stage has three substages. The *fantasy* substage occurs from age 4 to 10 and involves the child role-playing various fantasies regarding the world of work, for example, playing doctor or nurse. The *interest* substage extends from age 11 to 12. During this period, a child's likes and dislikes have a major impact on career aspirations. The third substage is *capacity*, which takes place from age 13 to 14. The capacity substage is characterized by a more realistic view of the world of work as individuals consider their abilities and job requirements.

Super's second stage is the *exploration stage*, which spans from 14 to 24 years of age. This is a period of self-examination in relation to the world of work. During this time, the individual also begins to directly experience work by involvement in part-time jobs. Developmental tasks associated with the exploration stage include crystallizing, specifying, and implementing a career preference.

The exploration stage has three substages. The *tentative* substage extends from age 15 to 17 and involves identifying appropriate fields of work. The *transition* substage begins at age 18 and continues to age 21. During this substage, the individual may pursue special educational or vocational training related to a field of work or enter directly into the job market. The third substage is referred to as *trial-little commitment* and ranges from age 22 to 24. During this period, the individual usually begins a first job. The commitment is usually tentative as the person decides whether the career choice was appropriate.

The third major stage is the *establishment stage*, spanning from 24 to 44 years of age. During this stage, individuals have identified an appropriate field of work that they want to make a long-term commitment. The key developmental task involves consolidation and advancement.

Two substages are associated with the establishment stage. First is *trial-commitment and stabilization*, which occurs from age 25 to 30. During this substage, the individual either settles down with a particular occupation or becomes dissatisfied and begins to explore other occupational possibilities. *Advancement* is the second substage and extends from age 31 to 44. This is typically a time for stabilization, during which seniority is required. It also tends to be a very creative, productive period.

Super's fourth stage is the *maintenance stage*, which spans from 44 to 64 years of age. This is a time for the individual to enjoy the security of seniority while attempting to maintain status as a current and productive professional. The major developmental task is preservation of achieved status.

The final stage in Super's model is the *decline stage*, which begins at age 64. During this stage, the individual adjusts to retirement as well as declining mental and physical skills and abilities. The key developmental tasks are deceleration, disengagement, and retirement.

The decline stage is composed of two substages. First is *deceleration*, which occurs between 60 and 65 years of age. This is a time when the individual begins to adjust to impending retirement, perhaps pursuing part-time jobs as a transition from full-time work. *Retirement* is the second substage and usually begins at age 61 or later. During this time, the individual may continue some part-time work or discontinue work and devote time to leisure activities.

More recently, Super (1980, 1990) referred to his theory as a life-span, life-space approach to career development. Its purpose was to add role theory into the five-stage model to create a model composed of multiple-role careers (Super, 1990). According to this theory, "career is defined as the combination and sequence of roles played by a person during the course of a lifetime" (Super, 1980, p. 282). These roles vary as a person proceeds through the life span and include such possibilities as student, worker, husband, wife, and parent (Super, 1980).

Many research studies have tested various aspects of Super's theory. Osipow (1983) concluded that most of the literature has provided support for Super's model. More recently, Phillips, Cairo, Blustein, and Myers (1988, p. 122) noted that Super's model continues to generate a wide body of research investigation in such areas as "identity, self-concept, career exploration, general developmental progress, and occupational change."

Holland's Theory.   Holland's (1973, 1985a) theory suggests that career choice results in an attempt to obtain a satisfactory fit of the person with the environment. Job satisfaction results when there is a congruence of personality type and work environment. In addition, Weinrach and Srebalus (1990) noted several practical applications of Holland's theory in terms of career counseling instruments, for example, Holland's (1985b) Vocational Preference Inventory and Holland's (1985c) Self-Directed Search.

Holland's (1973, 1985a) theory is based on the following four assumptions.

1. *People tend to be characterized by one of six personality types.* Holland (1973) originally believed that people could be characterized by six personality types. Holland (1985a) expanded this conception of personality types to include the possibility of subtypes or patterns that would provide further differentiation of a person's personality characteristic. The original six personality types with brief descriptions are

   - *Realistic* individuals take a logical, matter-of-fact approach to life.
   - *Investigative* people use an investigative, analytic approach to problem solving.
   - *Social* individuals tend to be social, cooperative, and people-oriented.
   - *Artistic* people tend to be sensitive, creative, spontaneous, and nonconforming.
   - *Conventional* individuals are conforming, inhibited, and have a preference for structured situations.
   - *Enterprising* individuals tend to take an extroverted, aggressive approach to problem solving.

2. *There are six kinds of environments that correspond with the six personality types (realistic, investigative, artistic, social, enterprising, and conventional).* Most environments attract workers with corresponding personality types. For example, artistic people work in places such as the theater. A congruent person-environment fit tends to promote job satisfaction.

3. *People seek out work environments that enable them to use their skills, express their values, and enter into agreeable roles.* People are motivated to work in settings that have complementary personality structures.

4. *The interaction of the environment and personality determines behavior.* An individual's behavior, for instance, career choice and achievement, is determined by the nature of the person-environment fit.

Osipow (1987) noted that Holland's theory has generated more research activity than any other career development theory. Weinrach and Srebalus (1990) emphasized this point by observing that more than 450 studies of Holland's theory were conducted between 1959 and 1988. Fitzgerald and Rounds (1989) provided a literature review of some of these studies and concluded that Holland's congruence hypothesis relating to the person-environment fit has received the most empirical support. In addition, Brown (1987) noted that Holland's theory was well-defined and had substantial research support. Osipow (1987) suggested that Holland's (1985a) most current revision of his theory should generate another extended period of research investigation.

Roe's Theory.   The major principles of Roe's theory evolved from Maslowian and psychoanalytic theory (Roe, 1956; Roe & Lunneborg, 1990). Simply stated, Roe contends that unmet needs in childhood can have a major influence on career choice as an adult. In addition, her theory suggests that people can fulfill all basic and higher-order needs associated with Maslow's hierarchy in their careers. These include needs related to physiology, safety, love and belonging, self-esteem, and self-actualization.

Roe (1956) identified three types of parent-child relationships that could foster need satisfaction in particular careers. Osipow (1983) provided an overview of these relationships as follows.

1. *Overprotective or excessively demanding parents.* Parents who are overly protective or make excessive demands tend to satisfy physiological needs, but they may be less prone to gratify psychological needs such as love and self-esteem. These parents foster dependency within their children since gratification of psychological needs is contingent on children engaging in socially desirable or high-achieving behaviors. Their children grow into adults with an excessive need for recognition and approval. As a result, they may choose highly visible occupations, for instance, politics or a branch of the performing arts such as acting.

2. *Rejecting parents.* These parents either neglect or reject their children. Their children will tend to have many unfilled needs and may become suspicious or untrusting of others. They may therefore select careers where their needs can be met in activities that involve working with things, for example, computers, rather than people.

3. *Accepting parents.* These parents tend to be very accepting and loving toward their children. They engage in unconditional rather than conditional love. Their children's basic and higher-order needs are therefore met, promoting a sense of autonomy and independence in the children as they grow into adulthood. Since these individuals tend to feel secure with themselves, they may choose a profession such as teaching or medicine in which they can assist others in moving toward their own self-realization.

Osipow (1990) noted that Roe's theory is almost impossible to test empirically because of the subjective nature of the constructs on which the theory is based. Additional refinement of the theory and empirical investigation of its principles appear warranted.

Career Decision-Making Theories

Career decision-making theories provide another theoretical foundation for assisting with career counseling. These theories provide "guidelines for collection, processing, and utilization of information in order to improve decision making" (Gati, 1990a, p. 508). Several theories have been developed on career decision making. This section will provide an overview of decision-making theories based on cognitive dissonance theory, social-learning theory, and a multiple career decision-making theory.

Cognitive Dissonance Theory.   Hilton (1962) was one of the first to suggest that career decision making is based on the theory of cognitive dissonance. According to

Festinger (1957), cognitive dissonance occurs when an individual has two incompatible cognitions. For example, an individual may contend, "I don't like my job, and it has low pay." The person may then attempt to remove the dissonance by changing one of the cognitions or by aiding dissonance-reducing cognitions, saying, "I like my job even though it does not pay well."

Osipow (1983) identified the following implications of cognitive dissonance theory on career decision making.

- *It is important for counselors to identify factors that can increase occupational dissonance.* One example is a person with an interest in an occupation that has limited opportunities, for example, wanting to be a professor in a field that has few academic positions available. If the dissonance cannot be resolved, the counselor might advise the client to avoid that occupation.

- *Counselors should develop strategies to deal with dissonance.* This can involve a career counselor introducing "counter-dissonance agents." For example, the counselor might tell a premedical student who lacks the aptitude for medical study that being a physician involves long hours resulting in little time for family life.

- *Counselors can help clients avoid making a premature choice.* One way to accomplish this is by noting that modifying a choice in the future may cause excessive dissonance. This in turn can interfere with making a more appropriate choice in the future. For example, a person with a strong need to be perceived as having clear goals and objectives may decide to pursue a career as a computer analyst. After several courses on the topic, the person might discover an aversion to computers and want to consider other occupations. This would create dissonance with the need to be perceived as "having clear goals and objectives." To avoid such perceptions and reduce dissonance, this individual may then decide to continue working in an undesirable career.

a personal note

I entered college as a predental major. I had wanted to be a dentist because my father was a dentist. As part of my predental studies I had to take a lot of chemistry and biology courses, which I hated and in which I had limited ability. This created dissonance, since I thought I wanted to be a dentist but discovered I did not have the aptitude to do so.

I soon found myself changing my attitude toward becoming a dentist. Before I knew it, I began to think, "I don't want to be a dentist." I soon began to think of a lot of good reasons for not wanting to be a dentist, including not wanting to bend over all day and stick my hands in people's mouths. At this point, I had begun to resolve my dissonance by creating a new attitude. I was able to conclude, "I don't want to be a dentist, and I don't have the ability to become one." During my next semester at the university I was attending, I took a psychology course and quickly became interested in the subject. I also discovered that I had the aptitude to become a psychologist.

Social Learning Theory.   Krumboltz (1979) and Mitchell and Krumboltz (1990) developed a career decision-making model based on social learning theory. The social learning model contends that learning experiences play a key role in occupational selection. Krumboltz (1979) suggested that career choice is influenced by the following factors.

- Genetic endowment creates limits to career choice

- Environmental factors, such as the economy and educational requirements, will determine occupational choice to some degree

- Learning experiences, for example, being reinforced for pursuing intellectual endeavors, will influence one's interest and aspirations

- Task-approach skills, such as work habits and interpersonal skills, will affect one's ability to be successful in a particular occupation

Mitchell and Krumboltz (1990) expanded their model to include cognitive behavioral theory. From this perspective, career decision making is also influenced by cognitions and behaviors of clients. Mitchell and Krumboltz (1987) provided empirical support for the importance of cognitive behavioral strategies in career counseling. They found that cognitive behavioral approaches contributed to appropriate career decisions and also reduced anxiety regarding career decisions.

Multiple Career Decision-Making Theory.   Gati (1986) and Gati and Tikotzki (1989) developed a multiple career decision-making theory. They contend that all career decision-making theories can be described in terms of three major models. A detailed description and analysis of these models is provided by Gati and Tikotzki (1989), Carson and Mowsesian (1990), and Gati (1990a, 1990b). Reduced to their most basic elements, these three models can be summarized as follows.

- *Expected Utility Model.* This model suggests making separate evaluations of the advantages and disadvantages of various occupations and comparing them to other occupational alternatives. The individual then chooses the occupation with the highest overall value.

- *Sequential Elimination Model.* This model involves identifying attributes of an ideal occupation, for example, working outdoors, and ranking the attributes in terms of importance. Minimal levels of acceptability regarding these criteria are established. Occupations are evaluated on the basis of this criterion and sequentially eliminated if they do not meet the established criterion.

- *Conjunctive Model.* In this model, occupational alternatives are given consideration only when they meet basic occupational requirements, for instance, a minimal salary level.

Gati (1986) suggested that no single model of career development is superior to another. Instead, the models should be empirically investigated to determine the conditions that would be most appropriate for their use.

TREATMENT ISSUES

This section will provide an overview of several important treatment issues that relate to career counseling. Information will be provided on personal versus career counseling, assessment instruments, intervention strategies, and the process of career counseling.

Personal Versus Career Counseling

There appears to be a shift in interest from career counseling to personal counseling (Birk & Brooks, 1986; Spengler, Blustein, & Strohmer, 1990; Watkins, Lopez, Campbell, & Himmell, 1986; Watkins, Schneider, Cox, & Reinberg, 1987). For example, Birk and Brooks (1986) surveyed 300 members of the division of Counseling Psychology of the American Psychological Association (APA) on their attitudes toward various counseling activities. Personal counseling was ranked as the most important activity, whereas career counseling was ranked 10th. Watkins, Lopez, Campbell, and Himmell (1986) also surveyed members of the division of Counseling Psychology of the APA regarding their attitudes relating to career counseling. Results of this study showed that members in private practice spend 59.2% of their time conducting psychotherapy and only 3.5% of their time conducting career counseling. The study also suggested that counseling psychologists are minimally engaged in career counseling and view it as an uninteresting and unattractive alternative to personal counseling.

With career counseling receiving less interest than personal counseling, an apparent treatment bias in favor of personal counseling is not surprising. Spengler, Blustein, and Strohmer (1990) found that counselors who preferred personal counseling over career counseling engaged in diagnostic and treatment overshadowing. In this process, issues relating to personal counseling overshadowed the importance of diagnostic and treatment issues relating to career counseling. Other studies have shown that vocational problems receive poorer prognosis and less counselor empathy than personal problems (Hill, Tanney, & Leonard, 1977) and less of the core conditions and affective and exploratory responses (Melnick, 1975).

A recent trend in the literature suggests it is not necessary to conceptualize career counseling and personal counseling in dichotomous terms. Several authors have contended that career counseling should be integrated into nonvocational treatment approaches (Blustein, 1987; Phillips, Cairo, Blustein, & Myers, 1988). Blustein (1987, p. 794) provided a rationale for integration by noting that "separating work issues from other psychosocial concerns creates an artificial distinction between aspects of life that are clearly interrelated." In addition, the manner in which a person relates to career issues involves coping strategies similar to those utilized in other life concerns (Blustein, 1987).

Blustein (1987) provided guidelines for integrating career counseling with psychotherapy. He recommended that counselors take a first step of incorporating a detailed work history during the intake process to obtain important diagnostic considerations. The next step is to gain a comprehensive understanding of career devel-

Exploring personal issues can be an important dimension of career counseling.

opment and career decision-making theories to broaden one's understanding of human behavior. In this process, counselors could select career theories that are compatible with their theories relating to personal counseling. For example, Super's theory of career development with his emphasis on the self could supplement Rogers' person-centered approach. As another example, Krumboltz's social-learning theory might be used in conjunction with the cognitive-behavior school of counseling. Blustein (1987) also noted that it was important to integrate career counseling with personal counseling in cases that involve substance abuse problems, since clients with these problems often have trouble with work and personal issues.

Other individuals have attempted to integrate career counseling with personal counseling. Raskin (1987) integrated career counseling with interpersonally oriented schools of counseling; Yost and Corbishley (1987) conceptualized career counseling from a cognitive-behavior perspective; and Gysbers and Moore (1987) described career counseling within a broad framework that includes marriage and family counseling and cognitive psychology. It is hoped that this trend toward integration will promote more interest in career counseling so that these vital issues and concerns of clients will receive the attention they deserve.

Assessment Instruments

Career counseling has historically placed a major emphasis on assessing interests, abilities, and personality traits (Phillips, Cairo, Blustein, & Myers, 1988). These assessment procedures play a vital role in career planning and decision making by increasing self-understanding and providing information on careers and educational programs.

The most significant area of assessment in career counseling is related to the measurement of interests (Osipow, 1987). Several prominent interest instruments have been updated with new editions. Some of these are the Strong-Campbell Interest Inventory (Hanson & Campbell, 1985); the Kuder Occupational Interest Survey (Zytowski, 1985); and the Self-Directed Search (Holland, 1985c). These and other interest instruments are described in several sources. The Mental Measurements Yearbook (Mitchell, 1985) provides both a review and critical analysis of tests, and Tests Supplement (Sweetland & Keyser, 1984) lists tests by function and population.

One important assessment issue relates to possible cultural bias in testing, as discussed in Chapters 3 and 5. Several interest inventories have been evaluated to determine whether they are valid for ethnic minorities. Carter and Swanson (1990) conducted a literature review of studies that investigated the validity of the Strong Interest Inventory (Hanson & Campbell, 1985) for African-American clients. This review found little evidence of the validity of the Strong Interest Inventory for Blacks. These findings are particularly significant, because this instrument is the most frequently used interest inventory in college counseling centers (Zytowski & Warman, 1982). On a more positive note, Haviland and Hanson (1987) found that the Strong Campbell Interest Inventory (Hanson & Campbell, 1985) has adequate criterion validity for American Indian college students. Additional research on the cross-cultural use of interest inventories appears warranted.

Intervention Strategies

A wide range of intervention strategies can be used in career counseling. These include strategies associated with career planning and decision making, assisting with vocational adjustment, and helping clients overcome personal problems. Career counseling can also take place in a variety of formats, including individual, group, self-help, and computer-assisted programs.

A large body of research has evaluated the various forms of career interventions. These studies have been summarized in several annual reviews (Fitzgerald & Rounds, 1989; Morrow, Mullen, & McElvoy, 1990; Osipow, 1987; Phillips, Cairo, Blustein, & Myers, 1988; Savickas, 1989; Slaney & Russell, 1987). Oliver and Spokane (1983, 1988) conducted two meta-analyses of career counseling that have received considerable attention in the literature. Both studies provided support for the efficacy of career counseling. Their 1988 review involved an analysis of 58 studies on career counseling published from 1950 to 1982. It attempted to gain a more precise understanding of the variables associated with efficacy in terms of types of intervention, client characteristics, and outcome measures. Results of the study showed differences in type and intensity of intervention. In terms of type of intervention, individual career counseling produced the most gain per hour of any intervention strategy. Group career counseling and workshops were the least effective intervention per hour of treatment. The study also showed intensity of intervention to be important. Efficacy improved with increased length of sessions and number of sessions.

A study by Kivlighan and Shapiro (1987) also showed it is important to consider client characteristics when formulating treatment strategies in career counseling. This study found that the clients most likely to benefit from self-help career counseling were rated as realistic, conventional, and investigative on the Vocational Identity Scale of Holland's Vocation Situation (Holland, Daieger, & Power, 1980).

Oliver and Spokane (1988) suggested that future research on career intervention would gain a more realistic understanding of the counseling process by relying more on clients who have sought out career counseling and less on solicited clients who have responded to an ad. These authors also suggested that research efforts should include multiple outcome measures relating to career decision making, effective role functioning, and client satisfaction.

The Process of Career Counseling

Frank Parson was one of the first individuals to identify stages of career counseling. Parson (1909) described his three-stage approach as follows. To make an appropriate career decision, the person needs: "(1) a clear understanding of aptitudes, abilities, interests, ambitions, resources, limitations, and their causes; (2) a knowledge of the requirements and conditions of success, advantages and disadvantages, compensations, opportunities, and prospects in different lines of work; and (3) true reasoning on the relations of these two groups of facts" (Parson, 1909, p. 5).

Salomone (1988) added two stages to Parson's (1909) three-stage model. These additional stages focus on interventions that counselors can use after a client makes a career decision. The first stage involves helping the client implement educational and career decisions. This stage might involve helping the client with job-seeking skills and assisting with job placement. The second stage involves helping the newly employed individual adjust to the new job. This process might involve helping the client deal effectively with job stress, fear of failure, or other barriers to a successful job placement.

Salomone (1988) provided additional information on how to conceptualize these stages. He suggested that counselors did not necessarily have to proceed through these stages sequentially, but could work in several stages simultaneously. Salomone (1988) also noted that many counseling strategies are available for counselors to use in helping clients move through these stages. Some of these strategies are establishing a positive counseling relationship; helping clients assess their abilities and aptitudes regarding work, including promoting self-assessment; providing information about careers and the world of work: and offering assistance with career placement.

SPECIAL ISSUES

This section covers two special issues in career counseling: career counseling for women and computer-assisted career counseling.

Career Counseling for Women

A major criticism of career counseling is that the majority of its theories and approaches have been based on men and are therefore not sensitive to the special

Women's issues can create important considerations in career counseling.

issues of women (Brooks, 1990). Several recent theories have attempted to make career counseling more responsive to the special needs of women. This section will provide an overview of two theories and identify their implications for career counseling for women.

Self-Efficacy Theory.   Self-efficacy, as described in Chapter 8, is the belief in one's ability to successfully perform a particular behavior (Bandura, 1986, 1989). Self-efficacy has been related to what behaviors will be initiated, the amount of effort expended, and duration of engagement in the face of obstacles (Lent & Hackett, 1987). The origins of career self-efficacy can be traced to the work of Hackett and Betz (1981) and Betz and Hackett (1986). It can be broadly defined as the relationship between self-efficacy and various behaviors associated with career choice and adjustment (Lent & Hackett, 1987).

Hackett and Betz (1981) contend that self-efficacy theory has particular relevance to career counseling for women. A central factor to this position is that women and men acquire different efficacy expectations due to differential gender-role experiences and limited access to efficacy information (Lent & Hackett, 1987). This in turn can contribute to the limited position women hold in the labor force (Brooks, 1990).

Career self-efficacy has stimulated a wide range of research activity. Lent and Hackett (1987) conducted a literature review of the research on career self-efficacy. The authors concluded that research has provided consistent support for the notion that "self-efficacy beliefs are predictive of important indices of career entry behavior such as college major choices and academic performance in certain fields" (Lent & Hackett, 1987, p. 362).

Morrow, Mullen and McElvoy (1990) described two studies that identified gender differences in self-efficacy and career behavior. Matsui, Ikeda, and Ohnishi (1989) found that men reported equal levels of self-efficacy in male- and female-dominated occupations, whereas women had higher self-efficacy perceptions in female-dominated fields than male-dominated occupations. A second study showed women had lower self-efficacy perceptions than men in mathematical activities although mathematical accomplishments were equivalent for men and women with similar preparatory backgrounds (Lapan, Boggs, & Morrill, 1989).

Brooks (1990) described implications of self-efficacy theory for career counseling for women. She suggested its primary use could be to broaden career options for women and facilitate the pursuit of those options. Brooks (1990) also identified several counseling strategies that could be used to promote these outcomes. These include cognitive strategies to help clients view their abilities more realistically; reattribution training to enable clients to attribute success to internal rather than external causes (Fosterling, 1980); the use of incremental graded success experiences (Lent & Hackett, 1987); vicarious learning, which could be promoted by arranging experiences for clients to "shadow" successful career women; and desensitization procedures to reduce anxiety that relates to career choice and performance.

Gottfredson's Theory.   Gottfredson's (1981) theory of occupational operations was one of the major vocational theories to emerge in the 1980s (Hesketh, Elmslie, & Kaldor, 1990) and applies to both men and women (Brooks, 1990). Hesketh, Elmslie, and Kaldor (1990) noted that this theory is important to career counseling for women because it explains how compromise takes place in vocational decision making; identifies factors associated with social identity; and explores the difficulties that women face entering nontraditional careers.

Brooks (1990) identified the following major principles associated with Gottfredson's (1981) model.

- People differentiate occupations in terms of sex type (job preferences relating to gender), work level, and field of work.

- People determine the appropriations of an occupation in terms of their self-concept.

- Self-concept factors that have vocational reliance include gender, social class, intelligence, values, interest, and abilities.

- Vocationally relevant self-concept factors emerge in the following developmental sequence. From age 3 to 5, individuals understand the concept of being an adult; from age 6 to 8, they develop the concept of gender; from age 9 to 13, they understand the abstract concepts of social class and intelligence; and beginning at age 14, they refine their attitudes, values, traits, and interests.

- People reject occupations on the basis of self-concept as they proceed through the developmental stages.

- The reasons for rejecting occupations have the following hierarchy. Individuals reject occupations when they are not suitable: first, in terms of gender; second, for social class and ability reasons; and third, on the basis of interests and values.

- Occupational preferences result from compatibility between the job and self-concept and from judgments about job accessibility.

- Compromise in job choice follows a predictable pattern. People will first sacrifice their interests, then prestige, and finally sex type, or job preferences related to gender.

Gottfredson's (1981) theory has stimulated a wide range of research activity. Brooks (1990) identified several studies that provide general support for Gottfredson's (1981) model (Henderson, Hesketh, & Tuffin, 1988; Holt, 1989; Taylor & Pryor, 1985). Two more recent studies do not support Gottfredson's theory regarding the predictable nature of compromise in job choice. Leung and Plake (1990) found that prestige and not sex type was the most important factor in job choice. Hesketh, Elmslie, and Kaldor (1990) further challenged Gottfredson's (1981) position regarding the process of compromise. Results of their study suggest that interests incorporate attributes of prestige and sex type and is therefore the most important factor in job choice and compromise. These studies together indicate that the factors influencing compromise and job choice are much more complex than Gottfredson suggested.

Brooks (1990) identified several implications of Gottfredson's (1981) theory for career counseling for women. First, Gottfredson's model suggests that clients may experience problems with indecision when they do not have an awareness of the effects of sex type, prestige, and interests on career choice and compromise. Counselors can assist these clients by helping them clarify their vocational priorities regarding these factors. Second, clients may need assistance in identifying occupations that are acceptable in terms of their self-concept. Third, clients may have aspirations that are incongruent with their abilities or interests. In these instances, counselors can evaluate the client's aspirations to determine whether they are associated with self-defeating processes, such as trying to live up to other people's standards.

Computer-Assisted Career Counseling

Computer-assisted information and guidance programs have become an integral part of career counseling (Sampson, Shahnasarian, & Reardon, 1987). In fact, most career centers have at least one interactive system (Johnston, Buescher, & Heppner, 1988). These programs can be an important adjunct to direct counseling services by providing career information and assisting with career planning and decision making (Cairo, 1983).

Several authors have commented on the importance of including direct counseling services when utilizing computerized career counseling. Sampson, Shahnasarian, and Reardon (1987) identified the following problems that could occur when computerized career counseling is used without direct counselor contact: inappropriate clients can use the system; clients may not understand the purpose or operation of the system; and clients may not be able to integrate their computerized counseling experience into their decision-making process.

Table 12.1
Computerized Career Programs

Program Name	Publisher & Year	Program Overview	Special Features	Role of Counselor Client
Elementary Careers Software	Kansas Careers, 1988	Takes students on a tour of Careerville, traveling from building to building to explore different careers.	Suggestions for classroom activities are provided including games, puzzles, and practical problems relating to career issues.	Some aspects require assistance of a counselor or teacher.
Computerized Career Assessment and Planning Program (CCAPP)	Cambridge Career, 1989 (Updated every 2 years)	Assists with career assessment, selecting alternatives, career planning, and career exploration.	Information on over 1,200 occupations; a list of college majors or vocational courses relating to career interest; and an individual career plan and a job-hunting plan.	Some aspects can be used independently by client, but counselors explain how a counselor can use the program to assist the client.
The Perfect Career	James Couyes, Mindscope, 1988	Assists with personal assessment, decision making, occupational exploration, and career planning.	Contains an interest/ability inventory of 144 sample work activities; career analysis; and suggested career goals based on scores in 12 career fields.	Can be used with minimal counselor assistance.
C-LECT	Chronicle Guidance, (Updated annually) 1991	Assists with career awareness, exploration, decision making, and educational planning.	Connects 14 school subjects with over 700 occupations; describes 717 occupations; has 5 self-assessment options; provides information on financial aid; and answers questions on specific colleges and universities.	Can be used with minimal counselor assistance.

DISCOVER	The American College Testing Program, Version 4.3, 1990	Assists with career choice and decision-making skills; and enhances the general adjustment of the client.	Opportunities to take interest, ability, and value inventories, producing scores that are used to conduct job search and search for college majors or programs of study, provides information regarding various occupational fields and educational institutions.	Can be used with or without a counselor's assistance or in conjunction with career planning, curriculums or workshops.
The Guidance and Information System (GIS)	Riverside, Houghton and Mifflin, 1991	Provides information on 1,200 primary occupations and 3,000 related occupations. Grouped according to the U.S. Office of Educational Occupational Clusters and the Dictionary of Occupational Titles (DOT).	Accessibility through a telephone and teletypewriter or display terminal that receives signals and prints or displays copy, thus does not require an institution to have its own computer.	Not designed to be the sole source of career and educational information but can be a meaningful tool for the career counselor.

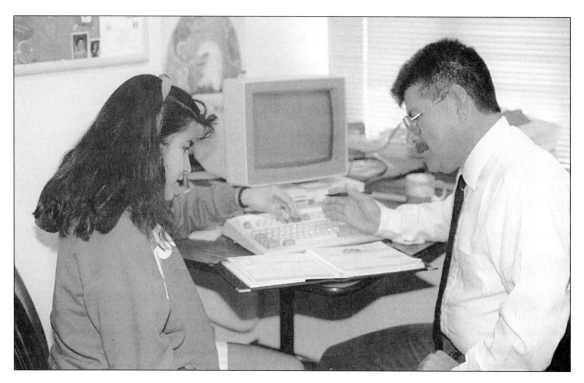

Computer programs can play an important role in career counseling.

In addition, Johnston, Buescher, and Heppner (1988) noted that ethical standards require orientation of information prior to and following administration of tests, including those utilized in computer-assisted career counseling programs. Dungy (1984) provided further support for the importance of direct counseling by noting that it enhanced the effectiveness of subsequent computer-assisted program use.

Numerous computerized career programs are currently available. Heppner and Johnston (1985), Maze (1984), and Zunker (1986) provide a description and comparative analysis of the major programs. Table 12.1 incorporates computer-assisted career programs described by Zunker (1986) and some of the most current programs available.

The wide variety of computer-assisted career programs can overwhelm counselors, making it difficult to select one for use. Maze (1984) provided the following guidelines for selecting the most appropriate program.

- *Obtain staff input.* Perform a needs assessment with the staff, identifying areas that could be improved by computerized programs.

- *Obtain relevant information about the programs under consideration.* Evaluate each program in terms of cost, software packages, hardware requirements, and user population.

- *Arrange for demonstrations of software programs.* If possible, preview all software before purchasing a program.

- *Evaluate samples of the system's output.* Review sample printouts produced from each module or component of the system before deciding on a program.

- *Determine the total cost of the system.* Calculate the total cost of each software and hardware system under consideration.

- *Determine the cost per user.* Calculate the maximum, minimum, and average estimates for potential users to determine the cost-effectiveness of the system.

- *Determine one-time charges and ongoing charges.* Examples of one-time charges are the cost of a printer and a telephone adapter. Ongoing charges include the costs of renewing software packages and maintaining equipment. There may also be ongoing expenses associated with mainframe or centralized systems that should be determined.

CHAPTER SUMMARY

Career counseling is a dynamic counseling specialty. This chapter provided an overview of its theoretical foundations in terms of theories of career development and decision making. It also described treatment issues relating to career counseling. These issues include the trend to integrate personal counseling and career counseling; assessment in career counseling, including interest measurement and cross-cultural issues; intervention issues and strategies; and the process of career counseling. Two special issues were also discussed: career counseling for women and computer-assisted career counseling. Two theories were presented that can help counselors formulate strategies for career counseling for women. Guidelines for selecting an appropriate computer-assisted program were also provided.

REFERENCES

Axelson, J. A. (1985). *Counseling and development in a multicultural society*. Belmont, CA: Wadsworth.

Bandura, A. (1986). *Several foundations of thought and action: A social cognition theory*. Englewood Cliffs, NJ: Prentice-Hall.

Bandura, A. (1989). Human agency in social cognitive theory. *American Psychologist, 44*(9), 1175–1184.

Betz, N. E., & Hackett, G. (1986). Applications of self-efficacy theory to understanding career choice behavior. *Journal of Social and Clinical Psychology, 4*, 279–289.

Birk, J. M., & Brooks, L. (1986). Required skills and training needs of recent counseling psychology graduates. *Journal of Counseling Psychology, 33*, 320–325.

Blustein, D. L. (1987). Integrating career counseling and psychotherapy: A comprehensive treatment strategy. *Psychotherapy, 24*, 794–799.

Brooks, L. (1990). Recent developments in theory building. In D. Brown, L. Brooks, & Associates (Eds.), *Career choice and development* (2nd ed.). San Francisco, CA: Jossey-Bass.

Brown, D. (1987). The status of Holland's theory of vocational choice. *Career Development Quarterly, 36*, 13–23.

Cairo, P. C. (1983). Evaluating the effects of computer-assisted counseling systems: A selected review. *Counseling Psychologist, 11*(4), 55–59.

Carson, A., & Mowsesian, R. (1990). Some remarks on Gati's theory of career decision-making models. *Journal of Counseling Psychology, 37*(4), 502–507.

Carter, R. T., & Swanson, J. L. (1990). The validity of the Strong Interest Inventory with Black Americans: A review of the literature. *Journal of Vocational Behavior, 36*, 195–209.

Dungy, G. (1984). Computer-assisted guidance: Determining who is ready. *Journal of College Student Personnel, 25,* 539–546.

Festinger, L. (1957. *A theory of cognitive dissonance.* Stanford, CA: Stanford University Press.

Fitzgerald, L. F., & Rounds, J. B. (1989). Vocational behavior, 1988: A critical analysis. *Journal of Vocational Behavior, 35,* 105–163.

Fosterling, F. (1980). Attributional aspects of cognitive behavior modification: A theoretical approach and suggestions for techniques. *Cognitive Therapy and Research, 24,* 27–37.

Gati, I. (1986). Making career decisions: A sequential elimination approach. *Journal of Counseling Psychology, 33,* 408–417.

Gati, I. (1990a). Interpreting and applying career decision-making models: Comments on Carson and Mowsesian. *Journal of Counseling Psychology, 32*(4), 508–514.

Gati, I. (1990b). Why, when, and how to take into account the uncertainty involved in career decisions. *Journal of Counseling Psychology, 37*(3), 277–280.

Gati, I., & Tikotzki, Y. (1989). Strategies for collection and processing of occupational information in making career decisions. *Journal of Counseling Psychology, 35*(3), 430–439.

Gottfredson, L. S. (1981). Circumscription and compromise: A developmental theory of occupational aspirations. *Journal of Counseling Psychology Monograph, 28,* 545–579.

Gysbers, N. C., & Moore, E. J. (1987). *Career counseling: Skills and techniques for practitioners.* Englewood Cliffs, NJ: Prentice-Hall.

Hackett, G., & Betz, N. E. (1981). A self-efficacy approach to the career development of women. *Journal of Vocational Behavior, 18,* 326–339.

Hanson, J. C., & Campbell, D. P. (1985). *Manual for the SVIB-SCII* (4th ed.). Palo Alto, CA: Consulting Psychologists Press.

Haviland, M. G., & Hanson, J. C. (1987). Criterion validity of the Strong-Campbell Interest Inventory for American Indian college students. *Measurement and Evaluation in Counseling and Development, 19,* 196–201.

Henderson, S., Hesketh, B., & Tuffin, K. (1988). A test of Gottfredson's theory of circumscription. *Journal of Vocational Behavior, 32,* 37–48.

Heppner, M. J., & Johnston, J. A. (1985). Computerized career guidance and information systems: Guidelines for selection. *Journal of College Students Personnel, 26,* 156–163.

Hesketh, B., Elmslie, S., & Kaldor, W. (1990). Career compromises: An alternative account to Gottfredson's theory. *Journal of Counseling Psychology, 37*(1), 49–56.

Hill, C. E., Tanney, M. F., & Leonard, M. M. (1977). Counselor reactions to female clients: Type of problem, age of client, and sex of counselor. *Journal of Counseling Psychology, 24,* 60–65.

Hilton, T. L. (1962). Career decision making. *Journal of Counseling Psychology, 9,* 291–298.

Holland, J. L. (1973). *Making vocational choices: A theory of careers.* Englewood Cliffs, NJ: Prentice-Hall.

Holland, J. L. (1985a). *Making vocational choices: A theory of vocational personalities and work environments* (2nd ed.). Englewood Cliffs, NJ: Prentice-Hall.

Holland, J. L. (1985b). *Manual for the vocational preference inventory.* Odessa, FL: Psychological Assessment Resources.

Holland, J. L. (1985c). *Professional manual self-directed search.* Odessa, FL: Psychological Assessment Resources.

Holland, J. L., Daieger, D. C., & Power, P. G. (1980). Some diagnostic scales for research in decision making and personality: Identity information and barriers. *Journal of Personality and Social Psychology, 39,* 1191–1200.

Holt, P. A. (1989). Differential effects of status and interest in the process of compromise. *Journal of Counseling Psychology, 36,* 42–47.

Johnston, J. A., Buescher, K. L., & Heppner, M. J. (1988). Computerized career information and guidance systems: Caveat emptor. *Journal of Counseling and Development, 57*(1), 39–41.

Kivlighan, D. M., Jr., & Shapiro, R. M. (1987). Holland type as a predictor of benefit from self-help career counseling. *Journal of Counseling Psychology, 34*(3), 326–329.

Krumboltz, J. D. (1979). A social learning theory of career decision making. In A. M. Mitchell, F. B. Jones, & J. D. Krumboltz (Eds.), *Social learning theory and career decision making.* Cranston, RI: Carroll.

Lapan, R. T., Boggs, K. R., & Morrill, W. H. (1989). Self-efficacy as a mediator of investigative and realistic general occupational themes on the Strong-Campbell Interest Inventory. *Journal of Counseling Psychology, 36,* 176–182.

Lent, R. W., & Hackett, G. (1987). Career self-efficacy: Empirical status and future divisions. *Journal of Vocational Behavior, 30*, 347–382.

Leung, S. A., & Plake, B. S. (1990). A choice dilemma approach for examining the relative importance of sex type and prestige preferences in the process of career choice compromise. *Journal of Counseling Psychology, 37*(4), 399–406.

Matsui, T., Ikeda, H., & Ohnishi, R. (1989). Relations of sex-typed socializations to career self-efficacy expectations of college students. *Journal of Vocational Behavior, 35*, 1–16.

Maze, M. (1984). How to select a computerized guidance system. *Journal of Counseling and Development, 63*(3), 158–162.

Melnick, R. R. (1975). Counseling responses as a function of method of problem presentation and type of problem. *Journal of Counseling Psychology, 22*, 108–112.

Mitchell, J. V. (1985). *Mental Measurements Yearbook* (Vols. 1, 2). Lincoln: University of Nebraska Press.

Mitchell, L. K., & Krumboltz, J. D. (1987). The effects of cognitive restructuring and decision-making training on career indecision. *Journal of Counseling and Development, 66*, 171–174.

Mitchell, L. K., & Krumboltz, J. D. (1990). Social learning approach to career decision making: Krumboltz's theory. In D. Brown, L. Brooks, & Associates (Eds.), *Career choice and development* (2nd ed.). San Francisco, CA: Jossey-Bass.

Morrow, P. C., Mullen, E. J., & McElvoy, J. C. (1990). Vocational behavior, 1989: The year in review. *Journal of Vocational Behavior, 37*, 121–195.

Oliver, L. W., & Spokane, A. R. (1983). Research integration: Approaches, problems and recommendations for research reporting. *Journal of Counseling Psychology, 30*, 252–257.

Oliver, L. W., & Spokane, A. R. (1988). Career-intervention outcome: What contributes to clients' gain? *Journal of Counseling Psychology, 35*(4), 447–462.

Osipow, S. H. (1983). *Theories of career development* (3rd ed.). Englewood Cliffs, NJ: Prentice-Hall.

Osipow, S. H. (1987). Counseling psychology: Theory, research, and practice in career counseling. *Annual Review of Psychology, 38*, 257–278.

Osipow, S. H. (1990). Convergence in theories of career choice and development: Review and prospects. *Journal of Vocational Behavior, 36*, 122–131.

Parson, F. (1909). *Choosing a vocation*. Boston: Houghton Mifflin.

Phillips, S. D., Cairo, P. C., Blustein, D. L., & Myers, R. A. (1988). Career development and behavior, 1987: A review. *Journal of Vocational Behavior, 33*, 119–184.

Raskin, P. M. (1987). *Vocational counseling: A guide for the practitioner*. New York: Teacher's College Press.

Roe, A. (1956). *The psychology of occupations*. New York: Wiley.

Roe, A., & Lunneborg, P. W. (1990). Personality development and career choice. In D. Brown, L. Brooks, & Associates (Eds.), *Career choice and development*. San Francisco, CA: Jossey-Bass.

Salomone, P. R. (1988). Career counseling. Steps and stages beyond Parsons. *Career Development Quarterly, 36*, 218–221.

Sampson, J. P., Jr., Shahnasarian, M., & Reardon, R. C. (1987). Computer-assisted career guidance: A national perspective on the use of DISCOVER and SIGI. *Journal of Counseling and Development, 65*(8), 416–419.

Savickas, M. L. (1989). Annual review: Practice and research in career counseling and development. *The Career Development Quarterly, 38*, 100–134.

Slaney, R. B., & Russell, J. E. A. (1987). Perspectives on vocational behavior, 1986: A review. *Journal of Vocational Behavior, 31*, 111–173.

Spengler, P. M., Blustein, D. L., & Strohmer, D. C. (1990). Diagnostic and treatment overshadowing of vocational problems by personal problems. *Journal of Counseling Psychology, 37*(4), 372–381.

Super, D. E. (1951). Vocational adjustment: Implementing a self-concept. *Occupations, 30*, 88–92.

Super, D. E. (1957). *The psychology of careers*. New York: Harper & Row.

Super, D. E. (1980). A life-span, life space approach to career development. *Journal of Vocational Behavior, 16*, 282–298.

Super, D. E. (1990). A life-span, life space approach. In D. Brown, L. Brooks, & Associates (Eds.), *Career choice and development* (2nd ed.). San Francisco, CA: Jossey-Bass.

Sweetland, R. C., Keyser, D. J. (1984). *Tests: A supplement*. Kansas City, KS: Test Corporation of America.

Taylor, N. B., & Pryor, R. G. L. (1985). Exploring the process of compromise in career decision making. *Journal of Vocational Behavior, 27,* 171–190.

Watkins, C. E., Jr., Lopez, F. G., Campbell, V. L., & Himmell, C. D. (1986). Contemporary counseling psychology: Results of a national survey. *Journal of Counseling Psychology, 33,* 301–309.

Watkins, C. E., Jr., Schneider, L. J., Cox, J. R. H., & Reinberg, J. A. (1987). Clinical psychology and counseling psychology: On similarities and differences revisited. *Professional Psychology: Research and Practice, 18,* 530–535.

Weinrach, S. G., & Srebalus, D. J. (1990). Holland's theory of careers. In D. Brown, L. Brooks, & Associates (Eds.), *Career Choice and Development* (2nd ed.). San Francisco, CA: Jossey-Bass.

Yost, E., & Corbishley, M. (1987). *Career counseling: A psychological approach.* San Francisco, CA: Jossey-Bass.

Zunker, V. G. (1986). *Career counseling: Applied concepts of life planning* (2nd ed.). Monterey, CA: Brooks/Cole.

Zytowski, D. G. (1985). *Kuder Occupational Interest Survey Form DD Manual Supplement.* Chicago: Science Research Associates.

Zytowski, D. G., & Warman, R. E. (1982). The changing use of tests in counseling. *Measurement and Evaluation in Guidance, 15,* 147–152.

PART
4

Professional Settings and Issues

Part Four addresses professional settings and issues. The art of counseling is reflected in the manner in which the profession adjusts to the changing fabric of society. Recent examples are the increased emphasis on legal and ethical issues and the rising incidence of drug and alcohol abuse and school dropout problems. The science of counseling provides counselors a tool for gaining an objective understanding of these issues and problems. This insight allows them to develop appropriate treatment approaches for the settings in which they work.

Part Four begins by describing the two most common settings in which counselors work: schools (Chapter 13) and mental health settings (Chapter 14). These two chapters include descriptions of the role and function of school and mental health counselors as well as information about the special issues facing counselors who work in each of these settings. The final chapter (Chapter 15) provides information on issues such as professional organizations, state licensure for counseling, and legal and ethical issues in counseling.

CHAPTER THIRTEEN

School Counseling

CHAPTER OVERVIEW

This chapter will provide an overview of the issues relating to school counseling. Highlights of the chapter include

- A comprehensive developmental model for guidance and counseling
- The role and function of school counselors
- Special skills and problems
- Future trends in school counseling

School counseling represents an important field for the counseling profession. According to the *Occupational Handbook*, approximately 63,000 individuals were employed as public school counselors in 1986, with the majority being secondary school counselors. Bergin, Miller, Bergin, and Koch (1990) noted a recent trend for states to mandate that elementary schools have counseling programs. Some examples are Arkansas, Florida, New Hampshire, Oregon, South Carolina, Tennessee, Virginia, West Virginia, and Vermont, as well as Washington, D.C. A large percentage of school counselors are members of the American School Counselors Association (ASCA), a division of the American Counseling Association. The ASCA has developed its own ethical standards (see Appendix D) and publishes two journals, *Elementary School Guidance and Counseling* and *The School Counselor*.

A COMPREHENSIVE DEVELOPMENTAL MODEL FOR GUIDANCE AND COUNSELING

The recent literature suggests that school counseling should be conceptualized in terms of a comprehensive developmental model (Myrick, 1987; Gysbers & Henderson, 1988). The term *comprehensive* refers to the notion that school counseling programs should function as an integrated part of a K–12 program, not as separate entities. The *developmental* focus suggests that school counseling programs should be organized from a life-span perspective.

Myrick (1987, p. 40) identified the following eight goals and objectives associated with comprehensive developmental guidance and counseling programs. Counselors should strive to

1. Understand the school environment
2. Understand themselves and others
3. Understand attitudes and behavior
4. Use decision-making and problem-solving skills
5. Use interpersonal and communication skills
6. Use school success skills
7. Have career awareness and use educational planning
8. Have community pride and involvement

These goals and objectives indicate that counselors assist with a variety of tasks, including personal and social development; decision making and problem solving; career education; and educational planning. Myrick (1987) also noted that school counselors should use the following approaches to meet the overall objectives of school counseling.

- Crisis intervention to gain control of a particular situation
- Remedial approaches that focus on deficiencies
- Preventive approaches that anticipate problems to prevent their occurrence

- Developmental approaches that help students acquire the necessary skills and experiences to be successful in school

Bergin et al. (1990) noted that several states have comprehensive K–12 developmental guidance programs: Arkansas, Illinois, Iowa, Missouri, New Hampshire, North Carolina, Ohio, Oklahoma, and Wisconsin. A limited amount of research has been conducted to evaluate these programs. A study by Bergin et al. (1990) evaluated a developmental guidance model called *Building Skills for Tomorrow* (Oklahoma State Department of Education, 1988) that was being implemented in a rural school district. The study found that the program elicited positive responses from parents, teachers, and community leaders.

A Developmental Perspective

The developmental perspective is central to the comprehensive developmental guidance and counseling model. This perspective represents a shift from an orientation of counselors as clinicians to a role of counselors promoting prevention (Gysbers & Henderson, 1988). In this role, counselors work closely with teachers to promote developmental guidance and counseling as an integral aspect of the overall school program. Myrick (1989) noted that the goals of developmental guidance and counseling can never be fully realized unless teachers take an active role in offering guidance activities in the classroom.

Several individuals have applied the developmental perspective to counseling theories, for example, Blocher's (1974, 1987) developmental counseling and Ivey's (1986) developmental therapy. These theories suggest that counselors should first identify a client's developmental level and then implement an approach that addresses the needs for that level. Developmental counseling approaches incorporate various theories of development. Ivey (1986) emphasized Piaget's (1955) theory of cognitive development, whereas Blocher (1974, 1987) focused on Havighurst's (1972) concept of developmental tasks and Erikson's (1963) psycho-social theory.

Blocher's (1974) model suggests that there are certain developmental tasks associated with each stage of development. In addition, clients must master coping skills to meet the challenges of these tasks to successfully move forward to the next developmental task. Blocher (1974) contended that counseling goals and strategies can be developed to help individuals master the necessary coping skills as they proceed through the life span.

According to Blocher (1974, 1987), elementary school students face the developmental tasks of industry and initiative. These tasks can be facilitated by counseling goals that help students implement activities on their own and feel competent when competing with peers. Counselors can promote industry and initiative in students by helping them value themselves and feel a sense of control over their environment. Counseling strategies that foster self-concept development and encouragement can be used to facilitate these counseling goals.

Blocher's (1974, 1987) theory can also be applied to middle school students. The main developmental task during these years is identity formation. Counseling goals can be developed to assist with this task, such as helping students enhance their self-awareness and clarify their values. Individual and group counseling can be used to address these issues as well as other problems that require attention.

The primary developmental task for high school students is intimacy. This task requires developing the skills necessary to establish close, trusting relationships with siblings, peers, parents, and others. The counseling goals associated with this task include promoting students' concern and interest in others and enhancing interpersonal relationship skills. Group counseling that focuses on social-skills training can be particularly useful as a strategy to promote interpersonal effectiveness.

An overview of these developmental tasks, counseling goals, and associated counseling strategies according to Blocher's model is provided in Table 13.1.

The developmental tasks and their associated counseling goals and strategies shown in Table 13.1 can be useful in providing a focus for counseling services. At the same time, counselors should not limit their programs to these tasks and related counseling strategies. A comprehensive developmental guidance and counseling program should address the wide array of issues that concern school-age children, for example, divorced parents, drug and alcohol abuse, and teen-age pregnancy.

ROLE AND FUNCTION OF SCHOOL COUNSELORS

One of the most controversial issues in school counseling has been the role and function of school counselors. The controversy has centered around the difficulties that school counselors have faced in trying to establish a clear professional identity (Aubrey, 1982; Peer, 1985; Cole, 1988) and what steps should be taken to overcome these problems. This section will address the central issues associated with the school counselor's role and function, such as counseling from a historical perspective, the current ASCA role statement, and the role and function of school counselors working in elementary, middle, and high schools and in rural schools.

A Historical Perspective

A historical perspective can be useful for understanding how the school counselor's role and function have evolved. Gysbers (1988) provided a description of the history of school counseling, and I have incorporated his observations into the following overview.

The period from 1909 to 1920 represents the beginning of school counseling as a specialty. Its origins can be traced to the pioneering work of Frank Parsons (1909), who provided vocational guidance services in schools.

During the 1920s the emphasis shifted from vocational guidance to assistance with personal adjustment.

The 1930s was an era in which there was an attempt to differentiate guidance from vocational guidance. The term *guidance* was broadly defined as assisting individuals with problems of adjusting to any aspect of life, including health or family and friends as well as work. *Vocational guidance* was more narrowly defined as helping people with choice, preparation, placement, and advancement in a vocation. During this period, school counselors also began to use more formal terms, for example, counseling, assessment, information, placement, and follow-up, to described what occurred in the helping process.

Table 13.1
Developmental Tasks, Goals, and Counseling Strategies *Erickson*

Age Level	Developmental Tasks	Counseling Goals	Counseling Strategy
Elementary School	Industry and initiative	Foster independence and self-autonomy	Individual and group counseling to promote self-concept development; encouragement strategies to help students believe in their capabilities and implement activities on their own; and self-control interventions for students whose impulse control interferes with their ability to complete tasks.
Middle School	Identity formation	Help students gain a clear understanding of who they are as individuals	Individual and group counseling to promote self-awareness and value clarification.
High School	Intimacy	Promote social interest and interpersonal effectiveness	Individual, group, and family counseling to promote social interest and compassion for others. Group counseling to foster interpersonal effectiveness. Career counseling to relate to the world of work.

The counseling profession experienced the initial impact of Carl Rogers' views of counseling in the 1940s. Rogers' (1942) *Counseling and Psychotherapy* had a dramatic effect on the role and function of the school counselor. His person-centered approach provided a theoretical framework for personal counseling and resulted in school counselors utilizing a clinical emphasis in their overall role and function. Rogers' work continues to have a major impact on contemporary school counselors as they attempt to assist students with an ever-increasing array of personal problems.

During the 1950s support for school counselors increased with the passage of Public Law 85–864, the National Defense Education Act. This act allocated funds for colleges and universities to train students to become secondary school counselors.

In the 1960s the focus shifted from guidance as adjustment to developmental guidance. Developmental guidance stressed the importance of understanding and working with students from a developmental perspective. It also placed greater emphasis on preventing the occurrence of problems rather than merely helping students adjust to their existing problems. School counselors continue to utilize the developmental perspective.

The 1970s involved an expansion of the developmental perspective to include a K–12 comprehensive developmental guidance model. During this period, there was also a national effort to integrate career education into the overall school program. This effort was met with resistance from some teachers and administrators, because they believed it took valuable time away from necessary academic endeavors. Career education therefore had limited success in terms of being integrated into the public schools. The passage of Public Law 94–142, the Education for All Handicapped Children Act, in 1975 (Public Law 94–142, 1975) also affected the role of the school counselor. As a result of this act, school counselors expanded their role to include coordinating the testing and placement of exceptional students and assisting with the development and implementation of individual education programs for each student. Another force that impacted the role and function of the school counselor during this period was the use of personal computers in scoring tests, scheduling, and career counseling. In addition, school counselors began to incorporate group counseling in their guidance and counseling programs in the early 1970s.

During the 1980s career guidance received renewed federal support. The Carl D. Perkins Vocational Education Act was passed in 1984 in response to the belief that public schools were not providing adequate preparation for students to obtain employment or continue post-secondary education. Several states have utilized funds from the Perkins bill to develop K–12 counseling and guidance programs. To qualify for these funds, states must provide opportunities for students to acquire employability skills. Another force that occurred in the 1980s was an awareness of the importance of multicultural issues in counseling. School counselors therefore began to modify their counseling approaches to include a multicultural perspective.

The decade of the 1980s was also a time of changes in the fabric of society that dramatically affected school-age children. During this period, school counselors witnessed substantial increases in divorce, suicides, drug and alcohol abuse, teen-age pregnancies, and eating disorders. School counselors invested increasing amounts of energy in implementing prevention and treatment programs addressing these complex issues. Some examples are drug prevention and awareness programs; group counseling for children of alcoholics and children of divorce; parent education; and family counseling. Also during this time, financially conscious educational systems began to scrutinize the effectiveness of school counseling. As a result, schools placed greater emphasis on counselor accountability.

As the decade of the 1990s begins, school counselors are attempting to meet the needs of a divergent student population in terms of culture, school readiness, and psychological stability.

The Current ASCA Role Statement

In 1990 the ASCA revised its role statement of 1981 (ASCA Role Statement, in press). A significant change in the revised statement was the absence of the earlier differentiation in the role and function of counselors working in elementary, middle, and high schools. Instead, the statement identified five interventions that apply to all school counselors. The motivation for this change was to promote a clearer and more concise understanding of the overall role and function of school counselors. Highlights of the current ASCA role statement are as follows.

In the statement, the ASCA recognized and supported the comprehensive developmental guidance and counseling model. In this regard, school counselors should adjust the counseling approach to the developmental levels of students as they progress through the educational system. The aim of school counseling is to promote educational, social, career, and personal development so that students can become responsible, productive citizens.

The statement also identified five basic interventions common to all school counselors. These are individual counseling; small-group counseling, which involves five to eight students; large-group guidance, which includes nine or more students such as in a classroom; consultation; and coordination of the counseling program. A promising movement regarding these interventions is developing at the state legislative level (Myrick, 1989). Some states, for example, Florida, have mandated that school counselors devote a majority of their time to providing the five basic interventions (Myrick, 1989).

Role and Function by Grade Level and Setting

The literature provides extensive information about the specific goals and strategies for school counselors working with students at various levels and in various settings. Although the current ASCA role statement did not emphasize these differences, this section identifies some of the special facets of counseling in elementary, middle, and high schools and in rural schools.

Elementary School Counseling. Elementary school includes students from kindergarten through the fifth grade. The emphasis of elementary school counseling is on prevention (Muro, 1981). In this regard, counselors spend a large percentage of their time consulting with teachers and parents to promote the child's mental health (Dinkmeyer, 1968).

Several authors have attempted to describe the role and function of elementary school counselors. Morse and Russell (1988) surveyed 130 elementary school coun-

All school personnel can play an important role in the school counseling program.

selors in terms of how they perceive their current role and their ideal role. Their findings are summarized in Table 13.2, with actual and ideal roles each shown in rank order of importance to counselors.

Three interesting observations can be made from the survey results shown in Table 13.2. First, three of the top five functions listed as actual roles involve consultation. Second, these counselors ranked the function of helping teachers understand students' needs first as an ideal role, but only fourth as a function they currently perform. Third, four of the top five ideal roles indicate these counselors want to engage in more group counseling involving activities such as social-skills training. Results of this study emphasize the importance of elementary school counselors obtaining skills in consultation and group counseling.

Ginter, Scalise, and Presse (1990) conducted a study that surveyed 313 teachers in terms of their perceptions of elementary school counselors' role and function. Results of this study showed teachers viewed elementary school counselors as functioning primarily with the dual role of helper and consultant. The helper role entailed activities such as individual and group counseling, assessment, interpreting tests, and conducting guidance activities. The consultant role involved providing technical advice and expertise to school staff and parents. The authors concluded that there appears to be congruence between how teachers and elementary school counselors view their role and function.

In another study, Miller (1989) surveyed teachers, principals, and parents to determine their views regarding the role and function of elementary school counselors. The survey identified 28 functions that elementary school counselors were

Table 13.2
Actual Versus Ideal Roles of Elementary School Counselors

Rank Order of Actual Role	Rank Order of Ideal Role
Assist students with special needs by making appropriate educational referrals	Assist the teacher to better understand the needs of individual students
Work with school psychologist and educational specialist to meet the special needs of individual students	Provide group counseling to help students learn effective social skills
Provide individual counseling for students to help them understand their feelings	Work with students in groups to promote a positive self-concept
Help teachers better understand the needs of individual students	Counsel students in groups to help them become aware of their feelings
Work with students individually to promote a positive self-concept	Conduct groups to help students learn problem-solving skills

Note. From "How Elementary Counselors See Their Role: An Empirical Study" by C. L. Morse and T. Russell, 1988, *Elementary School Guidance & Counseling, 23*(1), pp. 44–62. Copyright 1988 by Elementary School Guidance & Counseling. Reprinted by permission.

believed to fulfill. These functions related to six tasks: developmental or career guidance; consulting; counseling; evaluation and assessment; guidance program development; and coordination and management. Results of the survey showed that teachers, principals, and parents strongly endorse these six tasks as being relevant functions for elementary school counselors. Miller (1989) believed the study provided grass-roots support for a developmental model of elementary school guidance and counseling. These studies collectively show recognition of the importance of the developmental model of counseling and the necessity for elementary school counselors to develop skills in direct services such as group counseling.

a personal note

I enjoyed working as an elementary school counselor. I liked the diversity of activities, which included play therapy, counseling, consulting, and working with parents. I also found children fun and exciting to work with, because they are so open, spontaneous, and interested in exploring the world around them.

When I work with children, I feel a sense of optimism that real and lasting changes can be made. Their problems have usually not yet become well-established facets of their personality. I firmly believe that early intervention can prevent children's problems from blossoming into major mental disorders and prevent them from becoming school dropouts. I often think that more of the educational and mental health budget should be invested in elementary school counseling. In the long run, I think it would be the most effective approach.

Middle School Counseling.   The middle school phenomenon is a relatively recent occurrence. This level of schooling provides educational opportunities for students from sixth through eighth grades. This concept evolved from the junior high educational system, which encompassed Grades 7 through 9. The middle school concept represents an attempt to group students together as they make their transition from childhood to adolescence.

The literature shows that the role and function of the middle school counselor are just beginning to be formulated. As a result, it is not surprising that less research has been conducted on middle school counseling than on elementary and high school counseling (St. Clair, 1989). Bonebrake and Borgers (1984) conducted a study in which they compared the ideal role of middle school counselors as perceived by counselors and principals. Their results showed essential agreement between the perceptions of counselors and principals. Both groups ranked individual counseling first in importance. Other tasks ranked high by both groups included consultation, coordination of student assessment, interpretation of tests, and evaluation of guidance programs. This study suggests that middle school counseling is similar to elementary school counseling in terms of the emphasis on consultation and direct services. One difference is that middle school counseling appears to place emphasis on individual counseling, whereas elementary school counseling stresses the importance of group counseling.

Another source of information on middle school counseling is the *School Counselor* (January, 1986), which presented a special issue on counseling middle grade students. This issue provided information on the developmental tasks of middle school students (Dougherty, 1986; Thornburg, 1986); counselors taking a role in the school effectiveness movement (George, 1986); enhancing self-concept and self-esteem (Beane, 1986); and special stressors experienced by middle school students (Elkind, 1986). More recently, St. Clair (1989) reviewed research on middle school counseling interventions in terms of Lazarus's (1976) concept of the BASIC ID, an approach that addresses behaviors, affect, sensation, images, cognition, interpersonal relations, and biological functions.

Secondary School Counseling.   The origins of secondary school counseling can be traced to the vocational guidance movement that began in the early 1900s. Since that time, secondary school counseling has maintained a close identity with vocational and career guidance and counseling. The role and function of secondary school counselors have centered around assisting students in making the transition from public school to post-secondary education, acquiring vocational training, and entering the world of work.

Secondary school counselors tend to be assigned numerous clerical tasks, including scheduling and administrative functions such as assistance with the disciplinary program. The result has been a loss of clear mission (Aubrey, 1982) and a "role mutation" that has seriously damaged the professional image of school counselors (Peer, 1985). Hutchinson, Barrick, and Groves (1986) provided evidence of the role mutation phenomenon cited by Peer (1985) in a study that compared actual and ideal functions of secondary school counselors. According to the study, counselors believed they should ideally provide the traditional counseling activities of personal, academic, and group counseling. In actual practice, scheduling required more time than any activity except for personal counseling. The authors concluded that counselors were performing noncounseling activities at the expense of more important functions such as group counseling, career and life planning, and classroom guidance. Tennyson, Miller, Skovholt, and Williams (1989) provided support for this observation by noting that scheduling of students appeared to be taking a higher priority over the critical functions of promoting developmental guidance and counseling.

When high school counselors do engage in direct counseling services, they are often unable to invest the necessary time and energy because of the large numbers of students and conflicting role demands. Rowe (1989) surveyed the type and extent of involvement high school counselors have with senior high school students. He found that counselors had sessions with 80% of the students who went to college. The primary purpose of their contact was to assist with college plans. Unfortunately, counselors averaged only two sessions with each student for a total of 15 minutes. These students received the largest number of contacts—approximately five— regarding college planning from parents and friends. Results of this study suggest that high school counselors are not providing sufficient information about college planning, even though it is the main topic they are addressing with senior high school students (Rowe, 1989).

Rural School Counseling.   The role and function of school counseling varies not only according to educational level but also in terms of rural versus urban settings. Sutton and Southworth (1990) reported that rural counselors have fewer referral sources and must therefore rely on their own resources and become jacks-of-all-trades. This situation can contribute to rural counselors experiencing more job-related stress than urban school counselors (Sutton & Southworth, 1990). At the same time, they feel more freedom, strength, optimism, and happiness than urban counselors (Sutton & Southworth, 1990). In addition, rural school counselors tend to have more positive relationships with their principals than urban counselors (Sutton & Southworth, 1990). These relationships may result from rural counselors having more contact and involvement with their principals than urban counselors (McIntire, Marion, & Quaglia, 1990).

McIntire, Marion, and Quaglia (1990) noted that 40% of rural counselors do not work with other counselors and must therefore develop their own support systems. They also suggested that for counselors to be successful in rural settings, they must be aware of the special needs and circumstances of the community and become actively involved in the community.

SPECIAL SKILLS AND PROBLEMS

This section will discuss the special skills and problems associated with school counseling. These include consultation, counseling exceptional students, and some of the special problems that students face: drug abuse, teen-age pregnancy, divorced or single parents, and dropping out of school.

Consultation

Tharp and Wetzel (1969) described consultation as a triadic process: consultation services are provided (a) by a consultant (b) indirectly through a mediator or consultee (c) to a target (client, clients, or organizational system). The individual who functions as a mediator will vary according to the situation and may be a parent or teacher, for example, needing suggestions about how to apply effective discipline procedures with a child. The target can be a client, a group of clients, or an entire system such as an organization. An example of consultation at an organizational level is a school administrator (the mediator) acquiring the services of a counselor (the consultant) to assist in implementing the school's drug prevention program among students (the target).

Kurpius (1978) provided guidelines to the consultation process in the following nine stages.

Stage 1: Reentry. The consultant clarifies the values, needs, assumptions, and goals of people in the organization.

Stage 2: Entry. The consultation relationship is established and defined in terms of roles, ground rules, and a statement of the presenting problem.

Stage 3: Gathering information. Additional information is obtained to clarify the presenting problem.

Stage 4: Defining the problem. Information obtained from assessment is used to determine goals for change.

Stage 5: Determine a solution to the problem. Strategies such as "brainstorming" and setting priorities are used to identify the best solution to the problem.

Stage 6: Stating objectives. Outcomes are identified that can be accomplished and measured within a specific period of time.

Consultation with teachers is an integral aspect of school counseling.

Stage 7: Implementation of the plan.   The plan is implemented according to the established guidelines.

Stage 8: Evaluation.   Ongoing activities are monitored and evaluated through a process evaluation. Final outcomes are also measured through an outcome evaluation.

Stage 9: Termination.   The consultant discontinues direct contact with the consultee. The effects of the consultation process are expected to continue.

Models of Consultation.   The actual process of consultation will vary according to the situation and model utilized. Kurpius (1978) identified the following four modalities for consultation.

1. *Provision mode.* In this mode, consultees do not involve themselves because they lack the expertise, time, or interest to pursue the problem. As a result, the consultant has sole responsibility for handling the problem.

2. *Prescriptive mode.* In contrast to the provision mode, consultees are actively involved in trying to resolve a problem. Typically, they have developed a plan, and they utilize a consultant because they lack the necessary problem-solving skills or confidence to implement the plan. The role of the consultant is to diagnose what is wrong and prescribe what should be done to ameliorate the problem situation.

3. *Collaborative mode.* The consultant's role in this mode is to facilitate self-direction for consultees in problem-solving capacities. The consultant also collaborates with consultees in developing a realistic plan for dealing with the problem situation and helps consultees work together effectively.

4. *Mediation mode.* The distinction of this mode is that the consultant initiates contact and requests help with a problem situation, rather than consultees seeking help, as in the other modes. The role of the consultant is to define the problem, identify goals and intervention strategies, and then call together the people who can assist with implementation of the plan.

School Consultation.   Podemski and Childers (1980) suggested that school counselors are in a unique position to offer consultation services since they are expected to act in an advisory and supportive manner. Elementary school counselors have been particularly successful in incorporating consultation into their role and function.

As early as 1957, Patouillet suggested the primary function of the elementary school counselor was that of consultant. More recently, Miller (1988) noted that elementary school counselors rated consultation services as a higher priority than did middle or high school counselors.

To a large degree, the success of consultation in elementary school can be traced to the pioneering work of Don Dinkmeyer and Jon Carlson. They were able to demonstrate how Adlerian principles could be used effectively in consulting with teachers, administrators, and parents (Dinkmeyer & Carlson, 1973). Dinkmeyer (1971, 1973) developed a collaborative model of consultation called the "C" group model, which can be used with groups of parents and teachers. The "C" group model was designed to create a channel for communication regarding issues pertaining to children, for example, how to deal with children's misbehavior. It was so-called because the forces that operate in the group begin with the letter "C": collaboration, consultation, clarification, confrontation, communication, concern, caring, confidentiality, change, and cohesion.

Opportunities exist for school counselors to provide consultation services at all levels of public schools. Griggs (1988) suggested that school counselors should expand their consultation role to become facilitators of learning. Ferris (1988) also noted that consultation is needed to provide safe, secure, and positive learning environments. The effective utilization of consultation skills will play an important role in the future of school counselors in the 1990s and beyond.

Counseling Exceptional Students

Issues that relate to counseling exceptional students have had a major impact on school counseling. The term *exceptional* can be defined as applying to "any individual whose physical or behavioral performance deviates so substantially from the norm, either higher or lower, that additional educational and other services may be necessary to meet the individual's needs" (Hardman, Drew, Egan, & Wolf, 1990, p. 14).

The passage of Public Law 94–142, the Education for All Handicapped Children Act (Public Law 94–142, 1975) provided for public education within the least restrictive environment for all students with disabilities. Cole (1988) observed that this law has had a dramatic effect on the role of the school counselor. She observed that in many schools, the counselor has become the case manager for exceptional students. This new role has required counselors to devote enormous amounts of time to coordination activities such as handling paper work, attending meetings, and placing students. In addition, counselors have become more involved in providing counseling services to disabled students and their families. It has therefore become important for school counselors to be aware of the special issues associated with counseling exceptional students. This section will address some of these issues as well as provide guidelines for working with exceptional students.

Guidelines for Counseling Exceptional Students.   Perhaps the most basic guideline for counseling exceptional students is to consider that these individuals are more similar to those without disabilities than they are different (McDowell, Coven, & Eash, 1979). Exceptional students should therefore be treated as unique individuals first and people with special needs second. This focus can help counselors become sensitive to individual differences and avoid stereotyping clients in terms of a label.

A second guideline for counselors is being aware of the common problems that exceptional students face. Rotatori, Banbury, and Sisterhen (1986) suggest that exceptional students tend to have difficulty with self-concept, body image, frustration, and dependency. A review of these common problem areas will now be provided.

Bello (1989) suggested that students with disabilities tend to suffer self-concept problems as a result of a history of frustration and failure. These failure-oriented experiences can contribute to irrational beliefs such as: "I am not able to do school work"; "People think I'm dumb'"; and "In order to be successful, I must be able to do as well as nondisabled people" (Bello, 1989). Bello (1989) therefore recommended that cognitive approaches could play a key role in helping students overcome a failure orientation and improve their self-concept.

Exceptional students, whose bodies have physical abnormalities, may be particularly prone to interpersonal difficulties (Goldberg, 1974). In addition, parents tend to discourage these students from exploring their bodies, contributing to a sense of denial (McDowell, Coven, & Eash, 1979). Rotatori, Banbury, and Sisterhen (1986) therefore recommended that these students be encouraged to explore their bodies and accept their particular disabling condition.

Rotatori, Banbury, and Sisterhen (1986) suggested that exceptional students can become frustrated when they do not feel they can measure up to expectations; a disabling condition limits opportunities for participation; their confidence or competence are threatened; or they do not feel support. Frustration can lead to behavioral problems such as aggression (Talkington & Riley, 1971); sarcasm and cynicism (McDowell, Coven, & Eash, 1979); and stubbornness (Clarizio & McCoy, 1983). Counseling strategies can be directed at resolving the frustration by providing a means for venting the negative emotions and fostering competency skills that prevent frustration (Rotatori, Banbury, & Sisterhen, 1986).

It is not uncommon for parents and teachers to foster dependency in an exceptional student, because they believe the individual is incapable of functioning independently. Overdependent students can lack motivation and experience academic difficulties. They can also be easily influenced by peer pressure, resulting in inappropriate behavior (Rotatori, Banbury, & Sisterhen, 1986). Counseling strategies should be directed at helping these students feel capable, maximizing their self-confidence, and promoting self-reliance.

A third guideline for counseling exceptional students is to be aware of the special needs and counseling strategies associated with the various types of exceptionality. For example, mentally retarded students tend to experience social, and emotional problems due to rigid behavior. Behavior therapy has been proven effective with this population to teach self-help skills, enhance social skills, and eliminate inappropriate behavior. Table 13.3 incorporates information from Rotatori, Gerber, Litton, and Fox (1986) to provide a description of the special needs, counseling goals, and associated counseling strategies for nine categories of exceptionality.

Special Problems

Students do not have to be exceptional to encounter problems in school. They face an increasingly diverse array of problems and challenges as they progress through the school years. This section will describe some of these problems and suggest possible counseling approaches.

Drug Use and Abuse. In this discussion, the term *drugs* refers to alcohol, cigarettes, and illicit drugs such as cocaine, marijuana, or heroin. Drug use has declined steadily in the United States since 1980, yet the U.S. continues to have the highest rate of abuse among industrialized nations (Newcomb & Bentler, 1989). A recent survey showed that 57% of high school seniors have used illicit drugs, and

Table 13.3
Counseling Exceptional Children

Disorder	Special Needs or Problems	Counseling Goals	Counseling Strategies
Mentally retarded student (Litton, 1986)	High incidence of social-emotional problems due to their rigid behavior; restricted life experience; problems perceiving personal and social situations.	Improve social adaptation; enhance self-help skills; increase awareness of self and others; assist with development of interpersonal relations skills; promote a positive self-image.	Behavior therapy to teach self-help skills, enhance social skills, and eliminate inappropriate behavior.
Learning disabled student (Gerber, 1986)	Poor self-concept and self-esteem; tendency to be rejected by peers; a lack of self-appraisal skills; fear of failure; test anxiety; a lack of motivation.	Enhance the student's self-esteem and self-concept; promote effective social skills; help overcome fear of failure; promote a positive attitude toward the learning process.	Self-concept programs, interpersonal relations training, and cognitive-behavioral approaches to overcome a fear of failure.
Mildly behaviorally disordered students (Raiche, Fox, & Rotatori, 1986)	Problems with impulse control, aggression, and defiance; emotional problems, hyperactivity, and academic problems.	Increase frustration tolerance and self-restraint; help overcome academic difficulties; improve interpersonal relations skills.	Cognitive-behavioral techniques to teach anger control; play therapy and group counseling to assist with social emotional problems; interpersonal relations training to enhance social skills.
Speech- or language-disordered students (Kelley & Rotatori, 1986)	Interpersonal problems resulting from exclusion, overprotection, and ridicule; educational difficulties; self-esteem problems; anxiety.	Help develop coping mechanisms to deal effectively with negative remarks of peers; help broaden and adapt communication skills to various settings; improve interpersonal relation skills, enhance self-concept and self-esteem; overcome educational difficulties.	Cognitive-behavioral approaches to deal effectively with negative remarks; self-concept programs, and communication skill development in small groups.

Hearing impaired students (Sisterhen & Rotatori, 1986)	Language difficulties, including problems with articulation and voice quality, vocabulary, syntax, and grammar; social-emotional problems, such as social isolation, emotional immaturity, behavioral problems, difficulty with interpersonal relations, identity problems.	Assist with identity formation; encourage independence; help develop appropriate social skills (e.g., reduce tendencies to appear physically aggressive).	Behavioral counseling that incorporates social modeling (particularly effective since deaf children tend to follow example set by significant others); guidance programs that focus on self-concept development to promote identity formation.
Visually impaired student (Heinze & Rotatori, 1986)	Low self-confidence, low self-concept, self-criticism, and social isolation.	Increase self-confidence; improve self image; and reduce tendencies toward self-criticism and social isolation.	Assertiveness training to help increase self-confidence; cognitive behavioral approaches to reduce tendencies toward self criticism; interpersonal relations training to increase social interest.
Physically disabled students (Griffin, Sexton, Gerber, & Rotatori, 1986)	Problems vary according to disability type: some need assistance with basic functioning such as eating, personal hygiene, and locomotion; others need assistance in establishing intimate relationships (including sexuality) or dealing with ridicule.	Help identify personal strengths to overcome their physical disability; encourage becoming involved in self-advocacy to foster a sense of self-control over their life.	Adlerian counseling to help identify strengths to overcome weaknesses; existential approaches to help discover personal meaning in life; sex education and sex therapy to help deal with sexuality issues.

Table 13.3, *continued*

Disorder	Special Needs	Counseling Goals	Counseling Strategies
Health-impaired students (Griffin, Berger, & Rotatori, 1986)	Health problems such as leukemia, diabetes, asthma, or a seizure disorder, that can interfere with academic functioning or psychosocial development.	Alleviate anxiety, depression, and bodily discomfort; maximize bodily functioning; and assist with academic difficulties.	Cognitive-behavioral strategies for anxiety and depression; stress management techniques and an exercise program to maximize bodily functioning; family therapy to help with familial factors associated with a seriously ill individual.
Gifted students (Kaufmann, Castellanos, & Rotatori, 1986)	Difficulties with peer relations due to being singled out as the "brain of the class"; lack of motivation and under-achievement when not challenged.	Increase awareness of self and others; enhance problem-solving and decision-making skills; clarify values and personal aspirations; maximize intellectual potential.	Appropriate classroom placement to ensure adequate academic challenge; career counseling (including the use of a mentor) to encourage pursuing personal goals and aspirations; personal counseling to increase awareness of self in relation to others.
Abused students (Kennell & Rotatori, 1986)	Multitude of problems such as dependency, anger, depression, anxiety, self-blame, withdrawal, low self esteem, interpersonal relations; educational problems.	Improve self-image, promote positive interpersonal relations skills, assist with anger control, alleviate anxiety and depression, and help overcome educational difficulties.	Counseling strategies to focus on helping students realize that they were not responsible for what happened, that the abuse was wrong, and that it will stop; self-concept development programs; cognitive-behavioral approaches to promote anger control and alleviate depression.

Note. From *Counseling Exceptional Students* by A. F. Rotatori, P. J. Gerber, F. W. Litton, & R. A. Fox (Eds.), 1986, New York: Human Sciences Press. Copyright 1986 by Human Sciences Press. Reprinted by permission.

Adolescent drug abuse is a major concern for school counselors.

more than one third have used illicit drugs other than marijuana (Newcomb & Bentler, 1989). The use of alcohol and tobacco is even higher, with 66% of seniors reporting use within the previous month, and one fifth reporting daily use of cigarettes (Newcomb & Bentler, 1989).

Despite the national trend, drug use is increasing among young children. Between 1976 and 1986, drug use tripled for students in grades 1 through 6 (Bennett, 1986). In addition, Hubbard, Brownlee, and Anderson (1988) reported that most students initiate drug use during the middle school years. These statistics suggest that elementary and middle schools represent important targets for intervention efforts.

Newcomb and Bentler (1988) identified factors associated with drug use and abuse. High levels of drug use were related to limited educational pursuits and early marriages. Polydrug use, or the use of many drugs, among teen-agers was associated with their later difficulty as young adults in role acquisition, for example, as a spouse or employer. Heavy use of so-called hard drugs was associated with loneliness, drop in social support, psychoticism, and suicidal tendencies.

Newcomb and Bentler (1989) provided information on the etiology, or causes, of drug use and abuse. These authors noted that use is prompted most by peer influence, while abuse stems from internal psychological distress. They also identified risk factors associated with drug use and abuse. These include a personal history of drug use; use by peers; a lower socio-economic level; family dysfunction; a family history of abuse; poor school performance; low self-esteem; lack of abidance with the law; need for excitement; stressful life events; and anxiety and depression.

Children of alcoholics are a particularly high-risk group for developing drug abuse problems. Newlon and Furrow (1986) noted that one in five children belongs to an alcoholic family. In addition, children in these families apparently have a genetic predisposition to becoming alcoholics themselves (Buwick, Martin, & Martin, 1988). Children of alcoholics tend to experience negative emotions, including anger (Clair & Genest, 1987); low self-esteem (Werner, 1986); and an external locus of control (Werner, 1986). Brake (1988) suggested that group counseling that focuses on the special problems of children of alcoholics could be beneficial for this population.

Preventive programs for drug abuse have received much attention in the literature. Two studies conducted meta-analyses of the literature. Bangert-Drowns (1988) found none of the existing preventive programs had any appreciable effect on reducing drug use or abuse. Tobler's (1986) review of the research suggested that programs focusing on increased knowledge about drugs and alcohol were not effective in reducing use or abuse. On the positive side, Tobler (1986) found peer programs that included assertiveness, especially refusal skills, and social-skills training proved the most effective in preventing abuse.

Several programs are available to promote assertiveness and social skills. A program called *Children Are People* (Lerner & Naiditch, 1985) can be used at the elementary school level, and the SMART program (Pearson, Lunday, Rohrbach, & Whitney, 1985) applies to the middle school level. For teens who have drug abuse problems, the most effective programs were those that promoted alternative activities, such as camping and sports; enhanced confidence and social competence; and provided broadening experiences (Tobler, 1986).

Teen-Age Pregnancy.   Each year there are 750,000 unintended pregnancies among teen-agers in the U.S. (Gibson, 1989). The U.S. has one of the highest rates of unintended teen-age pregnancy for any industrialized nation (Harris & Liebert, 1987). The U.S. rate is 2 times those of England and France and 2 1/2 times the rate in Sweden (Wallis, 1985). One explanation for the low rates of teen-age pregnancy in Sweden could be the comprehensive family life program, which begins in elementary school and continues throughout high school. Sex education is integrated into the overall family life program, rather than taught separately.

Many American teen-agers seem to have a lackadaisical attitude about having babies. In one study, one third of males between the ages of 11 and 19 said they would not be "very upset" if they were responsible for getting a girl pregnant (Berger, 1988). In another study, about one fifth of pregnant teen-agers surveyed said they wanted to have a baby (Morrison, 1985).

Adolescents in the U.S. also tend to be ignorant about conception and how to prevent it. For example, Harris and Liebert (1987) reported that most teen-agers did not know what time of the month is relatively safe or risky to engage in sexual intercourse. Morrison (1985) found that many delude themselves into thinking that they will not get pregnant the first time they have sex or if they do not have an orgasm or do not want to have a baby. With such attitudes, it is not surprising that about two

The incidence of teen-age pregnancy is increasing.

thirds of teen-agers use few or no contraceptive practices (Dryfoos, 1982). Furstenberg (1976) reported that a reason for some teen-agers not using contraception is the belief that only "bad girls" plan to have sex, while it is acceptable for "good girls" to engage in sex if they get "carried away with the moment."

The effects of becoming pregnant during the teen-age years can be devastating for the life of the teen-ager as well as her baby. Conger and Peterson (1984) noted that teen-age mothers are twice as likely to drop out of school and less likely to get a job than female students who are not parents. They are also less likely to get married, and if they do, more likely to have a divorce. In addition, they have a greater risk of engaging in child abuse (Conger & Peterson, 1984). Teen-age mothers also tend to have significantly more problems with their babies, including low birth weight, birth defects, and even death (Harris & Liebert, 1987).

Preventive programs can address the special problems associated with teen-age pregnancy. Furstenberg, Brooks-Gunn, and Chase-Lansdale (1989) noted that the most promising forms of prevention of teen-age pregnancy are contraceptive and family-planning services. These authors concluded that other preventive programs that focused on sex education or attempting to change attitudes toward early sexual involvement have had limited success.

Several preventive programs that are implemented after a teen-ager becomes pregnant have been found to be successful. Prenatal programs have been shown to promote healthy babies for teens (Brooks-Gunn, McCormick, & Heagerty, 1988; Brooks-Gunn, McCormick, Gunn, Shorter, Wallace, & Heagerty, in press). Parent education programs have been used to enhance parenting skills as well as the development of the child (Clewell, Brooks-Gunn, & Benasich, in press). In Emmons' (1988) research on the effects of parent education, she used the PREP for Effective Family Living program (Dinkmeyer, McKay, Dinkmeyer, Dinkmeyer, & Carlson, 1985) in small groups with pregnant teen-agers. Emmons found that the PREP program increased the teen-agers' self-concept and fostered democratic parenting attitudes. MacGregor and Newlon (1987) found the most useful approaches for working with pregnant teen-agers included group counseling to provide necessary peer support; parent education after delivery of the baby, but not before; and creative, imaginative prenatal class presentations that encourage active involvement of participants.

Divorced or Single Parents.   There has been a dramatic increase in the rate of divorce and the incidence of single-parent families in the United States. Some studies estimate that 40% to 50% of marriages of young people end in divorce (Dworetzky, 1990). In addition, the incidence of single-parent families has increased by 400% since 1970 (Weinraub & Wolf, 1983). These trends indicate that about half of all children born in the past 10 years will spend some time reared in a single-parent home (Hetherington, Stanley-Hagan, & Anderson, 1989).

Researchers have conducted numerous studies to evaluate the effects of divorce and single parenthood on child development. I reported that during the first year following divorce, children tended to be "more aggressive, distractible, and demanding than children from intact families" (Nystul, 1987, p. 1043). Parish and Wigle (1985) found that divorce had a negative effect on children's self-concept. Divorce has also been associated with poor school performance (Wallerstein & Kelley, 1976; Guidubaldi & Perry, 1984).

Robson (1988) described variations in the effects of divorce according to the age of the child. Children up to 5 years of age tend to regress by developing feeding and toileting problems. Children from age 6 to 8 initially use denial to cope and later remain hopeful that their parents will get back together. From age 9 to 11, children typically react with shock, surprise, denial, and disbelief. In addition, these children can experience conflicts in loyalty to their parents, often viewing one parent as good and the other as bad. Adolescents from 13 to 18 years of age appear to have increased risk of mental health problems and a negative view of their future, their parents, and their environment. Adolescent females also tend to engage in early heterosexual behavior.

Group counseling has been found effective for dealing with the special issues associated with divorce, for example, alleviating guilt and dealing with anger and feelings of abandonment. Many different kinds of divorce groups have emerged (Bowker, 1982; Cantor, 1977; Hammond, 1981). These groups tend to focus on easing children's level of stress and enhancing their self-esteem. Hammond's (1981) program is typical of these group approaches. It utilizes a structured format that includes tapes, film strips, and exercises providing information on divorce as well as opportunities to process feelings. Burke and DeStreek (1989) found empirical support for Hammond's (1981) approach in terms of enhanced self-concept. Additional research on these groups appears warranted.

Dropping Out of School.   Another major problem of adolescence results from not completing high school. It is estimated that 26% of students in the U.S. dropped out of school in 1983 ("School Dropouts," 1985). After adolescents drop out of school, they often become unemployment statistics and turn to delinquency to procure income. The cost of the dropout phenomenon to society can be staggering. One study estimated that the 12,804 dropouts in Chicago in 1982 would end up costing taxpayers $2.5 billion (Hawkins, 1986). The cost of dropping out of school can also be devastating for the dropouts themselves in its effect on their self-esteem, their career aspirations, and personal meaning in their lives.

Several counseling strategies can address the school dropout phenomenon. Preventive programs can provide special counseling services for students who are at risk for dropping out of school. Bearden, Spencer, and Moracco (1989) found that males have a higher risk of dropping out of school than females. The authors identified other at-risk characteristics, including low socio-economic status; a history of previous failures; drug abuse; academic and behavioral problems; poor school attendance; and boredom. Gibson (1989) described several programs that have been used to work with at-risk students. For example, Florida's Dade County Public Schools uses peer counseling, academic support, and help with educational deficiencies (Dade County Public Schools, 1985). The Los Angeles Unified School District (1985) employs counseling, special tutoring, and vocational assistance. More recently Ruben (1989) recommended that preventive efforts should be geared to the elementary level by providing classroom guidance programs like Gerler and Anderson's (1986) program called *Success in Schools*.

FUTURE TRENDS IN SCHOOL COUNSELING

School counseling appears to be at the cross-roads. School counselors are needed more than ever as students experience a complex array of personal and social problems. Yet concerns persist that school counseling cannot deal effectively with these challenges.

Hays (1980) warned that unless significant changes are made, the American school counselor may face extinction—"like the buffalo, the dodo bird, and the whooping crane." More recently, Cole (1988) expressed concern about the future of school counseling. She warned with some irony that school counselors could be replaced by Macintosh computers if they do not define and perform their roles well.

The complex problems that school counselors face have no simple solutions. Several authors have formulated suggestions that may help the profession move forward successfully. For example, Cole (1988) identified the following issues that should be addressed to clarify the role and function of the school counselor.

- How far does the school's responsibility extend into the family or community?
- Are school counselors doing too much or too little?
- Should they become more specialized or more versatile?
- How does school counseling vary with different populations and diverse settings?
- How can technology be used as an adjunct to the school counseling program?
- What is the role of school counselors in adult education?
- What is their role with exceptional children?
- What is their role in the movement toward excellence in education?

The College Entrance Examination Board (1987) also concluded the profession was in trouble and in need of changes. Based on an examination of school counseling, its report recommended making better use of the school counselor's special skills rather than imposing clerical tasks such as scheduling; increasing support for federal programs that assist disadvantaged students; placing more emphasis on counseling programs at the elementary and middle school level to prevent problems from becoming more serious; and promoting greater involvement of parents in the school counseling program.

Russo and Kassera (1989) noted that school counselors have been unsuccessful in clearly communicating the importance of their services. These authors suggested that school counselors should establish a comprehensive ongoing accountability program to overcome these difficulties. They recommended that school counselors could use Wiggins' (1985) accountability program, which includes setting goals, assessing needs, setting priorities, evaluating outcomes, and reporting results.

Green (1988) suggested that image-building activities will play a key role in the future of school counseling. He suggested that school counselors must be accepted as practitioners with specialized knowledge before they can establish professional autonomy. Green (1988) identified the following activities that could be used to promote a sense of professionalism for school counselors.

- Conduct a survey among colleagues to determine how they perceive the role of the school counselor. This type of peer review is a necessary component of professional behavior.

- Compile a list of professional activities during the previous three years. Determine whether these activities have promoted a professional image, required the special skills of a counselor or simply duplicated services offered by other professionals, and educated others on the complexity of the counselor's role in these activities.

- Provide programs for parents on topics such as parent education, drug abuse, and student achievement.

- Publish a newsletter describing activities of the school counseling program as well as issues that interest students, teachers, and parents.

- Become active in conducting research and writing articles for publication in professional journals.

- Become involved in professional organizations.

- Schedule special consultation days for parents and staff to assist with special needs.

- Provide in-service training to teachers.

- Sponsor a community seminar on a topical issue, for example, teen-age pregnancy.

Several authors have commented that school counselors should take a more active role in recent educational reforms (Kaplan & Geoffroy, 1990; Thomas, 1989). These authors suggested that school counselors can play an important role by promoting a positive school climate. The activities they recommended include encouraging success orientation in the school, fostering self-esteem of teachers and students, and helping integrate cognitive and affective dimensions in the educational process.

Capuzzi (1988) emphasized that research has an essential role in the future of school counseling. He identified nine problem areas that students commonly face: self-esteem, eating disorders, child and adolescent suicide, depression, teen-age pregnancy, drug abuse, physical and sexual abuse, stress, and divorced parents. The author noted that a school counselor's expertise on these issues was critical because the problems presented roadblocks to children's psychosocial development. He suggested that additional research is required for school counselors to deal effectively with these problems.

Counselor educators can also play an integral role in helping school counseling successfully move forward. Sweeney (1988) noted that school counseling has been de-emphasized in most counselor education programs. The current focus appears to be on providing course work and skills for agency counselors and not school counseling. According to Sweeney (1988), counselor educators have also neglected research on school counseling. For example, the number of articles published in *Counselor Education and Supervision* on the role and function of school counseling has steadily declined. For example, 39 articles appeared on this topic from 1961 to 1968, but none from 1980 to 1988. Besides helping school counselors formulate a professional identity, counselor educators can provide more emphasis on the educational needs of students interested in school counseling.

These studies collectively suggest that school counseling is a profession at risk and in need of dramatic changes. Briefly, school counselors should

- Clarify their role and function by encouraging others to focus on their special skills and not on clerical tasks such as scheduling
- Incorporate image-building activities and an ongoing accountability program
- Encourage parents to involve themselves more in their children's counseling programs
- Advocate greater emphasis on elementary and middle school counseling
- Become more actively involved in the school reform movement
- Promote research efforts on special problems such as suicide and depression
- Convince counselor educators to place more emphasis on school counseling

CHAPTER SUMMARY

This chapter provided an overview of school counseling. This is a dynamic and challenging field in the counseling profession. School counseling can best be understood within the context of a comprehensive K–12 developmental model. In 1990 the ASCA supported this model in a revised role statement, suggesting also that school counselors engage in individual counseling, small-group counseling, large-group guidance, consultation, and coordination activities. Recent legislative activities in Florida have resulted in mandating that at least 75% of the school counselor's time be spent in providing direct services to students and 25% on indirect or nonguidance activities (Myrick, 1989). There appears to be much promise for the passage of similar legislation in other states. This could help school counselors promote counseling services rather than clerical functions in their programs.

The chapter also provided information on the special skills of school counselors and the special populations they serve. Particular attention was given to the role of consultation because of its increasing emphasis in school counseling. Guidelines for counseling exceptional students and students with the special problems of drug abuse, teen-age pregnancy, divorced or single parents, and dropping out of school were also provided.

School counseling appears to be at a crossroads. Several studies have suggested that changes are needed for school counseling to successfully move forward as a profession. Some of these are increasing direct services and reducing clerical activities; putting more emphasis on elementary and middle school counseling to maximize preventive effort; and engaging in image-building activities.

REFERENCES

ASCA Role Statement (in press). American School Counselor Association role statement. *The School Counselor*.

Aubrey, R. F. (1982). A house divided: Guidance and counseling in 20th century America. *The Personnel and Guidance Journal, 761*, 198–204.

Bangert-Drowns, R. L. (1988). The effects of school-based substance abuse education: A meta-analysis. *Journal of Drug Education, 18*, 243–264.

Beane, J. A. (1986). The self-enhancing middle-grade school. *The School Counselor, 33*(3), 189–195.

Bearden, L. J., Spencer, W. A., & Moracco, J. C. (1989). A study of high school dropouts. *The School Counselor, 37*, 113–120.

Bello, G. A. (1989). Counseling handicapped students: A cognitive approach. *The School Counselor, 36*, 298–304.

Bennett, W. J. (1986). *What works: Schools without drugs*. Washington, DC: U.S. Department of Education.

Berger, K. S. (1988). *The developing person through childhood and adolescence* (2nd ed.). New York: Worth.

Bergin, J. J., Miller, S. E., Bergin, J. W., & Koch, R. E. (1990). The effects of a comprehensive guidance model on a rural school's counseling program. *Elementary School Guidance & Counseling, 25*(1), 37–45.

Blocher, D. H. (1974). *Developmental counseling* (2nd ed.). New York: Roland Press.

Blocher, D. H. (1987). *The professional counselor*. New York: Macmillan.

Bonebrake, C. R., & Borgers, S. B. (1984, February). Counselor role as perceived by counselors and principals. *Elementary School Guidance & Counseling*, 194–199.

Bowker, M. (1982). Children of divorce: Being in between. *Elementary School Guidance & Counseling, 17*, 126–130.

Brake, K. J. (1988). Counseling young children of alcoholics. *Elementary School Guidance & Counseling, 23*, 106–111.

Brooks-Gunn, J., McCormick, M. C., & Heagerty, M. C. (1988). Preventing infant mortality and morbidity: Developmental perspectives. *American Journal of Orthopsychiatry, 58*, 288–296.

Brooks-Gunn, J., McCormick, M. C., Gunn, R. W., Shorter, T., Wallace, C. Y., & Heagerty, M. C. (in press). Outreach as casefindings: The process of locating low-income pregnant women. *Medical Care*.

Burke, D. M., & DeStreek, L. V. (1989). Children of divorce: An application of Hammond's group counseling for children. *Elementary School Guidance & Counseling, 24,* 112–118.

Buwick, A., Martin, D., & Martin, M. (1988). Helping children deal with alcoholism in their family. *Elementary School Guidance & Counseling, 23,* 112–117.

Cantor, D. (1977). School-based groups for children of divorce. *Journal of Divorce, 3,* 183–187.

Capuzzi, D. (1988). Personal and social competency: Developing skills for the future. In G. R. Walz & J. C. Bleuer (Eds.), *Building strong school counseling programs.* Alexandria, VA: American Association for Counseling and Development.

Clair, D., & Genest, M. (1987). Variables associated with the adjustment of offspring of alcoholic fathers. *Journal of Studies on Alcohol, 48,* 345–356.

Clarizio, H. F., & McCoy, G. F. (1983). *Behavior disorders in children.* New York: Harper & Row.

Clewell, B. C., Brooks-Gunn, J., & Benasich, A. A. (in press). Evaluating child-related outcomes of teenage parenting programs. *Family Relations.*

Cole, C. G. (1988). The school counselor: Image and impact, counselor role and function, 1960s to 1980 and beyond. In G. R. Walz & J. C. Bleuer (Eds.), *Building strong school counseling programs.* Alexandria, VA: American Association for Counseling and Development.

College Entrance Examination Board (1987). *Keeping options open: Recommendations, final reports of the commission on precollege guidance and counseling.* New York: Author.

Conger, J. J., & Peterson, A. C. (1984). *Adolescence and youth: Psychological development in a changing world.* New York: Harper & Row.

Dade County Public Schools. (1985). *Dropout prevention/reduction programs and activities* (p. 22). Miami, FL: Author.

Dinkmeyer, D. C. (1968). The counselor as consultant: Rationale and procedures. *Elementary School Guidance & Counseling, 3,* 187–194.

Dinkmeyer, D. C. (1971). The "C" group: Integrating knowledge and experience to change behavior. *The Counseling Psychologist, 3,* 63–72.

Dinkmeyer, D. C. (1973). The parent "C" group. *Personnel and Guidance Journal, 52,* 4.

Dinkmeyer, D., & Carlson, J. (1973). *Consultation: Facilitating human potential and processes.* Columbus, OH: Merrill/Macmillan.

Dinkmeyer, D., McKay, G., Dinkmeyer, D., Jr., Dinkmeyer, J. S., & Carlson, J. (1985). *PREP for effective family living. Student handbook.* Circle Pines, MN: American Guidance Service.

Dougherty, A. M. (1986). The blossoming of youth: Middle graders "on the grow." *The School Counselor, 33*(3), 167–169.

Dryfoos, J. G. (1982). Contraceptive use, pregnancy intentions, and pregnancy outcomes among U.S. women. *Family Planning Perspectives, 14*(2), 81–94.

Dworetzky, J. P. (1990). *Introduction to child development* (4th ed.). St. Paul, MN: West.

Elkind, D. (2986). Stress and the middle grades. *The School Counselor, 33*(3), 196–206.

Emmons, R. D. (1988). *The effects of "PREP" for effective family living on self-esteem and parenting attitudes of adolescents.* Unpublished master's thesis, New Mexico State University, Las Cruces, NM.

Erikson, E. H. (1963). *Childhood and society* (2nd ed.). New York: W. W. Norton.

Ferris, P. A. (1988). Future directions for elementary/middle school counseling. In G. R. Walz & J. C. Bleuer (Eds.), *Building strong school counseling programs.* Alexandria, VA: American Association for Counseling and Development.

Furstenberg, F. F., Jr., Brooks-Gunn, J., & Chase-Lansdale, L. (1989). *Unplanned parenthood: The social consequences of teenage childbearing.* New York: Free Press.

Furstenberg, F. F., Jr., Brooks-Gunn, J., & Chase-Lansdale, L. (1989) Teenaged pregnancy and childbearing. *America Psychologist, 44*(2), 313–320.

George, P. S. (1986). The counselor and modern middle-level schools: New roles in new schools. *The School Counselor, 33*(3), 178–188.

Gerber, P. J. (1986). Counseling the learning disabled. In A. F. Rotatori, P. J. Gerber, F. W. Litton, & R. A. Fox (Eds.), *Counseling exceptional students*. New York: Human Sciences Press.

Gerler, E. R., & Anderson, R. F. (1986). The effects of classroom guidance on children's success in school. *Journal of Counseling and Development, 65*, 78–81.

Gibson, R. L. (1989). Prevention and the elementary school counselor. *Elementary School Guidance & Counseling, 24*, 30–36.

Ginter, E. J., Scalise, J. J., & Presse, N. (1990). The elementary school counselor's role: Perceptions of teachers. *The School Counselor, 38*, 19–23.

Goldberg, R. T. (1974). Adjustment of children with invisible and visible handicaps. *Journal of Counseling Psychology, 21*, 428–432.

Green, R. L. (1988). Image-building activities for the elementary school counselor. *Elementary School Guidance & Counseling, 22*(3), 186–191.

Griffin, H. C., Sexton, D., Gerber, P. J., & Rotatori, A. F. (1986). Counseling the physically handicapped child. In A. F. Rotatori, P. J. Gerber, F. W. Litton, & R. A. Fox (Eds.), *Counseling exceptional students*. New York: Human Sciences Press.

Griggs, S. A. (1988). The counselor as facilitator of learning. In G. R. Walz & J. C. Bleuer (Eds.), *Building strong school counseling programs*. Alexandria, VA: American Association for Counseling and Development.

Guidubaldi, J., & Perry, J. (1984). Divorce, socioeconomic status, and children's cognitive-social competence at school entry. *American Journal of Orthopsychiatry, 54*, 459–468.

Gysbers, N. (1988). Career guidance: A professional heritage and future challenge. In G. R. Walz & J. C. Bleuer (Eds.), *Building strong school counseling programs*. Alexandria, VA: American Association for Counseling and Development.

Gysbers, N., & Henderson, P. (1988). *Developing and managing your school guidance program*. Alexandria, VA: American Association for Counseling and Development.

Hammond, J. (1981). *Group counseling for children of divorce: A guide for the elementary school*. Ann Arbor, MI: Cranbrook.

Hardman, M. L., Drew, C. J., Egan, M. W., & Wolf, B. (1990). *Human exceptionality* (3rd ed.). Boston: Allyn & Bacon.

Harris, J. R., & Liebert, R. M. (1987). *The child* (2nd ed.). Englewood Cliffs, NJ: Prentice-Hall.

Havighurst, R. J. (1972). *Developmental tasks and education* (3rd ed.). New York: David McKay.

Hawkins, S. L. (1986, March 3). The campaign to lure kids back to class. *U.S. News and World Report*, 77–78.

Hays, D. G. (1980). The buffalo, the dodo bird, and the whooping crane. *The School Counselor, 27*, 255–262.

Heinze, A., & Rotatori, A. F. (1986). Counseling the visually handicapped child. In A. F. Rotatori, P. J. Gerber, F. W. Litton, & R. A. Fox (Eds.), *Counseling exceptional students*. New York: Human Sciences Press.

Hetherington, E. M., Stanley-Hagan, M., & Anderson, E. R. (1989). Marital transitions: A child's perspective. *American Psychologist, 44*, 303–312.

Hubbard, R. L., Brownlee, R. F., & Anderson, R. (1988). Initiation of alcohol and drug abuse in the middle school years. *Elementary School Guidance & Counseling, 23*, 118.

Hutchinson, R. L., Barrick, A. L., & Groves, M. (1986). Functions of secondary school counselors in the public schools: Ideal and actual. *The School Counselor, 34*(2), 87–91.

Ivey, A. (1986). *Developmental therapy: Theory and practice*. San Francisco: Jossey-Bass.

Kaplan, L. S., & Geoffroy, K. E. (1990). Enhancing the school climate: New opportunities for the counselor. *The School Counselor, 38*, 7–12.

Kaufmann, F. A., Castellanos, Z. F., & Rotatori, A. F. (1986). Counseling the gifted child. In A. F. Rotatori, P. J. Gerber, F. W. Litton, & R. A. Fox (Eds.), *Counseling exceptional students*. New York. Human Sciences Press.

Kelley, R. H., & Rotatori, A. F. (1986). Counseling the language-disordered child. In A. F. Rotatori, P. J. Gerber, F. W. Litton, & R. A. Fox (Eds.), *Counseling exceptional students*. New York: Human Sciences Press.

Kennel, S. E., & Rotatori, A. F. (1986). Counseling the abused child. In A. F. Rotatori, P. J. Gerber, F. W. Litton, & R. A. Fox (Eds.), *Counseling exceptional students*. New York: Human Sciences Press.

Kurpius, D. J. (1978). Consultation theory and process: An integrated model. *Personnel and Guidance Journal, 56*, 335–338.

Lazarus, A. A. (1976). *Multimodal behavior therapy*. New York: Springer.

Lerner, R., & Naiditch, B. (1985). *Children are people*. St. Paul, MN: Children are People.

Litton, F. W. (1986). Counseling the mentally retarded clinic. In A. F. Rotatori, P. J. Gerber, F. W. Litton, & R. A. Fox (Eds.), *Counseling exceptional students*. New York: Human Sciences Press.

Los Angeles Unified School District. (1985). Dropout prevention and recovery. Los Angeles, CA: Author.

MacGregor, J., & Newlon, B. J. (1987). Description of a teenage pregnancy program. *Journal of Counseling and Development, 65*, 447.

McDowell, W., Coven, A., & Eash, V. (1979). The handicapped: Special needs and strategies for counseling. *Personnel and Guidance Journal, 58*, 228–232.

McIntire, Marion, & Quaglia, R. (1990). Rural school counselors: Their communities and schools. *The School Counselor, 37*, 166–172.

Miller, G. D. (1989). What roles and functions do elementary school counselors have? *Elementary School Guidance & Counseling, 24*, 77–88.

Miller, G. M. (1988). Counselor functions in excellent schools: Elementary through secondary. *The School Counselor, 36*, 88–93.

Morrison, D. M. (1985). Adolescent contraceptive behavior: A review. *Psychological Bulletin, 98*, 538–568.

Morse, C. L., & Russell, T. (1988). How elementary counselors see their role: An empirical study. *Elementary School Guidance & Counseling, 23*(1), 44–62.

Muro, J. J. (1981). On target—on top. *Elementary School Guidance & Counseling, 15*, 307–314.

Myrick, R. D. (1987). *Developmental guidance and counseling: A practical approach*. Minneapolis, MN: Educational Media.

Newcomb, M. D., & Bentler, P. M. (1988). *Consequences of adolescent drug use: Impact on the lives of young adults*. Newbury Park, CA: Sage.

Newcomb, M. D., & Bentler, P. M. (1989). Substance use and abuse among children and teenagers. *American Psychologist, 44*(2), 242–248.

Newlon, B. J., & Furrow, W. V. (1986). Using the classroom to identify children from alcoholic homes. *The School Counselor, 33*, 286–291.

Nystul, M. S. (1987). Single parenthood. In R. J. Corsini (Ed.), *Concise encyclopedia of psychology* (p. 1043). New York: John Wiley & Sons.

Oklahoma State Department of Education (1988). *Building skills for tomorrow: A developmental guidance model*. Oklahoma City: State Board of Affairs.

Parish, T., & Wigle, S. (1985). A longitudinal study of the impact of parental divorce on adolescent's evaluations of self and parents. *Adolescence, 20*, 239–244.

Parsons, F. (1989). *Choosing a vocation*. Boston: Houghton Mifflin.

Patouillet, R. (1957). Organizing for guidance in the elementary school. *Teacher College Record, 58*, 434–436.

Pearson, J., Lunday, B., Rohrbach, L., & Whitney, D. (1985). *Project SMART: A social approach to drug abuse prevention*. Unpublished curriculum guide, University of Southern California, Health Behavior Research Institute, Los Angeles, CA.

Peer, G. G. (1985). The status of secondary school guidance: A national survey. *The School Counselor, 32*(3),181–189.

Piaget, J. (1955). *The language and thought of the child*. New York: New American Library. (Original work published 1923)

Podemski, R. S., & Childers, J. H., Jr. (1980). The counselor as change agent: An organizational analysis. *The School Counselor, 27*, 168–174.

Public Law 94–142, *The Education for All Handicapped Children Act of 1975* is coded at 20 U.S.C. Sec. 613 et. seq. and its implementing regulations at 45 C.F.R. Part 121a. (1975).

Raiche, B. M., Fox, R., & Rotatori, A. F. (1986). Counseling the mildly behaviorally disordered child. In A. F. Rotatori, P. J. Gerber, F. W. Litton, & R. A. Fox (Eds.), *Counseling exceptional students*. New York: Human Sciences Press.

Robson, B. E. (1988). Changing family patterns: Developmental impacts on children. In J. Carlson & J. Lewis (Eds.), *Counseling the adolescent: Individual, family and school interventions*. Denver, CO: Love.

Rogers, C. R. (1942). *Counseling and psychotherapy*. Boston: Houghton Mifflin.

Rotatori, A. F., Banbury, M., & Sisterhen, D. (1986). Overview of counseling exceptional students. In A. F. Rotatori, P. J. Gerber, F. W. Litton, & R. A. Fox (Eds.), *Counseling exceptional students*. New York: Human Sciences Press.

Rotatori, A. F., Gerber, P. J., Litton, F. W., & Fox, R. A. (Eds.). (1986). *Counseling exceptional students*. New York: Human Sciences Press.

Rowe, F. A. (1989). College students' perceptions of high school counselors. *The School Counselor, 36*, 260–264.

Ruben, A. M. (1989). Preventing school dropouts through classroom guidance. *Elementary School Guidance & Counseling, 24*, 21–29.

Russo, T. J., & Kassera, W. (1989). A comprehensive needs-assessment package for secondary school guidance programs. *The School Counselor, 36*, 265–269.

School Dropouts, State by State. (1985, June 3). *U.S. News & World Report*, p. 14.

Sisterhen, D., & Rotatori, A. F. (1986). Counseling the hearing-impaired child. In A. F. Rotatori, P. J. Gerber, F. W. Litton, & R. A. Fox (Eds.), *Counseling exceptional students*. New York: Human Sciences Press.

St. Clair, K. L. (1989). Middle school counseling research: A resource for school counselors. *Elementary School Guidance & Counseling, 23*(3), 219–226.

Sutton, J. M., Jr., & Southworth, R. S. (1990). The effect of the rural setting on school counselors. *The School Counselor, 37*, 173–178.

Sweeney, T. J. (1988). Building strong school counseling programs: Implications for counselor preparation. In G. R. Walz & J. C. Bleuer (Eds.), *Building strong school counseling programs*. Alexandria, VA: American Association for Counseling and Development.

Talkington, L. W., & Riley, J. B. (1971). Reduction diets and aggression in institutionalized mentally retarded patients. *American Journal of Mental Deficiency, 76*, 370–372.

Tennyson, W. W., Miller, G. D., Skovholt, T. G., & Williams, R. C. (1989). Secondary school counselors: What do they do? What is important? *The School Counselor, 36*, 253–259.

Tharp, R. G., & Wetzel, R. (1969). *Behavior modification in the natural environment*. New York: Academic Press.

Thomas, M. D. (1989). The role of the secondary school counselor: The counselor in effective schools. *The School Counselor, 36*, 249–252.

Thornburg, H. D. (1986). The counselor's impact on middle-grade students. *The School Counselor, 33*(3), 170–177.

Tobler, N. S. (1986). Meta-analysis of 143 adolescent drug prevention programs: Quantitative outcome results of program participants compared to a control or comparison group. *Journal of Drug Issues, 16*, 537–568.

Wallerstein, J., & Kelley, J. (1976). The effects of parental divorce: Experiences of the child in later latency. *American Journal of Orthopsychiatry, 46*, 256–269.

Wallis, C. (1985, December 9). Children having children. *Time*. 78–90.

Weinraub, M., & Wolf, B. M. (1983). Effects of stress and social supports on mother-child interactions in single- and two-parent families. *Child Development, 54,* 1297–1311.

Werner, E. E. (1986). Resident offspring of alcoholics: A longitudinal study from birth to age 18. *Journal of Studies on Alcoholism, 47,* 34–41.

Wiggins, J. D. (1985). Six steps towards counseling program accountability. *NASSP Bulletin, 69*(485), 28–31.

CHAPTER FOURTEEN

Mental Health Counseling

CHAPTER OVERVIEW

This chapter provides an overview of mental health counseling. Highlights of this chapter include

- Professional issues for mental health counselors, including professional organizations and certification
- The role and function of the mental health counselor, including direct and indirect intervention strategies
- Categories of mental health services: "problems of living" and mental disorders
- Strategies for suicidal clients
- Strategies for clients with drug abuse problems

Mental health counseling is both an emerging counseling profession represented by mental health counselors and an amorphous job role performed by various members of the helping professions such as counselors, psychologists, psychiatrists, psychiatric nurses, and social workers.

PROFESSIONAL ISSUES

Mental health counselors can be defined as individuals whose "primary affiliation and theoretical basis is counseling and not psychiatry, psychology, or social work" (Palmo, 1986, p. 41). Mental health counselors represent the fastest-growing segment of the mental health field (Dingman, 1988). Burtnett (1986) reported that 57% of mental health agencies have a mental health counselor. These counselors handle some of the most difficult cases, including crisis intervention (Ivey, 1989), and have therefore become an integral aspect of the mental health delivery system.

Until relatively recently, mental health counselors did not have a professional organization to identify. In 1976, the American Association for Counseling and Development (AACD)—now called the American Counseling Association (ACA)—addressed this need by creating a special division called the American Mental Health Counselors Association (AMHCA). By 1985, the AMHCA had become the largest division of the AACD. Since its inception, the AMHCA has embarked on numerous activities that have contributed to the professional identity of the mental health counselor. Its most important contributions include creating a code of ethics for mental health counselors (see Appendix E); publishing the *Journal of Mental Health Counseling,* which provides information regarding the theory, research, and practice of mental health counseling; spearheading a movement for counselor licensure in all states; and setting up national standards for certification of mental health counselors.

The National Academy of Certified Clinical Mental Health Counselors has established the following requirements for certification: a master's degree from a regionally accredited university, with a major in mental health counseling or a related discipline; a minimum of 2 years of post-master's experience in a mental health setting, including 1,500 supervised clinical hours and 50 hours of documented face-to-face supervision each year; and a passing grade on a national certification examination.

More than 1,400 individuals have been endorsed as Certified Clinical Mental Health Counselors (CCMHC) by the National Academy of Clinical Mental Health Counselors since 1979 (Brooks & Gerstein, 1990). The academy based its standards on criteria deemed essential for independent practice as a mental health provider and also what would be acceptable standards to third-party insurance programs (Brooks & Gerstein, 1990). CCMHC providers have been recognized by the Civilian Health and Medical Program of the Uniformed Services (CHAMPUS) for third-party insurance reimbursement when clients are referred by a physician (Brooks & Gerstein, 1990).

Mental health counselors work in a variety of settings that include private practice, community mental health centers, hospitals, alcohol and drug centers, social service agencies, and business and industry (Brooks & Gerstein, 1990). Hershenson and Power (1987) noted an apparent shift in work settings for mental health counselors during the last decade. For example, Weikel and Taylor (1979) reported that in 1978, the highest percentage (39%) of AMHCA members worked in community mental health centers, 18% in private practice, and the remainder in a variety of other settings, including college counseling centers and as college teachers. Weikel (1985) noted that in 1985, a large percentage of AMHCA members worked in private practice (22%), 13% in private counseling centers, 13% in colleges and universities, only 11% in community mental health centers, and the rest in other settings, such as rehabilitation agencies and state and local government. The trend of private practice becoming the dominant work setting for AMHCA members continues in the 1990s (Brooks & Gerstein, 1990).

Several other studies have shown that a high percentage of mental health counselors work in substance abuse centers (Hosie, West, & MacKey, 1988; Richardson & Bradley, 1985). Hosie et al. (1988) reported the largest percentage of professionals working in substance abuse centers held a master's degree in counseling or a Master of Social Work (MSW) degree. In addition, Hosie et al. (1988) noted that mental health counselors were more likely to hold a position as program director than individuals from other disciplines.

THE ROLE AND FUNCTION OF MENTAL HEALTH COUNSELORS

Nicholas, Gerstein, and Keller (1988) noted that mental health counselors perform most of the same tasks as other mental health practitioners, such as marriage and family counselors, social workers, and psychologists. These tasks include psychoeducational services, clinical or direct services, supervision, administration, program development, and consultation. Two tasks that mental health counselors did not tend to engage in were program evaluation and research. These tasks were often performed by doctoral-level counselors and psychologists (Nicholas, Gerstein, & Keller, 1988).

Brooks and Gerstein (1990) noted that while mental health practitioners serve similar functions, they vary in terms of treatment philosophies. These authors found that typically mental health counselors utilize a psychoeducational, developmental, and psychopathological point of view; marriage and family therapists use a systemic orientation; psychologists rely on a psychopathological frame of reference; and social workers adhere to a sociological perspective (Brooks & Gerstein, 1990). Ivey (1989) also differentiated mental health disciplines according to philosophical orientation, noting that mental health counselors define themselves primarily within a developmental perspective, while psychologists adhere to a medical/therapeutic model and social workers focus on the environment. The mental health counselor's role and function can also be conceptualized in terms of direct and indirect intervention strategies.

Direct Intervention Strategies

Mental health counselors provide direct counseling services to clients with a wide range of mental disorders (West, Hosie, & Mackey, 1988). This section will address two commonly used direct intervention strategies: counseling and crisis intervention.

Counseling.   Mental health counselors utilize a wide range of direct counseling strategies such as individual counseling, group counseling, marriage and family counseling, and substance abuse counseling (NeJedlo, Arrendondo, & Benjamin, 1985; Spruill & Fong, 1990; West, Hosie, & Mackey, 1988). In addition, Spruill and Fong (1990) suggested that there appears to be a shift in emphasis in mental health counseling from preventive approaches to direct counseling services such as individual, group, and family counseling.

Crisis Intervention.   Mental health counselors also provide crisis intervention services (Ivey, 1989; West, Hosie, & Mackey, 1988). George and Cristiani (1990) suggested that crisis intervention is not the same as counseling, even though it is a helping strategy. Its focus is more narrow and superficial, its goals are more modest, and it has a briefer duration than counseling. The following is a four-step model for crisis intervention.

The first step is to determine whether the client is in crisis. To determine if crisis intervention is necessary, the counselor must first decide if the client is experiencing a personal crisis. Gilliland and James (1988, p. 3) defined a crisis as "a perception of an event or situation as an intolerable difficulty that exceeds the resources and coping mechanisms of the person." Puryear (1979) identified five factors associated with a crisis.

1. The symptoms of stress result in psychological and physiological discomfort.
2. The client feels intense emotions such as feelings of inadequacy, helplessness, panic, or agitation.
3. The client is more concerned with gaining relief from the symptom than with the problem that precipitated the symptom.
4. The client has a reduced ability to function efficiently.
5. The crisis occurs during a short period of time.

Gilliland and James (1988) recommended that the counselor should use listening skills during the initial phase of crisis intervention to gain a phenomenological understanding of the client. This practice can also help the counselor determine if the client is experiencing a crisis. At the same time, it will enable the counselor to establish rapport and communicate support to the client.

The second step in crisis intervention involves assessment, using two separate procedures. First, the counselor must assess the severity of the crisis in terms of the potential for serious harm to the client or others. Gilliland and James (1988) emphasized that the primary goal of crisis intervention is to avoid a catastrophe in which someone would be seriously injured. The second assessment procedure involves determining whether the client is mentally able to take an active role in resolving the crisis situation. A useful tool in this process is a mental status exam (Othmer & Othmer, 1989), which can help determine whether the client is orientated to person, place, and time; free of hallucinations; and capable of coherent thinking. When a client does not appear to be capable of realistic decision making, the counselor may need to take a more active role in the crisis intervention process.

The third step in the crisis intervention model involves action. During a crisis, some form of action will usually be required to restore equilibrium to the client. Providing the client with rest can be an important part of this process. For example, if the client is acutely suicidal, the counselor may work with family members to arrange for the client to be hospitalized. Once the client receives rest and equilibrium has been restored, counseling strategies can be implemented. The counselor can attempt to identify the precipitating factors associated with the crisis and help the client overcome these problems in the future.

The fourth and final step entails follow-up. Cavanaugh (1982) noted that clients can have delayed reactions to a crisis, which may occur weeks or even months after the precipitating event. It is therefore important to arrange for appropriate follow-up counseling services.

The following Personal Note provides an illustration of crisis intervention.

a personal note

Mary arrived at an outpatient mental health clinic where I was a counselor and said that she was having trouble sleeping and wanted sleeping pills. She appeared agitated and tearful, and she spoke in a monotone. It soon became clear that there was much more on her mind than her trouble with sleeping. She began to talk about an affair that her husband was having. She went on to say that "because of my religious beliefs," it was necessary for her to kill her three children and herself. Mary reasoned that since her husband had an affair, he had lost his right to have any more contact with his family.

I asked Mary what religion would want her to kill herself and her children. At this point, she seemed to ramble on incoherently. A brief mental status examination showed her to be orientated to person and place—she knew who and where she was—but not to time—she didn't know the day, month, or year. There was no evidence of hallucinations but some possibility of a delusion since she described herself as the "savior" of the family. She intended to kill herself and her children to "save" them all from the sins of her husband.

I then explored the seriousness of her suicidal and homicidal threat. I discovered that she had a gun and planned to use it. Since Mary had a plan and a method of carrying it through, I saw this as a crisis that required immediate action. I became very concerned about the safety of Mary and her children. I decided that it would be best if Mary were hospitalized so that she could receive mental health treatment and be protected from hurting herself or her children.

I emphasized to Mary that I wanted her to be hospitalized for her safety and the safety of her children. Since there was not a mental health code on the Indian reservation where I was working, I could not insist that she be hospitalized. Fortunately, Mary agreed to be admitted to the hospital for a couple of days. For the first 2 days, Mary slept "around the clock," only getting up occasionally for water. After she rested, she said she felt much better. Although Mary was still very angry with her husband, she realized that killing herself and her children would accomplish nothing. Before Mary was discharged from the hospital, she made an appointment with me for individual and marital counseling.

Indirect Intervention Strategies

Hershenson and Power (1987) identified six indirect activities associated with the mental health counselor's role and function. They can be considered indirect intervention strategies in that they provide an indirect form of treatment. An overview of these activities follows.

Prevention.   Prevention represents the inverse of coping with a crisis (Barclay, 1984). Prevention of mental disorders and the promotion of mental health have been an integral part of the community mental health movement (Matus & Neuhring, 1979). An example of a preventive focus is the holistic health movement, which promotes healthy lifestyles to prevent the development of illness.

Hershenson and Power (1987) identified three types of prevention: primary, secondary, and tertiary.

1. *Primary prevention* evolved from the public health model. It refers to strengthening the resistance of a particular population and offsetting harmful influences before they can make an impact (Caplan, 1964). Primary prevention takes place before a problem has manifested itself or when its symptoms are barely noticeable (Gilbert, 1982). Shaw and Goodyear (1984) noted that primary prevention reduces the number of individuals requiring mental health services and is therefore an important aspect of any comprehensive human services program. Unfortunately, primary prevention has historically taken a back seat to other strategies because resources are instead applied to people with existing problems.

2. *Secondary prevention* involves programs that attempt to identify individuals who are at risk for developing certain problems and then prescribing remedial activities to prevent those problems from occurring (McMurty, 1985). For example, there has been some interest in working with children of alcoholics to prevent them from becoming alcoholic.

3. *Tertiary prevention* attempts to avert further consequences of a problem that has already manifested itself (Hershenson & Power, 1987). The present mental health system puts most of its efforts in tertiary prevention, focusing on alleviating existing mental health problems.

Advocacy.   Advocacy is another indirect intervention strategy utilized by the mental health counselors. *Advocacy* means to plead the cause of another person and follow through with action in support of that cause (Tesolowski, Rosenberg & Stein, 1983). Hershenson and Power (1987) further explained that ". . . a mental health counselor-advocate is one who is the client's supporter, the advisor, the champion, and if need be, the client's representative in dealing with the court, the police, the social agency, and other organizations that affect one's well-being" (p. 246).

Advocacy is an action-oriented form of intervention whereby the counselor does something for the client. This can have a positive impact on the counseling relationship in that the client may perceive the counselor as someone who can get things done. Mental health counselors can function as advocates in many ways, such as working with a human services department to ensure that clients receive benefits to which they are entitled.

Hershenson and Power (1987) identified the following advocacy skills of mental health counselors.

- *Timing.*   Counselors must decide when to be an advocate and when to let the client take the initiative. As a basic rule, counselors should intervene when it becomes clear that the system is not working for the client or even appears to be working against the client.

- *Support.*   Counselors must have the support of the system to be capable of working effectively with that system. In this vein, it is important for counselors not to alienate themselves from co-workers. Counselors are more successful when they work in a cooperative manner and avoid being perceived as "blindly fighting for another cause."

- *Compromise.*   To maintain support from the system, counselors should be flexible and willing to compromise. A give-and-take approach can also yield creative solutions to complex problems.

- *Communication.*   Several communication skills can be useful in the role of advocate. It is important to be able to listen and communicate an understanding of different points of view regarding the client. This can promote a cooperative approach. Another communication skill that may be necessary is assertiveness. Occasionally, mental health counselors need to take an assertive position to obtain the desired results. Naturally, this must be done in a tactful, caring fashion to be effective.

Consulting.   Since the passage of the Community Mental Health Act in 1963, consultation has been an important aspect of the mental health worker's role and function (Kurpius, 1978). The act noted that consultation services were to become an essential part of community mental health programs of the future (Hershenson & Power, 1987). This legislation was viewed as an attempt to broaden mental health services to include more developmental and preventive approaches (Kurpius, 1978).

Caplan (1970) provided the following definition of mental health consultation:

> "A process of interaction between two professional persons—the consultant, who is a specialist, and the consultee, who invokes the consultant's help in regard to a current work problem with which he is having some difficulty and which he has decided is within the other's area of specialized competence" (p.19).

Hansen, Himes, and Meier (1990) noted that Caplan's definition of mental health consultation has been broadened to include professional consulting with a lay person, for example, a counselor consulting with a parent.

Mediation.   Mediation is one of the newest roles of mental health counselors. Many states now offer mediation services to assist individuals who are going through a divorce (Hershenson & Power, 1987).

Witty (1980) defined mediation as the "facilitation of an agreement between two or more disputing parties by an agreed-upon third party" (p. 4). Kessler (1979) and Koopman (1985) noted the following components of mediation: each party agrees to utilize the services of a mediator; the outcome is an agreement made by the disputants themselves; conflict resolution is cooperative instead of competitive; the focus is on "where we go from here" as opposed to fault-finding; self-disclosure and empathy are promoted in place of deception and intimidation; decisions are self-imposed instead of imposed by others; and creative alternatives are promoted rather than win-or-lose positions.

Kessler (1979) described the actual process of mediation as a structured decision-making process that usually lasts one to three sessions. Hershenson and Power (1987) identified the following three steps that a mental health counselor could use to provide structure to the mediation process.

1. The counselor initially provides the necessary structure by establishing a cooperative tone; setting the rules; obtaining a commitment to the process; and providing an overview of what is to come (Kessler, 1979).

2. In this strategic and planning phase, the mediator obtains an overview of the conflict by reviewing all pertinent information. Toward the end of this step, the mediator can begin to develop a specific plan of action with the disputants.

3. The third step is the problem-solving phase, in which the mediator works with the disputants to help them reach a specific agreement. The mediator may use a variety of tactics during this process, including negotiation, creative problem solving, joining meetings, and private caucuses. The final agreement is usually written out by the disputants so they will have a permanent record of the mediation process.

Mentoring.   Mentoring is another relatively new role and function for mental health counselors. Krupp (1982) defined *mentoring* as a process in which a trusted and experienced individual takes a direct interest in the development and education of a younger, less experienced individual. Numerous studies have shown that mentoring has a positive impact on the mentor, the less experienced individual, and the organization involved (Lynch, 1980; Vaillant, 1977).

Farren, Gray, and Kaye (1984) identified several guidelines for establishing a mentoring relationship: participation should be voluntary; there should be minimal rules and maximum freedom; the mentor and the less experienced individual should share and negotiate expectations; and mentors should be rewarded for their efforts.

Education.   The mental health counselor can also function as an educator; a role that may involve indirect and direct intervention strategies. Education is often an important facet of both types of strategies described in this section, as shown in the following examples.

- Counseling can help a client learn how to become more autonomous.
- Crisis intervention may teach a client how to avoid future crises.
- Prevention often occurs through programs that emphasize an educational component such as parent education.
- Advocacy can teach a client how to be assertive without alienating others.

- Consultation may involve inservice training programs that teach special skills, such as how to avoid burnout.

- Mediation can help a client learn how to resolve conflicts in a cooperative fashion.

- Mentoring provides opportunities for a less experienced individual to learn from a more experienced person.

CATEGORIES OF MENTAL HEALTH SERVICES

The majority of mental health services are directed at helping clients who are dealing with problems of living or who have mental disorders. This section provides an overview of the clinical issues associated with these two categories of problems clients typically face.

Problems of Living

Hershenson and Power (1987) defined *problems of living* as ". . . aberrations and/or natural rough spots as one moves through the course of the life-span development" (p. 87). Typical problems of living that clients face are relationship difficulties, such as marital problems; lack of meaning in life, such as not feeling valued at work; and problems associated with stress, such as psychosomatic illness. Although mental disorders may contribute to problems of living, a client can have these problems without a recognized mental disorder.

Counseling is the primary treatment strategy used to help clients deal with problems of living. Counseling can help the client deal with specific problems, prevent future problems, and cope with stress. Since problems of living typically do not involve mental disorders, the use of psychoactive drugs is usually not part of the treatment program.

Mental Disorders

A mental disorder can be broadly defined as a dysfunctional behavioral or psychological pattern associated with distress or disability (American Psychiatric Association, 1987). In 1984 the National Institute of Mental Health conducted a survey of mental health problems in the United States ("Mental Disorders," 1984). It was an in-depth study costing $15 million. The study estimated that 40 million people in the U.S. experience mental health problems at any given time. More specifically it found that

- One in five adults suffered from a recognized mental disorder.

- The three most common disorders in order of incidence were anxiety, substance abuse, and depression.

- Only one out of five people with a mental disorder sought professional help. Those who did tended to seek help from someone at their church or from a family physician.

- Women tended to suffer from phobias and depression, while men tended to have problems with alcohol and drugs and antisocial behavior.

- The rates for mental problems were higher for those under 45.

- College graduates tend to be less prone to mental disorders than those who did not graduate from college.

The results of this survey suggest that a large percentage of Americans suffer from mental disorders. Another important implication is that when people experience mental problems, they tend not to utilize mental health services. Instead, they often turn to other professionals, such as physicians or members of the clergy. A challenge for mental health counselors has been to overcome the stigma often associated with mental health services so that individuals will seek help when they need it.

Treating Mental Disorders.   Treatment approaches for mental disorders include the use of psychoactive drugs and counseling. Psychoactive drugs are used by psychiatrists primarily to treat psychosis, depression, and acute anxiety reactions. It is important to note that these medications do not cure a person of a mental disorder. They are used primarily to treat underlying brain chemistry dysfunctions and provide symptom relief such as alleviating depression or anxiety. There are potential dangers, for example, the possibility of clients becoming dependent on these medications, especially in the case of tranquilizers to treat anxiety. There can also be serious side effects, for instance, tardive dyskinesia, an irreversible neurological disorder that can result from the prolonged use of antipsychotic medications.

Although psychoactive medications can have drawbacks and inherent dangers, their benefits usually outweigh the risks. For example, a schizophrenic client who does not receive medication may be overwhelmed with threatening hallucinations, dangerous delusions, or a disruptive thought disorder. Although medication cannot remove these symptoms entirely, it can usually control them to the degree that the client can function in society. Antidepressant medications can also be an important aspect of a treatment program for severely depressed clients, who may require medication to be able to work and engage in daily activities. Medication can also be very useful in treating a severe anxiety reaction, since it can reduce anxiety to a point where the client can cope.

Counseling can also play a vital role in the overall treatment program for mental disorders (see the section on cognitive-behavioral approaches in Chapter 8). Counseling may not be indicated until a client has been medically stabilized by the psychoactive medication. A client can be considered *medically stable* when the symptoms associated with the mental disorder have been reduced to the extent that the client is capable of actively engaging in the counseling process.

Counseling can also be used, of course, to treat mental disorders that do not require medication. The actual counseling strategies will vary according to the unique needs of the client and the clinical indicators associated with the particular mental disorder. The following Personal Note describes some of the things I have learned about the treatment of mental disorders.

a personal note

Over the years, I have learned many important lessons from clients who had mental disorders. Several clients have said something in particular that I have never forgotten. As I reflect on these cases, their comments symbolize lessons that I learned. I will describe five cases, giving the client's statement, a brief description of the situation, and the lesson I learned from each person.

Client's Statement: "Someone said pull my eyes out and I did."

Description of Client's Situation.   The client who made this statement was a 25-year-old male who was in jail for theft. A psychiatrist had been asked to make an evaluation because the client was acting strangely. The psychiatrist made a provisional diagnosis of schizophrenia and arranged to have the client admitted to a psychiatric hospital.

The client was not given any antipsychotic medication and was to be transferred to the hospital the next day. That night, he began to hallucinate that he was hearing voices. A "voice" told him to take his eye out, and he did. Then a "voice" said to take the other eye out, and he took it out as well. He was standing and holding his two eyes when a jailer walked by and saw with horror what had happened. The client was immediately taken to a hospital and provided treatment. At the hospital, the client was diagnosed as schizophrenic. I met this man while I was at the hospital checking on several clients. He told me about the voices he had heard, asking him to take his eyes out when he was in jail.

What I Learned.   I learned that clients who are actively hallucinating can do serious harm to themselves. Antipsychotic medications must therefore be considered to help control the hallucinations and other psychotic symptoms.

Client's Statement: "Would you like to see the picture I painted?"

Description of Client's Situation.   The client was a 23-year-old woman who had a long history of severe depression. I had been providing counseling for the client for about 1 year. Although she had weekly appointments, she often missed them. I was actually surprised when she did make an appointment, because she always seemed so disoriented.

One day, the client walked into the counseling center and said she wanted to see me. She told me she had painted a self-portrait and asked if I would like to see it. I could not believe my eyes. She painted the most beautiful painting I had ever seen!

What I Learned.   This client made me realize never to "write off" a client. Regardless of how incapacitated I may think some clients are, I will always remember that they are still capable of doing fantastic things with their lives!

Client's Statement: "There were spiders crawling all over my face and voices telling me I was going to die. I was terrified!"

Description of Client's Situation: This was a 54-year-old female who had been an alcoholic for 26 years. The client was on a drinking binge for 2 weeks and then experienced alcohol hallucinosis, which involved spiders crawling on her face and hearing terrifying voices. The client came to the counseling center the next day and said she would never drink again. I provided weekly counseling services for her over the next year. During that time, the client did not drink. She later moved to another city.

Auditory hallucinations are common in schizophrenia.

What I Learned.   I discovered that the prognosis for overcoming alcoholism is good when the client decides that the costs outweigh the rewards of use. During the first few sessions, it became clear to me that this client had decided that drinking was just not worth it any more.

Client's Statement: "We just caught on fire."

Description of Client's Situation.   The client who made this statement was one of two brothers who caught on fire when they were sniffing gasoline. Both had a long history of inhalant abuse, spanning a 5-year period. I had been seeing them in counseling for 2 years prior to their accident with gasoline. During the years I worked with them, they were hospitalized on numerous occasions for treatment of acute lead poisoning. On one occasion, one of the brothers became psychotic, jumping out of a moving car and running down the street pounding on cars during the 8:00 a.m. rush-hour traffic.

What I Learned.   I learned several things from this case and similar cases involving inhalant dependency. First, I found these individuals have a very difficult time attempting to overcome inhalant dependency. My success rate has been very low with this population: only 1 out of 5 stopped using inhalants while I worked with them.

I soon discovered that lead poisoning can produce serious side effects. For example, both of the brothers I worked with showed significant intellectual impairment. Their overall IQ scores on the Wechsler Adult Intelligence Scale dropped 15 and 20 points respectively over a 12-month interval while they were using inhalants. I also discovered that gasoline sniffing can make a person psychotic. In addition, I learned that lead poisoning was very difficult to treat. I found out that when an individual inhales lead, the lead is absorbed into the bone structure as well as other parts of the body. Unfortunately, the lead tends to remain in the bone structure, gradually releasing lead into the body.

Client's Statement: "I got my meat, my flour, and my Jesus."

Description of Client's Situation.   This was a 45-year-old woman who had been suffering from chronic schizophrenia for 20 years. A residential program had just opened for people who were chronically mentally ill and had no relatives to assist them. I asked the client if she would like to be admitted into the program, and she said, "Yes."

Getting the client admitted into the program was a very long and drawn-out process. It involved filling out numerous forms and dealing with other seemingly endless aspects of the bureaucracy. I was finally told that my client could get into the program. I couldn't wait to tell her the good news.

When I told her she was accepted into the program, she looked puzzled. She then smiled and told me that she didn't want to go. She said, "I got my meat, my flour, and my Jesus." When I asked her what she meant, she said she had plenty of meat to eat and flour to make bread. Then she turned on her portable radio and played a religious station featuring a preacher giving a high-powered sermon. She pointed to the radio, smiled, and said, "That's my Jesus."

What I Learned.   I learned that freedom is essential to human dignity. Whenever possible, people need to have freedom of choice and be able to act on those choices. My job as a counselor was simply to help create choices. When I did create choices for this client, it seemed to bring more meaning to her existence—an existence that she already had.

STRATEGIES FOR SUICIDAL CLIENTS:

Mental health services must continually adapt to the changes in society. Two mental health problems requiring increasing efforts from mental health counselors and other members of the helping profession are suicidal clients and clients with substance abuse problems. To illustrate the contemporary issues and skills associated with mental health counseling, this section will provide an overview of suicide, and the next will cover drug abuse.

The rate of suicides per 100,000 people has increased steadily and dramatically over the past 30 years. In 1950 there were 4.2 suicides per 100,000; in 1974, 10.9; and 1984, 12.8 (Shneidman, 1984). Suicide rates are high across all levels of society. Among girls, the gifted have the highest rate of suicide nationally and are therefore considered to have an especially high risk (Taylor, 1979).

Capuzzi and Nystul (1986) provided a comprehensive overview of suicide—causes, myths, and treatment strategies. The remainder of this section is adapted from that work.

Causes

Shneidman (1984) identified four theoretical perspectives for understanding the motivation for attempting suicide.

Sociological.   Durkheim (1897) described sociological reasons for suicide that seem to have withstood the test of time. These reasons can be categorized as: (a) *egoistic,* when a person lacks a sense of belonging and therefore lacks a sense of purpose; (b) *altruistic,* when a person is willing to die for a particular cause (e.g., Japanese kamikaze pilots); (c) *anomic,* when people believe their relationship with society has been shattered (e.g., after being fired from a job); and (d) *fatalistic,* when individuals feel society does not offer any hope for a better future (e.g., people who feel trapped in poverty).

Psychodynamic.   Freud (1933) emphasized the role of unconscious forces in personality dynamics. In this regard, he believed that all people have an unconscious death wish that could contribute to suicidal behavior.

Psychological.   Shneidman (1976) provided a psychological perspective of suicide, suggesting that suicide is associated with the following psychological conditions: *acute perturbation,* when an individual is in a heightened state of unhappiness; *heightened inimicality,* the person has negative thoughts and feelings toward the self, such as self-hate and guilt; *constriction of intellectual focus,* characterized by a tunneling of thought processes resulting in an inability to see viable options; and *cessation,* when a person believes that suicide will make the suffering stop.

Constitutional or Biochemical.   The medical model suggests a link between depression and suicide and views depression as having an organic basis. In this model, therefore, suicide can be prevented by using psychoactive medication to restore an individual's biochemical balance.

Myths About Suicide

Numerous myths are associated with suicide. The following are some of the myths and the facts that counteract them, as provided by Capuzzi and Nystul (1988) and Gilliland and James (1988).

- *Suicide is only committed by people with severe psychological problems.* Studies have shown that most individuals who commit suicide had not been diagnosed as having a psychological disorder (Shneidman, Farberow, & Litman, 1976).

- *Suicide usually occurs without warning.* In fact, most suicides are preceded by warning signs. The nature of the warning signs may be a sudden change of behavior, self-destructive behavior, verbal threats of suicide, talk of hopelessness and despair, and depression.

- *People who are suicidal will always be prone to suicide.* In truth, most people who become suicidal do not remain in that state forever. They may be struggling through a temporary personal crisis. Once they work through the crisis, they may never be suicidal again.

- *Discussing suicide may cause the client to want to carry out the act.* The opposite is actually true. Talking with a caring person can often prevent suicide.

- *When a person has attempted suicide and "pulls out of it," the danger is over.* Actually, the greatest period of danger is usually during the upswing period, when the person becomes energized following a severe depression and has the energy to commit suicide.

Treatment Strategies

The best strategy for dealing with the suicidal phenomenon would appear to be prevention. One way to prevent suicide is to be aware of the factors associated with suicide. Gilliland and James (1988) identified several factors, which include: the client has a family history of suicide attempts; the client has attempted suicide before; the client has a plan for suicide and the means to carry out the plan; there is a history of unsuccessful medical treatment for a serious illness; or the client has recently experienced a loss through death, divorce, or separation. When several of these factors are present, especially a past history of suicide and a current plan for suicide, a client can be considered a high risk for suicide.

Capuzzi and Nystul (1986) described crisis intervention strategies and post-crisis strategies that could be used with suicidal clients. Crisis intervention strategies include the procedures described earlier in this chapter and may also involve consideration of hospitalization and psychiatric intervention. It may also be necessary to inform family members of the risk of suicide so the client can be monitored. Post-crisis counseling strategies can be implemented after the client is no longer suicidal. These procedures can include determining what caused the client to become suicidal; developing a treatment program to overcome the precipitating factors; and teaching coping skills to prevent problems in the future. The following Personal Note provides additional insights into the suicidal phenomenon.

a personal note

When I was the psychologist for an Indian reservation, I provided mental health counseling to more than 100 clients who attempted suicide. Most of these clients were female adolescents who tried to kill themselves by taking large amounts of pills they found in a medicine cabinet.

The thing that surprised me about these clients was that nearly all of them truly seemed to want to die. They did not appear simply to be making a "cry for help." Several nearly died when their hearts stopped. Each time, fortunately, the medical team was able to bring the client back from "the grips of death." When these young women regained consciousness, however, almost all of them immediately said something that expressed their disappointment that they had not died.

As I explored their reasons for wanting to die, the majority seemed to believe life had nothing to offer them. They had reached a dead-end, with nowhere to go. They felt if they did try to continue living again, things would probably just get worse. There were feelings of futility and sorrow in their words and tone of voice. Their desire for life seemed to be gone, and in its place grew a sense of apathy.

The focus of counseling with these clients was to help them discover some personal meaning in life. Together we worked to cultivate dreams and develop the means to turn those dreams into reality. This process required intensive individual counseling and psychotherapy. In addition, I often utilized couples counseling and family therapy as an important facet of the overall treatment program.

STRATEGIES FOR CLIENTS WITH DRUG ABUSE PROBLEMS

Drug abuse has become a major health problem in the United States as well as many other countries. Alcoholism is considered to be the third most prevalent public health problem in the U.S. (Pattison & Kaufman, 1982). For some cultures, such as Native Americans, alcoholism ranks first among all health problems (Harrar, 1984). Illicit drug use is also widespread in American society and includes use among children and adolescents, as discussed in Chapter 13. A 1982 survey estimated that 32 million Americans smoke marijuana at least once a year, and 20 million use it once a month; over 12 million use cocaine once a year; and several million use a variety of drugs, such as tranquilizers and stimulants, without medical supervision (Polich, Ellickson, Reuter, & Kahan, 1984).

Drug abuse has permeated all levels of society: approximately one fifth of all Americans have a problem with alcohol or drug abuse at some time in their lives, and one third of all psychiatric patients have alcohol or drug abuse problems (Frances, 1988). Counselors can therefore expect to come into contact with problems relating to drug abuse regardless of the counseling setting where they work.

Drug abuse counseling requires special skills and training.

This section will provide an overview of drug abuse, with information relating to diagnosis, special treatment issues, counseling goals, treatment strategies, and prevention of relapses. Since alcoholism is the most prevalent of these problems, particular attention is devoted to that issue.

Diagnosis

Counselors can diagnose drug, or substance, abuse problems using DSM-III-R (American Psychiatric Association, 1987), which recognizes two mental disorders associated with substance abuse: substance abuse and substance dependence. A diagnosis of substance abuse applies to a client with an impairment in social or occupational functioning. Substance dependence is considered a more serious disorder and is diagnosed when a client shows evidence of physiological withdrawal or tolerance. It is important to note that use of a particular substance like marijuana does not constitute abuse. Instead, the use of the substance must result in impairment in functioning before it should be considered abuse or dependence, a recognized mental disorder.

Questionnaires can also be used as a part of the diagnostic process to determine whether a person is an alcoholic or has a drug abuse problem. A commonly used questionnaire is the Michigan Alcohol Screening Test (Selzer, 1971). This test has 24 questions that require yes-or-no answers from the respondent.

Some dangers can result, however, from using the DSM-III-R system of diagnosis or a questionnaire to label a person as a drug abuser. These systems have either-or definitions of alcoholism in that they provide a result that a client either is or is not an alcoholic. This either-or definition could result in a counselor not providing needed services to a client with a borderline problem.

Pattison and Kaufman (1982) rejected the either-or perspective and instead conceptualized alcoholism as a multivariant syndrome. This position suggests that no two alcoholics are alike. Instead, alcoholics represent multiple patterns of dysfunctional use, varying personalities, numerous possibilities for adverse consequences, and various prognoses, and each individual requires a different type of treatment (Pattison & Kaufman, 1982).

According to Lewis, Dana, and Blevins (1988), the multivariant position suggests that drug abuse should be conceptualized on a continuum from nonuse to dependence (see Figure 14.1). Lewis, Dana, and Blevins (1988) note that the continuum model does not imply that people who develop problems will always move steadily

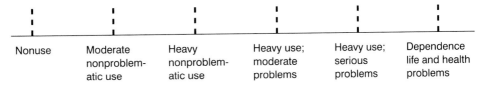

| Nonuse | Moderate nonproblematic use | Heavy nonproblematic use | Heavy use; moderate problems | Heavy use; serious problems | Dependence life and health problems |

Figure 14.1
Drug Abuse Continuum
Note. From *Substance Abuse Counseling* (p. 6) by J. A. Lewis, R. Q. Dana, and G. A. Blevins, 1988, Pacific Grove, CA: Brooks/Cole. Copyright 1988 by Brooks/Cole. Reprinted by permission.

along the continuum from left to right. The relationship to the continuum will vary from individual to individual. Some will stay at the same spot; others will move to the right, signifying more serious problems; and some will develop less severe problems, moving to the left on the continuum.

Lewis, Dana, and Blevins (1988) suggested that counselors can estimate the place where a person is functioning on the continuum by determining the number of problems the person has experienced in relation to drinking or drug abuse. Vaillant's (1983) Problem-Drinking Scale can be used to identify problems relating to drinking, including work-related problems, such as excessive tardiness or sick leave or being fired from work; family problems, such as complaints from family members or marital problems; legal problems, such as alcohol-related arrests; and health problems, such as medical disorders, blackouts, and tremors.

Special Treatment Issues

Most of the counseling theories and strategies described in this text can be applied to the treatment of clients with drug abuse problems. At the same time, some special issues should be considered when working with this population. In this regard, Lewis, Dana, and Blevins (1988) provided the following guidelines for drug abuse counseling.

- Conceptualize drug abuse problems on a continuum from nonproblematic to problematic rather than in dichotomous, either-or terms.
- Provide an individualized treatment program in terms of goals and methods.
- Incorporate a multidimensional treatment program that includes social and environmental aspects associated with long-term recovery.
- Select the least intrusive treatment for each client.
- Consider new methods and goals as research findings become available.
- Be sensitive to the individual differences and various needs of diverse client populations.

These guidelines provide a general theoretical framework for working with drug abuse. In addition, there are some unique counseling goals and treatment strategies associated with drug abuse counseling.

Counseling Goals

Considerable debate exists in the literature as to whether the primary goal of alcohol abuse counseling should be abstinence or controlled drinking (Fisher, 1982; Marlatt, 1983; Sobell & Sobell, 1984). Proponents of abstinence align themselves with the disease model of alcoholism, contending that alcoholism is a chronic and progressive disease and that abstinence is therefore the only solution. Alcoholics Anonymous (AA) and Narcotics Anonymous (NA) are among the proponents of this position. In contrast, supporters of controlled drinking conceptualize alcoholism from a behavioral perspective, believing that it results from maladaptive learning.

Miller and Munoz (1982) noted that controlled drinking will be appropriate only for approximately 15% of all alcohol abusers. In addition, Miller and Munoz (1982) identified conditions that should preclude any consideration of controlled drinking as a treatment goal. These include clients who have a medical problem such as a disease of the gastro-intestinal system (e.g., liver disease), heart disease, or other condition that may be made worse by drinking; are pregnant or trying to become pregnant; tend to lose control of their behavior when they drink; have been physically addicted to alcohol; take medication that is dangerous when combined with alcohol, such as antidepressants or tranquilizers; or are currently abstaining successfully, particularly if there is a family history of alcoholism or a personal history of serious drinking problems.

Counselors who want to consider controlled drinking as a goal for a client should first receive specialized training. Behavioral self-control training is one approach that has received considerable attention, reporting a success rate between 60% and 80% (Miller, 1980). This program is educationally oriented and can be used in an outpatient setting. It involves a variety of behavioral techniques, including training the client to identify environmental cues that increase the frequency of drinking, monitoring drinking consumption, and the use of self-reinforcement to control drinking rates.

Aside from the issue of abstinence versus controlled drinking, there are other, more specific goals that counselors should address in developing a comprehensive treatment program. Lewis, Dana, and Blevins (1988) noted that drug abuse tends to be associated with social, physiological, family, and financial problems. Considering these related problems, they identified the following goals that counselors could attempt to accomplish in drug abuse counseling. The counselor can help clients to

- Resolve legal problems
- Attain stability in marriage and family
- Establish and meet educational and career goals
- Improve interpersonal and social skills
- Enhance physical fitness and health
- Develop effective coping mechanisms to deal with stress
- Learn how to recognize and express feelings
- Develop effective problem-solving and decision-making skills
- Establish a social support system
- Develop positive self-esteem and self-efficacy
- Deal effectively with psychological issues such as anxiety and depression
- Create recreational and social outlets

Treatment Strategies

Treatment approaches in drug abuse counseling vary according to the counselor's theoretical orientation as well as the goals established by the counselor and client. The following overview presents some commonly used treatment approaches.

The Minnesota Model. This is the dominant approach for the treatment of alcoholism (Allen, 1989). It incorporates the disease model of alcoholism and focuses on treating the whole person—mind, spirit, and body. The model also emphasizes ongoing involvement in Alcoholics Anonymous.

The Alcoholics Anonymous (AA) Model.   AA is a major force in the treatment of alcoholism (McLatchie & Lomp, 1988). This model incorporates the disease model of alcoholism and is based on the 12 steps of AA, which have a strong religious context.

The medical model.   This approach also adheres to the disease model of alcoholism. Researchers are currently investigating genetic and organic factors, including brain function and physiology, in terms of etiology and treatment of substance abuse disorders (Frances, 1988). Several medical approaches are used to treat drug abuse problems, including anti-abuse, which causes a violent physical reaction if alcohol is ingested; methadone maintenance to block the withdrawal symptoms associated with heroin use while not producing the euphoric effects; and programs at detoxification centers and in hospitals to allow patients to overcome the withdrawal effects of alcohol under medical supervision.

Behavioral approaches.   According to Lettieri (1988), several behavioral approaches are used in drug abuse counseling. Some of these are anxiety and stress management, self-control training; extinction training with and without drugs; assertion training; and social-skills training.

Family-system therapy.   Family therapy has become an important treatment approach for drug abuse (DeMaio, 1989). The systemic perspective conceptualizes drug abuse as perpetuated and maintained by a dysfunctional family system. Marriage and family counseling have been shown "to decrease family behaviors that trigger or enable drinking and increase positive reinforcement of sobriety" (O'Farrell, 1989, p. 23).

Prevention of Relapses

A comprehensive treatment program for drug abuse should also include strategies to prevent or deal with a client's relapse, or uncontrolled return to drug or alcohol use. The potential for relapse is a serious problem in substance abuse counseling. Some estimates suggest that 90% of all clients have a relapse within 4 years following treatment (Polich, Armor, & Braiker, 1981).

Several factors have been related to drug abuse relapse. Svanum and McAdoo (1989) noted that differences in the outcome of a drug abuse treatment program were related to the presence or absence of a mental disorder besides the drug disorder. These researchers found that clients with no additional disorders tended to avoid relapse, as long as they complied with after-care treatment, especially an exercise program; had a satisfactory job; and had an adequate living arrangement. Clients with multiple mental disorders were more prone to relapse if their emotional disturbance continued after participation in a drug abuse program. Other factors such as exercise, work, or living conditions did not appear to be related to relapse for these clients. Since a substantial minority of drug abuse clients suffer from psychopathology such as anxiety and depression (Mirin, Weiss, Michael, & Griffin, 1988), drug abuse programs should include careful screening and treatment for these disorders as part of relapse prevention.

A second factor related to drug abuse relapse is the lifestyle imbalance that can result from certain life events. Cummings, Gordon, and Marlatt (1980) attempted to determine what types of events precipitated a relapse. They found that negative emotional states were associated with 35% of all relapses; interpersonal conflicts were related to 16%; and social pressures accounted for 20%.

Lewis, Dana, and Blevins (1988) incorporated Marlatt and Gordon's (1985) model of the relapse process into the flow chart shown in Figure 14.2. The flow chart suggests that the relapse process can begin with a lifestyle imbalance, as shown at left. This can occur when a client experiences a particular problem, such as a setback at work or a relationship problem. The imbalance may cause the client to feel the need for immediate stress release. The client may rationalize taking a drink by thinking, "I deserve a drink, with all that I'm going through." At this point the client may deny having a problem with alcohol and make apparently irrelevant decisions (AIDs). Without the necessary coping skills, the client will experience a decrease in self-efficacy, feeling unable to cope with the situation. This in turn will result in a slip— beginning to drink—creating an abstinence violation effect (AVE). The AVE further undermines the client's self-efficacy, reducing self-confidence. The client may think, "I'm just a hopeless drunk." Such negative thinking can create a self-fulfilling prophesy, leading to an increased probability of a relapse. The flow chart also shows how a drug abuse counselor can help prevent relapse. The key to preventing a relapse is to teach effective coping skills, such as stress management, which can increase self-efficacy and decrease the probability of relapse.

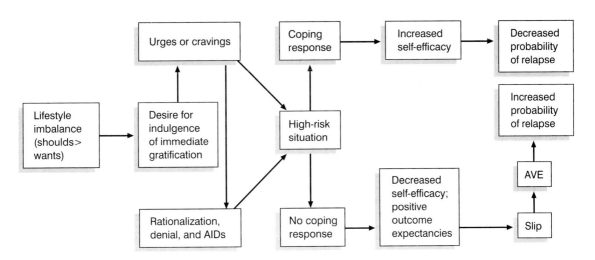

Figure 14.2
Relapse Process
Note. From *Substance Abuse Counseling* by J. A. Lewis, R. Q. Dana, and G. A. Blevins, 1988, Pacific Grove, CA: Brooks/Cole. Copyright 1988 by Brooks/Cole. Reprinted by permission.

SUMMARY

This chapter presented an overview of the issues associated with mental health counseling. Mental health counseling was described as both an amorphous job role performed by various members of the helping profession and an emerging profession for individuals who identify themselves as mental health counselors.

Information was provided on professional issues relating to mental health counselors such as professional affiliation and certification requirements. The role and function of mental health counselors was described in terms of direct and indirect services. Their primary function was then described as providing direct counseling services to clients who have either problems of living or mental disorders. The chapter concluded by addressing two mental health issues which are demanding increased attention by mental health counselors and other members of the helping profession: suicidal clients and clients with drug abuse problems.

REFERENCES

Allen, J. (1989). Overview of alcoholism treatment: Settings and approaches. *Journal of Mental Health Administration, 16*(2), 55–62.

American Psychiatric Association (1987). *Diagnostic and statistical manual of mental disorders* (3rd ed. revised). Washington, DC: Author.

Barclay, J. R. (1984, April). Primary prevention and assessment. *The Personnel and Guidance Journal,* 475–478.

Brooks, D. K., & Gerstein, L. H. (1990). Counselor credentialing and interpersonal collaboration. *Journal of Counseling and Development, 68,* 477–484.

Burtnett, F. E. (1986). *Staffing patterns in mental health agencies and organizations.* Unpublished report, American Association for Counseling and Development, Alexandria, VA.

Caplan, G. (1964). *Principles of preventive psychiatry.* New York: Basic Books.

Caplan, G. (1970). *The theory and practice of mental health consultation.* New York: Basic Books.

Capuzzi, D., & Nystul, M. S. (1986). The suicidal adolescent. In L. B. Golden & D. Capuzzi (Eds.), *Helping families help children: Family interventions with school-related problems,* pp. 23–32. Springfield, IL: Charles C. Thomas.

Cavanaugh, M. E. (1982). *The counseling experience.* Monterey, CA: Brooks/Cole.

Cummings, C., Gordon, J. R., & Marlatt, G. A. (1980). Relapse: Prevention and prediction. In W. R. Miller (Ed.), *The addictive behaviors.* New York: Pergamon Press.

DeMaio, R. (1989). Integrating traditional alcoholic treatment programs and family-systems therapy. *Family Systems Medicine, 7*(3) 274–291.

Dingman, R. L. (Ed.). (1988). *Licensure for mental health counselors.* Huntington, WV: Marshall University Press.

Durkheim, E. (1897). *Suicide: A study in sociology.* Glencoe, IL: Free Press.

Farren, C., Gray, J. D., & Kaye, B. C. (1984). Mentoring: A boom to career development. *The Personnel and Guidance Journal, 61,* 20–24.

Fisher, K. (1982, November). Debate rages on 1973 Sonell study. *APA Monitor,* pp. 8–9.

Frances, R. J. (1988). Update on alcohol and drug disorder treatment. *Journal of Clinical Psychiatry, 49*(9), 13–17.

Freud, S. (1933). New introductory lectures on psychoanalyses. In J. Strachey (Ed. and Trans.), The complete psychological works (Vol. 22). New York: Norton.

George, R. L., & Cristiani, T. S. (1990). *Counseling: Theory and practice* (3rd ed.). Englewood Cliffs, NJ: Prentice-Hall.

Gilbert, N. (1982, July). Policy issues in primary prevention. *Social Work,* 293–296.

Gilliland, B. E., & James, R. K. (1988). *Crisis intervention strategies.* Pacific Grove, CA: Brooks/Cole.

Hansen, J. C., Himes, B. S., & Meier, S. (1990). *Consultation: Concepts and practices*. Englewood Cliffs, NJ: Prentice-Hall.

Harrar, L. (1984). *Make my people live: The crisis in Indian health*. Public Broadcasting System: NOVA.

Hershenson, D. B., & Power, P. W. (1987). *Mental health counseling*. New York: Pergamon Press.

Hosie, T. W., West, J. D., & MacKey, J. A. (1988). Employment and roles of mental health counselors in substance-abuse centers. *Journal of Mental Health Counseling, 10*(3), 188–198.

Ivey, A. E. (1989). Mental health counseling: A developmental process and profession. *Journal of Mental Health Counseling, 11*(1), 26–35.

Kessler, S. (1979, November). Counselor as mediator. *The Personnel and Guidance Journal,* 194–197.

Koopman, E. J. (1985). The education and training of mediators. In S. Grebs (Ed.), *Divorce and family mediation*. Rockville, MD: Aspen Systems.

Krupp, J. (1982). *Mentoring as a means to personnel growth and improved school climate*: A research report. Colchester, CT: Project Rise.

Kurpius, D. (1978). Consultation theory and process: An integrated model. *The Personnel and Guidance Journal, 56,* 335–378.

Lettieri, D. J. (1988). Alcoholism treatment assessment: An overview of practical issues and methods. *Drugs and Society, 2*(2), 1–18.

Lewis, J. A., Dana, R. Q., & Blevins, G. A. (1988). *Substance abuse counseling: An individualized approach*. Pacific Grove, CA: Brooks/Cole.

Lynch, S. (1980). The mentor link: Bridging education and employment. *Journal of College Placement, 40,* 44–47.

Marlatt, G. A. (1983). The controlled drinking controversy: A commentary. *American Psychologist, 38,* 1097–1110.

Marlatt, G. A., & Gordon, J. R. (Eds.). (1985). *Relapse prevention*. New York: Guilford Press.

Matus, R., & Neuhring, E. M. (1979). Social workers in primary prevention: Action and ideology in mental health. *Community Mental Health Journal, 15,* 33–38.

McLatchie, B. H., & Lomp, K. G. E. (1988). Alcoholics anonymous affiliation and treatment outcome among a clinical sample of problem drinkers. *American Journal of Drug and Alcohol Abuse, 14*(3), 309–324.

McMurty, S. C. (1985, January-February). Secondary prevention of child maltreatment: A review. *Social Work,* 42–46.

Mental disorders may affect 1 in 5. (1984, October 3). *Washington Post,* p. A1.

Miller, W. R. (1980). Treating the problem drinker. In W. R. Miller (Ed.), *The addictive behaviors: Treatment of alcoholism, drug abuse, smoking, and obesity*. New York: Pergamon Press.

Miller, W. R., & Munoz, R. F. (1982). *How to control your drinking*. Albuquerque, NM: University of New Mexico Press.

Mirin, S. M., Weiss, R. D., Michael, J., & Griffin, M. L. (1988). Psychopathology in substance abusers: Diagnosis and treatment. *American Journal of Drug and Alcohol Abuse, 14*(2), 139–157.

NeJedlo, R. J., Arredondo, P., & Benjamin, L. (1985). *Imagine: A visionary model for the counselors of tomorrow*. Alexandria, VA: Association for Counselor Education and Supervision.

Nicholas, D., Gerstein, L., & Keller, K. (1988). Behavioral medicine and the mental health counselor. Roles and interdisciplinary collaboration. *Journal of Mental Health Counseling, 10,* 79–94.

O'Farrell, T. J. (1989). Marital and family therapy in alcoholism treatment. *Journal of Substance Abuse Treatment, 6,* 23–29.

Othmer, E., & Othmer, S. C. (1989). *The clinical interview: Using DSM-III-R*. Washington, DC: American Psychiatric Press.

Palmo, A. J. (1986). Professional identity of the mental health counselor. In A. J. Palmo & W. J. Weikel (Eds.), *Foundations of mental health counseling*. Springfield, IL: Charles C. Thomas.

Pattison, E. M., & Kaufman, E. (1982). The alcoholism syndrome: Definitions and models. In E. M. Pattison & E. Kaufman (Eds.), *Encyclopedic handbook of alcoholism* (pp. 3–30). New York: Gardner Press.

Polich, J. M., Armor, D. M., & Braiker, H. B. (1981). *The course of alcoholism: Four years after treatment*. New York: Wiley.

Polich, J. M., Ellickson, P. L., Reuter, P., & Kahan, J. P. (1984). *Strategies for controlling adolescent drug use*. Santa Monica, CA: Rand.

Puryear, D. A. (1979). *Helping people in crisis*. San Francisco: Jossey-Bass.

Richardson, B. K., & Bradley, L. J. (1985). *Community agency counseling: An emerging specialty in counselor education programs.* Alexandria, VA: American Association for Counseling and Development Foundation.

Selzer, M. L. (1971). Michigan alcoholism screening test: The quest for a new diagnostic instrument. *American Journal of Psychiatry, 127,* 1653–1658.

Shaw, M. D., & Goodyear, R. K. (1984, April). Introduction to special issues on primary prevention. *The Personnel and Guidance Journal,* 444–445.

Shneidman, E. S. (1976). A psychological theory of suicide. *Psychiatric Annals, 6,* 51–66.

Shneidman, E. S. (1984). Suicide. In R. Corsini (Ed.), *Encyclopedia of Psychology* (Vol. 3). New York: John Wiley.

Shneidman, E. S., Farberow, N. L., & Litman, R. E. (1976). *The psychology of suicide.* New York: Aronson.

Sobell, M. B., & Sobell, L. C. (1984). The aftermath of heresy: A response to Pendery et al.'s (1982) critique of "Individualized Behavior Therapy for Alcoholics." *Behavior Research and Therapy, 22,* 413–447.

Spruill, D. A., & Fong, M. L. (1990). Defining the domain of mental health counseling: From identity confusion to consensus. *Journal of Mental Health Counseling, 12*(1), 12–23.

Svanum, S., & McAdoo, W. G. (1989). Predicting rapid relapse following treatment for chemical dependence: A matched-subjects design. *Journal of Consulting and Clinical Psychology, 57*(2), 222–226.

Taylor, R. (1979). *The gifted and the talented.* CO: Educational Consultant Agency.

Tesolowski, D. G., Rosenberg, H., & Stein, R. J. (1983, July, August, September). Advocacy intervention: A responsibility of human service professionals. *Journal of Rehabilitation,* 12–17.

Vaillant, G. E. (1977). *Adaptation to life.* Boston: Little, Brown.

Vaillant, G. E. (1983). *The natural history of alcoholism.* Cambridge, MA: Harvard University Press.

Weikel, W. J. (1985). The American Mental Health Counselors Association. *Journal of Counseling and Development, 63,* 457–460.

Weikel, W. J., & Taylor, S. S. (1979). AMHCA: Membership profile and five journal preferences. *AMHCA Journal, 1,* 89–94.

West, J. D., Hosie, T. W., & Mackey, J. A. (1988). The counselor's role in mental health: An evaluation. *Counselor Education and Supervision, 27,* 233–239.

Witty, C. (1980). *Mediation and society: Conflict management in Lebanon.* New York: Academic.

CHAPTER FIFTEEN

Professional Preparation and Ethical and Legal Issues

CHAPTER OVERVIEW

This chapter will provide an overview of professional issues in counseling. The chapter covers important aspects of becoming a professional counselor and major ethical and legal issues. Highlights of this chapter include

- Becoming a professional counselor, including formal study and professional affiliation, certification and licensure, continuing education, and professional involvement
- Ethical issues, including client welfare, informed consent, and confidentiality
- Legal issues, including privileged communication and malpractice
- Special ethical and legal issues relating to marriage and family counseling, child counseling, group counseling, and AIDS
- Ethical decision making, including clinical examples

This chapter presents an overview of the major issues associated with becoming a professional counselor. Information is provided on topics such as certification and licensure and professional organizations. The chapter also addresses emerging ethical and legal issues in counseling. A description of these issues is presented along with guidelines for ethical decision making and clinical examples that illustrate some applications of ethical and legal principles.

BECOMING A PROFESSIONAL COUNSELOR

Deciding to undertake formal study in counseling constitutes the first step toward becoming a professional counselor. Being a professional counselor is an ongoing process that involves work, study, and commitment. This section describes four building blocks that characterize this process, as shown in Figure 15.1.

Formal Study and Professional Affiliation

Formal study in counseling usually involves working toward a master's or doctoral degree in the counseling field. There has been increasing pressure for graduate programs offering these degrees to obtain accreditation from one or more organizations: the American Counseling Association's (ACA) Council for the Accreditation of Counseling and Related Problems (CACREP); the American Psychological Association (APA); and, in some instances, the American Association of Marriage and Family Therapy (AAMFT). Accreditation helps insure that the programs will maintain an acceptable level of standards. In addition, some certification processes in counseling or psychology require a degree from an accredited program. A current list of graduate programs approved by the ACA, APA, and AAMFT can be obtained by writing directly to each organization at the following addresses.

The ACA: 5999 Stevenson Ave., Alexandria, VA, 22304

The APA: 1200 17th St., N.W., Washington, DC, 20036

The AAMFT: 1717 K Street, N.W., #407, Washington, DC, 20006.

Master's degree programs provide the necessary foundations for a career as a professional counselor. Students can also benefit from joining a professional organization,

Figure 15.1
The Building Blocks of
Professional Counseling

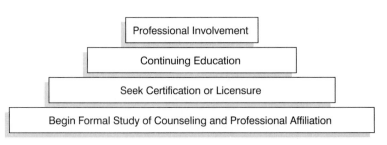

Professional Involvement

Continuing Education

Seek Certification or Licensure

Begin Formal Study of Counseling and Professional Affiliation such as the ACA or APA, as a student member. Student members can attend conventions and involve themselves in professional issues facing counselors and psychologists. They also receive journals and newsletters that address important counseling issues and receive a copy of the code of ethics that guides clinical practice.

The ACA and APA each have numerous divisions that may be of interest to counselors and psychologists. Selected divisions are listed in Table 15.1.

Certification and Licensure

Certification and licensure are important to all professions including counseling. They provide professional recognition as well as enabling members of the helping profession to utilize third-party insurance to help clients pay for counseling services. Certified or licensed psychologists can utilize third-party insurance in all 50 states. Counselors, on the other hand, are just beginning to be able to use third-party insurance programs. As of 1990, certified or licensed counselors could utilize third-party insurance in only four states: Montana, Virginia, Texas, and Vermont (Cummings, 1990).

Certification and licensure are similar processes whereby the applicant must meet certain requirements in education, training, experience, and clinical competence. Forester (1977) identified several differences between certification and licensure. Certification recognizes the competence of practitioners by authorizing them to use the title adopted by the profession. Unlike certification, licensure is authorized by state legislation and regulates the practice and title of the profession. Since licensure is a legal process, legal sanctions can be imposed on an individual who is licensed. Licensure also has more specific and comprehensive regulations, necessitating greater training and preparation than in the certification process (George & Cristiani, 1990).

Historically, most states have offered school counselors opportunities to be certified or licensed. Along with other school personnel, school counselors are traditionally certified by a state board of education. Most states also require counselors to be certified as teachers. Since 1977, all states have required that psychologists be either certified or licensed by a state board of psychologist examiners (Cummings, 1990).

More recently, there has been a trend to provide certification or licensure for counselors who wish to practice outside the school setting, for example, in mental health clinics, hospitals, or private practice. The counseling profession has made progress in passing legislation at the state level requiring certification or licensure. As of 1992, 35 states had passed certification or licensure laws for counselors, as listed in Table 15.2. Certification or licensure in counseling requires 30 to 60 graduate hours, depending on the state; a master's degree in counseling or a closely related field; 2 to 4 hours per week of supervised counseling experience, depending on the state; and passing an examination. There is some concern that current examination processes do not assess an applicant's clinical skills and are therefore in need of modification (Brooks & Gerstein, 1990).

The ACA has taken an active role in certification and licensure for counselors at the state and national levels (Brooks & Gerstein, 1990). For example, the ACA helped create the National Board for Certified Counselors (NBCC) in an attempt to identify national standards for professional counselors. Individuals wishing to obtain

Table 15.1
Selected Divisions and Affiliates of the ACA and APA

ACA	APA
1. American College Personnel Association (ACPA)	5 - Evaluation and Measurement
2. Association for Counselor Education and Supervision (ACES)	10 - Psychology and the Arts
	12 - Clinical
3. National Career Development Association (NCDA)	13 - Consulting
4. Association for Humanistic Education and Development (AHEAD)	14 - Society for Industrial and Organizational Psychology, Inc.
	15 - Educational
5. American School Counselor Association (ASCA)	16 - School
	17 - Counseling
6. American Rehabilitation Counseling and Development (ARCD)	18 - Psychologists in Public Service
7. Association for Measurement and Evaluation in Counseling and Development (AMECD)	19 - Military
	22 - Rehabilitation Psychology
	27 - Community Psychology
8. National Employment Counselors Association (NECA)	28 - Psychopharmacology
9. Association for Multicultural Counseling and Development (AMCD)	29 - Psychotherapy
	30 - Psychological Hypnosis
10. Association for Religious and Value Issues in Counseling	31 - State Psychological Association Affairs
	32 - Humanistic Psychology
11. Association for Specialists in Group Work (ASGW)	33 - Mental Retardation
12. Public Offender Counseling Association (Affiliate)	35 - Psychology of Women
13. American Mental Health Counselors Association (Affiliate)	36 - Psychologists Interested in Religious Issues (PIRI)
	37 - Child, Youth, and Family Services
14. Military Educators and Counselors Association	38 - Health Psychology
	39 - Psychoanalysis
15. Association for Adult Development	40 - Clinical Neuropsychology
16. International Association of Marriage and Family Counselors	42 - Psychologists in Independent Private Practice
	43 - Family Psychology
	44 - Society for the Study of Lesbian and Gay Issues
	45 - Society for the Study of Ethnic Minority Issues
	47 - Exercise and Sports Psychology

Table 15.2
States That Have Passed
Certification or Licensure Laws
for Counselors

State	Law Passed (Year)	State	Law Passed (Year)
Alabama	1979	Montana	1985
Arizona	1988	Nebraska	1988
Arkansas	1979	North Carolina	1983
California	1989	North Dakota	1989
Colorado	1988	Ohio	1989
Delaware	1987	Oklahoma	1985
Florida	1981	Oregon	1989
Georgia	1987	Rhode Island	1987
Idaho	1982	South Carolina	1985
Iowa	1991	South Dakota	1990
Kansas	1987	Tennessee	1987
Louisiana	1987	Texas	1981
Maine	1989	Vermont	1988
Maryland	1985	Virginia	1976
Massachusetts	1987	Washington	1987
Michigan	1988	West Virginia	1986
Mississippi	1985	Wyoming	1987
Missouri	1985		

recognition as an NBCC counselor must have a master's or doctoral degree in counseling or a closely related field; have at least 2 years of supervised professional counseling experience; and successfully complete a certification exam.

Counselors may also pursue certification in a specialty field. Some examples are National Certified Career Counselors, Certified Clinical Mental Health Counselors, and Certified Rehabilitation Counselors (Brooks & Gerstein, 1990).

Some animosity has developed among the members of various helping professions over the proper qualifications. In this debate, members of specialties such as psychiatry, psychology, and counseling emphasize the merits of their respective fields. For example, psychiatrists promote the need for medical training. Unfortunately, the real issue at hand appears to be gaining dominance and control. Some examples of this lack of cooperation are psychiatry's failure to support psychology; psychology's contempt for mental health counselors; and the counseling profession's (represented by the ACA) refusing to recognize the standards of the AAMFT as necessary to practice as marriage and family counselors (Cummings, 1990; Everett,

1990). Clearly, there is a need for more cooperation among the helping professions and less concern with special interests (Brooks & Gerstein, 1990; Cummings, 1990).

Continuing Education

Some form of continuing education is essential for the ongoing development of professional counselors. Most certification and licensure regulations also require counselors to take continuing education courses to maintain their professional credentials. This usually involves attending workshops or presentations at conferences or taking courses that have been approved for continuing education credits.

Other professional development activities can help counselors remain current and refine their clinical skills. Some of these are reading professional journals and books; attending inservice training programs; co-counseling with an experienced clinician; seeking ongoing supervision; and attending institutes for advanced training in a counseling specialty.

Professional Involvement

As mentioned, being a professional counselor requires ongoing work and effort. As individuals embark on a career in counseling, they initially draw help and guidance from the profession. As they advance in the profession, they find themselves in a position to make a contribution. Some ways that counselors can contribute are taking an active role in professional organizations; supporting efforts for certification and licensure; and writing in professional journals.

Professional involvement helps support and maintain the profession, but it also enriches the counselor. As counselors become professionally involved, they develop a network of friends who can often become an important support system. The experience can also diversify their interests and professional activities, which can be stimulating and professionally rewarding.

ETHICAL ISSUES

Ethical and legal issues have become increasingly important in the counseling profession (Krieshok, 1987; Paradise & Kirby, 1990). The emergence of these issues represents a response to the increased risk of malpractice suits against counselors (Corey, 1991) and to the AACD's (1988) statement that counselors should "respect the integrity and promote the welfare of clients" (Section B.1). Since several ethical and legal issues relate to counseling, a knowledge of these issues can be useful in clinical practice. This section presents information on ethical issues, and the next section covers legal issues.

Ethical codes have been formulated by the ACA and the APA (see Appendixes F & G). The ACA (1988) code of ethics relates to issues such as general topics of concern, the counseling relationship, measurement and evaluation, research and publication, consulting, private practice, personnel administration, and preparation standards.

The various ethical standards are guidelines rather than "black-and-white" rules for what a counselor can or cannot do. Each clinical situation is unique and may require an interpretation of the particular code of ethics. In this regard, the standards can be viewed as guiding principles that counselors can use to formulate a

Involvement in professional
organizations can play an important role in one's development
as a counselor.

clinical judgment. In addition, Mabe and Rollin (1986) noted that the codes of ethics
provide a framework for professional behavior and responsibility and serve as a
means for establishing professional identity.

Major Ethical Issues

Baruth and Huber (1985) identified three major ethical issues that influence clinical
practice: client welfare, informed consent, and confidentiality. An overview of these
issues follows.

Client Welfare.   The counselor's primary responsibility is the welfare of the client.
In this regard, the ACA and APA codes of ethics suggest that: the client's needs come
before the counselor's needs; counselors should practice within their area of competence; and counselors should terminate or refer a client who is no longer benefitting
from the service.

Table 15.3 provides excerpts from the ACA and the APA regarding client welfare
and conditions relating to client referral.

Informed Consent.   The ethical guidelines relating to informed consent require
counselors to provide each client with an overview of what counseling will entail so
the client can decide whether to participate. Table 15.4 lists excerpts on this topic
from the ACA and the APA. Mardirosian, McGuire, Abbott, and Blau (1990) noted

Table 15.3
Ethical Considerations Relating to Client Welfare and Referral

---

Client Welfare

ACA (1988):

"The member's primary obligation is to respect the integrity and promote the welfare of the client(s) whether the client(s) is(are) assisted individually or in a group relationship."

APA (1989):

"The maintenance of high standards of competence is a responsibility shared by all psychologists in the interest of the public and the profession as a whole. Psychologists recognize the boundaries of their competence and the limitations of their techniques. They only provide services and only use the techniques for which they are qualified by training and experience. In those areas in which recognized standards do not yet exist, psychologists take whatever precautions are necessary to protect the welfare of their clients. They maintain knowledge of current scientific and professional information related to the services they render."

Client Referral

ACA (1988):

"If a member determines an inability to be of professional assistance to the client, the member must either avoid initiating the counseling relationship or immediately terminate that relationship. In either event the member must suggest appropriate alternatives. (The member must be knowledgeable about referral resources so that a satisfactory referral can be initiated.) In the event the client declines the suggested referral the member is not obligated to continue that relationship."

APA (1989):

"Psychologists terminate a clinical or consulting relationship when it is reasonably clear that the consumer is not benefiting from it. They offer to help the consumer locate alternative sources of assistance."

---

that counselors can assist a client in making an informed consent by providing information on policies, goals, and procedures. In controversial issues such as pregnancy counseling, the authors suggested that counselors should inform the client of their moral-value position.

One way to give a client information to assist with informed consent is by providing a professional disclosure statement. McFadden and Brooks (1983) provided an example of such a statement, which has been incorporated into the professional disclosure statement shown in Table 15.5. The professional disclosure statement in Table 15.5 can be adjusted to reflect the counselor's professional identity and special theoretical orientation. For example, school counselors might mention that their approach includes consultation with parents and teachers and counseling with students individually and in small and large groups. In terms of theoretical orientation, school counselors might explain the importance of a developmental perspective in addressing the developmental tasks of children at different grade levels.

Table 15.4
Ethical Considerations Relating to Informed Consent

Informed Consent

ACA (1988):

"The member must inform the client of the purposes, goals, techniques, rules of procedure, and limitations that may affect the relationship at or before the time that the counseling relationship is entered. When working with minors or persons who are unable to give consent, the member protects these clients' best interests."

APA (1989):

"Psychologists fully inform consumers as to the purpose and nature of an evaluative, treatment, educational, or training procedure, and they freely acknowledge that clients, students, or participants in research have freedom of choice with regard to participation."

Confidentiality.   Confidentiality is a critical condition in counseling and psychotherapy (Paradise & Kirby, 1990). The client must feel safe in disclosing information to the counselor for the counseling process to be effective (Reynolds, 1976). Denkowski and Denkowski (1982) identified two purposes of confidentiality in counseling: (a) protecting the client from the social stigma often associated with being in therapy, and (b) promoting the client's vital rights that are integral to the client's welfare. The ACA and the APA provide guidelines relating to confidentiality, as shown in Table 15.6. The major exception to the principle of confidentiality is when clients pose a clear and imminent danger to themselves or others, such as a client who threatens to commit suicide or kill someone (Gross & Robinson, 1987). It is important to ensure that clients are aware of the limits regarding confidentiality before they begin counseling. This can be accomplished in several ways, including the use of a professional disclosure statement.

LEGAL ISSUES

Several legal issues that impact the practice of counseling relate to confidentiality. As mentioned, counselors are ethically obligated to maintain confidentiality unless clients pose a clear and imminent danger to themselves or others. A legal precedent for counselors to take decisive action to protect human life was set in the landmark case of Tarasoff versus the Board of Regents of the University of California (1974, 1976). The case involved a psychologist at the University of California at Berkeley who provided counseling services to a student. After the student threatened to kill his girlfriend, Tatiana Tarasoff, the psychologist failed to warn her of the threat. Two months later, the client killed the girl. Her parents filed suit against the university and won on the basis that the psychologist was irresponsible.

Corey (1991) identified three other situations when counselors are legally required to report information: (a) when the counselor believes that a client under the age of 16 is the victim of child abuse, sexual abuse, or some other crime; (b) if the counselor determines that a client is in need of hospitalization; and (c) if information is made an issue in a court action.

Table 15.5
Professional Disclosure Statement

Professional Disclosure Statement

(LETTERHEAD)

Milton H. Counselor, Ph.D.
333 Maple Street
Littletown, Alabama 36501
(205) 555-5347
Hours by Appointment

STATEMENT OF PROFESSIONAL DISCLOSURE

Ph.D., Counseling—Bigname State University, 1981
B.A., Group Communication /Psychology—Bigname State University, 1973
B.S., Psychology—Bigname State University, 1972

Certified Clinical Mental Health Counselor, 1980.
Certificate #609
Licensed Professional Counselor, 1980, License #576

Philosophical Base

I utilize a cognitive approach that emphasizes cognitive restructuring to alter affective states. This means that the way we feel and the way we behave are directly related to how and what we are thinking. The past and the future are not as important as living one's life to the fullest in the present. I view counseling as a process by which I facilitate my clients in exploration, clarification, and identification of their needs and help them make changes in their behavior that will result in the attainment of life satisfaction and self-acceptance.

Therapeutic Approach

I use an integrative approach. My core theory is Adlerian. I also utilize techniques and counseling procedures from other schools of counseling to meet the needs of my clients. In addition, I try to be especially sensitive to multicultural issues that may arise in counseling.

In individual counseling, I attempt to help clients focus their awareness on strengths rather than liabilities. Clients are encouraged to accept responsibility for initiating and maintaining change in their lives as those changes are identified through the counseling process.

In marriage counseling, I focus on developing a healthy independence and interdependence.

This is accomplished by using the techniques that help to develop self-awareness as well as improving the communication skills of both partners. I view group counseling as an adjunct to individual counseling rather than as a substitute for it. In my work in family counseling and the management of behavioral problems of children, I use an approach that involves encouragement, rational thinking, logical consequences, understanding misdirected goals, and improved parent-child communication. In all cases, I stress the effect of cognition on behavior and emotions and the need to develop control over this function.

Areas of Competency

Individual counseling	Drug abuse counseling
Marriage counseling	Career counseling
Family counseling	Values clarification and life planning
Child counseling	Organization development
Group counseling	Biofeedback and relaxation training

Ethical Standards

I subscribe to the codes of ethics of the following organizations. Copies are available and will be discussed with the client upon request.

American Counseling Association
American Mental Health Counselors Association
National Academy of Certified Clinical Mental Health Counselors
Alabama Board of Examiners in Counseling

Limits to Confidentiality

All information discussed in counseling will be treated as confidential except in instances when the client becomes a serious threat to self (e.g., suicidal) or others (e.g., homicidal) or when mandated by law (e.g., reporting of child abuse and neglect).

Professional Memberships

American Counseling Association
American Mental Health Counselors Association
Association for Specialists in Group Work
Alabama Association for Counseling and Development
Alabama Mental Health Counselors Association

Fees

Individual, marriage, or family counseling	$60 per session
Group counseling	$30 per session
Career counseling	Fees vary according to tests and services required.

(Ordinarily the above fee schedule will apply. Please feel free to discuss fees and special circumstances regarding fee payments at our first session.)

Please discuss any concerns about the counseling services you receive with me. If these concerns cannot be resolved between us, contact the Alabama Board of Examiners in Counseling, c/o Donald Schmitz, Chairman, Jacksonville State University, Jacksonville, AL 36265, or National Academy of Certified Clinical Mental Health Counselors, Two Skyline Place, Suite 400, 5203 Leesburg Pike, Falls Church, VA 22041.

Note. Adapted from Counseling Licensure Action Packet by J. McFadden and D. K. Brooks, 1983, Alexandria, VA: AACD. Copyright 1983 by AACD. Reprinted by permission.

Legal issues are becoming increasingly important to the practice of counseling.

Table 15.6
Ethical Considerations Relating to Confidentiality

Confidentiality

ACA (1988):
"The counseling relationship and information resulting therefrom must be kept confidential, consistent with the obligation of the member as a professional person."

APA (1989):
"Psychologists have a primary obligation to respect the confidentiality of information obtained from persons in the course of their work as psychologists. They reveal such information to others only with the consent of the person or the person's legal representative, except in those unusual circumstances in which not to do so would result in clear danger to the person or to others. Where appropriate, psychologists inform their clients of the legal limits of confidentiality."

Privileged Communication

Another legal issue that pertains to confidentiality is the notion of *privileged communication*. This term refers to a legal protection for clients, preventing a counselor from disclosing confidential communication in court without their permission (Herlihy & Sheeley, 1987). The privilege exists to protect the rights of the client and not the counselor. The client owns and controls the privilege (Herlihy & Sheeley, 1987) and can therefore determine whether or not a counselor may disclose confidential information in a court of law.

Corey, Corey, and Callanan (1988) identified the following exceptions when a client does not own and control the privilege and the counselor must provide information to the court. These instances are when

- A counselor is acting in a court-appointed capacity, such as conducting a psychological examination (Dekraai & Sales, 1982)
- A counselor determines that a client has a high risk of suicide (Schultz, 1982)
- A client initiates a lawsuit against a counselor (Denkowski & Denkowski, 1982)
- A client uses a mental condition as a claim or defense in a civil action (Denkowski & Denkowski, 1982)
- A counselor suspects that a client under the age of 16 is the victim of a crime such as child abuse or neglect (Everstine et al., 1980)
- A counselor determines that a client requires hospitalization for a mental or psychological disorder (Dekraai & Sales, 1982; Schultz, 1982)
- A client reveals an intent to commit a crime or is assessed to be dangerous to the self or others (Dekraai & Sales, 1982)

Laws relating to privileged communication between a client and a member of the helping profession vary considerably from state to state (Herlihy & Sheeley, 1987). Some states recognize privileged communication between psychologists and their clients but not between licensed counselors and their clients. Practitioners must therefore be aware of their state's laws regarding privileged communication.

Malpractice

Counselors have an increased risk of being sued for malpractice (Corey, 1991). It is therefore important for counselors to understand what malpractice is and what they can do to prevent legal difficulties.

Knapp (1980) defined malpractice as an act or omission by a counselor that is inconsistent with reasonable care and skill used by other reputable counselors and that results in injury to the client. Knapp (1980) noted that courts do not assume that malpractice exists if a counselor has made a mistake in judgment, since it is possible to make such a mistake and still exercise reasonable care. Keeton (1984) identified four conditions that must exist for malpractice to have occurred. Applied to a counseling situation, these are: (a) the counselor had a duty to a client; (b) the duty of care was not met; (c) the client sustained an injury; and (d) there was a close causal relationship between the counselor's failure to provide reasonable care and the resulting injury.

DePauw (1986) provided guidelines for avoiding ethical violations relating at each phase of the counseling process. These guidelines can minimize the risk of harm to clients and the incidence of malpractice suits for counselors.

Precounseling.   Issues during this phase include: accurately advertising services; making advance financial arrangements that are clearly understood and serve the best interest of the client; providing services within the counselor's parameters of competency; facilitating the client's informed choice of services; avoiding dual relationships; clearly indicating experimental treatment approaches and taking appropriate safety precautions; and identifying the limits to confidentiality.

Ongoing counseling.   Issues include maintaining confidentiality; seeking consultation as necessary; maintaining adequate client records; taking necessary action regarding clients who pose a clear and imminent danger to themselves or others; and complying with laws that relate to reporting child abuse and neglect.

Termination phase.   Issues at this point include: being sensitive to the client's termination and post-termination concerns; initiating termination or referral if the client is no longer benefitting from services; and evaluating the efficacy of counseling services.

SPECIAL ETHICAL AND LEGAL ISSUES

This section addresses some of the special ethical and legal issues associated with marriage and family therapy, child counseling, and group counseling. Information will also be provided on ethical and legal issues relating to Acquired Immunodeficiency Syndrome (AIDS).

Issues Relating to Marriage and Family Therapy

Huber and Baruth (1987) identified ethical and legal issues in marriage and family therapy in terms of client welfare, confidentiality, and informed consent (see Appendix B for American Association for Marriage and Family Therapy code of ethics).

Client Welfare.   The American Association for Marriage and Family Therapy's (AAMFT) (1988) ethical position relating to client welfare is:

> Marriage and family therapists are dedicated to advancing the welfare of families and individuals including respecting the rights of those persons seeking their assistance, and making reasonable efforts to ensure that their services are used appropriately.

The issue of client welfare can become complex in marriage and family therapy because the counselor is working with more than one client. Margolin (1982) noted that there can be a conflict in the goals of individuals seeking marriage and family therapy. This can occur in marriage therapy, for example, when one person wants a divorce and the other does not. Huber and Baruth (1987) suggested that a counselor can avoid these problems by utilizing a systems perspective rather than focusing on the problems of individual clients.

Confidentiality.   The AAMFT's (1988) ethical position on confidentiality is:

> Marriage and family therapists have unique confidentiality problems, because the "client" in a therapeutic relationship may be more than one person. The overriding principle is that marriage and family therapists respect the confidence of their client(s).

Respecting the confidence of clients in marriage and family therapy can often create an ethical dilemma, for example, being asked to keep information about a client's affair from the client's spouse.

Margolin (1982) noted that counselors tend to take one of two positions regarding confidentiality when working with couples and families. One position involves the counselor viewing each marital partner or family member as an individual client. In this approach, the counselor may routinely see the clients individually before seeing them together in couples or family therapy. A counselor who utilizes this approach needs to develop a clear position on confidentiality and communicate it to the clients. Typically, the counselor will either reserve the right to use professional judgment to maintain individual confidence or avoid disclosing sensitive information unless the client gives permission.

A second approach to confidentiality that Margolin (1982) described is based on nonsecrecy. From this perspective, the counselor does not feel any obligation to withhold information from the other marital partner or family member. A counselor who utilizes this position usually avoids seeing the clients individually. In addition, the counselor should inform the clients of the policy on confidentiality before they commence counseling.

Confidentiality can also vary in marriage and family therapy in terms of privileged communication. Huber and Baruth (1987) noted that the concept of privileged communication was originally developed within a context of one-to-one relationships, for example, doctor-patient or attorney-client. It is therefore not surprising that there have been conflicting legal precedents when this concept has been applied to situations involving more than one client.

Several legal cases have tested the validity of privileged communication for clients involved in marriage counseling. Herrington (1979) noted that a Virginia judge ruled that there was no confidentiality because statements were not made in private to a doctor, but were made in the presence of a spouse. Another case reported by Margolin (1982) provided support for privileged communication in marriage counseling. This case involved a man who decided to divorce his wife. He had his counselor subpoenaed to testify in court about statements his wife had made during their conjoint sessions. In this case, the husband was waiving his right of privileged communication, but the wife was not waiving her right. The judge ruled in favor of protecting the wife's right to confidentiality. In view of the varying litigation on this subject, it is important for counselors to determine the laws in their state regarding privileged communication in multiperson therapies (Gumper & Sprenkle, 1981).

Informed Consent.   The AAMFT (1988) provides the following ethical position relating to informed consent:

> Marriage and family therapists respect the right of clients to make decisions and help them understand the consequences of these decisions. Marriage and family therapists clearly advise a client that a decision on marital status is the responsibility of the client.

Applying the concept of informed consent can be more difficult in marriage and family therapy than in individual counseling. Margolin (1982) noted that the individuals who undergo marriage and family therapy together do not always begin therapy at the same time. It may therefore be necessary to repeat the procedures associated with informed consent as new clients begin the counseling process.

Issues Relating to Child Counseling

Child counseling can involve special ethical and legal issues in terms of informed consent, confidentiality, and reporting laws that relate to child abuse.

Informed Consent.   Corey, Corey, and Callanan (1988) noted that most states require parental consent for minors to receive counseling services. Some states permit minors to enter into a counseling relationship without parental permission in crisis situations, such as those involving substance abuse (Corey, Corey, & Callanan, 1988). Counselors should therefore be aware of the laws relating to informed consent in their state.

Confidentiality.   Ansell (1987) described confidentiality with minors as a gray area that requires the counselor to proceed with caution. Conflicts can result from the counselor's legal responsibility to respect a parent's right to be informed of counseling services and the ethical responsibility to maintain the confidentiality of the minor (Huey, 1986).

Ansell (1987) suggested that counselors establish guidelines with the parents and the minor regarding the nature of information that can be released to parents. The ACA's (1988) ethical code can be used to structure these guidelines: "When working with minors or persons who are unable to give consent, the member protects these clients' best interests" (Section B.8) The counselor can therefore suggest that confidential information will be released to parents when the counselor believes it is in the child's best interest.

Parents are also legally entitled to have access to their child's confidential records (Thompson & Rudolph, 1988). Personal notes are exempt from this requirement when they are kept separate from institutional files; they are not seen by anyone, including clerical staff; and they were not discussed with anyone in the process of decision-making (Thompson & Rudolph, 1988).

Child Abuse.   All states have laws relating to child abuse (Thompson & Rudolph, 1988) and most require counselors to report suspected abuse (Congdon, 1987). These laws usually "include penalties for failure to report and provide immunity for the reporter from criminal and civil liability" (Congdon, 1987). Counselors should limit their reporting of information to that which is required by law. Reporting additional information can make the counselor guilty of releasing privileged information (Congdon, 1987).

Issues Relating to Group Counseling

The Association for Specialists in Group Work (ASGW) revised its ethical standards in 1989 (ASGW, 1990) (see Appendix C). The highlights of the ASGW's ethical code follow.

Orientation.   Information is provided to prospective or new members on a variety of issues such as the length of group, role expectations for group members, goal of the group, potential risks, and fees.

Screening of members.   The counselor "selects group members whose needs and goals are compatible with the goals of the group; who will not impede the group process; and whose well-being will not be jeopardized by the group experience" (ASGW, 1990, p. 121).

Confidentiality.   Group counselors alert members of the limits to confidentiality before counseling begins. These limits relate to when a client poses a serious threat to self or others and when group members are minors. The counselors should also discuss potential problems of group members violating confidentiality.

Voluntary or involuntary participation.   "Group counselors inform members whether participation is voluntary or involuntary" (ASGW, 1990, p. 121). Informed consent should be obtained for both voluntary and involuntary groups. In addition, group counselors do not certify successful completion unless a member meets the defined group expectations.

Leaving a group.   "Provisions are made to assist a group member to terminate in an effective way" (ASGW, 1990, p. 122). Group members have the right to exit a group whenever they choose but should inform the counselor and group members prior to termination. The counselor should also discuss possible risks associated with premature termination.

Imposing counselor values.   Group counselors strive to become aware of their needs and values and the impact they may have on clients.

Equitable treatment.   "Group counselors make every reasonable effort to treat each member individually and equally" (ASGW, 1990, p. 123). Counselors also attempt to ensure that each group member has equitable use of group time.

Dual relationship.   "Group counselors avoid dual relationships with group members that might impair their objectivity and professional judgment, as well as those which are likely to compromise a group member's ability to participate fully in a group" (ASGW, 1990, p. 123).

Goal development.   Every effort is made to help each group member develop personal goals.

Consultation.   Policies regarding between-session consultation with group members are specified.

Termination from the group.   Group members are encouraged to terminate from the group in the most efficient period of time.

Evaluation and follow-up.   "Group counselors make every attempt to engage in ongoing assessment and to design follow-up procedures for their groups" (ASGW, 1990, p. 125).

Paradise and Kirby (1990) identified several legal issues relating to group counseling. They suggested that group counselors should take extra precautions regarding confidentiality. It is especially important to clarify the limits to confidentiality and privileged communication for members during pregroup orientation or the first session. Counselors could be sued for negligence if they have given the impression that confidentiality was guaranteed. In addition, group counselors should have all members sign a contract requiring confidentiality and stating that breach of confidentiality will result in the member being dropped from the group (Paradise & Kirby, 1990).

Legal problems in group counseling can also arise from issues relating to a counselor's duty to protect. As noted earlier in this chapter, the Tarasoff litigation (Tarasoff v. Board of Regents of the University of California, 1974, 1976) mandated that counselors have a legal responsibility to warn anyone who is the subject of a serious threat.

Corey, Corey, Callanan, and Russell (1982) noted that the incidence of verbal abuse and subsequent casualties is higher in group counseling than individual counseling, because of the intensity of group work and interaction between members. Paradise and Kirby (1990) therefore suggest that group counselors screen out potentially dangerous clients and continuously monitor clients to ensure their physical and psychological safety.

Issues Relating to AIDS

Many authors have addressed ethical issues that relate to providing counseling services to clients infected by the AIDS virus (Cohen, 1990; Gray & Harding, 1988; Melton, 1988). The main ethical question that emerges from the literature is, What should a counselor do when a sexually active client has AIDS and has not informed any partners of the illness? In these instances, the counselor's ethical dilemma would be whether to maintain confidentiality or inform the client's sexual partners that they are being exposed to the AIDS virus.

Gray and Harding (1988) believed there are both ethical and legal precedents for breaking confidentiality in these cases. In terms of ethics, the authors cited the ACA ethical standards, which state that confidentiality can be breached when there is a "clear and imminent danger" to self or others (ACA, 1988) (Section D.4). In addition, the Tarasoff case set forth a legal precedent regarding "duty to warn" (Tarasoff v. Board of Regents of the University of California, 1974, 1976). As a result of the Tarasoff case, professional counselors have a legal duty to warn a person if their client poses a serious threat.

Naturally, counselors should not arbitrarily break confidentiality in cases involving AIDS clients. Instead, they should only do this as a last resort. Gray and Harding (1988) and Cohen (1990) provided several guidelines that can assist counselors in dealing with these sensitive ethical dilemmas. Their recommendations are summarized as follows.

- Clients should be made aware of the limits to confidentiality before they begin counseling.
- Clients who have contracted the AIDS virus should be informed how the virus is spread and what precautions they can take to prevent its spreading.
- Clients should be encouraged to inform any sexual partner that they may have been exposed to the virus.

- If a client is unwilling to inform any partner who may be at risk, the counselor should first alert the client of the need to break confidentiality and then inform the sexual partner in a timely fashion.

- Counselors should limit disclosure of information to general medical information regarding the client's disease.

- Disclosures should only be made to the party at risk or to a guardian in the case of a minor.

- Disclosures should communicate willingness to provide counseling services to the client.

- Medical consultation and referral should be arranged as necessary.

ETHICAL DECISION MAKING

Huber and Baruth (1987) described four processes that could be used in ethical decision making by the professional counselor.

Process 1: Determining whether the situation requires an ethical decision. Counselors must first determine if an ethical decision needs to be made. This requires an awareness of ethical codes and how they may affect clinical practice, for example, the importance of confidentiality in counseling.

Process 2: Formulating an ethical course of action.   Once counselors establish that an ethical dilemma exists, they must determine what form of action to take. Consultation with one's supervisor can be an important first step in formulating a course of action. Suggestions from an experienced clinician can help identify potential problems and solutions associated with the ethical dilemma. Kitchener (1984, 1985) identified two levels of ethics that could be used to formulate a course of action: intuitive and critical-evaluative. The intuitive level addresses immediate feelings in response to the situation. An intuitive reaction can be useful in situations that require immediate action, such as crisis intervention.

The critical-evaluative level of ethical reasoning can be used in situations that do not require immediate action. Most situations requiring an ethical decision are complex, with no clear right or wrong way of proceeding. Kitchener (1984, 1985) suggests a three-tiered approach to critically evaluate a particular situation. The first tier involves referring to the code of ethics for guidelines pertaining to the ethical situation. If these guidelines are insufficient, counselors can move to the second tier and determine the philosophical foundations on which the ethical guidelines were based, such as the right to privacy or the right to make free choices. When counselors are still uncertain, they can proceed to the third tier and apply the principles of ethical theory. There are several noted ethical theorists who can help provide a rationale for ethical action (Ableson & Nielson, 1967; Baier, 1958; Toulmin, 1950). Huber and Baruth (1987) surveyed these theorists and identified suggestions that could be of help in ethical decision making. For example, counselors should do what they would want for themselves or significant others in a similar situation, or they should do what would result in the least amount of harm.

Some ethical dilemmas may
require consultation.

Process 3: Overcoming personal–professional conflicts.   This process recognizes
that a counselor's personal and professional values may be in conflict, thereby
inhibiting appropriate action. For example, a counselor may have a colleague who is
also a close friend. The counselor may become aware of unethical behavior on the
part of the colleague but may not want to take action because of their friendship.
One way for counselors to overcome such an impasse is to remember that they will
be acting unethically if they do not take constructive action.

Process 4: Implementing an action plan.   Once counselors have determined a
course of action and overcome possible personal-professional conflicts, they are in a
position to implement an action plan. This will require courage and the willingness
to accept personal responsibility for their actions. After implementing a plan of
action, counselors may wish to evaluate their professional functioning. Van Hoose
(1980) provided the following guidelines that counselors can use to determine
whether their actions were ethically responsible. Counselors have probably acted
ethically if they have maintained personal and professional honesty; had the client's
best interest in mind; acted without malice or personal gain; and could justify their
action as the best judgment according to the current state of the profession.

Clinical Examples

The following clinical examples provide an opportunity to practice ethical decision
making. Four ethical dilemmas are presented that relate to a variety of clinical situations. There is no right or wrong way of responding to these examples, but counselors should simply attempt to develop a response that reflects sound clinical judgment. I present each example followed by a description of the way I would respond.

Clinical Example #1.   You are a counselor at a community mental health center. A
young woman was convicted of drunk driving and told by the judge that she must

attend your alcohol treatment program to keep her driver's license. You are concerned about the issue of informed consent. What would you do in this situation if you were the counselor?

My Response.   Any situation that involves a client who has been court-ordered to undergo counseling creates an ethical dilemma. The ethical code regarding informed consent requires that this client must not be forced to attend counseling. In addition, the client should feel free to terminate counseling whenever she chooses. At the same time, the counselor must inform the judge if the client does not complete the alcohol program. Technically, the client is free to choose counseling and keep her driver's license or choose no counseling and lose her license. At the very least, if the client chooses counseling, she may be doing so under duress.

As the counselor, I would first discuss with the client what the alcohol treatment program entailed and give her a professional disclosure statement. The statement would provide information such as my background, my definition of counseling, and the limits to confidentiality. I would then explore with her the available options, that she may either lose her license or attend the alcohol program. If she did decide to participate in the alcohol program, I would recognize the duress she must be feeling and suggest that we both try to make the best of a difficult situation. I would tell her that she is free to terminate her participation in the program at any time. I would also emphasize that if she decided to do so, I would unfortunately be obligated to inform the judge that she did not complete the program successfully.

Clinical Example #2.   You are an elementary school counselor. After working at the school for a month, you identify several policies that conflict with your ethical code. Two examples of these policies are (a) You are told you must provide counseling services for certain students even if they don't want them; and (b) you are not allowed to maintain confidentiality because you must inform the principal about what certain students tell you during their sessions.

My Response.   The ACA (1988) code of ethics suggests that when an institution functions in a manner that conflicts with the counselor's code of ethics, the counselor should attempt to resolve the differences with the institution. If the institution in this example is not willing to make the necessary changes, you must resign. It would be important for you to remember that even when an institution asks you to act unethically, you cannot defend your action later by saying, "My supervisor told me to do it."

Clinical Example #3.   You are a mental health counselor in a community mental health center. After the second session with a male client, you decide he may be suffering from a serious mental disorder. You don't feel comfortable providing counseling services because you think the client requires help beyond your area of competence. You decide to refer the client to a psychiatrist. The client refuses to accept your suggestion and insists instead that you continue seeing him. What would you do if you were the counselor?

My Response.   The ACA (1988) and APA (1989) codes of ethics suggest that a counselor has an ethical responsibility to refer a client who requires help beyond the counselor's level of competency. Since the client refused to follow up on the referral and insisted on seeing the counselor, I would suggest that you kindly but firmly refrain from conducting any more counseling sessions but offer to remain available to help the client with the referral process.

Clinical Example #4.   You have a private practice specializing in marriage, family, and child counseling. You are seeing a married couple, Dan and Mary, in marriage counseling. Your approach to marriage counseling is to see the marital partners individually for 15 minutes each and then together for 30 minutes.

During the initial session, you first talk with Dan. He informs you that he and Mary have been married for 2 years. Before the marriage, he was an intravenous drug user, "shooting up" heroin at least twice a day for several years. Dan explains that he had been off drugs for 2 years, but 2 weeks ago he ran into some of his old buddies and started "using the needle again." He says that he will not tell Mary about his drug habit because he wants the marriage to work out. He fears that if she found out, she would leave him. What would you do in this situation if you were the counselor?

My Response.   As a counselor, I would want to help Dan with his drug problem and help Dan and Mary with their marital difficulties. In addition, I would be concerned about the potential ethical and legal issues, since current research suggests that intravenous drug users are a high-risk group for contracting the AIDS virus.

I also see a potential legal issue in this case in that the counselor is obligated to break the confidentiality if Dan poses a clear and imminent danger to himself or others. If Dan does not tell Mary, and she subsequently contracts AIDS from Dan, the counselor could be sued because of not warning her of the potential danger.

In weighing the various legal and ethical issues, I would first explain to Dan how the AIDS virus can be spread by sharing a needle among people who have AIDS or are HIV positive. I would then make sure he understood that he could transmit the AIDS virus to Mary if they had unprotected intercourse. In addition, I would request that Dan get an AIDS test; insist that Dan tell Mary about his drug habit before the end of our first session so that she could decide if she wanted to take the risk of having sex with him; warn him that if he did not tell her, I would, because I view his drug habit as posing a clear and imminent danger to Mary; recommend that Dan enter into a drug rehabilitation program as soon as possible; and continue marital therapy as necessary.

SUMMARY

This chapter described the professional issues that face counselors. The chapter began by exploring the four building blocks of professional counseling: formal study of counseling and professional affiliation, certification or licensure, continuing education, and professional involvement. This model encourages students to become involved in professional issues as soon as possible.

The remainder of the chapter focused on ethical and legal issues. Counselors and psychologists have codes of ethics such as the ACA, APA, and AAMFT to help guide their clinical practice. These ethical codes are not written in black-and-white terms but must be interpreted and applied to each particular clinical situation. Major ethical issues for counselors include client welfare, informed consent, and confidentiality. Special ethical issues relating to marriage and family therapy, child counseling, group counseling, and AIDS were also provided.

The chapter identified several legal issues that concern members of the counseling profession. For example, a counselor must break confidentiality when a client poses a clear and imminent danger to self or others. In addition, information relating to privileged communication was provided. Privileged communication exists to protect the rights of clients in terms of confidentiality in a legal proceeding. It was stressed that the privilege belongs to the client and not the counselor.

The chapter concluded with guidelines for ethical decision-making. It also presented several clinical examples, which provide opportunities to apply the various ethical and legal principles discussed in this chapter.

REFERENCES

Abelson, R., & Nielson, K. (1967). History of ethics. In P. Edwards (Ed.), *The encyclopedia of philosophy* (Vol. 3). New York: Macmillan.

American Association for Counseling and Development (AACD). (1988). *Ethical standards* (rev. ed.). Falls Church, VA: Author

American Association for Marriage and Family Therapy (AAMFT). (1988). *AAMFT code of ethical principles for marriage and family therapists.*

American Psychological Association (APA). (1989). *Ethical standards of psychologists* (rev. ed.). Washington, DC: Author.

Ansell, C. A. (1987). *Ethical practices workbook.* Santa Monica, CA: Association for Advanced Training in the Behavioral Sciences.

Association for Specialists in Group Work (ASGW). (1990). Ethical guidelines for group counselors. *The Journal for Specialists in Group Work, 15,* 2, 119–126.

Baier, K. (1958). *The moral point of view.* Ithaca, NY: Cornell University.

Baruth, L. B., & Huber, C. H. (1985). *Counseling and psychotherapy: Theoretical analyses and skill applications.* Columbus, OH: Merrill/ Macmillan.

Brooks, D. K., & Gerstein, L. H. (1990). Counselor credentialing and interprofessional collaboration. *Journal of Counseling and Development, 68,* 477–484.

Cohen, E. D. (1990). Confidentiality, counseling, and clients who have AIDS: Ethical foundations of a model rule. *Journal of Counseling and Development, 68,* 282–287.

Congdon, D. (1987). *Professional issues.* Santa Monica, CA: Association for Advanced Training in Behavioral Sciences.

Corey, G. E. (1991). *Theory and practice of counseling and psychotherapy* (4th ed.). Monterey, CA: Brooks/Cole.

Corey, G. E., Corey, M. S., & Callanan, P. (1988). *Issues and ethics in the helping profession* (3rd ed.). Monterey, CA: Brooks/Cole.

Corey, G., Corey, M., Callanan, P., & Russell, J. M. (1982). Ethical considerations in using group techniques. *Journal for Specialists in Group Work, 7,* 140–148.

Cummings, N. A. (1990). The credentialing of professional psychologists and its implication for other mental health disciplines. *Journal of Counseling and Development, 68,* 485–490.

Dekraai, M. B., & Sales, B. D. (1982). Privileged communications of psychologists. *Professional Psychology, 13,* 372–388.

Denkowski, K. M., & Denkowski, G. C. (1982). Client-counselor confidentiality: An update. *Personnel and Guidance Journal, 60,* 371–375.

DePauw, M. E. (1986). Avoiding ethical relations: A timeline perspective for individual counseling.

Journal of Counseling and Development, 64, 5, 303–310.

Everett, C. A. (1990). Where have all the "gypsies" gone? *Journal of Counseling and Development, 68*, 507–510.

Everstine, L., Everstine, D. S., Heymann, G. M., True, R. H., Frey, D. H., Johnson, H. G., & Seiden, R. H. (1980). Privacy and confidentiality in psychotherapy. *American Psychologist, 9*, 828–840.

Forester, J. R. (1977). What shall we do about credentialing? *Personnel and Guidance Journal, 55*, 573–576.

George, R. L., & Cristiani, T. S. (1990). *Counseling: Theory and practice* (3rd ed.). Englewood Cliffs, NJ: Prentice-Hall.

Gray, L. A., & Harding, A. K. (1988). Confidentiality limits with clients who have the AIDS virus. *Journal of Counseling and Development, 66*(5), 219–223.

Gross, D. R., & Robinson, S. E. (1987). Ethics, violence, and counseling: Hear no evil, see no evil, speak no evil? *Journal of Counseling and Development, 65*(7), 340–344.

Gumper, L. L., & Sprenkle, D. H. (1981). Privileged communication in therapy: Special problems for the family and couples therapist. *Family Process, 20*, 11–23.

Herlihy, B., & Sheeley, V. L. (1987). Privileged communication in selected helping professions: A comparison among statutes. *Journal of Counseling and Development, 65*(9), 479–483.

Herrington, B. S. (1979). Privilege denial in joint therapy. *Psychiatric News, 14*(1), 1–9.

Huber, C. H., & Baruth, L. G. (1987). *Ethical, legal, and professional issues in the practice of marriage and family therapy*. Columbus, OH: Merrill/Macmillan.

Huey, W. (1986). Ethical concerns in school counseling. *Journal of Counseling and Development, 64*(5), 321–322.

Keeton, W. P. (1984). *Prosser and Keeton on the law of torts*. (5th ed.). St.Paul, MN: West.

Kitchener, K. S. (1984). Ethics in counseling psychology: Distinctions and directions. *Counseling Psychologist, 12*, 15–18.

Kitchener, K. S. (1985). Ethical principles and ethical decisions in student affairs. In H. J. Canon and R. D. Brown (Eds.), *Applied ethics: Tools for practitioners*. San Francisco: Jossey-Bass.

Knapp, S. (1980). A primer on malpractice for psychologists. *Professional Psychology, 11*, 606–612.

Krieshok, T. S. (1987). Psychologists and counselors in the legal system: A dialogue with Theodore Blare. *Journal of Counseling and Development, 66*(2), 69–72.

Mabe, A. R., & Rollin, S. A. (1986). The role of a code of ethical standards in counseling. *Journal of Counseling and Development, 64*(5), 294–297.

Mardirosian, K., McGuire, J. M., Abbott, D. W., & Blau, B. I. (1990). The effects of enhanced informal consent in a prolife pregnancy counseling center. *Journal of Counseling and Development, 69*, 39–41.

Margolin, G. (1982). Ethical and legal considerations in marriage and family therapy. *American Psychologist, 7*, 788–801.

McFadden, J., & Brooks, D. K. (1983). *Counselor licensure action packet*. Alexandria, VA: American Association for Counseling and Development.

Melton, G. B. (1988). Ethical and legal issues in AIDS-related practice. *American Psychologist, 43*(11), 941–947.

Paradise, L. V., & Kirby, P. C. (1990). Legal issues in group work: Some perspectives on the legal liability of group counseling in private practice. *The Journal for Specialists in Group Work, 15*(2), 114–118.

Reynolds, M. (1976). Threats to confidentiality. *Social Work, 21*, 108–113.

Schultz, B. (1982). *Legal liability in psychotherapy*. San Francisco: Jossey-Bass.

Tarasoff v. Board of Regents of the University of California, 13 Cal. 3d 177, 529 P.2d 553 (1974), vacated, 17 Cal. 3d 425, 551 P.2d 334 (1976).

Thompson, C. L., & Rudolph, L. B. (1988). *Counseling children* (2nd ed.). Pacific Grove, CA: Brooks/Cole.

Toulmin, S. (1950). *An examination of the place of reason in ethics*. Cambridge, England: Cambridge University.

Van Hoose, W. H. (1980). Ethics in counseling. *Counseling and Human Development, 13*(1), 1–12.

Listening Skills

Becoming an effective listener is an art. It requires patience, work, and practice. Sometimes, by trying to use listening skills, a counselor can actually become a *less effective* communicator. This was discussed in Chapter two as the "monkey on the back syndrome," which is characterized as having one's spontaneity interfered with by avoiding "normal responses" and trying to do what has been taught. It is therefore important for the counselor not to be discouraged when attempting to incorporate these skills into an effective counseling style.

LISTENING SKILLS IN COUNSELING

Listening skills can be used during the various stages of the counseling process. For example, when a counselor takes time to really listen to a client, the client will tend to feel the counselor cares about him and is interested in his thoughts and feelings. Listening skills can also assist the counselor with assessment and enable the counselor to develop a phenomenological understanding of the client (i.e., understanding the client from the client's perspective). A counselor may utilize listening skills in formulating counseling goals by helping the client figure out what he wants out of counseling. Listening skills can also be particularly useful by

helping the client identify and explore issues and concerns that can be addressed in a problem-solving process.

Clearly, listening skills are vitally important to counseling. An overview of these skills follows.

Open-Ended Questions. These are questions such as, "What would you like to talk about?" or "How does this affect you?" These questions cannot be answered with a simple "yes" or "no," but encourage the client to elaborate on responses.

Paraphrasing. This can be useful after the client has talked at some length about a particular situation or problem. Paraphrasing allows the counselor to communicate that she has not only heard the client but understands what has been said. A paraphrase should be "tentatively" worded so the client can correct the counselor if necessary. Paraphrasing, like so many things, takes practice. A key to good paraphrasing is to keep it simple.

Paraphrasing often involves taking one or two key words that the client has said and finding analogous words. For example, if the client says, "I enjoy taking a run with my dog after work," a possible paraphrase is, "You like to jog with your dog." In this example, the counselor has found analogous words for enjoy (like) and run (jog). Another way to paraphrase is to repeat the client's overall message using slightly different words. For example, the client may say, "I like to take a jog after a stressful day, because it helps me unwind." A possible paraphrase would be, "Jogging is a good stress release for you."

Reflection of Feeling. This involves the counselor reflecting what he or she senses the client is feeling. It communicates that the counselor not only understands how the client is feeling, but also empathizes with the client. For example, if a client tells the counselor how her husband insults her in public, the counselor could respond by saying, "This really makes you mad." Again, as in paraphrasing, it is important to phrase the reflection of feeling statement tentatively so the client can correct the counselor if necessary.

It is also important to be specific in attempting to reflect the client's feelings. For example, the word "upset" is usually too general and may not communicate a clear understanding of the client's feelings. It is therefore useful for counselors to develop a broad repertoire of words associated with various emotional states. Cormier and Cormier (1991) provided a comprehensive list of words depicting various emotions (see Table A.1).

Minimal Encouragers. This technique allows the counselor to facilitate what the client is saying without changing the client's line of thought. Minimal encouragers include such words of acknowledgement as, "yes," "yeah," "oh," "ah-ha," and so forth.

Clarifying Remarks. This technique can be used when the counselor either did not hear or does not understand what the client has said. For example, the counselor could say, "I did not understand that," or "Could you go through that again?" Through the use of clarifying statements, the counselor communicates that she genuinely wants to understand what the client is saying.

Summarizing. This involves restating some of the major concerns the client has mentioned during a particular session. Obviously, this helps identify the client's areas of concern. Summarizing can also lead to a "perception check" and to the development of problem-solving strategies.

Perception Check. This technique helps the counselor determine what the client wants to work on. It follows the summary statement as illustrated in the following example: "You seem to be worried about your performance at school, your relationship with your wife, and your lack of money (the summary statement). I know all these problems concern you. I was wondering if you would like to focus on one of these areas, or is there something else that you haven't mentioned that you would like to talk about?"

The following dialogue provides an illustration of how these listening skills can be used in counseling.

Counselor: What would you like to talk about today? (open-ended)

Client: My daughter has me real worried.

Counselor: About what? (open-ended)

Client: She is dating someone too old for her.

Counselor: What concerns you about that? (open-ended)

Client: All kinds of things. Maybe he will put pressure on her to have sex, use alcohol, stay out late, or defy her parents. You name it. I'm worried.

Counselor: Yes, I can see you are afraid that all kinds of terrible things will happen. (reflection of feeling)

Client: Maybe I am overreacting. I just worry so. I don't know what to do.

Counselor: It's a real dilemma for you. (paraphrase)

Client: Yes. I would forbid her to see him, but that just might make her want to see him more. If I don't do something, I am afraid of the consequences.

Counselor: You feel pretty frustrated about what to do. (reflection of feeling)

Client: Yes, and panicky. Am I to blame?

Counselor: I'm not sure I understand what you mean by that. (clarifying)

Client: I mean, well, maybe I shouldn't have gotten a divorce. Maybe she is looking for a father figure.

Counselor: You think that her boyfriend is actually a father figure? (paraphrase)

Client: I don't know. It seems like my life has been such a failure.

Counselor: In what way? (open-ended)

Table A.1
Words Depicting Feelings

Level of Intensity	Happiness	Sadness	Fear	Uncertainty	Anger	Strength, potency	Weakness inadequacy
Strong	Excited	Despairing	Panicked	Bewildered	Outraged	Powerful	Ashamed
	Thrilled	Hopeless	Terrified	Disoriented	Hostile	Authoritative	Powerless
	Delighted	Depressed	Afraid	Mistrustful	Furious	Forceful	Vulnerable
	Overjoyed	Crushed	Frightened	Confused	Angry	Potent	Cowardly
	Ecstatic	Miserable	Scared		Harsh		Exhausted
	Elated	Abandoned	Overwhelmed		Hateful		Impotent
	Jubilant	Defeated			Mean		
		Desolate			Vindictive		
Moderate	"Up"	Dejected	Worried	Doubtful	Aggravated	Tough	Embarrassed
	Good	Dismayed	Shaky	Mixed up	Irritated	Important	Useless
	Happy	Disillusioned	Tense	Insecure	Offended	Confident	Demoralized
	Optimistic	Lonely	Anxious	Skeptical	Mad	Fearless	Helpless
	Cheerful	Bad	Threatened	Puzzled	Frustrated	Energetic	Worn out
	Enthusiastic	Unhappy	Agitated		Resentful	Brave	Inept
	Joyful	Pessimistic			"Sore"	Courageous	Incapable
	"Turned on"	Sad			Upset	Daring	Incompetent
		Hurt			Impatient	Assured	Inadequate
		Lost			Obstinate	Adequate	Shaken
						Self-confident	
						Skillful	
Weak	Pleased	"Down"	Jittery	Unsure	Perturbed	Determined	Frail
	Glad	Discouraged	Jumpy	Surprised	Annoyed	Firm	Meek
	Content	Disappointed	Nervous	Uncertain	Grouchy	Able	Unable
	Relaxed	"Blue"	Uncomfortable	Undecided	Hassled	Strong	Weak
	Satisfied	Alone	Uptight	Bothered	Bothered		
	Calm	Left out	Uneasy		Disagreeable		
			Defensive				
			Apprehensive				
			Hesitant				

From Cormier, W. H., & Cormier, L. S. (1991). *Interviewing strategies for helpers* (3rd ed.), p. 97, Brooks/Cole Publishing, Pacific Grove, California. Reprinted by permission.

Client: First, I failed with my husband, now I'm failing with my daughter

Counselor: You really seem down on yourself. (reflection of feeling)

Client: Yes, I guess I am, I just feel so inadequate.

Counselor: Well, it seems you are worried about your daughter, but you also have concerns about yourself as an individual. (summary)

Client: Yes, I guess you're right. There is more to this than concern for my daughter.

Counselor: Well, is there anything else you think I should know, or would you like to discuss one of these issues a bit more? (perception check)

Client: Yes, for now I want to figure out what to do about my daughter.

Counselor: Okay, let's explore this in more depth now to see what we can come up with. (The counselor and client are formulating a counseling goal that they can work toward.)

Effective Listening "Don'ts"

This section provides some helpful guidelines for effective listening. I have incorporated Dinkmeyer and McKay's (1989) "roadblocks to effective listening" into the following list of things to avoid.

Avoid moralizing or being judgmental. Imposing one's belief system onto the client can cause defensive reactions and be a demoralizing, dehumanizing experience.

Avoid premature analysis. Premature analysis involves identifying meaning behind the message such as motivational forces associated with a particular action. It can occur when the counselor uses the word "because" in her paraphrase. For example, if the client says, "No matter what I do, nothing seems to go right," a counselor engaging in premature analysis might respond with, "Nothing is going right because you lack confidence in yourself?"

When a counselor responds in this manner, the client may respond to the counselor's hunches (e.g., "Is nothing going right because I

lack confidence?"). This may result in redirecting the line of thought from client to the counselor. Once a counselor has gained a phenomenological understanding of the client, he may find it appropriate to analyze the content of the client's message and provide insights to the client (e.g., suggest that a lack of self-confidence may be a problem for the client).

Avoid "parroting." Parroting means repeating exactly what the client has said, just changing the order of the words. This communicates what the counselor has *heard* but may not understand (like a parrot). For example, if the client says, "I really like to jog after work," the counselor responding like a parrot might say, "After work, you really like to jog."

Avoid "gimmicky" phrases. Some counselors get into the habit of using a "lead in" phrase such as "Did I hear you say . . ." each time they paraphrase. This often sounds "gimmicky" to a client.

Effective Listening "Do's"

Decide to be in the role of the listener. Effective listening is a role the counselor must *decide* to take on. It involves utilizing a series of skills; focusing on the client; encouraging the client to freely express herself; and attempting to develop a phenomenological understanding of the client.

Try to sense the client's inner message: Communication is a complex process. It is important to learn to listen with a "third ear." The counselor needs to learn to go beyond the spoken word and try to listen to what is being communicated "between the lines."

Be aware of nonverbal communication. A large percentage of communication is nonverbal. It often provides the most authentic indicator of the client's emotional state.

Allow yourself to correct impressions. Being in the role of listener is a tentative process. It is a joint effort, whereby the counselor works with the client until she gains a clear understanding of the client's situation.

CONCLUDING REMARKS

Becoming an effective listener is an art that takes time to develop. One of the best ways to learn listening skills is to obtain a videotape critique of one's work from an experienced counselor. It can also be helpful to do co-counseling with an experienced counselor and obtain feedback from the counselor regarding one's counseling approach.

Developing listening skills can be discouraging. At times a counselor may even feel he is becoming a less effective communicator. During these times, the counselor could consider that he is in the process of becoming a more effective communicator. With practice, these new skills will become integrated into the counselor's natural mode of responding.

References

Cormier, W. H., & Cormier, L. S. (1991). *Interviewing strategies for helpers.* (3rd ed.). Monterey, CA: Brooks/Cole.

Dinkmeyer, D., & McKay, G. (1989). *Systematic training for effective parenting (STEP)* (3rd. ed.). Circle Pines, MN: American Guidance Service, Inc.

Ethical Code of the American Association for Marriage and Family Therapy

The Board of Directors of the American Association for Marriage and Family Therapy (AAMFT) hereby promulgates, pursuant to Article II, Section (1)(C) of the Association's Bylaws, the Revised AAMFT Code of Ethical Principles for Marriage and Family Therapists, effective August 1, 1988.

The AAMFT Code of Ethical Principles for Marriage and Family Therapists is binding on all Members of AAMFT (Clinical, Student, and Associate) and on all AAMFT Approved Supervisors.

If an AAMFT Member or an AAMFT Approved Supervisor resigns in anticipation of or during the course of an ethics investigation, the Ethics Committee will complete its investigation. Any publication of action taken by the Association will include the fact that the Member attempted to resign during the investigation.

Marriage and family therapists are encouraged to report alleged unethical behavior of colleagues to appropriate professional associations and state regulatory bodies.

1. RESPONSIBILITY TO CLIENTS

Marriage and family therapists are dedicated to advancing the welfare of families and individuals, including respecting the rights of those persons seeking their assistance, and making reasonable efforts to ensure that their services are used appropriately.

1.1 Marriage and family therapists do not discriminate against or refuse professional service to anyone on the basis of race, sex, religion, or national origin.

1.2 Marriage and family therapists are cognizant of their potentially influential position with respect to clients, and they avoid exploiting the trust and dependency of such persons. Marriage and family therapists therefore make every effort to avoid dual relationships with clients that could impair their professional judgement or increase the risk of exploitation. Examples of such dual relationships include, but are not limited to, business or close personal relationships with clients. Sexual intimacy with clients is prohibited. Sexual intimacy with former clients for two years following the termination of therapy is prohibited.

1.3 Marriage and family therapists do not use their professional relationship with clients to further their own interests.

1.4 Marriage and family therapists respect the right of clients to make decisions and help them to understand the consequences of these decisions. Marriage and family therapists clearly advise a client that a decision on marital status is the responsibility of the client.

1.5 Marriage and family therapists continue therapeutic relationships only so long as it is reasonably clear that clients are benefiting from the relationship.

1.6 Marriage and family therapists assist persons in obtaining other therapeutic services if a marriage and family therapist is unable or unwilling, for appropriate reasons, to see a person who has requested professional help.

1.7 Marriage and family therapists do not abandon or neglect clients in treatment without making reasonable arrangements for the continuation of such treatment.

1.8 Marriage and family therapists obtain written informed consent of clients before taping, recording, or permitting third party observation of their activities.

2. CONFIDENTIALITY

Marriage and family therapists have unique confidentiality problems because the "client" in a therapeutic relationship may be more than one person. The overriding principle is that marriage and family therapists respect the confidences of their client(s).

2.1 Marriage and family therapists cannot disclose client confidences to anyone, except: (1) as mandated by law; (2) to prevent a clear and immediate danger to a person or persons; (3) where the marriage and family therapist is a defendant in a civil, criminal or disciplinary action arising from the therapy (in which case client confidences may only be disclosed in the course of that action); or (4) if there is a waiver previously obtained in writing, and then such information may only be revealed in accordance with the terms of the waiver. In circumstances where more than one person in a family is receiving therapy, each such family member who is legally competent to execute a waiver must agree to the waiver required by sub-paragraph (4). Absent such a waiver from each family

member legally competent to execute a waiver, a marriage and family therapist cannot disclose information received from any family member.

2.2 Marriage and family therapists use client and/or clinical materials in teaching, writing, and public presentations only if a written waiver has been received in accordance with sub-principle 2.1(4), or when appropriate steps have been taken to protect client identity.

2.3 Marriage and family therapists store or dispose of client records in ways that maintain confidentiality.

3. PROFESSIONAL COMPETENCE AND INTEGRITY

Marriage and family therapists are dedicated to maintaining high standards of professional competence and integrity.

3.1 Marriage and family therapists who (a) are convicted of felonies, (b) are convicted of misdemeanors (related to their qualifications or functions), (c) engage in conduct which could lead to conviction of felonies or misdemeanors related to their qualifications or functions, (d) are expelled from other professional organizations, (e) have their licenses or certificates suspended or revoked, (f) are no longer competent to practice marriage and family therapy because they are impaired due to physical or mental causes or the abuse of alcohol or other substances, or (g) fail to cooperate with the Association at any stage of an investigation of an ethical complaint of his/her conduct by the AAMFT Ethics Committee or Judicial Council, are subject to termination of membership or other appropriate action.

3.2 Marriage and family therapists seek appropriate professional assistance for their personal problems or conflicts that are likely to impair their work performance and their clinical judgement.

3.3 Marriage and family therapists, as teachers, are dedicated to maintaining high standards of scholarship and presenting information that is accurate.

3.4　Marriage and family therapists seek to remain abreast of new developments in family therapy knowledge and practice through both educational activities and clinical experiences.

3.5　Marriage and family therapists do not engage in sexual or other harassment or exploitation of clients, students, trainees, employees, colleagues, research subjects, or actual or potential witnesses or complainants in ethical proceedings.

3.6　Marriage and family therapists do not attempt to diagnose, treat, or advise on problems outside the recognized boundaries of their competence.

3.7　Marriage and family therapists attempt to prevent the distortion or misuse of their clinical and research findings.

3.8　Marriage and family therapists are aware that, because of their ability to influence and alter the lives of others, they must exercise special care when making public their professional recommendations and opinions through testimony or other public statements.

4.　RESPONSIBILITY TO STUDENTS, EMPLOYEES, AND SUPERVISEES

Marriage and family therapists do not exploit the trust and dependency of students, employees, and supervisees.

4.1　Marriage and family therapists are cognizant of their potentially influential position with respect to students, employees, and supervisees, and they avoid exploiting the trust and dependency of such persons. Marriage and family therapists, therefore, make every effort to avoid dual relationships that could impair their professional judgment or increase the risk of exploitation. Examples of such dual relationships include, but are not limited to, provision of therapy to students, employees, or supervisees, and business or close personal relationship with students, employees, or supervisees. Sexual intimacy with students or supervisees is prohibited.

4.2　Marriage and family therapists do not permit students, employees, or supervisees to perform or to hold themselves out as competent to perform professional services beyond their training, level of experience, and competence.

5.　RESPONSIBILITY TO THE PROFESSION

Marriage and family therapists respect the rights and responsibilities of professional colleagues; carry out research in an ethical manner; and participate in activities which advance the goals of the profession.

5.1　Marriage and family therapists remain accountable to the standards of the profession when acting as members or employees of organizations.

5.2　Marriage and family therapists assign publication credit to those who have contributed to a publication in proportion to their contributions and in accordance with customary professional publication practices.

5.3　Marriage and family therapists who are the authors of books or other materials that are published or distributed should cite appropriately persons to whom credit for original ideas is due.

5.4　Marriage and family therapists who are the authors of books or other materials published or distributed by an organization take reasonable precautions to ensure that the organization promotes and advertises the materials accurately and factually.

5.5　Marriage and family therapists, as researchers, must be adequately informed of and abide by relevant laws and regulations regarding the conduct of research with human participants.

5.6　Marriage and family therapists recognize a responsibility to participate in activities that contribute to a better community and society, including devoting a portion of their professional activity to services for which there is little or no financial return.

5.7   Marriage and family therapists are concerned with developing laws and regulations pertaining to marriage and family therapy that serve the public interest, and with altering such laws and regulations that are not in the public interest.

5.8   Marriage and family therapists encourage public participation in the designing and delivery of services and in the regulation of practitioners.

6. FINANCIAL ARRANGEMENTS

Marriage and family therapists make financial arrangements with clients and third party payors that conform to accepted professional practices and that are reasonably understandable.

6.1   Marriage and family therapists do not offer to accept payment for referrals.

6.2   Marriage and family therapists do not charge excessive fees for services.

6.3   Marriage and family therapists disclose their fee structure to clients at the onset of treatment.

6.4   Marriage and family therapists are careful to represent facts truthfully to clients and third party payors regarding services rendered.

7. ADVERTISING

Marriage and family therapists engage in appropriate informational activities, including those that enable laypersons to choose marriage and family services on an informed basis.

7.1   Marriage and family therapists accurately represent their competence, education, training, and experience relevant to their practice of marriage and family therapy.

7.2   Marriage and family therapists claim as evidence of educational qualifications in conjunction with their AAMFT membership only those degrees (a) from regionally accredited institutions or (b) from institutions recognized by states which license or certify marriage and family therapists, but only if such regulation is accepted by AAMFT.

7.3   Marriage and family therapists assure that advertisements and publications, whether in directories, announcement cards, newspapers, or on radio or television, are formulated to make an appropriate selection. Information could include: (1) office information, such as name, address, telephone number, credit card acceptability, fee structure, languages spoken, and office hours; (2) appropriate degrees, state licensure and/or certification, and AAMFT Clinical Member status; and (3) description of practice.

7.4   Marriage and family therapists do not use a name which could mislead the public concerning the identity, responsibility, source, and status of those practicing under that name and do not hold themselves out as being partners or associates of a firm if they are not.

7.5   Marriage and family therapists do not use any professional identification (such as a professional card, office sign, letterhead, or telephone or association directory listing) if it includes a statement or claim that is false, fraudulent, misleading, or deceptive. A statement is false, fraudulent, misleading, or deceptive if it (a) contains a material misrepresentation of fact; (b) fails to state any material fact necessary to make the statement, in light of all circumstances, not misleading; or (c) is intended to or is likely to create an unjustified expectation.

7.6   Marriage and family therapists correct, wherever possible, false, misleading, or inaccurate information and representations made by others concerning the marriage and family therapist's qualifications, services, or products.

7.7   Marriage and family therapists make certain that the qualifications of persons in their employ are represented in a manner that is not false, misleading, or deceptive.

7.8   Marriage and family therapists may represent themselves as specializing within a limited area of marriage and family therapy, but may not hold themselves out as specialists without being able to provide evidence of training, education, and supervised experience in settings which meet recognized professional standards.

7.9   Only marriage and family therapist Clinical Members, Approved Supervisors, and Fellows—not Associate Members, Student Members, or organizations—may identify these AAMFT designations in public information or advertising materials.

7.10   Marriage and family therapists may not use the initials AAMFT following their name in the manner of an academic degree.

7.11   Marriage and family therapists may not use the AAMFT name, logo, and the abbreviated initials AAMFT. The Association (which is the sole owner of its name, logo, and the abbreviated initials AAMFT) and its committees and regional divisions, operating as such, may use the name, logo, and the abbreviated initials AAMFT. A regional division of AAMFT may use the AAMFT insignia to list its individual Clinical Members as a group (e.g., in the Yellow Pages); when all Clinical Members practicing within a directory district have been invited to list themselves in the directory, any one or more members may do so.

7.12   Marriage and family therapists use their membership in AAMFT only in connection with their clinical and professional activities.

Violations of this Code should be brought in writing to the attention of the AAMFT Committee on Ethics and Professional Practices at the central office of AAMFT, 1717 K Street, N.W., Suite 407, Washington, DC 20006.

Effective August 1, 1988.

APPENDIX

C

Ethical Guidelines for Group Counselors

PREAMBLE

One characteristic of any professional group is the possession of a body of knowledge, skills, and voluntarily, self-professed standards for ethical practice. A Code of Ethics consists of those standards that have been formally and publicly acknowledged by the members of a profession to serve as the guidelines for professional conduct, discharge of duties, and the resolution of moral dilemmas. By this document, the Association for Specialists in Group Work (ASGW) has identified the standards of conduct appropriate for ethical behavior among its members.

The Association for Specialists in Group Work recognizes the basic commitment of its members to the Ethical Standards of its parent organization, the American Association for Counseling and Development (AACD) and nothing in this document shall be construed to supplant that code. These standards are intended to complement the AACD standards in the area of group work by clarifying the nature of ethical responsibility of the counselor in the group setting and by stimulating a greater concern for competent group leadership.

The group counselor is expected to be a professional agent and to take the processes of ethical responsibility seriously. ASGW views "ethical process" as being integral to group work and views group counselors as "ethical agents." Group counselors, by their very nature in being responsible and responsive to their group members, necessarily embrace a certain potential for ethical vulnerability. It is incumbent upon group counselors to give considerable attention to the intent and context of their actions because the attempts of counselors to influence human behavior through group work always have ethical implications.

The following ethical guidelines have been developed to encourage ethical behavior of group counselors. These guidelines are written for students and practitioners, and are meant to stimulate reflection, self-examination, and discussion of issues and practices. They address the group counselor's responsibility for providing information about group work to clients and the group counselor's responsibility for providing group counseling services to clients. A final section discusses the group counselor's responsibility for safeguarding ethical practice and procedures for reporting unethical behavior. Group counselors are expected to make known these standards to group members.

ETHICAL GUIDELINES

1. *Orientation and Providing Information:* Group counselors adequately prepare prospective or new group members by

providing as much information about the existing or proposed group as necessary. Minimally, information related to each of the following areas should be provided.

a. Entrance procedures, time parameters of the group experience, group participation expectations, methods of payment (where appropriate), and termination procedures are explained by the group counselor as appropriate to the level of maturity of group members and the nature and purpose(s) of the group.

b. Group counselors have available for distribution a professional disclosure statement that includes information on the group counselor's qualifications and group services that can be provided, particularly as related to the nature and purpose(s) of the specific group.

c. Group counselors communicate the role expectations, rights, and responsibilities of group members and group counselor(s).

d. The group goals are stated as concisely as possible by the group counselor including "whose" goal it is (the group counselor's, the institution's, the parent's, the law's, society's, etc.) and the role of group members in influencing or determining the group's goal(s).

e. Group counselors explore with group members the risks of potential life changes that may occur because of the group experience and help members explore their readiness to face these possibilities.

f. Group members are informed by the group counselor of unusual or experimental procedures that might be expected in their group experience.

g. Group counselors explain, as realistically as possible, what services can and cannot be provided within the particular group structure offered.

h. Group counselors emphasize the need to promote full psychological functioning and presence among group members.

They inquire from prospective group members whether they are using any kind of drug or medication that may affect functioning in the group. They do not permit any use of alcohol and/or illegal drugs during group sessions and they discourage the use of alcohol and/or drugs (legal or illegal) prior to group meetings which may affect the physical or emotional presence of the member or other group members.

i. Group counselors inquire from prospective group members whether they have ever been a client in counseling or psychotherapy. If a prospective group member is already in a counseling relationship with another professional person, the group counselor advises the prospective group member to notify the other professional of their participation in the group.

j. Group counselors clearly inform group members about the policies pertaining to the group counselor's willingness to consult with them between group sessions.

k. In establishing fees for group counseling services, group counselors consider the financial status and the locality of prospective group members. Group members are not charged fees for group sessions where the group counselor is not present and the policy of charging for sessions missed by a group member is clearly communicated. Fees for participating as a group member are contracted between group counselor and group member for a specified period of time. Group counselors do not increase fees for group counseling services until the existing contracted fee structure has expired. In the event that the established fee structure is inappropriate for a prospective member, group counselors assist in finding comparable services of acceptable cost.

2. *Screening of Members:* The group counselor screens prospective group members (when appropriate to their theoretical orientation). Insofar as possible, the counselor selects group members whose needs and goals are compatible with the goals of the group, who will not impede the group process, and whose well-being will not be jeopardized by the group experience. An orientation to the group (i.e., ASGW Ethical Guideline number 1) is included during the screening process. Screening may be accomplished in one or more ways, such as the following:
   a. Individual interview,
   b. Group interview of prospective group members,
   c. Interview as part of a team staffing, and
   d. Completion of a written questionnaire by prospective group members.

3. *Confidentiality:* Group counselors protect members by defining clearly what confidentiality means, why it is important, and the difficulties involved in enforcement.
   a. Group counselors take steps to protect members by defining confidentiality and the limits of confidentiality (i.e., when a group member's condition indicates that there is clear and imminent danger to the member, others, or physical property, the group counselor takes reasonable personal action and/or informs responsible authorities).
   b. Group counselors stress the importance of confidentiality and set a norm of confidentiality regarding all group participants' disclosures. The importance of maintaining confidentiality is emphasized before the group begins and at various times in the group. The fact that confidentiality cannot be guaranteed is clearly stated.
   c. Members are made aware of the difficulties involved in enforcing and ensuring confidentiality in a group setting. The counselor provides examples of how confidentiality can non-maliciously be broken to increase members' awareness, and help to lessen the likelihood that this breach of confidence will occur. Group counselors inform group members about the potential consequences of intentionally breaching confidentiality.
   d. Group counselors can only ensure confidentiality on their part and not on the part of the members.
   e. Group counselors video or audio tape a group session only with the prior consent, and the members' knowledge of how the tape will be used.
   f. When working with minors, the group counselor specifies the limits of confidentiality.
   g. Participants in a mandatory group are made aware of any reporting procedures required of the group counselor.
   h. Group counselors store or dispose of group member records (written audio, video, etc.) in ways that maintain confidentiality.
   i. Instructors of group counseling courses maintain the anonymity of group members whenever discussing group counseling cases.

4. *Voluntary/Involuntary Participation:* Group counselors inform members whether participation is voluntary or involuntary.
   a. Group counselors take steps to ensure informed consent procedures in both voluntary and involuntary groups.
   b. When working with minors in a group, counselors are expected to follow the procedures specified by the institution in which they are practicing.
   c. With involuntary groups, every attempt is made to enlist the cooperation of the members and their continuance in the group on a voluntary basis.
   d. Group counselors do not certify that group treatment has been received by members who merely attend sessions, but did not meet the defined group expectations. Group members are

informed about the consequences for failing to participate in a group.

5. *Leaving a Group:* Provisions are made to assist a group member to terminate in an effective way.

   a. Procedures to be followed for a group member who chooses to exit a group prematurely are discussed by the counselor with all group members either before the group begins, during a pre-screening interview, or during the initial group session.

   b. In the case of legally mandated group counseling, group counselors inform members of the possible consequences for premature self-termination.

   c. Ideally, both the group counselor and the member can work cooperatively to determine the degree to which a group experience is productive or counterproductive for that individual.

   d. Members ultimately have a right to discontinue membership in the group, at a designated time, if the predetermined trial period proves to be unsatisfactory.

   e. Members have the right to exit a group, but it is important that they be made aware of the importance of informing the counselor and the group members prior to deciding to leave. The counselor discusses the possible risks of leaving the group prematurely with a member who is considering this option.

   f. Before leaving a group, the group counselor encourages members (if appropriate) to discuss their reasons for wanting to discontinue membership in the group. Counselors intervene if other members use undue pressure to force a member to remain in the group.

6. *Coercion and Pressure:* Group counselors protect member rights against physical threats, intimidation, coercion, and undue peer pressure insofar as is reasonably possible.

   a. It is essential to differentiate between "therapeutic pressure" that is part of any group and "undue pressure," which is not therapeutic.

   b. The purpose of a group is to help participants find their own answer, not to pressure them into doing what the group thinks is appropriate.

   c. Counselors exert care not to coerce participants to change in directions which they clearly state they do not choose.

   d. Counselors have a responsibility to intervene when others use undue pressure or attempt to persuade members against their will.

   e. Counselors intervene when any member attempts to act out aggression in a physical way that might harm another member or themselves.

   f. Counselors intervene when a member is verbally abusive or inappropriately confrontive to another member.

7. *Imposing Counselor Values:* Group counselors develop an awareness of their own values and needs and the potential impact they have on the interventions likely to be made.

   a. Although group counselors take care to avoid imposing their values on members, it is appropriate that they expose their own beliefs, decisions, needs, and values, when concealing them would create problems for the members.

   b. There are values implicit in any group, and these are made clear to potential members before they join the group. (Examples of certain values include: expressing feelings, being direct and honest, sharing personal material with others, learning how to trust, improving interpersonal communication, and deciding for oneself.)

   c. Personal and professional needs of group counselors are not met at the members' expense.

   d. Group counselors avoid using the group for their own therapy.

e. Group counselors are aware of their own values and assumptions and how these apply in a multicultural context.

f. Group counselors take steps to increase their awareness of ways that their personal reactions to members might inhibit the group process and they monitor their countertransference. Through an awareness of the impact of stereotyping and discrimination (i.e., biases based on age, disability, ethnicity, gender, race, religion, or sexual preference), group counselors guard the individual rights and personal dignity of all group members.

8. *Equitable Treatment:* Group counselors make every reasonable effort to treat each member individually and equally.

a. Group counselors recognize and respect differences (e.g., cultural, racial, religious, lifestyle, age, disability, gender) among group members.

b. Group counselors maintain an awareness of their behavior toward individual group members and are alert to the potential detrimental effects of favoritism or partiality toward any particular group member to the exclusion or detriment of any other member(s). It is likely that group counselors will favor some members over others, yet all group members deserve to be treated equally.

c. Group counselors ensure equitable use of group time for each member by inviting silent members to become involved, acknowledging nonverbal attempts to communicate, and discouraging rambling and monopolizing of time by members.

d. If a large group is planned, counselors consider enlisting another qualified professional to serve as a co-leader for the group sessions.

9. *Dual Relationships:* Group counselors avoid dual relationships with group members that might impair their objectivity and professional judgment, as well as those which are likely to compromise a group member's ability to participate fully in the group.

a. Group counselors do not misuse their professional role and power as group leader to advance personal or social contacts with members throughout the duration of the group.

b. Group counselors do not use their professional relationship with group members to further their own interest either during the group of after the termination of the group.

c. Sexual intimacies between group counselors and members are unethical.

d. Group counselors do not barter (exchange) professional services with group members for services.

e. Group counselors do not admit their own family members, relatives, employees, or personal friends as members to their groups.

f. Group counselors discuss with group members the potential detrimental effects of group members engaging in intimate inter-member relationships outside of the group.

g. Students who participate in a group as a partial course requirement for a group course are not evaluated for an academic grade based upon their degree of participation as a member in a group. Instructors of group counseling courses take steps to minimize the possible negative impact on students when they participate in a group course by separating course grades from participation in the group and by allowing students to decide what issues to explore and when to stop.

h. It is inappropriate to solicit members from a class (or institutional affiliation) for one's private counseling or therapeutic groups.

10. *Use of Techniques:* Group counselors do not attempt any technique unless trained in its use or under supervision by a counselor familiar with the intervention.

a. Group counselors are able to articulate a theoretical orientation that guides their practice, and they are able to provide a rationale for their interventions.

b. Depending upon the type of an intervention, group counselors have training commensurate with the potential impact of a technique.

c. Group counselors are aware of the necessity to modify their techniques to fit the unique needs of various cultural and ethnic groups.

d. Group counselors assist members in translating in-group learnings to daily life.

11. *Goal Development:* Group counselors make every effort to assist members in developing their personal goals.

a. Group counselors use their skills to assist members in making their goals specific so that others present in the group will understand the nature of the goals.

b. Throughout the course of a group, group counselors assist members in assessing the degree to which personal goals are being met, and assist in revising any goals when it is appropriate.

c. Group counselors help members clarify the degree to which the goals can be met within the context of a particular group.

12. *Consultation:* Group counselors develop and explain policies about between-session consultation to group members.

a. Group counselors take care to make certain that members do not use between-session consultations to avoid dealing with issues pertaining to the group that would be dealt with best in the group.

b. Group counselors urge members to bring the issues discussed during between-session consultations into the group if they pertain to the group.

c. Group counselors seek out consultation and/or supervision regarding ethical concerns or when encountering difficul-

ties which interfere with their effective functioning as group leaders.

d. Group counselors seek appropriate professional assistance for their own personal problems or conflicts that are likely to impair their professional judgment and work performance.

e. Group counselors discuss their group cases only for professional consultation and educational purposes.

f. Group counselors inform members about policies regarding whether consultations will be held confidential.

13. *Termination from the Group:* Depending upon the purpose of participation in the group, counselors promote termination of members from the group in the most efficient period of time.

a. Group counselors maintain a constant awareness of the progress made by each group member and periodically invite the group members to explore and reevaluate their experiences in the group. It is the responsibility of group counselors to help promote the independence of members from the group in a timely manner.

14. *Evaluation and Follow-up:* Group counselors make every attempt to engage in ongoing assessment and to design follow-up procedures for their groups.

a. Group counselors recognize the importance of ongoing assessment of a group, and they assist members in evaluating their own progress.

b. Group counselors conduct evaluation of the total group experience at the final meeting (or before termination), as well as ongoing evaluation.

c. Group counselors monitor their own behavior and become aware of what they are modeling in the group.

d. Follow-up procedures might take the form of personal contact, telephone contact, or written contact.

e. Follow-up meetings might be with individuals, or groups, or both to determine the degree to which: (i) members have reached their goals, (ii) the group had a positive or negative effect on the participants, (iii) members could profit from some type of referral, and (iv) as information for possible modification of future groups. If there is no follow-up meeting, provisions are made available for individual follow-up meetings to any member who needs or requests such a contact.

15. *Referrals:* If the needs of a particular member cannot be met within the type of group being offered, the group counselor suggests other appropriate professional referrals.

a. Group counselors are knowledgeable of local community resources for assisting group members regarding professional referrals.

b. Group counselors help members seek further professional assistance, if needed.

16. *Professional Development:* Group counselors recognize that professional growth is a continuous, ongoing, developmental process throughout their career.

a. Group counselors maintain and upgrade their knowledge and skill competencies through educational activities, clinical experiences, and participation in professional development activities.

b. Group counselors keep abreast of research findings and new developments as applied to groups.

SAFEGUARDING ETHICAL PRACTICE AND PROCEDURES FOR REPORTING UNETHICAL BEHAVIOR

The preceding remarks have been advanced as guidelines which are generally representative of ethical and professional group practice. They have not been proposed as rigidly defined prescriptions. However, practitioners who are thought to be grossly unresponsive to the ethical concerns addressed in this document may be subject to a review of their practices by the AACD Ethics Committee and ASGW peers.

1. For consultation and/or questions regarding these ASGW Ethical Guidelines or group ethical dilemmas, you may contact the Chairperson of the ASGW Ethics Committee. The name, address, and telephone number of the current ASGW Ethics Committee Chairperson may be acquired by telephoning the AACD office in Alexandria, Virginia at (703) 823-9800.

2. If a group counselor's behavior is suspected as being unethical, the following procedures are to be followed:

a. Collect more information and investigate further to confirm the unethical practice as determined by the ASGW Ethical Guidelines.

b. Confront the individual with the apparent violation of ethical guidelines for the purposes of protecting the safety of any clients and to help the group counselor correct any inappropriate behaviors. If satisfactory resolution is not reached through this contact then:

c. A complaint should be made in writing, including the specific facts and dates of the alleged violation and all relevant supporting data. The complaint should be included in an envelope marked "CONFIDENTIAL" to ensure confidentiality for both the accuser(s) and the alleged violator(s) and forwarded to all of the following sources:

1. The name and address of the Chairperson of the state Counselor Licensure Board for the respective state, if in existence.

2. The Ethics Committee
c/o The President
American Association for
Counseling and Development
5999 Stevenson Avenue
Alexandria, Virginia 22304

3. The name and address of all private credentialing agencies that the alleged violator maintains credentials or holds professional membership. Some of these include the following:

National Board for Certified Counselors, Inc.
5999 Stevenson Avenue
Alexandria, Virginia 22304

National Council for Credentialing of Career Counselors
c/o NBCC
5999 Stevenson Avenue
Alexandria, Virginia 22304

National Academy for Certified Clinical Mental Health Counselors
5999 Stevenson Avenue
Alexandria, Virginia 22304

Commission on Rehabilitation Counselor Certification
162 North State Street, Suite 317
Chicago, Illinois 60601

American Association for Marriage and Family Therapy
1717 K Street, N. W., Suite 407
Washington, DC 20006

American Psychological Association
1200 Seventeenth Street, N. W.
Washington, DC 20036

American Group Psychotherapy Association, Inc.
25 East 21st Street, 6th Floor
New York, New York 10010

Source: Approved by the Association for Specialists in Group Work (ASGW), Executive Board, June 1, 1989.

APPENDIX

D

Ethical Standards for School Counselors

PREAMBLE

The American School Counselor Association is a professional organization whose members have a unique and distinctive preparation, grounded in the behavioral sciences, with training in clinical skills adapted to the school setting. School counselors subscribe to the following basic tenets of the counseling process from which professional responsibilities are derived.

1. Each person has the right to respect and dignity as a human being and to counseling services without prejudice as to person, character, belief or practice.
2. Each person has the right to self-direction and self-development.
3. Each person has the right of choice and the responsibility for decisions reached.
4. The counselor assists in the growth and development of each individual and uses his/her highly specialized skills to ensure that the rights of the counselee are properly protected within the structure of the school program.
5. The counselor-client relationship is private and thereby requires compliance with all laws, policies and ethical standards pertaining to confidentiality.

In this document, The American School Counselor Association has identified the standards of conduct necessary to maintain and regulate the high standards of integrity and leadership among its members. The Association recognizes the basic commitment of its members to the Ethical Standards of its parent organization, the American Association for Counseling and Development, and nothing in this document shall be construed to supplant the code. The *Ethical Standards for School Counselors* was developed to complement the AACD standards by clarifying the nature of ethical responsibilities of counselors in the school setting. The purposes of this document are to:

1. Serve as a guide for the ethical practices of all school counselors regardless of level, area, or population served.
2. Provide benchmarks for both self-appraisal and peer evaluations regarding counselor responsibilities to pupils, parents, professional colleagues, school and community, self, and the counseling profession.
3. Inform those served by the school counselor of acceptable counselor practices and expected professional deportment.

A. RESPONSIBILITIES TO PUPILS

The school counselor:
1. Has a primary obligation and loyalty to the pupil, who is to be treated with respect as a unique individual.
2. Is concerned with the total needs of the pupil (educational, vocational, personal and

social) and encourages the maximum growth and development of each counselee.

3. Informs the counselee of the purposes, goals, techniques, and rules of procedure under which she/he may receive counseling assistance at or before the time when the counseling relationship is entered. Prior notice includes the possible necessity for consulting with other professionals, privileged communication, and legal or other authoritative restraints.

4. Refrains from consciously encouraging the counselee's acceptance of values, lifestyles, plans, decisions, and beliefs that represent only the counselor's personal orientation.

5. Is responsible for keeping abreast of laws relating to pupils and ensures that the rights of pupils are adequately provided for and protected.

6. Makes appropriate referrals when professional assistance can no longer be adequately provided to the counselee. Appropriate referral necessitates knowledge about available resources.

7. Protects the confidentiality of pupil records and releases personal data only according to prescribed laws and school policies. The counselor shall provide an accurate, objective, and appropriately detailed interpretation of pupil information.

8. Protects the confidentiality of information received in the counseling process as specified by law and ethical standards.

9. Informs the appropriate authorities when the counselee's condition indicates a clear and imminent danger to the counselee or others. This is to be done after careful deliberation and, where possible, after consultation with other professionals.

10. Provides explanations of the nature, purposes, and results of tests in language that is understandable to the client(s).

11. Adheres to relevant standards regarding selection, administration, and interpretation of assessment techniques.

B. RESPONSIBILITIES TO PARENTS

The school counselor:

1. Respects the inherent rights and responsibilities of parents for their children and endeavors to establish a cooperative relationship with parents to facilitate the maximum development of the counselee.

2. Informs parents of the counselor's role with emphasis on the confidential nature of the counseling relationship between the counselor and counselee.

3. Provides parents with accurate, comprehensive and relevant information in an objective and caring manner.

4. Treats information received from parents in a confidential and appropriate manner.

5. Shares information about a counselee only with those persons properly authorized to receive such information.

6. Follows local guidelines when assisting parents experiencing family difficulties which interfere with the counselee's effectiveness and welfare.

C. RESPONSIBILITIES TO COLLEAGUES AND PROFESSIONAL ASSOCIATES

The school counselor:

1. Establishes and maintains a cooperative relationship with faculty, staff, and administration to facilitate the provision of optimum guidance and counseling services.

2. Promotes awareness and adherence to appropriate guidelines regarding confidentiality, the distinction between public and private information, and staff consultation.

3. Treats colleagues with respect, courtesy, fairness, and good faith. The qualifications, views, and findings of colleagues are represented accurately and fairly to enhance the image of competent professionals.

4. Provides professional personnel with accurate, objective, concise and meaningful data necessary to adequately evaluate, counsel, and assist the counselee.

5. Is aware of and fully utilizes related professions and organizations to whom the counselee may be referred.

D. RESPONSIBILITIES TO THE SCHOOL AND COMMUNITY

The school counselor:

1. Supports and protects the educational program against any infringement not in the best interest of pupils.
2. Informs appropriate officials of conditions that may be potentially disruptive or damaging to the school's mission, personnel, and property.
3. Delineates and promotes the counselor's role and function in meeting the needs of those served. The counselor will notify appropriate school officials of conditions which may limit or curtail their effectiveness in providing services.
4. Assists in the development of (1) curricular and environmental conditions appropriate for the school and community, (2) educational procedures and programs to meet pupil needs, and (3) a systematic evaluation process for guidance and counseling programs, services and personnel.
5. Works cooperatively with agencies, organizations, and individuals in the school and community without regard to personal reward or remuneration.

E. RESPONSIBILITIES TO SELF

The school counselor:

1. Functions within the boundaries of individual professional competence and accepts responsibility for the consequences of his/her actions.
2. Is aware of the potential effects of personal characteristics on services to clients.
3. Monitors personal functioning and effectiveness and refrains from any activity likely to lead to inadequate professional services or harm to a client.

4. Strives through personal initiative to maintain professional competence and keep abreast of innovations and trends in the profession.

F. RESPONSIBILITIES TO THE PROFESSION

The school counselor:

1. Conducts herself/himself in such a manner as to bring credit to self and the profession.
2. Conducts appropriate research and reports findings in a manner consistent with acceptable educational and psychological research practices.
3. Actively participates in local, state, and national associations which foster the development and improvement of school counseling.
4. Adheres to ethical standards of the profession, other official policy statements pertaining to counseling, and relevant statutes established by federal, state, and local governments.
5. Clearly distinguishes between statements and actions made as a private individual and as a representative of the school counseling profession.

G. MAINTENANCE OF STANDARDS

Ethical behavior among professional school counselors is expected at all times. When there exists serious doubt as to the ethical behavior of colleagues, or if counselors are forced to work in situations or abide by policies which do not reflect the standards as outlined in these *Ethical Standards for School Counselors* or the AACD *Ethical Standards,* the counselor is obligated to take appropriate action to rectify the condition. The following procedure may serve as a guide:

1. The counselor shall utilize the channels established within the school and/or system. This may include both informal and formal procedures.
2. If the matter remains unresolved, referral for review and appropriate action should be

made to the Ethics Committees in the following sequence:

    local counselor association
    state counselor association
    national counselor association.

H. REFERENCES

School counselors are responsible for being aware of and acting in accord with the standards and positions of the counseling profession as represented in such official documents as those listed below. A more extensive bibliography is available from the ASCA Ethics Committee upon request.

Ethical Standards (1981). American Association for Counseling and Development, Alexandria, VA.

Ethical Guidelines for Group Leaders (1980). Association for Specialists in Group Work. Alexandria, VA.

Principles of Confidentiality (1974). ASCA Position Statement. American School Counselor Association. Alexandria, VA.

Standards for Educational and Psychological Tests and Manuals (1974). American Psychological Association. Washington, D.C.

Ethical Principles in the Conduct of Research with Human Participants (1973). American Psychological Association. Washington, D.C.

Ethical Standards for School Counselors is an adaptation of the ASCA *Code of Ethics* (1972) and the California School Counselor Association *Code of Ethics* (revised, 1984. Adopted by the ASCA Delegate Assembly March 19, 1984.)

Ethical Standards for Mental Health Counselors

PREAMBLE

Mental Health Counselors believe in the dignity and worth of the individual. They are committed to increasing knowledge of human behavior and understanding of themselves and others. While pursuing these endeavors, they make every reasonable effort to protect the welfare of those who seek their services or of any subject that may be the object of study. They use their skills only for purposes consistent with those values and do not knowingly permit their misuse by others. While demanding for themselves freedom of inquiry and community, mental health counselors accept the responsibility this freedom confers: competence, objectivity in the application of skills and concern for the best interests of clients, colleagues, and society in general. In the pursuit of these ideals, mental health counselors subscribe to the following principles:

PRINCIPLE 1. RESPONSIBILITY

In their commitment to the understanding of human behavior, mental health counselors value objectivity and integrity, and in providing services they maintain the highest standards. They accept responsibility for the consequences of their work and make every effort to insure that their services are used appropriately.

a. Mental health counselors accept ultimate responsibility for selecting appropriate areas for investigation and the methods relevant to minimize the possibility that their finding will be misleading. They provide thorough discussion of the limitations of their data and alternative hypotheses, especially where their work touches on social policy or might be misconstrued to the detriment of specific age, sex, ethnic, socio-economic, or other social categories. In publishing reports of their work, they never discard observations that may modify the interpretation of results. Mental health counselors take credit only for the work they have actually done. In pursuing research, mental health counselors ascertain that their efforts will not lead to changes in individuals or organizations unless such changes are part of the agreement at the time of obtaining informal consent. Mental health counselors clarify in advance the expectations for sharing and utilizing research data. They avoid dual relationships which may limit objectivity, whether theoretical, political, or monetary, so that interference with data, subjects, and milieu is kept to a minimum.

b. As employees of an institution or agency, mental health counselors have the responsibility of remaining alert to institutional pressures which may distort reports of counseling findings or use them in ways counter to the promotion of human welfare.

c. When serving as members of governmental or other organizational bodies, mental health counselors remain accountable as individuals to the Code of Ethics of the American Mental Health Counselors Association (AMHCA).

d. As teachers, mental health counselors recognize their primary obligation to help others acquire knowledge and skill. They maintain high standards of scholarship and objectivity by presenting counseling information fully and accurately, and by giving appropriate recognition to alternative viewpoints.

e. As practitioners, mental health counselors know that they bear a heavy social responsibility because their recommendations and professional actions may alter the lives of others. They, therefore, remain fully cognizant of their impact and alert to personal, social, organizational, financial or political situations or pressures which might lead to misuse of their influence.

f. Mental health counselors provide reasonable and timely feedback to employees, trainees, supervisors, students, clients, and others whose work they may evaluate.

PRINCIPLE 2. COMPETENCE

The maintenance of high standards of professional competence is a responsibility shared by all mental health counselors in the interest of the public and the profession as a whole. Mental health counselors recognize the boundaries of their competence and the limitations of their techniques and only provide services, use techniques, or offer opinions as professionals that meet recognized standards. Throughout their careers, mental health counselors maintain knowledge of professional information related to the services they render.

a. Mental health counselors accurately represent their competence, education, training and experience.

b. As teachers, mental health counselors perform their duties based on careful preparation so that their instruction is accurate, up-to-date and scholarly.

c. Mental health counselors recognize the need for continuing training to prepare themselves to serve persons of all ages and cultural backgrounds. They are open to new procedures and sensitive to differences between groups of people and changes in expectations and values over time.

d. Mental health counselors with the responsibility for decisions involving individuals or policies based on test results should know and understand literature relevant to the tests used and testing problems with which they deal.

e. Mental health counselors and practitioners recognize that their effectiveness depends in part upon their ability to maintain sound interpersonal relations, that temporary or more enduring aberrations on their part may interfere with their abilities or distort their appraisals of others. Therefore, they refrain from undertaking any activity in which their personal problems are likely to lead to inadequate professional services or harm to a client, or, if they are already engaged in such activity when they become aware of their personal problems, they would seek competent professional assistance to determine whether they should suspend or terminate services to one or all of their clients.

f. The mental health counselor has a responsibility both to the individual who is served and to the institution with which the service is performed to maintain high standards of professional conduct. The mental health counselor strives to maintain the highest levels of professional services offered to the individuals to be served. The mental health counselor also strives to assist the agency, organization or institution in providing the highest caliber of professional services. The acceptance of employment in an institution implies that the mental health counselor is in substantial agreement with the general policies and principles of the institution. If, despite concerted efforts, the member cannot reach agreement with the employer as to acceptable standards of conduct that allow for changes in institutional policy conducive to the positive growth and development of counselees, then terminating the affiliation should be seriously considered.

g. Ethical behavior among professional associates, mental health counselors and non-mental health counselors, is expected at all times. When information is possessed which raises serious doubt as to the ethical behavior of professional colleagues, whether Association members or not, the mental health counselor is obligated to take action to attempt to rectify such a condition. Such action shall utilize the institution's channels first and then utilize procedures established by the state, division, or Association.

h. The mental health counselor is aware of the intimacy of the counseling relationship and maintains a healthy respect for the personhood of the client and avoids engaging in activities that seek to meet the mental health counselor's personal needs at the expense of the client. Through awareness of the negative impact of both racial and sexual stereotyping and discrimination, the member strives to ensure the individual rights and personal dignity of the client in the counseling relationship.

PRINCIPLE 3. MORAL AND LEGAL STANDARDS

Mental health counselors' moral, ethical and legal standards of behavior are a personal matter to the same degree as they are for any other citizen, except as these may compromise the fulfillment of their professional responsibilities, or reduce the trust in counseling or counselors held by the general public. Regarding their own behavior, mental health counselors should be aware of the prevailing community standards and of the possible impact upon the quality of professional services provided by their conformance to or deviation from these standards. Mental health counselors should also be aware of the possible impact of their public behavior upon the ability of colleagues to perform their professional duties.

a. To protect public confidence in the profession of counseling, mental health counselors will avoid public behavior that is clearly in violation of accepted moral and legal standards.

b. To protect students, mental health counselors/teachers will be aware of the diverse backgrounds of students and, when dealing with topics that may give offense, will see that the material is treated objectively, that it is clearly relevant to the course, and that it is treated in a manner for which the student is prepared.

c. Providers of counseling services conform to the statutes relating to such services as established by their state and its regulating professional board(s).

d. As employees, mental health counselors refuse to participate in employer's practices which are inconsistent with the moral and legal standards established by federal or state legislation regarding the treatment of employees or of the public. In particular and for example, mental health counselors will not condone practices which result in illegal or otherwise unjustifiable discrimination on the basis of race, sex, religion, or national origin in hiring, promotion or training.

e. In providing counseling services to clients mental health counselors avoid any action that will violate or diminish the legal and civil rights of clients or of others who may be affected by the action.

f. Sexual conduct, not limited to sexual intercourse, between mental health counselors and clients is specifically in violation of this code of ethics. This does not, however, prohibit the use of explicit instructional aids including films and video tapes. Such use is within accepted practices of trained and competent sex therapists.

PRINCIPLE 4. PUBLIC STATEMENTS

Mental health counselors in their professional roles may be expected or required to make public statements providing counseling information, professional opinions, or supply information about the availability of counseling products and services. In making such statements, mental health counselors take full account of the limits and uncertainties of present counseling knowledge and techniques. They represent, as objectively as possible, their professional qualifications, affiliations, and functions, as well as those of the institutions or organizations with which the statements may be associated. All public statements, announcements of services, and promotional activities should serve the purpose of providing sufficient information to aid the consumer public in making informed judgements and choices on matters that concern it.

a. When announcing professional counseling services, mental health counselors limit the information to: name, highest relevant degree conferred, certification or licensure, address, telephone number, office hours, cost of services, and a brief explanation of the other types of services offered but not evaluative as to their quality or uniqueness. They will not contain testimonials by implication. They will not claim uniqueness of skill or methods beyond those acceptable and public scientific evidence.

b. In announcing the availability of counseling services or products, mental health counselors will not display their affiliations with organizations or agencies in a manner that implies the sponsorship or certification of the organization or agency. They will not name their employer or professional associations unless the services are in fact to be provided by or under the responsible, direct supervision and continuing control of such organizations or agencies.

c. Mental health counselors associated with the development of promotion of counseling device, books, or other products offered for commercial sale will make every effort to insure that announcements and advertisements are presented in a professional and factually informative manner without unsupported claims of superiority and must be supported by scientifically acceptable evidence or by willingness to aid and encourage independent professional scrutiny or scientific test.

d. Mental health counselors engaged in radio, television or other public media activities will not participate in commercial announcements recommending to the general public the purchase or use of any proprietary or single-source product or service.

e. Mental health counselors who describe counseling services or the services of professional counselors to the general public accept the obligations to present the material fairly and accurately, avoiding misrepresentation through sensationalism, exaggeration or superficiality. Mental health counselors will be guided by the primary obligation to aid the public in forming their own informed judgements, opinions and choices.

f. As teachers, mental health counselors ensure their statements in catalogs and course outlines are accurate, particularly in terms of subject matter to be covered, bases for grading, and nature of classroom experiences.

g. Mental health counselors accept the obligation to correct others who may represent their professional qualifications or associations with products or services in a manner incompatible with these guidelines.

h. Mental health counselors providing consultation, workshops, training, and other technical services may refer to previous satisfied clients in their advertising, provided there is no implication that such advertising refers to counseling services.

PRINCIPLE 5. CONFIDENTIALITY

Mental health counselors have a primary obligation to safeguard information about individuals obtained in the course of teaching, practice, or research. Personal information is communicated to others only with the person's written consent or in those circumstances where there is clear and imminent danger to the client, to others or to society. Disclosures of counseling information are restricted to what is necessary, relevant, and verifiable.

a. All materials in the official record shall be shared with the client who shall have the right to decide what information may be shared by anyone beyond the immediate provider of service and to be informed of the implications of the materials to be shared.

b. The anonymity of clients served in public and other agencies is preserved, if at all possible, by withholding names and personal identifying data. If external conditions require reporting such information, the client shall be so informed.

    c.   Information received in confidence by one agency or person shall not be forwarded to another person or agency without the client's written permission.

    d.   Service providers have a responsibility to insure the accuracy and to indicate the validity of data shared with their parties.

    e.   Case reports presented in classes, professional meetings, or in publications shall be so disguised that no identification is possible unless the client or responsible authority has read the report and agreed in writing to its presentation or publication.

    f.   Counseling reports and records are maintained under conditions of security and provisions are made for their destruction when they have outlived their usefulness. Mental health counselors insure that privacy and confidentiality are maintained by all persons in their employ or volunteers, and community aides.

    g.   Mental health counselors who ask that an individual reveal personal information in the course of interviewing, testing or evaluation, or who allow such information to be divulged, do so only after making certain that the person or authorized representative is fully aware of the purposes of the interview, testing or evaluation and of the ways in which the information will be used.

    h.   Sessions with clients are taped or otherwise recorded only with their written permission or the written permission of a responsible guardian. Even with guardian consent one should not record a session against the expressed wishes of a client.

    i.   Where a child or adolescent is the primary client, the interests of the minor shall be paramount.

    j.   In work with families, the rights of each family member should be safe guarded. The provider of service also has the responsibility to discuss the contents of the record with the parent and/or child, as appropriate, and to keep separate those parts which should remain the property of each family member.

PRINCIPLE 6. WELFARE OF THE CONSUMER

Mental health counselors respect the integrity and protect the welfare of the people and groups with whom they work. When there is a conflict of interest between the client and the mental health counselors employing institution, the mental health counselors clarify the nature and direction of their loyalties and responsibilities and keep all parties informed of their commitments. Mental health counselors fully inform consumers as to the purpose and nature of any evaluative, treatment, educational or training procedure, and they freely acknowledge that clients, students, or subjects have freedom of choice with regard to participation.

    a.   Mental health counselors are continually cognizant both of their own needs and of their inherently powerful position "vis-a-vis" clients, in order to avoid exploiting the client's trust and dependency. Mental health counselors make every effort to avoid dual relationships with clients and/or relationships which might impair their professional judgement or increase the risk of client exploitation. Examples of such dual relationships include treating an employee or supervisor, treating a close friend or family relative and sexual relationships with clients.

    b.   Where mental health counselors work with members of an organization goes beyond reasonable conditions of employment, mental health counselors recognize possible conflicts of interest that may arise. When such conflicts occur, mental health counselors clarify the nature of the conflict and inform all parties of the nature and directions of the loyalties and responsibilities involved.

    c.   When acting as supervisors, trainers, or employers, mental health counselors accord recipients informed choice, confidentiality, and protection from physical and mental harm.

d.   Financial arrangements in professional practice are in accord with professional standards that safeguard the best interests of the client and that are clearly understood by the client in advance of billing. This may best be done by use of a contract. Mental health counselors are responsible for assisting clients in finding needed services in those instances where payment of the usual fee would be a hardship. No commission or rebate or other form of remuneration may be given or received for referral of clients for professional services, whether by an individual or by an agency.

e.   Mental health counselors are responsible for making their services readily accessible to clients in a manner that facilitates the client's ability to make an informed choice when selecting a service provider. This responsibility includes a clear description of what the client may expect in the way of tests, reports, billing, therapeutic regime and schedules and the use of the mental health counselor's Statement of Professional Disclosure.

f.   Mental health counselors who find that their services are not beneficial to the client have the responsibility to make this known to the responsible persons.

g.   Mental health counselors are accountable to the parties who refer and support counseling services and to the general public and are cognizant of the indirect or long-range effects of their intervention.

h.   The mental health counselor attempts to terminate a private service or consulting relationship when it is reasonably clear to the mental health counselor that the consumer is not benefitting from it. If a consumer is receiving services from another mental health professional, mental health counselors do not offer their services directly to the consumer without informing the professional persons already involved in order to avoid confusion and conflict for the consumer.

i.   The mental health counselor has the responsibility to screen prospective group participants, especially when the emphasis is on self-understanding and growth through self-disclosure. The member should maintain an awareness of the group participants' compatibility throughout the life of the group.

j.   The mental health counselor may choose to consult with any other professionally competent person about a client. In choosing a consultant, the mental health counselor should avoid placing the consultant in a conflict of interest situation that would preclude the consultant's being a proper party to the mental health counselors' efforts to help the clients.

k.   If the mental health counselor is unable to be of professional assistance to the client, the mental health counselor should avoid initiating the counseling relationship or the mental health counselor terminates the relationship. In either event, the member is obligated to suggest appropriate alternatives. (It is incumbent upon the mental health counselors to be knowledgeable about referral resources so that a satisfactory referral can be initiated.) In the event the client declines the suggested referral, the mental health counselor is not obligated to continue the relationship.

l.   When the mental health counselor has other relationships, particularly of an administrative, supervisory, and/or evaluative nature, with an individual seeking counseling services, the mental health counselor should not serve as the counselor but should refer the individual to another professional. Only in instances where such an alternative is unavailable and where the individual's situation definitely warrants counseling intervention should the mental health counselor enter into and/or maintain a counseling relationship. Dual relationships with clients which might impair the member's objectivity and professional judgement (such as with close friends or relatives, sexual intimacies with any client, etc.) must be avoided and/or the counseling relationship terminated through referral to another competent professional.

m.   All experimental methods of treatment must be clearly indicated to prospective recipients, and safety precautions are to be adhered to by the mental health counselors instituting treatment.

n. When the member is engaged in short-term group treatment/training programs e.g., marathons and other encounter-type or growth groups, the member insures that there is professional assistance available during and following the group experience.

PRINCIPLE 7. PROFESSIONAL RELATIONSHIP

Mental health counselors act with due regard to the needs and feelings of their colleagues in counseling and other professions. Mental health counselors respect the prerogatives and obligations of the institutions or organizations with which they are associated.

a. Mental health counselors understand the areas of competence of related professions and make full use of other professional, technical, and administrative resources which best serve the interests of consumers. The absence of formal relationships with other professional workers does not relieve mental health counselors from the responsibility of securing for their clients the best possible professional service; indeed, this circumstance presents a challenge to the professional competence of mental health counselors, requiring special sensitivity to problems outside their area of training, and foresight, diligence, and tact in obtaining the professional assistance needed by clients.

b. Mental health counselors know and take into account the traditions and practices of other professional groups with which they work and cooperate fully with members of such groups when research, services, and other functions are shared or in working for the benefit of public welfare.

c. Mental health counselors strive to provide positive conditions for those they employ and they spell out clearly the conditions of such employment. They encourage their employees to engage in activities that facilitate their further professional development.

d. Mental health counselors respect the viability, reputation, and the proprietary right of organizations which they serve. Mental health counselors show due regard for the interest of their present or prospective employers. In those instances where they are critical of policies, they attempt to effect change by constructive action within the organization.

e. In the pursuit of research, mental health counselors give sponsoring agencies, host institutions, and publication channels the same respect and opportunity for giving informed consent that they accord to individual research participants. They are aware of their obligation to future research workers and insure that host institutions are given feedback information and proper acknowledgment.

f. Credit is assigned to those who have contributed to a publication, in proportion to their contribution.

g. When a mental health counselor violates ethical standards, mental health counselors who know first-hand of such activities, if possible, attempt to rectify the situation. Failing an informal solution, mental health counselors should bring such unethical activities to the attention of the appropriate state, and/or national committee on ethics and professional conduct. Only after all professional alternatives have been utilized will a mental health counselor begin legal action for resolution.

PRINCIPLE 8. UTILIZATION OF ASSESSMENT TECHNIQUES

In the development, publication, and utilization of counseling assessment techniques, mental health counselors follow relevant standards. Individuals examined, or their legal guardians, have the right to know the results, the interpretations made, and where appropriate, the particulars on which final judgement was based. Test users should take precautions to protect test security but not at the expense of an individual's right to understand the basis for decisions that adversely affect that individual or that individual's dependents.

a.   The client has the right to have and the provider has the responsibility to give explanations of test results in language the client can understand.

b.   When a test is published or otherwise made available for operational use, it should be accompanied by a manual (or other published or readily available information) that makes every reasonable effort to describe fully the development of the test, the rationale, specifications followed in writing items analysis or other research. The test, the manual, the record forms and other accompanying material should help users make correct interpretations of the test results and should warn against common misuses. The test manual should state explicitly the purposes and applications for which the test is recommended and identify any special qualifications required to administer the test and to interpret it properly. Evidence of validity and reliability, along with other relevant research data, should be presented in support of any claims made.

c.   Norms presented in test manuals should refer to defined and clearly described populations. These populations should be the groups with whom users of the test will ordinarily wish to compare the persons tested. Test users should consider the possibility of bias in tests or in test items. When indicated, there should be an investigation of possible differences in validity for ethnic, sex, or other subsamples than can be identified when the test is given.

d.   Mental health counselors who have the responsibility for decisions about individuals or policies that are based on test results should have a thorough understanding of counseling or educational measurements and of validation and other test research.

e.   Mental health counselors should develop procedures for systematically eliminating from data files test score information that has, because of the lapse of time, become obsolete.

f.   Any individual or organization offering test scoring and interpretation services must be able to demonstrate that their programs are based on

appropriate research to establish the validity of the programs and procedures used in arriving at interpretations. The public offering of an automated test interpretation service will be considered as a professional-to-professional consultation. In this the formal responsibility of the consultant is to the consultee but his/her ultimate and overriding responsibility is to the client.

g.   Counseling services for the purpose of diagnosis, treatment, or personalized advice are provided only in the context of a professional relationship, and are not given by means of public lectures or demonstrations, newspapers or magazine articles, radio or television programs, mail, or similar media. The preparation of personnel reports and recommendations based on data secured solely by mail is unethical unless such appraisals are an integral part of a continuing client relationship with a company, as a result of which the consulting clinical mental health counselor has intimate knowledge of the client's personal situation and can be assured thereby that his written appraisals will be adequate to the purpose and will be properly interpreted by the client. These reports must not be embellished with such detailed analyses of the subject's personality traits as would be appropriate only for intensive interviews with the subjects.

PRINCIPLE 9. PURSUIT OF RESEARCH ACTIVITIES

The decision to undertake research should rest upon a considered judgment by the individual mental health counselor about how best to contribute to counseling and to human welfare. Mental health counselors carry out their investigations with respect for the people who participate and with concern for their dignity and welfare.

a.   In planning a study the investigator has the personal responsibility to make a careful evaluation of its ethical acceptability, taking into account the following principles for research with human beings. To the extent that this appraisal, weighing scientific and humane values, suggests a deviation from any principle, the investigator incurs an increasingly serious obligation to seek ethical advice and to observe more stringent safeguards to protect the rights of the human research participants.

b.   Mental health counselors know and take into account the traditions and practices of other professional groups with members of such groups when research, services, and other functions are shared or in working for the benefit of public welfare.

c.   Ethical practice requires the investigator to inform the participants of all features of the research that reasonably might be expected to influence willingness to participate, and to explain all other aspects of the research about which the participant inquires. Failure to make full disclosure gives added emphasis to the investigator's abiding responsibility to protect the welfare and dignity of the research participant.

d.   Openness and honesty are essential characteristics of the relationship between investigator and research participant. When the methodological requirements of a study necessitate concealment or deception, the investigator is required to insure as soon as possible the participant's understanding of the reason for this action and to restore the quality of the relationship with the investigator.

e.   In the pursuit of research, mental health counselors give sponsoring agencies, host institutions, and publication channels the same respect and opportunity for giving informed consent that they accord to individual research participants. They are aware of their obligation to future research workers and insure that host institutions are given feedback information and proper acknowledgment.

f.   Credit is assigned to those who have contributed to a publication, in proportion to their contribution.

g.   The ethical investigator protects participants from physical and mental discomfort, harm and danger. If the risk of such consequences exists, the investigator is required to inform the participant of that fact, secure consent before proceeding, and take all possible measures to minimize distress. A research procedure may not be used if it is likely to cause serious and lasting harm to participants.

h.   After the data are collected, ethical practice requires the investigator to provide the participants with a full clarification of the nature of the study and to remove any misconceptions that may have arisen. Where scientific or humane values justify delaying or withholding information the investigator acquires a special responsibility to assure that there are no damaging consequences for the participants.

i.   Where research procedure may result in undesirable consequences for the participant, the investigator has the responsibility to detect and remove or correct these consequences, including, where relevant, long-term after effects.

j.   Information obtained about the research participants during the course of an investigation is confidential. When the possibility exists that others may obtain access to such information, ethical research practice requires that the possibility, together with the plans for protecting confidentiality be explained to the participants as a part of the procedure for obtaining informed consent.

PRINCIPLE 10. PRIVATE PRACTICE

a.   A mental health counselor should assist where permitted by legislation or judicial decision the profession in fulfilling its duty to make counseling services available in private settings.

b.   In advertising services as a private practitioner the mental health counselor should advertise the services in such a manner so as to accurately inform the public as to services, expertise, profession, techniques of counseling in a professional manner. A mental health counselor who assumes an executive leadership role in the organization shall not permit his/her name to be used in professional notices during periods when not actively engaged in the private practice of counseling.

The mental health counselor may list the following: Highest relevant degree, type and level of certification or license, type and/or description of services and other relevant information. Such information should not contain false, inaccurate, misleading, partial, out-of-context, or deceptive material or statements.

c.   The mental health counselors may join in partnership/corporation with other mental health counselors and/or other professionals provided that each mental health counselor of the partnership or corporation makes clear the separate specialties by name in compliance with the regulations of the locality.

d.   A mental health counselor has an obligation to withdraw from a counseling relationship if it is believed that employment will result in violation of the code of ethics, if their mental capacity or physical condition renders it difficult to carry out an effective professional relationship, or if the mental health counselor is discharged by the client because the counseling relationship is no longer productive for the client.

e.   A mental health counselor should adhere to and support the regulations for private practice of the locality where the services are offered.

f.   Mental health counselors are discouraged from deliberate attempts to utilize one's institutional affiliation to recruit clients for one's private practice. Mental health counselors are to refrain from offering their services in the private sector, when they are employed by an institution in which this is prohibited by stated policies reflecting conditions for employment.

g.   In establishing fees for professional counseling services, mental health counselors should consider the financial status of clients and locality. In the event that the established fee structure is inappropriate for a client, assistance should be provided in finding services of acceptable cost.

PRINCIPLE 11. CONSULTING

a.   The mental health counselor acting as a consultant must have a high degree of self-awareness of his/her own values, knowledge, skills and needs in entering a helping relationship which involves human and/or organizational change and that the focus of the relationship be on the issues to be resolved and not on the person(s) presenting the problem.

b.   There should be understanding and agreement between the mental health counselor and client for the problem definition, changed goals and predicted consequences of interventions selected.

c.   The mental health counselor must be reasonably certain that she/he or the organization represented has the necessary competencies and resources for giving the kind of help which is needed now or may develop later and that appropriate referral resources are available to the consultant, if needed later.

d.   The mental health counselor relationship must be one in which client adaptability and growth toward self-direction are encouraged and cultivated. The mental health counselor must maintain this role consistently and not become a decision maker or substitute for the client.

e.   When announcing consultant availability for services, the mental health counselor conscientiously adheres to professional standards.

f.   The mental health counselor is expected to refuse a private fee or other remuneration for consultation with persons who are entitled to these services through the members' employing institution or agency. The policies of a particular agency may make explicit provisions for private practice with agency counselees by members of its staff. In such instances, the counselees must be apprised of other options open to them should they seek private counseling services.

PRINCIPLE 12. CLIENT'S RIGHTS

The following apply to all consumers of mental health services, including both in- and outpatients in all state, county, local, and private care mental health facilities, as well as patients/clients of mental health practitioners in private practice.

The client has the right:

a. to be treated with consideration and respect;

b. to expect quality service provided by concerned, competent staff;

c. to a clear statement of the purposes, goals, techniques, rules of procedure, and limitations as well as potential dangers of the services to be performed and all other information related to or likely to affect the on-going counseling relationship;

d. to obtain information about their case record and to have this information explained clearly and directly;

e. to full, knowledgeable, and responsible participation in the on-going treatment plan, to the maximum feasible extent;

f. to expect complete confidentiality and that no information will be released without written consent;

g. to see and discuss their charges and payment records; and

h. to refuse any recommended services and be advised of the consequences of this action.

PROCEDURES FOR HANDLING COMPLAINTS OF UNETHICAL CONDUCT

I. Procedures for Handling Complaints (Consumer and Peer) of Unethical Conduct

A complaint concerning the behavior of a member of the American Mental Health Counselors Association shall be in writing, dated, and signed by the complainant and will be sent by certified mail to the Chairperson of the AMHCA Ethics Committee. The chairperson shall inform both the consumer or peer who filed the complaint, and the member against whom the complaint was filed, of the due process procedures and his or her right to appeal any forthcoming action to the AMHCA Board of Directors.

II. Procedures for Handling Allegations by Ethics Committee

A. Ethics Committee Chairperson will:

1. Receive and file communication alleging or inferring unethical conduct.

2. Within 15 days of receipt of the complaint, send to the consumer or peer a letter informing them of receipt of the complaint and steps to be taken.

3. Determine the membership status of the member on which the complaint is being made.

4. Send to the member against whom the complaint has been made a copy of the Procedures for Handling Complaints of Unethical Conduct and a copy of the complaint and request the member to prepare a written response to the complaint and send by certified mail, within 30 days of receipt of the complaint, the response to the Chairperson of the AMHCA Ethics Committee.

5. Conduct initial investigation to ascertain whether or not an ethical violation has occurred.

B. Ethics Review Panel:

1. If the complaint is found to warrant review by the Ethics Review panel, the Ethics Chairperson will take action to establish the panel in accordance with section III of this document.

2. The Ethics Review Panel (ERP) shall review the complaint and the response of the member. Such a review can take place through the mail, by phone, or in person.

3. The ERP may take up to 60 days of additional time to further investigate the complaint, permitting both sides to provide additional information. Upon conclusion of their investigation, the panel will take action to implement its decision.

4. The ERP may find that:

a. The complaint is without merit and dismiss it.

b. The complaint has been sustained and the member will be notified within 15 days after the ERP has reached a decision. The Chairperson of the Ethics Committee will inform by certified mail, the consumer or peer who filed the complaint and the member against whom the complaint was filed of the panel's action. Possible actions include:

1. Admonishment and request to cease the objectionable behavior.
2. Formal reprimand.
3. Suspension from membership for a specific period of time.
4. Expulsion from the Association.
5. The Ethics Review Panel will notify the AMHCA Board of Directors of its decision and the Board will take action to implement the decision.

III. Ethics Review Panel

The Ethics Review Panel shall consist of the AMHCA Ethics Committee Chairperson, the AMHCA Professional Affairs Committee Chairperson, the AMHCA President, and two voting members of the Association selected and appointed (one each) from a list of members presented to the Ethics Committee from the member and the complainant. (If dealing with a consumer complaint, only one association member shall be selected from a list submitted by the member, and the remaining panel member shall be either the Chairperson of the AMHCA Licensure Committee or the Chairperson of the Accreditation and Standards Committee or their designate who must be a committee member.)

IV. Appeal Procedure

A. Within 15 days of the receipt of action by the Ethics Review Panel, the member must file written notice with the chairperson of the AMHCA Ethics Committee of his or her appeal.
B. Suspended or expelled members shall be denied all membership privileges pending the appeal.
C. The appeal shall be heard at the next scheduled meeting of the AMHCA Board of Directors.
D. The members shall have the right to be heard, present his or her evidence, and be represented by legal counsel.
E. Presentation of evidence and arguments for the AMHCA shall be made by the President or a member of his or her choice.
F. A two-thirds (2/3) vote of the members of the Board present shall be required to alter the decision of the Ethics Review Panel. The Board can recommend the same actions available to the Ethics Review Panel (See Section II, B, 4-a. & b.).

Ethical Standards for the American Counseling Association

PREAMBLE

The Association is an educational, scientific, and professional organization whose members are dedicated to the enhancement of the worth, dignity, potential, and uniqueness of each individual and thus to the service of society.

The Association recognizes that the role definitions and work settings of its members include a wide variety of academic disciplines, levels of academic preparation, and agency services. This diversity reflects the breadth of the Association's interest and influence. It also poses challenging complexities in efforts to set standards for the performance of members, desired requisite preparation or practice, and supporting social, legal, and ethical controls.

The specification of ethical standards enables the Association to clarify to present and future members and to those served by members the nature of ethical responsibilities held in common by its members.

The existence of such standards serves to stimulate greater concern by members for their own professional functioning and for the conduct of fellow professionals such as counselors, guidance and student personnel workers, and others in the helping professions. As the ethical code of the Association, this document establish- *es principles that define the ethical behavior of Association members. Additional ethical guidelines developed by the Association's Divisions for their specialty areas may further define a member's ethical behavior.*

SECTION A: GENERAL

1. The member influences the development of the profession by continuous efforts to improve professional practices, teaching, services, and research. Professional growth is continuous throughout the member's career and is exemplified by the development of a philosophy that explains why and how a member functions in the helping relationship. Members must gather data on their effectiveness and be guided by the findings. Members recognize the need for continuing education to ensure competent service.

2. The member has a responsibility both to the individual who is served and to the institution within which the service is performed to maintain high standards of professional conduct. The member strives to maintain the highest levels of professional services offered to the individuals to be served. The member also strives to assist the agency, organization, or institution in providing the highest caliber of professional services. The acceptance of employment in an insti-

419

tution implies that the member is in agreement with the general polices and principles of the institution. Therefore, the professional activities of the member are also in accord with the objectives of the institution. If, despite concerted efforts, the member cannot reach agreement with the employer as to acceptable standards of conduct that allow for changes in institutional policy conducive to the positive growth and development of clients, then terminating the affiliation should be seriously considered.

3. Ethical behavior among professional associates, both members and nonmembers, must be expected at all times. When information is possessed that raises doubt as to the ethical behavior of professional colleagues, whether Association members or not, the member must take action to attempt to rectify such a condition. Such action shall use the institution's channels first and then use procedures established by the Association.

4. The member neither claims nor implies professional qualifications exceeding those possessed and is responsible for correcting any misrepresentations of these qualifications by others.

5. In establishing fees for professional counseling services, members must consider the financial status of clients and locality. In the event that the established fee structure is inappropriate for a client, assistance must be provided in finding comparable services of acceptable cost.

6. When members provide information to the public or to subordinates, peers, or supervisors, they have a responsibility to ensure that the content is general, unidentified client information that is accurate, unbiased, and consists of objective, factual data.

7. Members recognize their boundaries of competence and provide only those services and use only those techniques for which they are qualified by training or experience. Members should only accept those positions for which they are professionally qualified.

8. In the counseling relationship, the counselor is aware of the intimacy of the relationship and maintains respect for the client and avoids engaging in activities that seek to meet the counselor's personal needs at the expense of that client.

9. Members do not condone or engage in sexual harassment, which is defined as deliberate or repeated comments, gestures, or physical contacts of a sexual nature.

10. The member avoids bringing personal issues into the counseling relationship, especially if the potential for harm is present. Through awareness of the negative impact of both racial and sexual stereotyping and discrimination, the counselor guards the individual rights and personal dignity of the client in the counseling relationship.

11. Products or services provided by the member by means of classroom instruction, public lectures, demonstrations, written articles, radio or television programs, or other types of media must meet the criteria cited in these standards.

SECTION B: COUNSELING RELATIONSHIP

This section refers to practices and procedures of individual and/or group counseling relationships.

The member must recognize the need for client freedom of choice. Under those circumstances where this is not possible, the member must appraise clients of restrictions that may limit their freedom of choice.

1. The member's primary obligation is to respect the integrity and promote the welfare of the client(s), whether the client(s) is (are) assisted individually or in a group relationship. In a group setting, the member is also responsible for taking reasonable precautions to protect individuals from physical and/or psychological trauma resulting from interaction within the group.

2. Members make provisions for maintaining confidentiality in the storage and disposal of records and follow an established record retention and disposition policy. The counseling relationship and information resulting therefrom

must be kept confidential, consistent with the obligations of the member as a professional person. In a group counseling setting, the counselor must set a norm of confidentiality regarding all group participants' disclosures.

3. If an individual is already in a counseling relationship with another professional person, the member does not enter into a counseling relationship without first contacting and receiving the approval of that other professional. If the member discovers that the client is in another counseling relationship after the counseling relationship begins, the member must gain consent of the other professional or terminate the relationship, unless the client elects to terminate the other relationship.

4. When the client's condition indicates that there is clear and imminent danger to the client or others, the member must take reasonable personal action or inform responsible authorities. Consultation with other professionals must be used where possible. The assumption of responsibility for the client's(s') behavior must be taken only after careful deliberation. The client must be involved in the resumption of responsibility as quickly as possible.

5. Records of the counseling relationship, including interview notes, test data, correspondence, tape, recordings, electronic data storage, and other documents are to be considered professional information for use in counseling, and they should not be considered a part of the records of the institution or agency in which the counselor is employed unless specified by state statute or regulation. Revelation to others of counseling material must occur only upon the expressed consent of the client.

6. In view of the extensive data storage and processing capacities of the computer, the member must ensure that data maintained on a computer is: (a) limited to information that is appropriate and necessary for the services being provided; (b) destroyed after it is determined that the information is no longer of any value in providing services; and (c) restricted in terms of access to appropriate staff members involved in the provision of services by using the best computer security methods available.

7. Use of data derived from a counseling relationship for purposes of counselor training or research shall be confined to content that can be disguised to ensure full protection of the identity of the subject client.

8. The member must inform the client of the purposes, goals, techniques, rules of procedure, and limitations that may affect the relationship at or before the time that the counseling relationship is entered. When working with minors or persons who are unable to give consent, the member protects these clients' best interests.

9 In view of common misconceptions related to the perceived inherent validity of computer-generated data and narrative reports, the member must ensure that the client is provided with information as part of the counseling relationship that adequately explains the limitations of computer technology.

10. The member must screen prospective group participants, especially when the emphasis is on self-understanding and growth through self-disclosure. The member must maintain an awareness of the group participants' compatibility throughout the life of the group.

11. The member may choose to consult with any other professionally competent person about a client. In choosing a consultant, the member must avoid placing the consultant in a conflict of interest situation that would preclude the consultant's being a proper party to the member's efforts to help the client.

12. If the member determines an inability to be of professional assistance to the client, the member must either avoid initiating the counseling relationship or immediately terminate that relationship. In either event, the member must suggest appropriate alternatives. (The member must be knowledgeable about referral resources so that a satisfactory referral can be initiated.) In the event the client declines the suggested referral, the member is not obligated to continue the relationship.

13. When the member has other relationships, particularly of an administrative, supervisory, and/or evaluative nature with an individual seeking counseling services, the member must not serve as the counselor but should refer the individual to another professional. Only in instances where the individual's situation warrants counseling intervention should the member enter into and/or maintain a counseling relationship. Dual relationships with clients that might impair the member's objectivity and professional judgment (e.g., as with close friends and relatives) must be avoided and/or the counseling relationship terminated through referral to another competent professional.

14. The member will avoid any type of sexual intimacies with clients. Sexual relationships with clients are unethical.

15. All experimental methods of treatment must be clearly indicated to prospective recipients, and safety precautions are to be adhered to by the member.

16. When computer applications are used as a component of counseling services, the member must ensure that: (a) the client is intellectually, emotionally, and physically capable of using the computer application; (b) the computer application is appropriate for the needs of the client; (c) the client understands the purpose and operation of the computer application; and (d) a followup of client use of a computer application is provided to both correct possible problems (misconceptions or inappropriate use) and assess subsequent needs.

17. When the member is engaged in short-term group treatment/training programs (e.g., marathons and other encounter-type or growth groups), the member ensures that there is professional assistance available during and following the group experience.

18. Should the member be engaged in a work setting that calls for any variation from the above statements, the member is obligated to consult with other professionals whenever possible to consider justifiable alternatives.

19. The member must ensure that members of various ethnic, racial, religious, disability, and socioeconomic groups have equal access to computer applications used to support counseling services and that the content of available computer applications does not discriminate against the groups described above.

20. When computer applications are developed by the member for use by the general public as self-help/stand-alone computer software, the member must ensure that: (a) self-help computer applications are designed from the beginning to function in a stand-alone manner, as opposed to modifying software that was originally designed to require support from a counselor; (b) self-help computer applications will include within the program statements regarding intended user outcomes, suggestions for using the software, a description of the conditions under which self-help computer applications might not be appropriate, and a description of when and how counseling services might be beneficial; and (c) the manual for such applications will include the qualifications of the developer, the development process, validation data, and operating procedures.

SECTION C: MEASUREMENT AND EVALUATION

The primary purpose of educational and psychological testing is to provide descriptive measures that are objective and interpretable in either comparative or absolute terms. The member must recognize the need to interpret the statements that follow as applying to the whole range of appraisal techniques including test and non-test data. Test results constitute only one of a variety of pertinent sources of information for personnel, guidance, and counseling decisions.

1. The member must provide specific orientation or information to the examinee(s) prior to and following the test administration so that the results of testing may be placed in proper perspective with other relevant factors. In so doing,

the member must recognize the effects of socioeconomic, ethnic, and cultural factors on test scores. It is the member's professional responsibility to use additional unvalidated information carefully in modifying interpretation of the test results.

2. In selecting tests for use in a given situation or with a particular client, the member must consider carefully the specific validity, reliability, and appropriateness of the test(s). General validity, reliability, and related issues may be questioned legally as well as ethically when tests are used for vocational and educational selection, placement, or counseling.

3. When making any statements to the public about tests and testing, the member must give accurate information and avoid false claims or misconceptions. Special efforts are often required to avoid unwarranted connotations of such terms as IQ and grade equivalent scores.

4. Different tests demand different levels of competence for administration, scoring, and interpretation. Members must recognize the limits of their competence and perform only those functions for which they are prepared. In particular, members using computer-based test interpretations must be trained in the construct being measured and the specific instrument being used prior to using this type of computer application.

5. In situations where a computer is used for test administration and scoring, the member is responsible for ensuring that administration and scoring programs function properly to provide clients with accurate test results.

6. Tests must be administered under the same conditions that were established in their standardization. When tests are not administered under standard conditions or when unusual behavior or irregularities occur during the testing session, those conditions must be noted and the results designated as invalid or of questionable validity. Unsupervised or inadequately supervised test-taking, such as the use of tests through the mails, is considered unethical. On the other hand, the use of instruments that are so designed or standardized to be self-administered and self-scored, such as interest inventories, is to be encouraged.

7. The meaningfulness of test results used in personnel, guidance, and counseling functions generally depends on the examinee's unfamiliarity with the specific items on the test. Any prior coaching or dissemination of the test materials can invalidate test results. Therefore, test security is one of the professional obligations of the member. Conditions that produce most favorable test results must be made known to the examinee.

8. The purpose of testing and the explicit use of the results must be made known to the examinee prior to testing. The counselor must ensure that instrument limitations are not exceeded and that periodic review and/or retesting are made to prevent client stereotyping.

9. The examinee's welfare and explicit prior understanding must be the criteria for determining the recipients of the test results. The member must see that specific interpretation accompanies any release of individual or group test data. The interpretation of test data must be related to the examinee's particular concerns.

10. Members responsible for making decisions based on test results have an understanding of educational and psychological measurement, validation criteria, and test research.

11. The member must be cautious when interpreting the results of research instruments possessing insufficient technical data. The specific purposes for the use of such instruments must be stated explicitly to examinees.

12. The member must proceed with caution when attempting to evaluate and interpret the performance of minority group members or other persons who are not represented in the norm group on which the instrument was standardized.

13. When computer-based test interpretations are developed by the member to support the assessment process, the member must

ensure that the validity of such interpretations is established prior to the commercial distribution of such a computer application.

14. The member recognizes that test results may become obsolete. The member will avoid and prevent the misuse of obsolete test results.

15. The member must guard against the appropriation, reproduction, or modification of published tests or parts thereof without acknowledgement and permission from the previous publisher.

16. Regarding the preparation, publication, and distribution of tests, reference should be made to:

    a. "Standards for Educational and Psychological Testing," revised edition, 1985, published by the American Psychological Association on behalf of itself, the American Educational Research Association and National Council of Measurement in Education.

    b. "The Responsible Use of Tests: A Position Paper of AMEG, APGA, and NCME," *Measurement and Evaluation in Guidance,* 1972, 5, 385–388.

    c. "Responsiblities of Users of Standardized Tests," APGA, *Guidepost,* October 5, 1978, pp. 5–8.

SECTION D: RESEARCH AND PUBLICATION

1. Guidelines on research with human subjects shall be adhered to, such as:

    a. *Ethical Principles in the Conduct of Research with Human Participants,* Washington, D.C.: American Psychological Association, Inc., 1982.

    b. Code of Federal Regulation, Title 45, Subtitle A, Part 46, as currently issued.

    c. *Ethical Principles of Psychologists,* American Psychological Association, Principle #9: Research with Human Participants.

    d. Family Educational Rights and Privacy Act (the Buckley Amendment).

    e. Current federal regulations and various state rights privacy acts.

2. In planning any research activity dealing with human subjects, the member must be aware of and responsive to all pertinent ethical principles and ensure that the research problem, design, and execution are in full compliance with them.

3. Responsibility for ethical research practice lies with the principal researcher, while others involved in the research activities share ethical obligation and full responsibility for their own actions.

4. In research with human subjects, researchers are responsible for the subjects' welfare throughout the experiment, and they must take all responsible precautions to avoid causing injurious psychological, physical, or social effects on their subjects.

5. All research subjects must be informed of the purpose of the study except when withholding information or providing misinformation to them is essential to the investigation. In such research the member must be responsible for corrective action as soon as possible following completion of the research.

6. Participation in research must be voluntary. Involuntary participation is appropriate only when it can be demonstrated that participation will have no harmful effects on subjects and is essential to the investigation.

7. When reporting research results, explicit mention must be made of all variables and conditions known to the investigator that might affect the outcome of the investigation or the interpretation of the data.

8. The member must be responsible for conducting and reporting investigations in a manner that minimizes the possibility that results will be misleading.

9. The member has an obligation to make available sufficient original research data to qualified others who may wish to replicate the study.

10. When supplying data, aiding in the research of another person, reporting research

results, or making original data available, due care must be taken to disguise the identity of the subjects in the absence of specific authorization from such subjects to do otherwise.

11. When conducting and reporting research, the member must be familiar with and give recognition to previous work on the topic, as well as to observe all copyright laws and follow the principles of giving full credit to all to whom credit is due.

12. The member must give due credit through joint authorship, acknowledgement, footnote statements, or other appropriate means to those who have contributed significantly to the research and/or publication, in accordance with such contributions.

13. The member must communicate to other members the results of any research judged to be of professional or scientific value. Results reflecting unfavorably on institutions, programs, services, or vested interests must not be withheld for such reasons.

14. If members agree to cooperate with another individual in research and/or publication, they incur an obligation to cooperate as promised in terms of punctuality of performance and with full regard to the completeness and accuracy of the information required.

15. Ethical practice requires that authors not submit the same manuscript or one essentially similar in content for simultaneous publication consideration by two or more journals. In addition, manuscripts published in whole or in substantial part in another journal or published work should not be submitted for publication without acknowledgement and permission from the previous publication.

SECTION E: CONSULTING

Consultation refers to a voluntary relationship between a professional helper and help-needing individual, group, or social unit in which the consultant is providing help to the client(s) in defining and solving a work-related problem or potential problem with a client or client system.

1. The member acting as consultant must have a high degree of self-awareness of his/her own values, knowledge, skills, limitations, and needs in entering a helping relationship that involves human and/or organizational change and that the focus of the relationship be on the issues to be resolved and not on the person(s) presenting the problem.

2. There must be understanding and agreement between member and client for the problem definition, change of goals, and prediction of consequences of interventions selected.

3. The member must be reasonably certain that she/he or the organization represented has the necessary competencies and resources for giving the kind of help that is needed now or may be needed later and that appropriate referral resources are available to the consultant.

4. The consulting relationship must be one in which client adaptability and growth toward self-direction are encouraged and cultivated. The member must maintain this role consistently and not become a decision maker for the client or create a future dependency on the consultant.

5. When announcing consultant availability for services, the member conscientiously adheres to the Association's Ethical Standards.

6. The member must refuse a private fee or other remuneration for consultation with persons who are entitled to these services through the member's employing institution or agency. The policies of a particular agency may make explicit provisions for private practice with agency clients by members of its staff. In such instances, the clients must be apprised of other options open to them should they seek private counseling services.

SECTION F: PRIVATE PRACTICE

1. The member should assist the profession by facilitating the availability of counseling services in private as well as public settings.

2. In advertising services as a private practitioner, the member must advertise the services in a manner that accurately informs the public of

professional services, expertise, and techniques of counseling available. A member who assumes an executive leadership role in the organization shall not permit his/her name to be used in professional notices during periods when he/she is not actively engaged in the private practice of counseling.

3.   The member may list the following: highest relevant degree, type and level of certification and/or license, address, telephone number, office hours, type and/or description of services, and other relevant information. Such information must not contain false, inaccurate, misleading, partial, out-of-context, or deceptive material or statements.

4.   Members do not present their affiliations with any organization in such a way that would imply inaccurate sponsorship or certification by that organization.

5.   Members may join in partnership/corporation with other members and/or other professionals provided that each member of the partnership or corporation makes clear the separate specialties by name in compliance with the regulations of the locality.

6.   A member has an obligation to withdraw from a counseling relationship if it is believed that employment will result in violation of the Ethical Standards. If the mental or physical condition of the member renders it difficult to carry out an effective professional relationship or if the member is discharged by the client because the counseling relationship is no longer productive for the client, then the member is obligated to terminate the counseling relationship.

7.   A member must adhere to the regulations for private practice of the locality where the services are offered.

8.   It is unethical to use one's institutional affiliation to recruit clients for one's private practice.

SECTION G: PERSONNEL ADMINISTRATION

It is recognized that most members are employed in public or quasi-public institutions. The functioning of a member within an institution must contribute to the goals of the institution and vice versa if either is to accomplish their respective goals or objectives. It is therefore essential that the member and the institution function in ways to: (a) make the institutional goals specific and public; (b) make the member's contribution to institutional goals specific; and (c) foster mutual accountability for goal achievement.

To accomplish these objectives, it is recognized that the member and the employer must share responsibilities in the formulation and implementation of personnel policies.

1.   Members must define and describe the parameters and levels of their professional competency.

2.   Members must establish interpersonal relations and working agreements with supervisors and subordinates regarding counseling or clinical relationships, confidentiality, distinction between public and private material, maintenance and dissemination of recorded information, work load, and accountability. Working agreements in each instance must be specified and made known to those concerned.

3.   Members must alert their employers to conditions that may be potentially disruptive or damaging.

4.   Members must inform employers of conditions that may limit their effectiveness.

5.   Members must submit regularly to professional review and evaluation.

6.   Members must be responsible for inservice development of self and/or staff.

7.   Members must inform their staff of goals and programs.

8.   Members must provide personnel practices that guarantee and enhance the rights and welfare of each recipient of their service.

9.   Members must select competent persons and assign responsibilities compatible with their skills and experiences.

10.   The member, at the onset of a counseling relationship, will inform the client of the member's intended use of supervisors regarding the disclosure of information concerning this

case. The member will clearly inform the client of the limits of confidentiality in the relationship.

11. Members, as either employers or employees, do not engage in or condone practices that are inhumane, illegal, or unjustifiable (such as considerations based on sex, handicap, age, race) in hiring, promotion, or training.

SECTION H: PREPARATION STANDARDS

Members who are responsible for training others must be guided by the preparation standards of the Association and relevant Division(s). The member who functions in the capacity of trainer assumes unique ethical responsibilities that frequently go beyond that of the member who does not function in a training capacity. These ethical responsibilities are outlined as follows:

1. Members must orient students to program expectations, basic skills development, and employment prospects prior to admission to the program.

2. Members in charge of learning experiences must establish programs that integrate academic study and supervised practice.

3. Members must establish a program directed toward developing students' skills, knowledge, and self-understanding, stated whenever possible in competency or performance terms.

4. Members must identify the levels of competencies of their students in compliance with relevant Division standards. These competencies must accommodate the paraprofessional as well as the professional.

5. Members, through continual student evaluation and appraisal, must be aware of the personal limitations of the learner that might impede future performance. The instructor must not only assist the learner in securing remedial assistance but also screen from the program those individuals who are unable to provide competent services.

6. Members must provide a program that includes training in research commensurate with levels of role functioning. Paraprofessional and technician-level personnel must be trained as consumers of research. In addition, personnel must learn how to evaluate their own and their program's effectiveness. Graduate training, especially at the doctoral level, would include preparation for original research by the member.

7. Members must make students aware of the ethical responsibilities and standards of the profession.

8. Preparatory programs must encourage students to value the ideals of service to individuals and to society. In this regard, direct financial remuneration or lack thereof must not be allowed to overshadow professional and humanitarian needs.

9. Members responsible for educational programs must be skilled as teachers and practitioners.

10. Members must present thoroughly varied theoretical positions so that students may make comparisons and have the opportunity to select a position.

11. Members must develop clear policies within their educational institutions regarding field placement and the roles of the student and the instructor in such placement.

12. Members must ensure that forms of learning focusing on self-understanding or growth are voluntary, or if required as part of the educational program, are made known to prospective students prior to entering the program. When the educational program offers a growth experience with an emphasis on self-disclosure or other relatively intimate or personal involvement, the member must have no administrative, supervisory, or evaluating authority regarding the participant.

13. The member will at all times provide students with clear and equally acceptable alternatives for self-understanding or growth experiences. The member will assure students that they have a right to accept these alternatives without prejudice or penalty.

14. Members must conduct an educational program in keeping with the current relevant guidelines of the Association.

G

Ethical Principles of Psychologists

PREAMBLE

Psychologists respect the dignity and worth of the individual and strive for the preservation and protection of fundamental human rights. They are committed to increasing knowledge of human behavior and of people's understanding of themselves and others and to the utilization of such knowledge for the promotion of human welfare. While pursuing these objectives, they make every effort to protect the welfare of those who seek their services and of the research participants that may be the object of study. They use their skills only for purposes consistent with these values and do not knowingly permit their misuse by others. While demanding for themselves freedom of inquiry and communication, psychologists accept the responsibility this freedom requires: competence, objectivity in the application of skills, and concern for the best interests of clients, colleagues, students, research participants, and society. In pursuit of these ideals, psychologists subscribe to principles in the following areas: 1. Responsibility, 2. Competence, 3. Moral and Legal Standards, 4. Public Statements, 5. Confidentiality, 6. Welfare of the Consumer, 7. Professional Relationships, 8. Assessment Techniques, 9. Research With Human Participants, and 10. Care and Use of Animals.

Acceptance of membership in the American Psychological Association commits the member to adherence to these principles.

Psychologists cooperate with duly constituted committees of the American Psychological Association, in particular, the Committee on Scientific and Professional Ethics and Conduct, by responding to inquiries promptly and completely. Members also respond promptly and completely to inquiries from duly constituted state association ethics committees and professional standards review committees.

PRINCIPLE 1: RESPONSIBILITY

In providing services, psychologists maintain the highest standards of their profession. They accept responsibility for the consequences of their acts and make every effort to ensure that their services are used appropriately.

a. As scientists, psychologists accept responsibility for the selection of their research topics and the methods used in investigation, analysis, and reporting. They plan their research in ways to minimize the possibility that their findings will be misleading. They provide thorough discussion of the limitations of their data, especially where their work touches on social policy or might be construed to the detriment of persons in specific age, sex, ethnic, socioeconomic, or other social groups. In publishing reports of their work, they never suppress disconfirming data, and they acknowledge the existence of alternative hypotheses and explanations of their findings. Psychologists take credit only for work they have actually done.

b.   Psychologists clarify in advance with all appropriate persons and agencies the expectations for sharing and utilizing research data. They avoid relationships that may limit their objectivity or create a conflict of interest. Interference with the milieu in which data are collected is kept to a minimum.

c.   Psychologists have the responsibility to attempt to prevent distortion, misuse, or suppression of psychological findings by the institution or agency of which they are employees.

d.   As members of governmental or other organizational bodies, psychologists remain accountable as individuals to the highest standards of their profession.

e.   As teachers, psychologists recognize their primary obligation to help others acquire knowledge and skill. They maintain high standards of scholarship by presenting psychological information objectively, fully, and accurately.

f.   As practitioners, psychologists know that they bear a heavy social responsibility because their recommendations and professional actions may alter the lives of others. They are alert to personal, social, organizational, financial, or political situations and pressures that might lead to misuse of their influence.

PRINCIPLE 2: COMPETENCE

The maintenance of high standards of competence is a responsibility shared by all psychologists in the interest of the public and the profession as a whole. Psychologists recognize the boundaries of their competence and the limitations of their techniques. They only provide services and only use techniques for which they are qualified by training and experience. In those areas in which recognized standards do not yet exist, psychologists take whatever precautions are necessary to protect the welfare of their clients. They maintain knowledge of current scientific and professional information related to the services they render.

a.   Psychologists accurately represent their competence, education, training, and experience. They claim as evidence of educational qualifications only those degrees obtained from institutions acceptable under the Bylaws and Rules of Council of the American Psychological Association.

b.   As teachers, psychologists perform their duties on the basis of careful preparation so that their instruction is accurate, current, and scholarly.

c.   Psychologists recognize the need for continuing education and are open to new procedures and changes in expectations and values over time.

d.   Psychologists recognize differences among people, such as those that may be associated with age, sex, and socioeconomic and ethnic backgrounds. When necessary, they obtain training, experience, or counsel to assure competent service or research relating to such persons.

e.   Psychologists responsible for decisions involving individuals or policies based on test results have an understanding of psychological or educational measurement, validation problems, and test research.

f.   Psychologists recognize that personal problems and conflicts may interfere with professional effectiveness. Accordingly, they refrain from undertaking any activity in which their personal problems are likely to lead to inadequate performance or harm to a client, colleague, student, or research participant. If engaged in such activity when they become aware of their personal problems, they seek competent professional assistance to determine whether they should suspend, terminate, or limit the scope of their professional and/or scientific activities.

PRINCIPLE 3: MORAL AND LEGAL STANDARDS

Psychologists' moral and ethical standards of behavior are a personal matter to the same degree as they are for any other citizen, except as these may compromise the fulfillment of their professional responsibilities or reduce the public trust in psychology and psychologists. Regarding their own behavior, psychologists are sensitive to prevailing community standards and to the possible impact that conformity to or deviation from these standards may have upon the quality of their performance as psychologists. Psychologists are also aware of the possible impact of their public behavior upon the ability of colleagues to perform their professional duties.

a.   As teachers, psychologists are aware of the fact that their personal values affect the selection and presentation of instructional materials. When dealing with topics that may give offense, they recognize and respect the diverse attitudes that students may have toward such materials.

b.   As employees or employers, psychologists do not engage in or condone practices that are inhumane or that result in illegal or unjustifiable actions. Such practices include, but are not limited to, those based on considerations of race, handicap, age, gender, sexual preference, religion, or national origin in hiring, promotion, or training.

c.   In their professional roles, psychologists avoid any action that will violate or diminish the legal and civil rights of clients or of others who may be affected by their actions.

d.   As practitioners and researchers, psychologists act in accord with Association standards and guidelines related to practice and to the conduct of research with human beings and animals. In the ordinary course of events, psychologists adhere to relevant governmental laws and institutional regulations. When federal, state, provincial, organizational, or institutional laws, regulations, or practices are in conflict with Association standards and guidelines, psychologists make known their commitment to Association standards and guidelines and, wherever possible, work toward a resolution of the conflict. Both practitioners and researchers are concerned with the development of such legal and quasi-legal regulations as best serve the public interest, and they work toward changing existing regulations that are not beneficial to the public interest.

PRINCIPLE 4: PUBLIC STATEMENTS

Public statements, announcements of services, advertising, and promotional activities of psychologists serve the purpose of helping the public make informed judgments and choices. Psychologists represent accurately and objectively their professional qualifications, affiliations, and functions, as well as those of the institutions or organizations with which they or the statements may be associated. In public statements providing psychological information or professional opinions or providing information about the availability of psychological products, publications, and services, psychologists base their statements on scientifically acceptable psychological findings and techniques with full recognition of the limits and uncertainties of such evidence.

a.   When announcing or advertising professional services, psychologists may list the following information to describe the provider and services provided: name, highest relevant academic degree earned from a regionally accredited institution, date, type, and level of certification or licensure, diplomate status, APA membership status, address, telephone number, office hours, a brief listing of the type of psychological services offered, an appropriate presentation of fee information, foreign languages spoken, and policy with regard to third-party payments. Additional relevant or important consumer information may be included if not prohibited by other sections of these Ethical Principles.

b.   In announcing or advertising the availability of psychological products, publications, or services, psychologists do not present their affiliation with any organization in a manner that falsely implies sponsorship or certification by that organization. In particular and for example, psychologists do not state APA membership or fellow status in a way to suggest that such status implies specialized professional competence or qualifications. Public statements include, but are not limited to, communication by means of periodical, book, list, directory, television, radio, or motion picture. They do not contain (i) a false, fraudulent, misleading, deceptive, or unfair statement; (ii) a misinterpretation of fact or a statement likely to mislead or deceive because in context it makes only a partial disclosure of relevant facts; (iii) a statement intended or likely to create false or unjustified expectations of favorable results.

c. Psychologists do not compensate or give anything of value to a representative of the press, radio, television, or other communication medium in anticipation of or in return for professional publicity in a news item. A paid advertisement must be identified as such, unless it is apparent from the context that it is a paid advertisement. If communicated to the public by use of radio or television, an advertisement is prerecorded and approved for broadcast by the psychologist, and a recording of the actual transmission is retained by the psychologist.

d. Announcements or advertisements of "personal growth groups," clinics, and agencies give a clear statement of purpose and a clear description of the experiences to be provided. The education, training, and experience of the staff members are appropriately specified.

e. Psychologists associated with the development or promotion of psychological devices, books, or other products offered for commercial sale make reasonable efforts to ensure that announcements and advertisements are presented in a professional, scientifically acceptable, and factually informative manner.

f. Psychologists do not participate for personal gain in commercial announcements or advertisements recommending to the public the purchase or use of proprietary or single-source products or services when that participation is based solely upon their identification as psychologists.

g. Psychologists present the science of psychology and offer their services, products, and publications fairly and accurately, avoiding mis-

representation through sensationalism, exaggeration, or superficiality. Psychologists are guided by the primary obligation to aid the public in developing informed judgments, opinions, and choices.

h. As teachers, psychologists ensure that statements in catalogs and course outlines are accurate and not misleading, particularly in terms of subject matter to be covered, bases for evaluating progress, and the nature of course experiences. Announcements, brochures, or advertisements describing workshops, seminars, or other educational programs accurately describe the audience for which the program is intended as well as eligibility requirements, educational objectives, and nature of the materials to be covered. These announcements also accurately represent the education, training, and experience of the psychologists presenting the programs and any fees involved.

i. Public announcements or advertisements soliciting research participants in which clinical services or other professional services are offered as an inducement make clear the nature of the services as well as the costs and other obligations to be accepted by participants in the research.

j. A psychologist accepts the obligation to correct others who represent the psychologist's professional qualifications, or associations with products or services, in a manner incompatible with these guidelines.

k. Individual diagnostic and therapeutic services are provided only in the context of a professional psychological relationship. When personal advice is given by means of public lectures or demonstrations, newspaper or magazine articles, radio or television programs, mail, or similar media, the psychologist utilizes the most current relevant data and exercises the highest level of professional judgment.

l. Products that are described or presented by means of public lectures or demonstrations, newspaper or magazine articles, radio or television programs, or similar media meet the same recognized standards as exist for products used in the context of a professional relationship.

PRINCIPLE 5: CONFIDENTIALITY

Psychologists have a primary obligation to respect the confidentiality of information obtained for persons in the course of their work as psychologists. They reveal such information to others only with the consent of the person or the person's legal representative, except in those unusual circumstances in which not to do so would result in clear danger to the person or to others. Where appropriate, psychologists inform their clients of the legal limits of confidentiality.

a.   Information obtained in clinical or consulting relationships, or evaluative data concerning children, students, employees, and others, is discussed only for professional purposes and only with persons clearly concerned with the case. Written and oral reports present only data germane to the purposes of the evaluation, and every effort is made to avoid undue invasion of privacy.

b.   Psychologists who present personal information obtained during the course of professional work in writings, lectures, or other public forums either obtain adequate prior consent to do so or adequately disguise all identifying information.

c.   Psychologists make provisions for maintaining confidentiality in the storage and disposal of records.

d.   When working with minors or other persons who are unable to give voluntary, informed consent, psychologists take special care to protect these persons' best interests.

PRINCIPLE 6: WELFARE OF THE CONSUMER

Psychologists respect the integrity and protect the welfare of the people and groups with whom they work. When conflicts of interest arise between clients and psychologists' employing institutions, psychologists clarify the nature and direction of their loyalties and responsibilities and keep all parties informed of their commitments. Psychologists fully inform consumers as to the purpose and nature of an evaluative, *treatment, educational, or training procedure, and they freely acknowledge that clients, students, or participants in research have freedom of choice with regard to participation.*

a.   Psychologists are continually cognizant of their own needs and of their potentially influential position vis-à-vis persons such as clients, students, and subordinates. They avoid exploiting the trust and dependency of such persons. Psychologists make every effort to avoid dual relationships that could impair their professional judgment or increase the risk of exploitation. Examples of such dual relationships include, but are not limited to, research with and treatment of employees, students, supervisees, close friends, or relatives. Sexual intimacies with clients are unethical.

b.   When a psychologist agrees to provide services to a client at the request of a third party, the psychologist assumes the responsibility of clarifying the nature of the relationships to all parties concerned.

c.   Where the demands of an organization require psychologists to violate these Ethical Principles, psychologists clarify the nature of the conflict between the demands and these principles. They inform all parties of psychologists' ethical responsibilities and take appropriate action.

d.   Psychologists make advance financial arrangements that safeguard the best interests of and are clearly understood by their clients. They contribute a portion of their services to work for which they receive little or no financial return.

e.   Psychologists terminate a clinical or consulting relationship when it is reasonably clear that the consumer is not benefiting from it. They offer to help the consumer locate alternative sources of assistance.

PRINCIPLE 7: PROFESSIONAL RELATIONSHIPS

Psychologists act with due regard for the needs, special competencies, and obligations of their colleagues in psychology and other professions. They respect the prerogatives and obligations of the institutions or organizations with which these other colleagues are associated.

a.   Psychologists understand the areas of competence of related professions. They make full use of all the professional, technical, and administrative resources that serve the best interests of consumers. The absence of formal relationships with other professional workers does not relieve psychologists of the responsibility of securing for their clients the best possible professional service, nor does it relieve them of the obligation to exercise foresight, diligence, and tact in obtaining the complementary or alternative assistance needed by clients.

b.   Psychologists know and take into account the traditions and practices of other professional groups with whom they work and cooperate fully with such groups. If a psychologist is contacted by a person who is already receiving similar services from another professional, the psychologist carefully considers that professional relationship and proceeds with caution and sensitivity to the therapeutic issues as well as the client's welfare. The psychologist discusses these issues with the client so as to minimize the risk of confusion and conflict.

c.   Psychologists who employ or supervise other professionals or professionals in training accept the obligation to facilitate the further professional development of these individuals. They provide appropriate working conditions, timely evaluations, constructive consultation, and experience opportunities.

d.   Psychologists do not exploit their professional relationships with clients, supervisees, students, employees, or research participants sexually or otherwise. Psychologists do not condone or engage in sexual harassment. Sexual harassment is defined as deliberate or repeated comments, gestures, or physical contacts of a sexual nature that are unwanted by the recipient.

e.   In conducting research in institutions or organizations, psychologists secure appropriate authorization to conduct such research. They are aware of their obligations to future research workers and ensure that host institutions receive adequate information about the research and proper acknowledgment of their contributions.

f.   Publication credit is assigned to those who have contributed to a publication in proportion to their professional contributions. Major contributions of a professional character made by several persons to a common project are recognized by joint authorship, with the individual who made the principal contribution listed first. Minor contributions of a professional character and extensive clerical or similar nonprofessional assistance may be acknowledged in footnotes or in an introductory statement. Acknowledgment through specific citations is made for unpublished as well as published material that has directly influenced the research or writing. Psychologists who compile and edit material of others for publication publish the material in the name of the originating group, if appropriate, with their own name appearing as chairperson or editor. All contributors are to be acknowledged and named.

g.   When psychologists know of an ethical violation by another psychologist, and it seems appropriate, they informally attempt to resolve the issue by bringing the behavior to the attention of the psychologist. If the misconduct is of a minor nature and/or appears to be due to lack of sensitivity, knowledge, or experience, such an informal solution is usually appropriate. Such informal corrective efforts are made with sensitivity to any rights to confidentiality involved. If the violation does not seem amenable to an informal solution, or is of a more serious nature, psychologists bring it to the attention of the appropriate local, state, and/or national committee on professional ethics and conduct.

PRINCIPLE 8: ASSESSMENT TECHNIQUES

In the development, publication, and utilization of psychological assessment techniques, psychologists make every effort to promote the welfare and best interests of the client. They guard against the misuse of assessment results. They respect the client's right to know the results, the interpretations made, and the bases for their conclusions and recommendations. Psychologists make every effort to maintain the security of tests and other assessment techniques within limits of legal mandates. They strive to ensure the appropriate use of assessment techniques by others.

a.   In using assessment techniques, psychologists respect the right of clients to have full explanations of the nature and purpose of the techniques in language the clients can understand, unless an explicit exception to this right has been agreed upon in advance. When the explanations are to be provided by others, psychologists establish procedures for ensuring the adequacy of these explanations.

b.   Psychologists responsible for the development and standardization of psychological tests and other assessment techniques utilize established scientific procedures and observe the relevant APA standards.

c.   In reporting assessment results, psychologists indicate any reservations that exist regarding validity or reliability because of the circumstances of the assessment or the inappropriateness of the norms for the person tested. Psychologists strive to ensure that the results of assessments and their interpretations are not misused by others.

d.   Psychologists recognize that assessment results may become obsolete. They make every effort to avoid and prevent the misuse of obsolete measures.

e.   Psychologists offering scoring and interpretation services are able to produce appropriate evidence for the validity of the programs and procedures used in arriving at interpretations. The public offering of an automated interpretation service is considered a professional-to-professional consultation. Psychologists make very effort to avoid misuse of assessment reports.

f.   Psychologists do not encourage or promote the use of psychological assessment techniques by inappropriately trained or otherwise unqualified persons through teaching, sponsorship, or supervision.

PRINCIPLE 9: RESEARCH WITH HUMAN PARTICIPANTS

The decision to undertake research rests upon a considered judgment by the individual psychologist about how best to contribute to psychological science and human welfare. Having made the decision to conduct research, the psychologist considers alternative directions in which research energies and resources might be invested. On the basis of this consideration, the psychologist carries out the investigation with respect and concern for the dignity and welfare of the people who participate and with cognizance of federal and state regulations and professional standards governing the conduct of research with human participants.

a.   In planning a study, the investigator has the responsibility to make a careful evaluation of its ethical acceptability. To the extent that the weighing of scientific and human values suggests a compromise of any principle, the investigator incurs a correspondingly serious obligation to seek ethical advice and to observe stringent safeguards to protect the rights of human participants.

b.   Considering whether a participant in a planned study will be a "subject at risk" or a "subject at minimal risk," according to recognized standards, is of primary ethical concern to the investigator.

c.   The investigator always retains the responsibility for ensuring ethical practice in research. The investigator is also responsible for the ethical treatment of research participants by collaborators, assistants, students, and employees, all of whom, however, incur similar obligations.

d.   Except in minimal-risk research, the investigator establishes a clear and fair agreement with research participants, prior to their participation, that clarifies the obligations and responsibilities of each. The investigator has the obligation to honor all promises and commitments included in that agreement. The investigator informs the participants of all aspects of the research that might reasonably be expected to influence willingness to participate and explains all other aspects of the research about which the participants inquire. Failure to make full disclosure prior to obtaining informed consent requires additional safeguards to protect the welfare and dignity of the research participants. Research with children or with participants who have impairments that would limit understanding and/or communication requires special safeguarding procedures.

e.   Methodological requirements of a study may make the use of concealment or deception necessary. Before conducting such a study, the investigator has a special responsibility to (i) determine whether the use of such techniques is justified by the study's prospective scientific, educational, or applied value; (ii) determine whether alternative procedures are available that do not use concealment or deception; and (iii) ensure that the participants are provided with sufficient explanation as soon as possible.

f.   The investigator respects the individual's freedom to decline to participate in or to withdraw from the research at any time. The obligation to protect this freedom requires careful thought and consideration when the investigator is in a position of authority or influence over the participant. Such positions of authority include, but are not limited to, situations in which research participation is required as part of employment or in which the participant is a student, client, or employee of the investigator.

g.   The investigator protects the participant from physical and mental discomfort, harm, and danger that may arise from research procedures. If risks of such consequences exist, the investigator informs the participant of that fact. Research procedures likely to cause serious or lasting harm to a participant are not used unless the failure to use these procedures might expose the participant to risk of greater harm, or unless

the research has great potential benefit and fully informed and voluntary consent is obtained from each participant. The participant should be informed of procedures for contacting the investigator within a reasonable time period following participation should stress, potential harm, or related questions or concerns arise.

h.   After the data are collected, the investigator provides the participant with information about the nature of the study and attempts to remove any misconceptions that may have arisen. Where scientific or humane values justify delaying or withholding this information, the investigator incurs a special responsibility to monitor the research and to ensure that there are no damaging consequences for the participant.

i.   Where research procedures result in undesirable consequences for the individual participant, the investigator has the responsibility to detect and remove or correct these consequences, including long-term effects.

j.   Information obtained about a research participant during the course of an investigation is confidential unless otherwise agreed upon in advance. When the possibility exists that others may obtain access to such information, this possibility, together with the plans for protecting confidentiality, is explained to the participant as part of the procedure for obtaining informed consent.

PRINCIPLE 10: CARE AND USE OF ANIMALS

An investigator of animal behavior strives to advance understanding of basic behavioral principles and/or to contribute to the improvement of human health and welfare. In seeking these ends, the investigator ensures the welfare of animals and treats them humanely. Laws and regulations notwithstanding, an animal's immediate protection depends upon the scientist's own conscience.

a.   The acquisition, care, use, and disposal of all animals are in compliance with current federal, state or provincial, and local laws and regulations.

b.   A psychologist trained in research methods and experienced in the care of laboratory animals closely supervises all procedures involving animals and is responsible for ensuring appropriate consideration of their comfort, health, and humane treatment.

c.   Psychologists ensure that all individuals using animals under their supervision have received explicit instruction in experimental methods and in the care, maintenance, and handling of the species being used. Responsibilities and activities of individuals participating in a research project are consistent with their respective competencies.

d.   Psychologists make every effort to minimize discomfort, illness, and pain of animals. A procedure subjecting animals to pain, stress, or privation is used only when an alternative procedure is unavailable and the goal is justified by its prospective scientific, educational, or applied value. Surgical procedures are performed under appropriate anesthesia; techniques to avoid infection and minimize pain are followed during and after surgery.

e.   When it is appropriate that the animal's life be terminated, it is done rapidly and painlessly.

This version of *Ethical Principles of Psychologists* was adopted by the American Psychological Association's Board of Directors on June 2, 1989. On that date, the Board of Directors rescinded several sections of the Ethical Principles

that had been adopted by the APA Council of Representatives on January 24, 1981. Inquiries concerning the substance or interpretation of the *Ethical Principles of Psychologists* should be addressed to the Administrative Director, Office of Ethics, American Psychological Association, 1200 Seventeenth Street, N.W., Washington, DC 20036.

These Ethical Principles apply to psychologists, to students of psychology, and to others who do work of a psychological nature under the supervision of a psychologist. They are intended for the guidance of nonmembers of the Association who are engaged in psychological research or practice.

The Ethical Principles have previously been published as follows:

American Psychological Association. (1953). *Ethical Standards of Psychologists,* Washington, DC.

American Psychological Association. (1958). Standards of ethical behavior for psychologists. *American Psychologist, 13,* 268–271.

American Psychological Association. (1959). Ethical standards of psychologists. *American Psychologist, 14,* 279–282.

American Psychological Association. (1963). Ethical standards of psychologists. *American Psychologist, 18,* 56–60.

American Psychological Association. (1968). Ethical standards of psychologists. *American Psychologist, 23,* 357–361.

American Psychological Association, (1977, March). Ethical standards of psychologists. *The APA Monitor,* pp. 22–23.

American Psychological Association. (1979). *Ethical Standards of Psychologists,* Washington, DC: Author.

American Psychological Association. (1981). Ethical principles of psychologists. *American Psychologist, 36,* 633–638.

Request copies of the *Ethical Principles of Psychologists* from the APA Order Department, P.O. Box 2710, Hyattsville, MD 20784; or phone (703) 247-7705.

Name Index

Subject Index